Acclaim for DAVID S. REYNOLDS's

WALT WHITMAN'S AMERICA

"Fascinating. . . . For anyone who wants to learn more about the manners and mores of a century that ineluctably shaped our own, this book is essential reading."
—*San Francisco Examiner*

"It opens many windows on Whitman's makeup. . . . More than his predecessors, Reynolds places Whitman in the complex context of his times."
—*The New York Times*

"Reynolds's extraordinarily detailed exhumation of the Whitman experience is utterly fascinating. . . . A powerful incentive to turn again to Whitman's work itself."
—*Detroit Free Press*

"Superbly researched and systematic. . . . It greatly enriches our reading of Whitman."
—*New York Review of Books*

"An astounding feat of good scholarly writing."
—*Atlanta Journal-Constitution*

"Absorbing and minutely researched. . . . It will not be superseded for years to come."
—*Seattle Times Post-Intelligencer*

"The great merit of Reynolds's exceptionally informed and aptly titled book is that it examines the sources of Whitman's revolution."
—*Los Angeles Times*

"Once you have followed Reynolds around the nineteenth-century streets, you see Whitman with a sudden new clarity."
—*The New Yorker*

"A new and coherent portrait . . . vibrant and fully human. It sheds a tremendous amount of light on the poems. . . . Whitman has inspired a lot of first rate books. This may be the best."
—*Washington Times*

DAVID S. REYNOLDS

WALT WHITMAN'S AMERICA

David S. Reynolds is Distinguished Professor of American
Literature and American Studies at Baruch College and the
Graduate School of the City University of New York. Born
and raised in Rhode Island, he received his B.A. from
Amherst College and his Ph.D. from the University of
California, Berkeley. He has previously taught at Rutgers
University, New York University, Barnard College, and
Northwestern University. He is the author of the monumen-
tal *Beneath the American Renaissance: The Subversive
Imagination in the Age of Emerson and Melville*, winner of the
Christian Gauss Award. His other publications include *Faith
in Fiction: The Emergence of Religious Literature in America*;
George Lippard; and *George Lippard, Prophet of Protest:
Writings of an American Radical, 1822–1854* (edited antho-
logy). He is the editor of George Lippard's novel *The Quaker
City; or, The Monks of Monk Hall* and the author of numerous
articles and reviews in the field of American literature and
culture, including "Of Me I Sing: Whitman in His Time"
(*New York Times Book Review*).

WALT WHITMAN'S AMERICA

WALT
WHITMAN'S
AMERICA

A Cultural Biography

DAVID S. REYNOLDS

VINTAGE BOOKS

A DIVISION OF RANDOM HOUSE, INC.

NEW YORK

FIRST VINTAGE BOOKS EDITION, MARCH 1996

Copyright © 1995 by David S. Reynolds

All rights reserved under International and Pan-American Copyright
Conventions. Published in the United States by Vintage Books, a division of
Random House, Inc., New York, and simultaneously in Canada by Random House
of Canada Limited, Toronto. Originally published in hardcover
by Alfred A. Knopf, Inc., New York, in 1995.

The Library of Congress has cataloged the Knopf edition as follows:
Reynolds, David S.
Walt Whitman's America : a cultural biography / by David S. Reynolds.
p. cm.
Includes bibliographical references (p.) and index.
ISBN 0-394-58023-0
1. Whitman, Walt, 1819–1892.
2. Whitman, Walt, 1819–1892—Contemporary United States.
3. United States—Civilization—19th century.
4. Poets, American—19th century—Biography. I. Title.
PS3231.R48 1995
811'.3—dc20
[B] 94-12841
CIP
Vintage ISBN: 0-679-76709-6

Manufactured in the United States of America
10   9   8

To my wife, Suzanne, and our daughter, Aline,

with love and thanks

CONTENTS

Illustrations follow page 210.

ACKNOWLEDGMENTS

A scholar inevitably owes a great debt to research libraries. I especially thank the professional, helpful staffs at the Library of Congress, the American Antiquarian Society, the New York Public Library, the New-York Historical Society, the Museum of the City of New York, the Long Island Historical Society, the Smithtown Historical Society, Hofstra University Library, the Walt Whitman Birthplace Association, the Walt Whitman Association in Camden, and the libraries of the City University of New York.

A yearlong fellowship from the National Endowment of the Humanities supported part of the work on this project, as did a series of small research grants from Baruch College and the City University of New York.

Among the colleagues who helped me in various ways are Ed Folsom, Jerome Loving, Gay Wilson Allen, Sean Wilentz, and Michael Black. The latter's scrupulous comments on my manuscript were of great use. P. Marc Bousquet, my research assistant in one phase of this project, was particularly useful in gathering data on the Whitmans in early Brooklyn and on certain aspects of America's musical and theatrical culture. Special thanks go to Katherine Molinoff, who loaned me useful materials about Whitman's teaching days. I also thank Nancy Swertfager, David Swertfager, and James Bitses, who helped me on the Southold story. My editor at Knopf, Jane Garrett, has been encouraging from start to finish. Like others working on Whitman, I am deeply indebted to the Whitman scholars who have preceded me. In particular, the work of Gay Wilson Allen and Roger Asselineau remain invaluable resources.

I began this book in Camden, New Jersey, Whitman's last home and resting place, and finished it in Old Westbury, Long Island, not far from the poet's birthplace. All the while, I have had the loving support and encouragement of my wife, Suzanne Nalbantian, who was also working on a book at the time. My appreciation to her is unbounded. Our little daughter, Aline, couldn't wait till this book was done, but while it was in process she cheerfully tolerated my long hours of research and writing.

INTRODUCTORY NOTE

It has proven easier for critics to theorize about literary history than to write it. "Cultural studies" are often discussed but are rarely supported by the wide-ranging research that alone can bring alive a culture in its many dimensions. Literary texts are intricate tapestries whose threads can be followed backward into a tremendous body of submerged biographical and cultural materials.

Walt Whitman is a case in point. "No one can know *Leaves of Grass*," he declared, "who judges it piecemeal." The problem with most critics, he stressed, was that they "do not take the trouble to examine what they start out to criticize—to judge a man from his own standpoint, to even find out what that standpoint is." Whitman's best poems do not fall into any single—or even double or triple—historical category. The current book tries to overcome piecemeal approaches to literary history by reconstructing the life and times of America's most representative poet.

With a figure as familiar as Whitman, a certain amount of recapitulation or synthesis of known information is inevitable, and I am indebted to many fine studies of him. But the interaction between his life and writings and their historical background has been reported only fragmentarily. Whitman constantly called attention to the historical origins of his poetry. "In estimating my volumes," he wrote, "the world's current times and deeds, and their spirit, must first be profoundly estimated." The poet fails, he wrote, "if he does not flood himself with the immediate age as with vast oceanic tides [. . .] if he be not himself the age transfigured."

In his own copious reading, he had an undying fascination for all aspects of a writer's contexts—what he called "the part enacted by environment, surroundings, circumstances,—the man's age, land—all that went before." Criticism failed, he believed, if it did not take into account the details of a writer's times in their specificity and historical fullness. It also failed if it did not make note of the special resonance and artistry of certain texts.

There are countless ways of expressing love for Whitman's poetry. Mine is to recreate his life and art in the historical context of his culture, the way *he* experienced it as a vital, sensitive journalist and poet. Whitman described himself as a poet "attracting [the nation] body and soul to himself, hanging on its neck with incomparable love,/plunging his seminal muscle into its merits and demerits." It is this unprecedented love of a poet for his country that is the focus of this book.

In reconstructing Whitman's life and times I have found much to admire as well as certain attitudes that are repellent. Such attitudes are not defensible, but they are historically explainable. In all matters, I have tried to adhere to the historical record instead of imposing today's views on the past.

WALT WHITMAN'S AMERICA

PROLOGUE

BLUSTERY WINDS SWEPT through Camden, New Jersey, on the afternoon of May 31, 1889, as a large crowd gathered at Morgan's Hall to celebrate Walt Whitman's seventieth birthday. Camden, the drab town across the Delaware River from Philadelphia, did not have much to boast of. The New York *Sun* had once joked that it was the refuge for those in doubt, debt, or despair. It is understandable, then, that nine of its citizens would organize a fete in its fanciest public hall for the famous poet who had lived there for sixteen years and who had made the town an unlikely mecca for a succession of traveling notables, including Oscar Wilde, Edmund Gosse, and Henry Wadsworth Longfellow.

The heavy skies that day threatened rain, but the atmosphere inside Morgan's was festive. Three long rows of dinner tables, two of them parallel with the third crossing them at the top, were the picture of elegance, with dazzling white tablecloths and flowers everywhere. Banners festooned the walls, and a band played from a platform. The guests, some of whom had come a long way, had paid a five-dollar attendance fee. Crisply printed dinner menus, titled *A Feast of Reason*, promised they would get their money's worth. Littleneck clams on the half shell and consommé royal soup were being offered as appetizers; fish with cucumber sauce, lamb, roast beef, and broiled chicken with mushrooms were the choice of entrées. For dessert there would be a tempting array of delectables, including bisque, fancy cakes, and ice cream, topped off by French coffee and cigars—right down to the proverbial nuts.

Whitman himself was not present when the crowd gathered at 5:00 p.m. It was a motley group. Offbeat writers like Hamlin Garland and Julian Hawthorne rubbed shoulders with stodgy Philadelphia lawyers and bankers. After dinner was cleared away, the air buzzed with anticipation of the poet's arrival. Soon a policeman cried, "He's coming!" The hall fell silent and all eyes were riveted on the entrance door.

Doubtless, many hearts sank at his pitiful condition. His large, once-robust frame was now slumped in a wheelchair pushed by a male nurse. He had famously boasted in a poem of his perfect health, but a series of strokes—"whacks," he called them—had partly paralyzed him, while digestive and excretive disorders gave him what he described as a "soggy, wet, sticky" feeling, as of tar oozing over him.

Still, the undeniable Whitman magnetism was there. He was wrapped in a blue overcoat, under which he wore a black dinner jacket, a natty departure from his usual plain gray one. His clean white shirt was open at the neck, and his round felt hat was pushed back on his head. His snowy hair and cascading beard created an impression of Jovian majesty. Tiny wrinkles seamed his face, but his pink complexion gave him a deceptive air of health. His gray-blue eyes, their large lids drooping, had a look of tired wisdom and stolid impassivity. The high-arched eyebrows made him seem slightly surprised.

He had reason to be surprised now. Although he had helped organize the event, he could not have anticipated the standing ovation that greeted him or the reverent silence that was maintained as he was wheeled to his head position at the axis of the tables. As his chair was pushed through the room by his nurse, Ed Wilkins, an African-American cook ran up to him and seized his hand, thanking him for having nursed her husband in the Civil War hospitals.

He had meant to make only a token appearance but ended staying two to three hours. He picked flowers from a bouquet in front of him, and his weary expression disappeared as he sipped champagne. As was his custom on public occasions, he said little, preferring to take in the speeches and toasts in his honor. After the speeches, letters and telegrams from distant well-wishers were read aloud. The list of those who had sent communications was impressive, including Alfred, Lord Tennyson, Mark Twain, William Dean Howells, John Greenleaf Whittier, Robert Ingersoll, and William Michael Rossetti. One of the most perceptive messages was from his British friend, the ex-Philadelphian Mary Smith Whitall Costelloe, who wrote: "You cannot really understand America without Walt Whitman, without 'Leaves of Grass.' . . . He has expressed that civilization, 'up to date,' as he would say, and no student of the philosophy of history can do without him."

But some of the day's tributes must have made him squirm with their conventionality. How could the literary innovator and erstwhile bohemian possibly stomach this saccharine tidbit, dished up by Henry L. Bonsall:

All hail to thee! Walt Whitman! Poet, Prophet, Priest!
Celebrant of Democracy! At more than regal feast
To thee we offer homage, and our greenest bay
We crown thee Poet Laureate on this thy natal day.

The fact was, Whitman only half enjoyed events like these, which filled his final years. True, he basked in the worldwide fame that had come to him in old age. The celebrities that trekked to Camden to see him; the heartfelt letters from strangers inspired by his poetry; the inner circle of friends who idolized him; the plaudits not only from literary people but from tycoons like Andrew Carnegie, who had contributed four hundred dollars to his support—all such encouragement was welcome, particularly in light of the ridicule and neglect he had endured earlier in his career. He even took amused pride that a tobacco company had brought out a cigar with his avuncular face as its logo (see fig. 46). "Smoke Walt Whitman Cigars," the box read, "Guaranteed Cuban Hand Made."

But fame of this sort had its downside, beyond annoyances like the constant letters requesting his autograph, most of which he used to light his wood fires. The real problem was that from the start he had aimed to be more than an American institution, more than another celebrity to be ogled and feted. He had intended to be an agent of social change. "The proof of a poet," he had written in the 1855 preface to *Leaves of Grass*, "is that his country absorbs him as affectionately as he has absorbed it." This was a ringing proclamation of what he regarded as a vital, symbiotic relationship between the poet and society. He had fulfilled his role in this relationship. But had America absorbed him? Fancy fetes, the Walt Whitman cigar, and money from Andrew Carnegie were hardly what he had in mind when he had envisaged being absorbed by his country.

To be sure, he had effected real change in the realm of literature. Stylistically, he had exploded conventional patterns of rhyme and meter, freeing the poetic line to follow the organic rhythms of feeling and voice. Thematically, he had introduced a new democratic inclusiveness, absorbing images from virtually every aspect of social and cultural life.

But there, exactly, was the rub. His expansiveness and inclusiveness had never been merely a literary exercise. "I think of art," he declared, "as something to serve the people—the mass: when it fails to do that it's false to its promises." About his own poetry he said, "If Leaves of Grass is not for the average man it is for nobody." The irony was that while he was appreciated by a growing number of the educated elite, he remained, as one of his contemporaries put it, "caviare to the multitude." He was largely unread by those vibrant American masses whose concerns, attitudes, and language had provided the basis for some of his greatest poems.

When he left Morgan's Hall that stormy May evening, he took with him a rose and the memory of a grand occasion. It was not long, however, before an underlying sense of dissatisfaction would resurface. He confessed to his friend Horace Traubel* that he could never get it through his old head that he was not popular. "The people: the crowd—I have had no way of reaching them," he said. "I needed to reach the people: . . . but it's too late now." He had needed to reach the people ever since he had started writing serious poetry. He had much to tell them, about America and about themselves.

This is the story of how he absorbed his country and how he tried to make his country absorb him.

---

*Traubel, who visited Whitman almost daily between 1888 and 1892, taking extensive notes of the poet's conversations, is discussed on pp. 556–8.

1

"UNDERNEATH ALL, NATIVITY": LITERARY GENEALOGY, LITERARY GEOGRAPHY

WALT WHITMAN WAS BORN in a year of ill omens. In 1819 two phenomena destined to affect him profoundly—slavery and the economy—sprang into the national consciousness in frightening new ways. Missouri's application for statehood that year provoked the first national discussion of an issue that would eventually divide the country: Should the western territories be slave or free? A temporary solution would come the next year with the Missouri Compromise, which prohibited slavery in new territories above latitude 36° 30′, but political squabbling over the slavery issue would punctuate Whitman's childhood and prompt his heated involvement as a young politician and journalist. Deep divisions over slavery would shatter the parties, divide the churches, and lead to the bloodiest war in the nation's history. Whitman once said that the whole temper of American society before the Civil War could be summed up in one word: "convulsiveness." *Leaves of Grass* was, in part, his poetic effort to project these social convulsions while restraining them and redirecting them.

The year 1819 also witnessed the nation's traumatic awakening to the hard realities of the new market economy. Historians often point to the 1815–20 period as the time when the agrarian, household economy in America gave way to the capitalistic market system that eventually created mammoth corporations, huge private fortunes, and wide class divisions. The panic of 1819 was the first of several massive depressions in a boom-and-bust cycle that would destabilize Whitman's early years. Much of Whitman's poetry would try to come to terms with the dislocations resulting from rapid urbanization and the market revolution.

There is a strong nostalgic undercurrent in Whitman's writings, an impulse to revisit the period before his birth, when slavery and the economy were not yet problematic issues. In an 1857 newspaper article on the tumultuous state of America he called for a return to "the safe traditions of a better, a purer, and a wiser age." Elsewhere he recalled "the primitive simplicity and economy of former generations." Constantly in his poetry he returned to his family's and his nation's past in an effort to establish continuity with a bygone unified family structure and artisan work arrangements.

Personal Ancestry and National History

THE HISTORY OF the Whitman and Van Velsor families on Long Island became for him the quintessential touchstone of lost agrarian folkways. His nostalgia for his ancestors and their rural Long Island surroundings appeared early in his poetry and intensified as time passed. We may perhaps dismiss as a vagary of old age the signs of ancestor worship in the late Camden years: on his walls, the portraits of his parents and of an old Dutch ancestor from 150 years back, or poems like "Old Salt Kossabone" and "From Montauk Point" that re-created his Long Island background. But he had been looking backward long before that. He had underscored the importance of his genealogy in his 1856 poem "By Blue Ontario's Shore":

> Underneath all, Nativity,
> I swear I will stand by my own nativity.

It was in the third (1860) edition of *Leaves of Grass* that the nostalgic impulse became particularly visible. "O, to go back to the place where I was born," he wrote in one poem. "To hear the birds once more, / To ramble about the house and barn and over the fields once more, / And through the orchard and along the old lanes once more." He featured his Long Island roots in the poem "Proto-Leaf," which begins "fond of fish-shape Paumanok, where I was born." In the 1881 edition he added these autobiographical lines to "Song of Myself":

> My tongue, every atom of my blood, form'd from this soil, this air,
> Born here of parents born here from parents the same, and their
>   parents the same.

What is striking about these passages is their almost desperate affirmation of continuity with the past: "parents the same, and their parents the same." In truth, neither Whitman nor his parents were "the same" as their ancestors, for they were confronted by social complexities unknown to previous generations. His own family was typical of many nineteenth-century families disrupted by immense cultural changes, with a problematic father and siblings destined to become geographically dispersed and darkened by insanity, alcoholism, and early death.

Whitman's ancestors, by contrast, typified the unified stem family of America's rural past. It was this sense of family continuity that intrigued him. When at age sixty-two he revisited the old family burial hill on Long Island, he mused: "My whole family history, with its succession of links, from the first settlement down to date, told here—three centuries concentrate on this sterile acre." In both his life and his writings, Whitman showed a persistent instinct to keep strong this "succession of links" with his family's past.

Although some amount of idealization inevitably tinged his nostalgia, there had in fact been a certain symmetry to his genealogy that justified his longing for bygone stability. He often mentioned his dual ancestry—English on his father's side, Dutch on his mother's. Both the Whitman and the Van Velsor clans had settled in an area, central Long Island, where these two distinct cultures mingled: the island had been settled from the east by the English and from the west by the Dutch. Whitman identified certain traits within himself that he believed came from each side. From the "maternal nativity-stock" he thought he derived a "Hollandisk" firmness and endurance, from the "paternal English elements" a certain obstinacy and willfulness. Such racial stereotyping is important less for its accuracy than for what it tells us about his priorities. The words he used to describe his ancestors always connoted firmness, solidity, longevity. He could generalize that his ancestors as a whole were "a stalwart, massive, heavy, long-lived race."

When we look at his family tree, we find stem families typical of precapitalist American culture. Until about 1815 most Americans produced on their farms most of the goods they consumed and used, instead of buying them in an impersonal marketplace. This subsistence culture was characterized by large, cohesive families living in a central homestead that was passed down through the generations. Besides living off the land, the families remained geographically close. Although the family structure was patriarchal, women assumed a substantial role in the production of household goods. Family members were unified even in death, for they rested together in large family graveyards.

The Whitmans on Long Island were the prototypical stem family living in a subsistence arrangement. The poet traced his lineage to John Whitman, who came over from England on the *True Love* in 1640 and lived in Weymouth, Massachusetts. Also aboard the *True Love*, on the same voyage or a slightly later one, was John's brother Zechariah, who settled in Milford, Connecticut. Zechariah's son, Joseph, born about 1640 (presumably in England), had lived in Stratford, Connecticut, as early as 1655 and within five years relocated across the sound to Huntington, Long Island, where he established the Whitmans as a family of prominence. In Huntington he served variously as constable, grandjuryman, commissioner, and inspector of local leather. He also acquired large land-holdings. In 1672 the town leaders settled a dispute over lands along the border of Huntington and Smithtown by dividing them into "Ten Farms," one of which went to Joseph Whitman. This attractive property became known as Joseph Whitman's Great Hollow, later Whitmanvale, and finally Commack. Portions of this land would remain in the Whit-man family for 240 years, from 1672 to 1912. Joseph's holdings grew even larger in 1698 when, with three of his sons, he bought a deed to Baiting Place Purchase, later Lower Melville. Three other sons also accumulated lands in the area.

Small wonder that the Whitman ancestors would remain for Walt and his siblings the embodiment of bygone stability. Walt's neurotic sister Hannah, in an odd but telling fantasy, boasted late in life that the Whitmans had once "owned Long Island from neck to neck." Walt him-self, although less given than she to exaggeration, recalled with interest the prosperity the Whitman family reached with Joseph's grandson Ne-hemiah, who ran a farm of some five hundred acres in the West Hills area of Huntington. Describing Nehemiah, the poet wrote, "My father's grandfather was quite a large territorial owner in that part of Long Is-land, and also on the southern shore of that town."

Born in 1718 or '19, Nehemiah lived in what would become the fam-ily homestead, a heavily timbered story-and-a-half house with four fireplaces on the first floor. Across the road from the house was a barn and a huge orchard. The land sloped gently east and south, about a tenth of it wooded, with many old trees. Walt particularly enjoyed hearing about Nehemiah's wife, Phoebe (better known as Sarah), an energetic, determined woman who chewed tobacco, swore liberally, and rode through the farm on horseback, directing the slaves who tilled the land.

The last of the substantial Whitman landholders in West Hills was Nehemiah and Phoebe's son, Jesse W. Whitman, the poet's grandfather. Jesse inherited the farm and family home. His estate, left to his sons Jesse, Walter, and Treadwell and a daughter, Sarah, would be sold and dissipated by them. Walt never knew his grandfather Jesse but had fond recollections of his grandmother Hannah Brush Whitman, who lived un-til he was sixteen. Lively, attractive, and shrewd, she had once been a schoolteacher and was an accomplished needlewoman. An orphan, she had been given practical training by her aunt, Vashiti Platt, who had owned a large farm in eastern Long Island.

Whitman's distant genealogy on his mother's side is obscure. It is not known when or why the Van Velsors originally came to Long Island; according to one report, they descended from a Dutch noble family that fled Holland for America after the monarchy of William the Orange was overthrown. By the late eighteenth century the Van Velsors had established a large farm between the seaport town of Cold Spring Harbor and nearby Woodbury, not far from the Whitman land. The Van Velsor homestead was a rambling, gray-shingled house with sheds, pens, and a large barn. It was here that Walt's mother, Louisa Van Velsor, was born in 1795. Until late in life Walt vividly recalled the Van Velsor homestead, "where every spot had been familiar to me as a child and youth." His maternal grandmother, Naomi (Amy), was a mild, genial Quaker woman whose death in 1826 was one of the great sorrows of his youth. His grandfather, the jovial, red-faced Major Cornelius Van Velsor, with a booming voice and colorful personality, raised and bred horses, which the young Walt sometimes rode on Saturdays. Often as a boy Walt sat beside the major on his large farm wagon as he made the forty-mile ride across tortuous roads to Brooklyn to deliver produce.

Whitman's ancestry can be pointed to as a source not only of his poetic paeans to agrarian values and artisan labor but also of his interest in the American Revolution. From his grandmother Hannah Whitman he heard stirring stories of his ancestors' involvement with the patriot side in the war. Since Long Island was held by the British for the whole war, the Whitman and Van Velsor homesteads were in constant peril. Enemy squadrons anchored in nearby Huntington Harbor and camped all over the area, foraging whenever they chose. Hannah told Walt of "the most horrible excesses—enough to make one's blood boil." One day she was curtly told to get a bedroom in her home ready for a ranking British officer, who never showed up. The Van Velsor home was terrorized as well. Once British soldiers appeared there, demanding a horse. They went to the barn and took a sorrel mare. The enraged Cornelius, then a young man, was restrained from retaliating by his wife and sisters until he finally broke away and seized the horse by the reins as they were leading it off. The soldiers threateningly raised their rifles but then backed down.

By far the most important event in the Revolution for Whitman was the Battle of Brooklyn, the first avowed battle for independence in the war. Throughout his writings we find what may be called reified models: exemplary persons, events, or concepts that are repeatedly made concrete in literary images. The Battle of Brooklyn was one such model.

Whitman had a family connection to the battle. One of his granduncles, a son of Nehemiah Whitman, had fought and had died in the losing American effort. Whitman could feel, then, that the battle was virtually part of his family history.

Heroic martyrdom and national unity were the principal values he associated with the battle. For the Americans, the engagement had been doomed from the start. There was little prospect of victory for the heavily outnumbered patriots. The invading troops from England, Scotland, and the Germanic principalities numbered 45,000, the Americans under Washington only 12,000. In the summer of 1776 General Howe had anchored three hundred vessels—more than twice the number in the Spanish Armada—off Staten Island, where he established a huge military camp in preparation for a tremendous invasion, which he hoped would be a deathblow to the patriot cause. The invasion was launched on August 22 at Denyse Ferry and Gravesend Bay, and within five days the British had won. The main fighting occurred on August 27, when 15,000 British moved toward Jamaica Pass. The victory proved useful to the British, since it gave them control of Long Island for the duration of the war.

Symbolically, however, the rebels could claim a kind of victory. Though some of the American officers had made strategic mistakes, the troops, particularly the Maryland Brigade, had fought with sterling courage in the face of overwhelming odds. Their bombardment of the British from hill encampments like Fort Greene had inflicted heavy casualties. Aided by two days of bad weather that interfered with the British invasion, Washington organized one of the deftest retreats in military history. On the night of August 29, under the cover of heavy fog, the surviving 9,300 patriots were taken in fishing boats across the East River to Manhattan. Washington was the last to cross over. When he gathered his troops two days later, he did his best to console them.

Whitman relived this historical moment time and again in his writings, with an almost ritualistic fervor. In a corner of his capacious mind, it was always August 27, 1776; the British were always invading; the rebel troops were always dying bravely. He wrote at length about the battle in the *Brooklyn Daily Eagle*, arguing that August 27 should be as venerated a date as July 4. In "The Centenarian's Story," a poem written on the eve of the Civil War, he had a grizzly old Revolutionary War veteran describe the battle to a young soldier as they look down from Brooklyn Heights. The veteran re-created the battle as experienced by the heroic brigades from Maryland and Virginia. The poem dramatized in detail the slaughter of the battle, the Americans' anguished defeat, the retreat by night—all leading to a poetic coda that shows Whitman's undying fascination with the battle:

> See—as the annual round returns the phantoms return,
> It is 27th of August and the British have landed,
> The battle begins and goes against us, behold through the smoke
>   Washington's face,
> The brigade of Virginia and Maryland have march'd forth to
>   intercept the enemy,
> They are cut off, murderous artillery from the hills plays upon them,
> Rank after rank falls, while over them silently droops the flag,
> Baptized that day in many a young man's bloody wounds,
> In death, defeat, and sisters', mothers' tears.

It was mainly because of the Battle of Brooklyn that George Washington became one of Whitman's important models. Described in an early Whitman story as "one pure, upright character, living as a beacon in history," Washington assumed a central place in the major poem "The Sleepers," where his role in the battle and his later reunion with his troops are sentimentally embellished:

> Now of the older war-days, the defeat at Brooklyn,
> Washington stands inside the lines, he stands on the intrench'd hills
>   amid a crowd of officers,
> His face is cold and damp, he cannot repress the weeping drops, [. . .]
> The same at last and at last when peace is declared,
> He stands in the room of the old tavern, the well-belov'd soldiers all
>   pass through,
> The officers speechless and slow draw near in their turns,
> The chief encircles their necks with his arms and kisses them on the
>   cheek,
> He kisses lightly the wet cheeks one after another, he shakes hands
>   and bids good-by to the army.

Whitman was as obsessed by the grim aftermath of the battle as by the battle itself. After their victory, the British had used Brooklyn's Wallabout Bay as the mooring place for a dozen rotting hulks used as prison ships throughout the war. Conditions in these floating hells were atrocious. Starvation, disease, and lack of ventilation ravaged the American prisoners. Some twelve thousand died in the course of the war. Each morning the dead were passed out and taken to the Brooklyn shore for burial in shallow graves, often to be washed out by the next tide. As a boy in Brooklyn, Whitman sometimes came across the bones of prison-ship victims in the Wallabout sands.

The ships became the subject for some of Whitman's most jingoistic poetic passages. On July 2, 1846, as editor of the *Eagle*, he published an ode to the prisoners, intended to be sung at Independence Day celebra-tions to the tune of "The Star-Spangled Banner." The ode's repeated re-frain sang praise to "The battle, the prison-ship, martyrs and hill," with grisly emphasis on the prisoners' remains: "Mark well their crumbled-in coffins, their white, holy bones." By the time he reached old age, Whitman had come to regard the prison ships as little less than the source of American culture, as evidenced by his 1888 poem "The Walla-bout Martyrs":

> Greater than memory of Achilles or Ulysses,
> More, more by far to thee than tomb of Alexander,
> Those cart loads of old charnel ashes, scales and splints of mouldy
>   bones,
> Once living men—once resolute courage, aspiration, strength,
> The stepping stones to thee to-day and here, America.

Given Whitman's interest in the Battle of Brooklyn, it is understand-able that he was one of the chief activists for a monument commemorat-ing the event. It was largely due to his editorials in the *Eagle* in the late 1840s that public support for the monument gained momentum, re-sulting in 1855 in a public resolution to rebury the prisoners' bones. Eventually his efforts would be rewarded by the construction of the Prison Ship Martyrs' Monument, at 148 feet still the world's tallest Doric column.

The ultimate significance of the Battle of Brooklyn and other Revo-lutionary War moments for Whitman was that they embodied an ideal of union. The very use of the Revolution as a model event had power-fully unifying implications. During the pre–Civil War period one of the few things such disparate groups as Northern Free-Soilers and Southern fire-eaters, conservative Whigs and radical Locofocos, had in common was their retrospective veneration of the American Revolution. Hoping to affirm the American spirit of revolt while maintaining the integrity of the Union, Whitman in the 1855 preface harked back to "the haughty defiance of '76, and the war and peace and formation of the constitution . . . . the union always surrounded by blatherers and always calm and impregnable." The fact that Southerners and Northerners had fought side by side in the Revolution was important for Whitman, who took every opportunity in his poetry to affirm national unity to counteract sectional divisions. He deemphasized the often contradictory meanings that various groups drew from the Revolution; for instance, Southerners' use of it as a model for revolt against the North, versus Free-Soilers' use of it as a guide for challenging the Southern slave power. He established between the competing political interpretations of the Revolution a humanistic, poetic middle ground, stressing the bravery of Northerners and Southerners united against a common enemy, and the tears of a very human Washington as he gathered his soldiers in comradely embrace.

To Whitman privately, the Revolution signified an intersection of his private history with his nation's history. His granduncle's death in the Brooklyn engagement and his own viewing of the Wallabout prisoners' bones made the Revolution a pungent fusion of the private and the social. On this level, Washington hugging his troops becomes for Whitman a kind of ideal private father (a poetic substitute, perhaps, for his own less-than-ideal father), who at the same time was a father of the nation.

West Hills, Long Island

IF IN HIS POETRY Whitman was trying to reconnect with his ancestral and national past, he was also inscribing his own experience as one of eight children of Walter and Louisa Whitman in West Hills and Brooklyn.

Exploring Whitman's early physical environment and parentage contributes to an understanding of him, particularly since both factors were highlighted in the educational and scientific philosophies that he accepted and that shaped his poetry. He viewed his own childhood from the perspective of then-current theories about environmental and parental influence, much the way today one might view one's formative years through the lens of Freud. Modern critics have often turned the Freudian lens on Whitman, with mixed results. For an understanding of the familial images in his poetry from his own perspective, it is useful to resurrect the theories of childhood influence that were as much gospel to him as Freud or Lacan are to many today.

Progressive educational and psychological theorists in Whitman's time dismissed the Calvinistic doctrines of predestination and human depravity. Swept up in nineteenth-century liberalism, they embraced the idea of the perfectibility of human nature. For the educators, environment and training were the all-determining factors; for the scientists, inherited traits and parental self-regulation. The two views, though not mutually exclusive, came into competition in the late 1840s. Whitman, intimately aware of both, reconciled them in his poetry and used them to work out imaginatively some of the more problematic aspects of his immediate family history.

The geography of his childhood was a lifelong reference point for the poet who accepted the environmental theories of liberal educators. Locke's notion of tabula rasa became for the educators the rationale for an outlook that stressed the role of environment. Many of Whitman's newspaper editorials of the 1840s echoed this theory, calling for careful control of both physical and emotional factors affecting the child. Horace Mann, an educational leader Whitman greatly respected, had written of the effect of surroundings on the child: "Their influences are integrated and made one with the soul. They enter into spiritual combination with it, never afterwards to be wholly decompounded. They are like the daily food eaten by wild game,—so pungent and saporific in its nature, that it flavors every fibre of their flesh, and colors every bone in their body." This outlook reveals the same kind of sensibility as that behind these famous lines:

> There was a child went forth every day,
> And the first object he look'd upon, that object he became,
> And that object became part of him for the day or a certain part of
>   the day,
> Or for many years or stretching cycles of years.

What did the child Whitman see as he went forth every day? How was he formed by his surroundings?

Just as there had been a symmetry about Whitman's ancestry—two stem families of different backgrounds meeting in the same geographical area—so there was a centrality about the place where Whitman was born: at the very heart of Long Island. "[T]*he successive growth stages of my infancy, childhood, youth and manhood," he wrote, "were all pass'd on Long Island, which I sometimes feel as if I had incorporated." Although the family moved to Brooklyn just before he turned four, he spent many summers with his grandmothers on their Long Island farms, and over the years he tramped much of the island by foot. The island stretches 125 miles east of Manhattan, like a huge fish with its head pointed toward the city and its two tail fins (the North and South Forks) toward Europe. The north shore of the island is on the Connecticut

---

*Brackets around an individual letter usually, as here, signify a capitalization change from the original text, indicating that I have put a lower-case letter in upper case, or vice versa. In other instances, brackets indicate the addition of a letter not present in the original. For an explanation of brackets around ellipses, see Notes, p. 591.

Sound, with picturesque bays and areas of small, wooded hills. A sandy glacial plain slopes away from the hills to the south shore, which has long white beaches on the Atlantic, protecting a chain of bays.

The island's population in Whitman's time was an unusual mix of different cultures, combining elements from both Puritan New England and Dutch New York. In 1640 Puritans from New England had settled Southampton on the east end of the island and over the next century moved steadily west, establishing New England–like villages throughout what is now Suffolk County. Meanwhile, the Dutch who settled Manhattan and Brooklyn (then "Breuckelen") established farms and villages over the western half of the island.

Was there a distinct Long Island type? Whitman thought so. He once sketched plans for a poem to be written about "*Long Island Character.*— Draw the Long Island character different from the New England—the Middle states—or any of the Southern states—." From his journalism we can glean some qualities he saw in the Long Island character: gruffness, oddness, independence, geniality. He wrote that "the island was worthy of long study, and the folks too—queer folks with strong personalities." His lifelong habit of hailing everyone he met he attributed to a friendly Long Island custom. His brash yet warmly inclusive poetic persona doubtless owed much to the farmers and baymen he knew in his youth.

In his day Long Island was almost totally rural. For him it would always remain the virtual synonym of nature. "Me pleas'd, rambling in lanes and country fields, Paumanok's fields," he wrote in one poem. In 1820, a stage leaving the western village of Jamaica at 10:30 a.m. would not reach Oyster Pond (now Orient Point) on the east end, 105 miles away, until 6:00 p.m. the next day. It would pass through some Dutch farms into the huge expanse of meadow and grazing land known as the Great Hempstead Plain, and then, after a night's stopover in the wooded center of the island, proceed on to several other small villages until it reached Oyster Pond.

West Hills, three to four miles south of Huntington village, has a special importance in Long Island history because for many years it was a travelers' hub of the island. At West Hills the Old Post Road extending from Brooklyn to the east end intersected with the South Path connecting Huntington with Amityville and the south shore. Around 1810 the principal intersection was relocated slightly southward when a new road was built on a route similar to that of the present Long Island Expressway. But the old intersection through West Hills remained an important alternate route that provided easy access to other parts of the island. The singer of the open road was literally born near an open road.

He was also born near an important knoll. Not far from his birth-place was Jayne's Hill, at 428 feet the tallest spot on Long Island. The hill commanded a vista of the sound to the north, farms and hills to the east, the plains to the west, and, on clear days, a blue strip of the distant Atlantic to the south. The ocean's faint rumble could sometimes be heard at night. When the poet revisited West Hills in old age he gave this account of the hill: "I write this back again in West Hills on the high elevation (the highest spot on Long Island?) of Jayne's Hill which we have reached by a fascinating winding road. A view of thirty or forty or even fifty or more miles, especially to the east and south and southwest; the Atlantic Ocean to the latter points in the distance—a glimpse or so of Long Island Sound to the north."

The hill, the road, and the vista of his childhood give an autobiographical ring to this famous passage in "Song of Myself":

> [E]ach man and each woman of you I lead upon a knoll,
> My left hand hooking you round the waist,
> My right hand pointing to landscapes of continents and the public
>   road.

With its proximity to the island's main road and highest hill, West Hills was a kind of metonymy of the island itself, whose best features were within easy reach.

And the island, with its varied geography and pronounced mix of racial and religious groups, was a kind of metonymy of America. There was both a literal and metaphorical sense to Whitman's emblematic use of "Paumanok" in his poetry. He could slide with remarkable ease from the autobiographical to the fictive:

> Starting from fish-shape Paumanok where I was born,
> Well-begotten, and rais'd by a perfect mother,
> After roaming many lands, lover of populous pavements,
> Dweller in Mannahatta my city, or on southern savannas,
> Or a soldier camp'd or carrying my knapsack and gun, or a miner in
>   California,
> Or rude in my home in Dakota's woods [. . .]

In reality, Whitman never roamed "many lands" nor mined in California nor lived in the Dakota woods. But Long Island, with its racial and geographical diversity, had predisposed him to jump gleefully into such buoyant fictions. Symbolically, he was always "[s]tarting from fish-shape Paumanok," moving from the authentic "I" born at the center of Long Island to the representative "I" who embraced all America.

Long Island was a metonymy of America in more ways than one: it embodied its cruelties as well as its beauties. Here as elsewhere a rich Native American culture had been supplanted by encroaching Europeans. At one time, Long Island had been inhabited by many tribes: Canarsies, Rockaways, Nesquakes, Matinecocks, Setaukets, Patchogues, Shinnecocks, Montauks, Manhassets. Among the Native American names for the island were Sewanhacky (island of shells), Meitowax (country of the ear-shell), and Wamponamon (at the east). Paumanake (land of tribute) was the name used by some of the east end tribes. The original deed to the Easthampton settlers assigned this name to the island, and the chiefs of the Montauk and Shelter Island tribes were styled Sachems of Paumanacke. By Whitman's day, some of the tribes had been displaced; others had disappeared altogether. They left behind their names (to this day used as place-names throughout the island) and arrowheads that were unearthed by children at play.

Relations between Native Americans and whites, however, were not as strained on the island as in New England. The Dutch and English skirmished as their settlements neared each other, and each side tried to befriend the natives in order to enlist their support against the other side. Some of the tribes, especially the Montauks and Shinnecocks, remained active and visible through the nineteenth century and beyond. For Whitman, Native American culture had an intrinsic attraction because it embodied a closeness to the elements that much of his poetry tried to recover. The modern Native American poet Joseph Bruchac sees in Whitman "much which reminds me of the American Indian way of looking at the world, of *being* in the world and not just *observing* it." Bruchac points to Whitman's celebration of the earth, precise namings, and quality of incantation.

Many Romantic writers, of course, were drawn to the ideals of primitivism and the Rousseauesque noble savage. But few had been raised in an area so rich in Native American lore as Whitman's. The kind of simple subsistence culture he saw exemplified in his own ancestors was even more pronounced among Native Americans, who quintessentially exemplified the subsistence way of life. Their rootedness in the earth was enacted in picture-words like "Paumanok" and "Mannahatta" (originally "Manahatin," the hill island) that the poet adopted. The place of his birth was originally inhabited by the important Matinecock tribe, the name variously meaning "at the hilly land," "at the place of observation," and "at the place to search, to look around from." A poignant blending of Native American culture, his ancestry, and nostalgia for lost folkways appears in the passage in "The Sleepers" where he describes a Native American woman who once appeared at the old Van Velsor homestead, stayed the day with his mother, then disappeared into the woods.

Long Island was emblematic of America in yet another respect: it made allowance for the institution of chattel slavery. Whitman's acceptance of certain aspects of this institution can be explained in part by the background of slavery on Long Island. Slavery was introduced to the island in 1660 and was not abolished until 1828, when Walt was nine. As late as 1810, nearly every major Dutch landowner in Kings County owned one or more slaves. The same was true of most English farmers on the eastern half of the island. Manumission of slaves was far more common on Long Island than in the South. A slave was often granted freedom upon request at the owner's death. Slaves typically spoke the language of the family; most in western Long Island spoke Dutch.

Whitman had come to terms with the fact that several of his ancestors, like others on the island, were slave owners. He recalled, "We all kept slaves on Long Island—up to the early part of this century." His great-grandfather Nehemiah Whitman not only owned slaves but willed to his wife "the use of the negro girl during her lifetime and after her decease to be sold and the money divided as the rest of my moveable estate." Vashiti Platt, the woman who had raised Walt's grandmother Amy, owned sixteen slaves, preparing Amy herself to manage the slaves owned by Cornelius Van Velsor. As was generally true throughout Long Island, the Whitman and Van Velsor slaves generally stayed in the kitchens of the homesteads. Whitman's first biographer, John Burroughs, described the Whitman slaves grouped around the roaring fire and eating Indian pudding and milk. In old age Walt recalled that one of his closest companions in his youth was a liberated West Hills slave named Old Mose: "He was very genial, correct, manly, and [a]cute, and a great friend of my childhood."

The poet's nostalgia for his ancestors' ways would later make him tolerant of the South. His complex views of race and slavery, which are important to an understanding of his poetry, are contextualized elsewhere in this book. For now it is sufficient to note that, despite periods of antislavery activism, he always maintained a lurking sympathy for the South. He once said: "I must admit that my instinct of friendship towards the South is almost more than I like to confess." A reason for this sympathy was that the South remained an agrarian-based economy much longer than the North, where manufacturing and urbanization rose rapidly in the antebellum period. By extension, the South became blended in his mind with the social arrangements of his ancestors. These arrangements included slavery. Perhaps this is why sometimes in his poetry the South's peculiar institution takes on an agrarian, almost picturesque quality:

> There are the negroes at work in good health, the ground in all
>   directions cover'd with pine straw,
> In Tennessee and Kentucky slaves busy in the coalings, at the forge,
>   by the furnace-blaze, or at the corn-shucking,
> In Virginia, the planter's son returning after a long absence, joyful
>   welcom'd and kiss'd by the aged mulatto nurse.

Whitman was more troubled by slavery and his genealogy than such passages indicate. To see how he tried to accommodate gaps or contradictions in his background, it is useful to turn to his immediate family.

"Parentage Is Everything"

"THE TIME OF MY BOYHOOD was a very restless and unhappy one," Whitman once confessed. "I did not know what to do."

This was, to be sure, a generalization made in a sour moment; at various times he came up with happy memories of his youth. The profile that emerges is one of a family shaken by sudden social changes and a traumatized son who eventually sought explanation and solace in contemporary theories of childhood influence, theories that he redistributed in his poetry.

Parentage was an essential part of Whitman's self-identity largely because he accepted the findings of hereditarian science, a precursor of eugenics. In the late 1840s, just as he was discovering his poetic powers, the Lockean notion of environmental influence began to give way in scientific circles to the doctrine of the inheritability of acquired characteristics. For Whitman *both* environment and parentage were crucial shaping influences.

It is no accident that he particularly underscored the role of parentage in the first three editions of *Leaves of Grass*, for it was then that hereditarian science was in the first flush of its popularity. The New York scientific publishing house Fowlers and Wells, distributor of the first edition of *Leaves of Grass* and publisher of the second, had in the decade before 1855 published several books that gave high visibility to the notion of inherited traits. Orson Fowler's *Love and Parentage* (1851), which went through forty editions of a thousand copies each, put the doctrine unequivocally, capitalizing key words: "Education is something, but PARENTAGE is EVERYTHING; because it 'DYES IN THE WOOL,' and thereby exerts an influence on character almost infinitely more powerful than all other conditions put together." By what Fowler called the law of hereditary descent, "progeny *inherits* the constitutional na-

tures and characters, mental and physical, of parents, including . . . pre-
dispositions to consumption, insanity, all sorts of diseases, &c., as well as
longevity, strength, stature, looks, disposition, talents." To illustrate the
idea, Fowler devoted a whole book, *Hereditary Descent* (1847), to tracing
the family histories of scores of known and unknown people. Whitman,
who sold Fowlers and Wells books in his home bookstore in the early
1850s, doubtless came across Fowler's flattering portrait of one of his own
ancestors, John Whitman.

Along with this doctrine went a belief in the improvability of the
race through parental self-control. That is, parents could change them-
selves by regulating their own behavior, and this change would have
happy results in the moral and physical well-being of their children.
Another element of this outlook was that certain races had specific, iden-
tifiable characteristics.

Some version of all these tenets can be found throughout Whitman's
writings. Borrowing the vocabulary of hereditary descent, Whitman in
the 1855 preface writes, "To him the hereditary countenance descends
both father's and mother's." Traits like prudence and caution, he contin-
ues, are "parts of the greatest poet from his birth out of his mother's
womb and from her birth out of her mother's." On some level, parentage
was "everything" for him just as it was for the scientists. If in reality he
could not change his parents, in poetry he constantly reinvented them
and—by the law of hereditary descent—himself.

The checkered story of Whitman's immediate family is one that was
played out repeatedly in America in the opening decades of the nine-
teenth century. Several leading writers of the American Renaissance
had fathers who were either rigid, distant, or victims of early death.
One thinks of Emerson's father, who died when Waldo was eight, or Mel-
ville's, who died bankrupt and apparently insane when Herman was
thirteen, or Hawthorne's, dead by the time Nathaniel was four, or Dick-
inson's, who kept an authoritarian distance from the children. The phe-
nomenon extended well beyond literary circles. Among those who
suffered from cruel or distant fathers were some of the age's leading so-
cial or religious radicals, including William Lloyd Garrison, Andrew
Jackson Davis, Gerrit Smith, and James Freeman Clarke. Often, as was
true with Emerson, Melville, and Hawthorne, the failed father was com-
pensated for by supportive mothers and sisters. Typical was the reformer
Thomas Wentworth Higginson, whose father went bankrupt and died
young, leaving him in the hands of his mothers and sisters. Another radi-
cal, Henry Blackwell, spoke for many when he declared, "All that I am
I owe to women."

In Whitman's case as in many others, the phenomenon of the failed father and idealized mother had much to do with sudden changes brought about by the market revolution. The story of Walter and Louisa Whitman's experiences in rural Long Island and Brooklyn is a case history in early nineteenth-century dislocation.

Walter Whitman was born on July 14, 1789: Bastille Day. The coincidence was not lost on Walt, who took an interest in the revolutionary writers and thinkers of eighteenth-century France. His father's opinions of the French philosophes are unknown, but we can guess that they were positive, for he was a freethinking democrat attracted to rationalists like Thomas Paine and Fanny Wright. Raised in Huntington on what remained of the old Nehemiah Whitman lands, Walter by fifteen was apprenticed in Brooklyn to a relative who was a carpenter and woodworker. In three years he was back in West Hills housebuilding and chopping wood for local residents. He also took up farming. In June 1816 he was married to Louisa Van Velsor, and they moved into a house in West Hills he had built some six years earlier. A moderate-sized two-story house with cedar shingles, it had a kitchen wing and a barn and sheds nearby (see fig. 7). Three of their children were born there: Jesse, on March 2, 1818; Walter (later called Walt to distinguish him from his father) on May 31, 1819; and Mary Elizabeth on February 3, 1821. The house was on a tract of sixty acres that Walter Whitman at first leased and then bought at a sheriff's sale from Gilbert Valentine on April 21, 1821, three years before taking the family to Brooklyn.

Walter Whitman was a moody, taciturn man with a knack for ill success. A photograph of him (see fig. 5) shows a strong face with a large nose, full lips, intense eyes, hollowed cheeks. He looked a bit like Emerson, but there the resemblance stopped, for he had little of the Concord sage's equanimity. Walt once told his friend John Burroughs that his father had had periods of heavy drinking. Doubtless his temperament was at least partly captured in these famous lines:

> The father, strong, self-sufficient, manly, mean, anger'd, unjust,
> The blow, the quick loud word, the tight bargain, the crafty lure.

Some have suggested that Walt Whitman was locked in Oedipal conflict with his father and worked out his neuroses in his poetry. But his relationship with his father was more complicated than this. On some level, he felt a deep kinship with him. His brother George once declared, "His relations with his father were always friendly, always good." George's comments are borne out by Walt's own statements about his father, most of which were in fact affectionate. In old age he liked to repeat stories of his father's love for children and cattle; on trips from town he would load his wagon with children from the road and give them a lift. His artisan work habits had a lasting significance for the poet, who recalled, "My good daddy used to say: 'Oh! what a comfort it is to lie down on your own floor, a floor laid with your own hands, in a house which represents your own handiwork—cellar and walls and roof!'" The poet assimilated many of his father's freethinking and democratic sympathies; he liked to say his father had known Tom Paine in his youth.

The restlessness and unhappiness Whitman associated with his childhood had less to do with a uniformly hostile relationship with his father than with his family's unstable position in the changing economic and social order. The pressures of the market economy disrupted the American family, as a new emphasis was placed on mobility and risk. For the family of Walter Whitman these pressures were particularly great because the father was a man out of his times, a Jeffersonian rationalist in an age of ascendant religious revivalism, a lackluster businessman when shrewdness was the order of the day. The "tight bargain" and "crafty lure" mentioned in Whitman's poem are descriptive less of his father than of the often brutal market realities he faced.

When on May 27, 1823 (four days before Walt's fourth birthday), Walter Whitman took his pregnant wife and three young children from West Hills to seek fortune in Brooklyn, he had every reason to anticipate success as a builder of small frame houses. Brooklyn was in the early phase of its rapid expansion from a rural village to a major American city. Real estate in the village was valued at more than two million dollars. Housing starts for frame dwellings averaged more than 130 a year and were rising. To meet the demands of a growing population, cheap houses were erected on small lots. Skilled carpenters were in demand. In the nation as whole, carpenters would fare well during the antebellum period.

Why, then, did Walter Whitman fail? Fail he did, perhaps even more dramatically than has been heretofore acknowledged. Previous biographers have described a "buy, build, and sell" pattern in Walter Whitman's business dealings, suggesting that through speculation he at least kept his head above water. Real estate records show that the picture was not that rosy. Between May 1823, when the Whitmans arrived in Brooklyn, and the summer of 1833, when they went back to the country, they moved at least seven times. But in this period there were only two recorded *purchases* of land by Walter Whitman; the rest of his transactions were leases or subleases. Both purchases occurred early in the period and were only six months apart, on September 1, 1824, for a lot on Johnson Street and on March 1, 1825, for another on Tillary and Adams. Even these transactions were ill fated. As Walt would recall, the houses his father built on the Johnson and Tillary streets lots "were mortgaged and we lost them." Walter Whitman's failure to buy other real estate indicates severe financial distress, particularly since by 1831 he seems to have been renting the Tillary Street property he had owned and lost.

These failures may never be fully explained, but they can be seen in context. The building trade was going through momentous changes just at the time Walter Whitman was trying to establish himself. The past approach to housebuilding, by which construction parts were custom designed by an individual builder for each unit, gave way in the 1820s to the more modern technique of prefabricated parts installed by specialized workers who were often coordinated by contractors. The movement toward prefab design would accelerate in the thirties with the advent of balloon framing, involving vertical studs and crosspieces quickly installed by framers. Prefab construction made entry into the building craft far easier than before and opened the way for canny contractors who scrambled for cheap labor in specialized areas like window installation, framing, and so on. The poet's memory of his father's delight in living in a house whose floor, roof, cellars, and walls were all built with "your own hands" and represented "your own handiwork" points to Walter Whitman's devotion to the personalized building techniques that were becoming fast outmoded in the 1820s.

There were larger reasons for Walter Whitman's travails. He was a blunt-spoken worker accustomed to honest self-sufficiency in a time when the market was calling for new traits: slickness and self-promotion, with more than a dash of craft. He might love cattle, children, and living under his own roof, but what he needed in the new environment was an eye for the deal. Like his poet son, he seems to have had his head always half-turned backward at his ancestors' subsistence way of life. Indeed, he would abandon the busy Brooklyn scene in the 1830s, return to Long Island, and resume farming and carpentering in tiny villages, eventually to return to Brooklyn to make another half-hearted stab at housebuilding. The poet's nostalgia for the premodern artisan economy was on some level linked with affection for his father. A difference between the two was that Walt would learn well those devices of self-advertisement which the modern way demanded and which his father, either by inability or disinclination, did not adopt.

For the young Walt, his father's economic vacillations gave him an early exposure to issues of class and politics that later would flower in his political journalism and, differently, in his poetry. The economic depression that coincided with Walt's birth signaled the advent not only of a new kind of economy but also of a new kind of politics.

Few social phenomena would affect Whitman so deeply as the Second Party System, whose origins can be traced to the year of his birth. In the three years before 1819, the old division between the agrarian Jeffersonian Republicans and the business-oriented Hamiltonian Federalists had dwindled during the so-called Era of Good Feelings. James Monroe, the colorless Virginian who was president from 1817 to 1825, oversaw in 1817 the nation's first protective tariff and the charter of the Second Bank of the United States. In the flush years that followed, America was on an inflationary binge caused by overexpansion of the paper-money system. Soon, however, the Era of Good Feelings collapsed into a season of hard times. The dire events of 1819 would be played out repeatedly during the boom-and-bust antebellum period. While American paper money inflated, world commodity prices suddenly collapsed. Public disenchantment with paper currency caused a run on the banks for redemption in "specie," or hard money. Banks failed, and businesses followed. Unemployment and misery were widespread. The urban poor were devastated, and even rural villages had their coatless parents and naked, starving children. A New Jersey farmer expressed the general discontent: "Go where you will, your ears are continually saluted with the cry of *hard times! hard times!*"

The panic of 1819, the first "modern" American depression, provoked widespread disaffection with government and the privileged elite. Political loyalties, which had been weak in the Era of Good Feelings, intensified along class lines. Party divisions were also sharpened by the Missouri crisis. The aging Thomas Jefferson could prophetically call the slavery issue "a firebell in the night" tolling "the knell of the Union," but party leaders, accepting the Missouri Compromise, temporarily swept the issue under the rug by placing party loyalty above sectional issues. In the 1820s a crude party polarity emerged, leading in the thirties to the consolidation of the Democrats versus the Whigs.

A new breed of populist politician, feeding on working-class resentments and dreams, emerged from the 1819 panic. The plainspoken, tempestuous Andrew Jackson, the first presidential candidate of nongentry origin, had emerged from a Carolina backcountry subsistence family to become a military hero, Indian fighter, and political champion of common folk. It was among the hardworking, often hard-luck farmers and artisans like Walter Whitman that the Jacksonians formed their political base, which extended throughout much of the South and West and reached into rural areas and poor city districts in the mid-Atlantic states. The twenties, writes Arthur Schlesinger, Jr., "were a decade of discontent, born in depression, streaked with suffering and panic, shaken by bursts of violence and threats of rebellion."

As one who felt the disruptions of the decade on his very nerve endings, Walter Whitman was naturally drawn to the defenders of workers against the economic elite. He and his wife paid homage to both threatened agrarianism and ascendant populism by naming one son Thomas Jefferson Whitman and another Andrew Jackson Whitman, nodding to the heroic past with George Washington Whitman. He exposed his family to the most radical thought of the day by subscribing to the *Free Enquirer*, edited by the militant reformers Robert Dale Owen and Fanny Wright. These and other labor radicals of the decade ushered in a rhetoric class conflict, defending "productive," virtuous workers against the "idle" rich and calling for laws to aid the poor.

Both emotionally and intellectually, then, the impressionable Walt was immersed in the political ambience of class awareness that would eventually make him responsive to working-class culture in all its manifestations.

If Whitman's father has been treated too harshly by biographers, his mother (see fig. 6) has been, in general, presented, justifiably, in a mixed light. It is difficult to locate the real Louisa Van Velsor Whitman beneath the snow cover of praise the poet heaped upon her. For him, she was little less than a paragon of virtue. In an 1881 poem he called her "the ideal woman, practical, spiritual, of all of earth, life, love, to me the best." While the father in "There Was a Child Went Forth" is angry and unjust, the mother is benign:

> The mother at home quietly placing dishes on the supper-table,
> The mother with mild words, clean her cap and gown, a wholesome
>   odor falling off her person and clothes as she walks by.

Given his belief in the law of hereditary descent, it is understandable he would want to prettify the facts. To write that the poet's traits come "from his birth out of his mother's womb and from her birth out of her mother's" places tremendous emphasis on the maternal stock. "The best part of every man," he once told Traubel, "is his mother." Walt's mother was partly a construction of his own wishful imagination.

What was Louisa Van Velsor Whitman really like? Attractive, lively, imaginative, a good housekeeper and family peacemaker—but also idiosyncratic and at times querulous, penny-pinching, nervous, hypochondriac. There's ample documentation of her old-age quirks in the form of letters she wrote Walt in the 1860s and 1870s. What she was like during his childhood and young manhood is less clear. Walt recalled that she was a good storyteller and had a gift for impersonation, attributes that surely contributed to his writing talents and his love of acting.

She faced hard circumstances: financial uncertainty, her husband's moodiness, the loss of a child (a five-month-old infant died on September 14, 1826), and problems with some of the children. The early history of most of Walt's siblings is unknown, but the later records are bleak. The poet's older brother, Jesse, would lose his mind and die in an insane asylum. His beloved sister, Hannah, became neurotic, possibly psychotic. His brother Andrew became an alcoholic who died young and whose indigent wife became a streetwalker. Although it's impossible to reconstruct these siblings' early behavior, that of another—Edward, the youngest—was erratic from the start. Eddy was retarded from birth, partly crippled, and possibly epileptic. He could do only the simplest of tasks, like rocking cradles and running errands. At meals he would not stop eating unless forced to do so. Walt called him "a poor, stunted boy almost from the first," one who had "infernal, damnable fits" and who "lived in darkness, eclipsed almost from the start."

Despite his family's failings and lack of appreciation for his poetry, Walt remained powerfully devoted to the ideals of family and parentage. He confessed that on one level his feelings toward his family were "wholly loyal, even sort of tribal." His mother may have had some problematic children, but she had four—George, Mary, Jeff, Walt himself— who approached normalcy. Perhaps her most important feature, in Walt's eyes, was simply that she was a fecund, caring mother in a time when he felt motherhood was threatened. As a result of economic change and family planning, fertility rates dropped precipitously during the nineteenth century. The number of children for white American women sank from more than 7 in 1800 to fewer than 6 by 1825, 5.42 by 1850, 4.24 by 1880, to 3.54 by 1900. Walt was painfully aware of the change. In an 1857 newspaper article he lamented "this alarming sterility," citing statistics showing that "the procreative capacity of foreigners is much greater than that of natives." Because he accepted the hereditarian idea that parentage is everything, he saw in his mother a model of fecundity. According to Orson Fowler, parentage was not just an option in life, a choice among other choices. It was an absolute duty, since it meant the perpetuation and, potentially, the improvement of the race. As Fowler wrote: "We are under a *moral obligation*, solemn and imperative, *to become parents*, and thus fulfill this high function, this exalted destiny of us all; nor can they attain the perfect stature of men and women, who do not."

Whitman, never inclined to marry, had little possibility of carrying out this dictum. But he idealized his fertile mother and showed a distinct parental strain in his own life. He once boasted he had fathered six children, an obvious prevarication that was part of the same impulse that led him to say another time that he envied married men not for their wives but for their children. His siblings became like surrogate children to him, as indicated especially in his autobiographical story "My Boys and Girls." He would assume a parental role with his young male friends, many of whom called him Father or Uncle or Old Man. He even had what seemed a motherly side. Burroughs noted in him a gentle, tender quality, "something indescribable in his look, in his eye, as in that of the mother of many children."

In his poetry he returned time and again to affirmations of procreation and parenthood. He loved to imagine himself as a fecund parent with vigorous offspring. In "A Song of Joys" he pretended to be a venerable patriarch: "O the old manhood of me, my noblest joy of all! / My children and grand-children, my white hair and beard." In the next passage he switched genders: "O ripen'd joy of womanhood! O happiness at last! / I am more than eighty years of age, I am the most venerable mother." His whole conception of the poet's relationship with the nation was expressed in a metaphor of procreation. In "By Blue Ontario's Shore" he described the poet "hanging on [the nation's] neck with incomparable love, / Plunging his seminal muscle into its merits and demerits." From his perspective, great poems were the products of the interpenetration of two "parents," the poet and the nation.

If he often played the role of surrogate parent, he also sought to establish links with imagined parental figures. The terms "mother" and "father" are scattered liberally throughout his poems, applied variously to the earth, the sea, the night, the flag, the Union. There is a good amount of imaginative re-creation even in his ostensibly factual writing about his own parents. In a notebook passage, typically referring to himself in the third person, he said the foundation of his character "doubtless comes from his English fatherhood, the emotional and liberty-loving, the social, the preponderating qualities of adhesiveness, immovable gravitation and simplicity, with a certain conservatism protestantism and other traits, are unmistakably from his motherhood, and are pure Hollandic or Dutch." In this syntactically garbled sentence, it's hard to tell which qualities supposedly stem from his father and which from his mother. In a sense, though, it doesn't matter. Here and elsewhere he is mythologizing his parents, finding security in the hereditarian idea that healthy traits have been passed from them to him.

Recoiling from the restlessness of his childhood, the idiosyncrasies of his parents, and the problems of his siblings, he would continue throughout his life to fabricate comforting parental figures, including himself.

2

A BROOKLYN BOYHOOD: SIGHTS, SURROUNDINGS, INFLUENCES

No AMERICAN CITY witnessed the effects of the market revolution as dramatically as Brooklyn. A nondescript rural village of four thousand in 1810, by 1855 it had become America's fourth-largest city, with a population above two hundred thousand. Even in a period of remarkable growth nationally, Brooklyn stood out for the rapidity of its development. Whitman spent twenty-eight years of his life residing in Brooklyn—more than in any other place—and absorbed all aspects of its daily life. Its strategic location between the almost statically rural Long Island and rapidly expanding Manhattan gave it a special importance for him. "I was bred in Brooklyn," he told Traubel, "through many, many years; tasted its familiar life." At his last birthday celebration, in 1891, he told his followers that his "preparatory and inauguratory life" was that "on which everything else rests,—New York and Brooklyn, experimentation, . . . actual life from New York and Brooklyn."

When we revisit his early Brooklyn years, we find not only a salubrious physical environment but also a unique blend of cultural influences that would contribute much to his later development. By sixteen, when he left for a teaching stint on Long Island, he had been exposed to fundamental religious, literary, and political issues that would provide him with a lifetime's food for thought—and fodder for culturally representative poetry.

The Brooklyn Scene

IN AN 1857 magazine article, published not long after the second edition of *Leaves of Grass*, Whitman looked fondly back at his boyhood days in Brooklyn. Those were "events and days altogether unknown to the busy and swarming crowds of modern Brooklyn," he wrote; three decades had changed "every aspect of Brooklyn."

He was right. The Brooklyn of his youth had a crude simplicity about it that would be quickly brushed aside in its expansion. (See fig. 8 for a representation of Brooklyn shortly before the Whitmans arrived there.) American life as a whole was in the 1820s primitive in ways that are sometimes forgotten. Water came from street pumps and was carried home in wooden buckets. Slops and refuse were thrown into street gutters. In the absence of central heating and hall stoves, fires had to be lit in individual rooms. The railroad would not come until 1829; rubber overshoes and brimstone matches were introduced in 1830, the street railway in 1831, the steam press for newspapers in 1835, the icebox and the daguerreotype in 1839. Throughout his life Whitman witnessed all such innovations with the curiosity of one who had been raised without them.

The primitivism of early Brooklyn stood out particularly because of its later status as a sprawling, congested city. Even parts of Manhattan at the time were quite rural. In 1820, when the tallest building in New York was only four stories high, one could stand on Brooklyn Heights (then Clover Hill) and look clear across Manhattan and beyond the Hudson River to the distant New Jersey shore (see fig. 9). As late as 1850 Manhattan had developed uptown only about as far as Thirty-fourth Street, above which were farms and open country; even the Twenty-third Street area had a rural feel, with apple blossoms tumbling down on dirt lanes.

Brooklyn in the twenties had characteristics of a country town. As Whitman recalled in the sixties, "Brooklyn had such a rural character that it was almost one huge farm and garden in comparison with its present appearance." Pigs and chickens crowded the public thoroughfares, rooting in the garbage that was thrown in the street for the lack of systematized waste disposal. The streets themselves were largely unpaved, becoming mud soup in the winter and dust bowls in the summer. Gas street lamps were introduced in 1828 on Fulton Street but weren't widely used until much later, so that at night people had to pick their way with lanterns along streets lacking both pavement and decent sidewalks. Sanitary conditions were so poor that cholera epidemics were regular occurrences. In the absence of fire pumps, huge fires often swept through the houses and sheds. There were no large buildings other than some of the churches and the Apprentice's Library, built in 1825. Old trees shaded village streets that rapidly became country lanes as they stretched eastward, passing through the outlying farms still operated by descendants of the early Dutch settlers.

In Whitman's mind, Long Island meant nature, Manhattan commerce and culture, and Brooklyn a propitious cross of both. Long Island, he wrote, "was fertile, beautiful, well-watered, and had plenty of timbers; while Manhattan was rocks, bare, bleak, without anything to recommend it except situation for commercial purposes, which is without rival in the world." Brooklyn was a middle ground between the two, with access to both. In his words, "Indeed, it is doubtful there is a city in the world with a better situation for beauty, or for utilitarian purposes." New York was fifteen minutes away by ferry. The names of many distant Long Island towns, half of them Indian and half of them English, were listed on a tremendous sign in Brooklyn that hung outside the Fulton Street tavern and stage house run by the stout, hearty Coe Downing; the sign was long an exotic memory for Whitman.

One of his main metaphors for the poet would be that of the joiner: joiner of sections of the nation, of different nations and peoples, of the past and the future. This metaphor of joining was rooted partly in his early experiences in Brooklyn. The years of his first stay in Brooklyn, 1823–35, were a moment of uneasy truce between Brooklyn and Manhattan, which over the years had a history of smoldering enmity.

Until 1816 Manhattan controlled the East River ferries and the Brooklyn shore as a result of a crown grant from colonial days. When Brooklyn incorporated as a village that year, it won some of these rights, but there remained a legacy of resentment against the domination of the city, and control of the ferry crossings would remain a vexed issue for a long time. New York pushed for corporate union with Brooklyn, but Brooklyn vigorously maintained its independence and was finally chartered as a city in April 1834. Union with New York would not come until 1898—the long delay resulting largely from continued hostilities between the cities. Brooklyn boosters viewed New York as a fountain of vice, while Manhattan enthusiasts saw Brooklyn as provincial. One Brooklyn leader stated flatly: "Between New-York and Brooklyn there is nothing in common, either in object, interest, or feeling—nothing that even apparently tends to their connexion, unless it be the waters that flow between them."

The waters that flow between them. It was exactly this common ground that Whitman would capitalize upon in his poem "Crossing Brooklyn Ferry," which pictures both cities from the improving perspective of the East River. In his journalism he would often play the Brooklyn booster, emphasizing the salubrity of his home city and calling New York "the Gomorrah across the river." He even proposed that Long Island be made the state of Paumanok with Brooklyn as its capital. Still, he was always aware of Manhattan's cultural and commercial superiority to

Brooklyn, and from a young age he made regular ferry crossings to the city. He became the first great urban poet by immersing himself totally in the daily life of both cities, extracting the best features of each while leaving behind what he saw as the worst, and achieving in his poetry a space of aesthetic mediation between the two.

His poetic role as joiner and mediator was facilitated by the fact that, in his vision, Brooklyn itself was a symbol of mediation between city and country. This was especially true in his boyhood. Although the opening of the Erie Canal in 1825 quickened Brooklyn's commercial life, it had a small-town atmosphere in the early days. Many future building lots were still open fields where the neighborhood children flocked to play. Whitman developed a lifelong love for baseball in the fields of Brooklyn. On Saturdays he joined other boys in a strange early form of the game in which a base runner was out when struck by a ball hurled by a fielder—a method that resulted in bruises all over the players' bodies. For bats, flat or round sticks picked up casually were used; for balls, stray pieces of cork or rubber hand-wrapped with old stocking yarn and glove leather. From an early age Walt was adept at baseball, which he would later call "America's game: has the snap, go, fling, of the American atmosphere."

An intimacy and camaraderie characterized even public celebrations and festivals. Whitman would be appalled in the 1850s when holiday celebrations began to be mass-oriented spectacles manipulated by professionals. One of his most famous poetic lines—"I celebrate myself"— can be taken, on one level, as an attempt to restore the idea of celebration, which was fast becoming coldly manipulative, to the personal and genuinely celebratory. It was this kind of personal celebration he had grown up with in Brooklyn. He later looked back nostalgically: "Then we had various sorts of 'celebrations'—sometimes of the Sunday Schools, sometimes the regular education establishments, sometimes of an anniversary of one kind or another." On New Year's Day the custom was for people to visit as many friends as possible in their homes; the streets were thronged with those coming or going from visits. Easter time was particularly lively. African-Americans flocked from all over Long Island for their annual saturnalia, called Pinkster, in which they drank, danced, and played practical jokes; their laughter rang through the entire village. The whites gathered on the streets for a celebration called Paas, which involved a communal cracking of eggs.

The model celebration in Whitman's memory was that surrounding the visit of the Marquis de Lafayette to Brooklyn on July 4, 1825. The Revolutionary War hero was on a triumphal tour of the United States, and his entrance to Brooklyn was a memorable event. He rode in an old-fashioned yellow coach drawn by four horses through town to the corner of Cranberry and Henry streets, where he laid the cornerstone for the Apprentice's Library building. There was no mass-produced fanfare, no fireworks or cannons, only a genuine show of emotion from the people who lined the streets, giving the celebration spontaneity and honesty. The whole affair, Whitman recalled, "had an air of simplicity, naturalness and freedom from ostentation or clap-trap—and not without a smack of antique grandeur"; "it was something very different," he emphasized, "from such a turnout of modern date." In two of his retellings of the event he said that Lafayette lifted several of the village children in his arms, among them the six-year-old Walt, whom he kissed on the cheek. Fanciful embellishment? Possibly, but it shows just how intimate these early celebrations seemed to Whitman in memory.

If Brooklyn's festivals were personal, its public education tended to be impersonal. Until 1827, there was just one public school in Brooklyn, District School No. 1, which was established in 1816 on Concord and Adams streets. This was the school Whitman attended from 1825 (possibly earlier) until 1830, when his family's straitened finances forced him to go to work. The school was held in ill repute as a place for "charity scholars." Still, Walt was better off than many; a fourth of Brooklyn's population of children between five and fifteen didn't attend school at all. Although a second district school was formed in 1827, even then there were only two teachers in the village for more than two hundred public-school children. Like most large schools of the time, Brooklyn's were run according to the rigid system that had been developed by the English Quaker Joseph Lancaster. In this system, a single teacher handled huge classes through a network of student monitors.

There was an authoritarian distance between teacher and students. Learning was by rote repetition. The school day began at 9 a.m. with Bible reading and moral instruction. For primary students, there was word dictation, arithmetic, spelling, geography, and writing. The upper classes got grammar, geometry, trigonometry, history, and a heavy dose of sciences, including zoology, physiology, astronomy, mineralogy, and natural history. Whitman was probably exposed to part but not all of the upper-class program, since he left school at eleven. Corporal punishment was part of the Lancastrian approach. Doubtless Whitman, whose first published story would condemn school flogging, witnessed thrashings at his school. Though he never left a record of his feelings toward the school, we can guess he felt out of place. His teacher, B. B. Hallock, recalled him as "a big, good-natured lad, clumsy and slovenly in appearance." Upon learning later on that Walt had become famous, he said, "We need never be discouraged over anyone." Like Emerson at Harvard and Hawthorne at Bowdoin, Whitman at District School No. 1 was apparently a mediocre student. His early exposure to the Lancastrian regime later impelled him to seek other, milder educational theories, which he would incorporate into his poetry.

More than any course or teacher, Whitman always remembered the fateful day, June 24, 1829, when he was sitting in class and heard a tremendous explosion that rattled the schoolhouse. A powder magazine of the frigate *Fulton*, a receiving ship moored off the Navy Yard, had been ignited by a novice gunner who had carried a candle into the forward hold. The explosion killed at least twenty-four seamen, whose blackened, mangled bodies were brought to the Navy Yard and put in coffins. Ten-year-old Walt was deeply moved by the public funeral of one of the officers whose coffin was carried through town to Greenwood Cemetery, with sailors marching two by two, black crepe banners billowing, bugles wailing mournfully, followed by merry jigs played by the same horns as the procession wended home after the burial.

City of Churches

BROOKLYN WAS PERHAPS the most important locale in America for new religious developments that occurred during the nineteenth century. It became known as the City of Churches for good reason. In Whitman's boyhood it was already the home of active, important churches of virtually all denominations; by 1855 it had more than 130 churches. Over the years its churches were led by a series of notable pulpit innovators. No city produced preachers more influential than Brooklyn's.

Whitman would say he couldn't "have written a word of the Leaves without its religious rootground," corroborating his statement in the 1872 preface to *Leaves of Grass* that his "one deep purpose" beneath all others was "the religious purpose." It will be seen that the religious and philosophical influences on *Leaves of Grass* were the products of a specific moment, the 1850s, when several radical religious and philosophical influences came together. But Whitman never would have responded to these influences if he had not been open to them.

Many of those who would prove most responsive to radical religious tendencies came from either freethinking or Quaker backgrounds. Whitman had *both* of these in his background and thus developed a liberated openness to all kinds of religious discourse. He did not have to struggle, as did Hawthorne or Dickinson, with a personal heritage of repressive Calvinism, although his boyhood visits to different churches did give him some exposure to gloomy religion, as is suggested by this late poem:

Silent and amazed even when a little boy,
I remember I heard the preacher every Sunday put God in his
     statements,
As contending against some being or influence.

Whitman's father did not attend church. His mother sometimes went to the humble wooden Baptist meetinghouse on Pearl Street. Walt recalled attending two Sunday schools and many different churches.

What stands out is the amazing variety of his youthful religious experiences. Above all, the religion of his poetry would be ecumenical, naming and embracing many different religions without lending absolute credence to any single one. To many orthodox readers in his day and ours, this has been a difficult attitude to swallow. How can a believing Catholic or Methodist or Jew accept one who places no faith in any single religion? As he himself expressed it, his was the greatest of faiths and the least of faiths—the greatest in his belief in God and everyday miracles, the least in his acceptance of any church's creeds.

But he had a very clear precedent in American history and in his own family for this radically ecumenical outlook: deism. He had every reason to be attracted to deism and to associate it with America. Two of his brothers were named after deists who had become American presidents, George Washington and Thomas Jefferson. The deist his father had known in youth, Thomas Paine, was also a revolutionary patriot whose pamphlet *Common Sense* had sparked the rebellion against England. Benjamin Franklin and several other founding fathers were deists. So was General Lafayette, who, Whitman liked to think, had consecrated him with a kiss. Lafayette's lover Fanny Wright (see fig. 28), one of Whitman's favorite women, was perhaps the most visible deist of the day. Whitman was struck by her winning looks and eloquence. The slim, chestnut-haired Wright lectured to much fanfare in New York's Park Theatre and Hall of Science in 1829, brilliantly presenting her radical views on religion, marriage, and class. She would return in the late 1830s. "I never felt so glowingly toward any other woman," he would say. "She possessed herself of my body and soul." Since so many heroes and patriots embraced deism, he could think of deism as being in the American tradition.

He recognized, however, that deism was absolutely reviled in orthodox religious circles, for it placed all churches on the same level and valorized human reason and nature. It had never been popular, even at its peak in the 1790s, and the number of its adherents dwindled steadily in the first half of the nineteenth century with the rise of evangelical Protestantism and Roman Catholicism. He witnessed countless quarrels over Tom Paine and Fanny Wright. With regard to Paine he recalled that "as a youngster I heard many, many, many a fight over him—warmest espousals, hottest denunciations—denunciations by preachers whose words got hot in the mouth." As for Wright, he knew of the torrent of abusive epithets, like Red Harlot of Infidelity, hurled at her by evangelicals. He would call Paine and Wright two of the superb, maligned figures in American history.

But he instinctively accepted deism's centrality to American thought. It was, after all, the free thought of Jefferson, Franklin, and others that made toleration of all religions a specifically American phenomenon. It was a short step from the deists' notion of the equality of all faiths to the venerated American institution of toleration. In *Leaves of Grass,* absorbing America meant absorbing a philosophy—deism— that both was and wasn't at the heart of the American culture.

Free thought also made him responsive to another powerful religious influence: Quakerism, which for him specifically referred to the views of the schismatic Quaker leader Elias Hicks (see fig. 25). There were family connections with Hicks. Whitman's paternal grandfather as a boy had gone on sledding parties with Hicks on the Jericho Plains on Long Island. His father, too, was a friend of Hicks. One evening in November 1829 his father came home, threw down his kindling blocks on the kitchen floor, and announced, "Come, mother, Elias preaches to-night." Walt would never forget being taken to Morrison's Hotel that evening and hearing the eighty-one-year-old Quaker leader speak. Tall, of middling build, with a ramrod posture and a deep voice, Hicks made an imposing presence as he stood on a raised platform in the hotel's handsome ballroom. He and a small group of nearby Quakers, with their characteristically drab garb, looked incongruous in the elegant hall amid the fashionable folk who had flocked to hear him. His blazing eyes swept the crowd, and he began, "*What is the chief end of man?* I was told in my early youth, *it was to glorify God, and seek and enjoy him forever.*"

So deep were Whitman's feelings about Hicks that through much of his life he felt destined to be his biographer. Hicks had traveled forty thousand miles by foot and horseback as a Quaker evangelist, going as far away as Indiana, Virginia, and Canada. He had endured terrible tragedy: only four of his eleven children survived childhood. Doctrinally he was an extreme liberal who created a schism in Quakerism by denying that Christ's blood was any better than that of a bull or a goat, a heresy even more extreme than Emerson's later rejection of the Unitarian communion. The division between orthodox and Hicksite Quakers occurred in 1827 but had been preceded by years of squabbling. Hicks's valuation of the inner light above all creeds and religious institutions struck orthodox Quakers as sacrilege.

Elias Hicks ushered Quakerism to the brink of a pre-Whitmanian religious vision. Intrinsically, Quakerism had more appeal to Whitman than deism because it made allowance for ecstasy and intuition, which the rationalistic deism did not. Hicks's extreme emphasis on the sanctity of the inner light resonated within the poet who would place total reliance on the voice of the self. The natural world for Hicks became imbued with mystical meaning. His statement that the godhead is "in every blade of grass" prefigures Whitman's loafing and observing a single spear of summer grass. His doctrine that heaven or hell is not a distant locale but a state of being is echoed in the line in "Song of Myself" asserting there is never "any more heaven or hell than there is now." There was also a strongly nationalistic and working-class aspect to Hicks, who as the plainspoken American had stood up against the London-based orthodox Quaker establishment. Whitman could believe that this latest rebellion against England had succeeded, for by 1828 Hicksites outnumbered orthodox Quakers by three to one in New York, Philadelphia, and Baltimore.

Hicks's eloquence was particularly affecting to Whitman, who placed him in a select group of American religious orators along with Father Taylor and Henry Ward Beecher. Indeed, if we rearrange some lines from a characteristic Hicks sermon we find rhythmic repetitions much like Whitman's verse:

> And the law of God is written in every heart, and it is there that he
>   manifests himself:
> And in infinite love, according to our necessities, states, and
>   conditions,
> And as we are all various and different from one another, more or
>   less,
> So the law by the immediate operation of divine grace in the soul,
> Is suited to every individual according to his condition.

Such pulsating, oracular statements, which, like Whitman's poetry after them, had a distinctly biblical resonance, explain why Hicks always stuck out in Whitman's mind as one of the great religious speakers of the age. There was a special democratic emphasis to the Quaker mode of oratory, which carried the Protestant notion of the priesthood of all believers to a radical extreme. Whitman called Hicks "the only real democrat among all religious teachers: the democrat in religion as Jefferson was the democrat in politics." In ordinary Quaker meetings, there were no official priests or sermons. Silence was maintained until members of the congregation felt compelled by the inner light to rise and speak. Hicks's eloquence, then, was potentially available to anyone who came under the inspiration of the inner voice—a message not lost on one who would one day sing himself for all the world to hear.

The pan-religious quality of deism and the democratic emphasis of Quakerism made an explosive, liberating combination for the young Walt. This combination freed him to be open to the uniquely varied religious influences in the City of Churches. Whitman would once say that his poetry was thoroughly religious but swept the foundations from under the churches. His deeply anticlerical, anticreedal heritage had prepared him for this position. In his case, the foundations were swept from under the churches right from the start, since both deism and Quakerism claimed to be religious but had nothing to do with church or creed.

As a churchgoer, Whitman was a catholic in the original sense of the word. In the early 1830s, under the guidance of different employers, he attended two very different kinds of Sunday school—Dutch Reformed and Episcopalian. He was exposed to rigid Calvinism at the Dutch church on Joralemon Street, a massive, narrow-windowed graystone structure that looked like a fortress. Its congregation came mainly from the old Dutch farms on the outskirts of Brooklyn. If this church had links to the rural, Calvinistic past, St. Ann's Episcopal was connected to the urban, capitalistic future. St. Ann's was supported by wealthy families such as the Pierreponts, Gleaveses, and Sands. It had been reconstructed in the 1820s under the Reverend Charles Pettitt McIlvaine, who quickly gained a reputation as a skilled orator.

Whitman also attended services in various denominations. He went, he would recall, "anywhere—to no one place: was a wanderer: went oftenest in my earlier life." He loved to attend wild evangelical revivals at the wooden Sands Street Methodist church, crowded with working-class young men and women ("and O what pretty girls some of them were!" he recalled). "The galleries of the church," he wrote, "were often sprinkled with the mischievous ones who come to ridicule and make sport; but even here the arrows of prayer and pleading sometimes took effect."

He would always keep a sharp eye on developments in American oratory, and pulpit oratory was among his special objects of interest. In the course of the nineteenth century, the theological rigor that had characterized Puritan sermons gave way to a style that was relaxed, anecdotal, humorous. Brooklyn would lead the way in the stylistic revolution. Its churches were the home of such famous pulpit innovators as J. N. Maffitt, Samuel Hanson Cox, George Bethune, Richard Salter Storrs, Henry Ward Beecher, and T. De Witt Talmage. As editor of the *Eagle*

Whitman kept a regular column on the style of Brooklyn preachers and developed a special attraction for the pulpit showmanship of Beecher. Whitman's casual fusion of earthly and divine images in his poetry owed much to the pulpit stylists he observed so closely.

The Literary and Cultural Scene

AS PROGRESSIVE as was Brooklyn from a religious standpoint, there was a crude simplicity about its literary and cultural life. When the Apprentice's Library was proposed in 1824, few Brooklyn residents wanted to give money for the project, so library representatives went from door to door with a wheelbarrow into which were thrown books, pamphlets, and almanacs that formed the basis for the library's collection. A similar haphazardness surrounded Brooklyn experiments in the theater, which were sporadic and ill fated. The void of public amusements drove many young people to self-education and the circulating libraries. As a boy Whitman had to seek out cultural enrichment on his own.

The first place he looked was books. One of his favorite authors in his youth was Walter Scott. "How much I am indebted to Scott no one can tell," he later declared. "If you could reduce the Leaves [of Grass] to their elements you would see Scott unmistakably active at the roots." He had a childhood infatuation with the romance and chivalry of Scott's novels, but his main love throughout life was *The Border Minstrelsy*, Scott's collection of old ballads, which first appeared in America in 1830. Whitman called this volume "the richest vein he ever worked," "an inexhaustible mine and treasury of poetic forage (especially the endless forests and jungles of notes)—has been so to me for fifty years."

On the surface, his attraction to these poems is surprising, since their tight rhymes, strict meter, and medieval subjects are worlds away from his free verse. A clue to their appeal for him lies in Scott's extensive notes and introduction, which Whitman said he especially loved to pore over. Scott discussed at length the primitive roots of poetry, which he said was originally linked with popular song. The connection between poetry and music was not lost on Whitman, who, like Scott, referred to the poets as "bards" and poems as "songs." The early ballads, Scott stressed, represented the very beginnings of poetry, written before the corruptions of civilization and the constraints of literary influence had arisen. The primitive poets, he continued, were typically fresh and rude, not refined. "Thus it happens," he wrote, "that early poets almost uniformly display a bold, rude, original cast of genius and expression." In his efforts to return to origins, Whitman found a model for his "barbaric yawp" in Scott, who stressed the lawlessness of early poets.

In reading *The Border Minstrelsy*, then, Whitman could feel he was traveling back to poetry's roots, just as in his own poetry he would try in many ways to conjure up a sense of primitive beginnings. "Stop this day and night with me and you shall possess the origin of all poems," he would write in "Song of Myself"—the kind of line that impelled Thoreau to call *Leaves of Grass* "a great primitive poem."

But there was good reason Whitman found more inspiration in Scott's notes than in his poems. In theory, Scott may have loved the wildness of primitive poetry, but his own poems were highly structured. In fact, Scott was a model to be supplanted as much as to be observed. In explaining his use of free verse, Whitman told Traubel that in former ages poetry had been orally transmitted, so that rhyme and meter had been necessary as mnemonic aids. With the rise of modern printing, this need for mnemonic devices had disappeared, and more relaxed verse forms were called for. His conception of early poetry as strictly structured and orally transmitted most likely came from Scott's ballads, which therefore stood as examples of outmoded poetic forms. Indeed, Whitman's poetry was in several respects the opposite of the old ballads: free-flowing rather than structured; fragmented, not narrative; modern as opposed to ancient.

Whitman was not alone among American writers who were calling for a rejection of rhyme and meter on behalf of a rhythmic prose-poetry. The Maine novelist and radical reformer John Neal did the same long before the publication of *Leaves of Grass*. Emerson in his essay "The Poet" would say that "it is not metres, but a metre-making argument that makes a poem," but he did not develop the idea to the extent that Neal had in his 1823 novel *Randolph*. Did Whitman read Neal? He knew him personally by 1843, when he worked for Neal's magazine *Brother Jonathan*, in which two of Whitman's early poems and one of his articles appeared. Whitman said that as a boy he had read "cartloads" of novels, which were "a most formative element in my education, nurture," so it is not unlikely that he read Neal, a leading American novelist of the twenties and one who influenced Poe and Hawthorne. In *Randolph* Neal presented a rationale for prose-poetry similar to the one Whitman would give. He had a character ask: "What is rhyme, and all the artificial constraints of poetry, but the vestiges of that barbarous taste, which formerly delighted in conundrums, acrosticks, riddles, and alliteration?" The character continues, "I do, in my heart, believe that we shall live to see poetry done away with—the poetry of form, I mean—of rhyme, measure and cadence." In an uncanny prediction of *Leaves of Grass*, he adds:

"A great revolution is at hand.—*Prose will take precedence of poetry:* or rather poetry will disencumber itself of rhyme and measure, and talk in prose—with a sort of rhythm, I admit."

Another key work in Whitman's youth was Fanny Wright's novel *Ten Days in Athens* (1822), which he said "was daily food to me: I kept it about me for years." The novel, set in ancient Greece, is mainly a dialogue between the philosopher Epicurus and several of his followers. This talky, plotless novel was never popular and probably would be lost from literary annals if it had not had great appeal for Whitman. What explains the appeal? For one thing, the novel may have taught Whitman that imaginative literature could be a serious vehicle for progressive ideas. In the novel, Wright's radical deism verges on materialism. In particular, Epicurus's teachings about the interchangeability of all matter prefigures Whitman's organic view of death. This view would reach full scientific development in the writings of the German chemist Justus Liebig, whom Whitman would read admiringly in the forties, but his mind had been earlier prepared by Wright. One of Wright's main themes is that although we have no physical evidence of God or an afterlife, we can still be confident that all matter is immortal, since material things, when they dissolve, become transformed into other things through an exchange of atoms. If Whitman would famously write "every atom belonging to me as good belongs to you," Wright had Epicurus argue that animals, vegetables, and all other things represent "only the different disposition of these eternal and unchangeable atoms," which are recombined in various ways. This notion stripped death of its terrors by making it a source of new life. The poet who would coin many fresh metaphors for the organic cycle—for instance, grass as "the beautiful uncut hair of graves" or "the resurrection of the wheat"—responded to Wright's thesis that death was powerless, since decomposing matter always created life. *Ten Days in Athens* made deistic materialism not only palatable but constructive and meaningful.

When we turn to cultural arenas other than literature, we find in the 1820s and 1830s the faint stirrings of the kinds of theatrical and musical activity that would later burgeon and profoundly influence Whitman. From a dramatic and musical standpoint, Brooklyn in Whitman's youth was backward. There were two attempts to establish a Brooklyn theater. The first came in March 1826, when the Brooklyn Theatre was started, showing a tragedy followed by comic songs and then a two-act farce. Two years after this venture flopped for lack of public interest, the barnlike Brooklyn Amphitheatre was established on upper Fulton, where a few pennies bought entrance to a show that included horses, Indian dances, a clown, and a melodrama. An attempt to make it a respectable play-house failed in the fall of 1828 when a bill was advertised and tickets were sold but no players appeared; disgusted ticket holders hurled furniture at the walls. Brooklyn could not compete with New York, where the number of theaters rose from one for the whole season in 1820 to five in 1836 and fourteen (with sixty minor places of amusement) by 1860.

Like other culturally curious Brooklyn folk, Whitman constantly ferried to Manhattan for theater and music. He attended theaters with an interest few could parallel. Describing his youth and early manhood, he said, "I spent much of my time in the theatres then—going everywhere, seeing everything, high, low, middling—absorbing theatres at every pore." Manhattan was not yet witnessing the explosion of talent, foreign and native, that would come in the forties and fifties. Still, it was undergoing a cultural quickening of life. Troupes of foreign actors and musicians began to tour the United States in earnest, almost always performing longest in New York. A certain class consciousness was already creeping into theater life, with the Park Theatre becoming associated with serious drama and the Bowery with melodrama. Also, tensions were rising between European and American performers. Anti-British riots greeted American appearances of three London actors: Edmund Kean in 1825, Joshua R. Anderson in 1831, and George P. Farren in 1834. Still, such signs of strain were inchoate and minimal when compared with the class-related, nationalistic warfare that would erupt in the forties, contributing to (among other things) Whitman's development.

For the time being, theater was for the young Whitman mainly an escapist pastime. His first theater-going period was from 1832 to '36, when he was thirteen to seventeen years old. He delighted in imported melodramas at the Bowery, such as Edward Fitzball's *Jonathan Bradford, or Murder at the Roadside Inn,* which, he recalled, filled the house week after week and "had a long and crowded run." The play involved a virtuous innkeeper and his wife falsely accused of a murder and saved from execution only by the repentant confession of the real villain. He also took pleasure in *Mazeppa,* an equestrian drama that featured a Cossack warrior tortured by being strapped to a wild horse that eventually aided his revenge, as he won by force the daughter of the man who had tortured him. A play that Whitman said "affected me for weeks; or rather I might say permanently filter'd into my whole nature" was John Howard Payne's *Brutus, or the Fall of Tarquin,* about a cruel tyrant whose son violently overthrew him after being cleverly disguised as an idiot. Among the British performers that appealed to him were Henry Placide, a master at eighteenth-century comedy, and Fanny Kemble, whose talents were highlighted in a drama of jealousy, *Fazio, or the Italian Wife,* which Whitman called "a rapid-running, yet heavy-timber'd, wrenching, passionate play." Among the Americans he enjoyed were James Henry Hackett, who introduced to the stage the characters of the backwoodsman and Rip Van Winkle; Thomas Hamblin, the manager of the Bowery Theatre, who was also a forceful actor of both Shakespeare and melodrama; Edwin Forrest, the stentorian actor whose muscular style made him a favorite with the street types known as the Bowery b'hoys; and, above all, Junius Brutus Booth, the Britisher-turned-Marylander whose lead role in *Richard III* Whitman considered the highest moment in American theater history.

As will be seen later, the techniques of these and other performers would set off creative sparks within Whitman, influencing his poetic voice and shaping his ideas of Americanism.

Publishing and Politics

AT ELEVEN WHITMAN was forced, apparently by his family's financial necessity, to seek employment. His job history over the next two decades would be amazingly varied, as he would hop from job to job with a kind of restless frenzy.

The meandering trail of his job history began around June 1830 when he worked as an office boy for two lawyers, James B. Clarke and his son Edward. Edward tutored the eleven-year-old Walt and sparked his interest in reading by providing him with a subscription to a circulating library. Walt was soon devouring Cooper's novels, the *Arabian Nights*, and other exotic, adventurous works. He clerked briefly in a doctor's office and then entered the world of newspaper publishing.

By the summer of 1831 he was apprenticed to Samuel E. Clements, the editor of the weekly Long Island *Patriot*, the Democratic paper to which Whitman's father had subscribed. Tall and lean, the hawk-nosed Clements was a Southern Quaker who wore a long blue-tailed coat with gilt buttons. He had a fast horse on which he would deliver papers to country subscribers. On Sundays the kindly Clements sometimes took his apprentices to the old Joralemon Street church. Not long after Whitman's arrival on the job, Clements became involved in a bizarre scandal. In response to a number of local people who wanted a bust of the recently deceased Elias Hicks, he and someone else (possibly the New York sculptor Henry Kirke Brown) went to Hicks's grave in Jericho, disinterred the body, made a mold of his face, and from the mold had several plaster busts made. But in an argument over distribution of profits, the molds and busts were smashed, and the affair came to naught. Clements got into a lawsuit and was fired from the *Patriot* in November 1831. To his former opponents' glee, the erstwhile Democrat was soon editing a Whig paper in Camden, New Jersey.

After Clements's departure, Walt continued his training under the *Patriot*'s foreman printer, William Hartshorne. Small, fragile-looking (though he would live to eighty-four), Hartshorne had been born the year before the outbreak of the American Revolution and was full of personal reminiscences of Washington and Jefferson. A sedate, cautious man who was always cheerful and kept his temper in check, Hartshorne had an old-school dignity that Whitman would in some respects emulate in manhood. Hartshorne initiated the young Walt into the mysteries of the printing trade, teaching him the painstaking process of setting type by hand.

In the summer of 1832 Walt worked briefly for Erastus Worthington, another dignified and aloof Brooklyn printer. This was a bad summer for cholera, causing thirty-five deaths in Brooklyn, and was followed by an economic downturn that evidently affected Whitman's already hard-pressed family, for by the next spring his parents moved back to Long Island country in the region of West Hills. Walt stayed on in Brooklyn, working as a compositor for the leading Whig weekly the *Long-Island Star*, run by the lively Alden Spooner. Born in 1810 in Sag Harbor, a descendant of John and Priscilla Alden and the son of a pioneering Vermont printer, Spooner was a former Jeffersonian who did a political flip-flop and became a staunch Whig. For years in the *Star* Spooner had parried with his main political opponent, the *Patriot*, using a witty, acidic style his foes could rarely match. A defender of Whig causes like temperance and the tariff, Spooner nonetheless treated Fanny Wright kindly in his paper and printed verses by the antislavery poet Lucy Hooper and the experimental McDonald Clarke, a poet who influenced Whitman. Walt worked for Spooner from the fall of 1832 until May 12, 1835, after which he spent a year as a compositor in Manhattan.

These early jobs were principally important for giving him firsthand exposure to the kind of simple artisan work arrangements that were being threatened by rapid changes in publishing technology. Printing and distribution techniques improved immensely over the early decades of the nineteenth century. Stereotyping, the use of metal plates to produce multiple editions of a work, was introduced in 1814. The cylinder press, which greatly sped up the printing process, was introduced the same year and improved in 1847 when New York's Robert Hoe added an automatic "fly" used for paper removal. The steam press for newspapers came in the thirties. With the advent of transportation improvements, especially the Erie Canal and the railroad, huge distant markets opened up on the American continent. Book and newspaper production soared. The $2.5

million worth of books published in America in 1820 reached $16 million by 1856. The 200 newspapers of 1800 paled in their cultural impact next to the 2,526 at midcentury.

Along with technological change went dramatic shifts in work arrangements within publishing houses. In a word, publishing became less personal over time as publishers oriented themselves to mass production. Early in the century, the head of a newspaper often served several functions at once: proprietor, editor, compositor, distributor. The proprietor had control over virtually every aspect of production, sometimes even including home delivery. In the 1830s and 1840s this unified job arrangement gave way to a far more diversified one, as varied specialists, hired by a proprietor and working under an editor, all performed different functions to keep the machine of the metropolitan daily going. The penny papers that exploded on the scene in the early thirties reached unprecedented circulation levels, resulting in a much larger production team than before. Similar changes were occurring in book publishing, as authors, who previously had great input into many aspects of production, were more and more alienated from the production process, which was left to experts.

Whitman entered the printing trade early enough to savor the relatively primitive, personal work arrangements that characterized artisan publishing. The *Patriot* and the *Star* were small political sheets printed on simple wooden bed-and-platen presses and run by forceful individuals who oversaw every aspect of production. This unified, single-person production technique is described by a historian of Brooklyn:

> In the early village years, the functions of printer, publisher, and editor were assumed by a single individual. In fact, the term *editor* did not come into use until the early 1830s, previously called proprietor or publisher. As a practical pressman and compositor, he was a mechanic; as owner and manager, he was a businessman; as an employer and maker of books, he was a capitalist; he was always a political partisan.

This was particularly true of the person for whom the young Walt worked longest, Alden Spooner. Whitman would never forget the painstaking care that the early publishing process required. Each letter had to be removed from a rack of fonts and placed carefully in metal guides to form words and sentences. The compositor worked closely with the proprietor. This experience left with Whitman a lifelong desire to control absolutely the production of his poetry.

In this sense, he would always be looking back to the early days when the various printing functions were performed by a single person. All six editions of *Leaves of Grass*, plus the three major reprints, had the strong controlling hand of Whitman himself in virtually every facet of publication. "I like to supervise the production of my own books," he explained to Traubel. He added elsewhere: "My theory is that the author might be the maker even of the body of his book—set the type, print the book on a press, put a cover on it, all with his own hands: learning his trade from A to Z—all there is of it." Appalled by the impersonality of modern publishing, he would declare that authors needed to be rescued from publishers. Self-publishing was not uncommon among nineteenth-century American authors—Longfellow, Prescott, and others tried it at various times. But no one pursued it with the fervor or persistency of Whitman, who never deviated from the artisan conception of authorship he had learned in his early newspaper days.

Besides immersing him in this tradition of personal authorship and publication, his *Star* and *Patriot* jobs exposed him to political changes in local and national life.

Historians would do well to explore Brooklyn's early political history, which is as yet unmapped in many of its dimensions. It is generally forgotten, for instance, that Brooklyn has importance in the history of women and African-Americans. Whitman was raised in a progressive political environment. The Brooklyn Collegiate Institute for Young Ladies, one of the nation's earliest women's institutions of learning, was opened in 1830. It was committed, in the words of the opening-ceremony speaker, to the ideal that women should be educated "as carefully, as substantially, and as liberally" as men. Whitman, who would write "I am the poet of the woman the same as the man," had thus been exposed early on to protofeminist activity in his home city.

African-Americans were a vital presence in early Brooklyn life. This presence was complicated by the area's legacy of slavery: as late as 1812, in a population of 4,500, Brooklyn counted 1,432 slaves. Although most Brooklyn slaves were freed long before New York's abolition of slavery in 1827, African-Americans faced the kinds of segregation and racism that were all but universal throughout the North. Most Brooklyn blacks were crowded in the ferry district, relegated to menial jobs and living in shanties. Largely in response to these disturbing conditions, African-Americans entered political and cultural life in ways that manifested independence and sometimes militancy. The Brooklyn African Woolman Benevolent Society was a black organization devoted to mutual aid. Brooklyn blacks attended the Sands Street Methodist church, but in 1819, repelled by the racism of its pastor, a group established the African Methodist Episcopal Church, whose minister, William Quinn, Whitman later remembered. The church became a center of abolitionist propaganda and part of the Underground Railroad. African-Americans even entered the performing arts. Brooklyn's second public performance was given in December 1825 by John Hewlett, a black actor from Rockaway who sang, played the hornpipe, and did scenes from Shakespeare. Blacks attended Whitman's school, although they were give a separate floor from the whites; in 1827 they formed their own school.

Surely the most dramatic event among New York–area blacks was the formation in Manhattan of an abolitionist society by several leading African-American orators, including Henry C. Thompson, James Pennington, and George Woods. This group published an abolitionist newspaper, *Freedom's Journal*, which first appeared in 1827, four years before William Lloyd Garrison's *Liberator*. In Brooklyn, antislavery activities widened when a public meeting for blacks was held on Nassau Street in a wooden building called African Hall. By 1833 Alden Spooner in the *Star* could refer to "the abolitionists of Brooklyn, composing the greater portion of the colored male population."

Whitman's sympathetic portraits of blacks in *Leaves of Grass*, which would win praise from the likes of Sojourner Truth and Langston Hughes, can be profitably viewed against this background of the African-American presence in Brooklyn. His childhood friendship with the freed slave Mose partook of the spirit of camaraderie that characterized many interactions between blacks and whites in Brooklyn.

At the same time, however, his mixed feelings about the abolitionist movement were rooted in the antiabolitionist fervor that crescendoed throughout his childhood. As late as 1830, antislavery activity was rare in America; by far the greatest number of antislavery societies were in the South, not the North. Most Northern antislavery activism was led by colonizationists, whose name referred to their efforts to relocate freed slaves to the African colony of Liberia or elsewhere. Colonization would long remain a force in American culture: for instance, it would influence Harriet Beecher Stowe. But a rising group of abolitionists, led in New York by the editors of *Freedom's Journal* and in New England by William Lloyd Garrison, attacked the colonizationists as conservative and called for immediate emancipation and integration of freed slaves into American life.

Whitman's longtime ambivalence about the slavery issue can be traced in part to the fact that colonization took hold strongly in Brooklyn, and abolitionism was generally opposed as divisive and disruptive. The kind of antiabolitionist violence that was flaring up all over the North erupted in nearby New York in 1833, when the homes and businesses of abolitionists, including the store of the wealthy philanthropist Arthur Tappan, were attacked by rioters. When Tappan moved to Brooklyn two years later and formed an abolitionist society, his efforts were vigorously resisted there too. Among those who denounced him was Whitman's employer at the *Star*, Alden Spooner.

Whitman, then, had a divided history on the issues of race and slavery: a spirit of African-American participation in Brooklyn life, confirmed personally by his friendship with Mose, but also an animus against abolitionists—a feeling he would share not only with most Brooklynites but also most Northerners throughout the antebellum period.

The young Whitman also internalized a twin set of paradoxes that was emerging in the early 1830s in Jacksonian democracy: the question of liberty versus power surrounding Jackson himself, and the larger question of states' rights versus nationalism that was raised by the so-called nullification crisis.

When Andrew Jackson made a presidential visit to Brooklyn in the summer of 1833, the fourteen-year-old Whitman saw a sight that would always be engraved in his memory. There was the wiry Old Hickory, his white hair brushed stiffly back from his weather-beaten face, waving his white beaver hat to the applauding crowds as he was drawn through Brooklyn in his open barouche. More important for Whitman than this vivid scene, however, were the notably mixed signals Jackson's whole presidency sent. Jackson was on the one hand the great egalitarian, the voice of the masses. He was on the other hand "King Andrew II," the almost totalitarian leader who dominated the American political scene for nearly two decades and who was considered a despot by his enemies.

As a poet, Whitman would embody these Jacksonian paradoxes. The link between Whitman and Jacksonian politics has often been vaguely made, but inevitably what gets emphasized is the poet's debt to the populist side of Jackson. True, there is a powerfully leveling tendency in Whitman's verse. But this egalitarian instinct would remain largely latent and unexpressed in Whitman until years after Jackson's death in 1845 and would burst forth poetically only in response to specific political events of the fifties. Besides, Whitman, like Jackson, would reveal a contrary strain, one toward despotism. The Latin American poet Pablo Neruda has called Whitman "the first totalitarian poet." Indeed, there is a despotic force in Whitman's theory and practice of poetry: "What I assume you shall assume." "The presence of the greatest poet conquers." "He does not stop for any regulation. . . . he is the president of regulation." In these and other passages Whitman controls, almost bullies, us, just as elsewhere he proclaims himself our friend and equal.

Was he imitating the egalitarian but despotic Andrew Jackson? He certainly knew Jackson's contradictory nature well enough to describe his different qualities. On the one hand, he insisted he was gentle and selfless: "Massive, yet most sweet and plain character!" he wrote. "Your great soul never knew a thought of self, in questions which involved your country." At the same time, he noticed his "FIXED WILL, around which faction howled in vain, and against whom all the fierce storms of baffled interest were ineffectual." A fundamental American paradox—a combined emphasis on liberty and power—had surfaced with Jackson and was differently manifested by several later political leaders Whitman observed. Under the pressure of calamitous events of the fifties, it would find poetic expression in *Leaves of Grass*.

A related political tension that emerged in the 1830s—states' rights versus nationalism—would have an equally lasting effect on the poet. Whitman would long remain haunted by a central question of American democracy: How can the rights of the individual be balanced against those of society? How does the "simple, separate person" fit into democracy "en-masse"? On a national level, this question was of crucial importance in antebellum America. Today's versions of the issue (for example, big government versus state autonomy) actually pale in significance to the issue as it applied in Whitman's time. The first dramatic confrontation over the problem came in 1832 when the state convention of South Carolina, led by Vice President John C. Calhoun, voted to nullify two national tariffs that had been passed by the Jackson-led forces in Washington. This nullification crisis led to a showdown between Calhoun and Jackson at a government party. Jackson toasted Calhoun: "Our Federal Union. *It must be preserved.*" Calhoun raised his glass to the president, glared, and said, "The Union: Next to our Liberty, most dear."

Liberty or Union? State sovereignty or national power? The individual or the mass? These were basic questions raised by the nullification crisis, questions that had momentous importance in a time when the central government was still relatively weak. The Bill of Rights had ensured many individual liberties, but it would not be until the Civil War that a series of laws and constitutional amendments would bring about a great strengthening of the central government. In the antebellum period, the threads holding together the Union were fragile and ill defined. The nullification crisis raised the frightening possibility that these threads could snap altogether. This was no passing issue, for although it was temporarily resolved by the passage of a compromise tariff, it would reemerge in different forms: the demands for the breaking up of the Union by both abolitionists and fire-eaters, the attempts to establish alternative societies by Fourierists and religious utopians, and, ultimately, the actual secession of eleven Southern states leading to war.

It would be some time before Whitman would recognize this tension between the individual and the mass as a central one in American life. Still, the nullification crisis left an indelible mark on him. In an 1842 article for the New York *Aurora* he praised Calhoun as vigorous and brilliant but did an instinctive double take: "But that nullification business—ah, there's the rub!" He wondered how Calhoun could dare jeopardize the "beloved Union." A few years later he again lamented "the nullification and withdrawing-from-the-union folly of a few hotheads at the south." The political events of the early thirties had set in motion a process that would eventually drag the nation into conflict and, at the same time, contribute to Whitman's profound meditations on the individual and society in *Leaves of Grass* and *Democratic Vistas.*

3

DARK PASSAGES: TEACHING
AND EARLY AUTHORSHIP

W HITMAN'S FIVE YEARS as a country schoolteacher and newspaper editor on Long Island, from 1836 to 1841, have often been viewed as a benign rural interlude before his entrance into the stormy New York political and publishing scene in the forties. Recently unearthed documents show a darker picture. Six letters Whitman wrote in 1840 to a friend from the village of Woodbury—the earliest extant letters by him—reveal a dissatisfied, gloomy young man who was in some kind of trouble with the townspeople. Evidence is also gathering that he may have endured traumatic public persecution when he taught in another Long Island village, Southold.

Did either of these incidents have anything to do with the great secret Whitman kept mentioning late in life? Every time the subject of his untold big story came up with Traubel, he trembled anxiously and put off full disclosure, explaining that "it involves so much—feeling, reminiscence, almost tragedy." Given the dearth of reliable documentation, we cannot say for certain what the great secret was or what the Woodbury and Southold incidents truly involved. His secret remains among the beguiling lacunae of American literary history, along with Henry James's obscure hurt, the identity of Emily Dickinson's beloved "Master," Hawthorne's secret, and the cause of Poe's death.

What can be said is that some terrible pain lurks behind his verse. He is, of course, the definitive poet of joy. But there are signs of personal trauma even in his most exuberant poems. "Crossing Brooklyn Ferry" contains dark suggestions of "hot wishes I dared not speak," with "the wolf, the snake, the hog, not wanting in me." "Song of the Open Road" has a long passage in which Whitman identifies with people who feel "a secret silent loathing and despair, / [...] death under the breast-bones, hell under the skull-bones."

It has not been previously noticed that this kind of pain entered Whitman's writing at a specific moment, the summer of 1841, with the publication of his first short story, "Death in the School-Room"—just after the Woodbury and Southold incidents seem to have occurred. Negativity and gloom had characterized some even earlier writings, but it was only with this tale about a country teacher who flogs to death an innocent student that negativity begins to be combined with gory violence and autobiographical overtones. Whitman's early fiction and poetry as a whole, sometimes dismissed as blandly conventional, is in fact scarred with suffering. His entrance into the field of authorship, then, was at least partly prompted by some terrible pain that his writings indirectly dramatized and perhaps helped to purge.

The nation, too, was in great pain during this period. The panic of 1837 led to the longest and deepest depression of the pre–Civil War period. From 1837 to 1843 business failures and unemployment were widespread. Hard times again hit Whitman's ever-struggling father, who in 1836 was forced to sell off the last of his landholdings in West Hills, snapping all direct links to the stem family of the past. A main theme of Whitman's early fiction would be the violent breaking up of families, a theme doubtless connected to the surrendering of the paternal estate.

A positive effect of the personal and public pain was that it turned Whitman toward reflection, creativity, and political sympathy with outcasts and losers, whose poetic champion he would one day become.

From City to Country

IN THE SPRING of 1835, his family having moved back to Long Island two years earlier, Whitman left Brooklyn and took his printing skills to Manhattan, where he worked for a year as a compositor. Whom he worked for and where he boarded are unknown. What can be established is that the relative stability he had enjoyed during his three years at Spooner's *Star* gave way to a sense of insecurity in the course of his year in New York. The great fire of 1835 and the early phases of the economic depression would make the aspiring printer and author take the rather desperate step of becoming a country teacher.

It is difficult today to comprehend the devastating effects of urban fires in Whitman's day. The competing volunteer fire companies who raced with their hand-hauled engines to fires had great enthusiasm but little organization or efficiency. The fire that swept through Manhattan's commercial district in December 1835 (see fig. 13) was particularly bad because of poor weather conditions. Subzero temperatures froze up the recently installed fire hydrants. In the few instances that the hydrants were operating, the water froze quickly in the hoses. Portable water brought in the fire engines met the same fate. As a result, the fire that began on December 16 raged out of control for two and a half days. A fifty-acre area in downtown Manhattan was wiped out, with the loss of twenty blocks of buildings. The damage was estimated at fifteen million dollars, a tremendous sum in those days.

Even more devastating than the fire, in the long run, were developments in the nation's economy. Crop failures in 1835 broke down the chain of payment from farmer to merchant to banker. As in the years before the panic of 1819, paper notes began to outstrip specie (hard money) at an alarming rate. The inflationary spiral reached a dizzying peak in the summer of 1836, when interest rates reached 24 percent. Prices soared. Flour and meat prices nearly doubled in two years. Bread became so expensive that a flour riot involving more than a thousand poor people erupted in Manhattan in February 1837. A drain of specie in England exacerbated America's problems. In the South, cotton houses that relied heavily on British markets failed, and Northern merchants, factories, and banks followed. In April 1837 world prices suddenly collapsed, causing a run on banks, many of which failed. The New York diarist George Templeton Strong wrote of the banks, "So they go— smash, crash. Where in the name of wonder is to be the end of it?" In the wake of the bank failures came further business collapse and widespread unemployment. The number of jobless reached half a million nationally in the winter of 1838. President Martin Van Buren, who assumed office in March 1837, was, in spite of his record as a dexterous manipulator, virtually helpless before an economy that sputtered to near collapse during the four years of his term. The depression dragged on for six miserable years, reaching a nadir in New York in 1842.

Whitman's years as a teacher, then, were spent against a bleak social background. In his mind, his turn to teaching would always be associated with the instability of his environment. He captured the quicksandlike circumstances of 1836 in his semiautobiographical portrait of the young Archibald Dean in his story "The Shadow and Light of a Young Man's Soul":

> When the young Archibald Dean went from the city—(living out of which he had so often said was no living at all)—went down into the country to take charge of a little district school, he felt as though

the last float-plank which buoyed him up on hope and happiness, was sinking, and he with it. But poverty is as stern, if not as sure, as death and taxes, which Franklin called the surest things of the modern age. And poverty compelled Archie Dean; for when the destructive New-York fire of '35 happened, ruining so many property owners and erewhile rich merchants, it ruined the insurance offices, which of course ruined those whose little wealth had been invested in their stock.

If poverty and the New York fire contributed to Whitman's insecurity, what can have been the effect of his father's selling off family land in West Hills? Walter Whitman, Sr., had managed in 1821 to retain a sixty-acre portion of what once had been the old Nehemiah Whitman homestead. Evidently he held on to the land during the Brooklyn years and had even gotten more acreage, probably through the death of his brother Jesse. But in March 1836 he and Louisa, then living in Hempstead, sold the West Hills parcel, now more than a hundred acres, for $2,250 to the farmer Richard Colyer, whose wife, Hannah, was the daughter of Walter's sister Sarah. When Walt Whitman and his father visited West Hills in the early 1850s, the home was inhabited by the poet's widowed Aunt Sarah and her daughter Hannah Colyer, also a widow. Showing some resentment over the loss of the family holdings, Walt in his notebook described his Aunt Sarah as one who "has very little regard for dress; but is craving for money and property."

The upshot of these tangled real estate dealings was that Whitman's immediate family relinquished its final connection to the old Whitman lands just at the moment, in spring 1836, when Walt himself was confronted with dire economic circumstances in Manhattan. Although he never directly commented on the loss of the family estate, some of his early fiction, written within a decade of the sale of the West Hills property, dramatizes the shattering of once-unified stem families and the loss of family property. Toward the beginning of his novel *Franklin Evans* he portrays an innkeeper who had been a hale farmer living with his wife and children on the old family farm until alcohol comes like "a great dark cloud, overhanging all, and spreading its gloom around every department of the business of that family, and poisoning their peace, at the same time that it debars them from any chance of rising in the world." He loses his farm and his family breaks up. The Native Americans in *Franklin Evans* also become symbolic of the collapsed family, for "they found themselves deprived not only of their lands and what property they hitherto owned, but of everything that made them noble and grand as a nation!"

If his fiction indirectly reflected his distress over his separation from his bygone stem family, it explicitly revealed his interest in constructing a strong sense of parenthood amid existing family members. His autobiographical story "My Boys and Girls" was published in 1844, but an early draft was probably written in the mid-1830s, when he could still think of his siblings as his "children." In 1836 his older brother Jesse may have already gone to sea; as for the others, Mary was fifteen, Hannah thirteen, Andrew nine, George six, Jeff almost three, and Eddy nine months.

He made clear his parental feelings toward the group: "Though a bachelor I have several boys and girls I call my own." He describes Hannah as "the fairest and most delicate of human blossoms," Jeff as "a fat, hearty, rosy-cheeked youngster," and he asks, "What would you say, dear reader, were I to claim the nearest relationship to George Washington, Thomas Jefferson and Andrew Jackson?" He tells of carrying "the immortal Washington" on his shoulders, teaching "the sagacious Jefferson" how to spell, and tumbling with Andrew Jackson.

The story shows not only a strong parental strain but also an instinct to freeze himself and his siblings in childhood, as though the passage to adulthood is viewed as intrinsically fraught with danger. The oldest sister, Mary, gets a tellingly mixed description, as Whitman sees in the beautiful but vain girl "misty revealings of thought and wish, that are not well." Mary's only real failing, it would seem, is that she is older than the others, for adulthood in this story is linked with pain. How dreary it is, Whitman writes, to look into these children's future "and see the dim phantoms of Evil standing about with nets and temptations." He continues:

> Alas! that there should be sin, and pain, and agony so abundantly in the world!—that these young creatures—wild, frolicsome, and fair—so dear to me all of them, those connected to blood, and those whom I like for themselves alone—alas that they should merge in manhood and womanhood the fragrance and purity of their youth!

One is tempted to say that the happy part of this story, describing his relationship with his siblings, was penned in 1835 or '36, before the time of his own severest traumas, and that the darker passages were added after they had occurred, as though he was projecting his own pain onto them.

Whatever the facts about the composition of the story, it can be safely said that Whitman's first impulse on abandoning Manhattan was to seek refuge in family. His first two teaching jobs were in Long Island villages, Norwich and Babylon, where his family was living successively in 1836.

His first post was one or two terms beginning June 1836 in Norwich, where his parents and younger siblings had been living for at least two years. A few miles south of the picturesque Oyster Bay in the north-central part of the island, Norwich (now East Norwich) was not far from the old Van Velsor homestead, which the seventeen-year-old Walt doubtless visited often during the beautiful summer months. In August his family moved to the south-central village of West Babylon, where his father apparently made another stab at farming. By the winter Walt had joined them, teaching in the Babylon school and helping out with the family.

His arrival at the island's south shore coincided with two terrible shipwrecks there that would always stand out in his memory. On November 21, 1836, the American ship *Bristol*, after a month at sea, was wrecked in a furious storm off Far Rockaway; some sixty to seventy people lost their lives. Six weeks later, another storm caused the wreck of the *Mexico* on Hempstead Beach, just west of the Babylon area where the Whitmans lived. One hundred and twenty lives were claimed by the *Mexico* disaster, which Whitman in *Specimen Days* said he was "almost an observer" of, though he wrongly recalled its having occurred in 1840. He gave a powerful rendering of the tragedy in "The Sleepers":

> I look where the ship helplessly heads end on, I hear the burst as she
> strikes, I hear the howls of dismay, they grow fainter and fainter.
> I cannot aid with my wringing fingers,
> I can but rush to the surf and let it drench me and freeze upon me.
>
> I search with the crowd, not one of the company is wash'd to us alive,
> In the morning I help pick up the dead and lay them in rows in a
> barn.

Whitman would soon move on to teaching posts in various other parts of the island, but Babylon would be home base for the immediate future, for his family remained there until May 1840.

Schoolteaching, which had been forced upon Whitman by hard times and ill luck, must have been a comedown for him. There was little glamour about the job of a country teacher in those days. Job security was minimal, since some schools were open only three months (the minimum required for public funding), some four, some six or nine, and a few twelve. Teachers usually drifted from school to school, teaching four terms of thirteen weeks each. Unlike today, when hard-pressed teachers can usually give at least two reasons for their line of work (July and August), vacations were virtually nil. There were no official holidays for

Christmas, Thanksgiving, or New Year's Day; teachers had only Sundays and every other Saturday off. Salaries were wretched. A country teacher might expect to make around $40 a term, or $160 a year, though expenses were reduced by the common practice of "boarding round," by which a teacher would spend a week or two living in the home of a student and then move on to another.

From our perspective, teaching in a one-room schoolhouse might appear to have been quaintly charming, but it rarely was. The little wooden structures were drab on the outside; inside there were typically only backless benches of varying height against the walls, with the teacher's desk in the center and a few benches near it for students called up for recitation. Furniture was made locally from rough-hewn lumber. There were no blackboards, few windows, and terrible ventilation. Conditions were not only primitive but, in cold weather, sometimes brutal. In most of the schoolhouses Whitman taught in, heating was supplied simply by a fireplace at one end of the room. A pail of water on the side of the room opposite the fire would freeze solid. Students had constantly to trade places near the fireplace to avoid shivering in the winter months.

Understandably, there was not a great rush to fill country teaching posts. As Whitman later explained in the *Brooklyn Star,* most who took jobs in the district schools were "*chance teachers*—young men during college vacations, poor students, tolerably intelligent farmers." The curriculum was almost as basic as the little structures in which it was taught. The three R's, with perhaps some science and occasionally a language or two, was the standard fare. It's doubtful that Whitman, who never knew more than a smattering of French and Spanish, taught languages.

In the early going, it seems that Whitman adapted well to the rigors of teaching. He was liked by both parents and students in Babylon. In one sense, his early jobs had a natural appeal for him, for he was reunited with his family in lovely surroundings. Babylon is on Great South Bay, the huge expanse of water and wetlands that stretches between the mainland and Fire Island, the distant strip of beaches beyond which lies the Atlantic. Whitman would never forget spearing eels through holes cut in the thick bay ice in winter or boating across the bay in summer to gather seagull eggs on the ocean beaches. He would recall, "The shores of this bay, winter and summer, and my doings there in early life, are woven all through L[eaves] of G[rass]."

We get a small but telling glimpse of Whitman's personality from an incident he said happened during his months in West Babylon. This story, based on a newspaper interview with Whitman in old age, could be apocryphal, though it jibes with other reports of his generally calm but sometimes explosive demeanor. One day he was fishing from a boat on a trout pond near the family property when he was harassed by Benjamin Carman, a boy who lived on the adjacent farm. Carman was throwing stones near the boat to disturb the fish. At last he got in his own boat and approached Whitman, who patiently ignored him and then struck up a cheerful conversation. When Carman's boat came within striking range, Walt seized his pole and thrashed the boy mercilessly, breaking the pole in the process. The beaten Carman went home, and soon his furious father brought charges of assault and battery against Whitman. News of the case spread like wildfire, and on trial day the courtroom was crowded. Whitman pleaded his own defense, admitting to the beating but insisting his vested rights had been violated. The case was dismissed. The courtroom exploded into laughter when the jury foreman, an Englishman, declared, "We find 'e did not 'it him 'ard enough."

The eighteen-year-old Whitman left the family home in spring 1837, just when the economy was going into a free fall. He briefly assumed a one- or two-term teaching post in Long Swamp, a village in the South Huntington area between West Hills and Dix Hills. By the fall he had relocated twenty miles to the east to Smithtown, a Suffolk County town of about 1,500. His Smithtown teaching job lasted three terms, including the fall and winter of 1837 and spring 1838. He got $72.50 for five months of teaching. At one point he had some eighty-five students aged five to fifteen. As usual, the schoolhouse was primitive, with a fireplace at one end and writing desks that faced three walls with their backs to the teacher's central desk. Its doors and three windows fronted the town's main street, and it was near the village green, where Walt played ball with the boys. For the lack of a janitor, the girls swept and cleaned the school, and the boys chopped wood. There was no bell or clock. The goose-quill pens were split and sharpened for all students by the teacher.

Walt boarded part of the time with Joseph Hull Conklin, a tall, robust man who drove the stage between Orient and Brooklyn. Conklin had lost an eye in a coach accident but had not lost his humor or high spirits; he was one of those hearty, direct types that Walt found characteristic of Long Island.

While in Smithtown he joined a local debating society with thirty members and served as the secretary of its first ten meetings. From the records of the society we get a sense of his social attitudes at this time. In his debates, he took positions against slavery as well as against the discouragement of foreign emigration to this country. He supported the abolition of capital punishment and argued that the maltreatment of Native Americans by the early colonists was not justifiable.

Even though his Smithtown experience seems to have been among

his most successful teaching posts, he must have felt frustrated and con-
fined by the exigencies of the schoolmaster's tasks, for in the spring of
1838 he abruptly left off teaching and reentered the world of newspaper
publishing. He went to Huntington and founded a weekly paper he
called the *Long-Islander*, the first issue of which probably appeared in
May. Later a major town, Huntington was then little more than two
sparse rows of wooden houses separated by a broad street and backed by
rolling fields and woods. In one field there was a windmill on whose
rotating arms the local children loved to swing. Whitman published his
paper in the upper floor of a small frame house facing the main street.
A hole was cut in the house's sloping roof to accommodate the large arm
of the printing press.

The *Long-Islander* was a throwback to old-time artisan publishing.
Whitman was publisher, editor, compositor, pressman, and distributor all
at once. His young brother George reportedly came to Huntington to
help out for a time, but the newspaper was essentially a one-person oper-
ation. Like Samuel Clements, his former employer at the *Patriot*, Whit-
man even did home delivery. Each week he made the thirty-mile circuit
on his horse, Nina, to nearby villages and as far as Babylon to the south
and Smithtown to the east. There are no extant early issues of his *Long-
Islander*, but a story titled "The Effects of Lightning," reprinted in the
Long Island Democrat, shows he was more than willing to print the kind
of sensational news that was coming to the fore in American journalism
in the thirties. The story told of a Northport farmer who unwisely carried
a pitchfork during a storm and was struck dead by lightning. In his later
newspaper writings, and to some degree even in his poetry, Whitman
would become a sensationmonger in competition with the rising penny
press.

Whitman ran the *Long-Islander* for ten months and then sold it in
the spring of 1839. It may have been a losing venture, though the reason
he abandoned it appears to have been related to a temperamental aver-
sion to entrepreneurship. His successor, E. O. Crowell, who revived the
paper on July 12, 1839, promised subscribers in his first issue: "[B]y in-
dustry and punctuality, he hopes to be enabled to overcome these disad-
vantages, and remove any prejudices that may exist in the minds of its
late patrons."

After leaving the *Long-Islander*, Whitman visited briefly with his
family in West Babylon before returning to Manhattan, where he unsuc-
cessfully sought a printer's job. Late summer found him back on the is-
land working as a typesetter for a weekly paper published in Jamaica,
the *Long Island Democrat*, edited by the Democratic partisan James J.
Brenton. For the *Democrat* he wrote a series of numbered articles with

the running title "The Sun-Down Papers." The earliest Whitman publications of note, "The Sun-Down Papers" merits more consideration than it has received. The first few numbers reveal an openness to popular cultural modes that would later became more pronounced.

Specifically, these early writings reveal his roots in reform literature and in a popular genre I have called elsewhere the visionary mode. The 1830s had witnessed the explosion of reform pamphlets linked with evangelical Protestantism and aimed at eradicating various bad habits, including intemperance, masturbation, smoking, and excessive meat eating. Whitman's major poetry would have a revolutionary sensuousness but also, curiously, a contrary tendency toward prudishness that sometimes became strident. When in "Song of the Open Road" he insisted that "No diseas'd person, no rumdrinker, or venereal taint is permitted here," or when in "Song of Prudence" he decried "Putridity of gluttons or rum-drinkers," "privacy of the onanist," and "seduction, prostitution," he was harking back to the kind of moralistic reform rhetoric that had surfaced in the thirties, a decade that produced best-selling tracts against vice, such as the Reverend John Todd's *The Student's Manual* (1835) and Sylvester Graham's *A Lecture to Young Men, on Chastity* (1837). In the fifth installment of "The Sun-Down Papers" Whitman struck the popular reform note in the most straightforward way, arguing against the use of tobacco, coffee, and tea. Sylvester Graham (best remembered today as the father of the graham cracker) had been making identical pleas for several years, so Whitman was saying little that was new.

Moralistic reformers like Graham and Whitman were responding to a heritage of bad habits in American life. In the opening decades of the century, tobacco chewing was almost universal among American men. Rarely could a woman take a walk on town streets without having her dress stained by yellowish-brown tobacco juice spit randomly by male promenaders. Cigar smoking was almost equally common, and, until the temperance movement began to take effect in the late thirties, alcohol consumption was astoundingly high. Whitman, then, was in step with the decade's reformers when he drew negative portraits of street loungers haloed by cigar smoke and drinking stimulating beverages.

He had obviously kept an eye on another vogue, the visionary tale, which since the 1790s had been a primary means for American writers to air progressive, sometimes dangerously skeptical ideas. For decades, freethinkers and religious liberals had packaged their heterodox notions in benign tales in which the protagonist had a dialogue with an angel who discoursed on some philosophical idea. The eighth number of Whitman's "Sun-Down Papers" was directly imitative of what I term the "dark visionary mode," in which philosophical skepticism bordered on relativism. In this almost pre-Melvillian piece, the protagonist dreams he searches for truth in all corners of the earth but cannot find it. The meaning of his fruitless quest is revealed to him by an angel, who shows him an allegorical vista of a huge mist-covered mountain viewed from a distance by throngs of people, all wearing different kinds of glasses. The mountain is truth, and the colored lenses are the purely subjective interpretations people of different creeds impose upon this always hidden truth. The fact that Whitman would write such a gloomy tale suggests that the deism and radical Quakerism of his youth had left nothing firm in their wake for him to believe in. Consolation would come to him only with religious and philosophical developments of the 1850s, which he would incorporate into his poetry.

Although Whitman continued to write pieces for Brenton's *Democrat* for another year, he soon left his printing job there and resumed teaching. He continued to board for a time with the Brentons, but Mrs. Brenton found him lazy, uncouth, and not fit to associate with her daughters. She recalled him lounging under her apple tree and dreaming the days away.

For six months Whitman taught at Jamaica Academy at Flushing Hill, between Jamaica and Flushing. His salary for this job was a typically meager eighty-two dollars. Then it was on to another school, at Little Bayside, where he taught for some months in 1839–40, and after that to nearby Trimming Square, about two miles from Hempstead.

Despite the rapid moves, this seems to have been a good period for him. One of his Little Bayside students, Charles A. Roe, later recalled him as a beardless, ruddy-faced young man who dressed in an old-style black frock coat, with a vest and black pants. He was a big eater and had a free, easy attitude toward his students, of whom he had between seventy and eighty. He used the kind of experimental teaching methods that were just then being introduced to American education. In the late 1830s the education reformer Horace Mann began to call for a rejection of the harsh, authoritarian methods of the past on behalf of milder, more creative approaches. The spirit of reform touched Bronson Alcott, who at his Temple School in Boston introduced progressive educational practices. Whitman's Little Bayside experience suggests that he too shared the creative new spirit. Instead of drilling his students, as under the old Lancastrian system, he drew them out through provocative questions. He concocted a game of twenty questions in which students learned through friendly competition. He had them memorize one of his own early poems, "The Punishment of Pride," part of which Charles Roe could still recite more than half a century later. When it came to punishment, Whitman, like Mann and Alcott, had a horror of the rod. He devised his own mild method of punishment: he told a story in which the identity of the guilty student was exposed indirectly.

His identification with the progressive teaching methods of the day would prove to be no short-lived phenomenon. It lasted through his life and had a direct impact on his poetry. As a journalist in the forties he wrote dozens of articles on education. In these pieces, he allied himself completely with the education reformers by emphasizing the role of a nurturing physical and emotional environment in the training of children. He argued that American schools should be well ventilated and clean, that punishment should be gentle, and that the curriculum should be widely expanded to include music, art, and gymnastics. In making these arguments he cited such innovative educators as Mann, Lyman Cobb, and Edward Everett. He kept up the identification with the new teaching methods when he became a poet. The breezy, ventilated feel of many of his major poems shows his effort to regulate his poetic space just as he had wanted to make the learning environment salubrious. If he drew out his students through creative questions, so in his poems he often questions his reader rhetorically: "Have you practis'd so long to learn to read? / Have you felt so proud to get at the meaning of poems?"

His whole conception of his role as a poet was linked to his education theories. "We consider it a great thing in education," he had written in an 1846 *Eagle* article, "that the learner be taught to rely upon himself." He reiterated the idea in an 1855 notebook entry calling for "an entirely new system, theory, & *practice* of education, viz: to do that which will *teach to think* everyone for himself." As a poet, he is both the firm teacher trying to guide us and the mild one inviting us to develop on our own, a paradox captured in lines like "I teach straying from me, yet who can stray from me?" or "He most honors my style who learns under it to destroy the teacher." He addresses his readers as "Élèves" and titles one poem "To a Pupil." After the first two editions of *Leaves of Grass* were published, he actually contemplated becoming a roving "public teacher," going all over the country and directly addressing the people.

Besides developing his teaching skills in 1840, Whitman kept a steady stream of publications coming out in the Long Island newspapers. Several installments of "The Sun-Down Papers" and a number of poems ran in the *Long Island Democrat* from the spring through the fall. It became clear in these pieces that his drifting, economically insecure life as a teacher and journalist had the positive effect of sparking his creativity. As deleterious as the panic of 1837 was on America, it actually contributed to what literary historians have called the nation's literary renaissance (which was really more of a nascence). Economic hard times snuffed out the family fur business of Herman Melville, forcing him to drift and eventually go to sea, an experience that formed the basis of his greatest fiction. Emerson, whose pioneering pamphlet *Nature* appeared in 1836, had his most creative period between 1837 and 1843, the years of the economic depression. Thoreau was forced in these years to define his relationship to the threatened financial world represented by his father's pencil business, opting for a contemplative, solitary life outside of trade. Whitman's literary aspirations, too, were fanned by hard times. In one of his "Sun-Down Papers" he expressed a desire that would one day come true: "I would compose a wonderful and ponderous book. . . . Yes: I *would* write a book! And who shall say that it might not be a very pretty book?"

His desire for literary distinction was directly linked to the economic and political realities of the time. He would become the most famous exponent of contemplative loafing. The activity of poetry would be for him largely a matter of relaxation, opening up his sensibilities to the natural and spiritual worlds: "I loafe and invite my soul, / I lean and loafe at my ease observing a spear of summer grass." Some have argued that his indolent, loafing persona stood in direct opposition to an increasingly capitalistic American culture where manhood was equated with pragmatic activity. To say this, however, is to ignore the way in which his poetry reflected a whole class of antebellum Americans with whom he identified deeply: the class of so-called loafers. These were mainly young working-class men and women who had been impelled by hard times to reject normal capitalist pursuits and find other means of gratification and amusement.

In terms of the party arrangement of the day, the Whigs were usually associated with the capitalist success ethic and the Democrats with loaferism. It was this distinction that George Templeton Strong had in mind when in an 1838 diary entry he said a Democratic meeting "looked like a convention of loafers from all quarters of the world" and when elsewhere he noted that while the Whigs attracted respectable types Democrats tended "to take in all the loaferism of the nation." So distinct a class did the loafers become that by 1856 the *New York Times* could note, "New York may be classified into Uppertendom, Loaferdom, and Shantydom," with the Bowery the center of Loaferdom. Urban versions of loaferism, especially street loungers known as the b'hoy and the g'hal, would attract Whitman when he became a city journalist. For the time being, his experience as a working-class Democrat set adrift in the unsteady world of country teaching made him contemplate loaferism as a viable alternative to a social system that had in many ways beaten him down, as it had many others. "I have sometimes amused myself with picturing out a nation of loafers," he wrote in a November 1840 essay.

"Only think of it! an entire loafer kingdom!" Adam, he says whimsically, was a loafer, and so were all the philosophers. The political underpinnings of his conception of loaferism were undeniable:

> Give us the facilities of loafing, and you are welcome to all the benefits of your tariff system, your manufacturing privileges, and your cotton trade. For my part, I had serious thoughts of getting up a regular ticket for President and Congress and Governor and so on, for the loafer community in general.

To contemporary readers, the political message of this passage would have been clear, since the supporters of the "tariff system" and "manufacturing privileges" were the Whigs, victorious in that year's presidential election. Whitman, as one of the defeated Democrats, seemed ready to drop out and become a full-time loafer. But the time was not yet ripe.

Purgatory Fields

THE YEARS 1840 AND 1841 would prove momentous and bizarre for America and for Whitman. On a national level, this was the period when presidential politics took on the combined qualities of excitement and claptrap, bravura and distortion, that have characterized many elections since. In the hoopla surrounding the Whig candidate William Henry Harrison the nation got its first heavy exposure to the image-over-reality syndrome that would later become commonplace in many areas of American life. It was appropriate that the political packaging of Harrison came only four years after the world's first large advertising campaign (for Brandreth's Vegetable Universal Pills, a cathartic that claimed to cure virtually all diseases) and five years after P. T. Barnum first hoodwinked the public with his exhibition of the aged African-American Joice Heth, who he insisted was the 161-year-old ex-nanny of George Washington.

The image of the Whig candidate lapped up by the American public in 1840 was about as authentic as Brandreth's pills or Joice Heth. The well-heeled Harrison was peddled in the campaign as just plain folk with the help of an image coined by his opponents. A Baltimore paper had disparagingly written that Harrison would forget the presidency and "would be entirely happy on his backwoods farm if he had a pension, a log cabin and a barrel of hard cider." Even though Harrison was a scion of Virginia plantation gentry and lived on an Ohio estate, his Whig supporters seized the opportunity and converted the criticism into political gold. Cider barrels and miniature log cabins suddenly popped up every-where—in earrings, on banners, at Whig rallies, on the streets. Rousing campaign songs reiterated the populist log-cabin motif, and the New York Whig Horace Greeley founded a newspaper, *The Log Cabin*, the forerunner of his influential *New York Tribune*. Harrison's military ser-vice was emphasized through the sobriquet Old Tippecanoe, and he and his nondescript Virginia sidekick John Tyler were swept into office to the tune of "Tippecanoe and Tyler too."

Democrats like Whitman did not have much to crow about in 1840. Andrew Jackson's handpicked successor Martin Van Buren had presided over the worst depression in the nation's history to that time. In stark contrast to the exuberant Whig rallies, the Democratic meetings were listless and directionless, almost as though defeat were foreordained. Whitman, despite his antipathy to the Whigs, enjoyed attending a spir-ited Whig rally in August 1840 where the speaker, as he put it in a letter, "cut capers, which certainly never before met the eye or ear of civilized man." The same Whigs who made the elitist Harrison seem a rough-hewn folk hero made Van Buren, the uneducated tavern keeper's son, appear to be a dandified aristocrat. Certain forward-looking thinkers cut through the prevailing distortions and made forceful, genuine pleas on behalf of the working class. Orestes Brownson's landmark essay "The Laboring Classes," published in the July issue of the *Boston Quarterly Review*, made a pre-Marxist appeal to workers to rise up against the rul-ing class. But such apocalyptic appeals could not hope to have any imme-diate effect during an economic depression. As in other depressed times in American history, organized-labor activity had been killed off by the panic.

The dire circumstances surrounding the Democrats in 1840 had been presaged by the fate of one of Whitman's political mentors, William Leg-gett. The man Whitman would revere had been in the thirties the most articulate and forceful promoter of the Jacksonian political philosophy. He had used the columns of William Cullen Bryant's Democratic paper the *New York Evening Post* and then his own *Plaindealer* to sound off on political and social issues. Like Whitman after him, Leggett was an ar-dent free trader who had no tolerance for tariffs or other forms of govern-ment interference with the economy. He impugned the social elite with a virulence that would be later amplified by the likes of Mike Walsh and George Lippard. He may be identified as the one who introduced the peculiar type of slashing political rhetoric that fed into various levels of radical discourse and had a profound impact on Whitman's theory and use of language. He was one of the original Locofocos, whose name came from an October 1835 Democratic meeting that was interrupted when opponents turned off the lights but that continued when the radicals lit locofoco matches. His populism was so strong that he viewed the plow-man farmer as the highest embodiment of virtue. Despite his visibility, Leggett failed miserably with the advent of the depression. His calls for working-class activism could have little effect when many were out of work. He alienated abolitionists by attacking them, and he became the victim of infighting within Democratic ranks. He had fallen out of favor by the time of his death in May 1839, though he soon became a cult figure worshipped retrospectively by many Democrats, including Whit-man. "Can we forget the career of the lamented Leggett?" Whitman later asked in the *Eagle*.

Despite the drooping fortunes of the Democrats in 1840, the election year prompted Whitman's first active involvement in politics. He served in the fall as the official Democratic electioneer for Queens County and entered political debates. He got an acidic reception in early October when he jousted verbally with John Gunn, a Whig opponent in Jamaica. In a report of the debate, the *Long Island Farmer* said that Gunn was eloquently persuasive while Whitman, "a well known loco foco of the town," made up for lack of proof with "the most false and scurrilous assertions," such as calling a local editor a "liar and blackguard." The *Farmer* warned Whitman: "We say *to him beware.... [A]nother* such provocation, *another* such encroachment on the decencies of life, and this loco foco, or any other, may meet with severe and deserved chas-tisement."

Although wounded in political frays and doubtless depressed over Democratic prospects in the November election, he had a deep-seated loyalty to the two-party system as it had developed in the previous de-cade. Until 1850 the ongoing conflict between the Democrats and Whigs would seem to him a primary illustration of the strength and soundness of the American system, which, he believed, would stand strong through all turbulence and disagreement. His faith in the integrity of the Union despite party quarrels was made clear in "The Columbian's Song," a poem he wrote for the *Democrat*. "Though parties sometimes rage, / And faction rears its form," he wrote, still "this heart-prized union band" would stay firm in the face of a foreign threat.

The defeat of Van Buren was, predictably, a source of sorrow to him. With other Democrats he had to look to the future. This became easier when Harrison died of pneumonia after a month in office and was suc-ceeded by "His Accidency," John Tyler, whose indecision in office would alienate even Whigs. In July 1841 Whitman told a rally of thousands gathered in a Manhattan park that the next Democratic candidate would be "carried into power on the wings of a mighty re-action." He was right, for the Democrat James Polk would be elected in 1844 by a large electoral margin.

There were other important developments in the 1840–41 period. In May 1840 his family moved from West Babylon to Dix Hills, where they would remain for five years. Walt's sister Mary was married that spring to a Farmingdale shipbuilder, Ansel Van Nostrand. Soon they were living in the North Fork whaling village of Greenport, where they would raise five children. Mary, the most conventional of Walt's siblings, apparently remained contented with the domestic life, though she would have periods of strain over her husband's habitual drinking.

More than any political setbacks or family changes, the pain that most powerfully affected Whitman pertained to his schoolteaching, which he resumed in the summer of 1840 in the midisland village of Woodbury. The little schoolhouse was on a knoll not far from the Van Velsor farm. Walt was a summer replacement for Scudder Whitney, who sneeringly remarked upon returning to his post in the fall that "the pupils had not gained a 'whit' of learning" under Whitman. Something was terribly askew in Woodbury. One of Whitman's students from around this time would recall that he "warn't in his element. He was always musin' and writin', 'stead of 'tending to his proper dooties." His letters that summer to a Jamaica friend, Abraham Paul Leech, written between July 30 and September 9, were unrelievedly negative.

He didn't identify the exact source of his discomfort, but he expressed utter contempt for the provincial villagers, whom he branded as "contemptible ninnies." In all the letters, he manifested boredom and exasperation with his routine. He reported being dragged on long huckleberry outings in the broiling sun. He detested a local diet that included greasy ham, boiled beans, and moldy cheese. His language about the Woodbury experience ranges from amused sarcasm to outright hatred. "O, damnation, damnation!" he writes, "thy other name is schoolteaching and thy residence Woodbury." He dubs Woodbury Devil's Den and Purgatory Fields, launching into impassioned tirades against the town:

> I am getting to be a miserable kind of dog; I am sick of wearing away
> by inches, and spending the fairest portion of my little span of life,
> here in this nest of bears, this forsaken of all Go[d]'s creation; among
> clowns and country bumpkins[,] flat-heads, and coarse brown-faced
> girls, dirty, ill-favored young brats, with squalling throats, and crude
> manners, and bog-trotters, with all the disgusting conceit, of ignorance
> and vulgarity.—It is enough to make the fountains of good-will dry
> up in our hearts, to wither all gentle and loving dispositions, when we

are forced to descend and be as one among the grossest, the most low-minded of the human race.—Life is a dreary road, at the best; and I am just at this time in one of the most stony, rough, desert, hilly, and heart-sickening parts of the journey.

The one who would become the quintessential singer of common folk here denounces the common folk as repulsive and ill bred. His commitment to Jacksonian politics had not yet instilled in him a real sympathy for the ordinary types Jackson championed. His snobbish demeanor in the Woodbury letters corresponds with his appearance in the first surviving daguerreotype of him, dating from the early 1840s (see fig. 1). In the picture he looks like a dandy, with a dark frock coat and vest, fashionable black hat, a heavy polished cane, and a look of slightly disdainful sophistication. In Woodbury, and indeed in his other teaching posts, the young man who had been bred in Brooklyn and exposed to the rich cultural life of Manhattan felt out of sorts in the company of simple country people.

Was he suffering some kind of persecution at the hands of the citizens of Woodbury? Beneath the contemptuous jocularity of the letters to Leech lurks real pain. The metaphors he uses to describe his relations with the townspeople suggest hellish torments and violence of various kinds. "Woodbury!" he writes, "Appropriate name!—it *would*-bury me!" He confesses a perverse desire to burn the schoolhouse and perform other evil deeds:

> The next you hear of me, I may possibly be arraigned for murder, or highway robbery, or assault and battery, at the least.—I am getting savage.—There seems to be no relief.—Fate is doing her worst.—The devil is tempting me in every nook and corner.

Biographers have always been puzzled by Whitman's abrupt abandonment of schoolteaching in 1841. The Woodbury letters may provide an explanation. Whatever trauma he suffered there, however, did not impel him to abandon either Long Island or teaching immediately. Although Woodbury remained an important nexus of pain that darkened his early writings, it appears that what drove him to Manhattan was an even sharper trauma that winter.

In his last letter to Abraham Leech from Woodbury, on September 9, 1840, he asked his friend to find him a teaching job in Jamaica. Evidently Leech was unable to do so, for Whitman spent the fall in the Jamaica area electioneering for Van Buren. What happened after Harrison's victory in November is the great mystery. Whitman himself, who never gave more than sketchy accounts of his teaching days, would once scribble in his notebook, "Winter of 1840, went to white stone [*sic*], and was there till next spring." Previous biographers have taken him at his word, saying that he went directly from Jamaica to teach at Whitestone.

But is that what happened? He was notoriously foggy about autobiographical data, and several times he would actually change or destroy data in an effort to cover up something. At any rate, the only surviving documentation of his presence in Whitestone dates from early spring 1841, including a March 25 letter to Leech and a March 30 recommendation he wrote for an assistant teacher, Clarissa Lyvere. The wording of the March 25 letter makes it sound as though he had arrived at Whitestone only recently. He reminded Leech of the letters he had written him from "Purgatory Place" (Woodbury) eight months earlier, and he gave an introductory overview of Whitestone, describing the locale and the people. Although he was, as usual, contemptuous of the villagers, he showed great relief over his current situation: "I have reason to bless the breeze that wafted me to Whitestone."

Could that reason have been that something terribly painful had happened between November and March? The answer may lie in an experience that seems to have taken place when he taught that winter in Southold, a fishing village on the northeastern end of Long Island.

Was the young Whitman run out of town by the enraged citizens of Southold after having been publicly charged with sodomy? This sensational story, which surfaced briefly in the 1960s, has never been told fully in a Whitman biography.

In those days it was not unusual for a male teacher boarding with his students' families to sleep in the attic with one or more of the boys. Whitman allegedly did more than sleep. As the story goes, one Sunday (January 3, 1841, is the probable date) he was publicly denounced by the Reverend Ralph Smith (see fig. 11) from the pulpit of Southold's First Presbyterian Church "because of his behavior to the children, and his goings on." (Later on, reports of "bloody bedding" would emerge.) Members of the congregation formed a furious mob and went to nearby Kettle Hill, where hot tar was always available for mending fishing nets. They hunted Whitman down at the home of George C. Wells, whose son Giles was later said by Judge Jesse Case to have been "one of Whitman's victims." Whitman fled to the nearby home of Dr. Ira Corwin, whose housekeeper, Selina Danes, known as "the orphan's friend," hid him in the attic. The pursuing townspeople found him there, hiding under "straw ticks" (summer mattresses). They seized him, plastered tar and feathers on his hair and clothes, and rode him out of town on a rail.

Eventually, he was rescued by the kindly Selina Danes, who cleaned him and nursed him back to health. His recovery took a full month, a period that suggests he had suffered severe injury at the hands of the infuriated citizens.

The school where he had taught, Locust Grove No. 9, was renamed "the Sodom School," by which name it was popularly known into the twentieth century.

The main details of this story were passed down through generations of Southolders to Wayland Jefferson, an African-American who was long the official historian of the town. Jefferson's story was printed in Katherine Molinoff's *Walt Whitman at Southold* (1966), a slim, privately printed pamphlet that received little publicity and seems to have been dismissed without further attempt at corroboration. Although Molinoff did not have documentary evidence of the scandal, she had the oral testimony of fourteen Southolders who had heard that Whitman had taught there. Half of them supplied information about his stormy expulsion from the town; the other half had heard simply of his having taught in Southold. She also found veiled references to the scandal in *Heritage,* a historical novel about Southold by George F. Hummel, a longtime resident of the town. One character in the novel reports that Whitman "had been in some kind of trouble" in Southold, and another, upon hearing Whitman's name, cries, "You mean that schoolteacher? Your grandfather reads you that man's stuff? That unspeakable vagabond! If I were you I wouldn't dream of letting my boys near anything that loafer ever wrote. How does he dare show his face among people?"

There are no Southold court records from this period and only scattered issues from the local paper, the Greenport *Republican-Watchman.* The most likely source of information, the church records, have been tampered with. Twelve pages of the Reverend Ralph Smith's sermon book were torn out, Molinoff believes, by two church elders who wanted to protect their family names from association with the scandal. Because Southold is an isolated village on the extreme eastern end of Long Island, news of the incident probably would not have appeared in papers published farther to the west.

Nevertheless, I have discovered documentation suggesting Whitman's presence in Southold, something neither Whitman himself nor his biographers have mentioned. A letter dated November 28, 1840, from a Southold resident, Giles C. Waldo, to a Washington lawyer, Charles C. Cragin, contains references to Whitman. Waldo writes, "I am most sincerely sorry that Whitman tho't it expedient to 'run a muck' under the chariot wheels of 'old Tip'—but hope he may escape unscathed." This cryptic statement evidently refers to Whitman's political activity, for "old Tip" was the Whig presidential candidate Harrison, against whom

Whitman had been campaigning that fall. This letter, written about a month before the alleged scandal, suggests that Whitman was indeed a familiar figure in the Southold area at the time. Four months after the alleged incident, Waldo had lost track of Whitman, for he wrote Cragin on May 3, 1841: "Have you heard from Whitman or from Fitchburg since you wrote last?" Another strong suggestion of Whitman's presence in Southold is the painting *Walt Whitman's School at Southold, 1840*, attributed to the Long Island artist William Sidney Mount (see fig. 10).*

There is a certain persuasiveness about the detailed nature of the Southold story. Most stories about Whitman's early life derive, like this one, mainly from hearsay, but few have the vivid exactitude of this. The image of Whitman cowering under "straw ticks" in Ira Corwin's attic, for instance, sounds too particular to be mere fabrication.

Confirmation of The Trouble, as the scandal came to be called locally, came to me from a living Whitman relative, a direct descendant of the poet's sister Mary. Over the years Whitman has been viewed ambivalently by certain family members specifically because of the Southold incident. Although the tarring-and-feathering part wasn't passed down through the family, the story about Walt and The Trouble has been passed down through the generations. Additional evidence, all of it indirect, has come to me from various people living in the Southold region.

It is not improbable that Whitman would show affection for his male students or that he would be persecuted for it in a town like Southold. He would later confess to a friend that a Long Island farmer with whom he was boarding reproved him for making a pet of his son, who returned the affection. His brother George would say, "I am confident I never knew Walt to fall in love with young girls or even to show them marked attention. He did not seem to affect the girls." Likewise, his Little Bayside student Charles Roe reported, "The girls did not seem to attract him. He did not specially go anywhere with them or show any extra fondness for their society." At the very least, Whitman's feelings for young men were particularly ardent expressions of the kind of same-sex passion that was common among both men and women in nineteenth-century America. Such ardor was in fact widely accepted in the street culture of Brooklyn and New York, but in a Puritan-based rural town

---

*Evidently, there was a cover-up related to the painting, whose title, revealed only by police X ray, was long obscured on the back of the painting by the word "Smithtown" superimposed over the word "Southold." Moreover, Smithtown was obviously false and misleading, since the structure depicted in the painting bears no resemblance to Whitman's Smithtown school, which still survives.

like Southold, a bastion of conservatism, it would have been frowned upon, whether or not it involved sexual contact.

Whitman once hinted of tensions with country folk when he wrote in an article, "Long Island Schools and Schooling," of rural teachers: "They are apt to be eccentric specimens of the masculine race—marked by some of the 'isms' and 'ologies'—offering quite a puzzle to the plain old farmers and their families." Whitman's alleged accuser, the Reverend Ralph Smith, was a Princeton-trained Calvinistic Presbyterian who had a reputation for being abrasive and paranoid. It is possible that his charges against Whitman were exaggerated by his own homophobia and that the behavior of the Southolders was the product of mob frenzy. Whatever the case, it is significant that Smith suddenly left Southold in 1841, after having served there for five years, and went far away, assuming a pastorship in Milton, Connecticut.

Whitman also went far away. He was distancing himself from Southold by going to Whitestone, on the opposite end of the island, just north of Brooklyn and within sight of Manhattan. Although he was initially happy at Whitestone, there is some evidence that he may have left there under a cloud too. In a letter that is undated but can be assigned to May 1841 he writes to his friend Leech, "I am still in this whereabouts, and here I shall probably remain for some time to come." But before the end of the month he had abandoned schoolteaching altogether and had plunged into the world of Manhattan journalism. Why the sudden departure from Whitestone when he had just told Leech he planned to stay there for a long time?

Unless fresh documentation comes to light, this question may remain unanswered. But the possibility that at least one great trauma happened to Whitman in the six months after November 1840 is further reinforced by a huge, hitherto unremarked gap in his literary output. In the seven months leading up to November 28, 1840, he had written steadily for the Long Island papers, producing eleven separate works: six poems and five installments of "The Sun-Down Papers." Then suddenly his writing ceased completely. As far as is known, nothing of his appeared in print between November 28, 1840, and June 22, 1841. In July 1841 his output resumed its former pace. Between then and the following March he wrote ten pieces: five short stories, the rest poems and essays. Those "lost" seven middle months lend credence to the notion that he experienced some numbing blow that incapacitated him emotionally and perhaps physically.

There was also a significant change in the nature of his writings over the period. The five works he published up to August 4, 1840 (that is, up to the early Woodbury period), were conventional works that showed little angst. They included "Sun-Down Paper" No. 5, the prudish protest against tobacco and stimulating drinks; two exotic poems, "The Inca's Daughter" and "The Spanish Lady"; and two other poems, "The Love That is Hereafter" and "We Shall All Rest at Last," which were meditations on death after Bryant's "Thanatopsis."

With the appearance of the sixth "Sun-Down Paper," published on August 11 in the midst of Whitman's Woodbury debacle, his writing darkens. This "Sun-Down" installment is a gloomy essay that commends the strewing of children's coffins with flowers because the young die before "Guilt and Wretchedness yet had dominion over them." With almost Hawthornesque gloom he writes, "When a man dies, who can say what deep stains may have rested, at one time or another, upon his soul? what crimes (untouchable, perhaps, by the laws of men or the rules of society) he has committed, either in evil wishes or in reality?"

Was the pain of his Woodbury experience seeping into his writings? Had Whitman himself committed untold crimes "either in evil wishes or in reality"?

The writings he produced in the three months just after Woodbury did not totally free themselves of this gloom. "The End of All," a poem published on September 22, argued that since pain and grief are universal, death is welcome. The eighth "Sun-Down Paper," which appeared on October 20, is the long, dark visionary tale discussed earlier, which expresses a kind of bleak relativism. Whitman was wounded that fall in political battles, had to confront the defeat of his party in the election, and began to crave literary fame in earnest. At the end of September he wrote of his wish to produce "a wonderful and ponderous book." In the ninth "Sun-Down Paper," published in November, he dedicated himself to loafing, whimsically fancying himself the leader of a nation of loafers.

One would think, in light of his stated desire to gain literary fame and to take up contemplative loafing, that his literary output would have actually increased after November. But not only did it cease for seven months, but when it resumed in Manhattan the next summer it became quite different from before. Four of his earliest works published in Manhattan were short stories that established a whole new tone in his writings and that seemed to resonate with recent personal trauma. All of them involved some kind of bloody, violent confrontation, usually between an adult authority figure and a male child or youth, often communicated in sadomasochistic language peppered with phallic images. Three of the stories used the rhetoric of moral reform, showing Whitman smuggling psychologically suggestive violence into a purportedly prudish framework.

The first story he published after the seven-month gap was titled, significantly, "Death in the School-Room." Appearing in the August issue of the *Democratic Review*, this story would go on to become one of his most popular works. It was reprinted six different times in his lifetime. Its appeal can be partly attributed to its combination of sensationalism and reform message. Americans of the 1830s and '40s were hungry for sensationalism in any form, but they felt especially comfortable with it when it was sugarcoated with some reformist intent. Whitman's chosen reform in "Death in the School-Room" was education reform. Horace Mann had been lecturing for several years against the excessive use of the rod in the classroom. Corporal punishment, Mann said in an 1837 lecture, should never be inflicted in a passion and should be done with a light rod rather than a ferule, below the loins or on the legs rather than upon the body or hand. Whitman adopted Mann's message but allied it with the popular technique of what I have termed "immoral reform": that is, the description of vice so vivid that the vice itself predominates over the ostensible moral. This device lay behind the immense controversy surrounding several reform works of the period, such as the sensational best-sellers *Magdalen Facts* (1831), by the antiprostitution reformer John McDowall, and *The Quaker City* (1844–45), by the Philadelphia firebrand George Lippard.

Whitman's story portrays a cruel, authoritarian country schoolteacher, Lugare, who brutally flogs a male student, Tim Barker, for refusing to confess to stealing fruit from a local farmer's garden. Barker has been wrongly accused. Lugare takes sadistic delight in thrashing the sickly boy, who is slumped over his desk apparently asleep but, Lugare finds to his horror, is in fact dead. The teacher has been pummeling a corpse.

Whitman makes sure to mention the reform message. "We are waxing toward the consummation," he writes, "when one of the old-fashion'd schoolmasters, with his cowhide, his heavy birch-rod, and his many ingenious methods of child-torture, will be gazed upon as a scorn'd memento of an ignorant, cruel, and exploded doctrine." But in light of his apparently traumatic experiences in the year preceding the publication of the story, there seem to be autobiographical overtones as well. One does not have to be a Freudian to see homoerotic connotations in the picture of a country teacher beating a supine boy's lower back with a rattan, a scene described in images suggestive of erection and forced penetration:

> Lugare lifted his rattan high over his head, and with true and expert aim he had acquired by long practice, brought it down on Tim's back

with a force and whacking sound which seem'd sufficient to awake a
freezing man in his last lethargy. Without waiting to see the effect of
the first cut, the brutal wretch plied his instrument of torture first on
one side of the boy's back, and then on the other, and only stopped at
the end of two or three minutes from very weariness.

There may be parts of Whitman himself in both the teacher-criminal
and the flogged victim of persecution. The story projects both guilt over
bad treatment of students and fear of savage punishment by an author-
ity figure.

Another story that involves violent confrontation between an adult
male and an innocent youth is "The Child's Champion," which appeared
in the November 20, 1841, issue of Park Benjamin's paper *The New
World*. If in "Death in the School-Room" Whitman used the education-
reform framework, here he turns to temperance reform. In the original
version, the temperance message was muted, but this tale of a virtuous
boy maltreated by a barroom ruffian was later revised slightly by Whit-
man and made into a temperance story, "The Child and the Profligate."
The ease with which Whitman retooled the story illustrates the fluid
exchange between sensationalism and reform in his day. In its various
forms, this story was reprinted more often than any other Whitman tale
except "Death in the School-Room." Having feasted for years on a spicy
diet of dark-reform works, the American public was attracted to this
mixture of melodrama and morality.

The tale involves a poor widow's son, Charles, who on his way to
work passes a bar where drunken frolic, dancing, and smoking are going
on. He enters the bar and is offered brandy by sailors but refuses, saying
his mother has warned him against drinking. A one-eyed drunken sailor,
angered at the boy's refusal to drink, seizes Charles and kicks him vio-
lently until he is stopped by the blow of an onlooker, John Lankton, a
once-dissipated man whose conscience has been aroused by the boy's ex-
emplary virtue. The newly reformed Lankton takes Charles to an inn,
where the two sleep together according to the common custom of the
day. Later the repentant Lankton helps out Charles's family financially.

Once again, within the moralistic frame we find psychologically res-
onant images. The tale presents another innocent boy who is assaulted
on the backside by an overeager man. The assault scene again has over-
tones of rape: "[The sailor] seized the child with a grip of iron; he bent
Charles half way over, and with a heavy foot gave him a sharp and solid
kick." The boy helplessly "hung like a rag in his grasp." Lankton's inter-
ference is rendered in terms of penetration; Whitman writes that his
"blow . . . had been suddenly planted in the ear of the sailor." But unlike

"Death in the School-Room," which ends abruptly with the grisly after-math of such violence, "The Child's Champion" moves toward moral affirmation. If the barroom scene shows the underside of homoeroticism, the inn scene where Lankton and Charles sleep together points toward its benign side. As Lankton lies in bed, "All his imaginings seemed to be interwoven with the youth who lay by his side; he folded his arms around him, and, while he slept, the boy's cheek rested on his bosom. Fair were those two creatures in their unconscious beauty." In the night, an angel comes down and kisses the innocent Charles; Lankton too is thenceforward a pure man. Whitman makes the common nineteenth-century practice of men sleeping together a means of reconciling his private desires with his reformist instinct toward virtuous conduct. The tale enables him to inscribe his recent traumas while imaginatively resolving them through an affirmation of pristine love and socially approved behavior.

If the confrontation between adult and child in these two tales suggests homoerotic violence, in two other stories of the period it resonates with parent-son tension. Had Whitman's parents caught wind of something shameful he had done in his teaching days? With the current lack of information, we cannot say for certain. But a painful or shameful meeting between a son and his parents is enacted in "Wild Frank's Return," published in the *Democratic Review* in November 1841, and "Bervance," which appeared the next month in the same magazine.

It is significant, given Whitman's problems in rural Long Island, that the bloody events of "Wild Frank's Return" take place "in a country town in the eastern section of Long Island." The story dramatizes a son's separation from the stem family, his subsequent plunge into dissolute habits, and his attempted contrite return for a reconciliation with his parents, a return foiled by a tragic accident. This plot indirectly fits the general pattern of Whitman's teaching years, which began with a cutting away from the family estate and a passage into murky behavioral territory over which there may have been family shame. "Wild Frank" Hall had abandoned the family farm two years earlier after his father had decided a quarrel between Frank and his brother in favor of the brother. Frank is now returning home after two debauched years. After stopping in a bar for a drink and a smoke, Frank rides toward the family farm but decides to take a rest, falling asleep on the ground after tying his horse's reins to his wrist.

While he is sleeping, a violent storm breaks out and terrifies the horse, which gallops off, dragging its master, who is nothing more than a bloody mass when the horse reaches home. The story culminates with Frank's mother coming out of the farmhouse and seeing "a mangled, hideous mass—the rough semblance of a human form—all batter'd and cut, and bloody." The horrid truth comes upon the mother as she gazes at "the fatal cord, dabbled over with gore," and she sinks into a deathlike swoon. The rope that kills Frank becomes a grim version of the umbilical cord, once the source of life to the son but now the cause of "death" for the mother. Was this a projection of the battered prodigal son Walt Whitman, after one of his traumatic experiences, returning home to his mother's shocked dismay?

His last tale of 1841, "Bervance; or, Father and Son," describes an initially happy widower who develops an uncontrollable aversion to his second son, Luke Bervance, whose eccentric behavior shows incipient insanity. Among other things, the father resents the son's attachment to his male tutor. He prohibits the excitable Luke from attending the theater and one night becomes enraged when Luke breaks the rule and goes to a play. A fight results in which the son fells the father with a violent blow. In revenge, the father has Luke put into an asylum, where the son actually goes insane. One day the father is looking in the mirror when he sees behind him the haggard form of Luke, who speaks wildly to him and then disappears. The father is forever haunted by the image of his insane son's visage in the mirror.

The situation here of a son alienated from a once-unified home as a result of his lawless behavior seems yet another variation on Whitman's downward pattern during his teaching years. Whitman himself was a second son who had reason to feel estranged from his family at the time he wrote the story. It is difficult not to hear Oedipal echoes in a narrative of growing hostility between a father and son that leads to fisticuffs and separation. But the father in the story is not just the stern Walter Whitman, Sr., but also, to some degree, the tormented young Walt Whitman looking at himself in a kind of specular gaze. The father's perturbation over the son's attachment to his tutor may indicate Whitman's guilty relationships with his own students. The mirror scene becomes a weird enactment of parent-son tension and of almost paranoid desperation in the face of outside assault. The crazed Luke says to his father:

> You are Flint Serpent. . . . Speak low, big eyes and bony hands are out there, and they would take me back again. But you will strike at them, Flint, and scatter them, will you not? Sting them with poison; and when they try to seize me, knock them down with your heart, will you not?

One is tempted to say that the conflict here between the phallic "Flint Serpent" and the grasping "bony hands" projects a confrontation between Whitman and some punitive authority figure (the Reverend Ralph Smith?), while the image of "Flint Serpent" scattering and knocking down enemies is a fantasy of Whitman being rescued from his pursuers.

Writing fiction for Whitman in 1841, then, was largely a means of purging inner demons through scenes of violence, homoeroticism, shattered families, as though the turbulent 1836–41 years had been rolled into an imaginative ball and hurled against a wall, leaving autobiographical traces and, more generally, giving an impression of someone projecting angst and coming to terms with trauma.

Never again would violence or blood so dominate his writings. As he distanced himself from the painful period, his fiction and poetry became less perfervid and traumatized. To be sure, pain would never disappear totally from his writings and would in fact form a vivid counterpoint to the prevailing optimism of his major poems. Some of the most moving portraits in his poetry are those of marginalized people—fugitive slaves, prostitutes, losers of all kinds—who are objects of severe persecution. Hence memorable lines like "I am the man, I suffer'd, I was there" or, "That I could forget the mockers and insults! / That I could forget the trickling tears and the blows of the bludgeons and hammers!" Was he drawing on personal experience? In "Trickle Drops," one of the dark poems of the homoerotic "Calamus" sequence, the very act of writing becomes a kind of ritualistic bloodletting:

> Trickle drops! my blue veins leaving!
> O drops of me! trickle, slow drops,
> Candid from me falling, drip, bleeding drops,
> From wounds made to free you whence you were prison'd,
> From my face, from my forehead and lips,
> From my breast, from within where I was conceal'd, press forth red
>   drops, confession drops,
> Stain every page, stain every song I sing, every word I say, bloody
>   drops.

Never would the purging of demons cease for Whitman. Still, over time his literary voice became increasingly more multifaceted than it was in 1841, embracing not only pain and suffering but also a multitude of other impulses and desires: rapturous sensuality, patriotism, mysticism, cheer, confidence, as well as love of nature and music and slang. All of these impulses and many more would feed into the remarkably polyvocal 1855 edition of *Leaves of Grass*. But before achieving this com-

prehensiveness, Whitman would experiment with many different popu-
lar genres that exposed him to the many voices of American culture and
society. It would be a long journey from horrific private dramas like
"Death in the School-Room" and "Bervance" to that triumph of expan-
sion and absorption, *Leaves of Grass.*

4

MANNAHATTA: THE LITERARY MARKETPLACE AND URBAN REALITY

WHITMAN ARRIVED in Manhattan during the early phase of a revolution in American popular culture. The combined forces of the economic depression and changing print technology resulted in a whole new kind of literature for the masses. The 1830s had seen the decline of the stodgy partisan six-penny newspapers of the past and the rise of the penny press. With the publication of Benjamin Day's New York *Sun* in 1833 and James Gordon Bennett's *New York Herald* two years later, American papers suddenly became mass oriented. The new Napier cylinder press facilitated the rapid production of newspapers published every day and costing just one or two cents. Lively, democratic, and often luridly sensational, the penny papers attracted the attention of nearly all observers of American culture, including the young journalist Whitman, who wrote of them: "Every where their influence is felt. No man can measure it, for it is immeasurable."

The same advances in print technology that affected journalism also brought about dramatic changes in book production. In the late thirties the American "mammoth weeklies" began publishing cheap editions of foreign novels by the likes of Dickens, Bulwer, and Marryat. Because of the absence of an international copyright, which would not come until 1892, foreign works were readily pirated in America. An effective resistance to the pirating phenomenon would later be launched by the major American publishing houses, but in the meantime American authors labored under a distinct disadvantage. Mass publishers tended to take the safe route by reprinting already successful foreign writings instead of taking chances on unproven American ones. Foreign competition spurred a jingoistic reaction among American authors. This period saw the flowering of the intensely nationalistic Young America movement, whose organ was John L. O'Sullivan's *Democratic Review.* The bracing winds of nationalism wafted to Concord, Massachusetts, where Ralph Waldo Emerson called upon American writers to strike an original relation to the universe.

Whitman got direct exposure to Young America and Emerson in the forties. Seven of his early short stories were published in O'Sullivan's magazine. He reported one of Emerson's lectures for the New York *Aurora* and another for the *Brooklyn Daily Eagle.*

With literary nationalism so much in the air, why did Whitman not produce his intensely nationalistic *Leaves of Grass* in, say, 1845 instead of 1855? After all, Emerson's essay "The Poet," published in 1844, seems at first glance a perfect job description for the one who would celebrate himself as America's bard.

But it took far more than exposure to Emerson to produce *Leaves of Grass.* Too often a line is drawn from Emerson to Whitman, as though *Leaves of Grass* was little more than "The Poet" realized. Whitman, however, twice denied that Emerson had any influence at all on his poetry. Even if we accept another of his remarks—"I was simmering, simmering, simmering; Emerson brought me to a boil"—we are forced to realize that Emerson was at most a catalyst for a poetic imagination that had long been gathering materials and stimuli. Emerson himself expressed curiosity about what he termed the "long foreground" of *Leaves of Grass.* Whitman would write it was "useless to attempt reading the book without first carefully tallying that preparatory background."

Which brings us back to Manhattan in the forties. Arriving in the city at the time when the depression hit bottom, Whitman was forced to struggle in the literary marketplace. There was not a single kind of popular periodical he did not serve either as an editor or a contributor. His novel *Franklin Evans* represented his immersion in popular culture in two ways: it was one of America's earliest "shilling novels," works for the masses that presaged the famous dime novels; it was also a quintessential expression of the themes and style of the Washingtonians, the new populist temperance movement that had recently exploded on the cultural scene. Whitman's other fiction and poetry of the period shows him tapping into a variety of other popular genres as well.

But he was not just writing for the masses. He was throwing himself into their midst, observing every facet of their lives. "The popular tastes and employments taking precedence in poems or anywhere," he would write in "A Song for Occupations." The rapidly urbanizing environment of Manhattan and Brooklyn resulted in important changes in both the physical landscape of America and the behavioral patterns of its people. Whitman observed these changes with an eagle eye. "Remember," he would say, "the book [*Leaves of Grass*] arose out of my life in Brooklyn and New York from 1838 to 1853, absorbing a million people, for fifteen years, with an intimacy, an eagerness, an abandon, probably never equalled." Before producing what he called "the idiomatic book of my land," he listened attentively to his land's many idioms.

He was not, however, an undiscriminating populist. He saw great promise but also profound defects in the American urban scene and in working-class behavior. His poetry would be a kind of wondrous filtration system, absorbing all the disturbing, vicious aspects of American life and creatively recombining them with other, more positive ones. His poetry was not mimetic but rather transformative and meliorative.

His experiences in Manhattan in the forties show him surveying American society, familiarizing himself with its possibilities and its flaws, and preparing himself to produce fully representative poetry. If, as he once said, his poetry was "a great mirror or reflector" of society, it was a mirror in which America would see itself artistically improved.

Writing for the Masses

AS CHANGEABLE as had been his career as a teacher, it was downright dizzying when he became a full-time author and journalist. After his arrival in New York City from Long Island in May 1841 he wrote for O'Sullivan's *Democratic Review*, which would continue to publish his works for years. In the fall he became a compositor for Park Benjamin's *New World*, a weekly magazine with a circulation of nearly twenty-five thousand. By January 1842 Whitman's writings were appearing in John Neal's magazine *Brother Jonathan*, which promised the "Cheapest Reading in the World." That spring Whitman edited the New York *Aurora*, a patriotic daily leaning to nativism. After being discharged from the *Aurora*, apparently for laziness, he worked on an evening paper, the *Tattler*, for which he wrote a bulletin of murders.

Next he became a penny-a-liner for the *Daily Plebeian*, a Democratic Party paper run by the fiery, red-haired Locofoco Levi D. Slamm. Whitman's most popular work, the temperance novel *Franklin Evans*, appeared in late 1842 as part of a weekly shilling-novel series. The next spring he edited the *Statesman*, a semiweekly Democratic paper, and that summer he covered the police station and coroner's office as one of eight reporters for Moses Beach's famous penny paper, the New York *Sun*. Early 1844 saw him writing for a time for the *New York Mirror*, the popular weekly edited by N. P. Willis and George Pope Morris. In July he briefly edited the *Democrat*, a daily morning paper that was supporting James Polk for president and Silas Wright for governor of New York. The following spring he was writing tales for Thomas Dunn English's magazine, *The Aristidean*. By August 1845, when his family returned to Brooklyn after five years in Dix Hills, Whitman left Manhattan for Brooklyn, where he would remain, with only brief periods away, for the next seventeen years. In the fall of 1845 he wrote nearly a score of articles for Alden Spooner's *Star*. He had gained enough visibility to be hired as editor of the Democratic organ of Kings County, the *Brooklyn Daily Eagle*, which he edited from March 1846 to early 1848.

His residency pattern during this period was almost as varied as his job history. In the Manhattan years he shifted quickly between various boardinghouses. In 1842 he was at a Mrs. Chipman's, a genteel boardinghouse where he could live quietly and eat in a central dining room with the other tenants. In the *Aurora* he told an amusing story of getting home late one night, finding himself locked out, and being forced to spend the night at a city shelter along with a crowd of snoring strangers. The peripatetic nature of his living situations is captured in this later notebook jotting:

> Fall and winter of 1842 boarded at Mrs. R. in Spring st.
> Spring of 1843 boarded at Mrs. Bonnard's in John st.
> Also at Mrs. Edgarton's in Vesey.
> Summer of '43 at Mary's and Brown's in Duane st.
> October 1843 commenced with the Winants'

Only in 1845, when he settled near his family in Brooklyn, would he gain domestic stability, though even in Brooklyn he would move seven times in seventeen years.

Just as he worked and lived on the run, so he dashed off writings at a furious pace. Before 1855 he wrote twenty-four pieces of fiction, nineteen poems, and countless journalistic pieces. Too often this apprentice work is quickly dismissed or neglected altogether by those who turn immediately to the major poetry or try to guess about the causes of Whitman's change from pedestrian journalist to major poet. Paul Zweig's biography, for instance, picks up the poet's life in 1848, after most of the early pieces had already appeared, and follows it up to the Civil War, without tracing his roots backward into popular culture. A typical assessment of the early poems and fiction is given by Thomas Brasher, who calls them "unoriginal, conventional, and poorly written" and says of Whitman's only novel: "[I]t is almost incredible that the man who wrote *Leaves of Grass* also wrote *Franklin Evans*."

Although it is true that Whitman produced no distinguished work before the 1855 edition of *Leaves of Grass*, he did experiment with a variety of popular genres that set the stage for his multifaceted poetry. Before 1855, no single work by Whitman brought together under a single literary roof many voices of native and foreign culture. But his early writings, surveyed as a whole, show him reaching out in many directions, confining himself to no single style or theme. His readiness to test out different popular modes distinguished him from other popular authors of the day, many of whom stayed in fairly narrow ruts. Some, like Timothy Shay Arthur, stuck to reformist or moral fiction; others, like Susan Warner, to domestic novels; others, like William Ware, to historical and biblical fiction; others, like George Thompson, to seamy sensational fiction. Whitman tried out all these popular modes and more, integrating autobiographical elements with each.

Previous commentators on Whitman have not placed his early poems and fiction against their popular background and have thus failed to see just how culturally representative they were. Most of his early works fit into well-established popular categories, each with its own history. Among his pre-1855 imaginative writings, fourteen (nine poems, five tales) were dark works about death or haunted minds; seven (five stories, two poems) were sensational and adventurous; four (two tales, two poems) were visionary works, picturing angelic visitations; six others (a poem, three stories, a novel, and a tale fragment) endorsed reform, especially temperance; four (two poems and two tales) were patriotic or nationalistic; four poems were political; three tales and one poem were moral; one tale was biblical.

The fact that nearly two-thirds of his early writings were dark or adventurous works accords with the preponderance of these kinds of works in antebellum America. Contrary to the once-held view that the antebellum literary scene was dominated by sentimental, "feminized" writings, about 60 percent of all fiction volumes published in America between 1831 and 1860 were highly wrought, adventurous, or satirical, while just over 20 percent were domestic or religious. About 70 percent of the volumes were by men, 23 percent by women, with 7 percent published anonymously. During the 1840s, the decade in which nearly all Whitman's apprentice work appeared, the numbers tilted dramatically toward the sensational. By far the largest number of the cheap pamphlet novels introduced to the American scene during the decade were sensational; many almost literally dripped with blood.

Whitman always had a tricky time positioning himself vis-à-vis this sensational literature. On the one hand, he knew full well its sudden popularity and its broad appeal among the American masses. Even in the fifties, after the first crest of sanguinary pamphlet novels had passed,

he could write a newspaper article noting the extreme popularity of
"blood and thunder romances with alliterative titles and plots of star-
tling interest." "The public for whom these tales are written," he noted,
"require strong contrasts, broad effects and the fiercest kind of 'intense'
writing generally." He conceded that such writing was "a power in the
land, not without great significance in its way, and very deserving of
more careful consideration than has hitherto been accorded it." As chief
editor of the *Eagle* and later the *Daily Times*, he accommodated to popu-
lar taste by printing horrid stories of crime and violence. On the other
hand, he would become outspoken in his opposition to excesses in such
sensational literature. In his major poems he would make a studied effort
to represent the sensational as an important element of the cultural
scene, while rechanneling it and combining it with uplifting images de-
rived from other cultural arenas.

In the early forties, however, he had not yet developed such reserva-
tions about sensational literature. Nearly all the periodicals he wrote for
were riding the wave of sensationalism. The fact that he reported mur-
ders for the *Tattler* and wrote police and coroner's stories for the *Sun*
suggests his willing participation in this sensational culture. Several of
his early poems and stories were sensational in a straightforward way,
like the plotty, action-driven, yellow-covered novels of the day. One of his
poems, "The Inca's Daughter," portrays an Inca maid who, after re-
maining stoically silent while being tortured on the rack by Spaniards,
stabs herself with a poisoned arrow and dies. Another, "The Spanish
Lady," pictures the lovely Lady Inez, who is sleeping in her castle room
when suddenly she is stabbed by "one whose trade is blood and crime."
Five short sketches Whitman wrote for the *Aristidean* in 1845, published
as "Some Fact-Romances," lean toward the sensational. In one, a Long
Island man tries to save his drowning sister but fails and thereafter is
haunted by the vision of her dying face; he wastes away and dies. In
another, a French emigrant whose wife has died becomes a helpless ma-
niac and is committed to an asylum. Another, which Whitman calls "a
disgusting story of villainy and deceit," involves an imprisoned forger,
and another gives a comic twist to sensationalism by describing a woman
terrified at night by a thumping sound that turns out to be a fallen basket
of peaches.

Although Whitman's exercises in sensationalism were never as
bloody as those by his popular contemporaries, he did not shy away from
gory scenes. Two of his other tales in the *Aristidean*, "Richard Parker's
Widow" and "The Half-Breed: A Tale of the Western Frontier," show him
catering to the popular appetite for the grisly. The former tale recounts
the aftermath of the 1797 *Nore* [sic] mutiny, whose leader, Richard

Parker, was hanged from the yardarm. In a scene suggestive of necrophilia, Parker's maddened widow disinters his coffin, opens it, and embraces the corpse. "She clasped the cold neck," Whitman writes, "and kissed the clammy lips of the object of her search!" She later has his body reburied at Whitechapel, but she is eventually reduced to wretched beggary. "The Half-Breed" is a darkly adventurous story with an improbable cast of characters, including a monk, a hunchback, a half-breed, and a blacksmith. The plot, typical of sensational narratives of the day, is too tangled to be summarized: suffice it to say that the blacksmith, Peter Brown, is apparently murdered but is really not, that the hunchback is the true villain but the wrongly accused half-breed is tragically hanged and dies just before the frenzied Brown can rescue him. As the Indian's corpse swings on the rope, Brown dashes through the woods "with wild and ghastly visage, and with the phrenzied contortions of a madman in his worst paroxysm" until "his blood-shot eyes were fixed upon a hideous object dangling in the air."

Like other American sensationalists of the day, Whitman sometimes combined bloody violence with indictments of the ruling class. Several sensationalists of the 1840s assumed the dual role of entertaining the masses and defending their political interests. In the wake of Andrew Jackson's assaults on the "Monster Bank" and diatribes against capitalists by William Leggett and Orestes Brownson, popular novelists like George Lippard lambasted bankers, lawyers, and other upper-class figures in their fiction. Whitman assumed this kind of antielitist posture in "One Wicked Impulse!," a story that first appeared in 1845 in the *Democratic Review* under the title of "Revenge and Requital; A Tale of a Murderer Escaped." The villain of this piece is the sly lawyer Adam Covert, who "gained more by trickery than he did in the legitimate exercise of his profession." He takes control of the estate of a dead relative named Marsh, whose children Esther and Philip he threatens to drive into poverty unless Esther accepts his hand in marriage. Her brother Philip is enraged by Covert's knavery and becomes doubly angered when one night he meets the lawyer and thinks "what base and cruel advantage he had taken of many poor people, entangled in his power." Having impugned the exploitative rich, Whitman then points the tale toward another favorite theme of reform-minded sensationalists: opposition to capital punishment. The frenzied Philip murders Covert but escapes detection. Long haunted by the image of "the cold roll of the murder'd man's eye" and "the shrill exclamation of pain," he becomes a figure of agonized remorse, heroically nursing victims of a cholera epidemic. Whitman emphasizes that hanging Philip would have done no good, whereas his repentant social work helps humanity.

Metaphysical angst characterizes many of Whitman's early writings. Here again he corresponded with popular tastes. It is sometimes said that antebellum popular literature was comfortingly pious and that dark authors like Hawthorne and Melville stood in opposition to an easily optimistic culture. Actually, though, much popular fiction and poetry of the time was riddled with doubt and sadness. Whitman felt so at home in this cultural scene that when he offered his gloomy tale "The Angel of Tears" to an editor he boasted, "My stories, I believe, have been pretty popular, and extracted liberally." Among his most popular works were stories, like "Death in the School-Room" and "Bervance," that involved violence or haunted minds.

We have seen that these and certain other Whitman tales of the period seem to have sprung from some severe personal trauma. Other works are more generally brooding and skeptical. Life is full of "useless, vexing strife," Whitman writes in the poem "The Love That Is Hereafter"; all dreams are invalidated by "hope dissatisfied," and since on earth there is "Nought but woe," the heart "must look above, / Or die in dull despair." "Time levels all," he reflects in "The End of All"; the brilliant, rich, and gay "Live out their brief and brilliant day" and then "unheeded pass away." "All, all know care," he points out in "Each Has His Grief," and since death ends human agony, none should fear "The coffin, and the pall's dark gloom." Hopes for immortality through earthly renown are foolish, he says in "Ambition," for most who desire fame don't get it, and even those who do "must sleep the endless sleep" and will soon be forgotten. A real fear of annihilation lurks behind the poem "Time to Come," in which he notes that "This brain, and heart, and wondrous form / Must all alike decay," and, as for the soul, "Will it e'en live?"

None of these thoughts, of course, are either original or originally expressed. One can point to all kinds of literary antecedents for this kind of death-obsessed poetry, including eighteenth-century graveyard verse and dark Romanticism. It is significant, though, that he who would become the great poet of cheer (William James would characterize him as the apostle of healthymindedness) began as a poet of gloom. Most of his poetry of the 1840s reveals a dark, preoptimistic Whitman who had faith neither in organized religion nor in the saving power of poetry.

In fact, at this stage he was inclined to associate poetry with pain rather than hope. From our perspective, it might seem as though a Gray or Keats might have been his prototype for the brooding writer, but the poet who loomed largest in his young imagination was McDonald Clarke, the so-called Mad Poet of Broadway.

McDonald Clarke is a virtually forgotten figure in American letters, and his influence on Whitman has never been appreciated. A large-eyed man with tousled hair and a hooked nose, Clarke was a street drifter and the author of several volumes of poetry. Born in 1798 in Bath, Maine, he lost his parents early and in 1819 moved to Manhattan, where he was married to an actress whose mother opposed the match. Eventually the mother succeeded in separating them. He had intervals of insanity and spent time in the asylum on Blackwell's Island, but for the most part he wandered up and down Broadway, scribbling dark Romantic verse. As early as 1822, in the preface to his volume *Elixir of Moonshine*, he called himself a "wild, worn, wretched" man who was "classed with the vilest vagabond and the red list of madness and debauchery—a dangerous and desolating thing for fond mothers to curse, and frail daughters to depre-cate." Almost a caricature of the literary outsider, Clarke wrote poems on temperance, on city life, on his ill-fated romance, on Byron (with whom he identified), often with a defiant smack of vernacular wit. On March 4, 1842, he was picked up destitute by a policeman and put into a city prison, where he was found dead in the morning, having drowned in water flowing from an open faucet. He was buried in Brooklyn's Greenwood Cemetery. His grave read simply, "Poor M'Donald Clarke."

Whitman was fascinated by Clarke's life and poetry. In the *Aurora* he said Clarke "possessed all the requisites of a great poet," explaining: "Whoever has the power, in his writing, to draw bold, startling images, and strange pictures—the power to embody in language, original, and beautiful, and quaint ideas—is a true son of song. Clarke was such an one; not polished, perhaps, but yet one in whose faculties that all im-portant vital spirit of poetry burnt with a fierce brightness."

In a sense, Clarke was an early sketch of Whitman: a literary rebel who dressed in defiance of custom, wearing his shirt collar open at the neck to expose his upper chest (as Whitman later did), and who broke poetic rules. Although he almost always used rhyme, he sometimes var-ied the length of his lines and mixed slang with high diction, devices Whitman would perfect. Whitman's androgynous persona, his ability to switch genders, was foreshadowed in Clarke's belief that "Woman's na-ture is mixed with man's, / In the temperament of the Poet—a deep, / Unebbing tenderness . . . " If Whitman advertised his cheerful egotism by writing, "I cock my hat as I please indoors or out," Clarke had written that he "always wore a full cock'd hat, / In presence of Despair." He even anticipated Whitman by summoning eroticism into poetry, as in a piece on the women of Broadway:

What prodigious queer feelings will leap in the breast,
And make us feel funny in more parts than one,

If a fine girl is only transparently drest,
And shows what would take a seraph to shun.

Although Clarke's poetic voice ranged from the playful to the erotic, he was mainly a figure of desolation and despair. He wrote of the world: "Its look is warm—its heart is cold, / Its accent sweet—its nature savage." Elsewhere he called life "A cold, and clouded wilderness," adding that all suns "Dawn, but to light us to distress."

Whitman's poem "The Death and Burial of McDonald Clarke" portrayed Clarke as a persecuted author who died alone and without friends. When Clarke died, Whitman wrote, none thought "Of the griefs and pains that craz'd him; / None thought of the sorrow that turn'd his head, / Of the vileness of those who praised him." Both Clarke's iconoclasm and his suffering struck home with the impressionable young Whitman.

Besides finding in Clarke an example of literary experimentation, Whitman dabbled in popular genres that had taken on certain progressive characteristics. For example, in his 1845 tale "Shirval: A Tale of Jerusalem" he followed in the wake of a number of American writers who were revolutionizing the literary treatment of the historical Jesus. Because of America's powerful heritage of Puritanism, it had long been considered sacrilegious to deal freely with biblical topics in fiction. Only in the opening decades of the nineteenth century did some liberal writers dare to picture the human Jesus in concretely described historical settings. The movement toward the humanization of Jesus would lead to daringly secular embellishments of the Bible in best-sellers like Joseph Holt Ingraham's *The Prince of the House of David* (1855) and Lew Wallace's *Ben-Hur* (1880).

Whitman's contribution to the genre, "Shirval," was daring in its own right. Set in ancient Judea, the story tells of a funeral procession for a recently deceased man, Shirval. When the procession reaches the city gates, it is met by a man "of middle stature and fair proportions, in every motion whereof was easy grace. His step was neither rapid nor very slow. His face was beautifully clear, and his eyes, blue as the sky above them, beamed benevolence and love." He commands the dead man to rise, a command that, to everyone's amazement, is obeyed.

Today, this tale seems blandly conventional, but in a time when American writers were still escaping Puritan restrictions against fictionalizing the Bible, it was actually bold. The realistic description of Jesus was unusual for its day. It showed Whitman participating in the movement toward a relaxed, familiar treatment of sacrosanct topics, a movement that also lies behind some of his casual treatments of biblical themes in his poetry, as in "Song of Myself," where he imagines himself "Walking the old hills of Judea with the beautiful gentle God by my side."

A tale like "Shirval" is at the opposite pole from Whitman's dark, sensational writings and reveals his awareness of the entire spectrum of popular culture. If the dark works present the world as sad and violent, the biblical tale seeks consolation in the example of a tender, inspiring human being. This contrast anticipates Whitman's strategy in *Leaves of Grass* of seeking humanistic alternatives to a social reality that he regarded as ugly and fractious. If biblical fiction provided the archetype of the human Jesus, another popular genre—"legends" of the American Revolution—fed into the sentimental patriotism that informs much of his poetry. To counteract the disruptions of modern life, several popular writers of the forties, particularly George Lippard and Joel Tyler Headley, wrote nostalgically patriotic stories about Washington addressing his troops, the ringing of the Liberty Bell, and so on.

Whitman was not immune to the often excessive veneration the popular writers of the forties showered on the founding fathers. His 1842 tale "The Last of the Sacred Army" was as jingoistic and lachrymose as anything by his fellow authors. Whitman writes, "The memory of the Warriors of our Freedom!—let us guard it with a holy care." The narrator of the story dreams he is thirty years in the future, in the midst of people thronging to view the last surviving member of Washington's army. The old veteran tells of the war days, and the crowds shove forward to touch his garments. He shows them a medal with the initials "G. W." on it, given to him by the "Great Chief" himself. When the dreamer asks if it is right to bestow such veneration on a human being, a philosopher replies, "The model of one pure, upright character, living as a beacon in history, does more than the lumbering tomes of a thousand theorists." The kind of sentimental patriotism that suffuses the tale would tinge Whitman's poems, as witnessed by patriotic pieces like "The Centenarian's Story" and his poetic pictures of the weeping, tender Washington.

Another popular cultural phenomenon that affected him deeply was temperance reform. In old age Whitman became embarrassed by his novel *Franklin Evans*, which he said was one of his rare efforts on behalf of temperance. But he wrote several works before and after *Franklin Evans* that endorsed temperance, and he commented regularly on the issue in newspaper articles well into the 1850s. The rhetoric of temperance also appeared in his poetry.

It may be hard to understand how Whitman could have been involved with temperance reform, particularly since he was a convivial (though not excessive) drinker. The reasons for his involvement become clearer when we take into account historical background. Temperance reformers were responding to a long history of high alcohol consumption in American life. Up until the third decade of the nineteenth century, alcohol was served at virtually all social gatherings. "Everybody asked everybody to drink," recalled the reformer Thomas Low Nichols of his youth. "There were drunken lawyers, drunken doctors, drunken members of Congress, drunkards of all classes." Whitman's old-age memories of the prevalence of alcohol in his youth were equally vivid. He told Traubel, "It is very hard for the present generation anyhow to understand the drinkingness of those years—how the 'gentlemen' of the old school used liquor: it is quite incommunicable: but I am familiar with it: saw, understood it all as a boy." Whitman had personal reasons for concern about the problem. By his own report, his father had bouts with the bottle, as did his brother-in-law Ansel Van Nostrand and his brother Andrew.

Between 1825 and the Civil War, temperance reform came in three general phases: what might be called the evangelical, the Washingtonian, and the prohibition phases. Evangelical preachers like Lyman Beecher began in the 1820s to inveigh against the evils of drinking. This kind of religiously based temperance reform spread widely with the rise of the Whig Party. These early temperance reformers tried to use warnings and persuasion to induce people not to drink. A pledge of partial abstinence, prohibiting hard liquor but not wine or beer, was replaced in the thirties with one of total abstinence.

A dramatic change in emphasis came with the rise of the Washingtonians. This movement began in April 1840 when six men drinking in a Baltimore bar sent some of their number to a temperance lecture that led to their repentance. These men became the core of a movement of reformed drunkards that grew with incredible rapidity, gaining 100,000 members by 1841 and half a million two years later. Working class in origin, the Washingtonians appealed to the masses by acting out the miseries of drunkenness and fostering temperance saloons, temperance hotels, temperance theaters, temperance festivals—in other words, an alcohol-free version of working-class life.

Temperance agitation did affect yearly liquor consumption, which fell from around 4 gallons of absolute alcohol per American in 1830 to just 1.8 gallons by 1845. There was justification for Whitman's statement in *Franklin Evans:* "A great revolution has come to pass within the last eight or ten years. The dominion of the Liquor Fiend has been assaulted and battered." But the theatrical tactics of the Washingtonians and notorious instances of backsliding led to its supplantation by another group, the Sons of Temperance, which demanded respectable dress, language, and comportment. By the late forties, the whole moral-suasion movement had fallen into disrepute. The large majority of those who had taken the total abstinence pledge in 1840 were drinking again. Prohibition was seen as the only sure answer to the alcohol problem. The first state prohibition law had been passed in 1838, and a decade later the movement took off. Thirteen states adopted so-called Maine laws between 1852 and 1855, with 1855 the peak year in the number of prohibition laws passed.

The populist Whitman was more strongly attracted to the Washingtonians than to other types of temperance reform. He loved the colorful festivals the Washingtonians put on. "Yesterday was a great time with the New York temperance societies," he wrote in the March 30, 1842, issue of the *Aurora.* "They had processions, and meetings, and orations, and festivals, and banners displayed, and music, and a grand blow out at night to cap the whole." He approvingly noted "the immense number of citizens, formerly intemperate men, but now worthy members of society."

He especially enjoyed the dramatic speeches of the greatest temperance orator of the day, John Bartholomew Gough. An ex-actor and reformed drunkard, Gough put his histrionic talents to good use on the lecture platform, delighting his hearers with spine-tingling accounts of alcohol-induced crimes and nightmarish visions spawned by delirium tremens. Gough's sensational tactics prompted critics to insist he was a mere showman and charlatan, a charge that took on weight when in September 1845 he disappeared for several days and was found in a drunken stupor in a whorehouse. Whitman did not let the Gough case shake his faith in the temperance cause. In one of his articles on Gough for the *Brooklyn Star* he argued, "If the temperance doctrine fell whenever one of its converts became a backslider again, sad indeed would be its fate! . . . So long as the endless and overwhelming train of all fact and argument founds the great cause of temperance as a rock immovable, it matters not much whether one, two, or twenty of its shining lights go out." Whitman hated the prohibition movement, arguing in the *Eagle* that reform could be achieved only through persuasion, not legislation. He kept this hope alive even in the fifties when prohibition became popular. Some of his poems used the language of persuasion, associating drunkards with impure or disgusting things. "A drunkard's breath," he wrote in "A Hand-Mirror," "unwholesome eater's face, venerealee's flesh, / Lungs rotting away piecemeal, stomach sour and cankerous, /

Joints rheumatic, bowels clogged with abomination." In "Song of the Open Road" he declared that "no rumdrinker or venereal taint is permitted here."

Such moments in his poems were remnants of the scare-tactic rhetoric of the Washingtonians, whose years of prominence had been from 1840 to 1845, just when Whitman had written temperance poems and fiction. His first temperance work, a poem of early 1840 titled "Young Grimes," was temperance writing of the most conventional variety, harking back to Lyman Beecher's conservative language and tame fiction of the 1820s like *Edmund and Margaret* and *The Lottery Ticket*, which had emphasized the rewards of virtue rather than the wages of vice. "Young Grimes" is about a man who gains prosperity and domestic happiness through clean living.

Only with the rise of the sensation-mongering Washingtonians did Whitman's temperance writings begin to darken. His story "Reuben's Last Wish," published in the New York *Washingtonian* in May 1842, was a grim portrait of a once-happy farmer driven by alcohol to brutalize his wife and children. The man repents only when his invalid son Reuben, whose illness has resulted from the drunkard's maltreatment, points in warning to an unsigned temperance pledge as he dies.

This kind of moralistic sensationalism, typical of the Washingtonians, was multiplied exponentially in *Franklin Evans*, the novel Whitman wrote for the movement in the fall of 1842. Whitman's most popular work during his lifetime (it sold some twenty thousand copies), *Franklin Evans* shows him identifying fully with the popular imagination.

Since the early 1830s, American reformers had created sensations by describing vice so vividly that they themselves were denounced as vicious and exploitative. The most highly publicized scandal was that surrounding the Manhattan antiprostitution reformer, the Reverend John R. McDowall. In 1832 McDowall published a detailed description of New York's whorehouses and their inhabitants, whose numbers he wildly exaggerated. Immediately, the conservative press branded McDowall as an obscene writer pandering to vicious tastes. Although McDowall insisted on his worthy intentions, he was finally brought to trial on obscenity charges and defrocked. Similar controversies in the thirties surrounded anti-Catholic novels of the decade, particularly Maria Monk's *Awful Disclosures* (1836), a tale of convent debauchery and infanticide that was widely condemned as obscene. The antimasturbation tracts by John Todd and Sylvester Graham also stirred up a storm. The noisiest brouhaha would be provoked by George Lippard's 1845 antiseduction novel *The Quaker City*. Although Lippard called it "pure" and "destitute of any idea of sensualism," the novel described fallen women and upper-class philanderers in such lip-smacking detail that it was widely condemned as filthy. In Lippard's words, it became "more attacked, and more read, than any work of American fiction ever published."

Since few reviews of Whitman's *Franklin Evans* have survived, there is no telling whether this sort of controversy accompanied its publication. But the many surviving reviews of *Leaves of Grass* show that Whitman's major poetry aroused similarly ambivalent responses, with some calling it obscene, others defending it as pure, and Whitman himself insisting on his moral intentions. These complexities in response and intention reflect the stormy reform climate in which Whitman was weaned. If *Leaves of Grass* was an "immoral reform" book on a large scale, *Franklin Evans* had been one on a small one. It helped sow the seeds for *Leaves of Grass,* because it showed Whitman experimenting with an ostensibly pure vehicle—temperance reform—to explore themes that veered quickly into the sensational and erotic. From his reform culture Whitman learned to explore taboo social and psychological areas.

Written at the peak of the Washingtonian frenzy, *Franklin Evans* embodied all the contradictions of the Washingtonian movement, contradictions that would cripple the movement and lead to its downfall.

On one level, the temperance message of *Franklin Evans* is sincere. The novel gives many examples of the dire results of drinking. The young orphan Franklin Evans bears witness to the ravages of alcohol. At the stage depot on eastern Long Island he meets a once-happy man who has lost his farm and his family due to his own drinking. When Evans reaches New York, he is taken to a bar and has his first drink. A string of tragic events follows. He is married to a wonderful woman who soon dies from maltreatment and neglect. He falls in with criminals and is arrested for robbery. The man who procures his freedom persuades him to sign the "old" temperance pledge, forbidding hard liquor but permitting beer and wine. This partial pledge does not prevent him from resuming drinking and falling into deeper troubles. He goes south, where after a drunken revel he marries a mulatto woman, Margaret, whom he soon comes to detest. Margaret eventually murders a rival and then kills herself in prison. These horrid events give Evans an impetus for reform that is strengthened when he hears the sad story of a dying man, Stephen Lee, whose two children have died as a result of his wife's drunkenness. Lee convinces Evans to sign the new total-abstinence pledge and rewards him by leaving him money.

The novel ends with a long paean to the Washingtonians, who are said to be rallying the whole country with their calls for reform. In a guarded reference to the histrionic sensationalism of the Washingtonian orators, Whitman writes, "It is true, that the dictates of a classic and most refined taste, are not always observed by these people." Their "want of polish, or grace," he argues, is made up for by their forcefulness and democratic emphasis.

But the Washingtonians, and Whitman as their mouthpiece, were caught in a bind. As sincere as they may have been in their calls for reform, they were forced to compete for an American working class that feasted on crime-filled penny papers, melodramas, dark-reforms exposés, and P. T. Barnum's freak shows. Small wonder that the Washingtonians' surge in popularity resulted largely from their horrific renditions of crimes and delirium tremens. A lot of dark theater was involved in their efforts to reach the masses.

Likewise, there was a good amount of exploitation and manipulation in Whitman's delivery of the temperance message in *Franklin Evans*. The novel was, in his italicized words, "written *for the mass*," and, like other reformers of the day, he knew that the mass liked sex and violence mixed with their morality. Much of *Franklin Evans* has little to do with temperance. Whitman's publisher promoted the novel by saying it would "create a sensation, both for the ability with which it is written, as well as the interest of the subject." Most who bought the twelve-and-a-half-cent pamphlet were doubtless looking for one more sensation to go along with their morning *Herald* and their latest visit to Barnum's museum.

The novel is filled with scenes that offered diversion to the public and, perhaps, purgation for Whitman. The story of a disillusioned young man leaving for Manhattan from the extreme eastern end of Long Island (whose inhabitants, Whitman writes ambiguously, are not "versed in city life") reflects Whitman's own flight to the city after his troubling experiences on the island. Homoerotic fantasy seems to enter into the description of the bar Evans is taken to: "It was indeed a seductive scene. Most of the inmates were young men; and I noticed no small number quite on the verge of boyhood." The standard Washingtonian theme that homes can be shattered by alcohol is dramatized no fewer than four times by Whitman, whose harping on the theme of ruined marriages may reflect his own ambivalence about heterosexual relationships.

Whatever the biographical meanings of the narrative, gratuitous violence and taboo behavior abound. Significantly, the novel was later reprinted in the *Eagle* under the nontemperance title *Fortunes of a Country-Boy; Incidents in Town—and His Adventures at the South*. The boundary between Washingtonian reform and mere sensationalism was thin indeed. This becomes glaringly evident in the interpolated tale in *Franklin Evans* about two members of rival Indian tribes who kill each other: at the end, a chief shot by a poisoned arrow "gave a wild shriek—his life-blood spouted from the wound," but with "hate and measureless revenge" he plunges his knife into his foe, who also dies. This story has nothing to do with temperance reform. Nor do most of the incidents surrounding Evans's marriage to the slave Margaret. The theme of miscegenation was a daring one that had been treated only by a handful of writers before Whitman. Not only does he deal with this risqué topic, but he revels in the perverse results of the flawed marriage, including murder and suicide. Toward the end of the novel Evans admits he has enjoyed reflecting upon even "the very dreariest and most degraded incidents which I have related in the preceding pages." He adds the narration has been "far from agreeable to me—but in my own self-communion upon the subject, I find a species of entertainment."

A species of entertainment. This, ultimately, is what the Washingtonian reform was for Whitman. He would later joke that he wrote *Franklin Evans* in three days for money under the influence of alcohol; the type of alcohol was variously reported as port, gin, or whiskey. Given the contradictions surrounding the Washingtonians, it is no more surprising that Whitman would write the novel while under the influence than that John Gough was found intoxicated in a bordello or that the Washingtonians as a whole would decline. Nor is it odd that Whitman went on to begin another dark temperance piece, "The Madman," the opening section of which appeared on January 23, 1842, in the New York *Washingtonian*. His main goal in all his temperance writings, besides airing private aggressions and fantasies, was to make a connection with the American masses. Peddled as the work of "a Popular American Author," *Franklin Evans* was, in Whitman's words, "not written for the critics, but for THE PEOPLE." He hoped the story might do some good, issued "in the cheap and popular form you see, and wafted by every mail to all parts of this vast republic."

The problem was that this was a tawdry way of reaching the masses. Whitman's verdict on the novel in old age would be unequivocal: "It was damned rot—rot of the worst sort—not insincere perhaps, but rot, nevertheless: it was not the business for me to be up to."

Before he could recognize the tawdriness of *Franklin Evans* he had to observe closely the behavior and preoccupations of the kinds of working-class readers this sort of novel appealed to. His later affinity with the masses was tried in the fire of his firsthand observation of rapidly changing Manhattan and Brooklyn.

The Journalist and the City

WHITMAN'S EARLY CAREER as a fiction writer and poet was brief and intense. Most of his apprentice work was done by 1846, after which he wrote just one tale and five poems until the appearance of *Leaves of Grass* in 1855. As his popular fiction and poetry dwindled, his journalistic output remained steady. His journalism shows that *Leaves of Grass*, far from being an unexplainable miracle, was the product of a mind fully engaged with the contemporary cultural and social scene.

His writings for the New York *Aurora* in spring 1842, the first substantial body of his journalism, give a capsule view of the range of his interests. As editor of the *Aurora*, Whitman promised "something *piquant*, and something solid, and something sentimental, and something humorous—all dished up in 'our own peculiar way.'" The *Aurora* was a two-penny daily that had been founded in 1841 by Anson Herrick and John F. Ropes. The paper's first editor, Thomas Low Nichols, had left the paper in February 1842 after printing a libelous article. On March 28 Herrick and Ropes announced they had "secured the services of Mr. Walter Whitman, favorably known as a bold, energetic and original writer, as their leading editor" and that he would "carry out their original design of establishing a sound, fearless and independent daily paper." By March 30 the *Brooklyn Daily Eagle* could see "a marked change for the better" in the *Aurora* since Whitman's arrival there, though it noted "a dash of egotism occasionally." Although the *Aurora*'s circulation did not vie with that of the largest penny papers, it more than held its own, achieving a sizable readership.

Whitman saw the penny papers as a democratizing influence that brought knowledge to the masses. "Among newspapers," he wrote, "the penny press is the same as common schools among seminaries of education." This positive attitude to the penny papers was reflected in "A Song for Occupations," where he mentions among things to be sung "The column of wants in the one-cent paper" and "Cheap literature, maps, charts, lithographs, daily and weekly newspapers."

The *Aurora* was located at 162 Nassau Street in an area later called Printing-House Square because all the Democratic papers were published near Tammany Hall, the headquarters of Manhattan's Democratic Party. Named after Chief Tammany, an eighteenth-century Indian hero, Tammany Hall was the fountainhead of the powerful ward bosses whose exploitativeness would be epitomized by William Marcy Tweed, the Democratic boss who in the 1860s would use money and intimidation to control virtually every aspect of Manhattan public life. In the early forties Tammany was already touched by financial scandals and by power struggles over the emerging question of immigrants, who were beginning to flock to America's shores in large numbers. A group of nativist Democrats vigorously opposed the foreigners, while mainstream Tammany Democrats, led by Levi Slamm, wooed them in an effort to win the increasingly important Catholic vote. Much of the controversy centered on John Hughes, the Manhattan bishop who demanded public funds for Catholic schools, an idea bitterly opposed by the nativists.

In his columns for the *Aurora*, Whitman began to perform the kind of strange dance on the nativist question that would characterize his later journalism and his major poetry. He took the nativist side on several key questions. He spared no vitriol in describing Bishop Hughes, whom he called "a false villain, who uses his pontifical robes to cover the blackest, most traitorous heart in the broad limits of the American republic." When the working-class agitator Mike Walsh and his Spartan gang disrupted an Irish rally and then stoned Hughes's home, Whitman wrote: "Had it been the reverend hypocrite's head, instead of his windows, we could hardly find it in our soul to be sorrowful." In the war of the Democrats for Tammany, Whitman took the nativist side. He insisted that Tammany needed a thoroughly American paper like the *Aurora* and branded Levi Slamm's *New Era* "a stupid, wishy washy Catholic paper." Using the sort of racist, paranoid imagery that filled anti-Catholic literature of the day, he expressed dismay at the idea of Tammany serving a "coarse, unshaven, filthy, Irish rabble" and asked: "[S]hall these dregs of foreign filth—refuse of convents—scullions from Austrian monasteries—be permitted to dictate what Tammany *must* do?" On the other hand, he resisted thoroughgoing nativism. He specifically denounced the emerging Native American Party, urged the government to treat immigrants kindly, and stated, "Let us receive these foreigners to our shores, and to our good offices." Already, the odd coupling of intense Americanism and sincere internationalism, both central to his poetry, began to be visible.

He described the sights and sounds of the city in a spirit that would be felt in his poetry. His appreciative sketch of "an auctioneer, standing on a table or barrel top, and crying out to the crowd around him, the merits of the articles, and the bids made for them" presaged his own exuberant cataloging of the marvels of common experience in a way that once led Emerson to compare him to an auctioneer. His report of a fire— a "horrible yet magnificent sight" that left behind "crumbled ashes" and shattered dreams—anticipated the lines: "I am the mash'd fireman with breast-bone broken, / Tumbling walls buried me in their debris, / Heat and smoke I inspired, I heard the yelling shouts of my comrades."

His picture of butchers who after work "amuse themselves with a jig, or a break-down" and explore "the mystery of a double shuffle" looked forward to the lines:

> The butcher-boy puts off his killing-clothes, or sharpens his knife at
>   the stall in the market,
> I loiter enjoying his repartee and his shuffle and break-down.

Other aspects of his poetry nurtured by his early journalism were his brash independence and his combative rhetoric. The newspaper world in which he found himself was an explosive one of colorful personalities and rough language. Newspaper editors often resorted to the bare-fisted tactics used also by the street gangs of the day. Whitman's political mentor William Leggett wrote flaming editorials that got him into trouble with the conservative editor James Watson Webb, who met Leggett on the street one day and pummeled him with his cane. James Gordon Bennett, whose *Herald* was the nation's most popular paper, made great capital of his battles with other editors. In the thirties he was attacked on the street no fewer than three times; he played up each incident in the *Herald*, regaling his sensation-loving readers with the details of each assault. In 1840 he deliberately fanned the flames of what came to be known as the Moral War. Bennett had used the words "petticoats" and "legs" in his paper instead of permissible euphemisms like "inexpressibles" and "limbs." When his prudish opponents expressed outrage, he flouted them by writing, "Petticoats—petticoats—petticoats—petticoats—there—you fastidious fools, vent your mawkishness on that." Other editors heaped abuse on him, and he fired back. "Obscene vagabond," "mass of trash," "loathsome and leprous slanderer and libeller," were some of the epithets traded in the mud-fest.

Whitman leaped gleefully into the cutthroat world of popular journalism. Despite his view of the penny press as a democratizing force, he knew well the brutal, sensational nature of American papers when compared with those abroad. He noted "the superiority of tone of the London and Paris press over our cheaper and more diffused papers," and conceded, "Scurrility—the truth may as well be told—is a sin of the American newspaper press." As a journalist he dipped into the mud many a time. Because of its nativist slant, the *Aurora* regularly attacked editors born abroad, such as Bennett, a native of Scotland, and Park Benjamin, who was from British Guiana. In the aftermath of the Moral War, it was open season on Bennett. Whitman dredged up the blackest terms to describe him:

A reptile marking his path with slime wherever he goes, and breathing mildew at everything fresh and fragrant; a midnight ghoul, preying on rottenness and repulsive filth; a creature, hated by his nearest intimates, and bearing the consciousness thereof upon his distorted features, and upon his despicable soul; one whom good men avoid as a blot to his nature—who all despise, and whom no one blesses—*all* this is James Gordon Bennett.

Even though Whitman had worked for Park Benjamin's *New World* before coming to the *Aurora*, he turned on his former employer, calling him a foreign infidel and "one of the most vain pragmatical nincompoops in creation."

Such slashing rhetoric was so common in the penny press that it is hard to say whether in Whitman's case it resonated with the recent traumas he appears to have suffered as a Long Island teacher. Still, it should be noted that many of his tirades in the *Aurora* contain images of painful persecution, and some refer to tarring and feathering. To express his rage at a Democratic senator who supported Bishop Hughes he wrote, "If ever any scoundrel deserved a coat of tar and feathers, this base senator is the one." In reference to the "reverend villain" Hughes himself, Whitman asserted, "In the west, where the statute books afford no remedy for outrage, the injured community takes the case into its own hands." In his images of the priest and his followers being tarred and feathered, was Whitman enjoying imaginative reprisal for the injuries against him by the Reverend Ralph Smith and his Southold congregation? Whitman's denunciations of ministers often had a vindictive ring, as in an article against capital punishment where he declared that when "clergymen call for sanguinary punishments in the name of the Gospel . . . my soul is filled with amazement, indignation, and horror, utterly uncontrollable. When I go by a church, I cannot help thinking whether its walls do not sometimes echo, 'Strangle and kill in the name of God!'"

Whether or not such pained language was related to his Long Island experiences, he faced new traumas in the newspaper world. His dismissal from the *Aurora* was surrounded by infighting and backbiting. Although he had written most of the copy and kept some ten compositors busy, in the May 3, 1842, issue of the paper the owners charged him with laziness. By May 16 they reported that Whitman had been disconnected from the paper for several weeks, calling him "the laziest fellow who ever undertook to edit a city paper." That summer Whitman sought revenge by printing in his next paper, the *Tattler,* insulting tirades against Herrick and Ropes clipped from the Hartford *Review.* A lively war followed. In late August the *Aurora* owners reported that an abusive article had appeared in "a small, 'obscure daily' now under the control of a 'pretty pup' once in our employment; but whose indolence, incompetence, loaferism and blackguard habits forced [us?] to kick him out of office." Whitman replied in kind. "There is in this city," he wrote, "a trashy, scurrilous, and obscene daily paper, under the charge of two as dirty fellows, as ever were able by the force of brass, ignorance of their own ignorance, and a coarse manner of familiarity, to push themselves among gentlemen."

Such journalistic jousting placed Whitman in the company of that master of withering invective, Mike Walsh (see fig. 12). This volatile editor and working-class politician has been a shadowy figure in previous Whitman biographies, mentioned at most only in passing. The omission is surprising, especially since there are verifiable links between Whitman and Walsh. One of Whitman's early poems, "Lesson of the Two Symbols," appeared in July 1843 on the front page of the first issue of Walsh's newspaper, the *Subterranean*. Whitman praised Walsh and his Spartan gang in the *Aurora* and mentioned him several other times in his journalism. When Walsh died in 1859, a long obituary, probably by Whitman, appeared in the *Brooklyn Daily Times*, which Whitman was editing at the time.

Cockiness and defiance of authority were what Mike Walsh embodied above all. His newspaper's motto, "Independent in everything—neutral in nothing," was characteristic, as was one of his mots: "Any dead fish can swim with the stream, but it takes a real live one to go against the current." One thinks of Whitman's poetic boasts, such as "I know perfectly well my own egotism." Born in Ireland around 1810, Walsh had come as a child to New York City, where his father started a mahogany yard. Mike was apprenticed to a lithographer and then became a journalist and defender of the working class. He slept summers in city parks, insisting the night air toughened him, and refused to wear an overcoat in the winter. He was the leader of the b'hoys of the Bowery, who rallied around him and reflected his muscle and pluck. The kind of pointed rhetoric introduced by Leggett and Bennett became in Walsh's hands a clublike weapon. In his speeches at Tammany Hall he ridiculed his opponents to their faces. The pages of his *Subterranean* were alive with trenchant one-liners. He dubbed a New York judge "one of the human stink weeds which are nurtured by the moral slime and putrefaction of that sink of iniquity, satirically denominated, the 'Halls of Justice.'" Predictably, he was twice jailed for libel. In his erratic career, he participated briefly in the Fourierist experiment at Brook Farm and then went on to defend Southern interests in the North as a congressman. With the rise of antislavery sentiment in the 1850s, he fell out of favor, drifted in an alcoholic haze through Europe, and died in Manhattan on March 18, 1859, under suspicious circumstances.

Whitman's aggressive, sometimes hypermasculine persona in *Leaves of Grass* seems a tempered version of Walsh's self-consciously virile pose. The obituary of Walsh in Whitman's *Daily Times* called him "a man of original talent, rough, full of passionate impulses, . . . but he lacked balance, caution,—the ship often seemed devoid of both ballast and rudder." The assessment was apt. Walsh's Tammany speeches verged on becoming riots. If opponents tried to slink out of the hall, he called them soft-spined cowards and challenged them to fisticuffs. Fights between opposing parties of his hearers often broke out. Whitman's description of himself in "Song of Myself" as "Turbulent, fleshy, sensual, eating, drinking, and breeding" is less true of Whitman (he was in fact few of these things) than of Walsh and his ilk. The sexual machismo Whitman projected, as in the line "You there, impotent, loose in the knees, / Open your scarf'd chops till I blow grit within you," had been anticipated by Walsh's pronouncements of potency and virility, as when he derided men who "are not lascivious, because they have not got stamina enough in their composition to keep their back-bone straight."

Equally important for understanding the Whitman persona as Walsh was the group that worshiped him: the b'hoys of the Bowery. Again, the *Daily Times* obituary of Walsh is suggestive. It read: "What a career! A New York b'hoy—up to all the smartness and deviltry of the east side of town—fond of his friends, and they idolising him—. . . . " Although Whitman himself was never one of the b'hoys, he carefully observed their ways and language. He mentioned the b'hoy several times in his journalism and once wrote a long description of one for the *New Orleans Daily Crescent.* "Mose Velsor," a pseudonym he used for some of his newspaper pieces, combined his Velsor ancestry and the most popular nickname among the b'hoys, Mose.

The b'hoy grew from urban popular culture and fed back into it. The source of the figure seems to have been popular plays based on British author Pierce Egan's urban sketches *Life in London* (1821), usually called *Tom and Jerry* in its dramatic adaptations. Two lead characters, Bob Logic and Corinthian Tom, were streetwise young men who toured the city in picaresque fashion. Although partly based on this British type, the b'hoy of New York's Bowery district quickly assumed distinctive characteristics.

Typically, the b'hoy was a butcher or other worker who spent after-hours running to fires with engines, going on target excursions, or promenading on the Bowery with his g'hal. The b'hoy and the g'hal had their own dress and habits. The b'hoy clipped his hair short in back, kept his long sidelocks heavily greased with soap (hence his sobriquet "soap-locks"), and perched a stovepipe hat jauntily on his head. He always had a cigar or chaw of tobacco in his mouth. He wore a red shirt fastened to one side with large white buttons, a black silk tie knotted carelessly under a rolling collar, and trousers that flared slightly over his high-heeled calfskin boots. The g'hal wore colorful multilayered clothes, carried a parasol on her shoulder, and walked with a swing and a smirk. Though of the working class, the b'hoy and the g'hal aped the customs and manners of the upper class. They loved melodramas and penny papers but also Shakespeare. Whitman's humorous description of the b'hoy caught this range of attitudes and interests:

> Whilst he puffs the smoke of a remarkably bad segar directly under-neath your nostrils, he will discourse most learnedly about the classical performances in the Chatham Theatre, and swear by some heathen god or goddess that "[James Hudson] Kirby was one of 'em, and no mistake." This was one of the "b'hoys of the Bowery." He strenuously contends that Mr. N. P. Willis is a humbug—that Mike Walsh is a "hoss," and that the Brigadier "ain't no where."

When absorbed back into popular culture, the b'hoy became a larger-than-life American figure on the order of Paul Bunyan and Davy Crockett. The b'hoy character was introduced to the American stage in an 1834 melodrama, *Beulah Spa; or Two of the B'hoys*. The craze really took off with Benjamin A. Baker's 1848 play *A Glance at New York*, followed by other plays about "Mose" and "Sikesey." There were *Mose in a Muss*, *Mose in California*, and many similar plays, most of them with the versatile actor Frank S. Chanfrau in the b'hoy role. So popular were these plays that by the late 1840s the b'hoy had replaced the frontier screamer as the most prominent figure in American humor. Onstage, the b'hoy gained superhuman powers. The gargantuan Mose used lampposts as clubs, swam across the Hudson with two strokes, and leaped easily from Manhattan to Brooklyn. Pamphlet novels like Ned Buntline's *The Mysteries and Miseries of New York*, *The G'hals of New York*, and *The B'hoys of Boston* popularized the b'hoy as irrepressibly pugnacious and given to violent escapades.

As a New Yorker who loved to fraternize with common people, Whitman mingled with the workers who made up the b'hoy population. He later recalled going to plays on the Bowery, and "the young shipbuilders, cartmen, butchers, firemen (the old-time 'soap-lock' or exaggerated 'Mose' or 'Sikesey,' of Chanfrau's plays,) they, too, were always to be seen in these audiences, racy of the East River and the Dry Dock." In his book on language, *An American Primer,* he recorded several slang expressions used by "the New York Bowery Boy" and praised "the splendid and rugged characters that are forming among these states, or have already formed,—in the cities, the firemen of Mannahatta, and the target excursionist, and Bowery Boy."

One of his goals as a poet was to capture the vitality and defiance of the b'hoy:

> The boy I love, the same becomes a man not through derived power,
>   but in his own right,
> Wicked, rather than virtuous out of conformity or fear,
> Fond of his sweetheart, relishing well his steak,
> Unrequited love or a slight cutting him worse than sharp steel cuts,
> First-rate to ride, to fight, to hit the bull's eye, to sail a skiff, to sing a
>   song or play on the banjo,
> Preferring scars and the beard and faces pitted with smallpox over
>   all latherers,
> And those well-tann'd to those that keep out of the sun.

His whole persona in *Leaves of Grass*—wicked rather than conventionally virtuous, free, smart, prone to slang and vigorous outbursts—reflects the b'hoy culture. One early reviewer opined that his poems reflected "the extravagance, coarseness, and general 'loudness' of Bowery boys," also with their candor and acceptance of the body. Another generalized, "He is the 'Bowery Bhoy' in literature."

Another street group Whitman watched with interest was variously called the roughs, rowdies, or loafers, a distinct class of gang members and street loungers who roved through Manhattan's poorer districts and often instigated riots. A typical description of them came in a contemporary account of the 1834 election riots: "The disorderly class, 'the roughs,' by their protracted drinking, became more and more maddened, and hence riper for more desperate action." Rival companies of roughs formed gangs with names like the Plug Uglies, the Roach Guards, the Shirt Tails, the Dead Rabbits. In a time of rapid urbanization and economic dislocation, gangs provided certain of the urban poor with a sense of identity and an outlet for violent impulses.

The urban rough intrigued yet disturbed Whitman. It has been often said that Whitman, the ultimate democrat, loved the masses and championed them in his poetry. Actually, his poems presented an improved version of street types whose tendencies to violence and vulgarity he frowned upon. One of the constant themes of his journalism was that rowdiness and bad habits were all too common among the street toughs of New York and Brooklyn. He may have once fantasized leading a nation of loafers, but by the 1840s he thought urban loafing was often mingled with viciousness. In an 1845 article he asked, "How much of your leisure time do you give to *loafing?* what vulgar habits of smoking cigars, chewing tobacco, or making frequent use of blasphemous or obscene language?" In "Rowdyism in Brooklyn," a piece he wrote for the *Eagle*, he lamented the anarchic violence and loud obscenities of roving youths. A decade later, he feared the situation had worsened. "Mobs and murderers appear to rule the hour," he wrote in 1857 in the *Brooklyn Daily Times*. "The revolver rules, the revolver is triumphant." "Rowdyism Rampant" was the title of an alarmed piece in which he denounced the "law-defying loafers who make the fights, and disturb the public peace"; he prophesied that "some day decent folks will take the matter into their own hands and put down, with a strong will, this rum-swilling, rampant set of rowdies and roughs." In Manhattan, street gangs became so prominent during the administration of Mayor Fernando Wood that Whitman called the city's ruling party the Dead Rabbit Democracy.

If he chastised the rowdies and loafers in his journalism, he presented an improved version of them in his poetry. "Already a nonchalant breed, silently emerging, appears on the streets," he wrote in one poem, describing the type in another poem as "Arrogant, masculine, naive, rowdyish / [. . .] Attitudes lithe and erect, costume free, neck open, of slow movement on foot." In a draft of another poem he wrote that he alone sang "the young man of Mannahatta, the celebrated rough." Early reviewers of *Leaves of Grass* saw the link between the poet and New York street culture. The very first review placed Whitman in the "class of society sometimes irreverently styled 'loafers.'" The second review likewise called Whitman "a perfect loafer, though a thoughtful, amiable, able one." Another said that he exhibited "the quality of the celebrated New York 'rough,' full of muscular and excessively virile energy, full of animal blood, masterful, striding to the front rank, allowing none to walk before him, full of rudeness and recklessness, talking and acting his own way, utterly regardless of other people's ways." So indelible was the image of Whitman as a street person that the decorous poet James Russell Lowell once warned a foreign visitor against going to see him by exclaiming: "Whitman is a rowdy, a New York tough, a loafer, a frequenter of low places, a friend of cab drivers!"

Some, however, realized that Whitman was a rough with a difference. Charles Eliot Norton called him in a review "a compound of New England transcendentalist and New York rowdy," and in a letter noted that he combined traits of "a Concord philosopher with those of a New York fireman." Those who saw Whitman's infusion of a philosophical, contemplative element into street types accurately gauged his poetic purpose. Appalled by squalid forms of urban loafing, he outlined new forms of loafing in his poems. "Walt Whitman, an American, one of the roughs, a kosmos": this famous self-description in "Song of Myself" uplifts the rough by placing him between words that radiate patriotism ("an American") and mysticism ("a kosmos"). Purposely in his poems Whitman shuttled back and forth between the grimy and the spiritual with the aim of cleansing the quotidian types that sometimes disturbed him.

A similar improving strategy governs his treatment of the city itself. Often celebrated as the first great urban poet, Whitman in fact had notably ambivalent feelings about a rapidly urbanizing America. Between 1810 and 1860 the population of the United States grew six times faster than the world average, reaching 30 million by the Civil War. The proportion of Americans living in cities grew from 6 percent to 20 percent of the total. New York City's population rose from 123,706 in 1820 to 515,000 in 1850, surpassing a million by 1860. Brooklyn's soared from 5,210 in 1820 to well over 200,000 by the Civil War.

Behind the statistics were dizzying changes in the physical landscape of the city. By the mid-1840s Whitman's Brooklyn, which had been largely rural in his childhood, was rapidly becoming a full-fledged city. Whitman wrote a long editorial for the *Eagle* about the rising congestion of Brooklyn, which, he said, was now little more than a conglomeration of frame houses squeezed onto twenty-five-by-one-hundred-foot lots. Manhattan was changing even faster, as a result of its varied social and cultural life. (The bustle of the city's streets is captured in figs. 14 and 34.) Identifying the "pull-down-and-build-over-again spirit" as the main characteristic of modern America, Whitman wrote that the attitude of urban real estate developers could be summed up in the words "Let us level to the earth all the houses that were not built within the last ten years; let us raise the devil and break things!" "Constant flux" was the descriptive term of the day. One journalist remarked that New York was never the same place for a dozen years together. Another described the effects of new construction this way: "Everything in the streets and on the walks is untied, unpacked, unrolled, unboxed. Doors, windows, walls, roofs ... daily come tumbling down." This gathering of "un" words casts light on one of Whitman's best-known lines. Who was better equipped than a poetic observer of rapid urban change to write: "Unscrew the locks from the doors! / Unscrew the doors themselves from their jambs!" The prevailing fluidity of Whitman's poetry stemmed not only from a fragmenting political situation but also from the very texture of urban experience in mid-nineteenth-century America.

Urban congestion accelerated in a time when sanitary conditions were atrocious. New York's Croton Aqueduct, opened in 1842, helped resolve the water and sanitation problems of that city, but Brooklyn lagged far behind in the disposal of waste materials. Sewage was primitive until the late fifties, and slops and garbage were thrown into the streets. Since drinking water still came from city pumps, Whitman feared Brooklynites were being slowly poisoned:

> Imagine all the accumulations of filth in a great city—not merely the slops and rottenness thrown in the streets and byways, (and never thoroughly carried away)—but the numberless privies, cess-pools, sinks and gulches of abomination—the perpetual replenishing of all this mass of effete matter—the unnameable and unmeasurable dirt that is ever, ever filtered into the earth through its myriad pores, and which as surely finds its way into the neighborhood pump-water, as that a drop of poison put in one part of the vascular system, gets into the whole system.

Manhattan and Brooklyn had a terrible problem with animals in the streets. Hogs rooted in the garbage that was heaped in the gutters. Efforts to remove them were repeatedly thwarted, because, in the absence of systematized garbage removal, they were useful as scavengers. The pigs of Manhattan became a byword among foreign visitors. The British mesmerist Robert Collyer reported of them: "These domestic animals are seen at every turn; they not only hold their dominion in the street, but upon the sidewalks, frequently stopping the pedestrian in his course, and not unfrequently tripping people of meditation upon their noses." Charles Dickens in *American Notes* drew an amusing sketch of trying to cross Broadway while negotiating with eight fat sows.

In addition to the pigs, there were cows that were regularly herded up public avenues to graze in outlying farm areas. The animal problem struck home to Whitman. Even his relatively clean home city, Brooklyn, provoked his editorial outburst in the *Brooklyn Evening Star:* "Our city is literally overrun with *swine,* outraging all decency, and foraging upon every species of eatables within their reach.... Hogs, Dogs and Cows should be banished from our streets. There is not a city in the United States as large as Brooklyn, where the *cleanliness* and *decency* of its streets is so neglected as here."

City streets were often ill paved and unlit, as he constantly complained. Unpaved streets rapidly turned into either mud or dust, depending on the weather. Manhattan for him was even worse: he once sourly said that those who came on the East River ferry from New York trailed dirt behind them all through Brooklyn.

Cobblestone and Belgian block paving made little improvement, since it created a long-forgotten kind of nuisance: the unceasing roar of omnibuses, wooden-wheeled carriages, and clattering horses.

Painfully aware of the city's darker side, he tried in his poetry to emphasize its beauty and exuberance. His best-known urban poem, "Crossing Brooklyn Ferry," views both Manhattan and Brooklyn from the improving distance of the East River. The poem cleanses the city through distancing and through refreshing nature imagery. Manhattan is not the filthy, chaotic "Gomorrah" of Whitman's journalism but rather "stately and admirable . . . mast-hemmed Manhattan." Brooklyn is not the hog-infested, crowded city of his editorials but rather the the city of "beautiful hills" viewed from the sparkling river on a sunlit afternoon.

If in his journalism he often lamented the city's filth and crime, in "Song of Myself" he turned to its dazzle and show: "The blab of the pave, tires of carts, sluff of boot-soles, talk of the promenaders." There was something intrinsically ennobling about his word "Mannahatta," which he called a "choice aboriginal name, with marvelous beauty, meaning." Although the name meant "the hill island," Whitman often used it as a synonym for "place of sparkling waters," perhaps influenced by philologists of the forties who wrongly traced its etymology to the rushing waters around Hell Gate. The water connotation became increasingly important to Whitman as urban squalor and political corruption grew in the late fifties. The word was first featured at length in the 1860 edition of *Leaves of Grass*. His poem "Mannahatta" takes delight in the name while it minimizes less admirable features of the city:

> Now I see what there is in a name, a word, liquid, sane, unruly,
>   musical, self-sufficient,
> I see that the word of my city is that word from of old,
> Because I see that word nested in nests of water-bays, superb,
> Rich, hemm'd thick all around with sailships and steamships, an
>   island sixteen miles long,
> Numberless crowded streets, high growth of iron, slender, strong,
>   light, splendidly uprising toward clear skies.

This was a far cry from his articles just a few years earlier in the *Daily Times* in which he had complained vociferously about the dirt and violence of New York, which he called "one of the most crime-haunted and dangerous cities in all of Christendom." Actually, though, his awareness of the city's dark side underlay the affirmations he made in the poem. The city here is not described in detail but instead is transformed into "a name, a word"—better yet, a "word nested in nests of water-bays, superb." The potentially negative image of "[n]umberless crowded streets" is prefaced by images of water and masts and followed by ones of heaven-aspiring buildings.

Throughout his poetry, the disturbing aspects of urban experience are nested between positive, refreshing ones. The leap from the grimy Manhattan of his journalism to the dazzling Mannahatta of his poetry was momentous for the writer who saw clearly the city's failings but sensed too its possibilities.

5

"THE UNITED STATES NEED POETS": THE POLITICAL AND SOCIAL CRISIS

O F ALL NATIONS the United States with veins full of poetical stuff most need poets and will doubtless have the greatest and use them the greatest."

This proclamation in the 1855 preface to *Leaves of Grass* is laced with conflicting feelings: confidence, despair, anticipation. Confidence stemmed from Whitman's awareness of the rich potential of American life—a potential he thought was particularly visible, as later chapters show, in the areas of oratory and music, religion and philosophy, gender relations, science, and the visual arts. Anticipation lay in his hope that the nation, by seeing both its best and its worst features reflected in the improving mirror of his poetry, would reverse its current downward course and discover new possibilities for inspiration and togetherness.

If it did not, he feared the worst. The possibility of the imminent failure of the American experiment runs as a dark vein through his writings. "Of all nations the United States . . . most need poets." When he wrote these anxious words, the phrase "the United States" was virtually an oxymoron. Sectional animosities had flared up in 1850 with the congressional debates over slavery and then had exploded into full view in 1854 with the passage of the Kansas-Nebraska Act, which repealed the Missouri Compromise and opened up the western territories for slavery. The states, soon to be at war, were hardly united.

Nor were the parties. The early fifties witnessed one of the most momentous phenomena in American political history: the collapse of the party system. The Whig Party, weak for years, broke up in 1854 as a result of sectional quarrels over slavery, and Whitman's Democratic Party became strife ridden as well. The party crisis aroused the poet's wrath against governmental authority figures. The presidencies of Millard Fillmore, Franklin Pierce, and James Buchanan eroded his confidence in the executive office. History shows that this period was a time of egregious presidential incompetency, mainly because of these leaders' soft-spined compromises on the slavery issue. Whitman branded the three presidencies before Lincoln as "our topmost warning and shame," saying they illustrated "how the weakness and wickedness of rulers are just as eligible here in America under republican, as in Europe under dynastic influences."

The 1850s was also a decade of unprecedented political corruption, a time of vote-buying, wire-pulling, graft, and patronage on all levels of state and national government. Class divisions were growing at an alarming rate. Dislocations created by the market economy widened the gap between the rich and the poor.

The political and social crisis provoked the ire of reformers, who introduced a stinging, vibrant rhetoric. Whitman for a time identified fully with one reform movement—the Free-Soil wing of the Democratic Party—and watched with interest more radical reforms as well. Although he eventually cut ties with reform groups, he absorbed from them a subversive spirit and rhetoric that added a bracingly rebellious spark to his poetry.

The very social forces that drove him to despair simultaneously opened up new vistas of self-empowerment. As authority figures collapsed, suddenly the individual self—sovereign, rich, complex—stood forth amid the ruin of the parties. His growing disillusionment with authority figures also sparked his deep faith in common people and in the power of populist poetry. He had come to view American society as an ocean covered with the "scum" of politicians, below which lay the pure, deep waters of common humanity.

In the turmoil of the 1850s the very idea of America was at stake. A conflict between states' rights and centralized power was fought fiercely on several levels and fed directly into what Whitman saw as the central paradox of American life—the relation between the individual and the mass—a paradox he tried to solve in his poetry. Two documents he held dear, the Declaration of Independence and the Constitution, were cast into debate, the former being cited to defend widely varying views, the latter coming under assault by extremists of both antislavery and proslavery camps. Like Lincoln after him, Whitman had to redefine the notions of "America" and "liberty" in the broadest possible terms. With central texts of American democracy losing stable meaning, he felt he had to create a new national text in which America was poetically reconstructed.

Was he experiencing severe private traumas at the same time the nation was in the throes of crisis? A dearth of documentation about his private life for the 1847–55 period, when he changed into a major poet, makes firm conclusions on this score impossible, though some curiously dark lines appear in his notebooks. It may be that the pain resulting from persecution or repression lies behind some of the negative, brooding passages in his poems. But personal trauma alone does not create great literature, as Whitman himself emphasized when he constantly called attention to the historical origins of his poetry.

If Whitman's inner demons of the forties had been projected in sensationalistic fiction, by the early fifties they were expressed in bitter political invective. Rapidly deteriorating social conditions directed his vision outward, toward an America he feared was on the brink of collapse. America, he came to believe, desperately needed a poet to hold together a society that was on the verge of unraveling. Poetry became his way of simultaneously healing himself and healing the nation.

The Journalist Observes the Nation

WHITMAN'S RETURN to Brooklyn in August 1845 after four years in Manhattan was a family reunion in more ways than one. He boarded on Adams Street, near Myrtle, not far from 71 Prince Street, the new home of his parents and five of his siblings, who had just returned after five years in the mid–Long Island village of Dix Hills. (His married sister Mary was raising a family in Greenport, and his older brother Jesse was probably at sea.) The Whitmans returned to Brooklyn just as it was entering a phase of expansion that would be as dramatic as that in the 1820s, when Walter Whitman, Sr., had first brought the family there.

Brooklyn life had been quickened by the completion in 1844 of the Long Island Railroad, the only rail route between Manhattan and Boston. The train, moving at the then-dizzying speed of twenty miles an hour, took five hours to go from Brooklyn to Greenport, where passengers boarded a ferry to Connecticut to complete the four-and-a-half-hour journey north. Gone were the slow, heavy wooden farm wagons that had once rumbled down Brooklyn's lanes. Now and then Whitman still saw one of the old-fashioned country-wagon men, but as he lamented in the *Eagle*, "He has no one to keep him in countenance: the Long Island Railroad has quelled the glory of his calling."

Now a network of stages fanned out from the ferry landings. Frame houses on tiny lots were popping up everywhere. Brooklyn's population would leap from 40,000 in 1845 to 100,000 five years later and then, after consolidation with four neighboring towns, to nearly a quarter of a million in 1855. By then Brooklyn, the third-largest city in the nation, would have more than a hundred churches, twenty-seven public schools with more than 30,000 students, and thirteen ferries connecting it to Manhattan.

Whitman's father resumed carpentering, to be joined at the trade over the next seven years by George, Andrew, and then Walt himself. In the meantime, Walt stuck to journalism. In the fall and winter of 1845 he wrote many articles on miscellaneous topics—temperance, education, popular music, and theater—for Alden Spooner's *Star*. By the next March he was editing the *Brooklyn Daily Eagle*, the Democratic Party organ of Kings County. Founded in 1841 by the ward boss Henry C. Murphy, the *Eagle* was owned by Isaac Van Anden, a member of the conservative, or "Hunker," wing of the Democratic Party. Under Van Anden's management the *Eagle* had gained a reputation for caution on volatile issues such as slavery and the annexation of Mexico. His Hunker views had been ably promoted by the editor William C. Marsh. When Marsh died of liver failure in February 1846, Van Anden chose as his successor the seasoned Democratic journalist Whitman, whose views on slavery, much to the owner's alarm, would soon veer from the moderate Hunker line. At the start, neither Van Anden nor Whitman could know that events on the national scene would thus change the complexion of the *Eagle* and, more significantly, contribute to the gestation of *Leaves of Grass*.

From his office on the second floor of the *Eagle* building at 30 Fulton Street, Whitman had a good view of the busy Fulton ferry and the East River beyond. Henry Sutton, a printer's devil with the *Eagle*, recalled Whitman as "a good man, a nice, kind man" who dressed conventionally and kept his dark beard trimmed short. Whitman generally kept to his editor's quarters upstairs, rarely coming into contact with the owner Van Anden, who worked in the business office on the first floor.

Whitman typically wrote editorials in the morning, took a walk after sending them to the composing room, and read proofs upon his return. After work in midafternoon he perambulated Brooklyn or took the ferry to Manhattan for entertainment or to see the city sights, walking sometimes with literary types like the *Evening Post* editor William Cullen Bryant. On warm days he went with Henry Sutton for a twenty-minute swim at Gray's Swimming Bath at the foot of Fulton Street. He liked to take the East Brooklyn stages, pulled by teams of four to six horses, that ran southwest to Fort Greene and Greenwood Cemetery. Sometimes he attended Sunday-school picnics in Jamaica, the sleepy Dutch village eight miles east. Each June he went to the so-called "flying pic-nic" sponsored by the Long Island Railroad, which took crowds of Brooklynites ninety miles east to Greenport or Riverhead for a summer party. He also took the stage to Coney Island for a swim. "The beautiful, pure, sparkling, sea-water!" he wrote. "One yearns for you (at least we do), with an affection as grasping as your own waves"—anticipatory of his poetic lines: "You sea! I resign myself to you also—I guess what you mean, / [...] Cushion me soft, rock me in billowy drowse, / Dash me with amorous wet, I can repay you."

Like most newspapers of the day, the *Eagle* was a four-page, multi-columned paper with editorials and news on the second page, the other three pages being filled with advertisements, real estate listings, and political announcements. Whitman wrote articles on almost every topic, storing up images and impressions that would later be useful to him as a poet. It is questionable, however, whether he would have felt impelled to make poetic use of them if the political events set in motion between 1846 and 1848 had not occurred. Although only about a quarter of his *Eagle* articles were political, it was his political pieces that revealed his profound engagement with the developing national crisis.

Early in his editorship he was very much a Democratic loyalist who had full faith in the party's leaders and in the soundness of the two-party system. The healthiness of party conflict had been emphasized by Thomas Jefferson and defended at length by the Democrats Martin Van Buren and Andrew Jackson. The Whig Party, on the other hand, had long been suspicious of party quarrels, fearing they threatened national harmony. Whitman took the Democratic line on the issue. When a Whig paper complained of the destructiveness of party squabbling, Whitman replied: "Why, all that is good and grand in any political organization in the world, is the result of this turbulence and destructiveness; and controlled by the intelligence and common sense of such a people as the Americans, it has never brought harm, and never can." Since America's parties and elections washed away all impurities, he wrote, long-term corruption was impossible. "Nor can the Democratic Party become essentially corrupt, either," he argued. "For true Democracy has within itself a perpetual spring of health and purity." Sometimes he expressed his party loyalty in unequivocal black-and-white terms: "The struggles of those who have any faith in democracy at all, must be made *in the frame and limits of our own party*.... As far as the Democrats of Brooklyn are concerned, they recognize but two great political divisions—themselves, and the men who are not themselves. These are *all*. Those who work not for us, work against us."

His devotion to the Democratic president James Polk shows his willingness to conform himself to the party hierarchy and structure. He called Polk "a truly noble Magistrate, without fear and without reproach—whose name will shine with quiet brightness for years to come in our most honored democratic galaxy!" He was on hand when Polk gave a speech in Brooklyn on June 26, 1847, praising Brooklyn and its patriotic past. He placed Polk in the company of two of his other president-heroes, Jackson and Jefferson, and praised the presidential office itself as "this Great Office," "the most sublime on earth," at a "towering height above all other human stations."

His admiration for Polk was understandable. Having succeeded the indecisive Whig John Tyler in 1845, the industrious Polk was destined to be one of the few presidents to accomplish virtually everything he set out to do. His four main objectives—acquisition of Mexican California, British acknowledgment of Oregon as American territory, an independent Treasury, and a reduced tariff—were accomplished during his term, which he announced was to be his only one. By acquiring huge new territories in the Southwest through financial dealings and war against Mexico, Polk put into action the expansionist spirit of "manifest destiny," the phrase that had been coined in 1845 by Whitman's friend, the *Democratic Review* editor John L. O'Sullivan.

There was, however, the nagging problem of slavery in the territories. Like other antebellum presidents, Polk waffled on the slavery issue. Many Northerners opposed the Mexican War because they saw it as part of a Southern plot to extend slavery westward. When in the summer of 1846 Polk asked Congress for two million dollars to negotiate with Mexico, a portly Democratic congressman from Pennsylvania, David Wilmot, proposed that the bill be passed only with the proviso that slavery be excluded from all newly acquired territories. Polk, who tried to distance himself from the slavery issue, denounced the Wilmot Proviso as "mischievous & foolish." Although never approved by Congress, the Wilmot Proviso was supported by resolutions in many Northern states. It suddenly made the question of slavery in the territories the most hotly debated political topic of the day.

Whitman came out strongly and early for the Wilmot Proviso in the *Eagle*. He had been guided in his thinking by one of his political heroes, Silas Wright. The large, blue-eyed Wright had been a congressman and governor of New York whose fierce opposition to slavery extension helped give rise to the Barnburners, a faction of the Democratic Party so named because they were compared to a Dutch farmer who burned down his barn in his effort to get rid of a few rats. Wright had been elected governor in 1844, but his administration had been plagued from the start by internal opposition from Hunker Democrats who opposed his liberal views. Whitman had editorialized heavily on behalf of Wright in July 1844 and electioneered for him in the state contest of 1846, serving as secretary of a mass meeting of Kings County Democrats on October 29.

But Wright lost the election, and there was a bitter split in the Democratic ranks, with Whitman taking the Barnburner side. Regarded by some historians as an early version of Lincoln, Wright was a plain, upright man of principle who enjoyed doing common jobs on his upstate New York farm. His sudden death in August 1847 was a terrible blow to liberal Democrats. Whitman, absolutely devastated, penned a long eulogy of Wright. He wrote: "Our hopes, in common with nearly all the members of the Democratic party of this state, and indeed of other states, were so identified with this man—relied so much upon him in the future—were so accustomed to look upon him as our tower of strength, and as a shield of righteous virtue—that we indeed feel pressed to the earth by such an unexpected blow!"

Wright was perhaps the last political leader Whitman would fully believe in until the advent of Lincoln in the 1860s. Although Whitman sustained his support of Polk's expansionist policies, the president's opposition to the Wilmot Proviso troubled him. Slowly, Whitman was beginning to sour on the party that had nurtured him and to ponder the institution that would rip apart the parties and lead to war: slavery.

Since Whitman's earliest notebook jottings in his characteristic free verse were dated 1847 (while he was at the *Eagle*) and pertained to slavery, it is essential to consider his attitude toward the institution. Whitman was an antiextensionist: one opposed to the extension of slavery into the western territories. As was true with many antiextensionists, his main concern in 1847 was not the slaves themselves but rather the disruptions of American institutions posed by the South's apparent effort to put its own interests above those of the nation. Party conflict, he believed, was healthy and cleansing. Sectional conflict, by contrast, was not, since it upset the delicate balance between state and national interests.

Anything that threatened this balance was anathema to him. He was, of course, hardly alone in pondering the issue, which was one of the central ones of the day. In antebellum America the role of the federal government in state affairs was ambiguous. The new Republic was seething with barely controlled individualistic and sectional impulses that were not yet firmly restrained by a central authority. The issue of states' rights versus nationalism raised its head at key moments: in the nullification crisis of 1832, when South Carolina threatened to disobey a federal tariff law; in the famous Boston abolitionist convention at Faneuil Hall in 1842, when several speakers cursed the American Union and the Constitution; and again in the debate over the Wilmot Proviso, which set the stage for the turmoil of the fifties. Although Whitman supported the proviso, he was not ready to take an extreme stance on it, for he feared the possibly cataclysmic results of any extreme stance. He vigorously denounced the opposing camps of proslavery Southern fire-eaters and Northern abolitionists. Both, he insisted, threatened to rip apart the Union. When the South Carolina senate proposed to establish an independent government should the Wilmot Proviso become law, he wrote angrily: "Of all follies, the nullification and withdrawing-from-the-union folly of a few hotheads at the South, has always appeared to us among the greatest."

Abolitionism came under his constant attacks for similar reasons. It is sometimes forgotten today that abolitionism—the movement for the immediate emancipation of slaves—was actually unpopular in the North. According to one estimate in 1847, while two-thirds of Northerners disapproved of slavery and opposed its extension, only 5 percent went along with the abolitionists. Immediate emancipation, it was widely feared, would flood the North with freed slaves, creating racial disharmony and economic turmoil. Moreover, few could accept the abolitionists' proposed alternative to immediate emancipation: disunion, or the peaceful separation of the North and the South. When the abolitionists cursed the Union for tolerating slavery and denounced the Constitution for obliging Americans to return "fugitives from labor" (including, presumably, fugitive slaves), hostility toward the abolitionists increased. Not many were prepared to accept outbursts against the existing order, such as this one by William Lloyd Garrison:

> Accursed be the AMERICAN UNION, as a stupendous republican imposture! . . .
> Accursed be it, as a libel on democracy, and a bold assault on Christianity!
> Accursed be it, stained as it is with human blood, and supported by human sacrifices! . . .
> Accursed be it, for all the crimes it has committed at home—for seeking the utter extermination of the red men for its wildernesses, and for enslaving one-sixth of its teeming population!
> Accursed be it, for its hypocrisy, its falsehood, its impudence, its lust, its cruelty, its oppression!

It was such assaults on the Union and the Constitution that especially annoyed Whitman. In an article titled "The Union, vs. Fanaticism" he blasted the abolitionists: "The effort to destroy our Constitution—the work of the wisest and purest statesmen ever assembled—and to dissolve the Union, is worthy only of a madman and a villain." Calling the abolitionists "a few and foolish red-hot fanatics," an "angry-voiced and silly set," he wrote: "The abominable fanaticism of the Abolitionists has aroused the other side of the feeling—and thus retarded the very consummation desired by the Abolitionist faction." Whitman made clear his hatred of both forms of "disunion," abolitionism and nullification: "Despising and condemning the dangerous and fanatical insanity of 'Abolitionism'—as impracticable as it is wild—the Brooklyn *Eagle* just as much condemns the other extreme from that."

Fearing extremes, he began tentatively testing out statements that balanced opposite views, as though simple rhetorical juxtaposition would dissolve social tensions. In a list of "Principles We Fight For" in the August 26, 1846, *Eagle* he juxtaposed the following:

> The freedom, sovereignty, and independence of the respective States.
> The Union—a confederacy, compact, neither a consolidation, nor a centralization.

Thus began what would become a long-term strategy of his: resolving thorny political issues by linguistic fiat. The issue of states' rights versus national power he would return to repeatedly for the rest of his life, often directly, often metonymically in his many poetic versions of the theme of the individual versus the mass.

As for the slavery problem, he was now realizing it demanded especially careful literary treatment. He was confronted with what he saw as extremists on both sides: slaveholders cursing the government for threatening to interfere with slavery extension; abolitionists cursing the government and the Constitution for permitting slavery. It began to dawn on him that the greatest balancing agent could be poetry—poetry that took both sides while at the same time releasing the steam of curses. In a notebook dated 1847 there appeared his first truly Whitmanesque verses, beginning with the topic of slavery and moving on to curses:

> I am the poet of slaves and of the masters of slaves, [. . .]
> I go with the slaves of the earth equally with the masters
> And I will stand between the masters and the slaves,
> Entering into both so that both shall understand me alike.
>
> . . . .
>
> I am a Curse
> Sharper than serpent's eyes or wind of the ice-fields

O topple down Curse! topple more heavy than death!
I am lurid with rage!

The first of these verses presents an "I" who, as a "poet," is able to "enter into" both slaves and their masters, identifying with both in such a way that the divisive slavery issue is imaginatively resolved. The second passage projects all the fire of those who curse (who for Whitman were usually ranting reformers) and funnels it through an "I" who, by becoming "a Curse," expresses a general rage without specifically targeting the American Union, as the extremists did.

Although Whitman steered a fairly moderate course on slavery in his *Eagle* editorials, his support of the Wilmot Proviso apparently got him into trouble with his employer, Van Anden, and by mid-January 1848 he had lost his job. A rival paper reported that Whitman had not only offended his conservative employer but had kicked a well-known politician downstairs from his editor's office. The *Eagle,* which returned to Hunkerism after Whitman's departure, replied caustically that Whitman was "slow, indolent, heavy, discourteous and without steady principles. . . . Whoever knows him will laugh at the idea of his *kicking any body,* much less a prominent politician. He is too indolent to kick a musketo."

Whitman was not long out of work. Within a few weeks he met, between acts at a play, a Southern newspaper owner, J. E. McClure, who hired him as a rewrite and clipping man for the *New Orleans Daily Crescent.* Whitman got two hundred dollars for traveling expenses, and soon he and his fifteen-year-old brother Jeff headed south. They went by train to Baltimore, and from there by train and stage across the Alleghenies to Wheeling, then by boat down to Cincinnati, Louisville, Cairo, and New Orleans. En route, Whitman was struck by the rugged independence of frontier people, the grandeur of snowy mountain landscapes, and the river at night, which inspired his haunting but didactic nature poem "The Mississippi at Midnight."

He and Jeff arrived at New Orleans on the steamer *St. Cloud* on Saturday, February 26. New Orleans was a bustling city of some 160,000, with an equally large floating population of visitors and sailors. From the cobblestone wharf, streets led away from the river at a gentle downward slope. Because of the high water level, there were no cellars, wells, or graves within the city limits. The Whitman brothers roomed at a boardinghouse in Lafayette, then a small suburb. Rarely home, Walt spent his time at the *Crescent* office at 95 St. Charles Street, or lounging around the markets, bars, hotels, or theaters (which, unlike theaters in the North, were open every night of the week). At the *Crescent* Walt and

Jeff were part of a staff of twelve to fifteen. They helped with office work and perhaps paper delivery. Besides clipping items from other papers, Walt wrote articles on current events and covered the Recorder's Office.

Since he was in slave territory (slaves were auctioned openly on the streets), he avoided controversial political articles. His pieces for the *Crescent* were, by and large, lighthearted sketches of colorful types he saw about town: Peter Funk, a con man who tricked tourists into bidding high at street auctions by making phony bids; Miss Dusky Grisette, a flower girl and streetwalker; John J. Jinglebrain, a wealthy fop with fine clothes but no soul; the oyster vendor Timothy Goujon and the Irish driver Patrick McDray; Daggerdaw Bowie-Knife, a pistol-packing Southern politician.

His journalistic style was more linguistically inventive than before. One of the distinctive features of his poetry would be its inclusion of slang, which he would come to regard as "the lawless germinal element . . . behind all poetry," showing that language "has its bases broad and low to the ground." In the *Crescent* he experimented for the first time with an intermixture of slang and standard prose, as when he described a lovesick man as "a 'gone hoss'" or a fop's hair as "'done to a turn' and slick as grease."

His New Orleans period was once viewed by biographers as a crucial transforming time because of an intense, liberating romance he supposedly had with a woman who bore him at least one child. Not a shred of solid evidence of such an affair has ever been found. It is more likely, in fact, that the romance was with a man, as suggested by his poem "Once I Pass'd Through a Populous City," which in its original version describes his affection for a man (later changed to a woman when the poem was retailored for the heterosexual "Children of Adam" sequence). He did take note, however, of the sexual attractiveness of the New Orleans women. In old age he still recalled the city's octoroons, "women with splendid bodies— . . . fascinating, magnetic, sexual, ignorant, illiterate: always more than pretty—'pretty' is too weak a word to apply to them." For the *Crescent* he wrote a sprightly fantasy of instant infatuation, writing that at a recent ball he fell in love with a woman who, as it turned out, was married.

In light of the mixed evidence, any thesis about the supposedly transforming effect of the New Orleans period is suspect, particularly since it would be seven years before *Leaves of Grass* appeared. Whatever his romantic entanglements, New Orleans seems to have deepened his sympathy for the South, which he would never totally lose. His poetry often personalized this affection: "O magnet-South! O glistening perfumed South! my South!"

But the New Orleans stay was hardly euphoric. Jeff was intermittently homesick and had bouts of illness. The approach of summer was cause for concern, since the city was known to be dangerous for visiting Northerners who had little resistance to the yellow fever that often came with the hot season. In May Walt had a falling out with the owners of the *Crescent* over money matters. He and Jeff left New Orleans on the steamer *Pride of the West* on Saturday, May 27. They went up to St. Louis and Chicago, across Lakes Michigan and Erie, through Buffalo, Niagara, and Albany, and down the Hudson to Brooklyn.

Upon his return home, the political issues he had temporarily evaded in New Orleans suddenly impinged on his consciousness. It was an election year, and there was great turmoil in both the Democratic and Whig parties. At the Democratic convention held in Baltimore in April, the Michigan senator Lewis Cass, a weak party hack opposed to the Wilmot Proviso, had been chosen as the presidential candidate, with William O. Butler of Kentucky as his running mate. The Whigs, meanwhile, chose as their candidate Zachary Taylor, the military hero with little political record. The prospect of either of these colorless compromisers assuming power was too much to bear for antiextensionists, who wanted to keep the territories free of slavery. In June, shortly after Whitman's return, a huge rally of Free-Soilers was held in Manhattan's City Hall Park. Plans were laid out for a national antislavery convention to be held later that summer. The heady rebelliousness of the Free-Soilers was fanned by daily news bulletins of the populist revolutions in Europe. The creation of a Free-Soil Party was proposed. Its nominating convention was to open in Buffalo on August 9. Whitman was one of fifteen delegates from Brooklyn chosen to represent Kings County at the convention.

He participated in one of the most thrilling events of the era. The Free-Soil convention at Buffalo had all the intensity and excitement of a religious revival. About twenty thousand people, attracted by a dazzling lineup of speakers and by rail fares slashed for the occasion, crowded inside a tremendous tent under a sweltering sun. For two days the crowd was kept at a fever pitch by forty-three speakers and antislavery songs performed by the popular Hutchinson family singers. Huge banners blazoned forth the mottoes "Free soil, free speech, free labor and free men!" and "No more slave states, no more slavery territory and no more compromises with slavery anywhere!" A party platform firmly denouncing the spread of slavery was read aloud. The ex-president Martin Van Buren was chosen to represent the Free-Soil Party in November.

At the Buffalo convention Whitman got to hear many of the leading antislavery orators of the day, including the African-Americans Frederick Douglass, Charles Redmond, Henry Highland Garnet, Henry Bibb, and Samuel Ringgold Ward. In the *Eagle* Whitman had reported Douglass's founding of a new antislavery paper, which he said would "of course cause a great sensation," and in the late fifties his *Daily Times* would compliment Douglass's oratorical abilities: "He has a splendid voice, loud, clear and sonorous, which would make itself heard in the largest open air assembly." He never mentioned having read Douglass's popular autobiographical *Narrative* (1845), but he heard the celebrated ex-slave speak at Buffalo.

The presence of Douglass and the other African-Americans at the convention brings up the key question of race. Douglass left the convention dissatisfied because the rights of blacks were not considered. Within a month of the convention he was berating the Free-Soil group because of its neglect of the racial issue. His complaint was justified. The Free-Soil agenda, as radical as it seemed to some, was in fact based on the racist presumption that whites must be preserved from association with blacks. The Buffalo platform stated that the western territories must be kept for "the hardy pioneers of our own land, and the oppressed and banished of other lands"—with no mention of blacks.

The whites-only plan reflected not only a fear of economic competition from slave labor but also racial prejudice. John L. O'Sullivan, the editor who had fueled expansionism with his phrase "manifest destiny," made it clear he had in mind the spread of Anglo-Saxon values: "It would seem that the White race alone received the divine command, to subdue and replenish the earth!" David Wilmot, the congressman who had sparked the Free-Soil movement, called his measure the White Man's Proviso, declaring, "I would preserve for free white labor a fair country, a rich inheritance, where the sons of toil, of my own race and color, can live without the disgrace which association with Negro slavery brings upon free labor." Most leading Free-Soilers accepted this outlook.

Including Whitman. At this point in his career, he was in full accordance with the Free-Soil program, without active resistance to its racial assumptions. The whole slavery issue, he had written in the *Eagle*, was "a question between *the grand body of white workingmen, the millions of mechanics, farmers and operatives of our country,* with their interests, on the one side—and the interests of the few thousand rich, 'polished,' and aristocratic owners of slaves at the south, on the other." "We call upon every mechanic [that is, workingman] of the north, east, and west," he continued—inserting a long list of workers including the carpenter, mason, stonecutter, blacksmith, shipbuilder, shoemaker, paver, and others— "to speak in a voice whose great reverberations shall tell to all quarters that the *workingmen* of the free United States, and their business, are not willing to be put on the level of negro slaves."

This seemingly racist comment is in fact a double indictment, as if to say: We mistreat the slave, and now we are ready to extend the abuse to white workers.

The hard truth is that racism was rampant in nineteenth-century America. It was almost an inescapable fact of life. It permeated scientific thought. It circulated in popular literature and entertainments, especially frontier humor and minstrel shows. It characterized, of course, the prevailing attitude of Southern whites. More surprising, it was strong in the North as well, even among ardent antislavery activists. Tocqueville thought racial prejudice was actually more pronounced in free states than in slave states. As George Fredrickson has shown, racism was the ironic corollary of republican beliefs: in order to sustain the institutions of the new Republic, including slavery, American whites clung to a belief in the intrinsic inferiority of blacks. If blacks were the equals of whites, how could the institution of slavery be tolerated? The answer, for most whites, was that the races were *not* equal. There was an emerging consensus among scientists and phrenologists that there was a hierarchy of races, with the Caucasian on top and all others, including the African, below. Until the 1830s, race was not frequently discussed, but the rise of abolitionism impelled Southerners to develop a defensive posture that in the fifties would be consolidated in two widely read proslavery works, George Fitzhugh's *Sociology for the South* and *Cannibals All.* The white-supremacist argument was that Southern society was superior to Northern society because it suppressed racial tension by engendering a kindly reciprocal relationship between the races, thereby avoiding the painful class divisions of the North.

Racism also underlay the two major forms of antislavery activism in the antebellum era: colonization and antiextensionism. Colonizationists argued that slaves should be emancipated (most thought gradually) and then relocated to the African colony of Liberia or elsewhere. Leading colonizationists like Henry Clay took it for granted that any effort to integrate the races in the United States would inevitably lead to racial strife. The antiextensionism that arose during the Mexican War was, as seen, based on the idea that white workers would be degraded by association with blacks. The third main antislavery element, abolitionism, had a more positive attitude toward race relations than the other groups, but partly for that very reason was widely regarded as subversive and threatening to the social order. The most consistent foes of racism were African-Americans who, in abolitionist speeches, slave narratives, or (as in the case of William Wells Brown and Harriet Wilson) fiction, pointed out that racial prejudice was common even among ostensibly progressive Northerners.

Even the Great Emancipator, Lincoln, steered a cautious course on slavery and race relations. Until the second year of the Civil War, Lincoln was a colonizationist and antiextensionist who thought that slaves, after being gradually freed, should be shipped out of the country. Like his political hero, Henry Clay, he doubted the races would mix well in America. In his debates with Stephen Douglas he said he didn't advocate the political and social equality of whites and blacks because of what he called "a physical difference between the two, which in my judgment will probably forever forbid their living together upon the footing of perfect equality." Although he eschewed the kind of overt racism shown by many of his contemporaries, he could call an adult black man "boy," and he enjoyed jokes about "niggers," "Sambos," and "pickaninnies."

Whitman's views on race and slavery were in several ways like Lincoln's. Both criticized abolitionism, which they feared threatened the Union. Both were more concerned about preventing the spread of slavery than about getting rid of it. Both expressed doubt that the races could be successfully integrated. In some respects, Lincoln was more conservative than Whitman. In 1848 Lincoln refused to join the Free-Soil Party and campaigned instead for the Whig Zachary Taylor, a slaveholder widely considered sympathetic to the South. On the other hand, Whitman's attitudes toward race did not progress as far as Lincoln's over time. A combination of overwhelming national events and a deep-seated hatred of slavery would eventually impel Lincoln to take a quite radical stance after the second year of the Civil War.

Whitman followed a kind of arc around center in his racial attitudes, starting fairly conservative, then becoming quite progressive (it was in this middle phase that the broadly democratic first edition of *Leaves of Grass* appeared), and finally settling into a deepened conservatism during and after the Civil War. One can only guess what his racial opinions were in childhood, although, as suggested earlier, the vibrant presence of African-Americans in Brooklyn in the twenties and his longremembered friendship with the ex-slave Mose suggest an openness to their culture. The rise of abolitionism in the thirties seems to have pushed him, like others, to a fearful conservatism. During Andrew Jackson's administrations (1828–37) the legal rights of white males increased while those of blacks, women, and Native Americans decreased. In most Northern states, blacks were not allowed to vote, use public transportation, serve in the military, or sit on juries. Even the distinguished African-American leader Frederick Douglass was treated insultingly. Once when he tried to sit down with a white person in a Boston restaurant, the hundred other patrons immediately cleared out, and the restaurant refused to serve him.

By the time Whitman wrote *Franklin Evans* (1842) he had adopted certain pro-Southern attitudes. He had his hero learn from a Virginia planter that slaves are "well taken care of—with shelter and food, and every necessary means of comfort" and that "they would be far more unhappy, if possessed of freedom," a hundred times less happy than poor whites in Europe. Whitman made the same point in "Black and White Slaves," an 1842 *Aurora* article in which he argued that the condition of white workers in England was far worse than that of slaves.

The rise of antiextensionism, culminating in the Buffalo Free-Soil convention, pushed him in a more radical direction. A month after the convention he founded a newspaper, the Brooklyn *Freeman*, that championed the Free-Soil cause. Only one issue of the *Freeman*, dated September 9, 1848, has survived. "Free Soilers! Radicals! Liberty Men!" he exhorted his readers. "All whose throats are not tough enough to swallow Taylor or Cass! Come up and subscribe for the *Daily Freeman!*" "Our doctrine is the doctrine laid down in the Buffalo convention," he announced. He warned readers against voting for any candidate who would add to the Union "a single inch of *slave land,* whether in the form of state or territory," and he strongly endorsed the Free-Soil slate of Van Buren and Adams. But he pointed out that the large majority of Southerners were decent. It was the small faction of rich plantation owners who had to be fought tooth and nail to prevent them from spreading slavery to the territories.

Neither the paper nor the Free-Soil Party, however, had a happy fate. Shortly after the first edition was published, a disastrous fire destroyed the *Freeman* office at 110 Orange Street and much of downtown Brooklyn as well. By the time Whitman resumed publication in November, the Free-Soil ticket had been roundly defeated in the presidential election. Van Buren did not carry a single state and got just 10 percent of the popular vote, and Zachary Taylor was swept into office.

Whitman continued to edit the paper until the following September, when, to his dismay, it was taken over by Hunker Democrats. Free-Soil enthusiasm was fizzling. Economic necessity and the dampening of the antislavery cause made him turn his attention elsewhere. In January 1849 he rented space in Brooklyn's Grenada Hall, where he opened a small shop selling miscellaneous items: pens, pencils, paper, inkstands, musical instruments, and a full supply of books, mainly those published by Fowlers and Wells, New York's leading publisher in the booming fields of phrenology and physiology. In October 1848 he had bought a building lot at 106 Myrtle Avenue for one hundred dollars. When the narrow three-story house was finished in April, he moved in with his family and transferred his store to a room on the first floor. It became both a print shop and bookstore, and he ran it with Jeff until he sold the house three years later.

He kept a hand in popular journalism by writing a series of light articles for the New York *Sunday Dispatch* describing excursions he took to the east end of Long Island. Late in 1849 he served briefly as editor of a new penny paper, the New York *Daily News*, which suspended publication the following February, probably because of its noble but economically unwise policy of avoiding sensational news.

Party Collapse, Poetic Growth

EVENTS ON THE NATIONAL SCENE in early 1850 jarred him back into political action. The acquisition of some 850,000 square miles of land in the Southwest and the population explosion in California in the wake of the gold rush made the issue of slavery in the territories tense once more. A seeming solution to the problem appeared in the compromise measures forged by the Southern Whig senator Henry Clay and endorsed by his fellow Whig from Massachusetts Daniel Webster. According to the compromise, California would be admitted to the Union a free state, but there would be no legal restrictions on slavery in Utah and New Mexico, where, Webster rationalized, the climate was not salubrious to slavery anyway. To satisfy the South, a stringent fugitive slave law would be enforced by which recaptured slaves would not be allowed jury trial and those who aided them would be subject to a thousand-dollar fine or six months in jail. Southerners and conservative Northerners were, in general, pleased with the compromise. But fierce complaints came from both sides, especially Northern antislavery activists who hated the fugitive slave law.

Whitman saw that the compromise threatened the political health of the American Republic. Conflict over principles between opposing parties, he had long believed, was essential to the nation's health. But now principles and party differences were being tossed into a gray middle ground of compromise. He was prophetic. The Second Party System, which had emerged the year of his birth and had nurtured him, was on the verge of extinction.

Whitman tried to stir things up. He published four poems between March and June that represented a whole new tone and style for him. These were angry, agitated poems, erupting with rebellious ideas and occasionally straining beyond normal rhythms toward free verse.

The first poem, "Dough-Face Song," showed that his main concern about the slavery issue was that the tepid atmosphere of compromise was snuffing out all sense of principle among party leaders. Adopting the popular epithet "doughface," referring to malleable Northerners who were like dough in the hands of Southern slave owners, he wrote sarcastically: "We are all docile dough-faces, / They knead us with the fist, / They, the dashing southern lords, / We labor as they list." Evasion and moral flabbiness, he pointed out, could very well destroy the parties and possibly even the nation:

> Things have come to a pretty pass,
>   When a trifle small as this,
> Moving and bartering nigger slaves,
>   Can open an abyss,
> With jaws a-gape for "the two great parties;"
>   A pretty thought, I wis! [...]
> . . . .
> Beyond all such we know a term
>   Charming to ear and eyes,
> With it we'll stab young Freedom,
>   And do it in disguise;
> Speak soft, ye wily dough-faces—
>   That term is "compromise."

His animus was less against the South than against Northerners like Daniel Webster who seemed to be betraying their past principles. Webster had once been an ardent critic of slavery and supporter of the Wilmot Proviso but was now making conciliatory gestures to the South. His momentous speech before the Senate on March 7 brought the wrath of antislavery Northerners down upon him. His support of a harsh fugitive slave law drove Whitman, like others, to a white fury. On March 22 there appeared in the *New York Tribune* Whitman's poem "Blood-Money," which compared supporters of the new law to Jesus's betrayer Judas Iscariot.

> Of olden time, when it came to pass
> That the beautiful god, Jesus, should finish his work on earth,
> Then went Judas, and sold the divine youth,
> And took pay for his body. [...]
>
> And still goes one, saying,
> "What will ye give me, and I will deliver this man unto you?"
> And they make the covenant, and pay the pieces of silver. [...]

Witness of anguish, brother of slaves,
Not with thy price closed the price of thine image;
And still Iscariot plies his trade.

He kept up the attack on the compromisers in "Wounded in the House of Friends," published in the *Tribune* on June 14. Southern slave owners, he declared, were far more admirable than Northern doughfaces:

Virginia, mother of greatness,
Blush not for being also the mother of slaves
You might have borne deeper slaves—
Doughfaces, Crawlers, Lice of Humanity—[. . .]
Muck-worms, creeping flat to the ground,
A dollar dearer to them than Christ's blessing; [. . .]

Hot-headed Carolina,
Well may you curl your lip;
With all your bondsmen, bless the destiny
Which brings you no such breed as this.

Whitman was hardly alone in his use of poetry to express outrage over the compromise. Whittier and Longfellow, for example, wrote poems denouncing the apostate Webster. Of Webster, Whittier wrote in his poem "Ichabod": "So fallen! so lost! the light / Withdrawn which he once wore! The glory / From his gray hairs gone / Forevermore!" Longfellow added his poetic lament: "Fallen, fallen, fallen from his high estate."

To quote such lines, however, is to see the way in which Whitman was already departing from poetic norms. Whittier's and Longfellow's poems protesting the compromise were restrained and conventional in their imagery. Whitman's poems, in contrast, were blackly humorous, darkly ironic. Unlike the other poets, Whitman was beginning to absorb the wildly subversive political rhetoric that had been used by American reformers during the forties. Mikhail Bakhtin has suggested that truly indigenous, national forms of writing are produced by authors who absorb what Bakhtin calls *skaz*, roughly translated as "current idiom" or "national voice." Whitman would develop a similar theory. Later dedicating himself to producing what he called "the idiomatic book of my land," he would write in 1856: "Great writers penetrate the idioms of their races, and use them with simplicity and power. The masters are they who embody the rude materials of the people and give them the best forms for the place and time."

As I show in *Beneath the American Renaissance,* one such popular idiom in mid-nineteenth-century America was a subversive style that combined Gothic images and fiercely antiauthoritarian rhetoric. This rhetoric had appeared in various genres during the turbulent 1840s: in the working-class speeches and editorials of Mike Walsh and other Tammany "slang-whangers"; in some of William Lloyd Garrison's speeches and writings; in the novels of George Lippard and George Thompson, who furiously excoriated America's ruling class. Lippard's *The Quaker City* (1845), America's best-selling novel previous to *Uncle Tom's Cabin,* was the quintessential example of the subversive style. Lippard portrayed elite types—bankers, lawyers, clergymen, editors—engaged in all kinds of debauchery and exploitative practices. More important than the details of the labyrinthine plot of *The Quaker City* was its style, which combined black humor, fierce egalitarianism, and sheer sensationalism.

It was this bizarre combination of stylistic features that characterized Whitman's political poems of the fifties as well as many of the political moments of his major poetry and his prose writings like "The Eighteenth Presidency!" and *Democratic Vistas.* The connection between Whitman and Lippard has not been made by previous biographers. It has not been remarked, for instance, that Lippard was one of the few popular American writers mentioned in Whitman's voluminous notebooks. In 1860, when Whitman was a regular at Pfaff's restaurant in Manhattan, he discussed Lippard with the Philadelphia writer Charles D. Gardette, to whom he had sent a copy of the 1860 *Leaves of Grass.* Whitman jotted these notes about the conversation:

Nov. 26, '60—Lippard
 Gardette account to me, (in Pfaff's) of George Lippards life,—was handsome, Byronic,—commenced at 18—wrote sensation novels—drank—drank—drank—died mysteriously either of suicide or mania a potu at 25
 —or 6—a perfect wreck—was ragged, drunk, beggarly—

Gardette had some things wrong: Lippard died of tuberculosis in 1854 at age thirty-one, and, unlike his friend Poe, did not have a drinking problem; nor was he ragged and beggarly. Still, the fact that Whitman was discussing Lippard six years after his death suggests his interest in this popular reformer and sensational novelist. Had this been a longstanding interest? Had Whitman known Lippard's works in the 1840s?

There are strong indications he had. There was a close parallel between Lippard's indictment of capital punishment in *The Quaker City* and three Whitman articles published shortly after the novel appeared. Lippard and Whitman both pointed out that by executing criminals society is not eradicating the roots of crime and is overlooking much worse crimes among its most highly respected citizens. Astounded by the incongruity of Christian ministers endorsing death by hanging, Lippard sprinkled ironic commentary about the cruel "gibbet" throughout his novel and devoted long sections to his blackly humorous protagonist Devil-Bug, who cheers savagely at the sight of a gallows: "Hurrah! The gallows is livin' yet! Hurrah!" Whitman picked up Lippard's wording in his 1846 *Eagle* pieces "Hurrah for Hanging!" and "Hurrah for Choking Human Lives!" In an 1845 *Democratic Review* article, "A Dialogue," he made the Lippardian comment that every time he passed a church he saw a gallows frame and heard the words "Strangle and kill in the name of God!" Several of Whitman's scribblings in his early notebooks also bear the impress of Lippard. The outlandish scene at the heart of *The Quaker City* in which Devil-Bug has a nightmarish vision of a skeleton-filled coffin propelled on the Schuylkill seems to be echoed in Whitman's equally strange jotting: "A coffin swimming buoyantly on the swift flowing current of the river."

By the time Whitman wrote his political protest poems of 1850 the slashing Lippardian style had been further popularized in a number of imitative working-class novels, such as George Thompson's *Venus in Boston* and Ned Buntline's *Mysteries and Miseries of New York*. By using in "Dough-Face Song" and "House of Friends" dark political irony and words like "lice," "crawlers," and "muck-worms," Whitman was ushering the idiom of the working-class reformers into poetry.

His most intense experiment in the Lippardian vein was "Resurgemus," the last poem of the 1850 group. "Resurgemus" has a special place in the Whitman canon because it was only one of two pre-1855 poems—the other was the equally Lippardian "A Boston Ballad" (1854)—absorbed into *Leaves of Grass*. The poem registers both excitement and frustration surrounding the European revolutions of 1848, which had led to the temporary toppling of several authoritarian governments, but whose effects had subsequently been reversed. Whitman's message is that the revolutions may have been put down for the time being, but the spirit of revolt was very much alive in the heart of the people, who someday would rise up in anger again. Critics have tried to locate sources for the Gothicized images of "Resurgemus," some pointing to Poe. But Poe was no revolutionary, and he avoided political commentary in his writings. A more likely source was Poe's radical friend Lippard. Just as Lippard had often portrayed workers as "slaves" victimized by lying, cheating upper-class figures, Whitman indicted social rulers as "liars" who have been inflicting "numberless agonies, murders, lusts" on the people and have been "Worming from his simplicity the poor man's wages." Just as Lippard had imagined an apocalyptic time when the shapes of the murdered, oppressed classes would rise in an eerie, vindictive procession behind the upper classes, so Whitman describes ruling-class exploiters and then warns:

> Yet behind all, lo, a Shape,
> Vague as the night, draped interminably,
> Head, front and form, in scarlet folds;
> Whose face and eyes none may see,
> Out of its robes only this,
> The red robes, lifted by the arm,
> One finger pointed high over the top,
> Like the head of a snake appears.

Unlike Lippard, however, Whitman moves beyond Gothicized protest to a positive, hopeful image of restoration:

> Not a grave of those slaughtered ones,
> But is growing its seed of freedom,
> In its turn to bear seed,
> Which the winds carry afar and resow,
> And the rains nourish.

In "Resurgemus" Whitman is using the popular subversive style but also moving toward the kind of affirmation that would characterize his major poetry. Formerly a loyal Democrat writing straightforward journalese, he had been driven by national and world events to a cynical view of society expressed in a rebellious style. In his image of the seeds of freedom being carried by the winds and nourished by the rains, he was beginning to forge a humanistic, artistic reconstruction on the ruins of his shattered political beliefs. And for the first time in print, he was using a form that approximated free verse. The seeds of *Leaves of Grass* were sown in the political crisis of 1850.

As the crisis deepened, Whitman temporarily backed off from poetic protest. The death of Zachary Taylor of typhoid fever on July 9, 1850, and the accession to the presidency of Millard Fillmore crushed the hopes of former Free-Soilers like Whitman. Taylor had opposed Webster's compromise, but Fillmore favored it and helped shepherd the various measures of the omnibus bill through Congress. The official enactment of the compromise virtually killed off the Free-Soil Party.

The fate of the western territories seemed sealed by law. For the time being, Whitman backed off from political activism.

The Equalizer of His Age and Land

H E H A D N O T given up his longtime dream of appealing to the masses through popular fiction. On June 17, just as he was putting the final touches on "Resurgemus" for the *Tribune,* he wrote Alfred and Moses Beach, editors of the popular New York *Sun,* about the possibility of their printing serially his abridged version of *The Sleeptalker,* a novel by a Danish author named Ingemann. He said he had pared down the novel to almost half its original size. He wrote, "The romance is a stirring and lively one, and it seems to me fitted to become very popular." Not shy about money matters, he added, "I desire but a moderate price. After running through 'The Sun,' it seems to me it would pay handsomely to print it in a neat 25 cent book form." Apparently nothing came of the project, for the novel never appeared.

He was still living with his parents and siblings in the Myrtle Street house, now valued at two thousand dollars. From his print shop in 1851 he issued a guidebook called *The Salesman and Traveller's Directory for Long Island,* but he must have tired of it, for it ceased publication after a few issues. He wrote more Long Island sketches under the title of "Letters from Paumanok" in Bryant's *Evening Post.* He spent much of his spare time in the studios of Brooklyn artists and sculptors. A familiar presence among artists, he was elected president of the short-lived Brooklyn Art Union. In an address to the group on March 31, 1851, he argued that aesthetic appreciation was crucial for the human spirit in an increasingly materialistic age.

One day he introduced his sister Hannah to the painter Charles Heyde. By 1852 the two were married. Whitman later regretted having introduced them to each other, for he came to detest Heyde. A skilled but limited landscapist in the Hudson River style, Heyde proved in time to be a neurotic man who could get the whole Whitman family into an uproar through his maltreatment of his wife. In the early going, though, Hannah appears to have been happy enough. She and Heyde traveled around Vermont as he sold paintings, living for brief periods in various towns until settling in Burlington. She missed her family, especially Walt and Jeff, but found the Vermont countryside ruggedly exotic. With childish excitement, she reported to her family in a letter of October 1852: "There is plenty of Bears and some Panthers, and plenty of Hedge Hoggs [*sic*], and snakes."

Whitman was now turning to his father's business of carpentry. Try-ing to capitalize on Brooklyn's expansion, he bought lots, built frame houses on them, and sold them. Before the economic downturn of 1854 he seems to have achieved some success. In May 1852 he sold the Myrtle Street property and that summer built two three-story frame houses on Cumberland Street. He moved into one of the houses on September 1, renting out the other. Late in the year a "Carpenter and Builder" sign hung outside. By the next spring he had sold the two houses and was living in a little two-story house nearby on the same street. The family lived there a year before selling once again and moving to a house he had built on Skillman Street. But entrepreneurship was not the forte of one with a track record of contemplative indolence. His practical brother George, who worked with him at the time, would later recall, "There was a great boom in Brooklyn in the early fifties, and he had his chance then, but you know he made nothing of that chance."

Occupied as he was in Brooklyn, Whitman was drawn inevitably into dramatic events on the national stage. The fugitive slave law was arous-ing fury in the North. In response, Free-Soil activism, which had almost died out in 1850, made a resurgence. In the presidential campaign of 1852, the Democrats chose a dark horse, Franklin Pierce, an amiable but shallow man of uncertain opinions on slavery. Free-Soilers feared that, if elected, he would give in to proslavery forces—a prediction that proved accurate. His opponent, the pompous, aging General Winfield Scott, was also equivocal on slavery. Given this unsavory choice of candidates, Free-Soilers reorganized as the Free Democratic Party. At their convention in Pittsburgh, the New Hampshire senator John P. Hale was seriously considered as the Free Democratic presidential candidate. Hale was re-luctant to accept the nomination, since the chances for victory in No-vember seemed slim. He was wavering. In his moment of indecision he received a letter from "Walter Whitman" of Brooklyn urging him to accept the nomination.

Whitman had long admired Hale. He had heard him speak at the Buffalo convention and several times after that. Until late in life he would refer to Hale as one of his favorite speakers. Hale had begun as an antislavery Democrat who later became a leading Republican and served under Lincoln. What Whitman may have found especially appealing about Hale in 1852 was that he was a strong foe of slavery who nonethe-less was well liked by leading Southerners. Like another politician Whit-man often singled out for praise, Senator Cassius M. Clay, Hale was one of a small handful of Free-Soil advocates who, through force of personal-ity, managed to maintain friendly relations with the South despite their strong antislavery views. He was no weak doughface but rather a man of principle who embodied a spirit of togetherness and comradeship. In his August 14 letter Whitman commended Hale for "that temper of rounded and good-tempered moderation which is peculiar to you."

His letter to Hale is an important transitional document revealing his growing disgust with the established parties and his turn toward humanistic alternatives to the party system. His mentality was still, at this point, within the framework of the political process, for he expressed hope that under Hale "a real live Democratic party" would arise, "a renewed and vital party, fit to triumph over the effete and lethargic organization now so powerful and so unworthy." Expressing his disillusion with the current parties, he asked Hale "to make personal addresses directly to the people, giving condensed embodiments of the principal ideas which distinguish our liberal faith from the drag-parties and their platforms." Whitman stressed that current legislators were out of touch with "the great mass of the common people." He confessed he did not know "the great men" of Washington, "But I know the people. I know well (for I am practically in New York,) the real heart of this mighty city—the tens of thousands of young men, the mechanics, the writers, &c. &c. In all this, under and behind all the bosh of the regular politicians, there burns, almost with fierceness, the divine fire which more or less, during all ages, has only waited a chance to leap forth and confound the calculations of tyrants, hunkers, and all their tribe."

Hale was his last hope for party renewal. Perhaps influenced by Whitman's flaming words, Hale did accept the Free Democrat nomination and campaigned enthusiastically in the fall. But the November election was dismal for the Free Democrats, who got just 5 percent of the national vote—half of what the Free-Soil Party had polled in 1848. Whitman's hopes for "a renewed and vital party" were dashed. Worse yet, the party to which he had once been loyal, the Democrats, had put into office Franklin Pierce (see fig. 15).

On the surface, there were things about Pierce Whitman might have found attractive. The kind of antiparty hero of the common person Whitman saw in Hale was exactly how Pierce had presented himself in the presidential campaign. Moreover, Pierce was an expansionist Democrat who hoped America would acquire Cuba and even Central America and Mexico. "On to Cuba!" was one of the rallying cries of his campaign. This idea became a bane of his administration, since acquiring Cuba was widely seen as part of a Southern plot to extend slavery. Surprisingly enough, Whitman, despite his supposedly antiextensionist beliefs, actually favored the proslavery idea of Cuban annexation. In his poetry he included Havana as one of the cities America would one day include, and in a newspaper piece of the 1850s he stated directly: "It is impossible to say what the future will bring forth, but 'manifest destiny' certainly points to the speedy annexation of Cuba by the United States." He had not totally surrendered the jingoistic expansionism he had absorbed from Polk and the Young America movement of the forties.

The devotion to expansion was one of the few things he carried over from his old Democratic days. The central beliefs of Jacksonian democracy had run into the stone wall of slavery. Early pillars of the Democratic Party were either dead or had been driven into activity that seemingly contradicted their egalitarian principles. The erstwhile party of Jackson, once the defender of the common people, became under Pierce widely viewed as the defender of slavery. The charming but pliable Pierce rapidly became the tool of proslavery forces within the party. Several Jacksonians Whitman had known in the forties, including John L. O'Sullivan, Thomas Low Nichols, and Mike Walsh, had become promoters of the South.

No one embodied the current spirit of the Democratic Party more than the Illinois senator Stephen A. Douglas, known as the Little Giant because his domineering presence belied his diminutive stature. Whitman felt a kinship with the pugnacious senator and in the late fifties would actually take his side in his political maneuvering against Abraham Lincoln (though later Whitman claimed to have voted for Lincoln in 1860). A Democratic expansionist to the hilt, Douglas was a hero among the roughs and b'hoys with whom Whitman fraternized.

But Whitman could not tolerate the bill Douglas introduced to Congress on January 4, 1854, a bill that would overturn the Missouri Compromise by permitting settlers of the Kansas and Nebraska territories to decide for themselves about slavery. When President Pierce signed the bill into law as the Kansas-Nebraska Act on May 30, the North erupted in rage. Antislavery sentiment, which had been growing in the wake of the fugitive slave law of 1850 and the publication of *Uncle Tom's Cabin* two years later, now became remarkably widespread in the North, as the spread of the South's "peculiar institution" seemed all but certain.

The Democratic leadership for whom Whitman may have retained some residual respect suddenly seemed to him corrupt and beyond redemption. Surveying all antebellum presidents, Whitman would call Pierce "the weakest,—the very worst of the lot" (he made a similar statement about Pierce's equally malleable successor, James Buchanan [see fig. 16], whom he branded "perhaps the weakest of the President tribe—the very unablest"). Like many other Northerners, he seized on the fugitive slave law as a symbol of wrongheaded government intervention into the affairs of free society. For him as for other antislavery activists, the capture and retrieval of the slave Anthony Burns in Boston became the archetypal example of corrupt government.

Anthony Burns, the property of Charles T. Suttle of Alexandria, Virginia, had escaped from slavery on a Boston-bound ship early in 1854. On May 24 he was arrested by a federal marshal and confined in a Boston courthouse. After a weeklong trial, the judge of probate, Edward G. Loring, ruled that he be taken back to Virginia. Several leading antislavery agitators, including Wendell Phillips and Theodore Parker, led a rally where they championed Burns as a helpless martyr and impugned Loring and the fugitive slave law. Because most Bostonians were strongly opposed to Loring's decision, federal troops, a thousand strong with fifes and drums, were called in to conduct the chained Burns through the streets of Boston to the ship waiting to carry him back to captivity. The slow procession was performed amidst jeering crowds and buildings draped in black. On one building an enormous American flag hung up side down. On another was suspended a black coffin inscribed "Liberty."

Antislavery activists saw the seizure of Burns as an act of infamy. At a huge rally in Framingham on July 4 (a day the activists now celebrated only in irony) Henry David Thoreau gave his searing address "Slavery in Massachusetts." He denounced Judge Loring and declared: "My thoughts are murder to the State, and involuntarily go plotting against her." Equally angry speeches were given by Sojourner Truth, Wendell Phillips, and several others. William Lloyd Garrison burned copies of the Declaration of Independence and the Constitution as the crowd cheered grimly.

Garrison's gesture was highly symbolic. To thoughtful observers, the Burns case and others like it made the terms "America" and "liberty" contradictory. In the 1850s, 332 fugitive slaves were returned south, and only eleven were declared free. Each case gave antislavery people a rallying cause. The retrieval of Burns in particular drove many to view established American institutions with cynicism and disdain.

One such cynic was Whitman. Appalled by the Burns case, he wrote a poem, "A Boston Ballad," which, along with "Resurgemus," was one of the two pre-1855 poems incorporated into *Leaves of Grass*. The poem was a vigorous, sarcastic protest against the way the state and federal authorities handled the Burns case. Significantly, Burns himself is not mentioned in the poem. Whitman's emphasis is on the federal government's tyrannical violation of the idea of liberty. Picturing the government-authorized troops ushering Burns through the Boston streets, he writes ironically:

Clear the way there Jonathan!
Way for the President's marshal! Way for the government cannon!
Way for the federal foot and dragoons. . . . and the phantoms
    afterward.

I rose this morning to get betimes to Boston town;
Here's a good place at the corner. . . . I must stand and see the show.

I love to look on the stars and stripes. . . . I hope the fifes will play
    Yankee Doodle.

As in his political poems of 1850, he resorts to the kind of blackly
humorous, Gothic protest imagery popularized by George Lippard. The
central scene of Lippard's *The Quaker City* had been the terrible proces-
sion through the streets of a modern city in which haughty social rulers
led black and white slaves in chains; the procession went forward jaun-
tily, until suddenly there arose the phantoms of patriots and poor people
who followed and haunted the rulers. Whitman uses a strikingly similar
image in his bitter rendering of the Burns procession. He has the Boston
soldiers suddenly surrounded by the phantoms of old patriots who had
died for freedom and are now shocked by the betrayal of American ideals
in the retrieval of Burns. The patriot ghosts groan miserably and tremble
with anger at the horrid scene. The cynical narrator asks: "What troubles
you, Yankee phantoms? What is all this chattering of bare gums? / Does
the ague convulse your limbs? Do you mistake your crutches for fire-
locks, and level them?" He orders the helpless ghosts back to their graves
and whispers to the Boston mayor to send someone immediately to En-
gland to exhume the bones of King George III, bring them to America,
glue them together, and set up the king's skeleton as a centerpiece for
"the President's marshal" and all "roarers from Congress" to worship.

Among the messages of "A Boston Ballad" is that political power in
America has become so corrupt that it can be described only in savagely
subversive language. Whitman's image of the rising patriot ghosts may
derive specifically from Lippard, but the overall spirit of protest against
corrupt institutions was part of a larger reform rhetoric seen in many
activists of the day.

Whitman was adopting the spirit of agitation popularized by reform-
ers who were trying to arouse the moral conscience of the nation. The
Brooklyn preacher he most admired, Henry Ward Beecher, declared in
an antislavery speech of 1851: "Agitation? What have we got to work with
but agitation? Agitation is *the* thing in these days for any good." The next
year the abolitionist Wendell Phillips declared: "Only by unintermitted
agitation can a people be kept sufficiently awake not to let liberty be

smothered in material prosperity. . . . Republics exist only on the tenure of being constantly agitated." The antislavery leader Joshua Giddings used similar language: "Agitation is the great and mighty instrument for carrying forward . . . reforms. Agitation is necessary to purify the political atmosphere of this nation." And Whitman's correspondent and favorite speaker, John P. Hale, told the Senate, "I glory in the name of agitator. I wish the country could be agitated vastly more than it is."

Whitman was coming to think that he, above all, was the one chosen to agitate the country. He wrote in his 1856 notebook: "Agitation is the test of the goodness and solidness of all politics and laws and institutions.—If they cannot stand it, there is no genuine life in them, and shall die." He once declared, "I think agitation is the most important factor of all—the most deeply important. To stir, to question, to suspect, to examine, to denounce!" In the 1855 preface to *Leaves of Grass* he announced that in a morally slothful age the poet is best equipped to "make every word he speaks draw blood . . . he never stagnates." In a draft of a later preface he stressed that his poetry was meant to be bracing, rough, violent, "sharp, full of danger, full of contradictions and offence." Key lines in his poems echo this zestful tone: "I am he who walks the States with a barb'd tongue, questioning every one I meet"; "Let others praise eminent men and hold up peace, I hold up agitation and conflict." He would never give up the spirit of agitation he had shared with the antebellum reformers. "As circulation is to the air, so is agitation and a plentiful degree of speculative license to political and moral sanity," he wrote in *Democratic Vistas*. "*Vive*, the attack—the perennial assault!"

Like the reformers, he was ready to use black humor and Gothicized mudslinging to describe corrupt politicians. In his unpublished prose tract "The Eighteenth Presidency!" (1856) he spewed forth horrible epithets that suggested his profound disgust with the powers that be. Political leaders he compared to lice, corpses, maggots, venereal sores. This kind of reformist protest rhetoric runs as a sharp, needling voice through his poetry, as in "The Sleepers," where he writes, "I have been wronged. . . . I am oppressed. . . . I hate him that oppresses me, / I will either destroy him, or he shall release me," or in "Respondez!" which portrays a topsy-turvy society where churches are filled with vermin, criminals take the place of judges, God is pronounced dead, and so on for more than seventy scathingly subversive lines.

There was, in fact, historical justification for such language. The events in Kansas provoked Whitman's wrath. In November 1854 the Kansas congressional election was decided by some 1,700 border ruffians who crossed over from neighboring Missouri and cast illegal votes for the proslavery candidate. The following March, fraudulent voting by Missourians ensured the election of a proslavery territorial legislature in Kansas. Franklin Pierce's administration did little to oppose the bogus Kansas vote and in fact sanctioned its proslavery legislature. Fighting between pro- and antislavery forces broke out in what had come to be called Bleeding Kansas. Horrified by these turns of events, Whitman in "The Eighteenth Presidency!" lashed out against the Kansas frauds and wrote of the Pierce administration: "The President eats dirt and excrement for his daily meals, likes it, and tries to force it on The States. The cushions of the Presidency are nothing but filth and blood. The pavements of Congress are also bloody."

There was also justification for Whitman's savage words about corruption in government. Corruption had long been entrenched in antebellum politics, especially in Whitman's New York. Beginning with the state elections of 1834, Tammany Hall began its long-standing practice of controlling the Manhattan vote through muscle tactics, bribery, and illegal voting. Throughout the 1840s and beyond, Tammany "runners" would meet immigrants at the New York docks, and, in return for giving them illegal naturalization papers and finding them homes and jobs, secure their vote. In a time of lax voter registration, liquor and money were freely given to "repeaters," or people hired to vote repeatedly under various names in different parts of the city. In the city election of 1854 Fernando Wood was elected mayor as result of vote fraud; in one ward, the so-called Bloody Sixth, there were actually four thousand more votes cast than there were voters.

Graft and money skimming were so common in New York state government that by 1850 one observer could write: "The State creeps all over, like an old cheese, & swarms of maggots are hopping & skipping about all the avenues to the Legislature. . . . Gross corruption appears to be the order of the day." In 1852 the infamous board of aldermen known as the Forty Thieves took power in Manhattan. The group began the practice (later to become rampant when one of its members, William Marcy Tweed, took over Tammany) of grossly overcharging the city for various projects and pocketing the profits.

Manhattan's political shenanigans were emblematic of what was happening in the nation as a whole. As Mark Summers has shown, during the 1850s corruption was common in other cities up and down the eastern seaboard and even in the federal government. In the early 1860s the reformer Thomas Low Nichols looked back in horror on the previous decade: "It is a matter of world-wide notoriety that during the past ten years whole legislatures have been bribed; that the state and national treasuries have been despoiled of millions; that members of Congress have sold their votes in open market to the highest bidder."

There was direct historical reference, then, for Whitman's venomous diatribes, as in the 1855 preface where he impugned the "swarms of cringers, suckers, doughfaces, lice of politics, planners of sly involutions for their own preferment to city offices or state legislatures or the judiciary or congress or the presidency."

Another alarming social phenomenon was the growing inequality between the rich and the poor. Class differences in America widened far more rapidly between 1825 and 1860 than either before or after this period. In 1774 the richest 1 percent of free wealth holders had owned 12.6 percent of the nation's assets and the top 10 percent a little less than half. By 1860 these numbers had leaped to nearly 30 percent for the wealthiest percentile and 73 percent for the top decile. The cost of living for poor people increased notably, peaking in 1855, when the ratio of cost of living of poor to rich was 111.3 percent. Fewer than half of free white males in America owned real estate at midcentury. By the Civil War the poorest half of Americans owned just 1 percent of all assets.

A powerful discourse of working-class protest accompanied these growing class divisions. Novels by George Lippard, George Thompson, and Ned Buntline depicted upper-crust figures like bankers and lawyers involved in nefarious schemes while poor people starved. Whitman absorbed the language of working-class protest. Like the popular writers, he used in his journalism the term "upper ten" to describe the privileged few. In his notebook he denounced the "vast ganglions of bankers and merchant princes." He could sound just like Lippard or Thompson characterizing the grotesque rich: "I see an aristocrat / I see a smoucher grabbing the good dishes exclusively to himself and grinning at the starvation of others as if it were funny, / I gaze on the greedy hog." His poem "The Sleepers" included a similar image: "The head of the money-maker that plotted all day sleeps, / And the enraged and treacherous dispositions, all, all sleep." In "Song of Myself" he repeated the oft-made charge that the "idle" rich cruelly appropriated the products of the hardworking poor:

> Many sweating, ploughing, thrashing, and then the chaff for
>   payment receiving,
> A few idly owning, and they the wheat continually claiming.

Although he shared the concerns and language of the radical agitators of the day, he did not go as far as many did in their efforts to overthrow or supplant the American system. He took only passing interest, for instance, in the utopian socialist movement that swept the nation in the forties. Some twenty-seven utopian communities, many of them modeled on the phalanxes of the French socialist Charles Fourier, were established across the North between 1841 and 1855 in the hope of replacing the increasingly unfair capitalist system with one of cooperative ownership and shared living arrangements. Whitman wrote in 1848 in the *Crescent,* "We don't know much about Fourierism—that we confess," though he commended the ubiquity of music in one socialist community. He learned more about Fourierism when he opened his Brooklyn bookstore, which carried the full list of the progressive publications of Fowlers and Wells, including their translations of Fourier. But it was Fourier's ideas of "passional attraction" and brotherhood, not his economic plan, that most appealed to him. Throughout his life he resisted the programs of socialists and labor activists, saying that as a poet he was a socialist only "intrinsically, in my meanings." In New York he often spotted America's leading Fourierist, Charles Brisbane, describing him in an amusing newspaper sketch as a thin, long-chinned man with an awkward gait and an abstracted air.

As socialism gave way in the early fifties to more individualistic reforms, he seems to have taken greater interest. This was the time of the great flowering of American anarchism. Not far from Whitman's birthplace on Long Island, there was established in 1851 the utopian community of Modern Times led by a group of reformers who practiced the doctrine of individual sovereignty, by which every individual was pronounced the "absolute despot or sovereign" of his or her own life, without reference to outside laws or governments. The leading anarchist, Stephen Pearl Andrews, advanced his doctrine in a widely read series in the *New York Tribune* in 1852. Andrews wrote: "This is preeminently the age of Individualism (it would hardly be polite to say Egotism), where 'the Sovereignty of the Individual'—that is, the right of every one to do nearly as he pleases—is already generally popular, and is visibly gaining ground daily." Gleefully celebrating himself, he announced: "I claim individually to be my own nation. I take this opportunity to declare my national independence, and to notify all other potentates, that they may respect my sovereignty." Thoreau's *Walden* in 1854 gave further impetus to this individualistic reform.

In a decade when government authority was proving to be corrupt, individual authority seemed suddenly paramount. All the individualistic reformers explicitly or implicitly paid homage in their writings to the great enunciator of self-reliance, Ralph Waldo Emerson. Whether or not Whitman read Emerson in the fifties, Emerson's ideas flooded the reformist air in a decade when the individual seemed far more worthy than the state. Whitman's celebration of himself in egotistical poetry was right in step with the times. Frequently in the 1855 and '56 editions this timely individualism breaks forth: "I celebrate myself"; "Going where I list, my own master total and absolute"; "Each man to himself and each woman to herself." Like the individualistic reformers, he was impelled by chicanery among America's rulers to put the individual above the state. In "Song of the Broad-Axe" he imagines a society "Where outside authority enters always after the precedence of inside authority, / Where the citizen is always the head and ideal, and President, Mayor, Governor and what not are agents for pay."

Individualistic expression even came to characterize clothing fashions in the fifties, a decade of great creativity and latitude in American dress. For women, the liberating Bloomer costume—a tunic belted at the waist with a knee-length skirt and billowing pantaloons—was a brief rage, followed by a multilayered outfit of crinolines, hoopskirts, and multicolored dresses. Men also had sartorial flexibility. As one contemporary later recalled, "The ten years ending in 1860 will always be remembered as a period when styles and fabrics for men's wear were of greater variety than ever before or since." Before and especially after the fifties men's dress was more restrained and conventional. Whitman's dress habits followed the overall pattern. As late as 1847, when he edited the *Eagle,* he was still a conservative dresser. During and after the Civil War he would assume the black or gray clothes that then became the fashion (though he always gave an idiosyncratic twist with his large hat and open shirt).

It was in the flamboyant fifties that his dress was most individualistic. After the American tour of the Hungarian patriot Louis Kossuth in 1851, the "Kossuth hat," a dark fur cap with a feather, became the fashion. Whitman saw Kossuth make his grand entrance in Manhattan and met him several times. Thereafter, several offbeat variations of hats, including the Italian alpine and Mexican sombrero, were allowed for men. Whitman adopted his round felt hat at this time. Men's fashions followed the kind of do-your-own-thing mentality that would reappear in the 1960s, when the natural-dressing Thoreau and Whitman would become hippie icons. Wealthy men of the 1850s favored unusual, splashy colors and hyperelegance—the kind of showiness Whitman derogated in an 1855 article describing a "painted" Broadway dandy. Writers and artists, like those who gathered at Pfaff's restaurant, had virtually free choice in what they could wear. Some, like Whitman, adopted republican attire in the wake of Grahamite dress reformers who were calling for plain, loose-fitting apparel.

Whitman's dress expressed his political views. Since he now thought that beneath the "scum" of social rulers lay the hearty goodness of average workers, he adopted variations on the working man's garb. In the famous engraving in the 1855 edition of *Leaves of Grass* he appears in plain, common clothes, with white shirt open at the neck and rough, rumpled pants, with his round hat tilted in cocky defiance (fig. 2). Several who knew him in the midfifties noted his distinctive costumes that could include rough trousers tucked inside heavy cowhide boots, a checked shirt and red undershirt, heavy overcoat with large pockets, and large gray or black hat. Worker's trousers and colorful shirts and scarves remained his preferred garb until the early years of the Civil War, after which he dressed more conservatively.

Radicalism and Tradition

SUBVERSIVE RHETORIC aimed at social rulers; profound disgust with the party system; willing participation in the individualistic attitudes of the 1850s—all of these facets of Whitman fed into his rebelliousness as a poet and person. We are so accustomed, however, to think of Whitman as a revolutionary that we are liable to forget his conservative side. He loved to say: "Be radical, be radical, be radical—be not too damned radical." Although he associated with reformers of all stripes and absorbed their subversive spirit, he adopted none of their programs for social change. He once confessed, "I am somehow afraid of agitators, though I believe in agitation." He had vehement arguments with his abolitionist friends, who, he recalled, got "hot" with him for not espousing the abolitionist cause. He also shied away from joining the women's rights movement, the free love movement, and the labor movement, though he observed them all with interest. Some have expressed dissatisfaction at his failure to become a social activist. D. H. Lawrence pointed out that it is one thing to sympathize with slaves, as Whitman does in his poetry, but quite another thing to agitate for their emancipation. Henry Miller, likewise, complained that Whitman never took on the causes of those very oppressed peoples he ostensibly championed.

But there are all kinds of activism that work in different ways. In Whitman's day the lines between "conservatism" and "radicalism" were not clear. Harriet Beecher Stowe, for instance, took a fairly conservative stance on slavery, since she believed that blacks, once liberated, should be "civilized" and sent back to Africa. Yet her portrayal of slaves' suffering in *Uncle Tom's Cabin* was so powerful that Lincoln called her the woman who caused the big war. Lincoln himself, as seen, was in some ways conservative; yet he has justifiably gone down in history as the bold emancipator. An activist like Horace Greeley was vigorously antislavery, feminist, and Fourierist but at the same time reactionary on the issues of prohibition and prostitution.

Whitman feared what then was called ultraism, or any form of extreme social activism that threatened to rip apart the social fabric. He was concerned with assaults made on America's central documents, the Constitution and the Declaration of Independence. With respect to the Constitution, he faced a major crisis. The abolitionists called it "a covenant with death and a compact with hell" because of its return-of-fugitives clause. Even more mainstream types were dismissing it. In a famous Senate speech of 1850 the Whig leader William Seward, opposing slavery in the territories, had declared there was "a higher law than the Constitution"—meaning moral or religious principle. America's most famous preacher, Henry Ward Beecher, chimed in with his protest: "Not even the Constitution itself will make me unjust." Anti-Constitutional feeling became remarkably widespread after May 1854, which brought the twin indignities of Kansas-Nebraska and Anthony Burns.

Venerating the Constitution, Whitman did a balancing act: he excoriated the fugitive slave law but said fugitive slaves must be returned to their owners because the Constitution demanded it. "MUST RUNAWAY SLAVES BE DELIVERED BACK?" he asked in "The Eighteenth Presidency!" His answer: "They must. . . . By a section of the fourth article of the Federal Constitution." In the very next paragraph, though, he declared: "As to what is called the Fugitive Slave Law, . . . [it] is at all time to be defied in all parts of These States, South and North, by speech, by pen, and, if need be, by the bullet and the sword."

"I contradict myself, I contain multitudes," we almost hear him saying. The contradiction was meaningful. Although he hated the treatment of Anthony Burns and other returned fugitives, he could not give up his faith in the Constitution, which he called "a perfect and entire thing, . . . the grandest piece of moral machinery ever constructed" whose "architects were some mighty prophets and gods."

He was also confronted with problems related to the Declaration of Independence. The terminology of the document had been appropriated by a confusing array of groups: proslavery Southern fire-eaters, Northern abolitionists, radical feminists, Fourierists. These and other groups found in the Declaration support for their sometimes contradictory views. The South used it to defend its instinct to revolt against national authority and to assert the rights of individual states. It was this logic that led the Southern states to secede from the Union in 1860–61. The North, on the other hand, appealed to it to rebel against what it saw as the tyranny of the Southern "slave power" and to assert the rights of independent white laborers.

What was the "real" Declaration? How could a proper balance be achieved between the rights of individual states and the power of the federal government?

For Whitman, the problem was a momentous one, at the very heart of American life. In a prose work he said that one of his main poetic objectives from the start was to solve "the problem of two sets of rights," those of "individual State prerogatives" and "the national identity power—the sovereign Union." The issue was between the centrifugal forces of liberty and individual rights, on the one hand, and the centripetal ones of union and national power.

He shied away from movements that seemed to upset that delicate balance, and he tried mightily to restore that balance in his poetry. On this theme, the message of his poems was simple: balance and equipoise by poetic fiat. The kind of balance he asserted in his 1847 notebook jotting—"I am the poet of slaves and of the masters of slaves"—became far more crucial with the disturbing occurrences of the fifties, especially after the party collapse and the Kansas debacle. The poet was to be the balancer or equalizer of his land. "He is the arbiter of the diverse and he is the key," Whitman emphasizes in the 1855 preface. "He is the equalizer of his age and land. . . . he supplies what wants supplying and checks what wants checking."

With the possibility of resolution through normal political channels now dead, all the more reason, he saw, to forge a new resolution in his poetry. Seeing that the national Union was imperiled, in the 1855 preface he affirmed "the union always surrounded by blatherers and always calm and impregnable." The basic problem of the conflicting rights of the individual and the mass, to appear on many levels throughout his poetry, was resolved by poetic fiat in the ringing opening lines of the 1855 edition:

I celebrate myself,
And what I assume you shall assume,
For every atom belonging to me as good belongs to you.

He knew that Southerners and Northerners were virtually at each others' throats, so he made a point in his poems constantly to link the opposing groups. He proclaimed himself "A Southerner soon as a Northerner, a planter nonchalant and hospitable down by the Oconee I live, / [. . .] At home on the hills of Vermont or in the woods of Maine, or the

Texan ranch." When he directly addressed the issues of sectionalism and slavery in his poetry, he also struck a middle ground. In the 1855 preface he assures his readers that the American poet shall "not be for the eastern states more than the western or the northern states more than the southern." He writes of "slavery and the tremulous spreading hands to protect it, and the stern opposition to it which shall never cease till the speaking of tongues and the moving of lips cease." The first half of this statement gently embraces the Southern view; the second half airs sharp antislavery anger but leaves open the possibility that it may be a very long time before slavery disappears—a gradualist view confirmed by Whitman's statement in an 1857 *Daily Times* article that slavery would probably disappear in a hundred years.

Fearing the sectional controversies that threatened disunion, he represented the Southern point of view in his poetry, as when he described a plantation: "There are the negroes at work in good health, the ground in all directions is cover'd with pine straw." Even some racial attitudes of his day infiltrate his poems. Occasionally African-Americans are ghettoized by being placed in the company of disagreeable people or things. In "Song of the Open Road" he writes that "The black with his woolly head, the felon, the diseas'd, the illiterate person, are not denied." In the original version of "Assurances" he states, "I do not doubt there is far more in trivialities, insects, vulgar persons, slaves, dwarfs, rejected refuse, than I have supposed."

Such apparent lapses, though, are historically explainable. For his day, these lines were actually liberal. He was seeing worth in people and objects ordinarily cast aside by society. His attitude was more compassionate, for example, than that of an antislavery editor who wrote: "No slaveholders and no niggers in the territories. . . . Nigger slaves shall not be allowed to work among, associate nor amalgamate with white people." Whitman in his poetry struggled to free himself of these almost universal racist assumptions.

He was most successful in doing so in the broadly inclusive first edition of *Leaves of Grass*. His view was close to that of antislavery activists of the fifties who were emphasizing the humanity of African-Americans. The radicalism of *Uncle Tom's Cabin* lies in its powerful portrayal of African-Americans as vibrant, emotional human beings. The humanity of blacks was a chief point among black abolitionists. Frederick Douglass, appalled by the dehumanization of blacks in America, pointed to the humanity and nobility of the African-American:

> He stands erect. Upon his brow he bears the seal of manhood, from the hand of the living God. Adopt any mode of reasoning you please

with respect to him, he is a man, possessing an immortal soul, illuminated by intellect, capable of heavenly aspirations, and in all things pertaining to manhood, he is at once self-evidently a man, and therefore entitled to all the rights and privileges which belong to human nature.

Whitman takes this radically humanitarian view toward blacks several times in the 1855 edition. The opening poem, later titled "Song of Myself," contains a long passage in which the "I" takes an escaped slave into his house and washes and feeds him, keeping his firelock ready at the door to fend off possible pursuers. In another passage he actually becomes "the hounded slave," with dogs and men in bloody pursuit. In a third he admires a magnificent black driver, climbing up with him and driving alongside him. "I Sing the Body Electric" presents a profoundly humanistic variation on the slave auction, as the "I" boasts how humanly valuable his slave is: "There swells and jets a heart, there all passions, desires, reachings, aspirations, / [. . .] In him the start of populous states and rich republics."

Such passages help explain why his poetry has won favor among African-American readers. The ex-slave and abolitionist lecturer Sojourner Truth (fig. 30) was rapturous in her praise of *Leaves of Grass*. When she heard someone reading Whitman's verse aloud, she asked who wrote it but then added, "Never mind the man's name—it was God who wrote it, he chose the man—to give his message," and thereafter requested to hear it read aloud often. Such sentiments were shared by an African-American man who visited Whitman late in life, telling him, "You will be of great use to our race." The Harlem Renaissance writer Langston Hughes could talk of Whitman's "sympathy for Negro people," and poet June Jordan said, "I too am a descendant of Walt Whitman."

To Heal a Nation

IN SEVERAL SENSES, the first two editions of *Leaves of Grass*, published in 1855 and 1856, were poetic versions of the leading ideas of the two parties that dominated the North's political scene in these years, the Know-Nothings and the Republicans. Several of Whitman's central themes—extreme valuation of the common person, intense Americanism, a cleansing impulse—tie him to these parties.

Both the Know-Nothings and Republicans, besides being opposed to slavery, presented themselves as fresh, populist alternatives to previous parties, which were viewed as rotten to the core. They grew with amazing rapidity between 1854 and '56 partly because, with the disappearance of the Whig Party and the proslavery apostasy of the Democrats, they advertised a fresh beginning, a new world of political purity in a time of overriding ugliness and corruption. As Alexander H. Stephens, who moved, like Whitman, out of the Democratic Party into the Republican, wrote at the end of 1854: "Old parties, old names, old issues, and old organizations are passing away. A day of new things, new issues, new leaders, and new organizations is at hand." Whitman caught the spirit of the time when he wrote in the first paragraph of the 1855 preface that America "has passed into the new life of the new forms."

The old party leaders, insisted the Know-Nothings and Republicans, were grotesque representatives of a party system that had grown corrupt and detached from the people. Below the corruption of America's rulers lay the genuineness of average Americans whose values should be the basis of political action. One Know-Nothing typically called for a leader who was "fresh from the loins of the people." The two Republican presidential nominees of the fifties—the hardy explorer John Frémont and the Illinois rail-splitter Abraham Lincoln—epitomized this populist, antiparty impulse. In the 1856 race Frémont was pushed as "a new man, fresh from the people and one of themselves." Among his supporters was Whitman, whose whole family abandoned the Democrats and turned Republican.

Whitman shared the new populist impulse. He had once been snobbish, as witnessed by his snide aspersions of the simple Woodbury villagers in his 1840 letters to Abraham Leech. His sympathy for the masses had increased between 1846 and '48 with the rise of the Free-Soil movement, when the territorial dispute led him to praise publicly American working people whose values he suddenly championed. But he had then still been very much within the framework of the party hierarchy, and he retained an almost sheepish veneration of the presidency and the party leadership. With the corruption and political collapse of the fifties, however, his veneration for entrenched rulers disappeared and his respect for common people increased exponentially.

He espoused a dialectical mode of thinking that was new to him, one that lay behind the parties of the midfifties, involving fierce rejection of entrenched authority coupled with equally intense praise of simple artisan values. In his notebook he wrote: "I know that underneath all this putridity of Presidents and Congressmen that has risen to the top, lie pure waters a thousand fathoms deep." Eric Foner has shown that the Republican Party rose to prominence in large part because of its appeal to the ideology of free labor, epitomized in average workers such as independent shopkeepers, farmers, and artisans of all kinds, whose values were posed as preferable to those of exploitative moguls and politicians. Whitman shared this outlook. His tract "The Eighteenth Presidency!" follows the Republican dialectic. In it he unsparingly attacks the powers that be and sings praise to "the true people, . . . mechanics, farmers, boatmen, manufacturers, and the like." He hopes some "healthy-bodied, middle-aged, beard-faced American blacksmith or boatman" will "come down from the West across the Alleghanies, and walk into the Presidency."

A similar dialectic runs through the early editions of *Leaves of Grass.* In 1847 he had written in the *Eagle* that the presidency was the most sublime office on earth. Now his attitude was exactly reversed. The people, he stressed in the 1855 preface, should not take off their hats to presidents: it should be the other way around. The president would no longer be the people's referee: now the poet would be. The genius of the United States, he wrote, was not in presidents or legislatures but "always most in their common people," as it was better to be a poor free mechanic or farmer than "a bound booby and rogue in office." His early poems are full of long catalogs of average people at work. The party collapse and the devaluation of authority figures, in other words, had fueled his ardent populism, just as it had helped give rise to the new party organizations.

He also shared with the new parties an intense Americanism that tended toward jingoism. It has often been thought that his nationalistic instinct derived from the Young America movement or from Emerson. But by the early fifties the Young America movement had turned sour. Its intense Americanism, which had in the early forties engendered literary nationalism, had been swept up in the politics of expansionism, which by the fifties was allied with the proslavery forces. Two great champions of Young America, John L. O'Sullivan and Stephen Douglas, had by the fifties become defenders of the South. The organ of Young America, the *Democratic Review,* which had published several of Whitman's early stories, ceased publication in 1852. As for Emerson, it is likely that he directly influenced the nationalistic stance of Whitman's poetry, despite Whitman's later denials. It is important to note, however, that at the only two *documented* moments of Whitman's awareness of Emerson—in 1842 and 1847—the Concord sage had no fertilizing effect on his imagination. It was only after Whitman had escaped the shackles of party and had experienced the political crisis of the fifties that he gave literary form to the Americanism Emerson represented. The timing of Whitman's intense nationalism coincided exactly with the dominance of that most nationalistic of all political movements, the Know-Nothings.

After the collapse of the Whig Party in early 1854, the strongly pro-

American Know-Nothings suddenly became the most powerful new party in the nation. The Know-Nothings (probably so named because they started as a secret order whose members professed ignorance of it) tapped into long-smoldering nativist sentiment in the North. As a result of developments abroad, especially the Irish potato famine, immigrants were arriving in America at a pace never known before or since. Between 1845 and 1855, 3 million foreigners swarmed to America's shores, peaking in 1854, when 427,833 arrived. This was the largest proportionate increase in immigrants at any time in American history. The large majority were Roman Catholic. The Know-Nothings responded to a deep-seated fear that Catholic foreigners would infiltrate American institutions and possibly even take over the government. Since many foreigners, particularly the Irish, supported slavery, the Know-Nothings appealed to antislavery activists. They also incorporated defenders of the working class.

Above all, they were the party of intense, unabashed Americanism. "America for Americans" was their motto, the Star-Spangled Banner was their emblem, and in 1855 "American Party" became their public name. Their success in the Northern elections of 1854 and '55 was stunning. They elected eight governors, more than a hundred congressmen, mayors in three major cities, and thousands of other local officials. Their height of popularity was reached in June 1855, the month before *Leaves of Grass* appeared, with their number at about 1.5 million members.

Whitman later recalled that the Know-Nothings were "the great party of those days." Although he said he did not join the organization (but then, what Know-Nothing would say?), he had a history of flirtation with nativism. In 1842 he had come out strongly against Bishop John Hughes on the issue of public funding for Catholic schools, an issue that came back with redoubled fury in the fifties and fueled the Know-Nothing debate. The politician in the 1850s he most admired, John P. Hale, was an ardent nativist. Since the Know-Nothings in 1854 and early '55 were championing his favorite causes—antislavery, temperance, and rights for working people—he may have found the American Party appealing.

At any rate, the jingoistic moments in his early poetry smacked of nativism. In one poem he wrote, "America isolated I sing; / I say that works here made in the spirit of other lands, are so much poison to these States," adding, "Bards for my own land only I invoke." In the first two editions, at the peak of the nativist frenzy, he identified himself in his signature poem as "Walt Whitman, an American"—changed later, in less nativist times, to "Walt Whitman, of Manhattan the son." Trying to appeal to the nativist readership, he began a self-review of his poetry by boasting, "An American bard at last!" redoubling the boast in another self-review: "No imitation—No foreigner—but a growth and idiom of America."

If he was a nativist, though, he was one with a difference. His first woman reviewer, Fanny Fern, saw this when she called him "this glorious Native American" but specified that he was "no Catholic-baiting Know Nothing." On the one hand, he did adopt some of the attitudes of the Know-Nothings, to the extent that he would once say that America's digestion was strained by the "millions of ignorant foreigners" coming to its shores. Sketching plans for a lecture to be given to a Protestant group, he sounded like a Know-Nothing when he wrote that Catholics were sufficiently numerous to put all American enterprises in their grasp. He warned, "Beware of churches! beware of priests!" and wondered what America had to do with "all this mummery of prayer and rituals."

On the other hand, as was true with his attitude toward antislavery groups, he wanted to avoid extremes and in fact extended a friendly hand to foreigners in his poetry. In "Song of Myself" he announced himself "Pleas'd with the native and pleas'd with the foreign." In another poem he wrote, "See, in my poems immigrants continually coming and landing." His claim elsewhere that his poetry does not separate "the white from the black, or the native from the immigrant just landed at the wharf" in fact has validity, as is evidenced particularly by his poetic paean to international friendship, "Salut au Monde!" The American Party, while it stimulated his nationalism, became one more narrow political group he rejected. It made him wish to wrest the word "American" from partial definitions and seek the largest possible applications for the term.

Time would tell he had good reason to do so. The American Party rapidly fell prey to the same kind of sectional divisions that had killed off the Whigs. The ascendant Republicans, meanwhile, spent more energy attacking the Southern slavocracy than on representing the interests of Northern workers. Both the problems and the proposed solutions of the parties were addressed to specific, practical needs of the moment.

For Whitman, American's problem was far deeper than the immigrant explosion or the Southern slave power. Corruption in America was not superficial or easily removed. It was, he wrote, "in the blood." His disgust with the political process was more profound than that of any other commentator of the fifties. He wrote that the parties had become "empty flesh, putrid mouths, mumbling and squeaking the tones of these conventions, the politicians standing back in the shadow, telling lies." Those responsible for selecting America's leaders came "from political hearses, and from the coffins inside, and from the shrouds inside the coffins; from the tumors and abscesses of the land; from the skeletons and skulls in the vaults of the federal almshouses; from the running sores of the great cities."

The final effect of the dramatic political changes of the fifties was to drive him beyond parties altogether. In his 1856 notebook the former party loyalist could proclaim himself "no[t] the particular representative of any one party—no tied and ticketed democrat, whig, abolitionist, republican,—no bawling spokesman of natives against foreigners."

The history of parties and reforms had shown him that the former led to institutionalized corruption, the latter to narrow views and sometimes wild fanaticism. He now reminded himself, "We want no *reforms*, no *institutions*, no *parties*—We want a *living principle* as nature has, under which nothing can go wrong—This must be vital through the United States." He had once believed the American system would perpetually purify itself through party debates and periodic elections. But with the party system having collapsed in a morass of bad principle and outright knavery, he had to look elsewhere for purification and ennoblement.

If the political and social crises represented the grim aspects of American life, there were other cultural arenas that offered hope and restoration. Even as he had lost confidence in politics as usual, he had been surveying more positive, fruitful areas of cultural life. His omnivorous imagination profited from recent developments in popular performance, science, literature, sexual discourse, and the visual arts—all of which, along with freshly fashioned nature imagery, could remind Americans of the extraordinary potential of their nation.

In 1855 Whitman believed that the United States, cut adrift from its original ideals, desperately needed poets. He was confident too that America's veins were full of poetical stuff.

AMERICAN PERFORMANCES:
THEATER, ORATORY, MUSIC

A THIN ACTOR in a bejeweled, purple velvet shirt and a fur-trimmed cloak walks center stage at New York's Bowery Theatre. The audience waits in agonized anticipation as he ruminates with head bent. Nervously he kicks his sheathed sword. Suddenly he stops, his blue eyes fiercely sweeping the auditorium. In low, firm tones that crescendo he delivers the opening soliloquy of *Richard III*. The effect is electric. For more than three hours the audience is swept on waves of emotion. So impassioned is his delivery that in the sword-fight scene in Act 5 the other actors actually fear for their lives. The audience, overwhelmed, shows its appreciation noisily throughout.

A dark-haired, broad-browed clergyman walks out onto a pulpit platform that reaches well forward into the congregation. With a look of winning benignity, he surveys the nearly three thousand people who have traveled to Brooklyn's Plymouth Church to hear him. He has no script, no notes. He begins his sermon with a joke and a story. His listeners are enthralled. They laugh and cry their way through the sermon.

A family singing group—three brothers and a sister—mount the stage of the cavernous Broadway Tabernacle after the abolitionist lecturer has sat down. They launch into a spirited rendition of their antislavery song "Get Off the Track." When they reach the rousing chorus, about the unstoppable train *Emancipation* barreling across America, thousands in the audience sing along heartily.

The actor was Junius Brutus Booth, the clergyman Henry Ward Beecher, the singing group the Hutchinsons (see figs. 19, 20, 23, and 26). All were important elements of the performance culture Whitman loved. What they had in common, with each other and with his poetry, was a participatory spirit that permeated American life before the Civil War.

Whitman's poetry was the highest flowering of that participatory culture.

The forces unleashed by American republicanism changed the style of popular performances. The freewheeling, often raucous spirit of American popular culture affected those who entertained or instructed the masses. What came to be regarded as an "American" style of acting was developed by performers catering to audiences who feasted on sensations. Evangelical preachers, in the wake of the frenzied revivals during the Second Great Awakening, became so stylistically adventurous that they had to defend themselves against charges of theatricality and gimmickry. Political oratory enjoyed what some have called its golden age, featuring a style that was at once grandiloquent and familiar. Popular music came to reflect social issues and actual American experience to a degree never before seen.

As important as developments within these individual areas were the ways in which boundaries between them dissolved. In the carnivalized atmosphere of antebellum America rigid cultural hierarchies did not yet exist. Now-familiar separations between high, popular, and middlebrow culture would not begin to solidify until after the Civil War, when America became institutionalized. Before the war, there was a fluid exchange between different cultural idioms. Lawrence Levine has shown how Shakespeare's plays, far from being put on a pedestal, were regularly performed along with minstrels, farces, songs, and so on.

This phenomenon of mixed cultural categories was visible in other ways too. Political rallies, for instance, were rarely just political: they also included religious exhortations, poetry readings, musical performances. Holiday celebrations mixed the poetic and the pedestrian. Musical culture was shared in a way that has been lost. The gap between classical and popular music was narrow in a time when popular songs were often derived from operas and when classical compositions incorporated American folk music. Acting and popular oratory likewise drew off each other.

The differences between the prewar and postwar scenes can be highlighted by a quick comparison of the utopian experiment at Brook Farm in the 1840s and the utopian society portrayed by Edward Bellamy in his 1888 novel *Looking Backward*. At Brook Farm, as at many other antebellum utopian communities, concerts, poetry readings, *tableaux vivants*, and other communal entertainments were part of daily life. In Bellamy's futuristic society, life is far more passive and impersonal: music is piped into separate living compartments, workers join an Industrial Army, and much of the work is done by machines.

One doesn't have to look at utopias, however, to find differences. The very texture of everyday life in antebellum America was characterized by an interpenetration of different modes and styles. Many of the stories Whitman gave of his daily experiences were typical. In a July 1841 newspaper piece he told of going on a Long Island clam dig where there were readings from Shakespeare as well as stories and songs. His later reports of beach parties for the *Eagle* again highlighted lively mixtures of plays, songs, stories, games. In a day before passive spectatorship and the mass media, entertainment was supplied by actual people—not just paid performers but also ordinary people alone or in groups. Whitman's picture in "I Hear America Singing" of average people singing their "varied carols" was more than just a metaphor. It reflected a pre-mass-media culture in which Americans often entertained themselves and each other. Whitman's spouting Shakespeare atop omnibuses, declaiming Homer and Ossian at the seashore, and humming arias on the street typified these performances in everyday life.

His poetry tried to keep alive this participatory, dialogic spirit. No other writer challenges so many boundaries as he: boundaries between author and reader, between poetry and music and oratory, between high diction and slang, between different religions and social classes. This boundary-dissolving aspect of his verse can be tied to a populist performance culture that, in its various manifestations, had a cumulative impact on him that was perhaps as great as any other force.

"The Part That Looks Back on the Actor or Actress"

WHEN WHITMAN SAID he spent his young manhood "absorbing theatres at every pore" and seeing "everything, high, low, middling," he revealed his complete identification with the carnivalized culture of antebellum America. Like Lincoln, Whitman had eclectic tastes when it came to popular performances. Both took equal delight in Shakespeare and minstrel shows. Shortly before the election of 1860 Lincoln attended a minstrel show and loved it so much that he clapped longer and louder than anyone else. When the band played a new song, "Dixie," he yelled, "Let's have it again! Let's have it again!" Lincoln knew Shakespeare so well that he could recite pages by heart without making a mistake.

Whitman was even more open minded than Lincoln in his response to popular performances. His main theatergoing periods were from 1832–36, when he was a teenager in Brooklyn and Manhattan, and 1842–49, when he was back in the New York area as journalist and author. In the first period he generally had to pay his own way and therefore sat in the cheap third tier, or gallery, along with roughs and prostitutes. The theater was thus associated for him with galitarianism and populism. He once joked that he considered it a fall from grace when, in his journalism days during the forties, he got press passes to sit among more sophisticated types on the parquet, or first level, of the New York theaters.

The relationship between the theater and social class became an increasingly important one. Throughout the 1820s and 1830s the New York theater was in several senses truly democratic. The identification of the Park Theatre with elite culture and the Bowery Theatre with unadulterated sensationalism would not come until later. In fact, the Bowery pulled off a great coup in the thirties by wooing two of the era's best actors, Junius Brutus Booth and Edwin Forrest, away from the Park.

Whitman would long remember the primitive early theaters, with their dark entrances and the stark rows of plain wooden benches where the audience sat. Men usually did not remove their hats during plays (like them, the "I" of "Song of Myself" wears his hat "indoors and out"). Food was brought along and freely eaten during performances. Working-class viewers in the upper tier regularly tossed bones and other dinner remains onto those seated below.

By far the most important aspect of the theater experience for Whitman was the interaction between audience and performers. Although there was a kind of class distinction in the seating arrangement of the early theaters (the wealthy and respectable gravitated to the boxes on the second tier, with the less respectable above them and a mixed crowd below), these distinctions were in fact often erased by the noisy enthusiasm shared by all during performances. There was a fine line in antebellum public life between enthusiastic applause and uncontrolled mob frenzy. Rarely was the line so thin as in the theater. The b'hoys and roughs of the gallery went to the theater as much to engage in deviltry as to see plays. They expressed their praise and displeasure with the greatest possible noise. It was not unusual for the din of clapping, yelling, cheering, or hissing to drown out the actors. At the slightest provocation, unruly elements in the audience would throw things onto the stage.

Whitman became so accustomed to such audience outbursts that he was upset by theatergoers who did not express themselves loudly. Audience involvement reinforced his notion of the relationship between the artist and the people in a democracy. He applauded this relationship when it was intensely personal and intimate; he denounced it when it became cold or distant. He fondly recalled "those long-kept-up tempests of handclapping peculiar to the Bowery—no dainty kid-gloved business, but electric force and muscle from perhaps 2,000 full-sinew'd men."

His interest in audience-performer intimacy explains his attraction to performers who crossed the boundary between themselves and their listeners. Few crossed this boundary in so many ways as Junius Brutus Booth, his favorite actor and the leading tragedian of antebellum America. Booth is another of the unappreciated figures in Whitman biography. The omission is particularly surprising, since Whitman often expressed his indebtedness to the actor. "His genius," said Whitman, "was to me one of the grandest revelations of my life, a lesson of artistic expression." "He had much to do with shaping me in those early years," he added. Although Whitman did not know Booth personally, he attended many of his performances, saw him often on the streets, and discussed him with the Brooklyn actor and photographer Gabriel Harrison, a close mutual friend.

Doubtless Whitman knew something of Booth's checkered life. It was generally known that Booth was mad. Today, he would most likely be diagnosed as manic-depressive. THE MAD TRAGEDIAN HAS COME TO OUR CITY, the newspaper headlines read. Booth was born in England in 1796 and before he was twenty rivaled Edmund Kean as a Shakespearean actor. He was married to a Brussels woman but subsequently took up with a London flower girl who became the love of his life. With her he went to America in 1821, settling on a 150-acre farm near Baltimore. They had ten children, among them Edwin, later the renowned tragedian, and John Wilkes, Lincoln's assassin. Booth's wife caught wind of the affair and went to America, publicly denouncing him as a bigamist and the father of bastards. Eventually a divorce was filed. In the meantime Booth had earned a reputation as America's foremost actor—and as a drunk with a crazy streak. Theater managers around the country learned to lock him up before performances so that he wouldn't run to the local tavern. Once he was so intoxicated while performing that he fell off the front of the stage as the audience booed. One time, aboard a Charleston-bound ship, he reached the place where an actor friend had committed suicide; announcing he had a message for his friend, he jumped overboard and had to be rescued.

Although Booth's neuroses made him an erratic actor, Whitman did not dwell on his failings. Like another well-known madman, the poet McDonald Clarke, Booth was for Whitman an inspired genius who defied convention and established a new style. Whitman declared that "he stood out 'himself alone' in many respects beyond any of his kind on record, and with effects and ways that broke through all rules and all traditions."

The aspect of Booth that most impressed Whitman was his powerful expression. "I demand that my whole emotional nature be powerfully stirred," Whitman generalized about acting. No one could satisfy this craving more than Booth, who was a key figure in the development of an intense American style of acting. Whitman explained, "The words fire, energy, *abandon*, found in him unprecedented meanings." Short, slight, and bowlegged, he hardly had a magisterial physique. But his richly expressive voice and his piercing eyes made up for his shortcomings. He was especially effective as Shakespeare's villains and madmen: Richard, Iago, Lear, Othello. To these and other tragic roles he brought an unprecedented fervor.

Two schools of acting had emerged in the early decades of the century. The so-called Teapot School, epitomized by the decorous British actor Charles Kemble, was elegant and refined. The actor strove for subtlety, not drama, and typically kept one hand on the hip while making circular motions with the other. In rebellion against this stiff approach, two other British performers, George Frederick Cooke and Edmund Kean, introduced a tempestuous style. When transferred to America, the Cooke-Kean style became increasingly exaggerated. The exigencies of dramatic performance in America, where actors had to compete with ranting revivalists, ebullient blackface shows, and the popular frontier screamer character, notably intensified the vehement style.

Booth was more adept at this style than most because he knew how to calibrate his performances. He did not attack his roles with sledge-hammer heaviness but rather passed from valleys of restraint to peaks of near frenzy. It was the peaks for which he became known. "When he was in a passion," Whitman wrote, "face, neck, hands, would be suffused, his eye would be frightful—his whole mien enough to scare audience, actors; often the actors *were* afraid of him." In his rejection of the staid Teapot style, Booth moved into the uncertain realm of idiosyncratic interpretation. Even Whitman had to concede his acting could be "inflated, stagy." This unevenness, however, did not bother Whitman. His favorite article on acting, George Joseph Bell's "Mrs. Siddons as Lady Macbeth," argued that the special delight of acting was its unpredictability and evanescence. In a time before recordings, every performance was unique, never to be duplicated. Booth's off nights could be attributed to his well-known personal problems. Everyone considered his good nights well worth waiting for.

One such night Whitman saw him in *Richard III* at the Bowery Theatre. Whitman never forgot the night. Booth, of course, had played the role countless times before. It had been his first role upon arriving in America, and he had played it often in New York (see fig. 20). There was something distinctive about the performance Whitman witnessed. More than two decades later, Whitman called it "a night that formed an era in the experience of theatre-goers, for years afterward, and indeed down to this day."

Booth took to an extreme the total identification with the role that in the twentieth century would be associated with the Stanislavsky technique. So utter was his absorption in a role that he challenged the very boundaries between life and art. He could become so carried away as Othello trying to suffocate Desdemona with a pillow that he had to be pulled away by other actors for fear he would actually kill her. As the sword-wielding Richard he sometimes inflicted real wounds. Many times he pursued the terrified Richmond of the evening clear out of the theater and into the streets, once into a nearby tavern where he had to be disarmed forcefully. Nor did he surrender his stage realism in daily life. He appeared in a Cincinnati church dressed in the rich robes of Cardinal Richelieu; those present were genuinely honored that a foreign prelate was visiting them. He walked the streets as Shylock or Richard, flinging coins to people who paraded after him.

Such behavior might be dismissed as a laughable vagary if it didn't have larger ramifications in nineteenth-century American culture. This kind of intermingling of life and art contributed, tragically, to the murder of Abraham Lincoln and, happily, to the gestation of Whitman's *Leaves of Grass*. Booth's violent acting style was carried on, and even amplified, by his son John Wilkes Booth. Like most Southerners, John Wilkes Booth viewed Lincoln as a tyrant who was destroying American life. What made Booth unique was that he was a forceful Shakespearean actor, who, like his father, came to identify with the roles he played. After he shot Lincoln with a derringer in the presidential box in Ford's Theater, he leaped twelve feet down onto the stage, cried "Sic semper tyrannis!," and made a quick exit to a horse waiting outside. The whole event was theatrical to the hilt. Among the vindictive stage characters he compared himself with was Brutus, the assassin of the tyrant Caesar, a role he had played many times.

The intersection of life and art in Lincoln's assassination would not escape Whitman, who always saw the event as a towering, tragic drama. He had been prepared to interpret the event by his immersion in the emotional acting style of John Wilkes Booth's father. When Whitman said Junius Brutus Booth shaped him in his early years, he was referring to the intense emotionalism that made Booth seem not an actor but a real person. As Whitman put it, Booth "not only seized and awed the crowded house, but all the performers, without exception."

In several senses, Whitman himself was an actor, in daily life and in his poetry. "I have always had a good deal to do with actors: met many, high and low," he said. Obviously they shared trade secrets with him.

Not only did he declaim passages from plays on the streets and at the seashore, but he took pride in subtleties of interpretation. Thomas A. Gere, an East River ferry captain, recalled that he would regale passengers with Shakespearean soliloquies, stop himself in the middle, and say "No! no! no! that's the way bad actors would do it," and then begin again. "In my judgment," Gere said, "few could excel his reading of stirring poems and brilliant Shakespearian passages." He had a special fondness for stormy scenes from *Richard III, King Lear,* and *Coriolanus.* His "spouting" of loud Shakespearean passages on the New York omnibuses reflected his participation in the zestful turbulence of American life. As he explained to his friend Traubel while leafing through a copy of *Richard III:*

> How often I spouted this—these first pages—on the Broadway coaches, in the awful din of the street. In that seething mass—that noise, chaos, bedlam—what is one voice more or less: one single voice added, thrown in, joyously mingled in the amazing chorus?

He developed a theatrical style in his daily behavior. When he grew his beard and adopted his distinctive casual dress in the fifties, people on the street, intrigued by his unusual appearance, tried to guess who he might be: Was he a sea captain? A smuggler? A clergyman? A slave trader? If Booth walked the streets as Richelieu or Shylock, he walked them as Walt Whitman, gray-bearded, oddly dressed, with slouched hat and open shirt. One of his friends, William Roscoe Thayer, called him "a poseur of truly colossal proportions, one to whom playing a part had long before become so habitual that he ceased to be conscious that he was doing it."

Nowhere did he act so much as in his poetry. The "I" of *Leaves of Grass* has proven puzzling to critics. Some have seen it as autobiographical and have taken his poetry as a confession or sublimation of private anxieties and desires. Others see it as a complete fiction, with little reference to the real Whitman, as indicated by the many differences between the poetic persona and the man. Such confusions can be partly resolved by recognizing that the "real" Whitman, as part of a participatory culture, was to a large degree an actor, and that his poetry was his grandest stage, the locus of his most creative performances. When developing his poetic persona in his notebooks, he compared himself to an actor onstage, with "all things and all other beings as an audience at a play-house perpetually and perpetually calling me out from behind the curtain." In the poem "Out from Behind This Mask" he calls life "this drama of the whole" and extends the stage metaphor by describing "This common curtain of the face contain'd in me for me, in you for you" and "The passionate teeming plays this curtain hid!" Few personae in literature are as flexible and adaptable as Whitman's "I." In "Song of Myself" alone he assumes scores of identities: he becomes by turns a hounded slave, a bridegroom, a mutineer, a clock, and so on. He is proud of his role-playing ability: "I do not ask the wounded person how he feels, I myself become the wounded person." "I become any presence or truth of humanity here."

This flexibility itself was reflective of Whitman's performance culture. The lack of distinction between cultural levels in the new Republic was manifested not only in the fact that Shakespeare was played alongside cruder material. Actors and actresses too showed an unusual flexibility. One of Whitman's favorite actors, the Bowery manager Tom Hamblin, was equally at home in Shakespeare and tawdry melodramas. This was true too of Edwin Forrest, who excelled in Shakespeare but also in mass-oriented spectacles. The quick-change stunt of assuming many different roles in the same play became the rage after 1835, particularly at the Franklin Theatre on Chatham Square. Ada Webb sustained five parts in one play and six in another. A play called, appropriately enough, *Fast Women of the Modern Time* featured an actress taking seven parts and another six. Frank Chanfrau played four parts in the satirical *Mr. McGreedy.* Whitman's friend Adah Isaacs Menken broke all records in *The Three Fast Women, or the Female Robinson Crusoe,* in which she assumed no fewer than nine roles. Such flexibility challenged boundaries of gender. Several actresses Whitman praised—Menken, Charlotte Cushman, Clara Fisher—were known for their ability to assume male roles like Romeo and Hamlet. Cushman, Whitman's favorite actress, had plain but expressive features; with her tall, full body, she was said to be "dashed strongly with masculineness." Once when she played Romeo, a commentator wryly observed, "Miss Cushman is a very dangerous young man."

The shape-shifting, androgynous persona of Whitman's poetry, then, was not unusual. In a time of flexible role players, Whitman proved himself as flexible as any, ready to absorb himself at will into many identities, regardless of gender. "I am the actor, the actress, the voter, the politician," he announces in "The Sleepers." In "Crossing Brooklyn Ferry" he says he has "Play'd the part that still looks back on the actor or actress, / The same old role."

His responses to stage performers were always measured in emotional terms. He recalled the acting of one fiery actress who "knock'd us about, as the scenes swept on like a cyclone!" He liked the style of James

Henry Hackett, who introduced to the stage the wild frontier screamer. Even a minor actor named Charles Thorne he called "a sudden revelation," with the "power of an avalanche."

Though the intensely emotional acting style had originated abroad, it took on a specifically American character and was one of the contributing factors behind Whitman's nationalism. A conflict developed between a "British" style, which was popularly associated with tameness and snobbishness, and an "American" style, linked with fervency and democracy. The main figures in this hyped-up cultural war were the British actor William Charles Macready and the American Edwin Forrest. The climactic battle was the famous Astor Place Riot, in which conflicting acting styles and national loyalties collided.

Anti-British sentiment had often boiled over in theaters before the Astor Place Riot. The riots surrounding the American appearances of Edmund Kean (1821), Joshua R. Anderson (1831), and George P. Farren (1834) were among the stormiest incidents involving British actors who were reported to have derogated America and who were hissed or bombarded when they tried to perform. These events, however, were just minor rehearsals for the Astor Place Riot of 1849. The ascendancy of Edwin Forrest in the 1830s fanned the flames of nationalism. A committed Jacksonian Democrat who doubled as a political orator, Forrest (see figs. 21 and 22) became the era's most popular actor with his turbulent, muscular style. He had particular appeal for the b'hoys of the Bowery. Thickset and athletic, he was variously nicknamed the Bowery B'hoy's Delight, the Mastodon of the Drama, and the Ferocious Tragedian. By the forties his vehement style had come to be called American, partly because of a contretemps with the British Macready, who became his arch-opponent. Macready was a skilled actor who prided himself on subtlety and who had little tolerance for Forrest's "robustious" style, which he thought reflected the crudeness of American life. "*He is not an artist,*" Macready wrote of Forrest during a tour of America. "Let him be an American actor—and a great American actor—but keep him on this side of the Atlantic, and no one will gainsay his comparative excellence." The American intelligentsia liked Macready's "mental" style, while common folk preferred Forrest's wildness. This was both a cultural and a class war, with Macready adhering to the rules and Forrest breaking them on behalf of egalitarianism and individual personality.

In the clash of styles, Whitman at first leaned strongly toward Forrest but then came to have second thoughts. "After Booth was Forrest— a masterly man," he declared. "I watched his career," he said, "with both my eyes." He was attracted by Forrest's great strong voice and what he called his "massive freshness." Macready, in contrast, had little appeal for him: "I could never enter into the enthusiasm over him—never. He never seemed to address himself to me."

Still, Whitman can only have had a mixed response to the Astor Place Riot, that orgy of rowdiness and jingoism that drove Macready from the American stage. He never gave a full account of his reaction to the event, but he considered it important enough to make this jotting on a scrap of paper:

"Mem[orandum] *for Life*"
The Macready riot occurred on the
night of May 10, 1849

—I was then publishing
"the Freeman"
Cor[ner of] Middagh & Fulton sts.
Brooklyn
had returned from
N[ew] O[rleans]

When Traubel showed him this scrap late in life Whitman said, "Such little reminders sometimes open a very big door of reminiscence." The event had intrinsic interest for him, since it involved both class-related and cultural conflict. When the Astor Place Opera House had opened in November 1847, it quickly became the place where the bon ton went to show off their elegant clothes and white kid gloves. A stigma of upper-class snobbery soon surrounded it. Small wonder that trouble would arise when the anti-American Macready was announced to appear in *Macbeth* there in May 1849 when Forrest was to play the same role in the populist Broadway Theatre. The enmity between the two had smoldered since March 1846, when Forrest hissed Macready during a *Hamlet* performance in Edinburgh, after which Macready declared publicly, "I feel I cannot *stomach* the United States as a nation." Macready became a despised figure among Forrest's working-class followers, who took the occasion of the simultaneous *Macbeth* performances to display their anger.

Macready's opening performance, on May 7, was a virtual dumb show due to hissing and yelling among rowdies in the audience, many of whom had been given free tickets distributed by the actor's opponents. In the opening act Macready was pelted with rotten eggs, potatoes, pennies, even chairs. The performance had to be stopped. To prevent a similar fracas at Macready's May 10 performance, a force of citizen militia was posted outside the theater, barring entry to rough types. When the theater doors were locked and the play began, a screaming mob of more than ten thousand surrounded the theater and hurled paving stones through the windows with yells of "Burn the damned den of aristocracy!" and "You can't go in there without kid gloves on!" The alarmed militia fired into the air in warning and, when that failed, into the crowd. Twenty-two were killed and fifty wounded in the bloody fray. The performance was suspended, and Macready was spirited away in disguise. He soon left New York in disgust, never to return to America again.

A number of New York's leading citizens—among them Herman Melville, Evart Duyckinck, and Washington Irving—signed a public document expressing their disapproval of those who had participated in the riot. Whitman, then living in Brooklyn, did not sign, but it can be assumed he would have had he been asked. His love of audience-performer interaction did not take him so far as to approve of mob violence. The Astor Place Riot was a watershed moment when explosive elements within American culture collided with restraining, conservative ones. Macready had always been favored by respectable types, including Emerson and Longfellow, who saw his subtle style as a bulwark against frenzied, uncontrolled forces within American society. Forrest, in contrast, was beloved by figures, including the sensational novelist Ned Buntline and the Bowery b'hoys, who had come to embody these violent forces.

Whitman's attitudes toward these conflicting acting styles reflected his feelings about the American working class as a whole: he admired turbulent energy but detested violent excess. In the 1840s Forrest's style had been taken to an extreme he found disagreeable. In the *Eagle* he editorialized against "a sort of American style of acting. . . . We allude to the loud mouthed ranting style—the tearing of every thing to shivers," with "the loudest exhibition of sound, and the most distorted gesture" and "all kinds of unnatural and violent jerks, swings, screwing of the nerves of the faces, rolling of the eyes, and so on."

His taste in theaters changed too. In the thirties he had preferred the Bowery Theatre to the more aristocratic Park. He would always remember the way the crude green curtain at the Bowery jumped up and down like a rabbit, in contrast to the pompous, slow-moving painted canvas at the Park. By the early forties, however, the Bowery had become notably vulgarized. Prostitutes, always a presence in the upper tier of nineteenth-century American theaters, became so numerous at the Bowery that it became known as a den of iniquity. The plays performed there had always inclined to the sensational, but after 1840 it became "permanently the house of sensation," as a theater historian puts it. Whitman recalled that shortly after 1840 "the character of the Bowery completely changed. Cheap prices and vulgar programmes came in." In 1845 he announced he was "completely nauseated" by the plays at the Bowery. Two years later in an article titled "Miserable State of the Stage" he wrote: "Of all 'low' places where vulgarity (not only on the stage, but in front of it) is in the ascendant, and bad-taste carries the day with hardly a pleasant point to mitigate the coarseness, the New York theatres (except the Park) may be put down (as an Emeralder may say,) as the top of the heap! We don't like to make these sweeping assertations in general— but the habit of such places as the Bowery, the Chatham, and the Olympic theatres is really beyond all toleration."

It is understandable that after 1849, the year of the Astor Place Riot, his interest in the theater declined, to be replaced by other cultural interests such as vocal music and the visual arts. He could accept neither the senseless violence of the popular b'hoy plays nor the increased staidness which, as Richard Butsch shows, characterized elite theater after 1850.

Still, the theater left an indelible mark on him. In particular, the emotional peaks of the early editions of *Leaves of Grass* seem to reflect the style of the actor he most admired, Junius Brutus Booth. Neither Booth nor Whitman was particularly demonstrative in private. Booth, when sober, was quiet in his daily demeanor. Whitman, though capable of temper tantrums, was known to have a calm personality and to be a better listener than talker at social functions. But when performing— Booth on stage, Whitman in his poetry—both were volcanic. Whitman's identification with emotionally charged characters led him to near-melodramatic peaks. "O Christ! My fit is mastering me!" "You laggards there on guard! look to your arms! / In at the conquer'd doors they crowd! I am possess'd!" "You villain touch! what are you doing? my breath is tight in its throat; / Unclench your floodgates, you are too much for me." Like the actor who shaped him, Whitman as poetic performer took passionate expression to new heights.

"O the Orator's Joys!"

WHEREAS WHITMAN'S MAIN THEATERGOING PERIODS were brief, his attraction to popular orators was a lifelong phenomenon. In old age he declared: "It has always been one of my chosen delights, from earliest boyhood up, to follow the flights particularly of American oratory." As was true with the theater, his tastes in oratory were eclectic. He once wrote that he was "born, as it were, with propensities, from my earliest years, to attend popular American speech-gatherings, conventions, nominations, camp-meetings, and the like." It was natural that one so attracted to acting would also be fond of oratory, since the two were intertwined in his day. Edwin Forrest, whose stentorian stage style was influenced by the fiery speeches of Andrew Jackson and Henry Clay, gave rousing Democratic addresses in the thirties. The subtle, studied speaking style of the South's chief defender, John C. Calhoun, was compared by contemporaries with the restrained technique of William Charles Macready.

The period from the American Revolution through the Civil War has been called the Golden Age of Oratory, to give way later to showmanship and spectacle. American orators from Patrick Henry to Abraham Lincoln strode the lecture platform with an air of greatness later lost. Lecture styles varied, from Daniel Webster's pompous grandiloquence to John Calhoun's rapierlike logic to the furious harangues of Mike Walsh and his fellow "slang-whangers." What linked the speakers was the age's overall veneration of oratory. Thomas Low Nichols was justified in generalizing that during the two decades just before the Civil War lectures became "a national and pervading institution. Never, probably, had the lecturing system such development; nowhere has the platform such a powerful influence." Although popular entertainments were on the rise, the inundation of the average American's consciousness with profit-driven spectacles and images would not come until after the Civil War. Before the war, Americans attended to oratory with a seriousness and eagerness that would be frittered away with the advent of "show business," a term introduced in 1850 but not widely used until the late sixties.

The driving forces behind oratory in the antebellum years were populist politics and the lyceum movement. Political and reform oratory enjoyed its heyday in the three decades before 1865. Political speakers gained a wide audience at a time when, to use one historian's words, "politics seemed to enter into everything." With the rise of Jacksonian democracy, politics was populist in ways not seen before or since. Participation in the political process was unprecedented. Voter turnout in the presidential election of 1840 was a remarkable 83.4 percent, and the elections from 1848 to 1872 averaged a very high 75.1 percent—in contrast to the 1932–92 period, when it averaged only 56.3 percent. Political meetings were noisy and turbulent, with banners, flags, cheering, singing, and reading of poetry and religious passages.

The American lyceum, the brainchild of the Connecticut farmer's son Josiah Holbrook, began in 1826 and gathered popularity during the following decades, cresting in the early fifties, just as Whitman was writing his major poetry. Answering the hunger for varied knowledge and information on the part of a highly literate American public, the lyceum movement coordinated the appearances of lecturers in the arts, the sciences, religion, philosophy, and literature. In a time when the average American town had few theaters or concert halls, traveling lecturers appearing in local lyceums had immense appeal. An article in Whitman's *Brooklyn Daily Times* identified the years 1853–55 as the time when "The lecture system reached its culminating point. . . . Then it was a perfect *furor*. Lectures almost usurped the place of theatres and other amusements of the kind."

Given the high visibility of orators on the American scene, it is understandable that Whitman, who loved to test out popular fads, would try his hand at oratory. In fact, his instinct to lecture predated his instinct to write. "When I was much younger," he would tell Traubel, "—way back: in the Brooklyn days—and even behind Brooklyn—I was to be an orator—to go about the country spouting my pieces, proclaiming my faith. . . . I thought I had something to say—I was afraid I would get no chance to say it through books: so I was to lecture and get myself delivered that way." According to his brother George, at the peak of the lyceum craze, in the early fifties, "he had an idea he could lecture. He wrote what his mother called 'barrels' of lectures." Although apparently just one lecture (his March 31, 1851, address to the Brooklyn Art Union) has survived, both his notebooks and his poetry of the 1850s are filled with references to oratory. His conception of the national poet's role was related to his devotion to oratory. In his notebook he jotted this free-form reflection: "American Lectures / New sermons / America-Readings— Voices Walt Whitman's Voices." The great advantage of lecturing, he saw, was direct contact with the people. In a letter of 1857 he announced his plan to become "a public Speaker, teacher, or lecturer," trying "always to hold the ear of the people." He went so far as to write in a notebook that lecturing was "henceforth my employment, my means of earning my living," and he sketched out a circular titled *Walt Whitman's Lectures,* announcing his availability as a speaker for the modest fee of a dime per person.

Time would show that he was ill equipped to be a great orator, with a voice that had range and expression but that did not project well to large crowds. He admired America's successful orators, whose techniques are felt in his poetry. He was influenced by both the serious and the spontaneous forms of antebellum oratory. There was a grandeur about serious orators like Daniel Webster and Edward Everett. What some have called the oratorical style of Whitman's poetry refers particularly to his "grand," rolling lines with their rhythmic repetitions and vocal inflections. Among antebellum orators, the chief exponent of this style was the Whig statesman Daniel Webster. The strong-shouldered, craggy-faced Massachusetts senator could be dull or fiery on the lecture platform, given his mood and the amount of alcohol he had drunk. At his best he was, in Emerson's words, "the great cannon loaded to the lips." His awe-inspiring presence seemed to hover over the political landscape. Although Whitman, as an ardent Democrat, did not accept Webster's Whig views, he strongly felt his magnetism as a speaker. He said he saw him "often—heard him deliver some of the greatest of his political speeches." He was impressed less by anything he said than by what he called his "grandeur of manner, size, importance, power." In several of Webster's speeches we find the kind of rhythmic, repetitive speech patterns that would appear in Whitman's oratorical poetry. If sentences from a typical Webster speech (his famous celebration of the Bunker Hill monument on June 17, 1843) are arranged as free verse, they have a Whitmanesque feel:

> Woe betide the man who brings to this day's worship feeling less
>   than wholly American!
> Woe betide the man who can stand here with the fires of local
>   resentments burning, or the purpose of local jealousies and the
>   strifes of local interests festering and rankling in his heart!
> Union, established in justice, in patriotism, and the most plain and
>   obvious common interest,—
> [U]nion, founded on the same love of liberty, cemented by blood shed
>   in the same common cause,—
> [U]nion has been the source of all our glory and greatness thus far,
>   and is the ground of all our highest hopes,
> This column stands on Union.

The highest example of this kind of rhythmic oratory would be Lincoln's Gettysburg Address, whose stylistic roots, as Garry Wills shows, can be traced back through the carefully honed speeches of Edward Everett to classical orations by Pericles and Demosthenes. But both Lincoln and Whitman were indebted to less elite orators as well. If the Gettysburg Address shows Lincoln's kinship with Everett and the Greeks, another of his memorable oratorical performances—his debates with the Illinois senator Stephen A. Douglas—reveal his roots in a more free-wheeling, raucous brand of personal oratory. In the seven debates, Lincoln and Douglas gave alternating speeches punctuated by humor and stories while surrounded by enthusiastic crowds that hung on their every word and interjected constantly with cries of "That is so!" or "Hit him again!"

This interactive, personal lecture style was a distinctive feature of much antebellum oratory, and it held special appeal for Whitman. One reason his style sounds oratorical is its air of spontaneity, of being spoken aloud. His method of composition was spontaneous. Suddenly seized with an impression or image, he would scribble it quickly on any handy scrap of paper, trying, as he explained, "to write in the gush, the throb, the flood, of the moment—to put things down without deliberation." He kept separate scraps in an envelope, later bringing them together as poems after careful revision. He was never far from what he called vocalism. Of his poems he told Traubel, "I like to read them in a palpable voice: I try my poems that way—always have: read them aloud to myself." Writing for him was closely allied to speaking.

The seeming spontaneity of his poetic vocalisms placed him in the company of several prominent speakers who cultivated an extemporaneous form of oratory. His favorite Brooklyn minister, Henry Ward Beecher, would jot notes an hour or so before a sermon but dispense with them on the pulpit platform, preferring to speak from the heart. The temperance lecturer who most enthralled him, John Gough, also spoke without notes, as did the era's leading revivalist, Charles Grandison Finney, and several women reformers Whitman heard, especially Lucretia Mott, Ernestine L. Rose, and Abby Kelley. Mott merits special mention. Grounded, like Whitman, in Quakerism, this genial feminist orator delivered stirring appeals for women's rights that sprang spontaneously from within. She disdained notes and said the inner light would guide her "to speak as the spirit giveth utterance." Whitman, who often heard her, called her "a great grand woman" with a "majestic sweet sanity."

Often impromptu, the personal style was also lively and participatory. Many lecturers of the day tried hard to bridge the gap between themselves and the audience, projecting themselves amid their listeners and parrying with them. The Whig senator Henry Clay made a point of standing as near as possible to his auditors. The lawyers William T. Barry and Rufus Choate advanced and retreated while they were speaking. "And I have seen poor imitators of such men," said one observer, "use not only the forward advance, but a side vibration as well, like a chained coon or bear; and even come down from the platform, like a Methodist preacher at a camp-meeting revival, among the auditors." To be sure, none of the antebellum speakers reached the theatrical extremes of later orators like Billy Sunday, the athletic evangelist who would strip off his shirt in front of his congregation and slide into an imaginary base in order to "score" for God. But these kinds of histrionics were prepared for in the antebellum years. John Gough, who gave hundreds of lectures between 1842 and the Civil War, gesticulated, leaped and pounced, told stories and jokes, and pounded the rostrum until he was black and blue.

Whitman singled out for praise lecturers who specialized in the participatory style. He heard all the great orators—Everett, Webster, Phillips, Garrison—"yet," he wrote, "I recall the minor but life-eloquence of men like John P. Hale, Cassius Clay, and one or two of the old abolition 'fanatics' ahead of all those stereotyped fames." Recalling "the huge annual conventions of the windy and cyclonic 'reformatory societies'" at the Broadway Tabernacle, he described the speakers as "tough, tough" and added: "I went frequently to these meetings, May after May— learn'd much from them—was sure to be on hand when J. P. Hale or Cash Clay made speeches." Hale, the antislavery Democrat from New Hampshire, was tall and stout, with sparkling blue eyes and a roguish sense of humor. He was a dazzling speaker who loved, as a friend noted, "to *spout* before an awe-struck assembly." As seen in Chapter 5, Whitman thought so highly of Hale that in 1852 he wrote him a fervent letter encouraging him to accept the Free Democrat nomination for the presidency. Although Hale came in a distant third in the election, he thereafter became a favorite on the lyceum circuit. According to his biographer, "He was a stump speaker *par excellence,* a master orator with a common touch. He spoke in a language that even the humblest New Hampshire farmer could understand, but with force and polish few could match and in a voice whose resonance and power was truly extraordinary."

The other political speaker Whitman mentioned most often, Cassius Marcellus Clay, was an eccentric, pugnacious orator who had turned against slavery after witnessing its horrors in childhood on his father's Kentucky plantation. A Whig turned Republican, who in 1860 would be a leading candidate for the vice presidency under Lincoln, Clay addressed countless thousands in the forties and fifties on the superiority of free society to slave society. Always armed with a bowie knife and pistols, he was a rough-and-tumble political fighter known to carve off opponents' ears and gouge out eyes in gory combat. A skilled stump speaker, he matched sallies with his hearers and caused horrified shudders with his accounts of narrow escapes from would-be assassins. He said he liked to be "as near my audience as possible—preferring to have my rostrum not higher than the heads of my auditors." His speeches were quintessential examples of the antebellum participatory style. His rousing antislavery address in January 1846 at the Broadway Tabernacle attracted one of the largest audiences in Manhattan history. It was interrupted throughout by a chorus of hisses from proslavery listeners and equally loud cheers from antislavery ones. His ongoing dialogue with his

church, Manhattanites joked, take the ferry to Brooklyn and follow the
crowd. When the church burned down after two years, Beecher directed
its reconstruction, stipulating that his new pulpit extend well forward
into the congregation (see fig. 27). "I want the audience to surround me,"
he told the architect, "so that I shall be in the centre of the crowd, and
have the people surge all about me." Not only did he perfect the tech-
niques of personal oratory, but he made them the vehicle of a liberal
theology based on divine love and human warmth. He spoke out on all
kinds of social issues, particularly slavery, and urged his listeners to seek
divine worth in their own lives. Like Whitman's poetry, his sermons were
full of "I" and "you." "Do you suppose I study old, musty books when I
want to preach?" he asked his hearers. "*I study you!* When I want to
deliver a discourse on theology, *I study you!*" Extemporaneous and dra-
matic, his sermons elicited every kind of emotion.

Whitman, who ran a regular column in the *Eagle* on the pulpit style
of local preachers, was enraptured by Beecher when he heard him in
1849. "He hit me so hard," said Whitman, "fascinated me to such a de-
gree that I was afterwards willing to go far out of my way to hear him
talk." Like Whitman, Beecher was an indolent, genial man whose swag-
gering public persona masked private insecurities. In Beecher, Whitman
found a stylistic adventurer who combined machismo and tenderness,
qualities also commingled in Whitman's poetry. After hearing Beecher
at an antislavery rally in 1850, Whitman wrote that it was "refreshing
that his bold masculine discourses were *without* that prettiness and cor-
rectness of style that, say what we will, is very often accompanied by
emptiness and something very akin to effeminacy." Whether or not the
two imitated each other on the personal level, they shared an interest
in the new oratorical style based on audience-performer interaction. If
Beecher told his hearers he was studying "you," Whitman expressed a
similar eagerness to develop what he called an "animated *ego-style*" of
oratory with "direct addressing *to you.*" If Beecher wanted his hearers to
surge all around him, Whitman wrote poetry of unexampled intimacy,
telling his readers:

Come closer to me,
Push close my lovers and take the best I possess, [. . .]

I was chilled with the cold type and cylinder and wet paper between
    us.

I pass so poorly with paper and types. . . . I must pass with the contact
    of bodies and souls.

Although attracted to the personal, emotional style of antebellum orators, Whitman was repelled when this style was carried to an extreme. He was notably ambivalent, for example, about the fiery Whig senator from Kentucky, Henry Clay. Thin, tall, and stooped, with a large head and a tremendous mouth, Clay was an imposing presence on the lecture platform. His speeches could lack logic, but never fire. He took his audiences by storm, pounding his fists, stamping his feet, giving full expansion to his sonorous voice. Whitman called Clay "a splendid politician" but thought he had "little caution." "His forte," Whitman wrote, "is a bold, dashing kind of warfare. He resembles some fire brained political Murat, riding gallantly into the midst of the enemy, pressing on their very bayonet points, with cuts and thrusts to the right and left, but fearing nothing and heeding no warning, whether it come from friend or foe."

When Whitman sketched out in a notebook his own lecturing plans, he told himself to maintain verve without wildness, passion without excess. He wanted, he wrote, to develop a lecture style that was "far more direct, close, animated and fuller of live tissue and muscle than any hitherto." But he warned himself: "Be bold! be bold! be bold! Be not too bold! With all this life and on the proper emergency, vehemence, care is needed not to run into any melodramatic, Methodist Preacher, half-inebriated, political spouter, splurging modes of oratory." The Methodist preacher criticized here was probably the rambunctious itinerant John Newland Maffitt, known for his pulpit wildness. The political spouter was most likely Henry Clay or perhaps Mike Walsh and other working-class "slang-whangers" like Ned Strahan or Alex Wells, whose speeches often created sheer bedlam. He recoiled from such undisciplined orators. As he put it, "Not hurried gabble, as the usual American speeches, lectures, &c. are, but with much breath, such precision, such indescribable meaning, slow and with interior emphasis." What was needed, then, was breadth, strength, interiority.

He presented in his poetry the kind of oratorical style he had in mind. Never a successful orator himself, he nonetheless gained vicarious satisfaction in experiencing the effect that the most powerful American speakers had on their hearers:

O the orator's joys!
To inflate the chest, to roll the thunder of the voice out from the ribs
    and throat,
To make people rage, weep, hate, desire, with yourself,
To lead America—to quell America with a great tongue.

This passage makes explicit Whitman's impulse to make the participatory style an instrument of power and control. He was surrounded by orators who gained high visibility (and sometimes great power) through their ability to sway emotions. A large part of him wanted to be like them. He wanted to "make" people rage and desire with him, to "lead" his country, to "quell" it with a "great tongue." This near-totalitarian impulse, paradoxically coupled with intense egalitarianism, runs through his early poetry and reflects the mixed stance of his age's leading orators. It was, after all, the likes of Andrew Jackson and Henry Ward Beecher who gained great social influence through the power of their tongues. It would be Abraham Lincoln who sprang to prominence after his debates with Douglas and who would almost literally redirect American political philosophy in that most powerful of speeches, the Gettysburg Address.

Whitman would never surrender his goal of becoming a popular speaker. This goal was accomplished with only partial success late in life, with his annual lectures on Lincoln's death. But his highest oratorical legacy was his poetry. C. Caroll Hollis has shown that the poems of the first three editions of *Leaves of Grass* are characterized by oratorical devices such as exclamations, rhetorical questions, negations, parallelism, and addresses to a "you." Christopher Burnham, likewise, calls the controlling technique of the first three editions of *Leaves of Grass* "the oratorical style." This style made some fastidious commentators uncomfortable. Rossetti, for example, found in his verse outbursts "fitted for a Yankee stump orator, but forbidden to a poet." For Whitman, however, oratorical technique was a culturally accepted mode of making contact with the American public. He was writing oratorical poetry at a time when oratory was at a peak of popularity and influence. In 1855 the *Boston Transcript* noted that the lecture system "was never so universally adopted as at present." Whitman changed the participatory lecture style into a new participatory poetics. If the performers and speakers he admired challenged boundaries between themselves and their hearers, he tried to demolish such boundaries altogether. He coaxed, badgered, seduced the reader, reaching, as it were, right through the page.

His theory of poetry was by definition participatory and agonistic. "The reader will always have his or her part to do," he wrote, "just as much as I have mine." Reading he called a gymnast's struggle in which the reader grapples with the author. Absorbed into poetry, the antebellum personal style erases the boundary between performer and listener, between writer and reader:

Camerado, this is no book,
Who touches this touches a man.

"I Hear America Singing"

SURVEYING ALL THE ENTERTAINMENT EXPERIENCES of his young manhood, Whitman wrote, "Perhaps my dearest amusement reminiscences are those musical ones." Music was such an all-pervasive force for him that he saw himself less as a poet than as a singer or bard. "My younger life," he recalled in old age, "was so saturated with the emotions, raptures, up-lifts of such musical experiences that it would be surprising indeed if all my future work had not been colored by them."

The effect of music on him is gauged partly by the remarkable number of musical terms and devices in his poems. As Robert Faner points out, among the titles of his poems seventy-two different musical terms appear. In the poems themselves twenty-five musical instruments are mentioned, including the violin, the piano, the banjo, the oboe, and the drums. One poem, "Proud Music of the Storm," sings praise to virtually all kinds of music, popular and classical, even mentioning by name specific operas and symphonies:

> I hear those odes, symphonies, operas,
> I hear in the *William Tell* the music of an arous'd and angry people,
> I hear Meyerbeer's *Huguenots,* the *Prophet,* or *Robert,*
> Gounod's *Faust,* or Mozart's *Don Juan.*

The dominant musical-image group in his poetry derives from vocal music. As was true with his response to theater and oratory, he was stirred especially by what he called "the great, overwhelming, touching human voice—its throbbing, flowing, pulsing qualities." Of the 206 musical words in his poems, 123 relate specifically to vocal music, and some are used many times. "Song" appears 154 times, "sing" 117, and "singing" and "singers" more than 30 times each.

Such numbers point up music's powerful impact on Whitman, but they don't capture the social and cultural meanings music had for him. He regarded music as a prime agent for unity and uplift in a nation whose tendencies to fragmentation and political corruption he saw clearly. Even more than oratory, music offered a meeting place of aesthetics and egalitarianism. If, in Whitman's eyes, urban roughs gravitated to anarchic violence and politicians to shysterism, all could be potentially redeemed by their common love for music. For all the downward tendencies he perceived among contemporary Americans, he took confidence in the shared love of music. In the 1855 preface to *Leaves of Grass* he mentioned specifically "their delight in music, the sure symptoms of manly tenderness and native elegance of soul." Music allowed for sensuous release and emotional expression without the excesses he saw elsewhere in popular culture. As he explained in an 1855 magazine article: "A taste for music, when widely distributed among a people, is one of the surest indications of their moral purity, amiability, and refinement. It promotes sociality, represses the grosser manifestations of the passions, and substitutes in their place all that is beautiful and artistic." By becoming himself a "bard" singing poetic "songs" he hoped to tap the potential for aesthetic appreciation he saw in Americans' positive responses to their shared musical culture.

The emergence of his poetic sensibility corresponded closely with dramatic developments on the Manhattan music scene. During the 1840s there was an explosion of music on both the elite and popular levels. At first he was disturbed by what he saw as a gap between classical or operatic music, associated with upper-class sophistication, and more popular music forms that appealed to the working class. But he witnessed the increasing intermingling of these two levels, with the rise of the singing families and minstrel groups in the midforties, followed by Jenny Lind's sensational tour and Stephen Foster's popular songs in the early fifties, and then the triumphant tours of several great opera singers, including his all-time favorite, the Italian contralto Marietta Alboni. He came to see that opera, once the province of snobs, could be popular: he saw the way Alboni had strong appeal for all classes, and in his 1855 article "The Opera" he presented the dazzling spectacle of an operatic performance so as to make it intriguing to the mass audience.

Whitman's poetic yoking of images from various cultural levels— his alternation between aria motifs and minstrel-show antics, for instance, or his combination of high diction and slang—was reflective of the varied performance culture that surrounded him. Vocal music, both the opera and the music of the singing families he loved, became an important component of his poetic scheme of elevating the masses while catering to their interests. Classical instrumental music, particularly that of the period's most authentically American composer, Anthony Philip Heinrich, was a rich meeting place of high and low genres, as Heinrich and others adventurously combined sophisticated strains with popular melodies. Leading bands like Dodworth's Band also embodied this mixture of levels, as they played variously at religious services, political events, dances, or military drills with simple changes of instruments. Ballroom dancing was quickened in the forties by the introduction of lively polkas and the galop, complementing the more staid waltzes and quadrilles already popular in American ballrooms; it was surely one of these frenetic new dances Whitman had in mind when he wrote in "The

Sleepers": "I am a dance—play up there! the fit is whirling me fast!"

Whitman's immersion in his contemporary musical culture followed distinct phases. An invasion of foreign virtuosos in the early forties piqued his interest in music but, at the same time, drove him to embrace the simpler, more heartfelt indigenous music of the American families and minstrel troupes. His appreciation of these popular forms, in turn, opened the way to a transformed vision of elite styles, which in the fifties actually came close to being popular.

Shortly after his arrival in Manhattan in 1841, significant changes occurred in the music scene. In 1842 the New York Philharmonic Society, to become the longest lived American orchestra with a history of continuous performances, was established. Also that year Anthony Philip Heinrich was featured for the first time in a "Grand Musical Festival" at the Broadway Tabernacle. Whether Whitman attended the festival is unknown, but he did mention Heinrich in a laudatory note on American music in the *Eagle*. Now regarded as America's leading classical composer before the Civil War, Heinrich was born in Bohemia in 1781 and relocated in 1813 to the Kentucky backwoods, devoting his remaining forty-eight years to writing enormous quantities of music for voice, piano, and orchestra. He spent the years 1837–57 composing and performing in New York.

Rebelling against the symmetries of Mozart and Haydn, he imported into his music indigenous American idioms and a rambling, episodic form linked stylistically to frontier humor and the tall tale. Sometimes called the Beethoven of America, he was a committed populist who preferred the nickname the Log-House Composer of Kentucky (just as Whitman liked to be considered "one of the roughs"). Heinrich was the leading exponent of what music historians call the music of democratic sociability—a joyous, egalitarian brand of music that mixed the classical with the vernacular. Other antebellum composers in this mode included Richard Hoffman and Charles Grobe.

Heinrich was particularly daring in his experimental combinations. In the early fifties, when Whitman was composing experimental poetry, he wrote an intriguing long composition, *Barbecue Divertimento*, containing a premodern section called "The Banjo," a free-form extravaganza that juxtaposes staid European-based passages with snatches from "Turkey in the Straw" and "Yankee Doodle." That Whitman envisaged strikingly similar mixtures of "high" European music and vernacular American music is shown in this note: "*American opera.*—put three banjos, (or more?) in the orchestra—and let them accompany (at times exclusively,) the songs of the baritone or tenor—." Heinrich, shocking to many of his contemporaries, lived in near poverty and has been resurrected in modern times as a precursor of musical innovators like Charles Ives, who similarly tapped popular culture.

Because of a dearth of documentation, little more than an analogical relation can be drawn between Whitman and Heinrich, both forward-looking experimenters who used a free-flowing style and made unusual couplings of elite and popular images. What can be affirmed is that in music Whitman looked for exactly the combination of populism and artistry Heinrich represented.

In the early going, he wasn't sure such a combination was possible. He was ambivalent about the European classical musicians who flooded Manhattan in 1843, a watershed moment in American musical history. The New York theaters were at last recovering from the economic doldrums of 1837–43, and the rapid development of the transatlantic steamship made travel to America far easier than before. Manhattan was in a frenzy over the European superstars. There arrived Ole Bull, the tall, elegant violinist known as the Norwegian Paganini; the great Belgian violinist Henri Vieuxtemps; the Irish violin and piano master William Vincent Wallace; and many others. Whitman heard Bull, and two years later he heard the Austrian pianist Leopold de Meyer, called the Lion Pianist because of his aggressive style. He was also aware of vocalists like the Italian contralto Rosina Pico and the Scottish tenor John Templeton.

Aware, but not altogether impressed. At this point he showed little enthusiasm for classical music and in fact reacted strongly against the foreign performers, whom he associated with artificiality and pomposity. In the early forties he was writing for the strongly nationalistic *Democratic Review*, and the nativist tone of some of his journalism suggests his partial sympathy with the pro-Americanism that then swept through New York and resulted in the election of the nativist James Harper in the mayoral election of 1844. Whitman's politics seemed to have prevented him from fully embracing the foreign musical masters. What he sought was music that sprang from native soil and embodied the idioms and concerns of average Americans.

He discovered such music in the family singers and minstrel troupes that attained immense popularity in the midforties, just as the initial enthusiasm for the imported superstars was dwindling.

Singing families were not a uniquely American phenomenon. An Austrian family group from the Tyrol, the Rainers, with their Alpine costumes and Alpine songs, had initiated the craze for family singing in their 1839 American tour. Over the next five years there arose a breed of American family groups who embodied American ideas and styles. In a series of newspaper articles written from 1845 to 1847, Whitman rejoiced over what he saw as the distinctly American qualities of the new family singers. The Cheneys, a quartet of three brothers and a sister from New Hampshire, thrilled him when he first heard them in November 1845 at Niblo's Theatre. In an article for the *Brooklyn Star* entitled "American Music, New and True!" he raved: "For the first time we, on Monday night, heard something in the way of American music, which overpowered us with delightful amazement." Using the Cheneys as a weapon against the foreign musicians, he declared that they "excel all the much vaunted foreign artists, not excepting Templeton, whom we saw there." He deemed this article so important that he revised and expanded it four times in the next year to include comments on other singing families, particularly the Hutchinsons. It was published under different titles in three different newspapers. In all its versions, the message was the same: what he termed the "art music" of the foreign musicians was overly elaborate and fundamentally aristocratic, while the "heart music" of the American families was natural, democratic.

The sudden popularity of the family singers fueled his dream that a thoroughly American musical style would overthrow the European:

> Simple, fresh, and beautiful, we hope no spirit of imitation will ever induce them to engraft any "foreign airs" upon their "native graces." We want this sort of starting point from which to mould something new and true in American music; if we are not greatly mistaken the spirit of the Hutchinson's and Cheney's singing will be followed by a spreading and imitation that will entirely supplant, as far as this country is concerned, the affected, super-sentimental, kid-gloved, quavering, flourishing, die-away-in-demnition-faintness style of music which comes to us from Italy and France.

For a time it seemed this dream would come true, for a number of family groups attained great popularity. In his final version of the article, published in the *Eagle* in April 1846, he gave his blessing to many of them: "We have now several American vocal bands that in *true* music really surpass almost any of the *artificial* performers from abroad: there are the Hutchinsons, the Cheneys, the Harmoneons, the Barton family, and the Ethiopian serenaders—all of them well trained, and full of both natural and artistic capacity."

Here and elsewhere, he mentioned first the Hutchinsons, his and America's favorite singing family (see fig. 23). As editor of the *Eagle* he regularly ran notices of their Brooklyn and New York appearances, and he singled them out for praise in his articles on popular music. The most popular family group before the Civil War, the Hutchinson singers consisted of three brothers—Judson, John, Asa—and their younger sister Abby, part of a talented family of thirteen boys and girls from Milford, New Hampshire. Having had little formal training, they were naturally gifted vocalists who accompanied themselves with stringed instruments. They gave their first public concert in Milford in 1839, and three years later they went on tour. Their first New York appearance was in May 1843. With additions and substitutions of different family members, they remained popular for nearly four decades. They became international celebrities and played to packed houses everywhere. They were invited to perform at the White House by President Tyler, and their circle of friends included Frederick Douglass, William Lloyd Garrison, Edwin Forrest, Longfellow, and, eventually, Lincoln. Their catchy songs ran the gamut of popular idioms, from the sentimental to the sensational, and promoted a variety of reforms, particularly temperance and antislavery.

Since Whitman came to see himself above all as an American "singer," it is worthwhile to look closely at the group he thought epitomized American singing. In his poetry he would strive for naturalness and what he called "a perfectly transparent, plate-glassy style, artless," characterized by "clearness, simplicity, no twistified or foggy sentences." It was exactly this kind of artlessness he saw in the Hutchinsons. "Elegant simplicity in manner," he wrote of them, "is more judicious than the dancing school bows and curtsies, and inane smiles, and kissing of the tips of a kid glove a la [Rosina] Pico." He was not alone in emphasizing their naturalness. One reviewer admired their "perfect freedom from all affectation and stage grimace." Another wrote, "We like their music, because it is so simple and unadorned." Whitman's connection between their simplicity and Americanness was also made by others. One of their first reviewers called them "genuine children of the rugged New Hampshire soil, ... strong, simple characters" who "brought into the atmosphere of the concert room a freshness and native sweetness of melody." Their distinctly American quality was emphasized by a British commentator: "After the *staccatos* and runs of Italianised vocalism ... it is pleasant to hear music divested of its extraneous ornament" and assuming the "winning garb of simple and unadorned harmony."

Whitman also valued the fact that the Hutchinsons sang about common American experience and the ordinary lives of average individuals. In the *Eagle* he noted that they "are true sons of the old granite state; they are democrats." This comment suggests, among other things, his awareness of the Hutchinsons' signature song, "The Old Granite State," a song with a significant history in light of his later singing of himself. When one of the Hutchinson brothers, Jesse, wrote the first version of the song in 1841, the other members of the group refused to sing it since it seemed shockingly personal, tracing the family's New Hampshire roots and giving all the siblings' names along with their convictions and political views. Nothing even remotely like it had ever been sung on the American platform. John Hutchinson commented, "The song seemed the essence of egotism to us, and we wondered that Jesse could have written it." To their amazement, however, the public cared very much for their private story, and it quickly became a necessary part of every one of their performances. A rousing, participatory song with repetitive words set to a Millerite hymn tune, "The Old Granite State," in both its performed and published versions, captivated thousands with its egotistical personalism and unabashed patriotism. Some of its verses went as follows:

We're a band of brothers,
And live among the hills. . . .

We have eight other brothers
And of sisters, just another,
Besides our father and mother,
In the "Old Granite State.". . .

Thirteen sons and daughters . . .
And their history we bring.

David, Noah, Andrew, Zephy,
Caleb, Joshua, Jess and Beny,
Judson, Rhoda, John, and Asa,
And Abby are our names.

We're the sons of Mary,
Of the tribe of Jesse,
And now we address ye
With our native mountain song. . . .

Now three cheers altogether,
Shout Columbia people ever,
Yankee hearts none can sever,
In the old sister states.

The premier song of Whitman's favorite group, then, made singing oneself and singing America commonplace in the public arena. Whitman may have hoped to strike a responsive chord when he wove specific autobiographical details into his poems: "Walt Whitman, an American, one of the roughs, a kosmos."

Ardent individualists, the Hutchinsons were also, like Whitman, reform-minded performers who used song as a vehicle for social change. Whitman's reform roots, of course, were far-reaching. But one aspect of his sensibility—his linkage of social activism with public "singing"—specifically had precedent in the kind of reformist music the Hutchinsons made famous. In the 1840s they espoused many of the causes that were then preoccupying him: temperance, antislavery, prison reform, women's rights. They pioneered the association between public entertainment and radical reform, thus prefiguring his combined radicalism and public singing as a poet. From the first they were close allies of all the leading abolitionists, including William Lloyd Garrison and Wendell Phillips. The ex-slave Frederick Douglass, with whom they toured on behalf of abolition, said the impact of their antislavery songs, such as "Get Off the Track" and "There's a Good Time Coming," was "almost miraculous." They were, declared Douglass, "indeed an acquisition to the anti-slavery cause and to all other good causes. . . . They sang for freedom, for temperance, for peace, for moral and social reform." In 1851 they also began singing at women's rights conventions. Firm feminists, they would later appear on behalf of Susan B. Anthony's Woman Suffrage Association. For Whitman, who poetically sang "the woman the same as the man" and who wrote that to "cheer up slaves and horrify despots" was part of his literary mission, the Hutchinsons' reformist singing was a powerful precursor.

They also developed the stylistic device of solo and group singing. Until about 1900, the solo/group variation remained a peculiarly American phenomenon. Although the origins of the device are obscure, it was the American singing families who popularized it. In the Hutchinsons' performances, male and female solos by each of the four singers were interspersed with tight choral harmonies. Stephen Foster's songs, which Whitman called America's best music, standardized the device, since they were all written with the verse set for a single voice and the chorus for two to four parts. Whitman was fascinated by the technique. He especially praised the female solos in both the Hutchinson and Cheney families, claiming they rivaled all the foreign prima donnas, and in one of his poems he directly mentioned the device: "I heard the soprano in the midst of the quartet singing."

By all reports, the varied solos and harmonies of the Hutchinsons were especially affecting. Judson, a high second tenor, often took the melody line. John, a versatile baritone, glided easily into a falsetto, while Abby sang a rich contralto and Asa a resonant bass. Individually, the voices were distinctive; together, they blended so harmoniously audiences could not distinguish the separate parts. One can only guess whether Whitman's alternate singing of himself and of the masses throughout *Leaves of Grass* reflected this popular device. The least that can be said is that he was powerfully stirred by the rich vocal mixtures the singing families introduced, a mixture best captured in his poem "That Music Always Round Me":

> [N]ow the chorus I hear and am elated,
> A tenor, strong, ascending with power and health, with glad notes of
>   daybreak I hear,
> A soprano at intervals sailing buoyantly over the tops of immense
>   waves,
> A transparent base shuddering lusciously under and through the
>   universe, [...]
> I hear not the volumes of sound merely, I am moved by the exquisite
>   meanings,
> I listen to the different voices winding in and out, striving,
>   contending with fiery vehemence to excel each other in emotion;
> I do not think the performers know themselves—but now I think I
>   begin to know them.

Another form of American music that appealed to Whitman was the minstrel song. In the antebellum North, the African-American experience was presented to the public chiefly through the performances of minstrel troupes, generally white performers in blackface who gave caricatured versions of African-American customs and dialects.

Although widely accepted in the North as an accurate portrayal of blacks, most minstrel shows had little to do with African-Americans, who were presented by the impersonators as rambunctious, lazy, sensual, and affably satirical. The shows raised few eyebrows in a culture where racism was rampant. Even the democratic Whitman confessed his weakness for what he called "nigger songs." The earliest minstrels were given by individual performers who sang oddly and danced wildly. In 1827 George Washington Dixon performed in blackface in Albany, and five years later Thomas Dartmouth Rice, whom Whitman saw, opened at New York's Bowery Theatre with the sensational "Jim Crow," a song-and-dance routine featuring nonsensical lyrics and a weird shuffling step and jump. In 1843 appeared the first minstrel troupe, the Virginia Minstrels (none of them from Virginia or even the South), which consisted of four musicians featuring "Negro" songs, dances, and comic sketches. Hundreds of imitators followed, and for decades America was inundated by touring groups with names like the Sable Minstrels and the Virginia Harmonists. The first troupe of actual African-Americans, the Georgia Minstrels, would not appear until 1865, and even they stuck to the format and racial stereotypes that had been popularized by the whites.

Whitman took avid interest in the minstrel troupes that proliferated in the midforties. In an 1846 article, "True American Singing," he confessed he liked a minstrel group called the Harmoneons almost as much as the Cheneys: "Indeed, their negro singing altogether proves how shiningly golden talent can be spread over a subject generally considered 'low.' 'Nigger' singing with them is a subject from obscure life in the hands of a divine painter: rags, patches, and coarseness are imbued with the great genius of the artist, and there exists something really great about them." When the well-known Christy's Minstrels played locally in April 1847, he noted in the *Eagle* that "the famous band of 'nigger singers'" was appearing two nights at Brooklyn's Gothic Hall. Whitman later generalized about the period: "Then we had lots of 'negro minstrels,' with capital character songs and voices. I often saw Rice the original 'Jim Crow' at the Park Theatre filling up the gap in some short bill— and the wild chants were admirable—probably ahead of anything since."

Regarded by some music historians as one of the first distinctively American genres, minstrels were rambling, improvisational compositions that introduced a new subject or character in each verse, sometimes each line. Stylistically, they were the musical counterpart to what Mark Twain identified as the most truly indigenous form of American writing—the tall tale—and to the subversive style of frontier humor, a defiantly quirky style characterized by improbable images strung together loosely by association. Whether or not the free-flowing, associational style influenced Whitman, it is significant that he took pleasure in minstrel music and considered it distinctly American.

Particularly intriguing is the possible relationship between Whitman and the leading minstrel songwriter, Stephen Foster. Whitman left no extensive record of his response to this popular songwriter, but he did make a tantalizing comment to Traubel that songs like Foster's "Old Folks at Home" were "our best work so far" in native music. The first American to earn a living from songwriting, Foster first gained wide popular success in 1847 with "Oh! Susanna," followed in the next five years with "My Old Kentucky Home," "Beautiful Dreamer," "Old Dog Tray," and many others.

Foster broke with the almost uniformly racist tone of previous minstrel fare, portraying African-Americans as capable of sorrow, fear, hope, pain, nostalgia. Frederick Douglass saw Foster's songs as real contributions to the antislavery cause because they humanized African-Americans. "They are heart songs," Douglass wrote in 1855, "and the finest feelings of human nature are expressed in them. 'Lucy Neal,' 'Old Kentucky Home,' and 'Uncle Ned,' can make the heart sad as well as merry, and can call forth a tear as well as a smile. They awaken sympathies for the slave, in which anti-slavery principles take root, grow and flourish." This gesture toward the humanization of blacks is also found in Stowe's *Uncle Tom's Cabin* and in Whitman's verse, when he wrote in "I Sing the Body Electric" of the "passions, desires, reachings, aspirations" of the auctioned slave.

With the rise of Foster, American music became popular and participatory in an unprecedented way. In the days before such passive entertainments as radio and television, musical culture was shared in ways that are sometimes forgotten. People would hear melodies and sing them constantly aloud to themselves, creating, as it were, their own musical programs. Whitman himself did this. Often when alone, he sang popular ballads or martial songs in a low undertone, and while sauntering he hummed snatches of popular songs or operas. An East River ferryboat worker in 1852 said that when passengers were few, Whitman liked to regale them with "pleasant scraps and airs" in his "round, manly voice." In this sense he was little different than most of his contemporaries. Songs from *The Bohemian Girl*, a popular operetta performed by the Seguins, a group he loved, typically became, as one journalist wrote, "established favorites . . . whistled by every boy and ground by every hand organ." The ballad "The Hazel Dell" (1852) was so popular that "the boys whistled it and the hand organs played it from Maine to Georgia."

It was Foster's music, however, that sprang most naturally from Americans' lips in the early 1850s. The song Whitman mentioned to Traubel, "Old Folks at Home" (with the famous lyrics, "Way down upon the Swanee River"), became the national favorite of 1852, sung by virtually everyone. As the *Albany State Register* reported:

> Pianos and guitars groan it night and day; sentimental young ladies sing it; sentimental young gentlemen warble it in midnight serenades; volatile young "bucks" hum it in the midst of their business and their pleasures; boatmen roar it out stentorially at all times; all the bands play it; amateur flute players agonize over it at every spare moment; the street organs grind it out at every hour; the "singing stars" carol it on the theatrical boards, and at concerts; the chamber maid sweeps and dusts to its measured cadence; the butcher's boy treats you to a strain or two of it as he hands in the steaks for dinner; the milk-man mixes it up strangely with the harsh ding-dong accom-

paniment of his timeless bell; there is not a "live darkey," young or old, but can whistle, sing, dance, and play it.

Says the music historian Charles Hamm of Foster's impact: "Never before, and rarely since, did any music come so close to being a shared experience for so many Americans."

There was ample justification, then, for Whitman's confidence that music was commonly loved and even performed by many Americans. The lines he wrote to express music's near-universal presence in American daily life were a kind of poetic gloss on the newspaper reports of the day: "I hear America singing, the varied carols I hear, / Those of mechanics, each one singing his as it should be blithe and strong"—and so forth, as he goes on to describe the singing of the mason, the boatman, the shoemaker, the woodcutter, the wife, all "singing with open mouths their strong melodious songs."

Americans' shared love for popular music by the singing families and the minstrels was predictable, given the simple, egalitarian nature of this music. Far less likely was mass appreciation of the opera, which has historically appealed almost exclusively to the sophisticated. To some degree, this was true in antebellum America. Opera never gained truly widespread popularity. Before 1847, theater managers tried to maximize its appeal by mainly presenting English compositions or translated Italian ones. The first "Englished" Italian opera, *The Libertine,* was performed at the Park Theatre in 1817. At the peak of his enthusiasm for the family singers, Whitman had little nice to say even about English operas, which in 1845 he called "a mass of unintelligible stuff."

Several forces worked to lessen the public's hostility to the opera. The popularity of the singing families opened the door to an appreciation for opera. Unlike today, when most popular music is rooted in soul, jazz, or country forms, the music of the family singers was closely linked to the opera. Most of the leading antebellum songwriters were heavily steeped in operatic and classical music. The Rochester composer Henry Russell, who had the strongest impact on American popular song before Stephen Foster, wrote songs dealing with homespun American themes but retaining the melodic ariosolike lines, varied recitatives, and arpeggiated accompaniments associated with the Italian opera. Many of his songs, including "The Maniac," "The Gambler's Wife," and "Woodman, Spare That Tree," became staples of the family singers Whitman loved. Similarly, many of Stephen Foster's ballads, with their diatonic but expressive lines, were rooted in Italian music. A recent recording of a group reenacting the Hutchinsons has a distinctly operatic sound, albeit simplified. The most massively popular antebellum music, then, was never distant from the operatic style.

By the same token, in an increasingly commercialized performance culture, most "elite" musicians gave adventurously varied programs in the hope of catching the masses. Nearly all the virtuosos Whitman heard, such as Ole Bull and Leopold de Meyer, inevitably included on their programs popular songs like "Hail Columbia" and "Yankee Doodle" along with classical pieces. Some repertory companies, like the New York Philharmonic, did remain consistently elitist by performing only proper, "scientific" European standards; but, customarily, even the greatest musicians accommodated the demands of the Barnumesque performance environment.

Nothing revealed the mixture of elite and popular cultural levels as vividly as the American tour of the Swedish singer Jenny Lind in the early 1850s. The "Swedish Nightingale" was a dexterous, classically trained vocalist with an astonishing range and a thrilling natural tremolo. To reach the broad American audience, she gave a remarkably varied program that juxtaposed high arias with a grab bag of popular ballads, comic songs, folk tunes, and patriotic numbers. Her whole tour was a combination of craftsmanship and hype unequaled in American musical history, orchestrated by none other than P. T. Barnum. The American public was whipped to a frenzy of anticipation when Barnum filled the newspapers with glowing puffs about her and publicized his guarantee to pay her $1,000 for each of her 150 scheduled American appearances. When her boat arrived at New York's Canal Street dock on September 1, 1850, more than thirty thousand screaming people greeted her. In her opening performance at the Castle Garden she was almost drowned out by the constant shouting and clapping. She went on to give a two-year, ninety-three-concert tour that grossed more than $700,000, far beyond what Barnum himself had envisaged.

The darling of the public, Jenny Lind did not fare as well with reviewers, among them Whitman. Her dazzling vocal pyrotechnics bothered a reviewer for the *Albion*, who said her mission seemed to be "to dazzle and astonish, but not to delight or soothe." Whitman, who caught her last New York concert, felt much the same way. "The Swedish Swan," he wrote, "with all her blandishments, never touched my heart in the least. I wondered at so much vocal dexterity; and indeed they were all very pretty, those leaps and double somersets. But even in the grandest religious airs, genuine masterpieces as they are, of the German composers, executed by this strangely overpraised woman in perfect scientific style, . . . it was a failure."

What the Jenny Lind phenomenon showed was that serious vocal music could be popular. What Whitman wanted, though, was music that was at once sophisticated and soulful, that had both "art" and "heart."

He found such music in the great opera singers who came to America in the early fifties. The opera rage began in April 1847 when the famous Italian company from Havana, managed by "Senor" Francisco Marty y Torens, opened at the Park. That year also saw the opening of the Astor Place Opera House, with its 1,500 seats America's largest theater until the opening of the even larger New York Academy of Music in 1854. New York was graced by a succession of opera stars who came in the wake of the Havana company. Whitman enjoyed the musical quickening. Once averse to the opera, in 1847 he declared in the *Eagle* that "the *Italian opera* deserves a good degree of encouragement from us." He heard at least sixteen of the major singers who made their New York debuts in the next eight years, including the Italian baritone Cesare Badiali, the tenor Allesandro Bettini, the sopranos Giula Grisi and Balbina Steffanone, the contralto Marietta Alboni, and the English soprano Anna De La Grange.

Among the male singers, the ones he most admired were Badiali and Bettini. The large, broad-chested Badiali, who first appeared in New York in 1850, Whitman called "the superbest of all the superb baritones in my time—in my singing years." Bettini, especially as the male lead in Donizetti's *La Favorita*, made it clear to him that art music need not be distinct from heart music. "The fresh, vigorous tones of Bettini!" Whitman wrote in 1851. "His voice has often affected me to tears. Its clear, firm, wonderfully exalting notes . . . have made my very soul tremble. . . . [T]he singing of this man has breathing blood within it; the living soul, of which the lower stage they call art, is but the shell and sham." It was almost certainly Bettini to whom he paid tribute in this passage in "Song of Myself": "A tenor large and fresh as the creation fills me, / The orbic flex of his mouth is pouring and filling me full." Another tenor he heard in the early fifties, Pasquale Bignole, remained so vivid a memory that upon Bignole's death in 1884 he wrote a eulogistic poem, "The Dead Tenor," reviewing by name his major operatic roles and re-creating the effect of his singing:

> How much from thee! the revelation of the singing voice from thee!
> (So firm—so liquid-soft—again that tremulous, manly timbre!
> The perfect singing voice—deepest of all to me the lesson:—trial
>   and test of all) [. . .]
> *Fernando's* heart, *Manrico's* passionate call, *Ernani's,* sweet *Gennaro's,*
> I fold thenceforth, or seek to fold, within my chants transmuting.

Among all the opera stars, the one that shone brightest for him was Marietta Alboni, the great contralto who also sang soprano roles (see fig. 24). "For me," he told Traubel, "out of the whole list of stage deities of that period, no one meant so much to me as Alboni, as [Junius Brutus] Booth: narrowing it further, I should say Alboni alone." A short, plump woman with a low forehead and black hair, Alboni had been coached in Italy by Rossini and, after several European tours, arrived in New York in the summer of 1852. Her opening on a sweltering June 23 at Metropolitan Hall was a complete triumph. She had sung only two lines when shouts of "bravo, bravo" swelled from the audience as her strong, sumptuous tones filled the air. At the end, she laughed giddily at the long, tumultuous cheering and waving of hats and handkerchiefs. "There was never a more successful concert," raved the next day's *Herald*. "There was not—there could not be—any difference of opinion about her, as there had been about Jenny Lind. The characteristics of her voice are great power, strength and volume, not only without coarseness, but of the finest, softest, and richest texture, depth and great purity, with a most remarkable sympathetic touching quality." In the months that followed, the triumph continued. The normally exacting Richard Grant Dwight wrote in the *Courier and Enquirer:* "Alboni's performances are as purely and absolutely beautiful as it is possible for anything earthly to be." Between that summer and the next spring she appeared in ten operas and gave twelve concerts of operatic selections in Manhattan. She also toured other cities and states. Whitman later wrote that he heard her "every time she sang in New York and vicinity." "She used to sweep me away as with whirlwinds," he said.

It was not Alboni's talent alone that stood out. Several divas of the 1850s, such as Henrietta Sontag and Anna De La Grange, were reviewed as enthusiastically as she. What made her special was her combined artistry, soulfulness, and egalitarianism. A consummate artist, she was nonetheless down-to-earth and thoroughly human in her delivery. Whitman never forgot the way she got so caught up in her roles that real tears poured down her cheeks. Some critics sniffed that she could lapse on high notes, but for Whitman she was beyond cavil. In opera history, Alboni is remembered as one of the great representatives of bel canto, the flowing, simple line interrupted by vocal scrollwork that has an unearthly, almost orgasmic quality. Stylistically, it was this voluptuous, mystical aspect of her singing that Whitman had in mind when he referred to her impact on his poetry. A contemporary described the effect of Alboni's bel canto singing: "There is an indefinable something more delicate than expression, yet akin to it, which makes her song float like a seductive aroma around her hearer, penetrating to the most delicate fibres of his being, and pervading him with a dreamy delight." Whitman's verse often resonates with a bel canto feeling, even in passages where music is not directly mentioned:

> Smile O voluptuous cool-breath'd earth!
> Earth of the slumbering and liquid trees!
> Earth of departed sunset—earth of the mountains misty-topt!
> Earth of the vitreous pour of the full moon just tinged with blue!

The rapture Alboni inspired in him had more direct poetic ramifications as well. "I hear the trained soprano (what work with hers is this?)," he writes in "Song of Myself. "The orchestra whirls me wider than Uranus flies, / It wrenches such ardors from me I did not know I possess'd them." Although he included in his poems the names of several operas, opera characters, and classical composers, he named just one singer:

> (The teeming lady comes,
> The lustrous orb, Venus contralto, the blooming mother,
> Sister of the loftiest gods, Alboni's self I hear.)

As much as anything, he was intrigued by Alboni's appeal to all classes. He had long sought a music that was at once sophisticated and populist, and he found it at last in Alboni. "All persons appreciated Alboni," he noted, "the common crowd as well as the connoisseurs." He was fascinated to see the upper tier of theaters "packed full of New York young men, mechanics, 'roughs,' etc., entirely oblivious of all except Alboni." She managed to have broad appeal without resorting to hype; she was not promoted by Barnum, as Jenny Lind had been (though the lack of professional publicity shortened her American tour).

The possibility for aesthetic appreciation of music, which he had long considered inchoate in the American masses, seemed actualized in operatic performance whose appeal transcended class lines. Opera was now his chosen preference in music, and he did what he could to enhance its appeal for the general public. He knew he had a lot of persuading to do when many still turned to minstrel troupes or family groups for their music and, worse, to sensation novels, crime-filled penny papers, melodramas, and freak shows for other entertainment. "All of the amusements of the majority of nearly grown and just grown lads, about Brooklyn and New York, are injurious," he wrote in 1858. Opera, above all, possessed the purifying and refining influence he thought music should have on society.

One way of exciting the average American about opera was through catchy journalism, like his article "The Opera" published in 1855 in *Life Illustrated*, a New York magazine he often wrote for. A gimmicky piece of you-are-there reportage, the piece was written in the New-York-by-gaslight mode that had been popularized by working-class writers like George Foster. Whitman's undisguised goal in the piece was to instill in the unsophisticated a love for opera.

To do so, he resorted to the decade-old tricks of urban journalists. He devoted most of the article to describing the physical trappings of an opera performance: the arriving coaches with their sleek horses, the fancy people in elegant clothes, the streaming gaslight, the splendid hall. He didn't shrink from using naïvely hyperbolic language about the upper-class environment: "What a magnificent spectacle to see so many human beings—such elegant and beautiful women—such evidence of wealth and refinement in costume and behavior!" He knew that opera was still far less popular than other musical forms, and so he warned the uninitiated, "It is novel, of course, being very far different from what you were used to—the church choir, or the songs and playing on the piano, or the nigger songs, or any performances of the Ethiopian minstrels, or the concerts of the different 'families.'" Then, finally, he got to the music itself: "A new world—a liquid world—rushes like a torrent through you." He ended the piece by calling for an American music that might rival Europe's: "This is art! You envy Italy, and almost become an enthusiast; you wish an equal art here, and an equal science and style, underlain by a perfect understanding of American realities, and the appropriateness of our national spirit and body also."

An artistic music "underlain by . . . American realities." This is what he had been searching for all along in his musical experiences. He had found it, to some extent, in the popular families and in the minstrels, but, in light of the new musical vistas opened up by the opera, he knew he would have to forge a new kind of singing, one that highlighted American themes but also integrated operatic techniques. "Walt Whitman's method in the construction of his songs is strictly the method of the Italian Opera," he would write in 1860, and to a friend he confided, "But for the opera I could not have written *Leaves of Grass*." As Robert Faner has shown, opera devices do indeed run through his poetry. Many of the emotionally expressive, melodic passages, such as the bird's song in "Out of the Cradle Endlessly Rocking" or the death hymn in "When Lilacs Last in the Dooryard Bloom'd," follow the slow pattern of the aria. The more expansive, conversational passages in his poetry follow the looser rhythm of the operatic recitative.

To assign Whitman's poetic patterns to a single performance mode, however, is delimiting and misses the social significance of his imagery and style. In antebellum America, boundaries between different performance genres and cultural levels were permeable. Popular singers borrowed directly from the opera and from oratory. Actors and lecturers cribbed from each other. Artists in various fields mingled the high and the low. Whitman learned from them all. His verse enacted this permeability of modes. In one passage he could sound like an actor, in another like an orator, in another like a singer. The same was true in his daily life: he would by turns declaim, orate, sing. As both man and poet, Whitman simultaneously heard the thousand varied carols, knew the orator's joys, and played the part that looked back on the actor and actress.

7

"SEX IS THE ROOT OF IT ALL": EROTICISM AND GENDER

SHORTLY AFTER THE FIRST EDITION of *Leaves of Grass* appeared in 1855, Whitman was walking with a friend in Manhattan when he spotted a teenager hawking pornographic books. "That's a New York reptile," he snarled. "There's poison about his fangs, I think."

Five years later, when he was in Boston preparing the third edition of his poems, he got an earful from Ralph Waldo Emerson as they walked under the elms on Boston Common. The subject was sex. Emerson used every weapon in his rhetorical arsenal to try to persuade him to remove sexual images from his poems. Whitman listened to the Concord sage in respectful silence but rejected the advice. Sex, he believed, had to be treated openly. Agreeing to disagree, they went to dinner.

Which was the real Whitman? The antipornographer, or the daring defender of sex in literature?

In a crucial sense, both. At bottom, his distaste for pornography was linked to his hostility to prissiness and sexual repression. The scabrous and the repressed, he thought, were two sides of the same cultural coin. Both reflected skewed visions of womanhood and manhood.

He made clear his outlook in his article "A Memorandum at a Venture," in which he discussed the two prevailing attitudes toward sexual matters. The first he called "the conventional one of good folks and good print everywhere, repressing any direct statement of them" and giving off a scent "as of something sneaking, furtive, mephitic." The second— "by far the largest," he emphasized—was visible in "the wit of masculine circles, and in erotic stories and talk" aiming "to excite, express, and dwell on [a] merely sensual voluptuousness."

The time had come, he announced, for "a new departure—a third point of view," one consistent with recent advances in physiological science, art, and women's rights. Sexual passion, "while normal and unperverted," was a legitimate subject for the modern writer. "Indeed," he wrote, "might not every physiologist and every good physician pray for the redeeming of this subject from its hitherto relegation to the tongues and pens of blackguards, and boldly putting it for once, at least, if no more, in the demesne of poetry and sanity—as something not in itself gross or impure, but entirely consistent with highest manhood and womanhood, and indispensable to both?" He identified "the current conventional, prurient treatment of sex" as the main obstacle to women's social and political equality.

Whitman has normally been seen as a sexual rebel whose poetry stood in opposition to an absurdly proper Victorian America. Gay Wilson Allen distinguishes his work from the "characteristically sentimental and romantic" popular literature of the period. F. O. Matthiessen, likewise, insists that Whitman differed from "every other writer of the day" by realizing "the power of sex," and Paul Zweig has him railing against a "relentlessly moralistic" society.

True, there was an ice cap of conventionality Whitman was trying to pierce. In polite circles, piano legs were decorously covered with frilly stockings; undergarments were called "inexpressibles," shirts "linen," arms and legs "limbs" or "branches." In popular religious and domestic writings designed for the parlor, sex was rarely mentioned.

But just as today we see curious cultural contradictions—for example, political pronouncements on family values on the one hand and a thriving porn industry on the other—so there was a seamy underside to Whitman's America.

The sexual atmosphere before the Civil War was far more varied than is commonly believed. From a governmental standpoint, this was a hands-off period when, despite sporadic crackdowns by local authorities, moral regulations were few. There was no government-authorized moral police of the Anthony Comstock type, which after the Civil War crusaded against all kinds of explicit material, including Whitman's poetry. Before the war there were individual moral-reform groups, but none was longlasting and several actually came into disrepute because of their sensational tactics. Only four states had obscenity laws, and obscenity cases were rarely heard by American courts. In 1842 a ban was imposed on the importation of obscene pictures, but printed matter was left untouched, so that by 1847 Whitman could lament the "cataracts of trash" flowing from abroad. The same printing improvements that sped the production of mass-oriented sensational newspapers also permitted the growth of an underground industry of pornography, much of it foreign but a growing amount of it written indigenously and peddled in railway stations and at street bookstalls.

Both the prudish and the pornographic treatment of sex, Whitman thought, demeaned women and threatened to keep them in suppression. Two of the principal female stereotypes opposed by today's feminists, the retiring household angel and the manipulated sex toy, were already promoted in his time, the former in conventional literature, the latter in sensational writings. What he oxymoronically called the "conventional, prurient" sexual attitude was visible in the contrasting (but related) popular forms that either put women on pedestals or treated them as sex objects.

This was more than just a literary problem. It was part of everyday experience in an increasingly urbanized and capitalistic environment. In some ways, sex was more public than it would be in the twentieth century. Prostitutes, who would become "invisible" in the era of the high-rise and the telephone, were then seen everywhere in cities: on the streets, in theaters, saloons, restaurants, and oyster houses. Like others, Whitman was startled by the ubiquity of prostitutes in the forties and fifties. He extended a friendly hand to them in his poem "To a Common Prostitute" and elsewhere in his poetry, and at the same time wrestled with their plight in his journalism.

He believed that prostitution, like pornography, signaled larger problems in relations between the sexes. Keenly aware of the social and economic causes of prostitution, he protested in newspaper articles against economic injustice to women, and he affirmed woman's equality with man in his poetry. He befriended several women, including Paulina Wright Davis and Nelly O'Connor, committed to the women's rights movement. He also was concerned with male behavior in the new commercialized sexual environment. Alarmed by the habits of the emerging class of "fast" young men—habits that included not only whoring but also swearing and reading pornographic books—he castigated such behavior in prose and presented a sanitized alternative to it in his poetry.

In seeking such an alternative, he profited from developments in the areas of physiology, marriage reform, and the visual arts. Leading physiologists of the day called for an open, honest attitude toward sex to counteract the extremes of sickly repressiveness and gloating salaciousness. Marriage reformers, associated with the women's rights and free love movements, demanded a wholesale redefinition of gender relations by which women would be liberated from virtual enslavement and marriage would be reestablished on the basis of true passion and mutual respect. American artists like Horatio Greenough and Hiram Powers showed that the human body could be treated frankly without sacrificing aestheticism and nobility.

Determinedly avoiding both reticence and obscenity, Whitman in his poetry brought to all kinds of love a fresh, passionate intensity.

"The Tongues and Pens of Blackguards"

WHAT KIND OF SEX LIFE did the poet of sex have?

This question has been asked either directly or indirectly ever since *Leaves of Grass* first appeared. The first biography of Whitman, written in the 1860s by his friend John Burroughs and authorized by him, said that between 1837 and 1848 "he had sounded all the experiences of life with all their passions, pleasures, and abandonments."

Despite the digging of countless scholars, hard knowledge of his sexual activities has not gone much beyond Burroughs's maddeningly vague statement. His sister Mary had five children: although next to nothing is known about her, we know for certain five more things about her sex life than about Walt's.

In his own time, the most common insinuation made about his private life was that he was a womanizer. To some contemporaries, his poetry proved him a Don Juan. An 1860 parody of his poetry gave this typically rakish version of his persona:

Yes, Women.
I luxuriate in women.
They look at me, and my eyes start out of my head; they speak to
    me, and I yell with delight; they touch me, and my flesh crawls
    off my bones.
Women lay in wait for me, they do. Yes, Sir.
They rush upon me, seven women laying hold of one man.

In the decades just after his death, his supposed womanizing was viewed as a positive, liberating force. In 1905 the British scholar Henry Bryan Binns introduced the story of Whitman's alleged affair with a New Orleans woman, an affair that Binns thought opened his sensibility to the sensuous side of life and thus set the stage for his poetry. A later biographer, Emory Holloway, made much of the supposed affair and devoted himself to chasing down Whitman's phantom lovers and mythical children. Holloway built his case on indirect evidence, pointing to the poet's old-age references to a former girlfriend and illegitimate children as well as to a few earlier notebook entries suggesting sexual liaisons.

Holloway and several others have tried to prove Whitman's "normality" in sexual matters in part to refute those claiming Whitman was a homosexual. Whitman's poetry prompted scattered gay readings in the 1870s, and then in a now-famous letter of 1890 the British writer John Addington Symonds asked Whitman point-blank: "In your conception of comradeship, do you contemplate the possible intrusion of those semi-sexual emotions & actions which no doubt occur between men?" Whitman's flat denial of Symonds's queries, which he called "morbid inferences" that were "damnable" and "disavow'd by me," has been seen by many as an evasion, particularly since Whitman told Symonds he had sired six children—almost certainly a lie. Over the years, attitudes toward Whitman's attraction to men have changed with the times. For a while, this attraction was viewed as a source of self-torture, a "peculiar" inclination he repressed or sublimated. More recently, it has been seen as the source of sometimes anguished but ultimately triumphant poetic passages written in defiance of a prudish and homophobic society.

None of these interpretations quite fits the facts. Whitman's journal does suggest he had an affair or two, but he was certainly no womanizer, even though his poetry can make him sound like one. But he did have an eye for female beauty and a great respect for women. "Indeed," he told Traubel, "I think the best women are *always* the best of all: the flower—the justification of the race—the summit, crown." What today would be called heterosexuality was an essential part of his poetic program. When Americans talked of sex in his day, they were referring to sex between men and women. This is what Whitman meant when he declared: "Sex is the root of it all: sex—the coming together of men and women: sex: sex."

As for his relations with men, they can be best understood as especially intense manifestations of the kind of same-sex passion that was seen everywhere in antebellum America. Whatever we are to make of his denial of Symonds's inferences, there is reason to heed his warning to Symonds that his poetry about male love must be read only "within its own atmosphere and essential character." In the free, easy social atmosphere of pre–Civil War America, overt displays of affection between people of the same sex were common. Women hugged, kissed, slept with, and proclaimed love for other women. Men did the same with other men.

Gender roles, in other words, were fluid, elastic, shifting in a time when sexual types had not yet solidified. No one embodied this fluidity in sexual outlook more than Whitman. James Miller's claim that Whitman was neither uniformly homosexual nor uniformly heterosexual but flexibly "omnisexual" is perceptive, though it should also be pointed out that his omnisexuality betokened his awareness of the full range of sexual attitudes of his day. The search for details of Whitman's private sexual activities may be doomed to failure, but his role as a far-ranging observer of the sexual mores and literature of his time is more to the point, given his stated goal of absorbing his country. Significantly, one of the most vivid sexual images in his writings is the one in "By Blue Ontario's Shore" describing the poet "Attracting [the nation] body and soul to himself, hanging on its neck with incomparable love, / Plunging his seminal muscle into its merits and demerits." The image transfers the question of sex from the private to the public. Acutely aware, as we have seen, of America's social problems, Whitman felt compelled to fertilize his nation with the transforming power of his poetic imagination. Whatever he did in private, he "made love" in public to a nation he feared was going profoundly awry. One of the largest deficiencies, he felt, was in the area of sexuality and gender relations. We may never know the complex relationship between the "I" of his poetry—at times hetero-erotic, at times homoerotic, at times autoerotic—and the private Whitman. But we can reconstruct the social context of his sexual images to show that here, as in other areas, his poetry was, in his words, "the age transfigured."

Even some of his most daring and seemingly confessional poetic passages—those relating to masturbation—resonate with the language and feelings of antebellum sexual discourse. Masturbation, then called "the solitary vice," was a major concern of purity reformers. The leading campaigner against masturbation, Sylvester Graham, estimated that 60 to 70 percent of twelve- and thirteen-year-old boys masturbated, with some going to what Graham called "the still more loathsome and criminal extent of an unnatural commerce with each other!" (probably a reference to mutual masturbation). In 1844 Whitman's phrenologist friend Orson Fowler put the percentage of boys eleven and up who masturbated at 90 percent, while he said girls were "dying by thousands" because of the vice, which was thought to cause all kinds of disease. In Graham's eyes, masturbation resulted in "a blighted body—and a ruined soul"; the onanist not only loses physical health but, "Filled with self-contempt, and disgust, and reproach, he is sick of himself and everything around him."

Several masturbatory moments in Whitman's poetry communicate the intensity of the solitary vice while retaining elements of the moralis-

tic language of the purity reformers. A climactic moment in "Song of
Myself" begins as a paean to the wondrous sense of touch but rapidly
takes on autosexual overtones:

> Is this then a touch? quivering me to a new identity,
> Flames and ether making a rush for my veins,
> Treacherous tip of me reaching and crowding to help them, [. . .]
>
> The sentries desert every other part of me,
> They have left me helpless to a red marauder,
> They alone come to the headland to witness and assist against me.
> I am given up by traitors,
> I talk wildly, I have lost my wits, I and nobody else am the greatest
>   traitor,
> I went myself first to the headland, my own hands carried me there.

Critics have noted that the last words ("my own hands carried me
there") strongly suggest masturbation. Passages like this are sometimes
cited to show that Whitman's bold sexual frankness contrasted with the
prudery of his time and culture. But the language he uses here is in
line with that of the purity reformers. What begins as a half-painful re-
creation of the excitement of touch turns into a Grahamite masturbatory
nightmare. Just as Graham had said that masturbation leads to self-
reproach and hatred of everyone, so Whitman's "I" speaks of the phallus
as the "treacherous tip of me" and is pushed to a sense of paranoid isola-
tion: "They alone come to the headland to witness and assist against
me. / I am given up by traitors." Just as Graham and others had said that
masturbation leads to a ruined soul and mind, so the "I" ends up talking
wildly, losing his wits, and feeling himself to be "the greatest traitor."
Little wonder, given the moralistic framework in which Whitman is op-
erating, that this passage is followed by one in which touch is associated
with villainous, threatening things: "You villain touch! [. . .] / sheath'd
hooded sharp-tooth'd touch!"

Another central passage with masturbatory overtones using a similar
kind of rhetoric occurs in the 1855 version of "The Sleepers." Among
the first sleepers the "I" sees in his nighttime vision are "the sick-gray
faces of onanists," recalling Graham's statement that masturbators' faces
take on "a sickly, pale, shrivelled, turbid and cadaverous aspect." Shortly
thereafter the "I" himself has, as Stephen A. Black and Edwin Haviland
Miller suggest, what seems the experience of an adolescent learning
about sex through masturbation:

> My hands are spreading forth . . . I pass them in all directions, [. . .]

O hotcheeked and blushing! O foolish hectic!
O for pity's sake, no one must see me now! . . . . my clothes were
    stolen while I was abed,
Now I am thrust forth, where shall I run? [. . .]

Pier out from the main, let me catch myself with you and
    stay. . . . I will not chafe you;
I feel ashamed to go naked about the world,
And am curious to know where my feet stand. . . . and what is this
    flooding me, childhood or manhood. . . . and the hunger that
    crosses the bridge between.

The persona here seems to be crossing the bridge between youth and adulthood in an excited but confused and self-reproachful way. Like the "I" of the "touch" passage, so this "I" is driven to a kind of frantic paranoia: "O hotcheeked and blushing! O foolish hectic! /[. . .] no one must see me now!" The "I" feels alone, exposed in naked shame to the world, even to the extent that self-arousal blends impressionistically into a sense of wandering outdoors on a phallic "pier."

This kind of solitary shame is likewise manifested by the masturbatory young man in "Spontaneous Me":

The young man that wakes deep at night, the hot hand seeking to
    repress what would master him,
The mystic amorous night, the strange half-welcome pangs, visions,
    sweats,
The pulse pounding through palms and trembling encircling fingers,
    the young man all color'd, red, ashamed, angry.

Whitman comes to the verge of recognizing the pleasurable aspects of masturbation ("strange half-welcome pangs, visions, sweats"), perhaps as a gesture to the large percentage of his readers who, according to the reformers, masturbated regularly. But, as in the other passages, he couches the excitement in the reformers' remonstrative language, as the young man ends up "ashamed, angry." Sometimes Whitman comes close to taking a positively prudish stance on masturbation, as in "I Sing the Body Electric," where he describes "fools" of both sexes who corrupt themselves:

Have you seen the fool that corrupted his own live body? or the fool
    that corrupted her own live body?
For they do not conceal themselves, and cannot conceal themselves.

His moralistic attitude toward masturbation carried over to his views on such habits as swearing, pornography, and whoring. Because of the prevailing image of Victorian America as a laughably proper time, we tend to forget that swearing and the reading of indecent books were widespread, particularly among young men. To some degree, this was a class phenomenon: the working-class rowdies and roughs gravitated to the sexually explicit, middle- and upper-class types to the guarded.

But just as rowdiness intermingled with respectability in American theaters, so vulgar habits crossed class lines. As Whitman noted in the *Daily Times:* "A general laxity of morals—a general indifference to the old standards of right and wrong, by which our fathers regulated their lives, pervades all classes." One of the physiological books he admired, Mary S. Gove's *Lectures to Women on Anatomy and Physiology,* pointed out that masturbation was "fearfully common" even among even the most apparently respectable women, an idea vivified in George Thompson's novel *New-York Life,* which said of middle-class women: "They fancy that they are virtuous, and pass for the very paragons of perfection, when they scarcely pass a day without some secret violation of the laws of chastity," as their physical problems typically come "from the secret indulgence of passions which they would have people think they are too pure to possess."

Others observed that repressively puritanical environments were especially fertile breeding grounds for interest in the salacious. Whitman's point in "Memorandum at a Venture" about a "sneaking, furtive, mephitic" odor coming from the supposedly pure was also made by another writer in an 1855 article, "Fast Young Men," in *Life Illustrated.* The main point of this piece was that many of the sexually promiscuous "sporting" or "fast" men of the day were products of pious environments. The boundaries between prudery and sexual indulgence were hardly rigid; the latter often fed off the former. As the writer explained, "It is notorious that the sons of clergymen are apt to be of the fast species. . . . Where we see a man who makes it a sin to dance or take a walk on Sunday, we see a man whose children are almost *sure* to wring his heart by their dissipation and disobedience." To illustrate his conviction that excessive piety causes a backlash, he told of his experience as an adolescent in a religious boarding school. The school had all the trappings of middle-class propriety, with endless Bible readings, sermons, restricted books, and so on, but for that very reason created an interest in swearing and pornography. Nowhere, the writer pointed out, "was there so low a moral tone, so much outrageous wickedness, so little regard for the rights of others, such habitual nastiness of conversation, such a proclivity for all that is most hateful, vulgar, and suicidal" than in that religious school. "In two days we learned more evil in that school than in all our previous life. *The* subject of conversation was one which can not be named. The vilest books were secretly circulated."

When Whitman said he wanted to wrest the topic of sex from "the tongues and pens of blackguards," he was referring to the kind of language and habits this writer described. Though Whitman used slang words and swore on occasion, he had such a distaste for habitual obscenity that some of his closest friends never heard him swear. "No man ever lived who loathed coarseness and vulgarity in speech more than he," declared Ellen O'Connor Calder, "and I am witness that on two occasions he reproved men, supposed to be gentlemen, for their license in that respect." The alienist Richard Maurice Bucke, his closest friend in his later years, declared that Whitman's "speech and thoughts were, if possible, cleaner, purer, freer from taint or stain than were even his body or his linen." To be sure, he wasn't as pure as all that. In his conversations with Traubel he sometimes let out with a "hell" or a "damn" (though John Burroughs claimed most such words were added by Traubel for color). Once he laughed until he cried after joking he wanted to ram a needle up the rear of a recreant Philadelphia publisher. But this kind of language was innocent compared with that he had heard as young man on the streets of Brooklyn and New York. In a newspaper article of 1845 he upbraided young men's habits, which included "making frequent use of blasphemous or obscene language." Elsewhere, he similarly scolded those "indulging in low conversation, licentious jokes," and wrote: "Profanity is a mark of low breeding." He would often go to the store and hear men telling what he later called "vile, obscene stories and jokes" that made him want to show in poetry that "all in nature is good and pure."

This cleansing impulse also characterized his response to indecent books. Surveying the popular literature of the antebellum period, he said he saw "In the pleantiful [*sic*] feast of romance presented to us, all the novels, all the poems, really dish up only one figure, various forms and preparations of only one plot, namely, a sickly, scrofulous, crude amorousness." In *Democratic Vistas* he complained that in "the prolific brood of the contemporary novel, magazine-tale, theatre-play, &c.," he found "the same endless thread of tangled and superlative love-story." He was puzzled that some inferred from his poetry that he would take an interest in what he called "all the literature of rape, all the pornograph of vile minds." He sharply distinguished *Leaves of Grass* from this material: "No one would more rigidly keep in mind the difference between the simply erotic, the merely lascivious, and what is frank, free, modern, in sexual behavior, than I would: no one."

His distaste for obscene writings had surfaced first in the late 1840s, just when advances in publishing techniques and book distribution were making such writings available to the American masses. Typically, sensational novels appeared as yellow-covered pamphlets emblazoned with large black lettering and melodramatic woodcuts picturing violent or erotic scenes. Whitman had a deep ambivalence toward such writings. As a newspaper editor trying to please his readers, he often printed shocking and violent stories with titles like "Horrible—A Son Killed by His Father" or "Scalded to Death." He even made a tawdry appeal to lovers of sensational yellow-covered novels in the headline he authorized for a June 1847 story about a man mesmerized and put in a coffin: CAPITAL FOUNDATION FOR A SHILLING ROMANCE, IN YELLOW COVERS, WITH A TERRIFIC [WOOD]CUT ON THE OUTER PAGE.

Such sensationalism, however, was chiefly an obligatory gesture to an American public that was being fed a spicy diet of sex and horror in the penny press and cheap novels. The popular literature he most often praised belonged to that category I have elsewhere designated as conventional: religious and domestic works designed for the parlor. In many issues of the *Eagle* he raved wildly about the new *Harper's Illustrated Bible*, which today seems the epitome of Victorian rococo but which to him seemed the height of elegance and taste with its lavish gilt filigree and numerous illustrations of Bible scenes. He had a penchant for parlor-table works in gilt binding, a penchant that contributed to his conception of *Leaves of Grass* as a "New Bible" to be presented to the public, initially, in lavish gilt bindings.

When it came to the content of popular literature, he was careful to praise morality and denounce obscenity. He admired the novels of the didactic writer Joseph Alden, saying they "always inculcate a moral." The domestic novels in the Harper's Fireside Library also pleased him with their fine appearance and contents: "In tasty colored covers, and with gilt edging, and clean, spaced type, this series will surely gain a footing among the welcomed arrivals at parlors, and in the domestic circle." By contrast, a sensational story by William Gilmore Simms he found "in exceedingly bad taste" because of a "revolting drunken scene." He attacked venomously "the perfect cataracts of trash" produced by foreign sensational writers like Eugène Sue, Frederick Marryat, William Harrison Ainsworth, and Charles Paul de Kock. In a long article of July 11, 1846, he denounced these writers by name, expressing wonder that "the vulgar coarseness of Marryatt" and "the nastiness of the French Paul de Kock" attained high popularity in America while a worthy writer like Hawthorne was ignored (this was four years before Hawthorne became famous with *The Scarlet Letter,* his own novel of illicit sex compared by some to French fiction). "Shall real American genius shiver with neglect while the public run after this foreign trash?" he asked. He said that American sensational writers like Joseph Holt Ingraham ("their name is legion") had "quite as much genuine ability as these coiners of unwholesome reading from abroad."

How popular was pornography in antebellum America? Exact figures are impossible to obtain, but it seems that it was far more pervasive than is usually thought. When the moral reformer John McDowall in 1833 investigated pornographic articles in Manhattan, he was astounded by the number of books, prints, music boxes, and snuffboxes he uncovered. At a meeting before several hundred clergymen, he declared that "our country was flooded with these obscene articles," many of which he said were sold to adolescents when their parents were out. A police raid on Henry R. Robinson's store on Cortlandt Street in 1842 revealed thousands of indecent books and prints. Although imported pornographic pictures decreased after the legal ban imposed that year, there emerged a thriving trade in books with titles like *The Lustful Turk* and *The Confessions of a Voluptuous Young Lady of High Rank.* In 1843 one New York paper said nearly every sidewalk stand sold "libidinous books with the most revolting and disgusting contents," and two years later another lamented "all the trashy and disgusting fictions with which our country is flooded, and which has done so much to degrade our literature and corrupt our morals as a nation." For Henry Ward Beecher the popularity of obscene writings had by 1846 reached almost biblical proportions:

> The Ten Plagues have visited our literature; water is turned to blood; frogs and lice creep and hop over our most familiar things,— the couch, the cradle, and the bread-trough. . . . This black-lettered literature circulates in this town, floats in our stores, nestles in the shops, is fingered and read nightly, and hatches in the young mind broods of salacious thoughts.

Whitman was hardly alone, then, in sounding the alarm on what he called literary trash. Many American popular writers were following in the footsteps of the Europeans. In the wake of Eugène Sue's immensely popular exposé *The Mysteries of Paris* (1842–43), scores of lurid novels about the "mysteries" of American cities appeared. Titles included George Lippard's *The Quaker City; or, The Monks of Monk Hall,* Ned Buntline's *Mysteries and Miseries of New York,* and the many novels about city life by the New York sensationalist George Thompson. By 1857, as editor of the *Daily Times,* Whitman could generalize: "Within the last ten or fifteen years a new school of literature has come into existence. We refer to what has aptly been called the 'sensation novel.'" So popular was this genre that he identified the love of sensationalism as America's leading characteristic: "If there be one characteristic of ourselves, as a people, more prominent than the others, it is our intense love of excitement. We must have our sensation, and we can no more do without it than the staggering inebriate can dispense with his daily dram."

Although not explicit by today's standards, antebellum sensational fiction oddly combined sex and violence, and sometimes became daring, particularly in the hands of George Thompson, who churned out nearly a hundred pamphlet novels in the forties and early fifties. Thompson dealt with all kinds of sex: group sex, child sex, and miscegenation. He specialized in frustrated, lustful women, such as the wife of a lawyer in his novel *Venus in Boston* who cries: "How long must I remain here pining for the embraces of fifty men, and enduring the impotent caresses of but one?" In the same novel a veiled scene of lesbianism occurs, as twelve partly naked whores take a woman into a room and fondle her: "Each of the embryo Cyprians kissed the intended victim, some did it almost passionately, as if their libidinous natures derived gratification even in kissing one of their own sex." At one point Thompson takes us to a squalid hovel in the Five Points slum of New York where "the crime of *incest* is as common among them as dirt! I have known a mother and her son—a father and his daughter—a brother and sister—to be guilty of criminal intimacy!"

Given the popularity of sensational fiction, it is understandable that after Whitman's *Leaves of Grass* was criticized by some for its sexual openness, several of Whitman's defenders were quick to point out its relative purity when compared with the mass literature of the day. His friend William Douglas O'Connor asserted that the eighty or so sexual lines in Whitman did not merit his being lumped with "the anonymous lascivious trash spawned in holes and sold in corners, too witless and disgusting for any notice but that of the police." It was Whitman's special achievement, he claimed, "to rescue from the keeping of blackguards and debauchees, to which it has been abandoned, ... the great element of amativeness or sexuality, with all its acts and organs." Similarly, John Burroughs insisted, "Of the morbid, venereal, euphemistic, gentlemanly, club-house lust, which, under thin disguises, is in every novel and most of the poetry of our times, he has not the faintest word or thought—not the faintest whisper."

These friends of Whitman did not mention, of course, that when he was financially pinched, he was tempted to write the same kind of steamy potboilers that were filling the pockets of sensational writers and their publishers. At a particularly hard-pressed moment in the late fifties he actually began writing a city mystery novel titled *Proud Antoinette: A New York Romance of To-day,* involving a young man lured away from his virtuous girlfriend by a passionate prostitute who causes his moral ruin. Nor did Whitman's defenders mention that as the editor of the *Brooklyn Daily Times* he printed regular reports of rapes, murders, incest, and one case of homosexual rape.

They were right, though, in bringing attention to the comparative cleanness of his poetry, which was written partly as a response to the popular love plot, with its fast young men and depraved women. In planning his sexual cluster of poems, "Children of Adam," he specified in his notebook that he wanted to present "a fully-complete, well-developed man, eld, bearded, swart, fiery" as "a more than rival of the youthful type-hero of novels and love poems." Later on he wrote: "In my judgment it is strictly true that on the present supplies of imaginative literature—the current novels, tales, romances, and what is called 'poetry'—enormous in quantity and utterly unwholesome in quality, lies the responsibility, (a great part of it anyhow,) of the absence in modern society of a noble, stalwart, and healthy and maternal race of Women, and of a strong and dominant moral conscience." "Romances," a popular equivalent of novels in his day, became a word of opprobrium in his lexicon. "Great genius and the people of these states must never be demeaned to romances," he declared in the 1855 preface.

He incorporated his protest against romances into his poetry, most explicitly in "Song of the Exposition," where he wrote:

> Away with old romance!
> Away with novels, plots and plays of foreign courts,
> Away with love-verses sugar'd in rhyme, the intrigues, amours of
> idlers,
> Fitted for only banquets of the night where dancers to late music
> slide,
> The unhealthy pleasures, extravagant dissipations of the few,
> With perfumes, heat and wine, beneath the dazzling chandeliers.

"Of Physiology from Top to Toe I Sing"

HE FOUND A POWERFUL WEAPON against the perfervid sensuality of romances in the natural approach to sex and the body offered by the ascendant science of physiology. Popular physiologists like those associated with the scientific publishing firm of Fowlers and Wells stridently opposed pornography as one of several unnatural stimulants that threatened to disturb the mind's equilibrium by overexciting the brain's faculty of amativeness. Whitman became acquainted with the firm's publications when as editor of the *Eagle* he reviewed several of their books. In the store he ran from 1848 to 1852 he sold a wide range of Fowlers and Wells texts. He was so proud of the phrenological chart reading of his skull made by Lorenzo Fowler in July 1849 that he published it four separate times. When Lorenzo and his brother Orson Fowler, along with their brother-in-law and business partner Samuel R. Wells, agreed to serve as distributor of the first edition of *Leaves of Grass* and publisher of the second, they doubtless did so because they felt comfortable with a poet who denounced popular romances while singing of the sacredness of the body.

They had reason to feel comfortable with him, for, like other leading physiologists, they were calling for candid recognition of all bodily functions free of the distortions of the popular love plot. Like Whitman, the Fowlers were frank about the healthiness of sex but prudish about pornography. In one of their main books on physiology, carried by Whitman in his store, Orson Fowler emphasized, "Though the world is *full* of books attempting to portray this passion [love]—though tales, novels, fictitious writings, love-stories, &c., by far the most numerous class of books, are made up, warp and woof, of love, . . . yet how imperfectly understood is this whole subject!" Such stories, he argued, made the brain's organ of amativeness overactive by exciting imaginary love. In another book, in an admonitory chapter on "Yellow Covered Literature," the Fowlers unequivocally advised, "Read no love-stories unless you have health and sexuality to throw away." The earliest publishers of the nineteenth century's most sexually frank poet, therefore, had a deep-seated hatred of the kind of scabrous popular literature he also denounced.

The Fowlers were not alone among American physiologists who opposed indecent writings. Sylvester Graham declared: "The more perfectly scientific the young mind becomes in anatomy and physiology, the more strongly it is secured against undue influences of lewd associations; and learns to think, even of the sexual organs, with as little lasciviousness as it does of the stomach and lungs." John Scudder, one of nineteenth-century America's most explicit writers on the physiology of sex, condemned "this vicious traffic of obscene literature which is widely distributed throughout the country." Russell Trall, a leading physiological author in the Fowlers and Wells establishment, treated sex frankly and yet firmly denounced both pornography and bad language. He wrote: "Obscene novels and fictitious writings, specially addressed to the amative propensity, full of lewd images, impure conceptions, and lust-engendering narratives . . . are abundant in our literary markets." "Still worse," he noted, "is the general habit of low, vulgar, loose, and meretricious conversation," much of it "based on perverted ideas and depraved images relating to the sexual organs, and sexual commerce. With the gross and vulgar-minded this is the ever-present theme of the joke, and repartee, and anecdote, and song, and often, also, of fiction and falsehood."

By presenting himself in *Leaves of Grass* as one familiar with slang but avoiding obscenity, comfortable with sex but circumventing pornography, Whitman was placing himself in line with the physiologists who were trying to cleanse popular culture. He saw in the emerging class of popular physiological books on sex a healthy alternative to the prevalent lewdness of literature and conversation. In a review of Mary S. Gove's *Lectures to Women on Anatomy and Physiology* he wrote, "As respects physiological truths, . . . the more and wider these truths are known, the better." He also had high praise for Edward H. Dixon, the well-known physiologist, who he said was to medicine what Henry Ward Beecher was to preaching. He glowingly reviewed Dixon's book *Woman and Her Diseases*, which contained long, graphic discussions and pictures of all aspects of the female anatomy, including the breast and the uterus. He sold Dixon's medical journal *The Scalpel* in his store, and in the *Daily Times* he reprinted long excerpts from Dixon's writings.

The physiologists he read and associated with did not agree with each other on every particular regarding sex. Sylvester Graham, for instance, preached "spermatic economy," arguing that since both men and women lost vital forces through orgasm, sexual intercourse should occur fairly infrequently—Graham first advised once a week but then revised it to once a month. The physiologists connected with Fowlers and Wells, in contrast, generally advised regular, intense sexual relations as a means of providing healthy exercise to the faculty of amativeness. In 1853 Russell Trall wrote: "The reproductive function not only lies at the foundation of existence itself, but its integrity is essential to the proper development of the individual, as well as to the propagation of healthy and vigorous offspring."

It is Orson Fowler, the chief writer for Fowlers and Wells, whose attitude toward sex is especially instructive with regard to Whitman. In several best-selling works on physiology and phrenology Fowler argued that married couples must have regular sex to keep their systems in balance. This was one of the themes of books like *Amativeness* (1844), which reached forty editions of at least a thousand copies each, and *Love and Parentage* (1851), equally popular. It was almost certainly Orson Fowler who was responsible for taking on *Leaves of Grass* as a Fowlers and Wells book in the midfifties, since by then his views on sex accorded almost

exactly with Whitman's. Significantly, he broke with the firm at about
the same time as Whitman and over the same issue: sex. In 1855 Orson
left Fowlers and Wells (thereafter Fowler and Wells) to pursue a career
as a lecturer on sex. The firm's pragmatic businessman, Samuel Wells,
in effect forced him out by suppressing his new scientific book on sex,
published later in revised form as *Sexual Science; Including Manhood,
Womanhood, and Their Mutual Interrelations*. The next year Wells
cracked down on Whitman for a similar reason.

The nastiness was in the eye of the beholder, for both Orson Fowler
and Whitman had a deep-seated belief in the sacredness and purity of
sex when rightly treated. Both stood opposed to the desacralization of
sex in popular culture, and both hoped to reinstate sex as fully natural,
the absolute center of existence. In *Sexual Science* Fowler set out views
on sex that were very close to Whitman's. Sex is to people, he wrote,
"what steam power is to machinery—the prime instrumentality of its
motions and productions," the very "chit-function of all males and fe-
males"—close in spirit to Whitman's poetic lines "Sex contains all, bod-
ies, souls, / [. . .] Without shame the man I like knows and avows the
deliciousness of his sex, / Without shame the woman I like knows and
avows hers."

With Fowler as with Whitman, all organs and acts connected with
sex were holy. Both placed special emphasis on motherhood, the womb,
the phallus, and semen. Just as Whitman in his poetry virtually deified
mothers as initiators of life, so Fowler wrote, "She is the pattern woman
who initiates the most life, while she who fails in this, fails in the very
soul and essence of womanhood." Just as Whitman poeticized the folds
of the womb whence unfolded new life, so Fowler praised the womb as
"the vestibule of all life," insisting that "every iota of female beauty
comes from it." Just as Whitman in "A Woman Waits for Me" would
write that all is lacking in woman if sex is lacking, so Fowler underscored
the necessity for woman's full enjoyment of the sex act. PASSION ABSO-
LUTELY NECESSARY IN WOMAN, he headlined one section of his book. "The
non-participant female," he wrote, "is a natural abomination." Since rec-
iprocity was essential in sex, a woman must always be properly aroused.
The outlook of both Fowler and Whitman was sex based, womb cen-
tered, phallic centered, but also intensely religious. If Whitman's sexual
passages often soar quickly to the mystical, so do Fowler's. For instance,
the holiness Whitman saw in the "seminal milk" and "fatherstuff" was
seen also by Fowler, who wrote of the semen, "Great God, what wonders
hast Thou wrought by means of this infinitesimal sway!"

Among the methods the physiologists used to educate the American
public about the body and sex was the distribution of anatomical draw-

1. The dapper journalist
of the early 1840s

2. The rough of 1854

4. The elegant frontispiece of the
1860 edition of *Leaves of Grass*

3. The individualist of the 1850s

5. Walter Whitman   6. Louisa Van Velsor Whitman

7. Whitman's birthplace, West Hills, New York

8. *Winter Scene in Brooklyn* (C. 1817-20); painting by Francis Guy

9. *New York, from Brooklyn Heights* (1837); painting by John William Hill

10. *Walt Whitman's School at Southold, 1840*; painting
attributed to William Sidney Mount

11. The Rev. Ralph Smith,
who allegedly denounced Whitman
from the Southold pulpit

12. Mike Walsh, Bowery politician

13. *View of the Great Fire in New York, Dec. 16 & 17, 1835* (1836);
aquatint by Nicolino Calyo

14. *Broadway, New York* (1836); etching by Thomas Hornor

15. Franklin Pierce

16. James Buchanan

17. Abraham Lincoln

18. Andrew Johnson

19. Junius Brutus Booth

20. Junius Brutus Booth as Richard III

21. Edwin Forrest

22. Edwin Forrest as Macbeth

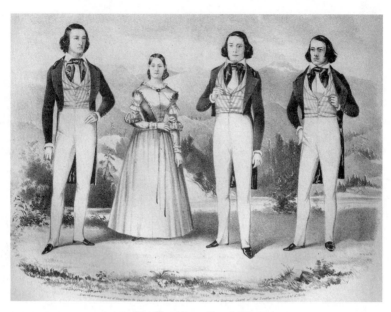

23. The Hutchinson Family Singers

24. Marietta Alboni

25. Elias Hicks

26. Henry Ward Beecher

27. Henry Ward Beecher preaching at Plymouth Church, Brooklyn

28. Frances Wright

29. Lucretia Mott

30. Sojourner Truth

31. Anne Gilchrist

32. Street
prostitution in
New York, 1850

33. The Crystal Palace, New York, 1853

34.
View of
Manhattan
street life,
1855

35. *The Trapper's
Bride* (1837); painting
by Alfred Jacob Miller

36. *Farmers Nooning* (1836); painting by William Sidney Mount

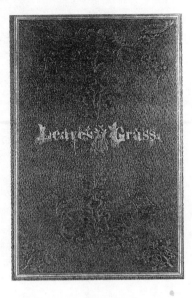

37. Front coverboard
of the 1855 edition
of *Leaves of Grass*

See next page of cover for Contents
of Walt Whitman's New Volume of
"Leaves of Grass."

LEAVES OF GRASS

IMPRINTS.

THAYER & ELDRIDGE,
Publishing House, 116 Washington St.

*To the Public.— In putting before you our new
and superbly printed electrotype edition of America's
first distinctive poetry, the "LEAVES OF GRASS,"
we offer the accompanying brochure as a circular to
all persons disposed to commence the study of the
Poems. We supply it gratuitously.*

The notices refer to the previous and partial
issues of the Poems. See the 2d page of Imprints
within. But all the pieces of previous issues are com-
prehended in our New Volume, with much additional
matter.

See last page for Publishers' advertisement.

BOSTON,

June, 1860.

Just Published.

WALT WHITMAN'S

LEAVES OF GRASS.

AN ELEGANT BOOK.

The publishers wish to call the attention of the reading
world to the superior manner in which they have pro-
duced the "LEAVES OF GRASS." The typography will be
found to vie in elegance with any thing ever issued from the
American or English press. The paper is thick, white, and
of superfine quality; the electrotyping from the Boston
Stereotype Foundry; the printing by Rand, has been done
with extreme care, with the best of ink; the binding is
substantial and unique; the steel portrait, by Schoff, (from
a painting by Charles Hine, of New York,) will enhance
the reputation of that first-rate artist.

The work, as a whole, will be found to be an ornament to
any book-shelf or table; and as such the publishers confi-
dently claim for it a recognition as

One of the finest specimens of modern book making.

We wish it distinctly understood that the inferior style of
print, typography, &c., spoken of in the notices in the fore-
going circular, refer altogether to the previous, temporary
and partial issues of the poems, and not at all to the superb
edition we now present to the public.

The work comprises 456 pages, 12mo.

Price $1.25.

Copies will be mailed to any address in the United
States, including California, postage paid, on
receipt of the retail price.

THAYER & ELDRIDGE, Publishers,

114 & 116 Washington St., Boston.

38 & 38A. Front and back covers of the 1860
promotional pamphlet *Leaves of Grass Imprints*

39.
William
Douglas
O'Connor

40. John Burroughs

41. Whitman and Peter Doyle

42. Horace Traubel

43. Around 1864

44. In 1879, with the son
and daughter of John Johnston

45. In 1878

46. Cigar box cover with Whitman logo

47. In 1891, amid the chaos of papers in his
bedroom at 328 Mickle Street, Camden

ings and artistic prints. The Greek Revival style that swept through American domestic architecture and cemetery design during this period was also manifested in the sculpture of Horatio Greenough and Hiram Powers. When Greenough's sculpture "Chanting Cherubs," a group of nude children, appeared in Boston in 1831, it aroused such an uproar that within three weeks city authorities had it draped in dimity aprons. But Greenough persisted in calling for an honest treatment of the nude, and his call was heeded by a number of artists, including Hiram Powers. Powers's *The Greek Slave*, a neoclassical study of a mournful, very naked slave woman whose chained hands fall strategically over the genital region, became by far the most famous American sculpture of the period. It was constantly copied and reproduced, and thousands of printed reproductions of it were distributed in the antebellum period, many of them by physiological firms like Fowlers and Wells, who saw in this naked but "chaste" work a vehicle of education about the body. Another such vehicle was life-sized anatomical drawings of the nude human body, in color and on rollers, which Fowlers and Wells sold to schools and sometimes individuals.

Whitman saw in such aesthetic and scientific works a model for his poetic treatment of the body. "I prefer the honest nude to the suggestive half-draped," he would tell Traubel. His attraction to the "honest nude" was stimulated in part by "The Greek Slave," which he thought even the most innocent could enjoy without being sullied. "We have scarcely witnessed a more pleasing sight than the visit of the young ladies belonging to the Brooklyn female seminary to the exhibition of the Powers' statue of the Greek Slave, in New York," he wrote in the *Eagle* in 1846. The aesthetic sensibility behind Powers's nude he also found in the "model artists," or *tableaux vivants,* which became the rage throughout the country in the late forties. In New Orleans he regularly attended model artist exhibitions, in which nude or lightly draped women and men enacted scenes from the Bible or classical myths. He denounced as "sickly prudishness" opposition to the model artists, which he thought revealed "Nature's cunningest work—the human frame, form and face."

His interest in such public exhibitions of the nude informed his treatment of the body in his poetry. In the 1855 preface he described the healthy effects of reproducing artistic nudes: "Clean and vigorous children are jetted and conceived only in those communities where the models of natural forms are public every day." He emphasized that Americans "shall receive no pleasure from violations of natural models" in sculptures or illustrations; specifically, "Of the human form especially it is so great it must never be made ridiculous." Such candid nudity was exemplified for him not only by sculptures and model artists but also by the physiologists' anatomical models. When planning in his notebook "a poem in which is minutely described the whole particulars and ensemble of a *first-rate Human Body*," he reminded himself: "Read the latest and best anatomical works/talk with physicians/study the anatomical plates."

Throughout his poetry, especially in the first three editions when he was heavily under the sway of the physiologists, he treated sex and the body in a physiological, artistic way as a contrast to what he saw as the cheapened, often perverse forms of sexual expression in popular culture. "Who will underrate the influence of a loose popular literature in debauching the popular mind?" he asked in a magazine article. Directly opposing the often grotesque versions of eroticism appearing in sensational romances, he wrote in the 1855 preface: "Exaggerations will be sternly revenged in human physiology[. . . .] As soon as histories are properly told, there is no more need for romances," a sentiment he repeated almost word for word in his 1860 poem "Suggestions." Priding himself, like the physiologists, on candid acceptance of the body, he announced in his first poem: "Welcome is every organ and attribute of me, and of any man hearty and clean." He sang the naturalness of copulation and the sanctity of the sexual organs: "Perfect and clean the genitals previously jetting, perfect and clean the womb cohering." In poems like "I Sing the Body Electric" and "Spontaneous Me" he listed the parts of the human body, including the sex organs, with the loving attention of a physiologist or sculptor:

> Head, neck, hair, ears, drop and tympan of the ears,
> Eyes, eye-fringes, iris of the eye, eyebrows, and the waking or
>   sleeping of the lids,
> Mouth, tongue, lips, teeth, roof of the mouth, jaws, and the jaw-
>   hinges, [slowly down the body to . . .]
> Hips, hip-sockets, hip-strength, inward and outward round, man-
>   balls, man-root,
> Strong set of thighs, well carrying the trunk above,
> Leg-fibres, knee, knee-pan, upper-leg, under-leg,
> Ankles, instep, foot-ball, toes, toe-joint, the heel.

If such lists sometimes seem a bit mechanical, it is partly due to his effort to present "natural forms" free of artifice and sensationalism, just as he saw them in the anatomical works of his day.

Several of his contemporaries saw the link between his sexual images and physiological science. Burroughs said that, unlike sensational authors, Whitman dealt with "the amative part of human physiology" with "physiological cleanliness, strength." Even those critical of Whitman made the science connection, like one commentator who wrote that his sexual passages "belong in a handbook of physiology." And a friendly reviewer noted that the "numerous class of prurient readers" who might buy *Leaves of Grass* for sexual titillation would be disappointed, since the poems were "not meant for obscenity, but for scientific examples, introduced as they might be as in any legal, medical, or physiological book, for purpose of instruction."

This kind of criticism Whitman liked. He always emphasized the physiological connection. "I have always made much of the physiological," he once told Traubel, explaining elsewhere that his best readers were "women, doctors, nurses: those who know the physiological man— the physiological spiritual man." After the first three editions prompted some adverse criticism because of their frankness, seemingly to ward off further attacks he wrote an opening poem, "Inscriptions," which placed his poetry in the clean realm of physiology:

> Of physiology from top to toe I sing,
> Not physiognomy alone nor brain alone is worthy for the Muse, I say
>   the Form complete is worthier far,
> The Female equally with the Male I sing.

Women's Roles, Free Love

IT IS SIGNIFICANT that the above lines move quickly from physiological praise of the body to a feminist assertion of woman's equality, for in Whitman's mind the two subjects were interconnected. "[O]nly when sex is properly treated, talked, avowed, accepted," he wrote, "will the woman be equal with the man, and pass where the man passes, and meet his words with her words, and his rights with her rights." Although repelled by the excesses of sensational novelists, he agreed with them that relations between the sexes were askew in an increasingly commercialized, urban environment. With women's rights activists of the day he shared a concern for the right of women to equal opportunity in society. Like advocates of free love, he thought relationships must be based on mutual attraction and respect rather than on money or one-sided desire. The language of magnetic bonding that fills his poetry shows his debt to the discourse of "passional attraction" used by the free lovers and other sex radicals of the day. The fact that he never actually joined the women's rights and free love movements reflects not complacency but rather his continual effort to take into account the full spectrum of women's roles offered by his contemporary culture. He once declared that *Leaves of Grass* was "essentially a woman's book, ... it is the cry of the right and the wrong of the woman sex." It was so, in the most far-ranging sense.

Whitman's treatment of women has disappointed some modern readers. D. H. Lawrence complains: "Whitman's 'athletic mothers of these States' are depressing. Muscles and wombs: functional creatures— no more." Like many of Lawrence's generalizations about American literature, this is a colorful half-truth. Whitman did stress motherhood and female athleticism in his poetry, but he by no means limited women to these roles. The "[m]uscles and wombs" Whitman was the physiological poet who, in accordance with medical theory, hoped to counteract a widely perceived decline in the physical and maternal powers of American women. As G. J. Barker-Benfield has shown, the medicalization of sexual discourse in the antebellum period was accompanied by an ever-increasing emphasis on the maternal role of women. Leading gynecologists helped popularize the idea that the womb was the all-defining part of woman; her sex organs, in effect, were herself, and reproduction was the great work of the sexes.

Ironically, more and more emphasis was being placed on motherhood in medical journals at a time when birthrates were falling precipitously. Whitman in *Democratic Vistas* lamented "the appaling depletion of women in their powers of sane athletic maternity, their crowning attribute." The "alarming sterility" of American women he wrote of in the *Daily Times* was an overstatement, but recent historians have found that the number of children per woman did decline by more than 50 percent during the nineteenth century. The reasons for the decline were both economic and demographic, associated with rising professionalism among women and the dissolution of the geographically stable stem family.

By emphasizing motherhood in his poetry, Whitman was simultaneously resurrecting the fertility of his own female ancestors and promoting the womb-centered vision of the physiologists. "W. W. himself makes much of the women in his ancestry," Burroughs wrote, and not the least of the qualities he admired in ancestors like his great-grandmother Phoebe Whitman and his own mother, Louisa Van Velsor Whitman, was their fertility. The women of the mid–nineteenth century, Whitman wrote, were "very far removed from the women of old times." He complained that "a healthy American female is rapidly becoming a *rara avis in terris*" and estimated that nine of ten "of our fair-featured, but frail-constitutioned sisters, wives, and mothers are weak, debilitated, and unfit for the burdens of life." He added in exasperation: "The mothers of the next generation!" This was a standard complaint among physiologists and reformers of the day, and his answer to the problem—athleticism and exercise for women—was a commonly prescribed solution.

For Whitman, there was great power and creativity in both motherhood and fatherhood. As seen earlier, he was surrounded by physiologists who believed, in Orson Fowler's words, that "PARENTAGE is EVERYTHING." The idea of the miraculous nature of parenting had a long history in scientific thought. In the late seventeenth century, European biologists had introduced preformation theory, based on the idea that all human beings were created by God in the beginning, enclosed one within the other, like Russian dolls that were unpacked generation after generation. Some scientists studying the semen under a microscope claimed to see tiny human beings, with arms and heads. Although by Whitman's time this notion had been discredited, several American scientists, most notably Henry Clarke Wright, retained the reverence for the sperm that preformation theory had instigated. Wright, around whom formed a fifties sexual reform group called the Wrightists, argued in his books *Anthropology* (1850) and *Marriage and Parentage* (1854) for open discussion of all sex matters, including the sperm, which he said contained the souls and character traits of future generations. Whitman often advanced a similar notion:

> This is not only one man, this the father of those who shall be
>   fathers in their turn,
> In him the start of populous states and rich republics,
> Of him countless immortal lives with countless embodiments and
>   enjoyments.
>
> How do you know who shall come from the offspring of his offspring
>   through the centuries?
> (Who might you find you have come from yourself, if you could trace
>   back through the centuries?)

Whitman here taps into the preformation theorists' idea that the semen grows from past existences and encases future ones. He also expresses a view similar to that of New York's foremost gynecologist, Augustus Kinsley Gardner, who argued that the father's patriotism could produce vigorous offspring. If Gardner envisaged "a new, scientifically bred race of patriotic giants," so Whitman says that the father has in him "the start of populous states and rich republics." Elsewhere he has his persona boast: "I pour the stuff to start sons and daughters fit for these States."

He found motherhood even more miraculous than fatherhood. The rise of embryology in the late eighteenth century had placed woman at the center of reproduction. The sperm cell, it was found, was not a miniature human being but produced one through union with the female egg. The physiologists and gynecologists around Whitman took embryological theory to an extreme. The mechanical, functional view of women Lawrence complained of in Whitman was actually far less pronounced with him than with gynecologists like J. Marion Sims, who said reproduction was just a matter of uniting the sperm and the egg, irrespective of passion or desire.

Far more attuned than Sims to sexually mystical theories discussed later, Whitman deified the womb as the emblem of almost divine power. He writes of women, "[Y]our privilege encloses the rest, and is the exit of the rest, / You are the gates of the body, and you are the gates of the soul." His 1856 poem "Unfolded Out of the Folds" sang praise to both the literal and metaphorical powers of the womb:

> Unfolded out of the folds of the woman man comes unfolded, and is
>   always to come unfolded,
> Unfolded only out of the superbest woman of the earth is to come
>   the superbest man of the earth, [. . .]
> Unfolded only out of the perfect body of a woman can a man be
>   form'd of perfect body, [. . .]
> Unfolded out of the strong and arrogant woman I love, only thence
>   can appear the strong and arrogant man I love,
> Unfolded by brawny embraces from the well-muscled woman I love,
>   only thence come the brawny embraces of the man, [. . .]
> Unfolded out of the sympathy of the woman is all sympathy;
> A man is a great thing upon the earth and through eternity, but
>   every jot of the greatness of man is unfolded out of woman;
> First the man is shaped in the woman, he can then be shaped in
>   himself.

Both the physiological and moral dimensions of motherhood are hyperbolically described here. Human life unfolds, as a fetus developing into a newborn, out of the "folds" of the womb. The child is then shaped in the maternal "fold," reaching satisfactory adulthood only to the extent that motherly nurturing is full and successful.

The piled-on superlatives of a poem like "Unfolded Out of the Folds"— the "superbest woman" with a "perfect body" who is the source of all greatness—have a ring of desperate affirmation, given Whitman's comments elsewhere about the "appalling depletion" of American women's maternal and physical powers. It was commonly pointed out in his day that the health of modern American women paled in comparison with that of previous generations or of women abroad. A physiological writer for *Life Illustrated* noted in an 1858 article: "It is notorious, all over the civilized world, that American females are unhealthy, and that the tendency to disease and infirmity is constantly increasing." Woman's ill health, the writer claimed, might prove "one of the leading causes of the ultimate degeneracy of the American people, and the final overthrow of our republican government, in the fact that the vitality of our females is running down."

In light of such apocalyptic warnings, Whitman's poetic paeans to what he called "sane athletic maternity" are explainable as attempts to present a model woman for all to observe. In establishing this model, he drew from several emerging theories of womanhood. One was related to the athletic woman. The physiologists of the day, believing women's health was declining, advised walking, running, calisthenics, and weight lifting for women. In a series of articles eventually published by Fowler and Wells in 1857 as *The Illustrated Family Gymnasium,* Russell Trall noted "the artificial *deformity* of many of the females" of New York and outlined a rigorous athletic regimen illustrated by pictures of women doing exercises and lifting barbells.

Such athletic prescriptions for women were common during a period when what has been called a cult of Real Womanhood was coming to the fore in American life and letters. American cultural historians long thought that as male and female spheres became separated with the rise of industrialism, men practiced aggressive values in the commercial marketplace while women, confined to the home, took on qualities such as passivity, piety, purity, and submissiveness. To be sure, as Ann Douglas and Barbara Welter show, the ideal of the angelic, submissive housewife was purveyed in many novels and advice manuals. But partly in response to the forces driving women to domesticity and debility, more vigorous roles for women were defined. Nina Baym and others have noted the sturdiness often exhibited by the heroines of domestic novels, and Jane P. Tompkins stresses the power and cultural work achieved by popular writers like Susan Warner and Harriet Beecher Stowe. Frances B. Cogan shows that to counteract signs of sickliness and passivity among women, antebellum health advisers and popular writers held up the ideal of the tough, active woman—what Cogan calls the Real Woman. In health literature, this movement flowered in works like Dr. Dio Lewis's *New Gymnastics for Men, Women and Children* (1863). In popular fiction, it gave rise to spirited heroines with the physical capabilities of men. For instance, the heroine of a Marion Harland story has "muscles like harpstrings" and at one point brags, "I can row six miles without fatigue, and walk ten. I can drive and swim, and ride twelve miles before breakfast on a trotting horse. I eat heartily three times a day, and sleep soundly for eight hours out of the twenty-four." Cogan points out that the Real Woman, although strong and economically self-reliant, believed in marriage and opposed political feminism.

Whitman's poetry was one of the period's clearest expressions of the Real Woman: athletic, sturdy, self-reliant yet also maternal, family based. Given the ideal of the Real Woman, there was no contradiction between the athletic and motherly roles he praised in his poetry. The woman in "Unfolded Out of the Folds," for instance, embodies tender maternal "sympathy" but also is "strong and arrogant," "well-muscled," and capable of "brawny embraces." It was natural that athletic womanhood was most prominent in the second (1856) edition of *Leaves of Grass*, for this edition was published by Fowler and Wells, prominent purveyors of the muscular ideal of Real Womanhood. Just as Fowler and Wells were printing articles recommending hardy exercise for women, so among the twenty new poems Whitman wrote for the second edition were several promoting female activity and adventurousness. One praised women who "know how to swim, row, ride, wrestle, shoot, run, strike, retreat, advance, resist, defend themselves." Another imagined America as a kind of utopia of Real Womanhood:

> I say an unnumbered new race of hardy and well-defined women are
>   to spread through all These States,
> I say a girl fit for These States must be free, capable, dauntless, just
>   the same as a boy.

The Real Woman was not the only current ideal of women he embraced. He also learned much from the women's rights movement, which became active and visible in America between 1848 and 1855, just when he was maturing as a poet. The world's first women's rights convention, held at Seneca Falls, New York, in July 1848, was a gathering of thirty-five women and thirty-two men who passed a declaration calling for recognition of women's social and political equality. Two years later the Rhode Island reformer Paulina Wright Davis, later one of Whitman's most appreciative readers and his close friend, organized the first of several national women's rights conventions that were held annually (except in 1857) until the Civil War. An even closer friend, Abby Price, was an activist for both free love and women's rights.

With his background in Quakerism and free thought, Whitman was predisposed to respond to the movement. The Quakers were the most progressive of America's larger religious denominations in their views of women, encouraging them to speak at meetings and ordaining them as ministers. The powerful women in Whitman's ancestry stood out particularly because of their association with Quakerism. The Quaker element, he told Traubel, was "altogether among the women, with my own dear mother, and grandmother and her mother again. It is lucky for me," he continued, "if I take after the women in my ancestry, as I hope I do: they were so superior, so truly the more pregnant forces in our family history." Quaker women were important in national history as well. Several of the women who organized the Seneca Falls convention, including Lucretia Mott, Jane Hunt, Martha Wright, and Mary Ann McClintock, were Quakers.

Among them, it was Lucretia Mott (fig. 29) with whom Whitman felt the deepest kinship. Lucretia and her husband James Mott were, like Whitman, associated with the liberal, Hicksite wing of the Quakers. They were active abolitionists whose home was busy in the Underground Railroad. Lucretia founded the first Female Anti-Slavery Society and, with Elizabeth Cady Stanton, laid the initial plans for Seneca Falls. A gentle woman with a high, slightly shrill voice, she typically wore a simple white dress and a little Quaker hat. Whitman heard her at reform meetings and got to know her a bit. He kept a photograph of her until the end of his life. Once when Traubel showed him the picture, he recalled "her majestic sweet sanity" and her smile: "Oh! it was sweet, winsome, attractive. It drew a fellow nearer and nearer." To him, she embodied the free-spirited nobility of all Quaker women. "Do you know the Quaker women?" he asked Traubel. "The women are the cream of the sect. It was not Lucretia Mott alone—I knew her just a little: she was a gracious, superb character, but she was not exceptional."

Woman's political entrance into public life was what Mott and others like her signified above all. Whitman was a close observer of woman's oratory and became a poetic celebrant of woman's new public role. The first lengthy political speech by a woman before a large audience in America had been given on July 4, 1828, by one of Whitman's favorite orators, Fanny Wright. The slim, chestnut-haired Wright had shocked conservatives with her electrifying appeals on behalf of women and workers. Whitman recalled her as "a brilliant woman, of beauty and estate, who was never satisfied unless she was busy doing good—public good, private good." Wright's meteoric career as a speaker peaked in 1828–29, after which there came a succession of women lecturers: the African-American Maria W. Stewart, one of the first women to promote both abolition and women's rights before mixed audiences of men and women; the peripatetic antislavery activists Sarah and Angelina Grimké, whose championing of women's rights led to a split in the abolitionist movement; the virulent crusader Abby Kelley, whose acidic rhetoric matched Garrison's; and Lucy Stone, who spoke boldly even when being pelted by rotten apples and tobacco juice.

Few were as controversial as Ernestine Rose, whom Whitman especially admired. The Polish-born Rose had arrived in America from England with her husband in 1836 and over the next two decades lectured on women's rights in twenty-three states. Because of her foreign accent, her Jewish ancestry, and her outspoken infidelity, she met with suspicion everywhere, but she won many to the feminist cause with a forceful delivery that belied her frail physique. "Oh! she was a splendid woman," Whitman recalled. "Big, rich, gifted, brave, expansive—in body a poor sickly thing: a strong breath would blow her away—but with a head full of brains—the amplitude of a Webster."

Feminist orators were not alone among women in making a dramatic entry into the public sphere. Women participated in parades, processions, and religious revivals in unprecedented numbers during this period. Whitman approvingly recorded women's suddenly public posture in "Song of the Broad-Axe," picturing a city "Where women walk in public processions in the streets the same as men, / Where they enter the public assembly and take places the same as the men."

Before the Civil War, women's rights activism centered not on suffrage, a main concern after the war, but on property holding, education, employment, and marriage. It was these issues that would always loom largest in Whitman's mind. His outlook was close to that of his fellow-Brooklynite Laura Curtis Bullard, a feminist novelist and broad-ranging activist whose special emphasis was woman's employment and social equality. Given their similar views, it is not surprising that Bullard loved *Leaves of Grass* from the beginning and told Whitman so in a letter of 1872, a letter he kept until his death.

His sympathy for the social and economic plight of women had first surfaced in his *Eagle* editorials. He was appalled by the wretched pay given for women's work. "Poor Payment for Toiling Women" was the title of a November 1846 piece in which he complained that "the payment for Women's labor—for female teachers, governesses, and so on, to the commonest house servant—is miserably poor." He gave added evidence of women's low wages in other articles, including one about a seamstress who supported five children on just fourteen cents a day and another about a woman who had worked forty years in a cotton mill but had managed to save only two thousand dollars. In the article "The Sewing-Women of Brooklyn and New York," he cited "the miserably low rate of wages paid for women's work" as the reason that four of five women in the New York area had to choose between poverty and prostitution.

He was also painfully aware of what happened to a woman's wages or property holdings in marriage: they were turned over to the husband. In marriage, early nineteenth-century American women forfeited their legal and economic existence. A wife could not sign a contract or make a will. Whatever property she owned could be sold by her husband without payment to her, and she lacked the power to sue in a court of law. Divorce was extremely difficult to obtain, and in the rare cases where it was granted, a woman could not recover money or property. The situation began to improve somewhat in 1839, when Mississippi passed a mild women's property law, followed two years later by Delaware and then by the New England states. Whitman jumped on the property-reform juggernaut. In the *Eagle* he supported a proposed Canadian law that would give married women exclusive right to their own property, and he commended American states that were passing marriage-reform laws. His enthusiastic support of property reform fed into the rising sentiment on its behalf in New York, where the Woman's Property Act was enacted in 1848.

These laws, however, were only halfway measures that left wives largely at the economic mercy of their husbands. The New York law, for instance, gave wives control over their property and real estate but left their earnings in the hands of their husbands. It would not be until the passage of a revised New York law in 1860, later imitated by other states, that wives gained full control over their wages and gained something like economic parity.

Before then the condition of wives was regarded as so bad in some quarters that they were compared with slaves. The women's rights activists Whitman knew emerged from one or more of three reforms that alerted women to their plight: abolition, in which the enslavement of African-Americans was associated with the status of women; "moral reform," in which the alarming increase of prostitution illustrated the sexual and economic exploitation of women; and temperance, which gave constant instances of women tied by law to drunken husbands. The legal restraints on women trapped them in ways that seemed to violate America's republican ideals. That divorce laws should be relaxed was a view held even by moderates, like the writer for *Life Illustrated* who wrote:

> No one is ignorant that evils of the most enormous and agonizing nature exist in the consequence of the perpetuity and exclusiveness of the matrimonial tie. . . . Many women are sold into eternal slavery. Many

women are linked for life to a man at whose presence their gorge rises; men whose lives are shameful, whose manners are brutal, whose persons are loathsome.

As a reform-minded writer in the 1840s Whitman showed that he was aware of such problems in relations between the sexes. The temperance fiction he wrote during this decade contained vivid scenes of wives and children brutalized by alcoholic husbands, and in the *Eagle* he printed a typical moral-reform poem about a heartless wealthy rake who regularly seduced women and thus drove them to prostitution.

Passion, Prostitution, Poetry

H E W A T C H E D with fascinated yet sometimes puzzled interest the various reforms that arose in response to flawed relations between the sexes. Antebellum America was an extremely fertile breeding ground for various religious and secular groups who practiced alternative lifestyles in an effort to put sexual relations on an entirely new basis. At one extreme were the Shakers, who practiced celibacy, at the other were free lovers, who called for the abolishment of marriage and the reestablishment of relationships on the basis of "passional attraction." In between were groups whose sexual adventurousness could vie with almost anything today. From 1848 onward the followers of the perfectionist leader John Humphrey Noyes at the Oneida community practiced "complex marriage" (many partners per woman) in the belief that women were sexually insatiable and had to be constantly satisfied, while men were supposed to avoid ejaculation to conserve vitality. In 1852 the Mormons in Utah instituted polygamy: Brigham Young apparently had between nineteen and twenty-seven wives.

Free love was the most pertinent of these movements with regard to Whitman. The association between him and free love was often made in his day. Emerson connected him with the free-love movement, as did James Harlan, Whitman's superior in the Interior Department who in 1865 fired him, reportedly, in the belief that he "was a free lover, deserved punishment, &c." When the 1881 edition of *Leaves of Grass* was banned in Boston, it was the New England Free Love League that publicly came to Whitman's defense and endorsed his sexual poetry. A member of the league, Benjamin Tucker, became his loyal friend.

Despite such connections, Whitman was deeply ambivalent about the free lovers. Like them, he saw profound defects in relations between the sexes. Also like them, he tried to repair these defects by appealing to natural passion and attraction. Just as they equated marriage with slavery, so the reason he gave for not marrying was "an overmastering passion for entire freedom, unconstraint" (though his attraction to men was a more likely reason).

But he shied away from what he saw as the free lovers' potentially disruptive effects on society. Despite his own disinclination to marry and his recognition of flaws in American marriages, he always venerated the marriage institution. In the *Eagle* he sharply criticized "single fools, the bachelors and maids who are old enough to be married—but who from appearances, will probably 'die and give no sign.'" He advised, "Young man reader! if you have good health, are over twenty-one years old, and nothing to 'incumber' you, go and get married." He viewed marriage as the very basis of all civilization: "When that goes, all goes," he wrote, emphasizing that "the divine institution of the marriage tie lies at the root of the welfare, the safety, the very existence of every Christian nation." He was firmly opposed to any kind of sexual experimentation that threatened marriage. As his friend Charles Eldridge recalled, "Anything like free love was utterly repugnant to his mind, and he had no toleration for the Mormons." When a Washington friend, Charles Howells, left his wife and children to follow the free-love leader Stephen Pearl Andrews, he excoriated Howells and called Andrews a Mephistopheles.

His ambiguous feelings about free love were registered in his response to radical conventions where free lovers were prominent. The famous gathering of two to three thousand reformers at Rutland, Vermont, in June 1858 attracted his interest. He described the conventioneers as "all sorts of odd-fishes . . . free-lovers, ultra-abolitionists, trance-media, female atheists, vegetarians, phrenologists, people in short possessed of all the 'isms' of the day." He was right to note the strange mixtures at Rutland, which was to the 1850s what Woodstock was to the 1960s, a grand outpouring of every kind of radical sentiment. Though hardly unified, the reformers at Rutland agreed on the idea of complete freedom, for women and slaves in particular. The free lovers dominated the lecture platform, arguing that the enslavement of women came from the marriage contract, in which woman lost control of her name, property, labor, person, affections.

For Whitman this was too much. He complained, "The marriage relation, in the opinion of these amiable lunatics, was a detestable humbug." But his attitude was not wholly negative. He thought the convention was part of "a grand upheaval of ideas and reconstruction of many things on new bases, not in the manner indicated by these excrescences who have just finished their pow-wow at Rutland, but on an infinitely larger, grander and nobler scale." He was less tolerant of another convention, held in Utica two months later, at which the free lover Julia Branch approved of having children out of wedlock. He decried "the contemptible lucubrations of the Free Love Convention," calling it a subversive attempt to free men and women "from every moral and social obligation or restraint." But he responded more positively to a similar gathering at North Collins, Erie County, of what he called "Free Lovers, Spiritualists, women's rights people." He admired the conventioneers' iconoclasm and wondered whether "these heterogenous elements are destined to coalesce at some period, distant or near, it matters not, and form a grand Heresy in religion and morals which shall number in its ranks millions of souls?"

What he wanted was the "passional" theory of the free lovers without their antimarriage proposals. The notion of passional attraction had been introduced by the French utopian socialist Charles Fourier, who conceived of an ideal society made up of cooperative communities whose members were bonded by an intrapersonal magnetic pull as powerful as gravity. Conventional marriage would be abolished in these communities, where passional attraction would operate as a subtle, constant force exhibited in various kinds of experimental sex.

Antebellum America was the main testing ground of Fourier's ideas. The passional theory did not take hold in most of the Associationist communities founded in the forties, where cooperative economics was not accompanied by cooperative sex. But with the rise of various interrelated radical movements in the late 1840s—spiritualism, mesmerism, Swedenborgianism, Harmonialism—the theory gained high visibility and surprisingly widespread acceptance. Between 1850 and 1855 America witnessed the formation of two free-love communities, at Modern Times, New York, and at Berlin Heights, Ohio, as well as various free-love clubs, journals, societies. At Modern Times, an anarchist and free-love community established in 1851 near Whitman's birthplace on Long Island, legal marriage was abolished. Couples signified their union by tying a colored thread to their finger and took it off when the passion fizzled.

Free love was a direct response to what was seen as the enslaving marriage institution. The foremost free-love writers of the early fifties, Marx Edgeworth Lazarus and Stephen Pearl Andrews, argued that marriage in America had become little more than legalized prostitution. Several books endorsing free love appeared, including Lazarus's *Love vs. Marriage* (1852), which argued that both men and women needed many different lovers since "monotony, monogamy, or exclusive constancy, are for love a true suicide." This book sparked a long public debate in the columns of the *New York Tribune* from November 1852 through February 1853, with Stephen Pearl Andrews taking the free-love side, Horace Greeley opposing him, and Henry James, Sr., taking a middle stance. Andrews insisted that "Our whole existing marital system is the house of bondage and the slaughter-house of the female sex," suggesting all love relationships should be established on the idea of attraction as elucidated by Fourier. But the free lovers did not emphasize promiscuity. Free love for them did not mean indiscriminate love but love freely given, freely shared. The precondition for sexual relations should be love, not marriage, and the woman should determine when sex took place. Thus the free lovers, though often castigated, considered themselves chaste and pure.

Because many spiritualists and Harmonialists adopted some version of the free lovers' views, the idea of passional attraction spread far beyond free love circles. In 1854 a British visitor found that "the passional theory" had "cropped out in all directions and in various forms" in America. One of these forms was Whitman's poetry. Some early reviewers of Whitman placed him among the faddish sex radicals. Rufus M. Griswold, one of the first to attack the 1855 edition of *Leaves of Grass*, connected him with recent sexual "progressionists" who suddenly seemed to be everywhere:

> There was a time when licentiousness laughed at reproval; now it writes essays and delivers lectures. Once it shunned the light; now it courts attention, writes books showing how grand and pure it is, and prophesies from its lecherous lips its own ultimate triumph.

There was reason for Griswold to link Whitman's poetry with current sexual theories, for the poetry was full of images of passional attraction. At a time when, as we have seen, the political parties were in chaos and sectional divisions loomed ominously, Whitman reached in many directions to offer models of bonding and togetherness to the nation. One model he found in passional theory, which he could have picked up almost anywhere in the early fifties—particularly in the New York papers and in the publications of Fowlers and Wells, who published a wide-ranging list that included translations of Fourier and books on free love, such as Lazarus's *Love vs. Marriage*. He also fell in with people who used the language of magnetic attraction. His close friend Sarah Tyndale was a Fourierist who in an 1856 letter to him said she hoped to see "men and women associating humanly in all the true brotherly relations of life, insensably [*sic*] imparting the magnetism of humanity to each other." Whitman could use similar language in his personal relations, as when he explained to a friend the presence of a boy by saying,

"I am trying to cheer him up and strengthen him with my magnetism."

It was in the poetry in the first three editions of *Leaves of Grass*, written when passional theory was at its peak of cultural influence, that the discourse of magnetic attraction was most pronounced. The gravity-like pull between humans expounded by Fourier and disseminated by the American reformers is felt at many moments in Whitman's poetry. "Crossing Brooklyn Ferry" asks: "What is more subtle than this which ties me to the woman or man that looks in my face? / Which fuses me into you now, and pours my meaning into you?" In "The Base of All Metaphysics" Whitman expresses hope that all groups of humans, from families to societies, will learn to be bonded magnetically: "The dear love of man for his comrade, the attraction of friend to friend, / Of the well-married husband and wife, of children and parents, / Of city for city and land for land." Sometimes his vocabulary of attraction seems straight out of passional theory:

> O to attract by more than attraction!
> How it is I know not—yet behold! the something which obeys none
>   of the rest,
> It is offensive, never defensive—yet how magnetic it draws.

Just as Fourier had discovered in passional attraction a human counterpart to the earth's gravity, so Whitman wrote:

> I am he that aches with amorous love;
> Does the earth gravitate? does not all matter, aching, attract all
>   matter?
> So the body of me to all I meet or know.

Passional attraction simultaneously permitted individual freedom, strong bonding between people of the same sex, and self-determination in heterosexual relations. The motto at the free-love community Modern Times, "Freedom, Fraternity, Chastity," linked these three instincts. For Whitman, too, passionate same-sex comradeship coexisted with a sense of liberation and a commitment to sexual self-regulation. It will be seen later how his comradely "Calamus" poems drew off the passional theory as well as other philosophies of friendship. In the realm of heterosexual love, passional theory aided Whitman in his effort to treat sex openly yet chastely. If chastity was a goal of the free lovers, so Whitman could write of "The great chastity of paternity, to match the great chastity of maternity, / The oath of procreation I have sworn."

Self-determination in sexual matters was the notion that free lovers had in common with a growing number of feminists and with Whitman.

The reason the free lovers called marriage legalized prostitution was their vision of countless wives bound by law to husbands whom they detested and yet who had free access to their bodies. The basic assumption was that capitalism had poisoned heterosexual relationships, making marriage an institution of entrapment. The "free" in "free love" meant freedom to regulate sex according to true feeling rather than exterior social codes, so that every individual heeded the inner call of his or her sexual voice. When Whitman in "A Woman Waits for Me" says that all is lacking in a woman if the moisture of "the right man" is lacking, he is advancing the idea of self-choice for women.

A great concern among marriage reformers of the day was that many American women were not married to "the right man," or, if they were, they could still become sexual slaves. Stephen Pearl Andrews thought American wives were little better off than whores. "Prostitution, in marriage and out of it, and solitary vice, characterizes society as it is," he wrote in 1852. An increasing number of women's rights activists claimed sexual self-determination as a central rallying point. It long remained a central issue for Whitman too, and by the 1880s he was gratified that women had gained more choice in sexual matters. Once when discussing free love with Traubel he declared, "I only feel sure of one thing: that we won't go back: that the women will take care of sex things—make them what they choose: man has very little do to with it except to conform."

All the flaws in relations between the sexes could be seen in that most public form of sex in antebellum America: prostitution. When Whitman emphasized in his journalism that economic injustices against working women drove many of them to streetwalking, he was getting at the combined economic and sexual exploitation that lay at the heart of antebellum women's culture. In the 1840s a young woman who could expect to make two or three dollars a week in a normal job could get between ten and fifty dollars for turning a single trick as a prostitute. As a result, sex was for sale everywhere in America's larger cities, especially in Whitman's New York.

Urbanization and the rise of market capitalism brought about the increasing commercialization of sex. (For one view of street prostitution in Manhattan, see fig. 32.) The numbers of brothels in New York tripled between 1820 and 1865, rising from around two hundred to more than six hundred. Because legal restrictions were nil and police crackdowns rare, prostitutes pursued their trade openly and ubiquitously. By 1855 prostitution in New York had become a $6.35 million business, second only to tailor shops when compared with legitimate forms of trade. As the easiest means for women to earn good money, prostitution was adopted by a remarkable number of them. According to a conservative estimate, from 1830 to 1860 some 5 to 10 percent of New York women between the ages of fifteen and thirty prostituted at one time or another. In bad times the number was pushed over 10 percent.

The proportion of men who visited prostitutes was even higher than this. Whitman noted in 1857 that the vast majority of men in American cities visited prostitutes regularly, many contracting sexual diseases. Nineteen of twenty urban men, he wrote, "are more or less familiar with houses of prostitution and are customers to them." Among "the best classes of Men" in Brooklyn and New York, he wrote, "the custom is to go among prostitutes as an ordinary thing. Nothing is thought of it—or rather the wonder is, how can there be any 'fun' without it."

Like others, he was appalled by the way prostitution was conducted in New York. In some areas of the city, such as the squalid Five Points district, prostitutes swarmed and traded oaths on the streets or in door-ways, sometimes with their dresses open and breasts in full view. As Whitman wrote, "You see the women half exposed at the cellar doors as you pass." In the poorer districts, where fifteen men, women, and children often shared three beds in a single room, sex became a public phenomenon. It was not unusual for someone passing by a brothel to see through a window a prostitute and her customer fornicating.

Prostitution proliferated in theaters. In 1843 one newspaper announced that some New York theaters had "degenerated into assignation houses—lounges for bawds and their victims—lust palaces." The upper or third tier was notorious for public sex, and one reporter described "males and females in strange and indecent positions in the lobbies, and sometimes in the boxes." Even respectable areas of the city had prostitutes. By 1851 the diarist George Templeton Strong declared New York a "whorearchy" and noted the extreme youth of some prostitutes: "No one can walk the length of Broadway without meeting some hideous groups of ragged girls, from twelve years-old down, . . . with thief written in their cunning eyes and whore on their depraved faces. . . . And such a group is the most revolting object that the social diseases of a great city can produce."

Whitman shared some of Strong's revulsion. In his walks about the city he reported seeing both the "notorious courtesan taking a 'respect-able' promenade" and the "tawdry, hateful, foul-tongued, harsh-voiced harlots." The question was: What to do? "If prostitution continues so," he asked, "and the main classes of young men merge themselves more and more in it, as they appear to be doing, what will be the result? A generation hence, what a scrofulous growth of children! What dropsies, feebleness, premature deaths, suffering infancy are to come!" To prevent the spread of disease and crime, he thought, prostitution should be regulated; he even suggested legalization. Imprisoning prostitutes he saw as counterproductive, since women in jail became better versed in vice. Vice campaigns, such as Captain John McManus's raid on the Five Points in 1850 or Fernando Wood's arrests of streetwalkers later in the decade, were too infrequent to have much effect. The economic and legal reforms that would most help women were slow in coming.

A good first step was full exposure of the problem and the cultivation of a sympathetic public attitude toward prostitutes. The prevailing attitude was one of derogation and censure. As Timothy Gilfoyle has shown, prostitutes actually were treated more harshly in antebellum America than were homosexuals. A kindlier attitude toward them emerged in moral reform circles and among the physiologists Whitman read. "Abandoned females are generally considered as constitutionally the scum and offscouring of mankind," wrote Orson Fowler in 1851. "But are they not human beings? Perhaps as good by nature as ourselves." Whitman warmly commended Dr. William A. Sanger's *History of Prostitution* (1858), which objectively gave the case histories of two thousand prostitutes without heaping opprobrium on them. Most prostitutes, Sanger pointed out, were driven to their trade by economic necessity or men's trickery. Sanger wrote: "Seduction; destitution; ill treatment by parents, husbands, or relatives; intemperance; and bad company, are the main causes of prostitution." Sanger recommended licensing prostitutes and providing them with regular medical checkups. Whitman praised Sanger for exposing "the great vice of the age—the vice most general, most costly, and most ruinous to health and morals."

One of Whitman's aims in his poetry was to extend a generous hand to the victims of deceitful men. Just as in the *Eagle* he had published someone else's poem about a seducer whose victims became prostitutes, so in the 1855 preface he refers to the "serpentine poison of those that seduce women" and in a poem he mentions "the treacherous seducer of young women." As for prostitutes themselves, he rose above his private distaste for them and made compassionate gestures. His first picture of a prostitute, in the 1855 version of "Song of Myself," retained traces of his revulsion but tried to communicate sympathy:

> The prostitute draggles her shawl, her bonnet bobs on her tipsy and
>   pimpled neck,
> The crowd laugh at her blackguard oaths, the men jeer and wink to
>   each other,
> (Miserable! I do not laugh at your oaths nor jeer you).

In later portraits he moved toward personal identification with them: "You prostitutes flaunting over the troittoirs or obscene in your rooms, / Who am I that I should call you more obscene than myself?"

His most famous sympathetic gesture was his 1860 poem "To a Common Prostitute":

> Be composed—be at ease with me—I am Walt Whitman, liberal
>   and lusty as Nature,
> Not till the sun excludes you do I exclude you,
> Not till the waters refuse to glisten for you and the leaves to rustle
>   for you, do my words refuse to glisten and rustle for you.
>
> My girl I appoint with you an appointment, and I charge you that
>   you make preparation to be worthy to meet me,
> And I charge you that you be patient and perfect till I come.
>
> Till then I salute you with a significant look that you do not forget
>   me.

Gone are all references to pimpled necks, blackguard oaths, or obscene behavior. The emphasis has shifted from the massive social problem that appalled Whitman to the poetic solution, embodied in refreshing nature images (the sun, the glistening waters) and the atmosphere of dignity and formality ("be worthy to meet me," "be patient and perfect," "I salute you with a significant look"). This "appointment" with a prostitute had little in common with the thoughtless, commercialized pairings Whitman saw everywhere in urban America. It was, instead, an ennobling appointment in which both parties profited, the "I" practicing democratic compassion, the prostitute being treated as a person rather than as a sex machine. Whitman gives a modern version of Christ's compassionate treatment of Mary Magdalene by fusing democratic sympathy with images of beauty and ennoblement.

All Together, Now

WHITMAN TRIED TO SUGGEST in his poems how not only prostitution but other forms of sexual exploitation and injustice could be overcome. Historians have shown that the decline of prostitution in the late nineteenth and early twentieth centuries was related to significant changes in attitudes toward sex and marriage. As time passed, the imbalances in gender relations of the antebellum period began to be rectified. Marriage became increasingly "companionate" and "democratized," with spouses starting to share household duties and improvements in household appliances softening the wife's burden. The advent of sexology in the 1880s was accompanied by a growing understanding of woman's sexual nature, so that the potential for mutual sexual satisfaction was increasingly a precondition for marriage. Premarital sex became more permissible, and the misogynist underpinnings of "sporting" male culture were challenged by the dissemination of feminist ideas.

In all these areas (including premarital sex, which he recommended in the *Daily Times*) Whitman had been remarkably prophetic. Culling positive, sympathetic attitudes toward sex, the body, and women from various cultural arenas, he presented powerful images that, when taken together, created a sexual program that held up the possibility of woman's social and personal liberation. Muriel Kolinsky has found that women are mentioned in at least a quarter of the 424 poems of *Leaves of Grass* and around half of its 403 pages. Whitman returned again and again to the woman's problem and through his imaginative fusion of different cultural images offered a pathway to freedom.

The woman question preoccupied him from the start. His earliest free-verse draft, in his notebook of 1847, contained the lines: "I am the poet of women as well as men. / The woman is not less than the man." Just as his poetic "I" interposed between slaves and their masters, so it affirmed woman's equality with man. This resolution of a thorny social problem by poetic fiat continued in the 1855 preface ("A great poem is [. . .] for a woman as much as a man and a man as much as a woman") and in the first poem:

> I am the poet of woman the same as man,
> And I say it is as great to be a woman as to be a man,
> And I say there is nothing greater than the mother of men.

This last line disconcerts some recent readers who want women's equality without the constrictions of motherhood. But in Whitman's day, women's rights and motherhood were not necessarily contradictory. Elizabeth Cady Stanton, whose career as a women's rights activist was longer lasting than anyone else's, was a devoted wife and mother who took pleasure in housekeeping. Several women in Whitman's circle were at once feminists and housekeepers. His Providence friend Paulina Wright Davis was a women's rights crusader who was nevertheless an affectionate mother. The same was true of his close friend Nelly O'Connor, who once confessed to him, "I have a great love of good housekeeping, care *too much*, I fear, for the trifles."

Without fear of contradiction, then, Whitman could praise simultaneously the ideas of motherhood and women's equality. Thus, his pronouncements on equality of the sexes can sound both feminist and familial:

> The wife, and she is not one jot less than the husband,
> The daughter, and she is just as good as the son,
> The mother, and she is every bit as much as the father.

He knew well enough, as his journalism shows, that in real life the wife, the mother, and the daughter were *not* treated as if they were "the same" or "every bit as much" as men. But he was dissatisfied with political activists' resolutions to the woman problem. His attitude toward agitation for women's rights had some of the same ambivalence as his feelings about abolitionism and free love. Seeing the prevalent tenor of the age as "convulsiveness," he shied away from the rising number of heterogeneous conventions that he thought threatened social stability. "What a queer medley of women's rights meetings at present!" he wrote in 1858 in the *Daily Times*. "Where but in New York could such a collection be got together? Women in breeches and men in petticoats—white, black, and cream-colored—atheists and free-lovers, vegetarians and Heaven knows what—all mixed together, 'thick and slab,' until the mixture gets a little too strong, we should think, even for metropolitan stomachs."

To some, his attitude toward women's rights seemed downright hostile. His Washington friend Charles Eldridge, for example, recalled:

> I have never heard him give any countenance to the contentions of the "Women's Rights" people; thought they were a namby-pamby lot as a whole, and he did not believe that woman suffrage would do any particular good. Susan B. Anthony was far from his ideal of a "fierce athletic girl." He delighted in the company of old fashioned women, mothers of large families preferred, who did not talk about literature and reforms.

This comment is deceptive. True, Whitman tended to retreat from militant spinsters like Susan Anthony and to befriend mothers, both feminists and nonfeminists, who had old-fashioned qualities he valued. What repelled him was the single-minded focus of certain feminists on individual issues. For instance, when he wrote in 1876 that he stood for "the radical equality of the sexes, (not at all for the 'woman's rights' point of view, however)," he seems to have been distancing himself from groups like Lucy Stone's American Woman Suffrage Association, which by then focused solely on winning the vote for women.

He believed women's equality could be gained only after wholesale changes in relations between the sexes. "Woman in the nineteenth century seems to be in a lamentably unsettled condition," he noted in the *Daily Times*, asking, "Why is not a candid and courageous course pursued by writers and speakers, upon the subject of sexuality?" He came to support woman's suffrage, but only as part of a more general reform that dealt with attitudes toward sex. In "A Memorandum at a Venture" he wrote:

> To the movement for the eligibility and entrance of woman amid new spheres of business, politics, and the suffrage, the current prurient, conventional treatment of sex is the main formidable obstacle. The rising tide of "women's rights," swelling and every year advancing farther and farther, recoils from it with dismay.

Whitman creates in his poetry a utopian space where "the current prurient, conventional treatment of sex" is overturned. Minimized in his poems are the flaws in gender relations he perceived all around him: declining health and fertility among women; trickery and misogyny on the part of men; legal discrimination against women; mockery of prostitutes; the contrasting extremes of prudish repressiveness and pornographic lasciviousness. Maximized are physiological acceptance of the body and sex; fertility and athleticism for both men and women; and an all-pervasive passional attraction.

These elements are scattered liberally through many poems and brought together in "A Woman Waits for Me." Like sex-oriented physiologists, Whitman in this poem emphasizes the pivotal importance of woman's frank recognition of her sexual nature. A woman in the poem shamelessly avows the deliciousness of her sex, just as a man avows his. The "I" dismisses "impassive women" and says he will stay "with those women who are warm-blooded and sufficient for me." Like popular writers who advanced the ideal of the Real Woman, he praises women who can row, wrestle, shoot, and so on. Like women's rights activists, he declares that women "are not one jot less than I am"; they are "ultimate in their own right" and "calm, clear, well-possess'd of themselves."

Sexual self-determination in the choice of partners is enforced in the lines about women who are aroused only by "the right man" and who "refuse to awake at the touch of any man but me." Embryological and gynecological veneration of the womb is reflected in his declaration to women: "Envelop'd in you sleep greater heroes and bards." Preformationist reverence for the sperm is suggested in the image of the "I" pouring stuff to start children "fit for These States" and the later line: "The drops I distill upon you shall grow fierce and athletic girls, new artists, musicians, and singers." This is preformation theory with a Whitmanesque twist, for the imagined future race is one of artists and bards, the types he thought could alone cleanse American culture and reverse its current downward course.

The "I" of the poem is Whitman's version of hardy, rough manhood, the ultimate match for the vigorous woman he embraces. The "I" has sexual machismo (almost too much so for modern taste, as in the lines "I do not hurt you any more than is necessary for you, / [. . .] I listen to no entreaties") but is still chaste in the physiological and free-love sense. He has practiced a kind of spermatic economy: he is depositing "what has so long accumulated within me" and lets loose "the pent-up rivers of myself." Whitman thus taps into the paradox represented by free love of sexual adventurousness and sexual purity. The poem presents neither lasciviously described sex nor indiscriminate sex but rather sex with a purpose, chaste sex for procreation.

The final line of the poem adds a mystical aura to the sexual message: "I shall look for loving crops from the birth, life, death, immortality, I plant so lovingly now." In Whitman, sexual passion is never far from religious vision. Rarely does he celebrate the body without affirming the soul. That is another part of the story.

8

EARTH, BODY, SOUL:
SCIENCE AND RELIGION

S OME SEE WHITMAN as the poet of nature and the body. Others consider him the poet of religion and the soul. Still others take both tendencies into account by coining phrases like "inverted mysticism" to describe his outlook.

The last are on the right track. Exclusive emphasis on either the physical or the spiritual Whitman misses his determined intermingling of the two realms. His earliest notebook poem contained the lines, "I am the poet of the body / And I am the poet of the soul," establishing at once the interpenetration and cross-fertilization between matter and spirit that is felt in virtually all his major poems. The earthly and the divine, the sensuous and the mystical, are never far from each other in his verse. His images flow rapidly from the minutiae of plant or animal life through parts of the human body to sweeping vistas of different times and places, often with affirmations of God's harmonious universe.

His physical spirituality, or spiritual physicality, was part and parcel of scientific and religious developments in mid–nineteenth century America. When he was composing the first three editions of *Leaves of Grass,* evolutionary and geological science was still in its pre-Darwinian phase. Scientists did not view species as combatants struggling fiercely for survival in an indifferent universe but as participants in an orderly plan visible in nature and following laws of progress. In an age before an emphasis on genetics, humans were thought to be able to control the physical and moral destiny of themselves and their offspring through regulation of environment and behavior.

The circle of scientists and pseudoscientists surrounding Whitman, most of them associated with his early distributor Fowlers and Wells, had a special role in popularizing and Americanizing such progressive, optimistic ideas. Phrenology, never more than an intellectual fad abroad, became in the hands of his friends Orson and Lorenzo Fowler an all-defining system of self-help that took into account all aspects of the human being, physical and spiritual. Mesmerism, another area the Fowlers specialized in, also became far more popular in America than in Europe, so that by the late forties the nation was flooded with mesmeric healers who used a language of magnetism, electricity, healing, and clairvoyance that Whitman incorporated in his poetry.

Also popular in America at midcentury were various religious and philosophical currents that brought together the earthly and the divine in sometimes startling ways. This was an extraordinarily fertile period in American religion, as the antinomian spirit unleashed by the Second Great Awakening led to the formation of several new denominations and sects, including Mormonism and various brands of millennialism. Whitman, who called *Leaves of Grass* "the new Bible" and said he wished to "inaugurate a religion," shared in this new creative spirit. His "religion" owed much to the sciences popularized by the Fowlers, to religious and philosophical authors he was reading, and particularly to the interrelated movements of spiritualism, Swedenborgianism, and Harmonialism. Taken together, these movements help explain the sometimes bizarre yoking of the erotic and mystical in his poems.

Science and Pseudoscience

"Lo! keen-eyed towering science, / As from tall peaks the modern overlooking," writes Whitman in "Song of the Universal." In the next breath he adds, "Yet again, lo! the soul, above all science."

These juxtaposed passages point to a characteristic movement in his poetry from the scientific to the spiritual. He struggled to bring together the two in his poetry, and he made use of popular approaches that made such couplings possible.

He fought constantly against a dark undercurrent of materialism that had appeared in eighteenth-century scientific thought and that came to him through his father's deism. The deists of the Enlightenment had an essentially secular outlook, viewing the universe as a vast machine originally set in motion by a God who had withdrawn, allowing the machine to run on its own. It was a short step from deistic secularism to atheistic materialism. The eighteenth-century philosophers Baron d'Holbach and Denis Diderot pictured a godless universe in which matter and physical laws were triumphant. American deists such as

Benjamin Franklin, Thomas Jefferson, and Thomas Paine gingerly circumvented atheism and materialism, though their secular outlook laid them open to frequent charges of infidelity. Paine in particular scandalized many with his argument in *The Age of Reason* (1793) that religion is the mere fabrication of humans and that nature is the highest object of study.

Whitman, as discussed earlier, got a heavy dose of deism through his early exposure to Paine and Fanny Wright; he also counted the deistic *Ruins* of Volney as one of his early texts. The legacy of deism was, to some extent, a positive force in his construction of a fresh philosophy. Like the deists before him, he denied the specialness of any single religion and forged a broadly ecumenical outlook that embraced all religions. He could sound much like Paine or Jefferson when imagining a simplified pan-religion. He wrote in his notebook that the well-developed mind passes through many religions to "the clear atmosphere above them—There all meet—previous distinctions are lost—Jew meets Hindu, and Persian Greek and Asiatic and European and American are joined—and any one religion is just as good as another." As he wrote several times, his was the greatest of faiths and the least of faiths. His ecumenical outlook engendered two long passages in "Song of Myself" in which he listed by name the major world religions, indicating that he respected and accepted them all. He surveyed them again in "With Antecedents" and affirmed: "I adopt each theory, myth, god, and demi-god, / I see that the old accounts, bibles, genealogies, are true, without exception."

Despite his professions of faith, however, he was never far from the skepticism that was the dark side of deism. He accepted all the churches but believed in none. It was particularly difficult for him to have faith in the churches at a time when he believed rising capitalism was tainting religion. Like other reformers of the day, he was upset by the intermingling of money and religion in America. New York's Grace Church became for him a primary symbol of the mixture of God and mammon. In the *Eagle* he pointed up the paradox of supposedly Christian churches like Grace basing membership on financial and social status. "We don't see how it is possible to *worship God* there at all," he wrote. "The haughty bearing of our American aristocrats (that most contemptible phase of aristocracy in the whole world!), the rustling silks and gaudy colors in which wealthy bad taste loves to publish its innate coarseness—the pompous tread, and the endeavor to 'look grand'—how disgustingly frequent are all these at Grace Church! Ah, there is no *religion* there." Similarly bitter observations on aristocratic churches were made by Melville in "The Two Temples" and by George Lippard in many novels. Like these authors, Whitman came to view much of mainstream religion as essentially godless.

On this score, they were aligned with the come-outers, a mixed group of reformers (many of them abolitionists or spiritualists) who "came out" from churches they felt had become poisoned by association with economic injustice or chattel slavery. Whitman excoriated the churches with the vigor of a come-outer. The prevailing spirit of the time, he asserted in his 1856 letter to Emerson, was, despite rising church membership, materialist and infidel. "The churches," he wrote, "are one vast lie; the people do not believe them, and they do not believe themselves; the priests are continually telling what they know well enough is not so, and keeping back what they know is so. The spectacle is a pitiful one." He made highly cynical comments on materialistic religion in his blackly humorous poem "Respondez!" in which he announced, "Let churches accommodate serpents, vermin, and the corpses of those who have died of the most filthy of diseases! / [...] Let there be no God!"

Often his doubts about the churches merged into doubts about larger matters. Deism had left him broadly tolerant but also bereft of a stable explanation of things. The grim, sometimes bleak ponderings of death that had filled his poetry in the early forties reappeared in later writings as outbursts of doubt. "O Mystery of Death," he lamented in a pre-1855 notebook, "I pant for the time when I shall solve you!" D. H. Lawrence calls Whitman the great poet of death and his poems "huge fat tomb-plants, great rank graveyard growths."

A reason for Whitman's obsession with death was the loss of life he saw around him in urban America. In a time when epidemics went virtually unchecked and the urban death rate rose dramatically, Whitman felt that the health of all Americans was in peril. In Manhattan, the annual death rate climbed from one in every forty New Yorkers in 1840 to one in twenty-seven by 1855. Even the completion of the Croton Aqueduct in 1842 did not improve sanitation sufficiently to stem the rising tide of yellow fever, measles, tuberculosis, and, beginning in the late forties, cholera. In 1847 Whitman noted in the *Eagle* that only half of the 450,000 children born annually in America lived to be twenty-one and that in large cities like New York and Boston the death rate was especially high. "As much as the present time is vaunted over the past," he wrote, "in no age of the world have so many influences been at work, averse to health and to a noble physical development, as are working in this age!" Eight years later he expressed amazement in the *Daily Times* about the ever-escalating suicides in modern life. Among his contemporaries, the high mortality rate contributed to a death-obsession variously visible in the custom of photographing the corpses of children, in the deaths that abounded in popular fiction (most notably those of Stowe's Eva and Uncle Tom), and in the popular graveyard verse Mark Twain would later satirize in his portrait of Emmeline Grangerford, the poetess who prided herself on reaching a corpse before the undertaker.

More frequently than any writer of his time, Whitman contemplated death in his writings. At moments he seemed to see nothing but death. "Not a day passes, not a minute or second without a corpse," he writes in one poem. "Slow-moving and black lines creep over the whole earth—they never cease—they are the burial lines." "The suicide sprawls on the bloody floor of the bedroom," he writes in "Song of Myself." "I witness the corpse with its dabbled hair, I note where the pistol has fallen." In "The Sleepers" he imaginatively enters a coffin: "A shroud I see and I am the shroud, I wrap a body and lie in the coffin." His poetry is scattered with the dead: the 412 soldiers slaughtered at Goliad, the heaped bodies of those killed during the sea battle, the drowned swimmer, the mashed fireman, the lost she-bird, Lincoln, the Civil War dead.

His contemplation of death brought him to the brink of doubt. He knew all too well, as he wrote in "Song of Myself," the feeling "That life is a suck and a sell, and nothing remains at the end but threadbare crepe and tears." He could use an almost Melvillian image when identifying with skeptics:

Down-hearted doubters dull and excluded,
Frivolous, sullen, moping, angry, affected, dishearten'd, atheistical,
I know every one of you, I know the sea of torment, doubt, despair
  and unbelief.

How the flukes splash!
How they contort rapid as lightning, with spasms and spouts of
  blood!

At times his vision seems as materialistic as d'Holbach's. In "Of the Terrible Doubt of Appearances" he presented life as a phantasmagoria uninformed by order or reason: "Of the uncertainty after all, that we may be deluded, / That may-be reliance and hope are but speculations after all, / That may-be identity beyond the grave is a beautiful fable only, / [. . .] How often I think neither I know, nor any man knows, aught of them."

What distinguished Whitman from his contemporaries were his

wide-ranging strategies for combating doubt. One strategy he found in physical science. He found reassurance even among some scientists who had little or nothing to say about God. Among the materialistic scientists who offered hopeful explanations of nature was the German chemist Justus Liebig, the founder of agricultural chemistry. When the American edition of Liebig's *Chemistry in Its Application to Physiology and Agriculture* appeared in 1847, Whitman raved about it in the *Eagle*. "Chemistry!" he wrote. "The elevating, beautiful, study. . . . Chemistry—which involves the essences of creation, and the changes, and the growths, and formations and decays of so large a constituent part of the earth, and the things thereof!" Liebig's fame, he noted, was "as wide as the civilized world—a fame nobler than that of generals, or of many bright geniuses."

Liebig presented a scientific rationale for what would become one of Whitman's main answers to cynics: even if matter were all, nature constantly regenerates itself and turns death into life through chemical transformation. The cyclical quality of all natural things was commonly emphasized by scientists of the day. Liebig gave the idea validity through the study of transferred chemical compounds. When an organism decomposed, its atoms were chemically recombined, immediately giving rise, in his words, "to another arrangement of the atoms of a body, that is, to the production of a compound which did not before exist in it." Every thirty years, he estimated, nearly a billion people and several billion animals died and were absorbed into the earth. Their atoms became transferred to the earth, rocks, and the varieties of plant life, whose atoms in turn became the source of new life. Whatever diseases they had were lost in the transforming process.

There seemed, then, to be an ongoing resurrection and a democratic exchange of substances inherent in nature. Just as Liebig wrote that "the active state of the atoms of one body has an influence upon the atoms of a body in contact with it," so Whitman announced in the second line of his opening poem that "every atom belonging to me as good belongs to you." As Liebig said that after death humans are changed into other things, so Whitman could write: "We are Nature [...] / We become plants, trunks, foliage, roots, bark, / We are bedded in the ground, we are rocks, / We are oaks." If Liebig envisaged an exchange of life-forms through decomposition and regrowth, so Whitman fashioned metaphors that vivified the idea of the ceaseless springing of life from death. "Tenderly will I use you curling grass, / It may be you transpire from the breasts of young men." "The smallest sprout shows there is really no death." "And as to you Corpse I think you are good manure, but that does not offend me, / I smell the white roses sweet-scented and growing, / I reach to the leafy lips, I reach to the polish'd breasts of melons." Liebig wrote that "the miasms and certain contagious matters [that] produce diseases in the human organism" become "not *contagious*" when the organism is absorbed into the earth. This becomes the central point of Whitman's poem "This Compost." He asks the earth in amazement: "Are they not continually putting distemper'd corpses within you? /...Where have you drawn off all the foul and liquid meat?" Then he provides the Liebigian answer:

> Behold this compost! behold it well!
> Perhaps every mite has once form'd part of a sick person—yet
>   behold!
> The grass of spring covers the prairies,
> The bean bursts noiselessly through the mould in the garden, [...]
> The resurrection of the wheat appears with pale visage out of its
>   graves, [...]
>
> What chemistry!
> That the winds are really not infectious,
> That this is no cheat, this transparent green-wash of the sea which is
>   so amorous after me, [...]
> That all is clean forever and forever.

The very title *Leaves of Grass,* and Whitman's constant play on foliage and leaves in his poetry, stem in part from propositions about plant life popularized by Liebig and others. For years after *Leaves of Grass* first appeared, Whitman heard complaints about its title. "What a fight I had for that name," he later recalled. "Who ever knew of a *Leaf* of Grass? There were *spears* of grass—but leaves? Oh! no!" But then a scientist assured him that "leaf" was the correct usage, saying that "whatever was the case in literature, in science *leaves* of grass there were and doubtless would be." Whether or not Whitman had originally chosen "leaves" for its scientific associations, at least one scientific writer he read, Liebig, had used the term broadly to signify the "green parts of all plants," including grass. Liebig underscored the essential function of leaves, which, he showed, constantly absorbed carbon to nourish "every part of an organism of a plant." When fused by Whitman with the literary pun on "leaves" (meaning the pages of a book), the scientific reference reflected his dream that the book, like grass leaves, would sprout in all regions and nourish its readers.

Whitman also found in science confirmation of his optimistic instincts about the origin and nature of humans and their place in nature. Although materialism lurked in the background of scientific thought, most scientists before Darwin were not pessimistic about nature and species. In the first half of the nineteenth century what might be called a progressive consensus emerged among naturalists and biologists. This consensus variously found expression in England's numerous *Bridgewater Treatises* in the 1830s, followed the next decade by several immensely popular books: *Vestiges of the Natural History of Creation* (1844) by the Edinburgh biologist Robert Chambers, *Old Red Sandstone* (1841) by the Scottish Hugh Miller, and the Prussian geographer Alexander von Humboldt's *Kosmos,* published in four volumes between 1845 and 1862. Not only were these works widely read in America, but in 1846 the Swiss naturalist Louis Agassiz relocated to the United States, devoting the remaining decades of his life to promoting an idealistic version of progressive science.

According to the progressive view, the earth and other astronomical bodies were originally formed from huge floating gaseous clouds, called nebulae, that rotated and condensed into matter. In Chambers's version of the theory in *Vestiges of Creation*, the universe was formed of gases that developed constantly toward man. (By a poetic metonymy, Whitman enacted this idea when he wrote in "Crossing Brooklyn Ferry," "I too had been struck from the float forever held in solution.") The earth was not young, as the Bible suggested and as previous scientists had believed, but instead was very old; the Scottish geologist James Hutton actually called it indefinitely old. Although the earth's extreme age seemed to contravene the Bible's teachings, scientists in general did not abandon religious faith.

On the contrary, they believed that every aspect of physical creation revealed a divine plan. They accepted the so-called argument from design, introduced in the late seventeenth century and given fresh life by William Paley's classic *Natural Theology* (1802), which taught that everything in the universe was so well adapted to its uses that it revealed God's benignity. The elegantly efficient joints of the hand and the intricate mechanism of the eye were the kinds of everyday miracles the scientists pointed to. When the Harpers brought out a new edition of *Natural Theology* in 1847, Whitman argued that it gave scientific proof of the sacredness of physical things. "If the undevout astronomer is mad, the undevout physiologist is equally so," he wrote. "For all the great harmony of purpose evinced in the structure and movements of worlds, is evinced—to our mind quite as wonderfully—in the structure and frame of animals and other growing life. Dr. Paley's 'Natural Theology' but systematises this great point."

The more idealistic scientists, like Chambers, argued that species were always progressing, with simple organisms always developing over time into complex ones, eventually becoming human beings and pointing even higher. Chambers echoed the idea, introduced in the 1760s by the Swiss naturalist Charles Bonnet, that humans have experienced many past incarnations in a series of ever-ascending organisms.

In Whitman's poems, the optimism of progressive science is figured forth as heady exuberance. No scientific idealist reveled in common natural experience to the extent he did. The "I" of "Song of Myself" announces that his armpit aroma is finer than any prayer, that his head is finer than all the churches and creeds, that a mouse is miracle enough to stagger sextillions of infidels. In another poem Whitman writes, "How beautiful and perfect are the animals! / How perfect the earth, and the minutest thing upon it!" All of these images argue from design with a vengeance. If the scientists called the earth indefinitely old, Whitman reveled in the sense of infinity: "A few quadrillions of eras, a few octillions of cubic leagues, [...] / They are but parts, any thing is but a part." Just as several scientists believed that people have evolved upward through many different organisms, he called life "the leavings of many deaths" and added, "No doubt I have died myself ten thousand times before." In one passage he gives what reads like a précis of Robert Chambers's evolutionary theory, complete with nebula and progress over time through varied forms:

> Cycles ferried my cradle, rowing and rowing like cheerful boatmen,
>   [...]
>
> Before I was born out of my mother generations guided me,
> My embryo has never been torpid, nothing could overlay it.
>
> For it the nebula cohered to an orb,
> The long slow strata piled to rest it on,
> Vast vegetables gave it sustenance,
> Monstrous sauroids transported it in their mouths and deposited it
>   with care.
>
> All forces have been steadily employ'd to complete and delight me,
> Now on this spot I stand with my robust soul.

In another passage he imagines climbing the evolutionary ladder, his feet striking "an apex of the apices of the stairs, / On every step bunches of ages." Having communicated this giddy message of evolutionary progress, he looks backward down time's ladder to "the huge first Nothing" and even envisages having rested for ages in the misty nebula:

I know I was even there,
I waited unseen and always, and slept through the lethargic mist,
And took my time, and took no hurt from the fetid carbon.

To communicate his sense of embodying all time and nature, Whitman fastened on the word "kosmos." The word was so important to him that it was the only one he retained in the different versions of his famous self-identification in "Song of Myself," which first read "Walt Whitman, an American, one of the roughs, a kosmos" and ended up as "Walt Whitman, a kosmos, of Manhattan the son." He also wrote a whole poem titled "Kosmos." The word, which had been popularized by the Prussian naturalist Alexander von Humboldt, epitomized the progressive scientists' vision of the universe. In 1834 Humboldt, who had published earlier studies of terrestrial magnetism and animal electricity, announced in a letter, "I have the crazy notion to depict in a single work the entire material universe, all that we know of the phenomena of heaven and earth, from the nebulae of the stars to the geography of mosses and granite rocks—and in a vivid style that will stimulate and elicit feeling." The first volume of his *Kosmos* appeared in 1845, when Humboldt was seventy-six, the second two years later, the third in 1850. *Kosmos* was spectacularly received; it was immediately translated into several languages—the English title was *Cosmos: A Sketch of a Physical Description of the Universe*—and by 1851 eighty thousand copies had sold.

Its appeal lay in its combination of factual data and comforting message. Providing descriptions of phenomena from the distant vastness of the Milky Way to the most minute organisms, it pictured nature not in chaos or conflict but as a source of calmness, always in equilibrium, with humans as the acme of creation. The scientist's pleasure, wrote Humboldt, is "the contemplation of all created things, which are linked together and form one *whole*, animated by internal forces." Cosmos he defined as a "harmoniously ordered whole" and nature as "a harmony, or blending together of all created things, however dissimilar in form and attributes, one great whole animated by the breath of life."

The infinite diversity but ultimate order suggested by the notion of cosmos is what made the word meaningful to Whitman. Several of his poems shuttle between distant expanses and minute phenomena, much the way Humboldt had. One thinks especially of the famous Section 5 of "Song of Myself," where, after lying on the grass with his soul, the "I" contemplates the vast creation and then turns his attention to ever-smaller things: the limitless leaves drooping in the fields, the brown ants underground, heaped stones, mullein and pokeweed. For Whitman as for

Humboldt, "cosmos" signified both the order of nature and the centrality of human beings. Humboldt said he wished to present nature not only in its "external manifestations" but "its image, reflected in the mind of man." He thus devoted the second volume of *Kosmos* to representations of nature in literature and painting, gauging what he called "the impressions reflected by the external sense on the feelings, and on the poetic imagination of mankind." Whitman was well aware of the centrality of humans in Humboldt's scheme. In the margin of an 1849 magazine article he wrote, "Humboldt, in his Kosmos, citing Schiller, has observed of the Greeks: 'With them the landscape is always the mere background, of a picture, in the foreground of which human figures are moving.'"

"Kosmos," then, was ready-made for poetic adaptation, since it gathered together nature, intuition, and art. Whitman in his poem "Kosmos" (he retained the "K" of the German) associated the word with a person in tune with all things, one

> Who includes diversity and is Nature,
> Who is the amplitude of the earth, and the coarseness and sexuality
>   of the earth, and the great charity of the earth, and the
>   equilibrium also, [...]
> Who, out of the theory of the earth and of his or her body
>   understands by subtle analogies all other theories,
> The theory of a city, a poem, and of the large politics of these States;
> Who believes not only in our globe with its sun and moon, but in
>   other globes with their suns and moons,
> Who, constructing the house of himself or herself, not for a day but
>   for all times, sees races, eras, dates, generations,
> The past, the future, dwelling there, like space, inseparable together.

This poem suggests that Whitman's sense of "kosmos" was deeply influenced by Humboldt. If Humboldt uses the word to present a theory of the earth and the heavens, so does Whitman. The earth-centered vision that later made Humboldt recognized as the father of modern geography is reflected in Whitman's repeated emphasis on the earth and the globe. Both the scientist and the poet are interested too in distant astronomical bodies—what Whitman calls "other globes with their suns and moons." Both include in "kosmos" a sense of the mystical and the aesthetic, and both use the term as an all-unifying force, making the most diverse things seem, in Whitman's closing words, "inseparable together." The all-embracing significance of the word was confirmed in Whitman's definition of "kosmos" in his notebook as "noun masculine or feminine, a person who[se] scope of mind, or whose range in a particular science, includes all, the whole known universe."

One might think, given Whitman's mind-set, that he would have been jarred by the advent of Darwinism, perhaps to the extent of removing some of the optimistic nature images from his poems. But Darwin didn't ruffle him. In old age he would declare, "I believe in Darwinianism and evolution from A to izzard." He didn't try to dismiss Darwin, as did, for instance, the idealistic Louis Agassiz. Nor was he driven to the kind of post-Darwinian gloom expressed by Melville in *Clarel.* His response was much like that of many American thinkers who qualified Darwin's vision of a violent, arbitrary universe with a more hopeful explanation derived from the early nineteenth-century evolutionist Jean-Baptiste Lamarck. Lamarck had introduced the doctrine of the inheritability of acquired characters: that is, traits acquired through effort were passed on to offspring. By emphasizing environment and nurture, Lamarck held up the hopeful prospect that humanity could constantly progress through self-control. Lamarckism became popular in America because it suggested that humans were not simply slaves of blind mechanical forces but could control their destiny.

Whitman probably did not read Lamarck in the early going but picked up his ideas secondhand. He may have read the 1852 article favoring Lamarck by Herbert Spencer, later the foremost popularizer of the idea of endless progress through self-improvement. A form of Lamarckism was interwoven with the phrenological teachings of Orson and Lorenzo Fowler. In their 1847 book *Hereditary Descent,* which mentioned one of Whitman's ancestors, the Fowlers stressed the importance of parental behavior on the physical and moral health of offspring.

The Fowler establishment in Manhattan was the center of virtually every scientific and pseudoscientific movement. We have seen how one movement, physiology, influenced Whitman's treatment of sex. An equally important movement for him was phrenology, the nineteenth century's version of psychology. Phrenology, the pseudoscience that taught that all beliefs and character traits were produced by specific brain "organs," had originated abroad with the Viennese scientist Franz Josef Gall and his pupil Johannes Gaspar Spurzheim. In August 1832 the tall, distinguished Spurzheim arrived in America to promote his doctrines, and though he died within four months of his arrival, he sparked a phrenology craze in America. The British writer Harriet Martineau declared, "When Spurzheim was in America, the great mass of society became phrenologists in a day, wherever he appeared." Emerson said he had one of the world's greatest minds. His ideas spread to Amherst College, where the students Henry Ward Beecher and Orson Fowler caught the fever. Four years later, Orson established the Phrenological Cabinet on Manhattan's Park Row, moving it the next year into Clinton Hall at 286 Broadway, where it remained until 1854. The Cabinet became a New York landmark, with its displays of plaster casts of murderers, thieves, hyenas, tigers, and a number of celebrities. The Fowlers also ran their publishing business and a skull-examining practice, with Orson doing most of the writing and Lorenzo the bump reading. They took phrenology on the road, lecturing to huge audiences all over the country and giving individual consultations for a price.

Whitman caught the phrenology bug in 1846, when he heard Orson Fowler lecture. Exulting in Fowler's idea that any mental faculty could be developed through exercise, Whitman wrote, "If the professor can, as he professes, teach men to know their intellectual and moral deficiencies and remedy them, we do not see that our people may long remain imperfect." In the *Eagle* he reviewed several phrenological books, including one by Spurzheim, and praised Fowlers and Wells: "Among the most persevering workers in phrenology in this country, must certainly be reckoned the two Fowlers and Mr. Wells." On July 16, 1849, Whitman went to Clinton Hall to have his head examined by the quiet, learned Lorenzo Fowler. In subjecting himself to phrenological analysis, he was doing nothing unusual. Among others who had their skulls read were Edgar Allan Poe, Margaret Fuller, Horace Greeley, Lydia Sigourney, Brigham Young, Hiram Powers, Lydia Maria Child, Edwin Forrest, and Mark Twain.

Whitman had reason to be pleased with the result of his skull exam. On a numbering system of 1 to 7 (with the high score of 7 indicating the largest size of a brain section), Whitman got a 6 to 7 in Self-Esteem and Caution and a 6 in Amativeness, Adhesiveness, Philoprogenitiveness, Concentrativeness, and Combativeness. He must have been cheered by Fowler's assessment, "You are yourself at all times," and a bit puzzled by his low scores of 4 in Tune and 5 in Language—not good signs for a budding bard. Lorenzo was dead wrong when he predicted that Whitman would marry young and only partly right when he said he loved children, home, and pets. But Whitman was sufficiently happy that he published his phrenological chart on four different occasions.

He also sprinkled phrenological terms throughout his poetry. In the 1855 preface he included the phrenologist among "the lawgivers of poets" and added phrenological force to his description of the poet by saying he has "large hope and comparison and fondness for women and children, large alimentiveness and destructiveness and causality." Phrenology taught that everyone possessed a unique blend of characteristics, an idea communicated in the first version of "Song of the Broad-Axe":

> Never offering others always offering himself, corroborating his
>   phrenology,
> Voluptuous, inhabitive, combative, conscientious, alimentive,
>   intuitive, of copious friendship, sublimity, firmness, self-esteem,
>   comparison, individuality, form, locality, eventuality.

In his notebook he associated various disorders with the size of brain segments, quoting Orson Fowler to say that morality and talent are influenced by physical habits. His interest in phrenology lasted long after the craze had died out, in spite of friends who kidded him about it. In old age he confessed, "I probably have not got by the phrenology stage yet."

The Fowlers had changed phrenology, mainly an intellectual concern abroad, into a popular program for self-help. In their efforts to Americanize phrenology, they simplified it and made it utilitarian, much to the chagrin of their counterparts in Europe, who dismissed them as panderers to the masses. Phrenology was often associated by its critics with materialistic fatalism, since it seemed to fix character in the brain, but this was not how the Fowlers saw it. The numbers they assigned to the various brain areas had a definite purpose: a low number suggested that a certain organ was too small and must be developed by exercise of that particular trait; a large number, by the same token, suggested that a trait had to be controlled so that it did not become dominant.

Above all, the Fowlers advised keeping the various brain sections and other bodily functions in equilibrium. Theirs was a holistic outlook that emphasized maintaining balance in every aspect of physical and mental being. Anything that threatened that balance could cause insanity or physical disease. It was not the brain alone that signaled well-being: all other bodily parts did too. Everything about a person—the walk, the laugh, the lips, eyes, skin, voice, gestures—betrayed character. Whitman echoed this holistic view in several poems, including "I Sing the Body Electric":

> [T]he expression of a well-made man appears not only in his face,
> It is in his limbs and joints also, it is curiously in the joints of his
>   hips and wrists,
> It is in his walk, the carriage of his neck, the flex of his waist and
>   knees.

Character imbalances, the Fowlers argued, sometimes made people look or act like animals. "Some men," they wrote, "closely resemble one or another of the animal species, in both looks and character; that is, have an eagle, or bull-dog, or lion, or baboon expression of face, and when they do, have the corresponding characteristics." When Whitman wanted to communicate moments of psychological imbalance, he used such imagery. Describing dark traits like anger and guile and lust in "Crossing Brooklyn Ferry," he used animal metaphors: "The wolf, the snake, the hog, not wanting in me."

What was most hopeful about the Fowlers' program was that they offered methods of repairing such imbalances. One was vigorous self-reprimand. If a person was on the verge of addiction to a certain vice or excess, he or she was enjoined to shout inwardly against that vice. In outlining a remedy for the widespread vice of masturbation, for instance, Orson Fowler used capitalization to suggest how one should talk to oneself:

> TOTAL ABSTINENCE IS LIFE; animal, intellectual, moral. INDUL-
> GENCE IS TRIPLE DEATH! RESOLUTION—DETERMINATION
> TO STOP NOW AND FOREVER—is your starting point; without
> which no other remedial agents will avail anything. ABSTINENCE
> OR DEATH is your only alternative. STOP NOW AND FOREVER, or
> abandon all hope.

Some of Whitman's most revealing notebook entries show that he had learned the technique of self-reprimand. In an entry of 1861 he announced: "I have resolv'd to inaugurate for myself a pure perfect sweet, cleanblooded robust body by ignoring all drinks but water and pure milk—and all fat meats late suppers—a great body—a purged, cleansed, spiritualised and invigorated body—." This was straightforward Fowlerian self-control. The Fowlers and their ilk regularly advised avoidance of meat, coffee, tobacco, and alcohol.

The most famous of all his notebook entries, the 1870 one in which he struggled to come to terms with his feelings toward his friend Peter Doyle, showed him again using the kind of self-reprimand the Fowlers had advised. For the Fowlers and for Whitman, adhesiveness, or friendship between people of the same sex, was an essential part of the human mind. A central tenet of phrenology was that humans were social beings who were healthy only when they maintained close relations with others. The social instincts of adhesiveness (friendship) and amativeness (love between the sexes) were thought to occupy a large section of the brain and thus had tremendous power for good or ill. When naturally developed, adhesiveness fostered intimacy of feeling or interest.

But when either adhesiveness or amativeness became overactive, the results on the mind could be disastrous. As Orson Fowler wrote, "When inflamed, fevered, dissatisfied, or irritated, [the social organs] inflame every other portion of the brain, throwing it into violent commotion, especially the *animal propensities;* but if their action is natural, if they are properly placed, they put to rest the other animal propensities."

When struggling with his feelings about Doyle in his diary, Whitman wrestled with such inflamed feelings:

TO GIVE UP ABSOLUTELY *& for good, from the present hour, this* FEVERISH, FLUCTUATING, *useless,* UNDIGNIFIED PURSUIT *of 16.4* [Peter Doyle]—*too long, (much too long)* persevered in,—so humiliating— —*It must come at last &* had better come now— *(It cannot possibly be a success)* LET THERE FROM THIS HOUR BE NO FALTERING, NO GETTING *at all henceforth,* (NOT ONCE, *under any circumstances*) —*avoid seeing her* [originally "him"], *or meeting her, or any talk or explanations* —or ANY MEETING WHATEVER, FROM THIS HOUR FORTH, FOR LIFE   July 15 '70

Outline sketch of a superb calm character [...]

His analogy is as of the earth, complete in itself, enfolding in itself
    all processes of growth effusing life & power, for hidden purposes

Depress the adhesive nature/
It is in excess—making life a torment/
Ah this diseased, feverish, disproportionate adhesiveness/

The most genuinely confessional of all Whitman's writings, this scrambled passage has been variously interpreted as an unequivocal expression of homosexuality and as a massive repression of the homosexual urge. But the vocabulary of modern psychology was not available to Whitman. He used instead the discourse of phrenological self-regulation, as popularized by his friends the Fowlers. Internalizing the language of the phrenologists, he says here that his "adhesiveness" has become "diseased, feverish, disproportionate" and warns himself to "Depress the adhesive nature." The main weight of his effort is to bring this inflamed inclination under control, to regain mental equilibrium. His first strategy, as with the Fowlers, is the strong self-reprimand. Just as they said that the first step toward self-correction was the "DETERMINATION TO STOP NOW AND FOREVER," so he tells himself "TO GIVE UP ABSOLUTELY" the pursuit of Doyle, warning sternly, "LET THERE FROM THIS HOUR BE NO FALTERING."

Interwoven with these strong resolutions are reminders of what a person in equilibrium is like. Whitman plans a sketch of "a superb calm character," echoing an earlier notebook entry in which he told himself to develop "A Cool, gentle (LESS DEMONSTRATIVE) MORE UNIFORM DEMEANOR" and "to live *a more Serene, Calm, Philosophic Life.—reticent, far more reticent*—yet cheerful, with pleased spirit and pleased manner." Behind these reminders lay the phrenological conviction that inner balance could be gained through exercise of the will. Whitman's generally calm demeanor, interrupted only sporadically by tempestuous outbursts, reflected his overall success in maintaining serenity.

He was always proud that his faculty of caution scored high on his phrenological chart. Explaining his temperament to a friend, he once declared, "I have always been very cautious—you know, the phrenologists put my caution at 6–7." If, as his diary entry on Doyle proved, he could be as inwardly convulsive as he claimed American society as a whole was, he could help calm both private and social turbulence by regulating his poetic persona in such a way that caution and detachment were highlighted. "Extreme caution or prudence" were the first qualities he assigned to the poet in the 1855 preface. He emphasized, "Caution seldom goes far enough." In his poetry his caution finds expression in a persona who, despite moments of extreme passion, remains ultimately self-possessed:

Apart from the pulling and hauling stands what I am,
Stands amused, complacent, compassionating, idle, unitary, [...]
Both in and out of the game, watching and wondering at it.

This posture of cool detachment was very possibly a cover for tumultuous feelings Whitman struggled to control, just as the "superb calm character" he outlines in the Doyle passage is at least partly an idealized self designed to counterbalance tendencies he called "diseased, feverish, disproportionate." His affirmations of equilibrium stemmed from the therapeutic programs presented by the scientific theorists of his time. Just as today many seek psychological counseling to restore balance to the mind and strength to the ego, so Whitman used the crypto-psychological approaches available to him in an effort to regain equilibrium.

Religion and Philosophy

SCIENCE, WHITMAN BELIEVED, could take humans only so far in explaining their origins and destiny. "Hurrah for positive science!" he writes in "Song of Myself." "Long live exact demonstration!" But then he says to scientists: "Your facts are useful, yet they are not my dwelling, / I but enter by them to an area of my dwelling."

Religion and philosophy helped address some of the larger questions left unanswered by science. Until fairly recently, it has been fashionable among twentieth-century critics to emphasize the more worldly aspects of his vision. For Whitman and his contemporary inner circle, however, neglect of his religious themes amounted to little less than sacrilege. In summing up his career in 1872, he generalized that from the start in his poetry "one deep purpose underlay the others, and has underlain it and its execution ever since—and that has been the religious purpose." The poet, in his words, was the "divine literatus" who replaced the priest. America, he constantly stressed, could be rescued from materialism and infidelity only by literature that pointed to the spiritual and moral. He clung to a faith in immortality. "I am not prepared," he told Traubel, "to admit fraud in the scheme of the universe—yet without immortality all would be sham and sport of the most tragic nature."

These were not just the pious meanderings of old age. True, as some have noted, Whitman's poetry became more spiritual over time, but a strong religious element had been there from the beginning. His Brooklyn friend Helen Price found his "leading characteristic" to be "the *religious sentiment* or feeling. It pervades and dominates his life." His Washington friend Peter Doyle confirmed that Whitman "had pretty vigorous ideas on religion" and, in particular, defended the idea of immortality. It was the religious element in Whitman's poetry that led to the formation of several Whitman-related cults. Richard Maurice Bucke, the Canadian alienist who was close to Whitman late in life, integrated Whitman's poetic religion into what he called a cosmic philosophy. The culmination of this religious appropriation of Whitman was the church founded on the poet's teachings in Bolton, England, where devotees gathered weekly and reverently read his verse aloud.

If the piety of Whitman's poetry was so clear to many of his contemporaries, why was it lost from view in much later commentary on him? Part of the explanation lies in the prevailing interest in the erotic and the psychological in our post-Freudian age. Many have preferred to contemplate Whitman as Oedipal father-hater and mother-lover or Whitman as homosexual rather than Whitman as religious seer.

But an even more significant explanation, one that gets at the heart of his religious purpose, is that the earthly and the spiritual are so closely intertwined in his verse that it is easy to miss the spiritual dimension altogether, or to dismiss it as window dressing. The religious and philosophical currents that influenced him themselves represented adventurous combinations of the physical and the mystical.

The distance between mainstream religion and progressive science was not great in his day. To the contrary, pre-Darwinian religious thinkers and philosophers made great efforts to align themselves with scientific theory in order to gain intellectual credibility. Several of the religiophilosophical currents that affected Whitman—particularly German idealistic philosophy, Boston Unitarianism, and Transcendentalism—were, in many respects, idealistic versions of an already religiously oriented scientific vision.

The close relation between the philosophical and scientific was exemplified by the essays in a philosophical volume Whitman loved, Frederic Henry Hedge's *Prose Writers of Germany,* which the poet called "a big valuable book." He owned a copy that was given him by a friend, F. S. Gray, inscribed August 29, 1862. But he had been aware of the volume long before that, perhaps as early as 1847, when it was first published, and almost certainly by 1852, when another edition appeared. Whitman did not have much firsthand exposure to European Romantic philosophy but received it through edited collections like Hedge's and through magazine articles he clipped. Although it was not until the 1860s that German philosophers, particularly Hegel, had a profound effect on him, their impact was visible in the early poems as well.

The major German thinkers of the eighteenth century and the Romantic era were represented in Hedge's volume. Some were connected with progressive science in direct ways. Immanuel Kant, for example, developed the nebular hypothesis later popularized by Chambers and poeticized by Whitman. All the philosophers in the volume accepted the argument from design that was an underpinning of progressive science. Sometimes their expression of the outlook approached a kind of pre-Whitmanian mysticism. The physiologist Johann Caspar Lavater emphasized the miraculous nature of apparently insignificant things: "Each particle of matter is an immensity; each leaf a world; each insect an inexplicable compendium." Whitman would write in the same vein that a tree toad is the chef d'oeuvre of the highest, a leaf of grass is the journeywork of the stars, and so on. Lavater also initiated the rhapsodic listing of body parts repeated by American physiologists and echoed by Whitman. If Whitman and his physiologist friends loved recording the interconnected particulars of the body from head to trunk to toe, that had all been presaged by Lavater, who sang praise to "The eye, the looks, the cheeks, the mouth, the forehead. . . . From the head to the back, from shoulder to the arm, from the arm to the hand, from the hand to the finger, from the root to the stem, the stem to the branch, the branch to the twig to the blossom and fruit, each depends on the other."

The German thinkers brought to physical science fresh speculation on the mind and spirit. Whitman once said that the most profound theme was "the relation between the (radical, democratic) Me" and "the (conservative) Not Me, the whole of the material objective universe." Kant was only partly helpful to him on this issue. Kant's argument that exterior reality was shaped by primary ideas within the mind gave rise to a subjectivism he felt uncomfortable with. Subjectivism ultimately made Emersonian Transcendentalism distasteful to him. Emerson had opened up possibilities of self-reliance and poetic creativity but had also taken Kant's subjectivism to what Whitman came to feel was a relativist extreme. More appealing to him than Kantian subjectivism was the synthetic idealism of Friedrich von Schelling and Friedrich Hegel. Schelling, he saw, conceived of analogies that brought matter and spirit into unity, while Hegel struck him as resolving the problem of evil. Hegel taught of a spirit pervading all phenomena, emerging from antagonistic forces. Whitman wrote that Hegel proved matter and spirit were "held together by a central and never-broken unity," radiations of "one consistent and eternal purpose." Anyone who did not see the unity but only darkness and despair Whitman called "the most radical sinner and infidel." Hegel accorded with Whitman's jingoism, since the all-resolving philosopher seemed to parallel the all-tolerating America.

Hegel's influence on Whitman's later poetry is undeniable. The 1865 poem "Chanting the Square Deific" posits the idea of a "Santa Spirita" absorbing heterogenous religions and even Satan himself, comparable to Hegel's all-pervading spirit resolving contradictions. A late poem titled "Roaming in Thought (*After Reading Hegel*)" has him thinking that "the vast all that is call'd Evil I saw hastening to merge itself and become lost and dead." Some elements of Hegelianism, such as an idealistic denial of the finality of evil, are present even in the original 1855 poems.

To mention the effect of German idealism on Whitman, however, is to neglect the specifically American characteristics of his vision. There was a radically egalitarian dimension to American Protestantism that he observed with interest. One of his favorite sermons was "Self-Culture" (1838) by the highly influential Unitarian leader William Ellery Channing. In the *Eagle* he wrote: "No terms are too high for speaking of this little work. . . . We have always considered it an unsurpassed piece, either as to its matter or manner." Like the German idealists and the progressive scientists, Channing brought attention to the miraculous nature of commonplace things. The idea of self-improvement, also central to the idealistic view, was reiterated in Channing's declaration that we all have the power of "acting on, determining, and forming ourselves." The powerfully egalitarian side of Channing's doctrine surely appealed to Whitman as he turned from veneration of social rulers to respect for everyday workers. "The truly great are to be found everywhere," Channing wrote—in the shop, in the field, in all the trades. Egalitarianism, which would spring forth in Whitman in reaction to the political crisis of the fifties, had assumed a distinctly religious aura in Channing's essay, an aura also felt in Whitman's images of the divine house framer, the mechanic's wife intervening for all mankind, and the snag-toothed hostler redeeming sins.

The secular, egalitarian liberal religion Channing represented increasingly characterized other forms of Protestantism in nineteenth-century America. No foreign country saw the explosion of working-class evangelical Protestantism that came in the wake of the Second Great Awakening in America. The evangelical groups that grew most dramatically, especially the Methodists and Baptists, were promoted by an intense zeal manifested in conversion "exercises" like running, barking, dancing, convulsions, a zeal captured in Whitman's line about a religious convert "Ranting and frothing in my insane crisis." Evangelical religion was spread by a vigorous, lively brand of preaching that made use of slang and humor. That Whitman thought some evangelists went too far in their preaching is suggested by a sketch he made for a story: "Introduce some scene in a religious revival meeting—Make a character of a ranting religious exhorter—sincere, but a great fool."

By the late 1840s this imaginative, anecdotal preaching had moved out of the frontier and into the cities. Brooklyn's Henry Ward Beecher made such extensive use of jokes and illustrations that he was once called a combination of Saint Paul and P. T. Barnum. As seen, Whitman was rapturous about Beecher when he saw him in 1849. For the *Eagle* he had written a regular column on the style of local preachers. In time, his fascination with popular preaching style made him susceptible to the pulpit eloquence of the homespun sailors' preacher Edward Thompson Taylor, whom he called America's "one essentially perfect orator," and later to Brooklyn's T. De Witt Talmage, whose lively sermons he enjoyed.

It might seem odd that Whitman on the one hand violently rejected American churches and on the other was vitally interested in American preaching and religion. But in a time when mainstream religion was becoming increasingly secular, promoters of religion could be thoroughly enjoyed without reference to the churches with which they were associated. Whitman wrote in his pre-1855 notebook, "The new theologies bring forward man," specifying later: "It is America that makes the radical change involving new stages many thousand years to come." Beecher and several other ministers became stars of the lyceum circuit. As a come-outer, Whitman separated someone like Beecher from church religion. "It was only fair to say of Beecher that he was not a minister," he said. "There was so much of him man there was little left of him to be minister." Beecher was emblematic of a larger secularizing tendency in American popular culture signaled also by the sudden explosion of religious fiction and poetry. The church leader William Ellery Channing conceded in 1841, "The press is a mightier power than the pulpit." Best-selling novels like Susan Warner's *The Wide, Wide World* and Maria Cummins's *The Lamplighter,* and hundreds of lesser-known works, promoted a simplified religion that had little to do with doctrine and much to do with feeling and behavior.

Whitman's advocacy of nondenominational "religion" in secular poetry, then, was not unusual, although some commentators, especially foreign ones, thought he went too far in combining the sacred and the secular. A British reviewer found his effort to imitate "our divine English Bible in poems where the jargon of the slums is mixed with Bible phraseology and bad Spanish and worse French is a sacrilege which every lover of the Bible finds it hard to condone."

But such linguistic mixtures were in keeping with the increasingly showmanlike nature of popular American religion. Not only did Whitman participate in the revolution in popular religious style, but *Leaves of Grass* in turn fed back into popular religion. Some of Whitman's images—such as the line in "Song of Myself," "I find letters from God dropt in the street, and every one is sign'd by God's name"—were picked up, predictably enough, by the era's leading preacher, Henry Ward Beecher. Such images were thoroughly compatible with Beecher's folksy style. Whitman called Beecher "a great absorber of Leaves of Grass," and he said he often met people who, having just heard Beecher preach, told him that "his whole sermon was you, you, you, from top to toe." Another preacher who cribbed from him was the Philadelphia liberal John Herbert Clifford, who, much to the poet's delight, read long passages from "Song of Myself" and "There Was a Child Went Forth" from the pulpit.

Whitman was in tune not only with the stylistic revolution but with other dramatic changes in American religion. Surging revivalism, the throes of the market economy, and the rise of mass print culture combined to make nineteenth-century America a remarkably fertile breeding ground of new religions. The Shakers, the Mormons, the Oneidan perfectionists, Phoebe Palmer's perfectionist Methodists, the Seventh-Day Adventists, the spiritualists, and the Harmonialists all sprang up between the Revolution and the Civil War, with Christian Science and New Thought coming later. Several of the new movements were based on freshly inspired sacred writings meant to supplant or complement the Bible. Most famously, in 1820 a young Vermont man, Joseph Smith, reportedly had directions from Jesus and God to found a new religion; he later claimed he had found golden plates, which he translated as *The Book of Mormon*, first published in 1830. Such illuminism, or direct illumination from God, informed other inspired texts such as Andrew Jackson Davis's *The Great Harmonia* (1850) and Mary Baker Eddy's *Science and Health with Key to the Scriptures* (1875). A form of illuminism touched secular writers as well, including Emerson, who in the famous "transparent eye-ball" passage in *Nature* announced himself "part or particle of God," and Harriet Beecher Stowe, who claimed it was God, not she, who wrote *Uncle Tom's Cabin*.

Whitman's role as a poetic seer writing a prophetic, supposedly inspired text with strongly biblical resonances was in keeping with the illuminist spirit of the era. If other Americans were founding new religions, so, in a sense, was he: a poetic religion based on progressive science and idealist philosophy that preached the miracle of the commonplace and the possibilities of the soul. In promoting religion in his poetry, he could sound much like a nineteenth-century showman peddling wares: "Magnifying and applying come I, / Outbidding at the start the old cautious hucksters," as he went on to review all the world religions and then proclaim the miraculous nature of the everyday world. He was conscious from the start about writing a supposedly inspired text. His messianic mission was made clear in the 1855 preface, in which he said of the poet, "The time straying toward infidelity and confections he withholds by his steady faith." He gave a recipe for salvation, including the command, "read these leaves in the open air every season of every year of your life." This mission became, if anything, stronger with time, as evidenced by his June 1857 notebook entry: "*The Great Construction of the New Bible* / Not to be diverted from the principal object—the main life work—." He saw that he was one of many who were initiating new religions. He confidently threw his hat into the ring:

> I too, following many and follow'd by many, inaugurate a religion, I
>   descend into the arena, [...]
> I say the real and permanent grandeur of these States must be their
>   religion,
> Otherwise there is no real and permanent grandeur.

To place him in the camp of nineteenth-century Americans who were inaugurating new religions is not to say that he was solely preoccupied with American religious developments. His notebooks of the late

1850s betray a real interest in foreign and historical religions as well. The religion of ancient Egypt represented for him the miracle of life, as in its worship of the beetle and the sun. India to him meant rhapsody, passiveness, meditation, and Greece the celebration of beauty and the natural world. Christianity stood for love, gentleness, morality, and purity, although he noted its history of harsh penances and religious wars.

The fact remains, however, that if he had much exposure to foreign religions before 1855, he apparently left few records of it. For example, when Thoreau asked him in 1856 whether he had read the Asian scriptures, he replied, "No: tell me about them." Of course, he could have learned about Asian and other world religions secondhand through Emerson, but his early knowledge of Emerson is itself wreathed in mystery. His friend O'Connor denied he had read Emerson before 1855, and the poet in old age repeated the statement.

To be sure, such denials were in part sour grapes on the part of Whitman and his circle, who became increasingly hostile to Emerson as the latter cooled to Whitman's verse. Actually, Whitman had been exposed to Emerson as early as March 1842, when six lectures given in New York by Emerson were reported in the *Aurora*. Probably Whitman attended at least some of these lectures, and he reported that one on poetry was "one of the richest and most beautiful compositions, both for its matter and style, we have heard anywhere, at any time." In the *Eagle* in December 1847 he reprinted the opening sentences of "Spiritual Laws," which he called "one of Ralph Waldo Emerson's inimitable lectures." Earlier that year he had clipped an article chiefly about Emerson from the *Democratic Review*. There is reason to believe his 1860 statement to John Townsend Trowbridge that while carpentering in Brooklyn in the early 1850s he often carried in his lunch pail a book and that one day the book was a volume of Emerson's essays. His statement to Trowbridge that he was "simmering" and Emerson brought him "to a boil" has a ring of truth. Certain aspects of his verse—especially his idealization of the poet and his proclamation of contradictions—seem to bear the Emerson stamp.

But there may have been reasons other than hurt feelings behind his later denial of Emerson's influence. Surveying the poetry of the first two editions of *Leaves of Grass*, we find many things that appear to echo Emerson but could just as easily have sprung from one or more of several interrelated popular movements that crested in the 1850s: mesmerism, spiritualism, Swedenborgianism, and Harmonialism. Emersonian Transcendentalism, never a popular movement, was in retreat by then, while these other movements were gaining millions of adherents. Whitman's confident declaration at the end of the 1855 preface—"The signs are effectual. There can be no mistake."—and his heady anticipation of being absorbed immediately by his country suggest his kinship with the popular currents of the decade. Also, Emerson's later disenchantment with his poetry, mainly because of its eroticism, indicates he was not as close as Whitman was to the earthy and sometimes sensuous versions of mysticism these movements represented.

Body Electric Speeding Through Space

IT IS DECEPTIVE to discuss the new movements separately, for by the midfifties they had become so closely intermeshed that they were barely distinguishable from each other. In fact, Whitman's poetry, which drew on all of them, reflected their convergence.

Still, each made its special contribution to his repository of images. Mesmerism, which began as hypnotic mind-control and developed into a system of healing, popularized the terminology of animal magnetism that lay behind his images of electricity and fluid energy. Spiritualism, which purported to prove immortality through contact with spirits, influenced his ideas about death and the soul. Swedenborgianism, in the antiecclesiastical form that made it popular among many Americans at midcentury, contributed to his notions of spiritual essences and sensuous mysticism. Harmonialism, an umbrella term referring to a broad religious outlook expounded most famously by Andrew Jackson Davis, drew together these and other movements to posit an eternal interchange between mind and matter. All the movements challenged boundaries of time and space in ways that anticipated the zanier moments in Whitman's poetry.

The supposedly scientific basis for several of the movements had been established in the late eighteenth century by the Viennese physician Franz Anton Mesmer. He argued that all physical and spiritual phenomena were linked by a magnetic, electrical ether or fluid, called by his followers the odic force. Certain people, called operators, had the ability to use their odic powers to magnetize, or place in a trance, other people, who thus became "subjects" or "mediums." By the 1830s mesmerism had become a popular tool in the hands of traveling showmen and would-be physicians. It was popularized in America by the French pseudoscientist Charles Poyen, who gave scores of mesmeric demonstrations from 1836 to 1839 in various states, putting about half his volunteers in a trance. Another traveling mesmerist, Robert Collyer of England, made a popular tour in 1839, and before long many American imitators sprung up in his wake. Whitman was at first skeptical about animal magnetism but then was won over. In August 1842 in the New York *Sunday Times* he said he had ceased being "a devout disbeliever in the science of animal magnetism," declaring that "it reveals at once the existence of a whole new world of truth, grand, fearful, profound, relating to that great mystery, in the shadow of which we live and move and have our being."

Little more than a minor curiosity among the aristocracy abroad, mesmerism joined phrenology as one of the great popular spectacles in the Barnumesque American 1840s. Just as the Fowlers and their ilk toured the nation reading heads, itinerant mesmerists fanned out over the nation giving exhibitions. According to one estimate, by 1843 there were between twenty and thirty thousand mesmerists lecturing in the Northeast alone. Many of them used their odic force to control the behavior and attitudes of their mesmerized subjects, to the wonder of audiences that often reached two or three thousand. Some were able to put their subjects into the highest, or third, degree of trance, in which their minds traveled to distant times and places. A good number used mesmerism for healing purposes. Sophia Hawthorne's treatment by the Boston mesmerist Cornelia Park was the most famous instance of a phenomenon that became widespread during the forties and that led eventually, in revised form, to the mind-cure movement.

The leading practitioner and theorist of mesmerism in antebellum America was John Bovee Dods. Whitman, who wrote an article on mesmerism in 1845, before Dods became prominent, almost surely came to know of the popular mesmerist, whose book *The Philosophy of Electrical Psychology* was part of a two-volume "Library of Mesmerism" published by Fowlers and Wells in 1850. In the book Dods recounted his experiences as a traveling mesmerist and presented an electrical theory that he claimed was the basis of all physical and spiritual things. Dods's mesmeric exhibitions, typical of the day, featured apparently miraculous occurrences that provide a backdrop to Whitman's adventurous poems.

The shape-shifting, sometimes sex-changing persona of Whitman's verse, which, as we have seen, owed something to the poet's observations of theater, was also reflective of the identity changes caused by the mesmerists. By putting a subject into a trance, an operator could make his or her identity shift rapidly. As Dods explained, "He can change the identity of certain individuals, making them imagine for the time being that they are persons of color, that they belong to the opposite sex, or that they are some renowned general, orator, statesman, or what-not." Like other healing mesmerists, Dods claimed to cure hopeless conditions such as deafness, blindness, dumbness, and paralysis. The ability of Whitman's persona to shift quickly between different identities, including those of blacks and women, and to emanate health to everyone approximated the mesmerists' posture.

His use of the vocabulary of animal magnetism and electricity also shows the mesmerists' influence. Dods's book was the period's most detailed presentation of the electrical theory. He converted the notion of a universal magnetic fluid into an all-explaining theory of creation. "Ever since 1830," he wrote, "I have contended that electricity is not only the connecting link between MIND and *inert* MATTER, but is the grand agent employed by the Creator." "Electricity," he continued, "as a universal agent, pervades the entire atmosphere," governing all the operations of nature and linking nature to God. The cause of disease, he wrote, is "*the electricity of the system thrown out of balance*." Balance could be restored either by mesmeric healing or by careful regulation of daily behavior.

Such ideas were widely accepted among the pseudoscientists in Whitman's circle. As Orson Fowler wrote in 1851: "Magnetism, or electricity, or galvanism, all only different names for the same thing differently applied, is now generally conceded to be the grand instrumentality of life in all its forms, all varieties of human, animal, and vegetable life included—all bones, muscles, organs, &c., being only the ropes, pullies, and tools, while this is the master workman, or grand executive, of every animal function and mental exercise."

So well attuned to the electrical theory was Whitman that at times his poetic persona seems like a bundle of electrical impulses coming into contact everywhere with electrically charged things. "I have instant conductors all over me whether I pass or stop," he writes in "Song of Myself," "They seize every object and lead it harmlessly through me." The doctrine of passional attraction, derived from Fourier, often becomes mixed in his poems with electrical magnetism, derived from the mesmerists. "O resistless yearning!" he writes in "From Pent-Up Aching Rivers," breaking immediately into the magnetists' language: "O for any and each the body correlative attracting! / O for you whoever you are and your correlative body! O it, more than all else, you delighting!"

His praise of the body took on a cleansing, mystical quality when expressed in electrical language:

I sing the body electric,
The armies of those I love engirth me and I engirth them,
They will not let go of me till I go with them, respond to them,
And discorrupt them, and charge them full with the charge of the
     soul.

This passage is framed by electrical images. Just as Fowler had written that "all bones, muscles, organs" were run by the "grand executive" of electricity, so Whitman sings the "body electric," setting the stage for his poetic listing of body parts later in the poem. The daring image of engirthing "[t]he armies of those I love" is converted in the last line into an act of magnetic healing, as the persona "discorrupt[s]" his lovers by "charg[ing] them full with the charge of the soul."

Because Whitman was always fighting the demon of doubt (in his words, the idea of "matter triumphant"), he took an interest in anything that offered liberation from chronological time and physical reality. There was precedent for such liberation in mesmerism and in the movement that blended with it, spiritualism.

In its popular form, spiritualism emerged in 1848 with the famous "Hydesville rappings" in upstate New York. Two impressionable girls, the fourteen-year-old Margaret Fox and her twelve-year-old sister Katherine, that year heard strange knocking sounds in their house in the village of Hydesville, near Rochester. They soon claimed the sounds were produced by a spirit that identified itself as Splitfoot. The case was sensationally reported in the press, and the Fox sisters became celebrities. In 1850 they were brought to New York City, where they gave public exhibitions of their ability to communicate with the dead. Among those who attended their séances were William Cullen Bryant, George Bancroft, James Fenimore Cooper, and N. P. Willis. It was not long before many were won over to spiritualism. The editor Horace Greeley, the ex-slave Sojourner Truth, and the abolitionists Sarah and Angelina Grimké and William Lloyd Garrison were among the converts.

There were soon thousands of spiritualist mediums in every state. The mediums held séances in which the presence of spirits was indicated by rappings, chair movings, table liftings, flying objects, and so on. A number of famous mediums, notably Cora Hatch and Anna Henderson, gave, while in a trance state, well-attended lectures on the afterlife. Previously, American trance religion had been confined to special individuals such as the Mormon prophet Joseph Smith or the Universal Friend Jemimah Wilkinson. But in the 1850s, trance writing and trance lecturing were performed by hundreds who claimed to have spiritual gifts. Several volumes of trance poetry were published, typified by E. C. Henck's *Spirit Voices: Odes, Dictated by Spirits of the Second Sphere, for the Use of Harmonial Circles* (1853) and Nathan F. White's *Voices from the Spirit-Land* (1854).

Whitman watched the spiritualist movement with genuine curiosity. He discussed the spiritualist Cora Hatch with his Swedenborgian friend John Arnold, and in 1857 in the *Daily Times* said that a recent trance lecture given by Hatch was "a singular compound of wisdom and blather, mixed with the most daring flights of scientific prophecy and knowledge." He saw "wildness and shallowness" in spiritualism but noted that the movement was "spreading with great rapidity." He estimated three to five million American adherents of spiritualism and wrote: "There can be no doubt, that the spiritual movement is blending itself in many ways with society, in theology, in the art of healing, in literature, and in the moral and mental character of the people of the United States."

One of the things it blended with was his poetry. In the 1855 preface he includes the "spiritualist" among "the lawgivers of poets." Spiritualist images are scattered throughout his early poetry. His repeated assurances about immortality retain the optimism of the spiritualists. It is just as lucky to die as to be born, he tells us in the opening poem. "I am the mate and companion of people, all just as immortal and fathomless as myself," he writes. "(They do not know how immortal, but I know.)" With the confidence of the spiritualist he announces, "I know I am deathless, [. . .] I laugh at what you call dissolution." This was a spiritualism without gimmickry, what he called a true spiritualism. In a self-review of the 1855 edition, he said of himself: "He is the true spiritualist. He recognizes no annihilation, or death, or loss of identity."

His interest in spiritualism increased with time. On some level, the poet became associated in his mind with the spiritualist medium. As he wrote in his notebook, "The poets are divine mediums—through them come spirits and materials to all the people, men and women." In an 1860 poem titled "Mediums" he says that a new race of mediums is arising that will "convey gospels" about nature, physiology, oratory, death. He used the vocabulary of spiritualism in other poems: "O! mediums! O to teach! to convey the invisible faith!" and "Something unproved! something in a trance!" In a Calamus poem he feels surrounded by "the spirits of dear friends dead or alive, thicker they come." Another 1860 poem describes "the rapt promises and luminè of seers, the spiritual world."

Closely associated in his mind with spiritualism was Swedenborgianism. In an 1857 *Daily Times* article he identified Emanuel Swedenborg as "the Spiritualist" and insisted that "his spiritual discoveries have special reference to America." He was perceptive in linking Swedenborg both with spiritualism and with America, for in the 1850s many American spiritualists claimed the Swedish mystic as their ancestor. Born in 1688 in Stockholm, Swedenborg had gained fame as a physical scientist before turning in the 1740s to spiritual matters. He hoped to prove the existence of the soul and the afterlife by applying science to metaphysical questions. He began having visions of angels and the afterlife, and before long he was holding regular converse with the dead. He reported being on familiar terms with the spirits of Saint Paul, Luther, and other notables. The remaining three decades of his life were devoted to expounding his philosophy in a series of weighty theological volumes. He laid down a doctrine of "correspondences," in which every material thing was said to have a spiritual counterpart, or "ultimate." His was a body-specific, erotic mysticism. He described God as the Divine Man, who speaks to humans through the head or heart by "influx," or "divine breath." Every human being, he argued, had an influx from heaven and an influx from hell, and by a simple decision of the will could turn from one to the other. The most controversial aspect of his teachings related to sex. The highest form of love he termed "conjugial love," or a "divine" marriage of spirits that lasted through eternity. Since conjugial love was rare on earth, he advanced a doctrine of "permissions," allowing for certain kinds of premarital sex and even, in some cases, adultery.

The New Church, established on Swedenborg's teachings, was founded in England in 1787 and not long after spread to the United States. Branches of the New Church were established in Manhattan in 1821 and in Long Island a decade later. Membership in this denomination was never large in America, reaching only 1,450 by 1850 and never exceeding 8,000 during the nineteenth century. But as a philosophy, Swedenborgianism had an extraordinarily widespread impact. It filtered into New England Transcendentalism, frontier revivalism, perfectionism, and spiritualism. Emerson, who derived many ideas from Swedenborg and mentioned him some eighty times in his writings, proclaimed in 1854, perhaps with a touch of envy: *"This age is Swedenborg's."*

Whitman's first exposure to Swedenborg's ideas (other than secondarily through Emerson) appears to have come in May 1846 when he heard two lectures by the New York University professor George Bush, one of the foremost American Swedenborgians. Bush had been ordained a Presbyterian minister in 1825 but was converted to Swedenborgianism in the early forties, a time when the philosophy was being actively promoted in New York by Reverend Benjamin Barrett. Bush went on to become the author of *Mesmer and Swedenborg* (1847) and, in 1852, the leader of the Society of Swedenborg in Brooklyn, though he was an anti-ecclesiast who rejected the New Church. When Whitman heard him lecture in 1846 on Swedenborg's doctrine of spirits existing around us at all times, he called him "a very clear and impressive preacher." Two years later Whitman referred to Swedenborg in the *Daily Crescent* in a sketch about an old man who seemed to be pondering "some beautiful idea collated from the philosophy of Emanuel Swedenborg."

His attraction to Swedenborg intensified in the fifties, a time when the Swede's ideas were given fresh life by a number of avid promoters and by the formation in 1850 of the American Swedenborg Printing and Publishing Society, which would publish two thousand volumes over the next three decades. Whitman had a friend who was close to Henry James, Sr., the intensely antiecclesiastical Swedenborgian who rejected the New Church but wrote a dozen books on Swedenborg. Whitman also mentioned in his notebook James John Garth Wilkinson, England's leading Swedenborgian, and William Fishbough, whose book *Macrocosm and Microcosm* was published by Fowlers and Wells in 1852. At the home of his Brooklyn friends the Prices, he had long, sometimes heated discussions with the Swedenborgian John Arnold. All this activity led to his *Daily Times* article on Swedenborg, in which he summarized the mystic's career, described Swedenborgian meetings in America, explained his main doctrines, and averred that Swedenborg would have "the deepest and broadest mark upon the religions of future ages here, of any man that ever walked the earth."

This was very strong praise. Whitman never commended any other religious figure so enthusiastically. What was it about Swedenborg he found attractive? For one thing, like Emerson and Henry James, Sr., he found appeal in the doctrine of correspondences. James took the doctrine to an extreme, insisting that absolutely every physical thing—a coat, a tree, anything—had its exact spiritual counterpart. Whitman, though never as doctrinaire as James, advanced a similar idea in his poetry. Like Swedenborg, and unlike the mind-cure people who came later, he did not deny the existence of evil. If Swedenborg said that everyone felt the pull of hell, he wrote in "Song of the Open Road" of everyone having "Another self, a duplicate of every one, skulking and hiding it goes, / [. . .] death under the breast-bones, hell under the skull-bones."

More typically, though, he found in the idea of correspondences a source of consolation. In his Swedenborg article he described the doctrine as "poetical." The Swedenborgian idea that even the most mundane things have spiritual essences is echoed in his lines in "Starting from Paumanok":

[H]aving look'd at the objects of the universe, I find there is no one
     nor any particle of one but has reference to the soul.

Was somebody asking to see the soul?

> See, your own shape, countenance, persons, substances, beasts, the
>   trees, the running rivers, the rocks and sands.

"Crossing Brooklyn Ferry" makes use of a similar idea, as the city and the commercial river traffic are called "dumb, beautiful ministers" of which "none else is perhaps more spiritual" and all "furnish your parts toward the soul." In "Song of Joys" Whitman emphasizes that his real self is spiritual, not physical: "Nor my material body which finally loves, walks, laughs, shouts, embraces, procreates." He went as far as James in "Song of the Redwood-Tree," in which he had a tree chant, *"For know I bear the soul befitting me, I too have consciousness, identity / And all the rocks and mountains have, and all the earth."* By far his longest and most fervent poem in this vein was "Eidólons," the title of which was his word for the Swedenborgian "ultimate." The poem outdoes Swedenborg or even James in its assertions of correspondences, as the poet looks everywhere and sees only the spiritual counterpart of every physical and emotional thing.

The brand of Swedenborgianism Whitman espoused had little to do with the New Church. Rather, it was one of many idiosyncratic offshoots, like James's and especially like Thomas Lake Harris's. Harris is another unappreciated figure in Whitman biography. Other than Floyd Stovall's comment that Whitman probably attended Harris's New York church in the early 1850s, few connections between the two have been made. Whitman discussed Harris in his notebook, and his eroticized mysticism was in several senses close to Harris's post-Swedenborgian vision.

The thin, soulful Harris had been a Universalist minister who in the 1840s turned to Swedenborgianism. For a time he was a member of the New Church but left it because it seemed too rigid and confining. He was swept up in the tide of mystical, illuminist American movements, especially mesmerism and spiritualism. In 1851 he established an independent Christian spiritualist church in New York, which was loosely associated with the New Church, although by 1857 he scandalized the church when he announced he was in regular, direct contact with God; orthodox Swedenborgians denounced his professions as blasphemous hubris. His conversations with God, however, were not unusual in the illuminist environment of antebellum America. Since the early fifties he had been combining spiritualism, mesmerism, and Swedenborgianism in mystical poetry that he wrote while in a trance state. Trance poetry and lecturing, as seen, was very common in the fifties, but Harris took the genre to new heights. In late 1853, in the presence of witnesses that included Carlos Stuart and William Fishbough (spiritualists Whitman knew), Harris fell into a series of trances in which he was guided by the spirit of Dante to chant verses that were copied by an amanuensis and published in 1854 as *An Epic of the Starry Heaven*. In the four-thousand-line poem, Harris's soul sped to vast reaches of space, beyond distant stars and suns to the highest or "seventh" sphere, where he saw a society of rapturously united conjugial lovers, a society of infinite love and brotherhood prefiguring a future Harmonic society on earth.

The strange time-space flights and the erotic spiritualism of Harris's poem showed what could happen when Swedenborgianism was mingled with other forms of popular American mysticism. Harris and others on the fringes of Swedenborgianism used a mystical language in which the union with the spiritual world was physical, sometimes sexual. Swedenborg's mysticism was inherently body specific, as believers were thought to communicate with God through particular parts of the body. The lungs were said to play a key role in spiritual communion. The "divine breath," also called the "influx" or "afflatus," was taken in from the spiritual atmosphere through the lungs, which in turn emanated an "efflux" of its own into the atmosphere. The Swedenborgian terms "influx," "efflux," and "afflatus" were picked up by several antebellum thinkers, including Emerson and several in Whitman's circle. Whitman's radical friend Sarah Tyndale, for instance, wrote him in a letter of 1856, "Thank God for the great influx of light, love, joy, and beauty which is every where manifest."

These Swedenborgian words are used in the early editions of *Leaves of Grass*. The "I" of "Song of Myself" calls himself the "Partaker of influx and efflux" and declares: "Through me the afflatus surging and surging.... through me the current and index." In "Song of the Open Road" Whitman writes: "Here is the efflux of the soul, / The efflux of the soul comes from within through embower'd gates, ever provoking questions." Like the post-Swedenborgians of the fifties, he could combine the notion of efflux with the "charge" and universal fluid of animal magnetism:

> The efflux of the soul is happiness, here is happiness,
> I think it pervades the open air, waiting at all times,
> Now it flows unto us, we are rightly charged.
>
> Here rises the fluid and attaching character.

The very act of breathing became, for the post-Swedenborgians, an act of participation in the divine life. "I inhale with equal ease the atmosphere of the three heavens," wrote Thomas Lake Harris, referring to his constant reception of the divine breath. There is a similarly giddy,

mystical aura to Whitman's description of breathing in the opening
verses of "Song of Myself," where he sings praise to "The smoke of my
own breath / [...] My respiration and inspiration, the beating of my
heart, the passing of blood and air through my lungs." Swedenborg sug-
gested to Whitman how the erotic and the mystical were linked. He told
Traubel, "I think Swedenborg was right when he said there was a close
connection—a very close connection—between the state we call reli-
gious ecstasy and the desire to copulate. I find it confirmed in all my ex-
perience."

Since the body was deeply involved in worship for the post-
Swedenborgians, they often came up with oddly physical metaphors for
prayer. At Harris's church, speeches were given by influx, which Harris
described as an act of bodily penetration: "When intelligence and faith
are treated of, it is through the left temple. When love to the Lord and
His Kingdom, through the head and extending to the heart and lungs.
When the Word is illuminated the influx is through the forehead." The
soul for the Swedenborgians was no rarefied essence but almost a palpa-
ble other self. The era's leading Swedenborgian, the British author James
John Garth Wilkinson (also mentioned in Whitman's notebooks), wrote
in 1851 that the soul was a comrade on equal and loving terms with the
self: "There is also ample space between soul and body, as between friend
and friend, and yet the ever-varying bond is all the closer, being found
upon interests of each, which have room for play in the wide interval
between them."

This cultural background of erotic mysticism casts light on the sec-
tion in "Song of Myself" in which the "I" describes lying with his soul
on the grass on a transparent summer morning. This passage, one of the
most famous in American poetry, has given rise to contradictory inter-
pretations. It was regarded by the poet's contemporary defenders as a
holy moment associated with a mystical experience Whitman suppos-
edly had in June 1853 or 1854. With the rise of Freudianism, the reli-
gious explanation was replaced with sexual ones, with some calling the
passage homoerotic, others autoerotic, others primal regressive. Lately,
room has been made for a renewed religious interpretation, but the pas-
sage has not been placed adequately in context. It merits being quoted
at length:

I believe in you my soul, the other I am must not abase itself to you,
And you must not be abased to the other.

Loafe with me on the grass, loose the stop from your throat,

Not words, not music or rhyme I want, not custom or lecture, not
    even the best,
Only the lull I like, the hum of your valvèd voice.

I mind how once we lay such a transparent summer morning,
How you settled your head athwart my hips and gently turn'd over
    upon me,
And parted the shirt from my bosom-bone, and plunged your tongue
    to my bare-stript heart,
And reach'd till you felt my beard, and reach'd till you held my feet.

Swiftly arose and spread around me the peace and knowledge that
    pass all the art and argument of the earth,
And I know that the hand of God is the promise [originally
    "elderhand"] of my own,
And I know that the spirit of God is the brother of my own,
And that all the men ever born are also my brothers, and the
    women my sisters and lovers,
And that a kelson of the creation is love.

The post-Freudian reader is apt to see all sorts of things in this passage, from regressive fantasy to fellatio. As in so many erotic passages in Whitman, an exact sexual interpretation is difficult, since even the gender of the sexual partner is unspecified. What is clear, though, is that the passage is framed by religious images. It begins with a religious statement—"I believe in you my soul"—and leads through rapturous union to an affirmation of the peace and joy and love of God's universe. Whatever the tangled sexual motivations behind the passage, the religious meaning is inescapable: the "I" begins by contemplating the soul and ends by contemplating God.

The mixture of the physical and the spiritual is established at the start, when the persona says that neither the soul nor the body should be abased to each other. The erotic scene that follows is thus prepared for by images that share the physical-mystical spirit of the period. Most mysticism, of course, has a sexual element; Foucault goes so far as to say that the language of the early Christian mystics was among the most erotic of all writing. In the post-Swedenborgian atmosphere of the American 1850s, the possibilities for erotic mysticism were greater than ever. If Harris could describe union with God as reception of the divine breath through the head or the chest, so Whitman could imagine the soul plunging its "tongue" to the "bare-stript heart" and spreading until it embraced the beard and feet. If Wilkinson could treat his soul as virtually another human being, Whitman was so successful in doing so that many modern critics have forgotten that the "you" referred to here is, on the literal level at least, the soul. The expansive aftermath of the erotic-mystical union also has Swedenborgian overtones. In Harris's *Epic of the Starry Heaven*, the soul, in its visionary flight to the divine world, encounters the spirits of countless men and women bound in love, and is told: "We all are Lovers in these pure dominions—/ [...] Love reigns in all—Love, the glorified." Similarly, Whitman's "I" feels that he is bonded eternally with all the men and women ever born and that "a kelson of the creation is love."

Whitman's attraction to men fits comfortably with post-Swedenborgian thought. For Swedenborg and his followers, not only did the divine breath enter through specific body parts, but union with God was, literally, union with the Divine Man. In describing God, Swedenborg had written that the highest heaven extended from the Divine Man's head down to the neck, the middle heaven from the breast to the loins, the lowest from the feet to the soles and also from the arms to the fingers. Whitman similarly combined the anthropomorphic and the divine. His "I," in effect, gains access to all heavens simultaneously when the soul's tongue penetrates the chest while the hands spread upward to the face and down to the feet. Union with the divine becomes a human experience, as the "I" feels that God's "hand" is his own "elderhand" and God's spirit is his "brother." This post-Swedenborgian impulse to be joined with the Divine Man is visible in his description elsewhere of God as "The great Camerado, the lover true for whom I pine." In the original version of "Song of Myself" he writes, "As God comes a loving bedfellow and sleeps at my side all night and close on the peep of the day." In a later poem he addresses God as follows: "Thou, thou the Ideal Man,/ Fair, able, beautiful, content, and loving, / Complete in body and dilate in spirit, / Be thou my God."

His treatment of religious matters also had precedent in the Harmonial movement led by the famous Poughkeepsie Seer, Andrew Jackson Davis. Whitman discussed Davis at length with his friend John Arnold and doubtless was exposed to one or more of the best-selling Harmonial books that Davis wrote between 1847 and 1854. Davis was an unlearned cobbler's apprentice who was introduced to mesmerism in 1843 when a traveling mesmerist put him into a trance. Davis served as a medium for various mesmerists for four years until he developed a remarkable capacity to slip in and out of trances at will, without the aid of an outside operator.

While in a trance state, Davis could accomplish apparently miraculous things, such as reading books through walls and peering inside people's bodies to spot hidden diseases. His early champion and promoter, the post-Swedenborgian George Bush, reported that although Davis had not more than five months of formal schooling, he could, while entranced, speak fluent French, Greek, Hebrew, and Sanskrit. Davis constantly traveled mentally to distant places and times. In a typical trance state, his mind roamed beyond the walls of his home, looked through the roofs of surrounding houses and through the clothes of their inhabitants, and even saw backward into history and outward to the distant expanses of the heavens. Every particle of matter came alive in Davis's vision. Such mental time-space travel was common enough among American mesmerists of the day, but Davis popularized it and gave it a name: traveling clairvoyance. As he wrote, "The clairvoyant sometimes sees places not as they appear now, but as they existed many years ago," as "the angels unroll before the spiritual sight of the clairvoyant, a grand panorama of past scenes and events." Davis became identified with spiritualism, for he had constant intercourse with spirits.

He also initiated the craze of trance performances that swept the nation in the fifties. Between 1845 and '47 he had given over 150 lectures while in a trance state, setting the stage for the many other popular trance lecturers and trance poets. Several of the mystics that followed him became famous for feats of traveling clairvoyance. For instance, when Thomas Lake Harris was in a trance, according to one account, "there was no limit to his vision. The most solid substances were transparent as ether; immeasurable distances opposed no barrier to his observations; the forgotten Past was unveiled before him, and he had power to unlock the mysterious Future, and to read from the page of Destiny!"

Whether or not Whitman had a trancelike mystical experience, as his friend and biographer Bucke claimed, he was a cultural ventriloquist who gave expression to the mass interest in trances and spiritualism. The midfifties, when he produced his mystical poetry, was a kind of watershed moment for popular mysticism. Whitman participated in the popular trend. In a notebook entry of the period he wrote, "I am in a mystic trance exultation / Something wild and untamed—half savage." In a later entry he described being "in a trance, yet with all senses alert" and with "the objective world suspended or surmounted for a while, & the powers in exaltation, freedom, vision."

The early editions of *Leaves of Grass* are filled with his versions of traveling clairvoyance. A prominent stylistic feature of his poems is their constant shuttling between different images, often different times and places. He outdid even Harris or Davis in his adventurous gamboling with time and space. In "Song of Myself" he writes: "My ties and ballasts leave me, I travel, my elbows rest in sea-gaps, / I skirt the sierras, my palms cover continents, / I am afoot with my vision." If the trance writers mentally traversed history and space, so Whitman jumped rapidly between historical events (for example, "Walking the old hills of Judea with the beautiful gentle God at my side") and distant places ("Speeding through space, speeding through heaven and the stars").

Sometimes his visionary perspectives produced images like those used by the space-traveling popular mystics. If Harris described himself flying through "seven spheres" representing "seven links from God to man," so Whitman's persona is "Speeding amid the seven satellites and the broad ring and the diameter of eighty thousand miles."

In several poems he makes time-space travel the basis for communication with future generations. The poet could declare himself the highest medium because poetic language, unlike the ephemeral performances of most spiritualists, could stay alive in print to buoy up future readers. "It avails not, time nor place—distance avails not," he writes in "Crossing Brooklyn Ferry." "I am with you, you men and women of a generation, or ever so many generations hence." In the 1860 poem "So Long!" he can mollify the pain of saying good-bye to his contemporary readership, which he thought he had lost, by imagining a poetic-spiritualist absorption into a later readership. He feels he is headed toward "An unknown sphere more real than I dream'd," and he concludes the poem with an image that proclaims his authorial death but spiritual life: "I depart from materials, / I am as one disembodied, triumphant, dead."

The spiritually healing powers of his persona bore the impress of the Harmonial outlook as expounded by Davis. In his many books, Davis set forth a philosophy that he said came from pure inspiration but which in fact bore the combined imprints of the progressive scientists, Emerson, Fourier, the phrenological Fowlers, the spiritualists, Swedenborg, the mesmerists, and various health reformers—all mentioned in his writings. Davis offered an integrative theory of the individual, society, and the physical and spiritual universe. Electricity, he believed after the mesmerists, governed all things and was the connecting link between mind and matter. Mid-nineteenth-century America, he believed, was the place where an age of miracles was occurring. A new version of Jacob's ladder, which he said was "composed of magnetism and electricity," had been constructed in America so that humans could readily be in touch with distant physical and spiritual phenomena. Health and peace of mind, he argued after the Fowlers, could be easily attained by restoration of balance to both the mind and the body. For Davis, perfect health was perfect harmony; disease was discord and indicated imbalance. Health came with restoration of harmony with the laws of the physical and spiritual universe.

The Harmonialists thought that electrical magnetism was perfectly in balance in nature and that by plunging into nature people could be physically healed and spiritually refreshed. An almost erotic bonding with nature was seen as a prelude to healing. As the Harmonialist Marx Edgeworth Lazarus wrote in 1851: "We shall know that we are healed when calm and unreproved we can press our cheek to our mother's great breast, and feel our heart answer to the pulses of her life, as it leaps in the deer, warbles in the bird, glides in the stream, and trembles in the consciousness of its exquisite animation, through every breeze-kissed flower, and every leaf of the forest harp." Nature for the Harmonialists was not just a Wordsworthian or Emersonian reminder of spiritual truths (though it was that too); it was a life-giving force to be enjoyed physically as a source of magnetic power. Not only the water cure but many other kinds of immersion in nature were viewed as health giving. For instance, Lazarus wrote that "One of the most effectual restoratives of health into which the magnetism of animal sympathies enters largely, is the travel cure on horseback"; riding a fine horse in the country is "worth all the other cures put together."

The madly loving, sometimes sexual attraction to nature in the early editions of *Leaves of Grass* bears the Harmonial stamp. Whitman's persona embraces nature like a Harmonialist hungry for a magnetic charge:

> Press close bare-bosom'd night—press close magnetic nourishing
> 　　night!
> Night of the south winds—night of the large few stars!
> Still nodding night—mad naked summer night.

Such "magnetic nourishing" power is supplied by virtually every facet of nature the "I" embraces. "Smile O voluptuous cool-breathed earth!" he proclaims. "Smile, for your lover comes." "You sea! I resign myself to you also [...] / Dash me with amorous wet, I can repay you." As with the Harmonialists, the sights, sounds, smells, and touch of the physical world have magnetic reverberations in the poet's sensibility. If Lazarus equated health with pressing close to "our mother earth's great breast," Whitman casts his persona into the embrace of nature, often calling it a lover or parent. He even gives a version of "the travel cure on horseback" in his eroticized description of riding "A gigantic beauty of a stallion, fresh and responsive to my caresses."

The sun had high significance for both the Harmonialists and Whitman. For the popular mystics, the sun was a chief source of the electrical fluid that permeated nature and quickened life. As the highest recipients of this magnetic energy, humans were thought to be extensions of the

sun. Lazarus called man the Solar Ray and the sun the pivot of all terres-
trial things, the material counterpart of God. In Thomas Lake Harris's
poem, spirits in space congregate around suns and absorb odic force.
"Spirits who stand in the Sun-sphere," Harris explained, "perceive by
means of an odic emanation from the sun. They become negative at
times to other suns, and leaving odylic forms, traverse with inconceivable
rapidity the region to which they may be attracted, entering into any
given solar system."

Whitman's persona too is a "solar" man, responsive to the sun's spe-
cial power and emanating an odic sun-force himself.

> Dazzling and tremendous how quick the sun-rise would kill me,
> If I could not now and always send sun-rise out of me.

> We also ascend dazzling and tremendous as the sun,
> We found our own O my soul in the calm and cool of the daybreak.

He is able not only to "send sun-rise" out of him but to speed like one
of Harris's spirits through solar spheres: "I depart as air, I shake my locks
at the runaway sun, / I effuse my flesh in eddies, and drift it in lacy jags."
The conflation of the human and the solar is beautifully expressed in
"Crossing Brooklyn Ferry," where the ferry passenger has his "eyes daz-
zled by the shimmering track of beams" and watches "the fine centrifu-
gal spokes of light round the shape of my head in the sunlit water." Like
the Harmonialists, Whitman is not just appreciating nature but exhaling
its magnetic force.

He was trying to define a model person who could heal both social
and physical disease. Socially, Andrew Jackson Davis envisaged a Har-
monial society in which, as he wrote, "all men shall be ultimately joined
into one BROTHERHOOD; their interests shall be pure and reciprocal;
their actions shall be just and harmonious; they shall be as one *Body.*"
Harmonial society would balance what Lazarus called "the Centripetal
force," or individual expression and freedom, with "the Centrifugal
force," or "the magnetic impulse of the mass," or group.

Whitman, confronted with a complex social and political situation
whose tensions he felt on his very nerve endings, embraced the kind of
affirmations Davis and Lazarus offered. Haunted by the increasing con-
flict between the individual and the mass, as in the harsh sectional con-
flicts of the fifties, he created a kind of Harmonic social space in his
poems where individuality and togetherness flourished simultaneously.
Adopting the social language of the Harmonialists, he described his per-
sona as "One of that centripetal and centrifugal gang." The centrifugal

side of his vision was manifested in the loose, sprawling style of the poems, particularly the all-encompassing catalogs. The centripetal impulse came forth in the magnetic "I" at the heart of his poetry, attracting everything to himself. This "I" was the ideal Harmonial person, always ready to be absorbed into the mass but always himself—and, above all, always in balance. "He is the equalizer of his age and land," Whitman writes, the one who sees that beauty is "exact and plumb as gravitation." Both spiritually and physically, the "I" proclaims himself a Harmonial healer. "Of your soul I say truths to harmonize, if anything can harmonize you," he reassures us: life is not "chaos or death—it is form, union, plan—it is eternal life—it is Happiness." "I shall be good health to you," he says at the end of "Song of Myself," "And filter and fibre your blood."

At times, Whitman's Harmonial optimism leads him to a denial of evil. The Harmonial movement would eventually feed into New Thought, the later spiritual-cure movement that minimized the power of evil. It was this kind of all-affirming optimism that led one late-nineteenth-century reviewer to place him in the company of "all who proclaim panaceas and nostrums," including Mary Baker Eddy.

More characteristically, though, his poems of the fifties move through various kinds of disease and evil to an ultimately affirmative statement. Most of his poems have a negative center framed by optimistic images. His strategy is not denial but absorption and cleansing. His social program demanded full confrontation with all the disturbing aspects of American society. To combat social and private evils, Whitman used every weapon in his metaphysical arsenal, which was well supplied by the popular religious movements of his day.

His recuperative strategy is particularly visible in his 1855 poem "The Sleepers." This is a poem of healing that absorbs numerous diseased or outlawed types and uses every technique in the popular religious repertoire to redeem them. The "I" of the poem sees, among other things, "The wretched features of ennuyés, the white features of corpses, the livid faces of drunkards, the sick-gray faces of onanists." He also sees insane people, bloody battlefield soldiers, a condemned murderer, unrequited lovers, a plotting moneymaker, a drowning swimmer, a shipwreck. But all these negative images are countered by the consolation brought to them by the soothing "I," who has all the capacities of a mesmeric healer and Harmonial life-affirmer. The persona makes such a weird voyage amid varied persons and things that "The Sleepers" has been called "perhaps the only surrealist American poem of the nineteenth century, remarkable in its anticipation of later experiment." Its effects are indeed surrealistic, but they stem from equally strange popular movements in antebellum America.

In making his visionary voyage, the "I" is in a state of traveling clair-voyance, like that of trance mediums of the day. "I wander all night in my vision," he begins, "Stepping with light feet, swiftly and noiselessly stepping and stopping." If in his notebook Whitman could imagine him-self in a trance with all his senses alert, so throughout the poem the "I" is in a kind of trance state but is fully aware of people and things in different times and places. He is in what the mesmerists called the third degree of trance, which made possible mental voyages to distant times and places. He can leap easily back to the aftermath of the Battle of Brooklyn, with the weeping Washington consoling his troops, and to his own childhood, with his mother being visited on the old homestead by the beautiful squaw. He has the entranced person's ability not only to see but to experience the emotions of others. He not only sees the shroud around the corpse but says, "I am the shroud." At other times in the poem he says he is a dance whirling fast, an actor or actress, a woman awaiting her truant lover.

His mesmeric capacity for all-absorption is matched by his mesmeric capacity for healing. As though the "I" were an entranced healer mak-ing electrically charged passes with his hands over a diseased person, he declares: "I stand in the dark with drooping eyes by the worst-suffering and restless, / I pass my hands soothingly to and fro a few inches from them." By the end of the poem, he brings about a kind of mass healing. "The suffering of sick persons is relieved," he announces, with the insane becoming sane, the paralyzed supple, the consumptive freely breathing, and so on. Of course, the trope of the poem is that the universal, nightly ritual of sleeping is itself restorative and democratizing. But the sleep of the poem is more than the normal refresher we all know. It is a cure-all, analogous to the healing sleep of the mesmerist.

Moreover, it is a spiritualistic and Harmonial reminder of the soul and immortality. Sleep reminds the persona of "the myth of heaven," which in turn "indicates the soul," and: "The soul is always beautiful, / The universe is duly in order, everything is in its place." The Harmonial idea of balance and equipoise dominates the end of the poem. All parts of the body, Whitman writes, are "proportion'd and plumb," "The an-tipodes [. . .] are averaged now," the universe is in order. The poem has moved through disease and social disorder to a sense of Harmonial peace.

It is not surprising, however, that it was the disordered, sometimes bizarre qualities of Whitman's verse that caught the eye of some contem-poraries, several of whom associated him with the weird mystical move-ments of the time. An early reviewer commented that Whitman was fine when he kept his feet on the ground but that sometimes he ran toward chaos in rhapsodic time-space flights, "as in the rigmarole of trance-speaking mediums, and we are threatened on every hand with a period of mere suggestion in poetry, mere protest against order, and kicking at the old limits of time, space, the horizon, and the sky." A British reviewer similarly pointed out that Whitman's gamboling with time-space limits was odd to the foreign sensibility, "but perhaps not so to a nation from which the spirit-rappers sprung."

Reviewers inclined to accept the new mystical movements, on the other hand, felt comfortable with Whitman's religious vision. The leading Harmonial journal of the 1850s, the *Christian Spiritualist,* gave a long, glowing review of the first edition of *Leaves of Grass,* placing Whitman in a line of modern seers and mediums that had begun in the late eighteenth century with Swedenborg. The reviewer covered several forms of direct spiritual inspiration that had been manifested in recent years, declaring that *Leaves of Grass* was "a sign of the times, written, as we perceive, under powerful influxes; a prophecy and promise of much that awaits all who are entering with us into the opening door of a new era." The reviewer said Whitman represented a new "poetic mediumship," which through active imagination sensed the influx of spirits and the divine breath. As evidence of this, the reviewer quoted several passages from Whitman's poetry, including this one from "Song of Myself":

> Through me many long dumb voices,
> Voices of the interminable generations of slaves,
> Voices of prostitutes and of deformed persons,
> Voices of the diseased and despairing, and of thieves and dwarfs, [. . .]
>
> Voices of sexes and lusts . . . . voices veiled, and I remove the veil, and
> Voices indecent by me clarified and transfigured.

It was understandable that the reviewer featured this passage, for it reveals the mediumistic nature and healing powers of Whitman's poetic persona. "Through me many long dumb voices" partakes of the spiritualist communion with spirits. The embrace of the diseased, the outcast, the despairing, the trivial, show Whitman's Harmonial confidence that all could be set right if filtered through his prophetic imagination. All potentially negative elements of the universe can, according to his Harmonial assertion, be "clarified" and "transfigured" by the all-receiving, healing poet.

Such reassuring messages would explain the appeal of Whitman's verse for many of his contemporary admirers. After he gained fame late in life, by far the most common response to his poetry expressed in letters he received was that he was a healer and soul rescuer. To some close to Whitman, he could actually seem like a lay spiritualist. Helen Price, who called religion his leading trait, reported that when talking of death he once became "rapt, absorbed" and "appeared like a man in a trance." Whitman served as an unwitting spiritualist medium for J. W. Wallace, an English visitor to his Camden home in 1891. Wallace, overwhelmed by the magnetism of Whitman's presence, immediately had a vision of the spirit of his dead mother, reporting later that it seemed to him "indisputable that Walt was the link between us."

To be sure, Whitman was never a card-carrying spiritualist. Averse to doctrinaire positions, he viewed the various forms of popular mysticism with a certain skepticism and humorous detachment. In a long conversation with John Arnold in 1857, he discussed Andrew Jackson Davis's theory that matter preceded spirit and Cora Hatch's contrasting idea that spirit preceded matter. Whitman commented that both seemed "quite determined in their theories" and would be "much less determined" if they knew more. When in 1864 he attended a séance led by the famed medium Charles H. Foster, he found it "a shallow thing, & a humbug," with "some little things some might call curious perhaps" but mainly "table rappings & lots of nonsense." All the mystical movements were finally too confining for his expansive view, particularly as the decades passed. Spiritualism in time degenerated into a gimmicky movement that relied heavily on physical "evidences" of the afterlife, like spirit photographs. Harmonialism was replaced by the Christian optimism of Mary Baker Eddy, on the one hand, and the bland healthymindedness of Warren F. Evans and the mind-cure movement on the other.

Still, Whitman never surrendered his curiosity about the popular mystical movements. In an 1871 letter he reported that in a recent visit with a couple of friends "we had a capital good hour & a half—*talked Spiritualism*—I enjoyed it thoroughly—." In 1888 he could still write a poem, "Continuities," which he said was inspired by a conversation with a spiritualist. The language he used was one of spiritualist consolation, as he wrote that "Nothing is ever really lost, or can be lost, / No birth, identity, form—no object of the world, / Nor life force, nor any visible thing." To the end, his poetry reflected his long-standing interest in popular mysticism.

9

TOWARD A POPULAR AESTHETIC:
THE VISUAL ARTS

WHITMAN'S BELIEF that he would be absorbed by his nation was buoyed in part by his awareness that in many respects his ideas about art accorded with those of a broad spectrum of Americans.

In the two decades before the Civil War, the visual arts—particularly in the forms of photography, painting, and sculpture—were, like music and theater, a shared experience for people of different social classes. A democratic ethos, spurred by the new medium of photography, characterized the leading art styles, Hudson River painting and luminism, which tried to present the world naturally and directly, without many of the "high art" devices associated with European art. Egalitarianism was even more pronounced in the genre paintings of the day, especially those of William Sidney Mount and George Caleb Bingham, who presented lively, benign portraits of rural Americans engaged in common activities. Popular exhibitions of photographs and paintings also contributed to the democratization of art. The 1840s saw the rise of exhibition spaces such as Mathew Brady's daguerreotype gallery and the American Art Union, where a remarkably variegated mix of visual images dazzled viewers. Whitman was not only a regular at the galleries but also a chief celebrant of the long-running art and science exhibition that opened at New York's huge Crystal Palace in 1853, an exhibit conceived above all as an effort to make art available to the masses.

Whitman's appreciation of art dated at least from his *Eagle* days and intensified greatly in the early fifties, when he hobnobbed with Brooklyn artists and daguerreotypists. A third of his thirty-seven articles published between 1849 and 1855 commented on art, and five were devoted solely to it. So involved in the art scene did he become that he was invited to address the opening meeting of the Brooklyn Art Union in 1851 and was subsequently nominated for the presidency of the union. His Art Union address showed him trying to push the notion of art beyond the limits of visual representation to the realms of behavior and political action. He described as artistic all heroic action directed against corruption or tyranny, and he concluded the address with a long passage from one of his 1850 political-protest poems, "Resurgemus."

This political and social dimension was the substratum to his attraction to art, just as it was to his attraction to the opera and to popular mysticism. All promised transcendence, a new aesthetics, a means of balancing the physical and the spiritual—and, most notably, a strategy for coming to terms with the harsh social realities of the fifties. The fact that in his longest poem of the early fifties, "Pictures," he compared his head to a picture gallery in which were hung images of all kinds of people and things suggests how crucial the techniques of democratic art had become for him. He had been underscoring the social uses of art since the *Eagle* days, and in face of the political and social crisis the aesthetic element took on new importance.

The aesthetic theories of American artists gave him an ideal he believed could ameliorate deteriorating social conditions. Where he saw ugly materialism and corruption, they offered what he called "the gospel of beauty." Where he saw prurient sensationalism or sexual repression, they reinforced his notion of the sanctity of the body. Where he found ornamentation and artifice in literary style, they gave a rationale for an organic art based on natural rhythms and free forms.

"The Well-Taken Photograph"

SURROUNDED AS WE ARE TODAY by swirling images in the mass media, we may find it difficult to recapture the simple wonder photography elicited when it was publicly introduced by the Frenchman Louis-Jacques-Mandé Daguerre in August 1839. The world, it seemed, could actually be reproduced. Loved ones might die, but their images could be preserved. Distant places never visited could be enjoyed in daguerreotype. Art, death, space, time: all seemed changed by this apparently miraculous medium.

Photography put new demands on the artist and the writer. Since the world could now be captured "as is," what was the artist's role? The French painter Delaroche famously declared that the daguerreotype spelled the death of painting. This was, of course, an overstatement, but changes in painting and in many other kinds of representation did occur.

For one thing, a new realism was in order. A writer for *The Living Age* in 1846 said that the daguerreotype was "slowly accomplishing a great revolution in the morals of portrait painting"; artists could no longer flatter their subjects by making them appear beautiful or intelligent where a daguerreotype would tell them otherwise.

Photography's ability to reflect reality would always remain for Whitman its chief attraction. He once declared: "The photograph has this advantage: it lets nature have its way: the botheration with the painters is that they don't want nature to have its way." The more realistic moments in his poetry owed much to the vogue of the daguerreotype in America. "In these *Leaves* [*of Grass*] every thing is literally photographed. Nothing is poeticized," he wrote. This statement was perhaps too sweeping, but it pointed up the importance photography had for him.

Introduced in New York in 1839 by D. W. Seager, the daguerreotype achieved a popularity in America unmatched abroad, where legal restraints interfered with its commercialization. By 1853, there were more daguerreotype studios in Manhattan alone than in all of England, and more on Broadway than in London. By then, around three million daguerreotypes were produced annually in the United States.

American daguerreotypes could also claim superiority in quality. American pictures regularly won high honors in international competitions. In 1853 a British daguerreotypist conceded, "America produces more brilliant pictures than we do." The *New York Tribune* editor Horace Greeley boasted, "In daguerreotypes we beat the world." Whitman joined the chorus by announcing in the *Star*: "In New York, according to the unanimous verdict of the world, are taken far better daguerreotypes than in any other town or country." He registered photography's place in modern culture in his poems. In one he mentions "The implements for daguerreotyping," and in another he writes, "The camera and plate are prepared, the lady must sit for her daguerreotype." Even more important than such explicit references were ideas about popular art he absorbed from the daguerreotype scene.

Among those responsible for America's distinction in the new art form were three daguerreotypists he knew and admired: John Plumbe, Jr., Mathew B. Brady, and Gabriel Harrison. All three were prize-winning daguerreotypists who ran popular galleries he frequented.

The Welsh-born John Plumbe owned a chain of daguerreotype galleries in the East, including one at 251 Broadway, which Whitman loved to visit in the forties. Although the poet could not know it at the time, he was destined to owe a great debt to Plumbe, who solved the problem of reproducing daguerreotypes. Negatives would not come until colloidal photography was introduced in the midfifties. Since multiple copies of daguerreotypes could not be made, Plumbe began the practice of having their images copied by artists on lithographic plates, permitting reproduction. This was how the famous 1855 portrait of Whitman would be produced.

Through Plumbe Whitman got one his earliest exposures to the exhibition-gallery experience. After touring Plumbe's gallery in July 1846 he wrote: "You will see more *life* there, more variety, more human nature, more artistic beauty (for what can surpass that masterpiece of human perfection, the human face?) than in any spot we know of." Whitman felt he was in the presence of "an immense phantom concourse—speechless and motionless, but yet *realities*," and he added: "Time, space, both are annihilated, and we identify the semblances with the reality."

Such identification of semblance with reality became a chief reason for the prominence of photography in nineteenth-century America. The fad of photographing the corpses of family members sprang from the notion that loved ones were thus somehow kept alive. Henry Ward Beecher expressed a general view when he said of photography: "The world will never die after this. It will live in shadow. We shall have our uncles and aunts, our fathers and mothers, our children, and our children's children in every year's stage; and we can keep them." Photography seemed to provide a miraculous suspension of time and space by preserving the essence of individuals. Given this almost mystical outlook, it is not surprising that toward the end of the century photography would merge with spiritualism in the form of "spirit photographs," which often showed people in the presence of the spirits of their departed dear ones, as in the well-known photo of Mary Todd Lincoln backed by Abraham Lincoln's spectral image. Photography actually seemed able to reach beyond the grave!

This preservation of people's essential selves through pictures was a topic of conversation between Whitman and the era's leading photographer, Mathew Brady. Whitman often went to Brady's daguerreotype gallery on Broadway and in 1846 called him "a capital artist" whose "pictures possess a peculiar life-likeness." Whitman told Brady that he believed history could be best preserved through realistic portraits. "We had many a talk together," Whitman later recalled, about "how much better it would often be, rather than having a lot of contradictory records by witnesses or historians—say of Caesar, Socrates, Epictetus, others—if we could have three or four or half a dozen portraits—very accurate—of the men: that would be history—the best history—a history from which there would be no appeal." Whitman's compulsion in *Leaves of Grass* to have everything, in his words, "literally photographed" reflects his faith in the power of photography to absorb experience and hold it fast. In this sense, his poetic "I" was a kind of roving camera eye aimed at the world around him.

As the experiences of both Brady and Whitman would show, however, pictures do not reflect history in a straightforward way. Rather, they show the shaping hand of the photographer, who can include or exclude people or things according to a particular vision of the world. Although Brady photographed people of all social classes, his most famous achievements in the forties and early fifties was the photographing of so-called "illustrious Americans"—celebrities of all kinds, particularly political leaders. When people of different political stamps, often at each other's throats, were grouped together in daguerreotype dignity as illustrious Americans, a kind of visual utopia was created in which sectional hostilities and bitter personal rivalries were temporarily suspended. Brady's *Gallery of Illustrious Americans* (1850), published the year of the Compromise, showed the utopian possibilities of the daguerreotype. Juxtaposed in the volume were pictures of the Southern loyalist John C. Calhoun, the Northern antislavery editor Horace Greeley, the senatorial compromisers Henry Clay and Daniel Webster, and others of varied political views, all conjoined in pictorial stateliness.

For Whitman, this rather traditional version of the "illustrious Americans" harked back to his younger days, before the political crisis of the fifties shook his confidence in social rulers. Like Brady, Whitman would perform a delicate political balancing act in *Leaves of Grass,* in which proslavery types and their antislavery foes were "photographed" and put on exhibition. Whitman's "illustrious Americans," however, had little to do with the social leaders Brady had valorized. As seen in Chapter 5, between 1850 and 1854 incompetence and corruption in high places eroded public confidence in the powers that be. Whitman, like the emerging Republican Party, was fiercely rejecting entrenched authority and advancing a new kind of populism. As the Republicans would come up with the hardy western explorer John Frémont as their 1856 presidential candidate, so Whitman advertised himself as "one of the roughs," an image powerfully communicated in the frontispiece portrait of the casually dressed Whitman in the 1855 edition of *Leaves of Grass.*

Although it is perhaps the most famous author's portrait in American literary history, the 1854 picture has not been adequately discussed in context. The artist behind the picture, Gabriel Harrison, was well equipped to produce a working-class version of the illustrious American. The son of a Philadelphia bank-note engraver, Harrison was born in 1818, a year before Whitman. When he was six, his family relocated to New York. Before long the Harrison household became a hub for artists and stage people. Gabriel became a jack-of-all-trades and master of several. He was a landscape painter, actor, and stage manager as well as the author of six plays (one of them an adaptation of Hawthorne's *The Scarlet Letter*) and a number of poems, stories, and articles. He knew Poe, of whom he did a portrait. Above all, he was an expert daguerreotypist who won several medals for his work. He had worked with John Plumbe and M. M. Lawrence in the forties and then in 1852 opened his own spacious daguerreotype gallery at 283 Fulton Street in Brooklyn. Two years later, here he took the daguerreotype of Whitman that was the basis of the 1855 picture.

The picture represented a confluence of Harrison's and Whitman's sensibilities. Their eclectic interests overlapped. Both were vitally interested in various forms of writing and art. Both were attracted to the tempestuous acting style of the Bowery B'hoy's Delight, Edwin Forrest—Harrison was Forrest's close friend, wrote a book on him, and tried to emulate him in his own perfervid acting. Both Harrison and Whitman were ardent Free-Soil Democrats who attended the 1848 Buffalo convention and remained politically active after that. Whitman met Harrison in the forties, probably when the latter was at Plumbe's and certainly when he was at Lawrence's. When Harrison opened his Brooklyn studio, Whitman exulted in the *Star*: "New York has made over to Brooklyn her most perfect daguerreotype artist—Gabriel Harrison." He hailed Harrison as "one of the best Daguerrean operators probably in the world" and his pictures as "perfect works of truth and art."

Harrison had the appropriate experience to take a daguerreotype that was at once casual and larger than life. On the one hand, he was skilled in what were called occupationals, daguerreotypes of workers in daily dress holding tools of their trade. On the other hand, he was an innovator in "poetic" or allegorical daguerreotypes, such as *The Infant Savior Bearing the Cross*, with his son in the role of Jesus, or *Young America*, a romantic study of his open-shirted son. On a sweltering summer day in 1854 when he saw Whitman on Fulton Street coming home from his carpenter job, he summoned him into his studio, probably with the aim of producing an occupational daguerreotype. What he produced, as it turned out, combined the egalitarianism of the occupational with the resonance of the allegorical—an ideal combination for the poet who in 1855 wished to present himself as both the ordinary American and the messianic Answerer.

Whitman would later say that the picture (see fig. 2) bore a close resemblance to the way he actually looked in the midfifties, but there is such a studied representativeness about it that it is hard to see it as a direct representation of the real Whitman. A certain distancing resulted inevitably from the method of reproduction. Harrison's daguerreotype was copied by the Manhattan engraver Samuel Hollyer onto a litho-graphic plate and then reprinted opposite the title page in the 1855 edi-tion of *Leaves of Grass*. The engraving process most likely added depth to the daguerreotype, which has not survived. The resultant picture pos-sesses the democratic familiarity of occupational daguerreotypes with the representative quality of allegorical ones. Whitman stands with an air of "I am your equal," with his open shirt, rumpled pants, tilted hat, and grizzled face radiating egalitarianism. At the same time, there are unexpected depths and subtleties. The right hand is perched openly on the hip, but the left disappears into the pants, suggesting the bodily mys-teries Whitman will be exploring. The expression of the face is full of emotional shadings: insolence, arrogance, calmness, compassion, even a touch of sadness.

Whether or not the portrait accurately portrayed Whitman, it was just as subjective a construction as Brady's celebrity-oriented gallery of illustrious Americans. Whitman's picture showed an illustrious Ameri-can for the midfifties: individualistic, defiant, rooted in the working-class consciousness that seemed to offer redemption in a time of failed social rulers. It pointed to the gallery of "photographs" in the early poetry— vignettes of common life promoting the artisanal values Whitman was holding up to the nation. Photography was an essential metaphor behind his democratic aesthetic. Since it was believed that essences could be cap-tured in photographs, Whitman presented a montage of images that, he hoped, would preserve the principally working-class types he was valo-rizing. This impulse toward working-class portraiture, as will be seen, also had deep roots in the American genre paintings of the day.

Photography offered an ideal of a direct mimesis of reality, support-ing Whitman's oft-repeated aim of establishing an honest, personal rela-tionship with the reader. He once told Traubel that the superiority of photographs to oils was that "they are honest." In a sense, photography pointed beyond itself; it suggested that the reality captured artistically in well-crafted photographs could enhance everyday reality. Everyone knows the glow that lingers after a good film, intensifying common ex-perience. Such possibilities for intensification seemed particularly great in a time when photography was brand-new. As Gabriel Harrison wrote: "You cannot look upon anything in nature without being reminded of some peculiar and beautiful result if daguerreotyped; even the small blade of grass." Whitman made a similar point when he said he saw "more *life*" in a daguerreotype gallery than anywhere else. He wrote in a poem, "The well-taken photographs—but your wife or friend close and solid in your arms?" Here the photographic representation of the loved one is the catalyst for a fuller appreciation of the loved one's actual presence. The picture as a focusing of experience led back to life. In the age of the daguerreotype, it was easy to believe in the miracle of the commonplace.

The Gospel of Beauty

ALTHOUGH PHOTOGRAPHY CONTRIBUTED to Whitman's democratic aesthetic, popular paintings of the day had an even greater influence on him. With a few notable exceptions (such as John Quidor and some periodical illustrators) antebellum painters had the same ethos as daguerreotypists: they strove for mimetic realism. Theirs, however, was a spiritualized realism, one that accorded at once with Whitman's earthly and religious sides. Accepting, like Whitman, the harmonious vision of the physical creation advanced by progressive scientists such as Humboldt and Agassiz, they pictured nature in detail but still retained a mystical aura that led in the fifties to the emergence of luminism. The pendulum swing in Whitman's poetry from earthly minutiae to mystical suggestion had precedent in a painting style that was at once mimetic and transcendental.

As with music, Whitman saw in painting a means of refining and elevating the masses. In the *Eagle*, at a time when he had just begun to complain vociferously about urban vice and squalor, he wrote an article, "Polishing the Common People," in which he called for the widespread distribution of artworks. "We could wish the spreading of a sort of democratical artistic atmosphere, among the inhabitants of our republic," he wrote, sped by "the more frequent diffusion of tasty prints, cheap casts of statuary, and so on." Twelve years later, in a piece on art and music in the *Daily Times*, he made a similar argument: "It is a well known fact that to the refining and conservative influence of the fine arts society owes more than we can readily trace; nay, the very stability of good government and the well being of society rest on no surer foundation than when it is cemented by these ties that bind all men in one bond of sentiment and feeling kindled by the admiration excited within them at the glories of art."

He had reason to find an almost religious elevation in art, for the antebellum art scene was dominated by forms that affirmed the beauty and order of creation. The art exhibits he frequented were filled with life-affirming, nature-affirming works: the Hudson River paintings of Thomas Cole, Asher B. Durand, and Thomas Doughty; the Greek Revival sculpture of Horatio Greenough and Hiram Powers; the optimistic, intensely democratic genre paintings of William Sidney Mount and

George Caleb Bingham; the peaceful luminist landscapes of Fitz Hugh Lane, Sanford Gifford, and John F. Kensett; the grand, epic luminist canvases of Frederick Edwin Church.

Though often technically sophisticated, these paintings were presented as works for the masses. This period saw the rise of popular art exhibitions. Reviewing the entertainment scene in 1850, the Manhattan journalist George Foster wrote, "Another very popular feature of our public amusements is picture-seeing; and in this respect it is really incredible the progress we have made and the advantages with which we are provided." Like the Phrenological Cabinet and the daguerreotype galleries, the picture galleries represented a democratized visual experience, as paintings of all varieties were typically hung in layered rows on crowded walls. Whitman's eclectic catalogs, with their juxtapositions of widely assorted vignettes, may be said to have reflected the exhibition format, particularly since the first such catalog appeared in the early fifties poem "Pictures," introduced by these lines comparing his head to an art gallery:

> In a little house pictures I keep, many pictures hanging suspended—
>   It is not a fixed house,
> It is round—it is but a few inches from one side of it to the other
>   side,
> But behold! it has room enough—in it, hundreds and thousands,—
>   all the varieties.

The American paintings of the period were democratic in style and subject matter. In general, they minimized the painterly and stylized on behalf of the direct, the accessible, the transparent. Although inevitably more idealized than daguerreotypes, many of them paid photographic attention to small details and minimized obvious artistic interference between the viewer and the scene being viewed. Brushstrokes were muted; impressionism and conscious subjectivity were avoided. In nature paintings, the main effort was to enable the average viewer to experience God's creation afresh, particularly in the form of still landscapes tinged with luminist iridescence. In genre paintings, the effort was to enable ordinary folk to see slightly idealized versions of themselves in action, at work or at play.

There were many practitioners of these principles between 1830 and 1860 and several theorists, most notably the sculptor Horatio Greenough. Greenough elucidated what was a basic tenet of antebellum art: ornament must be stripped away, and artistic form should be natural rather than artificial. Greenough's ideas gained wide exposure when a collec-

tion of his magazine essays was published in 1852 and when Henry T.
Tuckerman's *Memorial of Horatio Greenough* appeared the next year.
Like Whitman, Greenough believed that America desperately needed
art and artists. "I speak of art now," he wrote, "because I think I see that
it is a want—a want widely, deeply felt—an intellectual want, a social
want, an economical want—and that to a degree which few seem to
suspect. I believe that these States need art as a visible exponent of their
civilization." He called for a democratic art that was simple, unembel-
lished. "The invariable development of embellishment and decoration is
more embellishment and decoration," he wrote, adding that "the first
downward step was *the introduction of the first inorganic, nonfunctional
element, whether of shape or color.*" Along with naturalness came experi-
mentation. He noted that in nature "there is no arbitrary law of propor-
tion, no unbending model of form," and so artists should "*encourage
experiment* at the risk of license, rather than submit to an iron rule." As
seen earlier, Greenough was also a chief figure in the American treat-
ment of the nude. He could write of "the human frame, the most beauti-
ful organization of earth, the exponent and minister of the highest being
we immediately know."

Whitman's search for a transparent, democratic style free of artifice
and close to nature's forms was akin to this artistic theory. In the 1855
preface he labeled "a nuisance and revolt" anything that "distorts honest
shapes," specifying that in paintings or illustrations or sculptures Ameri-
cans "shall receive no pleasure from violations of natural models and
must not permit them." Sounding like Greenough and other artists of
the day, he wrote, "Most works are beautiful without ornament." The
"transparent, plate-glassy style" he said he wished to develop reflected
not only the popular music he loved but the art as well. His aim to restore
poetry to nature's forms brought him close to Greenough in advocating
organic form. Just as Greenough argued that art should follow nature's
rhythms, so Whitman wrote, "The rhyme and uniformity of perfect
poems show the free growth of metrical laws and bud from them as un-
erringly and loosely as lilacs or roses on a bush, and take shapes as com-
pact as the shapes of chestnuts and oranges and melons and pears, and
shed the perfume impalpable to form." Following the democratic trend
to get directly back to the creation in art, Whitman gave the Adamic
promise of unadulterated, sun-washed nature and a return to origins:

> Stop this day and night with me and you shall possess the origin of
>   all poems,
> You shall possess the good of the earth and sun (there are millions of
>   suns left,)

You shall no longer take things at second or third hand.

At times, he could borrow directly from specific paintings. The artistic school he usually tapped was genre painting. The portrayal of rural folk in daily activities was not exclusively an American phenomenon: it had precedent, for example, in the genre works of the Scottish artist Sir David Wilkie and the French painter Gustave Courbet. But genre painting took on distinctly American attributes when it was taken up by artists of the new Republic intent on featuring native scenes and characters. For subject matter, the American genre painters looked to hearty outdoor types—farmers, hunters, trappers, and riverboat men. More often than not, these subjects were portrayed good-humoredly engaged in some form of leisurely, often prankish activity. In the hands of the genre painters, the raucous individualism of the American frontier was given a picturesque, ennobled quality. At the same time, genre painting was one of the few public arenas in which Indians and blacks were treated with less of the overt racism that permeated nearly every aspect of American society.

This latter aspect of genre painting had a real importance for Whitman, who struggled against racist stereotypes that bombarded him on all sides and sometimes infiltrated his own attitudes. In American art he found a means of combating racism within his culture and within himself. His relationship with two artists who treated Native Americans—George Catlin and Alfred Jacob Miller—is particularly telling. Catlin, the foremost antebellum artist of the American West and the Indians, struck Whitman as a strongly American artist whose works were a national treasure. In 1846 Whitman wrote a series of articles urging the government to purchase and preserve Catlin's Indian paintings, writing that "we shall never again have the opportunity of restoring to our country these paintings and memorials, so emphatically American, and of such decided importance to Art and to our national history." Whitman got to know Catlin, who before going to Europe gave him a painting of the Seminole chief Osceola and possibly another work. In old age Whitman pointed out the Osceola to Traubel: "That picture on the wall over there was his [Catlin's]: he gave it to me over forty years ago. He was an interesting old codger." Leafing through a catalog of Catlin's paintings, Whitman told Traubel that the paintings were most interesting not "from the art side, but from the human side, the side of experience, emotion, life."

The human side. The first step in overcoming the racial stereotypes in antebellum America was recognizing the human side of ethnic minorities, who in many cultural areas were depicted as subhuman. Catlin's

special contribution was his moving portrayals of one of the most perse-
cuted of all the tribes, the Florida Seminoles, and their leader Osceola.
The famed Tiger of the Everglades, Osceola was the talented, magnetic
chief whose grim fate epitomized the prevalent injustices against Native
Americans. In the Southern wars of the mid-1830s, he outmaneuvered
federal troops until he was tricked to surrender under a truce flag. He
was bound to his horse and imprisoned in a South Carolina fort, where
he soon died, a miserable victim of treachery. This tragic incident had
struck home to the young Whitman when it had occurred in 1838, and
it was kept alive in his mind by Catlin's painting of Osceola. In 1890
the tragedy of the betrayed chief at last flowered in a Whitman poem,
"Osceola." In the prose preface to the poem Whitman gave his opinion
that the captured chief had "literally died of 'a broken heart.'" In the
poem Whitman re-created the sorrow of the incident in his description
of the imprisoned Osceola pathetically donning his native garb and war
paint, grasping his tomahawk, extending his hands to his wife and chil-
dren, then dying.

The humanization of minorities in American art had influenced
Whitman's earlier poetry as well. The section of "Song of Myself" pic-
turing the marriage of the trapper and the Indian woman was based on
The Trapper's Bride, an 1837 painting by the Baltimore artist Alfred Ja-
cob Miller. This famous painting (see fig. 35) had gone through nine
lithographic versions and was often reproduced. Whitman had many op-
portunities to see it, either in the original or in reproduction. He proba-
bly also saw another genre study of a racially intermixed family unit,
George Caleb Bingham's *Fur Trader and Half Breed Son* (1845). Both
Miller and Bingham showed how the taboo topic of miscegenation could
be handled frankly and without apology. In Miller's rendering of the
theme, the trapper sits on a bank, lovingly touching his bride's hand as
her friends and family watch nearby. Whitman gives a picture that is
particularly close to Miller's in the original, 1855 version:

> I saw the marriage of the trapper in the open air in the far-west....
>   the bride was a red girl,
> Her father and his friends sat near by crosslegged and dumbly
>   smoking.... they had moccasins to their feet and large thick
>   blankets hanging from their shoulders;
> On a bank lounged the trapper.... he was dressed mostly in skins....
>   his luxuriant beard and curls protected his neck,
> One hand rested on his rifle.... the other hand held firmly the wrist
>   of the red girl,
> She had long eyelashes.... her head was bare.... her coarse straight

locks descended upon her voluptuous limbs and reached to her
feet.

It is notable that although Whitman often endorsed the institution
of marriage and mentioned husbands and wives in his verse, this is the
only extended wedding scene in his poetry, and it involves a racially
mixed couple. Miller's painting had opened up possibilities for racial
harmony and love, and Whitman emphasizes the theme of racial bond-
ing. His scene is framed by Indians in their native dress, calmly smoking
with an air of relaxation and peace. Racial interchange is communicated
by similarities between the Indians and the trapper: they are relaxing,
wrapped in blankets; he is lounging, dressed in skins and enveloped by
his flowing hair. The cruel historical record of mass killings and displace-
ment of Native Americans that began in earnest under Andrew Jackson
and worsened in the course of the century is countered here by the trap-
per's rifle, destined not for murder but for defending his Indian wife and
supplying for her. Whitman's pictorial passage of interracial togetherness
aptly ends with a description of the woman herself, whose statuesque
beauty and simple dignity are highlighted.

Another of Whitman's scenes of interracial harmony, the later passage
in "Song of Myself" about the African-American team driver, also had
precedent in genre paintings, particularly those of the Long Island artist
William Sidney Mount. The influential Mount, whose works crowded the
New York galleries in the forties and fifties, became famous in part be-
cause of his paintings of blacks. An article on Mount in the 1851 *Ameri-
can Whig Review* by W. Alfred Jones emphasized this aspect of his work:
"His heads of negroes ... are the finest Ethiopian portraits put on can-
vas." The same year, Whitman in an article on American art mentioned
having seen "Mount's last work—I think his best—of a Long Island
negro, the winner of a goose at raffle." The fact that Whitman could
speak comparatively of Mount's "last" and "best" painting suggests he
was aware of his fellow Long Islander's oeuvre. It is likely Whitman and
Mount knew each other, especially since the painting *Walt Whitman's
School at Southold, 1840*, attributed to Mount, had an unusually personal
title for a painter who rarely used persons' names in his titles.

If they did know each other, Whitman found in Mount an artist who,
like himself, was an ardent Jacksonian Democrat who disliked abolition-
ism and had mixed feelings about slavery but who nonetheless depicted
blacks possessing nobility and humanity. To be sure, Mount's African-
Americans exist in an Arcadian world insulated from the raging slavery
controversy. But even the artistic portrayal of blacks in joyous rural activ-
ities had its use in a time when they were caricatured in minstrel shows,

phrenological illustrations, and much popular fiction. The predominantly racist cultural pictures of blacks enraged Frederick Douglass, who noticed that in phrenological illustrations in the popular press the white was inevitably shown as beautiful and dignified, while "the Negro, on the other hand, appears with features distorted, lips exaggerated, forehead depressed—and the whole expression of the countenance made to harmonize with the popular idea of Negro imbecility and degradation." Although Mount's African-American portraits had little revolutionary content, they overcame the nearly ubiquitous racism in American illustrations that Douglass lamented.

Particularly suggestive among Mount's paintings in terms of Whitman's portrayal of blacks is *Farmer's Nooning* (1835) (see fig. 36). The painting shows five farmers—three white men, a white boy, and a large black man—resting by a tree and a haystack at noon hour. The black man is strategically foregrounded: he is the only adult lying in the sun rather than in the shade, and he is the only one whose full body and face are shown (the white adults are viewed from the back and the side). He is a massive, handsome man clad in a sparkling white, open shirt and tan pants. As he lies on the ground, his arms outspread, a young white boy playfully tickles his face with a piece of straw—a bit of interracial *jouissance* anticipatory of Huck Finn in his more affectionate moments with Jim. The theme of racial intermingling and comradeship is underscored by Mount's positioning of the figures. All the bodies blend into each other because they overlap on the canvas. Mount creates a picturesque moment of racial harmony.

Whitman evokes a similar spirit in his passage about the black team driver:

> The negro holds firmly the reins of his four horses, the block swags
>   underneath on its tied-over chain,
> The negro that drives the huge dray of the stone-yard, steady and tall
>   he stands pois'd on one leg on the string-piece,
> His blue shirt exposes his ample neck and breast and loosens over his
>   hip-band,
> His glance is calm and commanding, he tosses the slouch of his hat
>   away from his forehead,
> The sun falls on his crispy hair and moustache, falls on the black of
>   his polish'd and perfect limbs.
>
> I behold the picturesque giant and love him, and I do not stop there,
> I go with the team also.

The specifically pictorial quality of this passage is unmistakable. Whitman calls the driver "the picturesque giant" and emphasizes his aesthetic, ennobling features. Even more than Mount's massive black, Whitman's is foregrounded, since he is not framed by whites but stands tall and commanding in his driver's seat. As in Mount, his open shirt exposes his upper chest, and the sun suffuses his black body, highlighting its beauty and brawn. The gesture toward interracial harmony made in Mount's painting is repeated in Whitman's passage, which ends with the "I" sitting by the black man as he drives his team.

The theme of interracial bonding in genre painting was mingled with the related one of a radically egalitarian treatment of rural types at work or at play. Here again Mount stands out as a figure close to Whitman's sensibility. Whitman and Mount had much in common. Mount was born in 1807 in Setauket, a Long Island village about thirty miles northeast of the West Hills area, where generations of Whitmans had settled. Mount had a rural childhood on a Long Island farm and then entered Manhattan's artistic and literary circles in early adulthood—a life pattern similar to Whitman's. Both divided time between the Long Island countryside and the city, though Mount was far less tolerant of the city than Whitman and in fact has been characterized by one art historian as "the most prominent painter to respond to the nationalistic surge that proclaimed the superiority of New World innocence over Old World corruption as embodied in the dichotomy of country versus city." The tall, slight, buoyant Mount had certain tastes and character traits in common with Whitman. Both had reputations for indolence and slowness belied by their actual industriousness and prodigious output. Both dabbled in spiritualism—Mount more seriously than Whitman (he once claimed to have gotten two spirit-letters from Rembrandt, who told him he was America's best artist).

More significantly, both consciously sought to create original American art forms that made room for previously marginalized working-class types. Deeply rooted in rural Long Island, both had vivid memories of a rapidly disappearing artisanal and farm-based communal culture. They took it upon themselves to keep alive the zest and intimacy of this pre-industrial culture. Like Whitman, Mount felt an impulse toward originality and independence. As Mount put it, he was driven from the start by "the desire to be entirely original.... I launched forth on my sea of adventure with the firm determination to avoid the style of any artist and to create a school of my own." In the eyes of many contemporaries, he succeeded in doing so. His genre studies of rustic Americans were endlessly imitated. A typically laudatory reviewer called Mount "a follower of no school, an imitator of no master" and specified that his works were "of a strictly national character; the pride and boast, not only of his native Long Island, not yet of the State of New York solely, but of the whole country."

Whitman and Mount shared an interest in the homely details of everyday life and people, usually with an emphasis on the joyful activity of country or artisan types. Just as Mount liked to capture workers in moments of recreation or ease (for example, rural folk dancing or playing instruments or just idling), so Whitman chants of lazily contemplating the grass or of common workers singing songs. Just as Mount, with particular persistence, represents the activity and movement of common life, so Whitman captures varied subjects in the midst of everyday activities, relying heavily on active verbs or participles. The participial usages in the titles of typical Mount paintings—*Bargaining for a Horse, Farmers Nooning, Eel Spearing at Setauket, Ringing the Pig*—communicate the sense of activity that enlivens them and explains why they were enjoyed by antebellum Americans as colorful stories. When Whitman's friend John Burroughs described the poet's catalogs as "one line genre word paintings," he doubtless had in mind the kind of crisp, lively vignettes Mount had popularized.

Given their shared copious interest in ordinary activities, it is understandable that when Mount sketched plans for possible paintings he produced notebook passages comparable in spirit to Whitman's catalogs:

Two lovers walking out.

Walking out after marriage, one after the other, after the manner of Judse and Sam.

The husband two months after marriage, with a bag of grain on his shoulder going to mill.

A Whig after the Election.

A Clergyman looking for a sermon at the bottom of his barrel.

A Negro fiddling on the crossroads on Sunday.

Kite broke loose.

Clamming and fishing.

. . . .

Lovers Economical eating ice cream out of one glass, aint you glad you have come. Only one shilling—the waiter grinning behind.

A Country woman looking at some portraits for the first time.

Boys fighting.

A nurse amusing a baby with a looking glass. The child diverted with its own image.

A little girl pointing at you with her finger.

A camp meeting scene. Interior of a tent or ring—

The abundant details of average American experience flood Mount's consciousness. As with Whitman, even the most common activities take on interest for Mount. It is not far from his artistic sensibility to the one that generated catalogs like this:

> The one-year wife is recovering and happy having a week ago borne her first child,
> The clean-hair'd Yankee girl works with her sewing-machine or in the factory or mill,
> The paving-man leans on his two-handed rammer, the reporter's lead flies swiftly over the note-book, the sign-painter is lettering with blue and gold,
> The canal boy trots on the tow-path, the book-keeper counts at his desk, the shoemaker waxes his thread,
> The conductor beats time for the band and all the performers follow him,
> The child is baptised, the convert is making his first professions,
> The regatta is spread on the bay, the race is begun, (how the white sails sparkle!)

Elsewhere in this catalog Whitman writes, "The connoisseur peers along the exhibition-gallery with half-shut eyes bent sideways." Whitman's catalogs as a whole are a kind of exhibition gallery, reflecting the democratic eclecticism in the antebellum galleries where Mount and others exhibited. Mount was hardly alone among artistic precursors of Whitman's catalogs. The Missouri painter George Caleb Bingham, a western version of Mount, produced popular genre studies of frontier types that Whitman knew of. Bingham's *The Jolly Boatman* (1846), labeled by one reviewer "a death blow to all one's preconceived notions of HIGH ART" because of its vernacular treatment of frolicking flatboat men, was bought by the American Art Union, which distributed around eighteen thousand copies of the painting to its members. Among Whitman's vignettes are several similar to Bingham's, such as this picture: "Flatboatmen make fast toward dusk near the cotton-wood or pecan-trees, / Coon-seekers go through the regions of the Red river or through those drain'd by the Tennessee, or through those of the Arkansas."

There is also a similarity between Bingham's painting *Shooting for the Beef* (1850) and Whitman's account of a western turkey shoot. Bingham's painting was shown at the American Art Union from January 1851 to December 1852, and it is likely Whitman saw it either then or another time, for he reproduced its principal characters and action in these lines:

The western turkey-shooting draws old and young, some lean on
    their rifles, some sit on logs,
Out from the crowd steps the marksman, takes his position, levels his
    piece.

While genre painting contributed to the catalogs, in a larger sense
Whitman was committed to the union of matter and spirit, the real and
the ideal that informed antebellum painting as a whole. He responded
favorably to two leaders of the Hudson River School, Thomas Doughty,
whom he called "the prince of landscapists" and "the best of American
painters," and Asher Durand, about whom he wrote, "all he does is
good." These painters modified the ideal, allegorical style of their fellow
Hudson River artist Thomas Cole, turning to a near-photographic style
in the faith that nature in its unembellished details always pointed to-
ward God's harmonious universe.

An even more obvious spirituality came with the luminists of the
fifties. Luminism had precedent in the paintings of eighteenth-century
French artists like Claude Lorrain. The American painters who devel-
oped the luminist style went beyond the almost uniform gold of Euro-
pean art, picturing landscapes bathed in cool light tones ranging from
silver to bronze. Representative luminist paintings, such as Frederick
Edwin Church's *Twilight, "Short Arbiter Twixt Day and Night"* (1850)
and John Frederick Kensett's *Sunset, Camel's Hump, Vermont* (1851),
studied the prismatic refractions along the color spectrum emanating
from a single light source. The rise of luminism came at a time when
Melville in *Moby-Dick* was pondering the "colorless all-color" of the
white whale and when Thoreau in *Walden* contemplated the dazzling
colors produced by the pond's clear water and ice.

Whitman joined his contemporaries by picturing light and its pris-
matic refractions. The light that floods luminist painting, suggesting
God's immanence and man's goodness, is akin to the light that plays
through his poetry. A particular analogy can be made between him and
Frederick Edwin Church. Like Whitman, Church was inspired by the
effort of the Prussian scientist Humboldt to record "kosmos," or the full
scale of physical creation; Church actually followed in Humboldt's foot-
steps by twice visiting South America. Church and another American
painter, Albert Bierstadt, forged an epic luminism by depicting vast,
light-filled landscapes on huge canvases. These landscapes affirmed si-
multaneously the grandeur of the physical world and the ever-present
possibility for transcendence. Church's *Andes of Ecuador* (1855) typified
epic luminism, revealing a tremendous mountainscape filled with varied

colors produced by the light of the sun, whose rays suggest spirituality by forming a glowing cross in the upper middle of the canvas.

Whitman similarly registered the vast effects of light. "Give me the splendid silent sun with all his beams full-dazzling," he wrote. His poem "A Prairie Sunset" pictured an expansive landscape aglow with the full range of colors:

> Shot gold, maroon and violet, dazzling silver, emerald, fawn,
> The earth's whole amplitude and Nature's multiform power consign'd
>   for once to colors;
>
> The light, the general air possess'd by them—colors till now
>   unknown,
> No limit, confine—not the Western sky alone—the high
>   meridian—North, South, all,
> Pure, luminous colors fighting the silent shadows to the last.

Like Church, Whitman here transforms a colorful landscape into a metaphor for cosmic unity. The colors are incredibly varied, but they have a unifying effect because they encompass the entire scene and, by association, the whole world. There is "[n]o limit, confine" to them. They embody "earth's whole amplitude and Nature's multiform power," taking possession of "the general air" and stretching in all directions.

The luminist tendency to see an idealizing light everywhere enabled him to update the traditional religious image of the halo. In his poem "To You" he re-created Christian art in modern, luminist fashion:

> Painters have painted their swarming groups and the centre-figure
>   of all,
> From the head of the centre-figure spreading a nimbus of gold-
>   color'd light,
> But I paint myriads of heads, but paint no head without its nimbus
>   of gold-color'd light,
> From my hand the brain of every man and woman it streams,
>   effulgently flowing forever.

This passage states directly an implied message of much antebellum art: the potential divinity of mankind. The luminists, like the Hudson River painters before them, avoided bald expression of this idea, featuring nature rather than humans. Whitman, perhaps influenced by the Harmonial idea of the "Solar Man," is as interested in the light emanating from humans as in the light that suffuses nature. Here and elsewhere in his poetry, he paints the light he sees streaming forever from every man and woman.

In Search of a Democratic Art

DESPITE REAL AFFINITIES between Whitman and contemporary painters, there were important differences. He was ultimately dissatisfied with the exactitude and precision of much antebellum painting. There was a philosophical and social complacency behind the prevailing style, which seemed to announce that nature, God, and humanity could be neatly summed up and delivered to the viewer in optimistic packages. He knew the rough, turbulent aspects of American experience, and he saw that they were minimized by the main Hudson River painters. He wanted picturesqueness but also explosiveness, rebelliousness, suggestiveness.

Late in life he would discover these qualities in the French painter Jean-François Millet. He found in *The Sower* (1850), Millet's famous study of peasant life, "a sublime murkiness and original fury," reminding him of the explosive cultural forces behind the French Revolution. In Millet's works Whitman felt "the untold something behind all that was depicted—an essence, a suggestion, an indirection, leading off into the immortal mysteries." He felt such a kinship with Millet that he once said his poems were "really only Millet in another form—they are the Millet that Walt Whitman has succeeded in putting into words." There is no evidence, however, that he had been aware of Millet before he had produced the early editions of *Leaves of Grass*. Nor is there a record of his having known of another populist French artist, Gustave Courbet, although, as Albert Boime points out, there are tantalizing similarities between Courbet's rebellious, sometimes sexually explicit paintings and Whitman's poems.

Although Whitman did not find a Millet or a Courbet on the antebellum scene, he made what use he could of the artistic materials America had to offer. In the early fifties he actually enjoyed the company of artists more than that of writers. He spent a lot of time in the Brooklyn studio of the sculptor Henry Kirke Brown, whose work he had admired since the *Eagle* days. Brown had begun as a smoothly neoclassic sculptor but then had introduced naturalistic American motifs in vigorous, action-oriented works like *Indian and the Panther*. Whitman also befriended many other artists, including the young sculptor John Quincy Adams Ward, the landscapist and portrait painter Frederick A. Chapman, and the Hudson River landscapist Jesse Talbot. In Brown's studio he talked with many other artists who told him of their experiences in the art circles of France and Italy. He later recalled "one sparkling fellow" full of enthusiasm about the French painter Pierre de Béranger. Whitman apparently shared some of the enthusiasm, for he was nicknamed Béranger by the Brown group.

There was one American artist he thought showed especially great promise: the Brooklyn portrait painter Walter Libbey. He found in Libbey's work the texturing and suggestiveness that were absent from the prevailing hard-surfaced style. In an 1851 article on Brooklyn artists he brought attention to a recent Libbey portrait of a casually dressed country boy playing a flute while seated on a riverbank. "There is no hardness," Whitman wrote, "and the eyes are not pained by the sharpness of outline which mars many otherwise fine pictures. In the scene of the background, and in all the accessories, there is a delicious melting in, so to speak, of object with object; an effect that is frequent enough in nature, though painters seem to disdain following it." It was this "melting in" quality that Whitman missed in much American art and that he tried to attain in several artistic moments in his poetry. With all his attention to vivid particularities, he also strained toward vista and suggestiveness, as in this line: "A show of summer softness—a contact of something unseen—an amour of the light and air."

Whitman saw in Libbey not only a nascent impressionism but also a freshly democratic treatment of common life. Indeed, he made Libbey's painting the pretext for differentiating democratic American art from what he saw as its aristocratic European counterpart:

> Abroad, a similar subject would show the boy as handsome, perhaps, but he would be a young boor, and nothing more. The stamp of class is, in this way, upon all the fine European painters, where the subjects are of a proper kind; while in this boy of Walter Libbey's, there is nothing to prevent his becoming a President, or even an editor of a leading newspaper.

This notion of the worth and potential of common folk, which would burst forth in Whitman's poetry of the midfifties, had been given a picturesque quality in Libbey's work.

Whatever promise Libbey showed, though, was not destined to be realized. He died prematurely the year after Whitman wrote his article. He would remain in the poet's mind an example of talent unfulfilled. As he said to Traubel: "Libbey: he was quite young—a friend of mine: Walter Libbey: bright, versatile, full of promise, it was everywhere recognized: but died young with practically nothing accomplished—not even a name won." Whitman kept a Libbey portrait until the end of his life.

One wonders whether he would have been fully satisfied with Libbey's art even if Libbey had lived and matured. Like most antebellum artists, Libbey failed to absorb the wild, agitated, radical idioms that represented the more subversive elements of American society and politics. Whitman took it upon himself to push American art theory toward a broad, inclusive realm that had room for the full range of experience, from the placidly beautiful to the rebellious and explosive.

His two main efforts in this direction were his 1851 Brooklyn Art Union address and his early fifties notebook poem "Pictures." Both of these pieces showed that Whitman viewed art as a powerful force for social redemption, whose full potential could be realized only if it took into account revolutionary aims and working-class expression.

His speech before the Brooklyn Art Union, delivered on March 31, 1851 (a month after his Libbey article), reiterated his idea that art was desperately needed by an increasingly materialistic society. "Among such people as Americans," he declared, "viewing most things with an eye to pecuniary profit—. . . ambitious of the physical rather than the intellectual; a race to whom matter of fact is everything, and the ideal nothing—a nation of whom the steam-engine is no bad symbol, he does a good work who, pausing in the way, calls to the feverish crowd that in life we live upon this beautiful earth, there may, after all, be something vaster and better than dress and the table, and business, and politics." He went on: "To the artist, I say, has been given the command to go forth unto all the world and preach the gospel of beauty." That gospel consisted of exposing people to the fresh, simple origins of creation: "[W]ith this freshness—with this that the Lord called good—the Artist has to do—And it is a beautiful truth that all men contain something of the artist in them."

So far, he was voicing ideas common in American art circles of his day. The Hudson River painters, after all, often argued that the artist's function was to arouse the aesthetic sense in people by returning them to nature's primal beauties.

Where he went beyond current artistic doctrine was in the closing section of his speech, in which he extended the idea of art to include all heroic actions, especially revolutionary or subversive ones. To be sure, he was not alone in identifying art with human behavior. Thomas Carlyle and Horatio Greenough, for instance, had argued that beauty and action were essentially one. Similarly, Whitman asserted: "I think of few heroic actions, which cannot be traced to the artistical impulse. He who does great deeds, does them from his sensitiveness to moral beauty. Such men are not merely artists, they are artistic material." What stood out was his revolutionary position. He gave as examples of artistic action the self-sacrifice of "all great rebels and innovators," mentioning the Hungarian revolutionary Kossuth, the exiled Italian rebel Mazzini, Commodore James Lawrence on the bloody deck of the *Chesapeake*, Washington in a crisis, Mary Stuart on the block. He continued: "Read how slaves have battled against their oppressors—how the bullets of tyrants have, since the first King ruled, never been able to put down the unquenchable thirst of man for his rights." He concluded the address with a recitation of the lines from his own poem "Resurgemus" about the corpses of murdered young rebels nurturing the seeds of freedom and revolt against tyrants all over the earth.

This was Whitman trying to bring social and political conscience to American art, which by and large in his day was politically complacent. As seen earlier, the early fifties was the time Whitman was assailing the American social system with irony and black humor. The fact that he ended his Art Union address with a passage from a political poem laced with the barbed rhetoric of working-class protest shows him trying to push American art in a new, radical direction.

His interest in the Art Union was part of his overriding desire to organize artists everywhere so that they might reform American society. In his Libbey article he had estimated there were some ten thousand artists in America but noted they had little social impact because they were not organized. "They want a strong hand over them," Whitman wrote. "Here is a case for an imperial scepter, even in America. . . . What a glorious result it would give, to form of these thousands a close phalanx, ardent, radical and progressive." He was integrating the Fourierist idea of the phalanx (the socialist community designed to supplant the capitalist system) with his dream of reorganizing American society along aesthetic rather than materialistic lines.

If he hoped that groups like the Brooklyn Art Union would contribute to this social reorganization, he soon learned otherwise. Although he was nominated for the presidency of the union in the spring of 1851, the group quickly fizzled. The union wanted to follow the example of the New York Art Union by holding painting lotteries to support itself. It was on the occasion of the first drawing of prizes, at the Brooklyn Institute on Washington Street, that Whitman addressed the union. But early in 1852, when the state banned art lotteries, which were regarded as a form of gambling, both the New York and Brooklyn Art Unions ceased to exist.

But Whitman's faith in the socially transforming powers of art did not die. To the contrary, it was given fresh life by the opening in the summer of 1853 of the world art and industry exhibition at New York's Crystal Palace. Inaugurated to great fanfare on July 14 by President Pierce and several members of his Cabinet, this long-running event was the culminating moment of antebellum exhibition culture.

In Whitman's eyes, the Crystal Palace itself was a work of art. Covering nearly five acres in the area of what is now Bryant Park, near Forty-second Street, the building was shaped like a tremendous Greek cross, with a towering dome at the intersection (see fig. 33). The upper walls and the ceilings were panes of glass—fifteen thousand in all—inlaid into cast-iron girders. Natural light flooded in from all sides, giving an open-air effect. The chief attraction was the central dome, 123 feet high and 100 feet in diameter, the largest dome in the United States.

Dazzled by the Crystal Palace, Whitman called it "an edifice certainly unsurpassed anywhere for beauty and all other requisites for a perfect edifice ... an original, esthetic, perfectly proportioned American edifice—one of the few that put modern times not beneath old times, but on an equality with them." He was equally taken with the multifaceted exhibit it housed. He was irresistibly attracted to it, recalling later, "*New York, Great Exposition open'd in 1853.* I went a long time (nearly a year)—days and nights—especially the latter."

He was doubtless excited by the radically democratic spirit that lay behind both the contents of the exhibit and the form of its presentation. The Crystal Palace was antebellum America's grandest attempt to make art available to the general public. The authors of the exhibition catalog wrote that "the power of Art to educate and refine the masses" would be realized only "when its works are no longer a monopoly, but an everyday possession, within the reach of the mechanic and the tradesman as well as the opulent and noble." The Crystal Palace promised to help fulfill Whitman's dream of transforming society through art, since, for the first time on a grand scale, the American masses could be exposed to art on a regular basis.

This was art in the most inclusive sense. On the one hand, there was a full range of paintings, daguerreotypes, and sculptures. Included among the sculptures were several nudes by Hiram Powers and W. C. Marshall as well as *Christ and the Twelve Apostles,* a group of thirteen large figures by the Dane Bertel Thorwaldsen. Whitman was particularly moved by the latter, a vignette of the risen Christ, his crucifixion wounds vividly visible, trying to console his startled apostles. Alongside such artworks were displayed elaborate chinaware and tapestries, the cotton gin, the electric telegraph, a fire engine, different pistols, the Adams printing press, and other instruments. It was a potpourri of the modern and the neoclassical, the artistic and the mechanical, that lent credence

to Whitman's idea that art could be defined flexibly and broadly. He saw
beauty and wonder in machines and liked to exhibit them in his poetry:

> The cylinder press . . the handpress . . the frisket and tympan . . the
>   compositor's stick and rule,
> The implements for daguerreotyping . . . . the tools of the rigger or
>   grappler or sailmaker or blockmaker, [. . .]
> The walkingbeam of the steam-engine . . the throttle and governors,
>   and the up and down rods.

That his catalogs are linked to antebellum exhibition culture is made
clear by the unfinished and uncollected pre-1855 poem "Pictures,"
which has survived in a faded notebook. Because the dating of the poem
is inexact, it is unclear whether or not it was inspired by the Crystal
Palace exhibit. But it outdid even that heterogeneous exhibit in the
eclecticism of its images. Whitman had long sought an organizing prin-
ciple—what he called in the Libbey article an "imperial scepter"—to
coordinate the wide range of people and things he viewed as artistic. He
was discovering that organizing principle in his poetic "I."

He begins the poem with the startling image of his own head as a
gallery with "many pictures hanging suspended" and repeats the motif
at the end: "And every hour of the day and night has given me copious
pictures." The picture gallery here is being internalized and identified
with the poetic imagination. The array of "pictures" in the poem are
analogous to antebellum exhibitions in their heterogeneity, but Whit-
man pushes the exhibition metaphor into new areas. He presents quick
vignettes from history—Adam in Paradise, Christ, a Hindu sage, Socra-
tes with his students, the Battle of Brooklyn—and even enters the spirit
world, describing "Phantoms, countless, men and women, after death,
wandering." Recent American history is included with pictures of
Jefferson and Emerson. He uses the exhibition trope to personalize his
yoking together of various geographical regions, as he speaks of "my"
Southern slave grounds, "my" Kansas life, "my" Oregon hut, and so on.
He introduces an urban element absent from most antebellum art by
celebrating "the young man of Mannahatta—the celebrated rough,"
adding emphatically: "The one I love so much—let others sing whom
they may—him I sing for a thousand years!"

The latter image is a reminder of his attempt to embrace idioms that
went far beyond what was permissible in most art of the day. The Hud-
son River School, genre painting, and luminism provided examples of
the aesthetic treatment of a vanishing artisanal, rural culture. These
schools appealed to the nostalgic Whitman, who wanted to preserve ele-

ments of his own and his nation's past, and to the scientific and religious Whitman, who wished to assert the unity of matter and spirit.

But the grittier, more turbulent aspects of American experience were, by and large, banned from polite art. As the art historian Theodore E. Stebbins notes, "The Hudson River school celebrated the vanishing wilderness of the West or pastoral places closer to home which progress somehow had spared. And the luminists went even farther to a pure and untroubled world indeed, where there is no sign of modern developments, . . . no steamboats, no cities, no factories—only the hush of a fragile moment suspended in time."

Such escapism and distancing are to some degree visible in Whitman too, but in his effort to be inclusive he also incorporated the rowdiness and turbulence of popular culture. There was a freakish, sensational side to popular exhibitions and working-class art forms that reflected this turbulence. P. T. Barnum, the Prince of Humbug, displayed in his famous museum on Broadway a razzle-dazzle lineup of freaks and oddities, including bearded ladies, mermaids, dwarves, two-headed calves, four-legged chickens, and so on. The grotesque and bizarre made its way into sophisticated art chiefly in the works of John Quidor, who, significantly, emerged from the fire companies of the New York Bowery b'hoys. Even more violent and bizarre than Quidor's paintings were the illustrations that appeared in many of the cheap pamphlets and newspapers of the day. The immensely popular Crockett almanacs—comic pamphlets featuring crude frontier humor and extreme violence—often had illustrations with presurrealistic effects, as when a clothed fly was pictured fishing on a riverbank with a human on the end of its line. Popular comic newspapers like *Yankee Doodle, John-Donkey,* the *Lantern,* and the *New York Picayune* pushed beyond the relatively restrained freakishness of English comic sheets like *Punch* in an effort to create a bumptious American humor frequently illustrated by pictures with distortions and odd juxtapositions, such as one in the *Picayune* of a man with dice as a head and scissors as a body.

Whitman was sufficiently aware of these bizarre effects in popular art to mention them in the 1855 preface and to present revised versions of them in his poetry. He attacks "that which distorts honest shapes" in any art, including "the illustrations of books or newspapers, or in any comic or tragic prints." But he knew that such distortions were prevalent in popular culture and particularly in the cheap literature that appealed to the same working-class types that also feasted on Edwin Forrest's boisterous acting style and Mike Walsh's slang-filled speeches. As a result, he included in his poetry not only rural genre vignettes and serene luminist pictures but also moments of pictorial distortion, as in these lines:

I find I incorporate gneiss, coal, long-threaded moss, fruits, grains,
  esculent roots,
And am stucco'd with quadrupeds and birds all over.

Here and elsewhere Whitman uses the kind of presurrealistic juxtapositions that abounded in popular culture. Two-headed cows and fishing flies had nothing over a man stuccoed over with quadrupeds and birds. The persona's rapid shifts in identity, influenced, as seen, by various elements of antebellum culture, intensify this wacky, sometimes disorienting effect.

Small wonder that his poetry was placed by some contemporaries among American freaks and oddities. The earliest printed notice of *Leaves of Grass,* by Charles A. Dana in the *New York Tribune,* said the volume would "awaken an interest in the lovers of literary curiosities." Another early review, by Charles Eliot Norton, noted the oddness of Whitman's juxtapositions and declared that "aside from America, there is no quarter of the universe where such a production could have had a genesis." A British reviewer associated Whitman's freakishness with famous oddities of American popular culture:

> We had ceased, we imagined, to be surprised at anything America could produce. We had become stoically indifferent to her Wooly Horses, her Mermaids, her Sea Serpents, her Barnums, and her Fanny Ferns; but the last monstrous importation from Brooklyn, New York has scattered our indifference to the winds.

This reviewer neglected to mention that if Whitman was an American freak, he was one with a difference. Unlike the Barnumesque illustrators of popular culture, he avoided freakishness for its own sake. His flowing montage of images juxtaposed bizarre moments reminiscent of Barnum with more natural, candid pictures allied to genre and Hudson River painters. Also, he redirected the bizarre. For example, the above lines about a person stuccoed with quadrupeds (arguably the strangest in his poetry) are visually odd but thematically reassuring. As Lawrence Buell notes, these lines follow the evolutionary ladder, as the images proceed from the inanimate gneiss through vegetables to animals. In other words, Whitman gives us what from one angle is a distorted image but from another reinforces his progressive-science view of evolution through varied forms. Characteristically, he absorbed the odd and pointed it toward the affirmative.

10

"I CONTAIN MULTITUDES": THE FIRST EDITION OF *LEAVES OF GRASS*

THE MID–1850S, WHEN THE FIRST TWO EDITIONS of Whitman's *Leaves of Grass* appeared, was a time of turmoil and upheaval.

Politically and socially, America was in some ways close to chaos. The old party system shattered, and a new one struggled to establish itself on the basis of a confusing array of splinter groups. Corruption in high places was rampant. Although a broad middle class was developing, the gap between the rich and the poor was wider than ever before. Immigrants arrived in unprecedented numbers, changing the nation's ethnic makeup and fanning antiforeign sentiment. Urban death rates soared. America's largest city, New York, could boast of its economic and cultural centrality, but it was also crowded, filthy, and infested by rowdy gangs and roving prostitutes—not to mention the ever-present swine on the streets.

The ship of state seemed poised to founder on the rock of slavery. After May 1854, when the Kansas-Nebraska Act was passed and the fugitive slave Anthony Burns was seized, disunion seemed a real possibility. The economy, which had been booming since the '48 gold rush, contracted sharply in late 1854, resulting in widespread unemployment and suffering. Even the weather did not cooperate. The winter of 1854 was one of the most brutal in memory. Frigid temperatures and wicked storms lashed the eastern seaboard, worsening the misery of thousands already stung by want.

Reactions to the social crisis ranged from anger and desperation to willed evasion. In the wake of the 1854 slavery debacles, William Lloyd Garrison publicly burned the Constitution and Henry David Thoreau spoke murder against the state. An ex-congressman from Illinois, Abraham Lincoln, declared that compromise between the North and South was now impossible. Frederick Douglass spoke for many when he wrote that year in his newspaper, "We now say, in the name of God, let the battle come." In the Manhattan mayoral elections of November 1854 Fernando Wood was elected on a promise to clean up a city he described as grubby and dangerous (ironically, it was quickly discovered that he had been elected by fraudulent balloting). On the national scene, the jingoistic Know-Nothings rose to bizarre prominence by promising to restore America to Americans. In the meantime, some disaffected groups—anarchists and free lovers in particular—dropped out of mainstream society altogether.

In the bubbling social cauldron of the midfifties, there were few who thought that the dis-United States could be made to cohere through normal political means. Certainly Walt Whitman did not. A decade earlier, he had been a dandyish Democratic journalist, sporting a vest and a polished cane, almost sheepishly loyal to political leaders and party principles. Now he was a roughly dressed carpenter who sneered at politicos and looked for redemption among common people. He was not alone in doing so. The Know-Nothings and the ascendant Republicans were also tapping into the antiauthoritarian, free-labor ideology of the midfifties. But Whitman's disenchantment with the social status quo was far deeper than theirs, and his strategies for cultural renewal far more wideranging.

His disenchantment would impel him, on occasion, to think even more murderously of the state than Garrison or Thoreau. The political "pimps," "excrement," and "serpentine men" of his prose tract "The Eighteenth Presidency!" sprang from the same sense of social doom that lay behind the "swarms of cringers, suckers, doughfaces, lice of politics" of the 1855 preface and the grotesque authority figures of "A Boston Ballad" and "Respondez!" At times his thoughts turned to revolution. When in 1856 corruption within the San Francisco city government resulted in its violent ouster by a vigilance committee of concerned citizens, Whitman wrote in his notebook that "These States need one grand national Vigilance Committee, composed of the body of the people" to overthrow the government.

Such anarchistic and revolutionary thoughts, however, were counterbalanced by his equally strong impulse to hold America together. The individual and the mass; states' rights and the Union; the centripetal and the centrifugal—tensions between these opposing tendencies had preoccupied politicians and social thinkers for decades and were especially pronounced when the national fabric seemed to be unraveling. In 1855, Whitman believed that resolution could be achieved through poetry that powerfully affirmed the individual while equally powerfully absorbing the mass.

Individualism was easy to come by in the dropout fifties, but no one took so radical a stand on it as Whitman. The almost dictatorial stance of his poetic "I" was echoed in notebook entries in which he emphasized the poet's commanding qualities: "The poets I would have must be a power in this state, and an engrossing power in the state."

This "I" was prepared to lead, but also to absorb. For Whitman, the times demanded a poet that could tyrannically survey the entire cultural landscape and give expression to the full range of voices and images America had to offer.

Having closely observed almost every aspect of American culture for years, Whitman realized that there were, after all, beliefs and tastes that many Americans shared, even in a time of division and confusion. There was the heritage of artisan labor and the unified stem family, still prevalent in agricultural areas and fondly recalled by many city dwellers, a shared memory that had special meaning for Whitman for his own family background in rural Long Island. There was also the reverence for the founding fathers and for the American Revolution, in which Northerners and Southerners had fought side by side against a common enemy. True, "democracy" in the old sense was a now-hollow word. The republicanism and egalitarianism of Jefferson and Jackson were by the fifties mocked by the grim realities of slavery and class divisions. In 1856 he wrote cynically: "I know nothing more treacherous than the position of nearly all the eminent persons in These States toward the Spirit of democracy."

But he saw that if democracy was under threat politically and socially, it was very much alive in other areas of American culture. The lively audience-performer interaction that characterized popular plays, music, and speeches had engendered a participatory style enjoyed by most Americans. Religion and progressive science, which mingled with the rise of Harmonialism and spiritualism, were other areas of widespread interest, as were popular visual media like the daguerreotype and genre painting.

The dissolving of boundaries between different occupational categories was very much part of the daily life for many antebellum Americans. Actors, musicians, lecturers, scientists, popular preachers, showmen, photographers, and painters—all borrowed from each other and appealed to an ever-widening audience. The 1855 edition of *Leaves of Grass* was a proclamation of these fertile cultural interactions, made in language that dissolved the boundaries between prose and poetry, between polite diction and slang.

His chosen medium—writing—had, he believed, a high potential for holding America together. America was a nation of readers, known worldwide for its high literacy rates. At midcentury, a full 90 percent of white American adults could read, as opposed to about 60 percent in England. Whitman crowed hyperbolically: "In regard to intelligence, education, knowledge, the masses of [English] people, in comparison with the masses of the U.S., are at least two hundred years behind us." Having witnessed the publishing boom of the first half of the century, he had an almost naïve faith in the power of the written word. "What a progress popular reading and writing has made in fifty years!" he exclaimed in his 1856 open letter to Emerson. He mentioned virtually every kind of popular writing—domestic novels, sensational novels, story papers, penny papers—and wrote that "all are prophetic; all waft rapidly on," each forming a "step to the stairs by which giants shall mount." There was justification for his excitement. American book production leaped some 800 percent between 1830 and 1850, growing ten times faster than the nation's population. Newspapers enjoyed a similar surge, increasing from 715 in 1830 to 2,526 two decades later.

Faced with fragmentation and what appeared to be impending social collapse, America might be saved, Whitman believed, by poetry in which it saw its best and worst features creatively recombined. "We need satisfiers, joiners, lovers," he wrote. "These heated, torn, distracted ages are to be compacted and made whole." The nation's "merits and demerits," as he called them, must be transformed in the crucible of poetry. Describing the poet's all-unifying role in "Song of the Answerer," Whitman announced: "One part does not counteract another part, he is the joiner, he sees how they join."

Poetry just might help restore the togetherness that politics and society had destroyed.

The 1855 Edition in Literary Context

THE FIRST EDITION of *Leaves of Grass* was a utopian document, suggesting that boundaries of section, class, and race that had become glaringly visible in America's political arena could be imaginatively dissolved by affirmation of the cross-fertilization of its various cultural arenas.

Whitman had been scribbling desultory passages of poetry for years, using paper scraps and a notebook, but when he brought the passages together, adding many new ones and a last-minute preface, he did so with a considerable amount of urgency. He surely dreamed, as Ezra

Greenspan suggests, that a large publishing firm would bring out the first edition. But conservative houses like the Harpers or the Appletons were not likely to show interest in proselike poetry that gave vent to the full range of personal and cultural impulses, including unconventional ones. A more appropriate publisher was Fowlers and Wells, which for more than a decade had found large markets for offbeat, experimental books in such fields as phrenology, free love, mesmerism, Fourierism, and spiritualism. But even this firm was not prepared to do more than advertise and distribute *Leaves of Grass*. At this stage, the poet who hoped to save America was very much on his own.

He did everything he could to get a hearing and to make himself attractive to a broad spectrum of readers. Because Whitman had a strong hand in printing, distributing, and promoting the volume, much can be learned from its publishing history.

Whitman hoped to be absorbed by his country, but in order to be absorbed, first he must be widely disseminated and read. Fowlers and Wells, with its large distribution network, made such wide dissemination a possibility. But before the firm would take him on seriously, he had to win some kind of cultural acceptance or approval.

As a solitary poet-publisher, he was facing formidable odds. Not many American poets reaped the benefits of the publishing boom of the antebellum period. Some, like Longfellow and Whittier, managed to reach a wide audience, but they were exceptions to the rule. A *Life Illustrated* article that Whitman clipped made this generalization: "All publishers are naturally shy of a new MS. of poetry, for they know by experience that the deadest of all dead books is a dead volume of poetry." America might *need* poets, as Whitman claimed in his preface, but it tended not to buy poetry volumes.

It was perhaps in part for this reason that the 1855 edition of *Leaves of Grass* was not, either outside or inside, like a normal poetry volume of the period. Whitman had it printed at the Brooklyn printing shop of James and Andrew Rome, Scottish immigrants he had known since he had run his own printing establishment in the late forties. In the early spring of 1855 he walked daily from his small frame house on Prince Street, where he still lived with his parents and several siblings, to the Romes' redbrick shop on the corner of Cranberry and Fulton, where he sat at a corner table and read the *Tribune* as the leaves of poetry came off the press. On May 15 he filed the book for copyright with the United States Court in the Southern District of New York.

This was hands-on, old-style artisan publishing, a throwback to the early days when authors had been directly involved in the publishing process. It established a pattern he would follow in preparing later editions. As Whitman recalled, the first edition was published "on very little different footing from the others. I always superintended, and sometimes undertook part of the work myself, as I am a printer and can use the 'stick,' you know."

In important ways, however, the 1855 *Leaves of Grass* drew off of modern publishing techniques. One was the publication of different formats of a book, variously priced, to reach as many audiences as possible. This diversified approach had become standard practice among American publishers in the thirties and forties as a result of advances in technology and distribution. Many American books were published in different formats. Longfellow's poetry, for instance, was available in formats ranging from expensive half-leather morocco to twenty-five-cent paperback. Of the 800 or so copies of *Leaves of Grass* printed by the Romes, about 295 were sent to the Brooklyn binder Charles Jenkins, who, for thirty-two cents a copy, set up a fancy green cloth jacket with "Leaves of Grass" stamped in gold leaf on both the front and back covers. This "first state" of the volume, priced at two dollars, was advertised for sale on July 5 at Fowlers and Wells outlets and other bookstores. The "second state" of the 1855 *Leaves of Grass*, still in green cloth but with less gilding and some prefatory promotional material, was put on sale at the reduced price of one dollar on September 25. Finally, in November there appeared a seventy-five-cent edition in pink or light-green paper wrappers.

Not only did Whitman try to cover all bases by steadily lowering the price of the three versions, but right from the start he combined elements of high culture and popular culture. The first issue of *Leaves of Grass,* elegantly bound and priced high, had the outside appearance of a fancy volume designed for the parlor (see fig. 37). Its subdued but ornate exterior announced, "Buy me because I am tasteful." Whitman clearly was trying to tap the growing audience for elegant books. In the *Eagle* he had often praised fancily printed books. He had gone into ecstasy, for instance, over the typography and binding of the Harper's Illustrated Bible, whose jacket he described as "inlaid with gilding, in a profusion of rich but chaste adornments." Other well-bound books drew similar responses from him. A poetry collection called *Sybil* was "printed in a fine sort, and bound with elegance and gilding." Of the Harper's Fireside Series he wrote: "In tasty colored covers, and with gilt edging, and clean, spaced type, this series will surely gain a footing among the welcomed arrivals for parlors, and in the domestic circle."

By 1854 America's taste for fancy books had grown to such a degree that Henry Ward Beecher could write:

Within ten years the sale of common books has increased probably 200 per cent., and is daily increasing. But the sale of expensive works, and of library-editions of standard authors in costly bindings, is yet more noticeable. Ten years ago, such a display of magnificent works as is found at the Appletons' would have been a precursor of bankruptcy. There was no demand for them. Now, one whole side of an immense store is not only filled with the most admirably-bound library books, but from some inexhaustible source the void continually made in the shelves is at once refilled.

The typical bookstore patron, Beecher pointed out, had become a connoisseur: "He studies the binding: the leather,—Russia, English, calf, morocco; the lettering, the gilding, edging, the hinge of the cover! He opens it, and shuts it, he holds it off, and brings it nigh. It suffuses his whole body with book-magnetism."

The 1855 *Leaves of Grass* was doubtless designed to exude the kind of "book-magnetism" Beecher described. It would have fit in naturally with the ladies' albums, illustrated Bibles, and domestic novels that adorned American parlors. It was a thin quarto, 8¼ inches wide by 11 ¼ inches high—about the size and shape of a current-day high school yearbook. Its dark olive-green jacket was pocked with ornamental leaf-and-vine designs. The gilding was not excessive, confined to its lettering and a triple-ruled frame, but was in its own way lavish. The "Leaves of Grass" stamped in gold on the front and back covers emphasized both rootedness and fecundity. Long roots, like tangled gold threads, stretched deep from the *L*, nearly obliterated the "of," and also emanated from the *G*, *a*, and second *s* in "Grass." Small sprouts of leaves came from a few of the letters, and a big sprout from the gold *G*.

Altogether, the jacket reflected the side of Whitman that wanted to reach the middle-class parlor. Explaining the reasons for the elegant appearance of several of the editions of *Leaves of Grass*, Whitman told Traubel, "People as a rule like to open books on center tables, in parlors, and so on and so on." When in 1889 he planned a fancy edition of his poems, he declared: "I think an edition, elegantly bound, might be pushed off for books for presents, &c., for the holidays, if advertised for that purpose. . . . I think it a book that would please women. I should expect it to be popular with the trade."

He was probably thinking along similar lines in 1855, when elegantly bound volumes of literary "leaves" were very popular. There had been Mary A. Spooner's *Gathered Leaves* (1848), Meta V. Fuller's *Leaves from Nature* (1852), and, most notably, Fanny Fern's *Fern Leaves from Fanny's Portfolio* (1853). Fern's volume sold more than 100,000 copies and became so popular with both men and women that a journalist in 1854 could report:

> We have met her Fern Leaves everywhere in our summer rambles. . . .
> We are not surprised to find the daughters of the family handling the
> portfolio and identifying its leaves, nor even the farmer's son stealing
> glances at night when the threshing was done and the cattle fed,—
> but it was strange to see the hardworking old man return at night, clad
> in the coarsest, homeliest attire, wipe his spectacles, look eagerly for
> the bundle of leaves, and then turn them over in his sun burnt fingers
> while the merry smile played on his lips, and the silent tear again and
> again glistened in his eye.

Whitman could reasonably expect, then, that his own tastefully packaged "leaves" would have popular appeal.

If *Leaves of Grass* was a parlor-table book, though, it was one with a difference. Its exterior announced elegance, but its interior announced utter democracy and rough simplicity. Opening the volume, one met a stripped-down title page, with "Leaves of Grass" in large black letters, "Brooklyn, 1855," below it, and the picture of the casually dressed Whitman opposite. Then came the twelve-page preface, untitled and printed in double columns and small type. The poetry itself was presented with typographical simplicity, almost primitivism. There were twelve poems, all untitled, with the first one (later "Song of Myself") longer than the rest together.

Everything about the book manifested Whitman's interest in dissolving boundaries between different cultural levels. If the jacket was designed for the parlor, the interior had resonances of the newspaper and the street. Whitman would say in 1856 that he found democracy in no current literature except "the cheap mass-papers," and the typeface of the first edition gave it a newspaper look. The preface, in particular, with its small type arranged in columns, resembled the multicolumned newspaper format. The picture of Whitman in street clothes intensified the proletarian effect. In his effort to challenge boundaries, Whitman abrogated normal rules of punctuation. Through much of the preface and the poetry he used ellipses instead of commas, periods, or semicolons. Lines never seemed to stop but rather flowed onward without interruption. Even the separate poems were barely differentiated from each other. One could easily read the volume as a single long poem broken only by double lines or the occasionally repeated title "Leaves of Grass."

Sometimes punctuation was sacrificed altogether. The interblending of cultural levels, for instance, was syntactically enforced by his statement in the preface that "the anatomist chemist astronomer geologist phrenologist spiritualist mathematician historian and lexicographer are not poets, but they are the lawgivers of poets, and their construction underlies the structure of every perfect poem." Whitman was always deliberate about punctuation. The correctly placed two commas here only highlight the all-fusing absence of commas earlier in the phrase.

Whitman's greatest stylistic innovation—the proselike nature of his verse—resulted mainly from the boundary-dissolving impulse. Whitman is often regarded as the father of free verse, but it is not sufficiently recognized that the loose structure of his poetry had precedent in a wide variety of cultural styles between which he was trying to negotiate. Already mentioned in this book as forerunners of Whitman's verse, Elias Hicks's cadenced sermons, Emerson's and Greenough's calls for organic form, and John Neal's predictions that prose and poetry would soon be conjoined. Others of the day were calling for free-flowing poetry devoid of strict rhyme or meter. An 1849 article in the *Edinburgh Review* that Whitman clipped and annotated contained many comments on poetry he underlined, including this: "With the merely technical rules of style poetry indeed has little concern." An unattributed piece on poetry, included by Whitman as part of the prefatory matter to the second issue of the 1855 edition, similarly called for "a new spirit through new forms" and asked: "Who does not tire of rhymes, anyhow—and of regularly continued metre?"

A relaxation of poetic form was discussed and, on occasion, acted on. Three popular poets who experimented with prose-poetry before Whitman were James Macpherson, Samuel Warren, and Martin Farquhar Tupper.

James Macpherson, a Scottish tutor, had in 1760 published *Fragments of Ancient Poetry*, which he claimed were translated from old Gaelic. The volume was instantly popular and went through many editions, among which the 1839 Philadelphia one, titled *The Poems of Ossian*, was in Whitman's book collection at his death. He recalled having "spouted" Ossian as a youth on the shores of Long Island. The poems were epic ones about the great Scottish chief Fingal, whose son Ossian sang his exploits and those of other national heroes. Whitman was probably attracted by the biblical, bardic nature of Macpherson's lines, which were called poems but in fact were emotive, rhythmic prose. Presaging Whitman, Macpherson was strong on declamation, as in these typical lines: "O thou that rollest above, round as the shield of my fathers! Whence are thy beams, O sun? thy everlasting light?"; "Rise, moon! from behind thy clouds. Stars of night, arise!"; "Father of heroes! O Trenmor! High dweller of eddying winds!" As early as 1847 Whitman was imitating Macpherson, about whom he wrote, "How misty, how windy, how full of diffused, only half-meaning words!" Macpherson's overreliance on windy exclamations lay behind Whitman's warning to himself, "*Don't fall into the Ossianic,* by any chance," though he also insisted "Ossian must not be despised," and he liked Macpherson's biblical cadences, which he would perfect.

Other prose-poems Whitman may have known were those in Samuel Warren's *The Lily and the Bee,* which also contained several devices— apostrophe, declamation, and catalog—associated with Whitman. A paean to the 1851 world's fair at London's Crystal Palace, this volume described the exhibit as "all marvelous and affecting,—past, present, future, linked together mystically." Warren often breaks into exclamations that have a Whitmanesque tone and a democratic reach: "Hail! Welcome! brethren, sisters all! come hither trustfully from every land and clime! All hail! ye loveliest! bravest! wisest! Of every degree! complexion! speech! One and the self-same blood in our veins! Our hearts, fashioned alike!" Also Whitmanesque are his lyrics praising science, which Warren says reveals "A world in every atom—a system in every star!" It may be that Whitman's ecstatic response to New York's Crystal Palace two years later was influenced by Warren's passionate apologue. Just as Whitman giddily soars through space and over the earth, so Warren says that science has liberated modern man, about whom he writes:

> He mounts into the air, and is dizzily hid in the clouds.
> He descends into the earth, and extorts its precious treasures.
> He sails around the globe, defiant of storm, commanding the wind and tide:
> He turns water into air, and air into water: the solid substance into fleeting vapor, and vapor again into substance.

The most visible prose-poet before Whitman was Martin Farquhar Tupper, with whom Whitman was often compared in his day. In the *Eagle* Whitman called Tupper "one of the rare men of the time." Among the books in Whitman's private collection at the end of his life was Tupper's gathering of prose-poems, *Proverbial Philosophy,* with blue-penciled underlinings and notations in Whitman's hand. *Proverbial Philosophy* had first appeared in 1838 and eventually sold more than 300,000 copies. It was a remarkable publishing phenomenon that showed how popular prose-poetry could be. An 1852 Boston edition of Tupper's complete poetry had a fancy red binding with gold-leaf vegetation on the cover and a gilt design on the spine—the kind of elegant touches Whitman hoped to achieve in the expensive first issue of the 1855 *Leaves*.

Tupper's poems had a free form analogous to Whitman's, with long lines running to prose and without fixed rhyme or meter. Sometimes his themes anticipated Whitman's, as when he pointed out the miraculous nature of small things. Whitman's expressed desire in "Song of Myself" to live among the animals and to find divinity in insects, for example, was prefigured by these lines in *Proverbial Philosophy,* which Whitman circled heavily in pencil:

> To watch the workings of instinct, the grosser reason of brutes,—
> The river-horse browsing in the jungle, the plover screaming on the
>   moor,
> The dog at his master's feet, and the walrus anchored to the iceberg;
> To trace the consummate skill that hath modelled the anatomy of
>   insects,
> Small fowls that sun their wings on the petals of wild flowers;
> To learn a use in the beetle, and more than a beauty in a butterfly;
> To recognize affections in a moth, and look with admiration on a
>   spider.

Tupper here brings attention to the miracle of the commonplace, an idea also illustrated in Whitman's lines in worship of the beetle and his discovery of significance in the noiseless, patient spider.

When Whitman's contemporaries identified precursors of his style, they mentioned Macpherson and Warren sometimes and Tupper often. Swinburne wrote that Whitman took "as his precursors and apparent models in rhythmic structure and style, Mr. James Macpherson and Mr. Martin Tupper." The London *Leader* commented that Whitman's style was "the same with which Mr. Martin Tupper has made us familiar in his 'Proverbial Philosophy,' and Mr. Warren in his 'Lily and the Bee.'" Henry James wrote of Whitman's verse: "It is more like Mr. Tupper's proverbs than anything we have met." The London *Saturday Review* said Whitman's reading had clearly been confined to "Mr. Tupper, his newspaper, and the semi-lyrical rhapsodies of the Boston transcendentalists." Another British paper, the *Examiner,* dubbed Whitman "a wild Tupper of the West," supposing Tupper was brought up an auctioneer, maddened by Carlyle and Emerson, and banished for a time to the backwoods.

The last two remarks, though snide, are suggestive, for they point out that Whitman's Tupper-like prose poetry had elements of Transcendentalism on the one hand and working-class and frontier expression on the other. Whitman's interest in yoking together disparate cultural levels made his poetry far more distinctive and wide-ranging than that of any of the previous prose-poets. The Transcendentalists Carlyle and Emerson provided precedent for Whitman's organic rhythms, aesthetic sensibility, and belief in the saving power of poetry. In the *Eagle* Whitman had recognized Carlyle as a beguiling stylistic liberator by describing his "rapt, weird (grotesque?) style" in *Heroes and Hero Worship*. Also in the *Eagle* he had quoted the opening paragraph of Emerson's essay "Spiritual Laws," in which Emerson stressed that even the ugliest aspects of experience took on beauty as time passed. If Whitman was indeed "brought to a boil" by Emerson, as he once claimed, he was probably most attracted to the aesthetic, beautifying aspects of Emerson's philosophy, which saw the poet as one who traversed the whole range of experience and uncovered analogies that changed the lowliest phenomena into things of beauty.

Traversing the range of experience meant for Whitman opening himself up to the daily idioms and styles that Emerson only touched on distantly. The grizzled rough who gazed with casual defiance from the frontispiece of *Leaves of Grass* had been exposed to the wildest players in American life. The street rowdies who swore, fought, and loved sensation novels and melodramas. The brash actors who introduced a stormy "American" style to the stage. The slang-whanging orators who jousted with their audiences. The reformers who agitated constantly. The blackface minstrels who parodied polite culture in free-flowing, disjointed songs. The native humorists, whose quirky style had interested Whitman since the late forties. The spirit-rappers, free lovers, mesmerists, and trance poets who paraded their odd marvels.

All these voices are heard in the 1855 *Leaves of Grass*. By integrating them into poetry, Whitman was showing how American literature could possess real Americanness. This topic had been debated for years, most stridently by the Young America group of the forties. Young America talked of literary democracy but shied away from the kind of untamed American idioms that would give Whitman's poetry its freedom and tang. Young America's leading spokesman, Cornelius Matthews, declared in an 1847 *Democratic Review* article Whitman clipped that American literature must possess "nationality and true Americanness . . . in its purest, highest, broadest sense. Not such as is declaimed in taverns, ranted off in Congress, or made the occasion of boasting and self-laudation on public anniversaries." Another prominent literary figure, Evert A. Duyckinck, likewise declared that national literature should be "immune from democratic enthusiasms, and from the wildness of American life." Matthews and Duyckinck were distancing themselves from those demotic, idiomatic modes of popular expression that Whitman reveled in.

American poets like Longfellow and Whittier also avoided these racy modes of expression. Longfellow once wrote, "We cannot yet throw off our literary allegiance to Old England." He demanded an American literature "without spasms and convulsions," one that gains universality by being "the result of culture and refinement." Longfellow himself had plenty of the latter. In his life and writings he was closely allied to Europe. Even his most famous "American" poem, *The Song of Hiawatha*, became notorious for its European associations: it was commonly charged that the poem's trochaic rhythm was borrowed from the Finnish epic *Kalevala*. It is misleading, of course, to neglect the fact that Longfellow brought alive Native American and New England cultures in popular verse. Still, it is true that the rowdiness and turbulence that fascinated Whitman had little appeal for the Harvard professor who studied three and a half years in Europe and among whose publications were about a hundred translations of works from eighteen foreign languages. There was justification for Whitman's charge that Longfellow was "essentially the scholar, translator, borrower—adaptor and adopter!" Whitman lamented the "want of racy nativity and special originality" in Longfellow, whom he called "the poet of melody, courtesy, deference," one who does not sing "jagged escapades" or "deal hard blows."

Whittier would seem to have had more in common with Whitman than Longfellow, for he was of Quaker background, and his poetry sometimes dealt with the kinds of working-class and reform themes that interested Whitman. Whittier had anticipated *Leaves of Grass* by ten years in "The Shoemaker," a poem extolling the working man that appeared in the August 1845 *Democratic Review*, an issue that also carried Whitman's tale "Revenge and Requital." Like Whitman, Whittier wrote poetic denunciations of the apostate Whig leader Daniel Webster in 1850 and of those who seized Anthony Burns four years later. But Whittier was even more wary of savage rhetoric than Matthews or Longfellow. A sedate man whose habitual calmness was reflected in the gentle rhythms of his poetry, he once complained that American democracy lacked "calmness and solidity, the repose and self-reliance which come of long habitats and settled convictions." Whitman said Whittier was a skilled writer of antislavery verse and rural genre bits but had "very few strings—very few—to his harp" and was not composite or universal.

He made similar comments about other American poets. James Russell Lowell he classed with "the disciples of form—of exquisite workmanship." Edgar Allan Poe, whom he had met once in New York in the midforties, he associated with "morbidity, abnormal beauty—the sickliness of all technical thought or refinement itself—the abnegation of the perennial or democratic concretes at first hand." William Cullen Bryant, the New York poet and editor with whom he took long walks around the city, always stood high on his list of American poets, but mainly as a perfecter of European forms. Bryant, said Whitman, "belonged to the classics: liked the stately measures prescribed by the old formulas." Although he thought Bryant handled these formulas "marvelously well," he judged that "after all his contribution was not novel—it was nature song, philosophy, of a rather formal cast."

What he thought was most lacking in American poetry was what he called "race"—a distinctive form of national expression. In an interview in the 1870s he would declare: "Although we have elegant and finished writers, none of them express America or her spirit in any respect whatever." In another interview he discussed his idea of race: "A wild strawberry, a wild grape has the very quality, the distinctive tang. Our poetry lacks 'race.' Most of it might have been written on England or on the Continent."

"Race" for Whitman was an inclusive word that took into account all that is associated today with race, class, and gender. He scoured working-class and African-American cultures in search of idioms and slang expressions ordinarily banished from polite literature. American street slang, as Irving Lewis Allen has shown, arose at a precise historical moment—the 1840s—when the linguistic texture of working-class life was changing due to rapid urbanization. In fact, the word "slang" itself was first used around 1850 to mean "illegitimate language." For Whitman and some others, slang was a new discovery, offered up freshly by the American masses for the use of writers and speakers. Now-familiar slang terms like "chum," "kick the bucket," "bender," "pal," and "blowout" were introduced by the Bowery youths Whitman fraternized with throughout the period. Whitman saw slang as "the lawless germinal element, below all words and sentences, and behind all poetry," revealing "a certain perennial rankness and protestantism of speech."

Although slang did not make its way into much American poetry besides Whitman's, it did enter popular speeches, sermons, and dictionaries. Kenneth Cmiel has demonstrated that popular orators of antebellum America, including Henry Ward Beecher and Abraham Lincoln, forged a "middling style" that combined polite and low diction, a style that would disappear after the Civil War as a more refined discourse came into vogue. This mixed style was also manifested in American dictionaries, most notably Noah Webster's *An American Dictionary of the English Language* (originally 1828), which in later versions went beyond its closest competitor, by Joseph E. Worcester, in its inclusion of simplified spellings and slang words. Whitman recognized its innovative comprehensiveness, calling it "the best *complete* dictionary that had yet been published for the people at large."

Still, he thought that even Webster did not go nearly far enough in incorporating the idioms of the people. He set out himself to write a book on language that would do so. Begun in the early fifties and written earnestly on scraps of paper after 1856, *The Primer of Words* was his loudest call for a radically inclusive language, though none at the time heard the call, since the volume remained unpublished until after his death. He criticized existing grammars and dictionaries and wrote that a new one was needed "to conform to our uses,—a far more complete dictionary to be written—and the grammar boldly compelled to serve the real genius underneath our speech, which is not what the school men suppose, but wild, intractable, suggestive." This "great dictionary of the future," as he called it, must contain, among other things, "strong coarse talk." He listed a number of slang expressions used by the b'hoys of the Bowery, including "So long!" which he later used as the title of a poem. He added: "Many of slang words among fighting men, gamblers, thieves, prostitutes, are powerful words." He imagined a language in which gender distinctions would be abolished: "hater" and "hatress," for instance, would become "hatist." Anticipating women's liberation, he wrote, "The woman should reserve her own name, just as after marriage as before." Anticipating another modern idea, he noted that the word "Indian" was a misnomer for a Native American, and he praised several words that had emerged from Native American culture.

He also had a close eye on African-American language. "In the South," he wrote, "words that have sprouted up from the dialect and peculiarities of the slaves.—the Negroes.—The south is full of negrowords.—their idioms and pronunciation are heard every where." Using the then-common word "nigger," he went on to make large claims for the African-American contribution:

> The nigger dialect furnishes hundreds of outre words, many of them adopted into the common speech of the mass of the people.— [. . .] The nigger dialect has the hints of a future theory of the modification of all words of the English language, for musical purposes, for a native grand opera in America.

The fact that Whitman here suggests that African-American dialect could bring about a revolutionary combination of language and music raises the possibility that the "race" he desired in American poetry was linked on some level to "race" as it is understood today—that is, in reference to ethnic identity. Shelley Fisher Fishkin's idea that the narrative voice of Mark Twain's *Huckleberry Finn* may have been influenced by African-American language perhaps has relevance to Whitman, who surely had extensive exposure to black dialect in the Manhattan and Long Island area and particularly in New Orleans in 1848. In the absence of documentation, a full account of the African-American influence on *Leaves of Grass* cannot be given. But at least in the above passage (written after the first two editions of *Leaves of Grass* had appeared) Whitman pays homage to the creativity of black dialect and, with striking prescience, anticipates the widespread influence of this dialect in twentieth-century popular culture, especially in the area of music.

Both slang and African-American dialect appealed to him because they were vital, spontaneous, and often violently antiauthoritarian. Whitman strongly objected to the era's most popular grammar book, Lindley Murray's *English Grammar*, which had first appeared in 1795 and gone through at least thirty editions by 1850. "Murray," wrote Whitman, "would make of the young men merely a correct and careful set of writers under laws.—He would deprive writing of its life—there would be nothing voluntary and insouciant left." What appealed to him in slang and dialect was their lawlessness and defiance. "I like limber, lashing, fierce words," he wrote, "I like them in newspapers, courts, debates, congress[;] . . . strong, cutting, beautiful rude words."

The kinds of native idioms that Matthews and the others purposely avoided, then, were an important part of Whitman's poetic agenda. One such idiom, Gothicized mudslinging at social rulers à la George Lippard and Mike Walsh, had accounted for the verbal energy of his 1850 political-protest poems, his published verse in his distinctive prose-like vein. The pressures of the gathering political crisis had made him resort to a violently subversive kind of language. Whatever moves toward free verse poets like Tupper or Warren had made, he was prepared to go much further than they, because he had opened himself up to the free forms of both popular and elite culture. On the popular side, these free forms included slang, dialect, sermons, speeches, humor, reform rhetoric, and mesmeric and spiritualist marvels. On the elite side, they included the organicism of the Transcendentalists and the fluid rhythms of Italian opera.

When they all came together in Whitman's poetry, they gave rise to a wholly new kind of writing.

Something for Everyone

BRINGING TOGETHER different cultural images was not mere literary exercise for Whitman. It was an act of extreme urgency, even desperation. Confronted with a social crisis and with a checkered private history, Whitman sought in poetry healing for both his nation and himself.

Signs of crisis or trauma lurk in many places in the first two editions of *Leaves of Grass*. These editions contain what may be called negative centers, both in the editions as a whole and in individual poems. Related to society and politics, these negative moments reflected Whitman's fear that the American experiment was an utter failure. Related to Whitman's private life, they resonated with metaphysical angst, family difficulties, and, it would seem, struggles with his sexual orientation. The fact that the final effect of his poems was triumphantly affirmative shows how successful he was in garnering all his cultural and creative resources to challenge the negative and imaginatively overcome it.

Negative centers in the 1855 edition are not difficult to find. Among the twelve poems in the edition, the eighth and ninth—revised versions of his protest poems "Resurgemus" and "A Boston Ballad"—gave reminders of the political crises that had unleashed Whitman's subversive rhetoric in the early fifties and that would remain in the background of his savage social commentary for decades. On the surface, "Resurgemus," the 1850 poem about the failed European revolutions, might appear to have been outdated by 1855, but there was good reason for its inclusion in the first edition. The images of ruling-class "liars" who "defile the people" and steal "the poor man's wages" had trenchant suggestiveness in the midfifties, with rising political corruption and class divisions darkening the social landscape. The idea of corrupt, failed rulers was brought decidedly up-to-date in the next poem, "A Boston Ballad," in which the federal marshals escorting Anthony Burns back to captivity are jeered by the phantoms of Revolutionary War troops who retrieve George III's bones as a monument to modern-day tyranny.

Negative figures from society and politics appear at many other moments in the first edition. There are "the moneymaker that plotted all day" and "him that oppresses me" of "The Sleepers," the "shaved blanched face of orthodox citizens" in "Faces," the "few idly owning" with the "many sweating, ploughing, thrashing" in "Song of Myself," and, in the preface, the swarming "lice of politics" and "planners of sly involutions for their own preferment to city offices or state legislatures or the judiciary or congress or the presidency." Such negative images reflect Whitman the social reformer who was swept up in the rising reform agitation of the fifties.

Also present in the first edition is the private Whitman, struggling with family problems and doubt. Some have seen *Leaves of Grass* as a massive act of compensation and wish fulfillment on the part of an anxious, tortured man. This interpretation is based largely on guesswork, since reliable primary documents about Whitman's pre-1855 life are scanty. Still, it is hard to read certain passages in the first edition without thinking of the more troubled aspects of his private experience. The "mean, angered, unjust" father of "There Was a Child Went Forth," who is ready with "The blow, the quick loud word," almost certainly has some linkage to Whitman's gruff father, just as the mental retardation and physical handicaps of his younger brother Eddy were registered in "Faces": "I knew of the agents that emptied and broke my brother." The skeptical pondering of death that had filled Whitman's early forties poems and that punctuated his notebooks is reflected in gloomy moments in the first edition, as when he identifies with those who feel life is just "a suck and a sell, and nothing remains at the end but threadbare crepe and tears." His expressions of psychological depression in his notebooks (such as "Every thing I have done seems to me blank and suspicious") doubtless lay behind brooding lines like these:

> The doubts of the daytime and the doubts of the nighttime. . . . the
> > curious whether and how,
> Whether that which appears so is so. . . . Or is it all flashes and
> > specks?

It is also possible, as several have suggested, that Whitman found in poetry a means of coming to terms with guilt or persecution resulting from his homosexual leanings. His notebooks of the midfifties are filled with long lists of men he has met in Brooklyn and New York. Most of these men were in their late teens or early twenties, and many were drivers, policemen, or other common workers. These notebook listings are, in general, so cursory that it is impossible to glean from them the exact nature of his relationships with the men or the extent to which these relationships resulted in the kind of suffering he appears to have experienced in his Long Island teaching days. Eventually, as my later discussion of the "Calamus" poems shows, Whitman developed ways of expressing homoerotic feelings while according with views of same-sex love widely sanctioned in his time. But the perception of Roger Asselineau and others that a certain amount of psychological pain was associated with Whitman's homoeroticism takes on validity when we think of an 1855 poem like "Song of Myself," which contains both homoerotic images and graphic passages in which Whitman identifies with traumatized or harshly persecuted types.

In the first edition of *Leaves of Grass* Whitman created an all-powerful "I" that tried mightily to relieve both social and private ills by tapping America's well-stocked reservoir of affirmative cultural images.

This "I" was partly autobiographical but largely fictive, a created self that served the restorative purposes of the poetry. Whitman brought attention to the dual functions—private and public—of his "I." In an 1856 self-review in the *Daily Times* he noted that his poetry was "an assertion of a two-fold individuality for the author: of himself personally, and of himself nationally." Explaining to Traubel his reason for keeping his name off the title page of most of the editions of *Leaves of Grass*, he declared: "It would be a sacrilege to put a name there—it would seem just like putting a name on the universe. It would be ridiculous to think of Leaves of Grass belonging to any one person: at the most I am only the mouthpiece.... I like the feeling of a general partnership—as if the Leaves was anybody's who chooses just as truly as mine." "The Walt Whitman who belongs in the Leaves," he added elsewhere, "is not a circumscribed Walt Whitman but just as well a Horace Traubel as any one else."

Whatever the tangled autobiographical components of this poetic "I," its public components are highlighted from the very start of the 1855 *Leaves of Grass*. The merging of cultural levels announced by the edition's binding and physical layout was made explicit in the preface and continued in the poems themselves.

The preface was a heady announcement of the total reciprocity of the poet and the nation. It began with the image of America absorbing the past and ended with the one about the nation absorbing the poet as affectionately as he has absorbed it. In between, Whitman gave a mélange of antebellum American society and culture, indicating the poet's crucial role in reshaping America.

There is no apparent structure to the preface; as with the poetry that follows, its very lack of structure enacts the free-flowing cultural interactions it announced. Still, it makes an argument that can be briefly paraphrased as follows. America desperately needs poets to repair its deficiencies and realize its potential. Its deficiencies include corrupt politicians on all governmental levels, the specter of disunion, widespread vice, failed relations between the sexes, and distortions in many popular romances and pictures. Its potential lies in the ideals of democracy and union, in free individual expression, in the nation's ample geography, and in cultural areas like music and art. The poet's role is one of restoration and reconciliation. In a time of failed social rulers, the poet announces himself superior to the president. He is "hungry for equals," who are found among common folk and outcasts rather than legislators. In the absence of a viable political democracy, the poet announces a new cultural democracy formed by various kinds of phenomena, from spiritualism to phrenology, from art to physiology. Because the poet lovingly absorbs virtually all of America's tastes, he in turn will be absorbed by his country.

The whole first edition of *Leaves of Grass* is buoyed by this faith in the reciprocity of the poet and his nation. "I celebrate myself," the first poem begins: but the "I," it turns out, is just as much America—or the average American—as it is the private Walt Whitman. D. H. Lawrence called Whitman "this poet with his private soul leaking out of him all the time. All his privacy leaking out in a sort of dribble, oozing into the universe." Denis Donoghue, likewise, points out that Whitman's "I" always has an equal sign after it. Whitman's archetypal democratic "I" flows in and out of images and personae from widely varying cultural arenas.

In "Song of Myself" especially, it does so with amazing ease and rapidity, as though Whitman had not only observed his culture's images and idioms but felt them along his very nerve endings. In "Song of Myself" and a few other poems of the first edition, Whitman doesn't *write about* his culture but actually *inhabits* it and *inscribes* it from within. Bakhtin's idea of *skaz*—the incorporation of national idioms into narrative voice—is usually applied to fiction but has relevance to Whitman's verse as well. When Whitman in the *Daily Times* said that great writers "embody the rude materials of the people and give them the best forms for the place and time" he was describing the all-assimilating process that lay behind "Song of Myself."

Few lines in the poem can be read as the expression of a single idea or viewpoint. Because Whitman is constantly negotiating between the personal and the social, his images are multilayered and resonant. The poem as a whole follows no discernible pattern. There have been nearly twenty different descriptions of a "structure" of "Song of Myself," most of them centered on the development of the private self, but these varying, sometimes contradictory explanations are Procrustean efforts to impose order on a poem whose free form is one of its main rhetorical points. The "convulsiveness" that Whitman said characterized antebellum America had found expression, as has been seen, in many kinds of free forms on both the popular and elite levels. By joining many of these forms together under one literary roof, Whitman was able to bring democratic zest to elite images and philosophical depth to popular ones. The cross-fertilization of different images, he hoped, might help to disperse the various ills he and the nation faced.

The famous opening lines of "Song of Myself" immediately resolve by fiat what had long been a basic problem in American life: how to balance the demands of the individual with those of the mass. This problem had raised its head in the nullification crisis of 1832 and had attained cataclysmic importance in the fifties, when the country was at a breaking point. If politically America was near disunion, Whitman offered a new poetic union based on the dissolving of cultural boundaries:

I celebrate myself,
And what I assume you shall assume,
For every atom belonging to me as good belongs to you.

I loafe and invite my soul,
I lean and loafe at my ease observing a spear of summer grass.

The tensions between liberty and power, states' rights and union, are here resolved by an "I" who proclaims both individuality and total equality with others. In the aftermath of Kansas-Nebraska and Anthony Burns, America in fact had difficulty in celebrating itself except with bitter irony. Whitman's representative "I" is the antiauthoritarian individual American of the fifties, mistrustful of power structures. He can celebrate himself and announce equality with others because he is attuned to the full range of unifying cultural possibilities. Celebrating "myself" instills personalism and purity to the idea of celebration, harking back to those intimate populist festivals of Whitman's childhood, so distant from the chilly, impersonal public celebrations he complained of in the fifties. When in the final version of the poem Whitman added the phrase "and sing myself," he was opening up another potential unifying force—music—that was also a key part of his poetic blend.

So powerful was his belief in the possibilities of cultural democracy in 1855 that he could take an almost totalitarian stance: "And what I assume you shall assume." The "I" of the 1855 edition asserts total control, because he wants to direct attention constantly to those aspects of experience he thinks most of his readers share. The next line—"For every atom belonging to me as good belongs to you"—plants the notion of sharing in the very process of nature. Echoing the ideas of two of his favorite authors, Fanny Wright and Justus Liebig, about a democratic interchange of atoms, he expresses the faith in the natural cycle that remains a major source of affirmation throughout the poem.

He is careful, however, to avoid materialism. "I loafe and invite my soul" proclaims the matter/spirit dualism that, in ways often allied to Swedenborgianism and spiritualism, is asserted insistently throughout the 1855 edition and that took on even greater prominence in later editions. This line also adds philosophical depth to the notion of loafing, which in Whitman's day (as his own newspaper pieces attested) was ordinarily associated with derelict behavior among the shiftless urban underclass. Having his loafer invite his soul has the same ennobling effect as the addition of the word "kosmos" to Whitman's later self-description as a "disorderly fleshy sensual" rough. Having him contemplate a spear of summer grass introduces the notion of the miracle of the commonplace, derived mainly from progressive science and Harmonialism, which is another key theme of the poem. Also, the valorization of the grass is a means of seeking resolution of the individual-versus-mass tension in nature itself: grass embodies simultaneously individualism, each spear a unique phenomenon, and radical democracy, as it is a common vegetation that sprouts everywhere, among all sections and races.

In his opening lines, then, Whitman presents a reconstructed democracy, one in which the self, culture, and nature fruitfully intermingle. If in his notebook he was declaring that "We want no *reforms*[,] no *institutions,* no *parties*" but "a *living principle* as nature has, under which nothing can go wrong," in "Song of Myself" he created a world in which many deficiencies of political and social life were imaginatively corrected. Throughout the poem the cross-penetration of cultural levels has an ameliorating effect.

Take that major preoccupation of antebellum Americans: sensationalism. The kind of blood and gore that filled much pre–Civil War popular literature (and entered Whitman's own apprentice writings) is not absent from "Song of Myself." To the contrary, the poem makes gestures toward satisfying readers who feasted on what Whitman called "blood and thunder romances with alliterative titles and plots of startling interest." One thinks especially of three sensational narratives at the heart of the poem. The first recounts the wreck of the steamship *San Francisco* in an Atlantic storm in the winter of 1853–54. The second describes the massacre of 412 American soldiers by Mexicans at Goliad, Texas, in 1836. The third recounts a dramatic sea battle between British and American frigates. Whitman does not shy from mentioning bloody details, such as the "maimed and mangled" bodies piled on each other at Goliad or the "dabs of flesh upon the masts and spars" after the sea fight. He knew well the popular appeal of these kinds of stories, as is shown by the fact that in 1854 he carefully preserved six *Tribune* clippings about the *San*

Francisco disaster and the subsequent rescue of its passengers by Captain Creighton. Given the prominence of such news in antebellum America, it is probable Whitman had sensation lovers in mind when he included grim images such as the suicide sprawled on the bloody bedroom floor or the amputated limb that falls horribly into the pail.

Still, there was justification for Whitman's statement to Traubel that *Leaves of Grass* "yields nothing for the seeker of sensations." Just as his early writings had never been as gory as those of many of his contemporaries, so the sensational moments in "Song of Myself" are not indulged in for their gratuitous shock value but rather are subsumed to a larger purpose. The sensationalism in the popular press reflected the wild side of antebellum America that at times threatened to degenerate into anarchy. Crimes against persons in New York rose 129 percent between 1848 and 1852, with a sixfold increase in murders. One of the papers Whitman read regularly, the *New-York Atlas,* reported in August 1854: "Horrible murders, stabbings, and shootings, are now looked for, in the morning papers, with as much regularity as we look for our breakfast." Elsewhere the *Atlas* reported, "Rowdyism runs rampant in the city, and bids likely to do so for some time. Scarcely a day passes that we do not hear of the most outrageous assault with a deadly weapon." There was a reason for Whitman's calling New York "crime-haunted and dangerous" and writing that "The revolver rules, the revolver is triumphant."

In "Song of Myself" Whitman tried to make sensationalism philosophically meaningful and socially restorative instead of anarchic or senseless. He believed that disasters had a potential for bonding people in sympathy and heroism. Even newspaper accounts of tragic events held interest for him, since they contributed to his overarching search for shared interests and cultural unity. When in 1857 more than four hundred people died in a sea wreck in the Caribbean, he philosophized in the *Daily Times:*

> "One touch of nature makes the whole world kin": The very sentence cannot but recur to the mind, when we take up the broad pages of the metropolitan sheets and see them filled with the most minute and detailed accounts of the last Great Disaster, when we remark how eagerly these details are seized upon, and devoured by millions who are entirely destitute of selfish and personal interest in the matter, and who are only moved by that mysterious sympathy which is the universal bond underlying all mankind. . . . Such great calamities . . . startle us from our paltry, apathetic selfishness, they elicit feelings better and higher than ordinarily moves us, they link us together, for a time at least, by the bonds of a mutual sentiment, they teach us that poor frail

human nature can deport itself bravely and well under circumstances the most appalling.

It is such togetherness, sympathy, and heroism that are featured in the disaster narratives at the heart of "Song of Myself." Sensational stories, he believed, if rightly treated, could be a strong force for togetherness and mutual sympathy. Whitman's notebook jotting in reaction to the *San Francisco* wreck emphasized these qualities: "Greater than wires of iron, or even strong mutual interests is S[y]mpathy.—When Creighton hove to for many days and nights and rescued the wrecked tho[u]sand on the San Francisco." In his poetic version of the disaster he emphasized Creighton's heroism:

> The courage of present times and all times;
> How the skipper saw the crowded and rudderless wreck of the
> steamship, and Death chasing it up and down the storm,
> How he knuckled tight and gave not back one inch, and was faithful
> of days and faithful of nights,
> And chalked in large letters on a board, Be of good cheer, We will
> not desert you,
> How he saved the drifting company at last,
> How the lank loose-gowned women looked when boated from the
> side of their prepared graves,
> How the silent old-faced infants, and the lifted sick, and the sharp-
> lipped unshaved men;
> All this I swallow and it tastes good, I like it well, it becomes mine,
> I am the man.... I suffered.... I was there.

Whitman here expects readers of all kinds to join in admiration for the skipper's courage and in sympathy for the passengers' plight. He tries to elicit similar feelings toward the stoical Americans murdered at Goliad and the staunch sea captain who snatches victory from the jaws of defeat. In yet another story in the poem—about the hounded slave whose blood and sweat ooze as he clutches the fence rail—he uses sensational details to evoke sympathy for blacks and horror at the fugitive slave law.

He is able to accentuate aspects of these and many other tragic phenomena because he had learned well strategies for absorption, affirmation, transcendence, and beautification from antebellum culture.

Absorption, influenced both by the new acting style and by the rapid identity changes of popular mesmerists, makes possible his treatment of tragedies as though they were roles to be played to their fullest and then dropped. "I am the ————," the persona asserts confidently, filling the blank with all kinds of suffering types from the mashed fireman to the old artillerist to the mutineer walking handcuffed to jail. Since agonies are, as he puts it, "one of my changes of garments," they can be donned with as much believability as they were by Whitman's favorite actor, Junius Brutus Booth, or by shape-shifting mesmeric performers. Then they could be shed, as though the essential self were untouched. The "I" can inhabit even the most wretched identities and yet stay unruffled: "All these I feel or am."

Affirmation, which Whitman learned largely from positive-thinking phrenologists and physiologists like the Fowlers, was another means of dealing with private and social ills in "Song of Myself." By simple positive declarations Whitman could free himself—and, by extension, America—of all kinds of problems. He scores a huge rhetorical victory in the opening thirty lines of the poem, in which the persona exudes health and cheer as he revels in nature: "The play of shine and shade on the trees as the supple boughs wag, / [...] The feeling of health, the full-noon trill, the song of me rising from bed and meeting the sun." By the time, about sixty lines into the poem, severe problems are mentioned, they can be blithely dismissed by a cheerful Fowleresque affirmation:

> The sickness of one of my folks—or of myself .... or ill-doing .... or
>   loss or lack of money .... or depressions or exaltations,
> They come to me days and nights and go from me again,
> But they are not Me myself.

The problems mentioned here appear to have specific topical reference to Whitman in 1854–55. "The sickness of one of my folks" could refer to the last illness of Whitman's father, who died on July 11, 1855, a week after *Leaves of Grass* was published. The "loss or lack of money" may be a reference to financial setbacks Whitman almost surely suffered in the panic of 1854, while the "depressions or exaltations" bring to mind the mood swings of some of his notebook entries. But all storm clouds on the personal horizon are dispersed by the simple affirmation: "But they are not Me myself." National storms could also be scattered by affirmation, as was shown when after the Civil War Whitman added this line after "depressions and exaltations": "Battles, the horrors of fratricidal war, the fever of doubtful news, the fitful events." Just as the Fowlers and other nontraditional therapists preached the possibility of gaining health and equanimity through firm exercise of the will, so Whitman wills himself and his nation into equilibrium. He announces in the next lines that he stands "Apart from the pulling and hauling" as a compassionate, unitary observer.

Affirmation of health had special relevance in the midfifties, because it was a period when America witnessed illness and death in startling new forms. The Asiatic cholera, which had not been seen in America since 1832, returned with a vengeance in 1849 and then annually for the next five years. Cities like Brooklyn and New York, where sanitation was still primitive, were natural hosts for cholera. Death from the disease was cruel and swift. Symptoms included diarrhea, vomiting, dizziness, and dehydration, causing a ghastly paleness. Whitman described it vividly in "Song of Myself":

> Not a cholera patient lies at the last gasp, but I also lie at the last
>   gasp,
> My face is ash-colored, my sinews gnarl. . . . away from me people
>   retreat.

Cholera was not the only health scourge of the era; measles, smallpox, yellow fever, and tuberculosis took heavy tolls as well, especially since population growth during this period far outstripped improvements in sanitation or medicine. With homicides and suicides also on the rise, death rates rose ominously. Whitman, who wrote alarmed articles about the rising death rate in both the *Eagle* and the *Daily Times*, mentioned death often in the 1855 edition, as in the passage in "To Think of Time" about "the burial lines" creeping slowly "over the whole earth."

Equally difficult to face as illness and death was a sense of malaise that afflicted many Americans. Tocqueville had noted that despite their activity and overall prosperity, Americans often experienced deep gloom. He described "the strange melancholy often haunting inhabitants of democracies in the midst of abundance, and of that disgust with life sometimes gripping them in calm and easy circumstances." Such dark feelings intensified with rapid urbanization and particularly with the political collapse of the fifties, which created widespread alienation and disenchantment. Michael Holt argues that "a genuine sense of crisis troubled Americans living in that decade."

Whitman's comments on America in his notebooks and articles support this dark view. "Our country seems to be threatened with a sort of ossification of the spirit," he noted around 1854. "For I do not believe the people of these days are happy. The public countenance lacks its bloom of love and its freshness of faith.—For want of these, it is cadaverous as a corpse." Three years later, in a *Daily Times* article called "Suicides on the Increase," he generalized: "There is something radically wrong in modern society: while wealth and luxury are on the increase, happiness and contentment are on the decrease." Just as Thoreau in *Walden* (1854) was commenting that the mass of men lead lives of quiet desperation, so Whitman was confronting the psychological traumas associated with urbanization, market capitalism, and disillusion with politics.

Both physical and psychological ills are challenged by the powerful "I" of "Song of Myself," who is equipped with a full range of life-affirming, health-giving restoratives from mid-nineteenth-century therapeutic thought. Up until the 1830s, American medicine had been dominated by so-called "regular" physicians who used all kinds of heroic physical measures—emetics, cathartics, and bleeding—to combat disease. Over the next three decades, the regulars and their drugs came into wide disrepute as more "natural" forms of healing came into vogue. Regulation of diet, exercise, ventilation, temperance, and other personal habits were thought to ensure mental and physical health, while drug therapy was considered dangerous and outmoded. Whitman was right in step with the times when he copied this quotation from Orson Fowler on a paper scrap: "Morality and talent are more affected by food, drink, physical habits, cheerfulness, exercise, regulated or ir-regulated amativeness than is supposed.—O. S. Fowler."

Regulation of habits in the name of health sometimes appears nega-tively in the 1855 edition in images like "the sick-gray faces of onanists," "the putrid veins of gluttons or rumdrinkers," and the "serpentine poi-son of those that seduce women." More often, however, it appears posi-tively, as affirmation of health and cheer made with the confidence of the midcentury natural therapist. To the end of his life Whitman would look upon regular doctors and their drugs with suspicion. Such suspicion lay behind his harsh portrait of a regular doctor in "Faces":

> This is a face of bitter herbs, this an emetic, they need no label,
> And more of the drug-shelf, laudanum, caoutchouc, or hog's lard.

While dismissing drugs, Whitman affirmed all the images associated with natural therapy. His opening image of inhaling pure air and going "undisguised and naked" by the riverbank summons up the idea of ven-tilation and water cure advised by the natural therapists. His welcome of "every organ and attribute of me, and of any man hearty and clean" resonates with the physiologists' frankness about the body and sex, as do statements like "Copulation is no more rank to me than death is." His exhilarating plunge into the ocean—"Cushion me soft, rock me in billowy drowse, / Dash me with amorous wet, I can repay you"—is a giddy rendition of water-cure therapy, which he had been advising since the *Eagle* days. Throughout "Song of Myself," the intermixture of images of pain or illness with ones of ventilation, water, and general exuberance in nature enhances the therapeutic effect Whitman is striving for. Toward the end of the poem, the "I" feels his healing power can overcome all diseases and even death:

> To any one dying . . . . thither I speed and twist the knob of the door,
> Turn the bed-clothes toward the foot of the bed,
> Let the physician and priest go home.
>
> I seize the descending man. . . . I raise him with my resistless will,
> O despairer, here is my neck,
> By God! you shall not go down! Hang your whole weight upon me.

The dismissal here of "the physician and priest" was typical of the natural therapists, who grouped together doctors and priests as hurtful authority figures. Natural therapy was egalitarian. Even a working-class rough like the "I" of "Song of Myself" could become an effective healer if he asserted health and cheer and encouraged others to do likewise. Because he stresses healthymindedness and immersion in the healing forces of nature, the "I" can declare, "I am he bringing health for the sick as they pant on their backs" and can conclude "Song of Myself" by affirming: "I shall be good health for you nevertheless, / And filter and fibre for your blood."

Transcendence is another ameliorating strategy in "Song of Myself," and here again he had a diverse array of cultural materials from which to draw. He expresses a Swedenborgian confidence throughout the poem, and through the whole edition, that everything physical has a spiritual counterpart:

> Clear and sweet is my soul. . . . and clear and sweet is all that is not
>   my soul.
>
> Lacks one lacks both. . . . and the unseen is proved by the seen, till
>   that becomes unseen and receives proof in its turn.

A Swedenborgian "partaker of influx and efflux," he is also the spiritualist who proclaims immortality, the progressive scientist who knows God has ferried his cradle for ages, and the Harmonialist who has a loverlike intimacy with nature and who revels in the senses. He is also the trance poet through whom speak "many long dumb voices" and who can say, "I am afoot with my vision." Transcendence permits him almost literally to fly away from problems when they start to cause him too much agony. For instance, after the dark middle section of the poem, in which he describes many suffering types from the Goliad victims to the cholera patient, he is able to transcend all the pain:

> I rise extatic through all, and sweep with the true gravitation,
> The whirling and whirling is elemental within me.

Just as mesmeric healers and trance poets felt the power to soar beyond physical reality, so he has an "elemental" capacity for "whirling and whirling" beyond pain and suffering.

If transcendence was facilitated by Whitman's awareness of the scientific and religious movements of the day, beautification was best exemplified by the visual arts. Whitman was never as escapist as the luminists, who retreated from the troubled fifties into idealized, light-filled landscapes. But his succession of sharply drawn "pictures" of everyday reality in "Song of Myself" drew from the widely enjoyed egalitarian art forms of the day.

"Song of Myself" was the only poem by a nineteenth-century American in which these and several other cultural phenomena came together under a single literary roof. Whitman himself never duplicated this triumph of cross-fertilization and fusion. Although I have discussed the various cultural threads in the poem separately, in fact they are interwoven with such fluidity that they can barely be separated. Many passages in the poem are densely layered collations of personal and cultural images, fused in a wholly new way. Take these lines:

> Magnifying and applying come I,
> Outbidding at the start the old cautious hucksters,
> Taking myself the exact dimensions of Jehovah,
> The most they offer for mankind and eternity less than a spirt of my
>   own seminal wet,
> Lithographing Kronos and Zeus his son, and Hercules his grandson,
> Buying drafts of Osiris and Isis and Belus and Brahma and Adonai,
> In my portfolio placing Manito loose, and Allah on a leaf, and the
>   crucifix engraved.

The general message is clear enough: I, as a modern-day American, am able to survey and embrace all historical religions. Whitman was tapping into his own and his nation's background of religious tolerance, which stemmed mainly from the deistic Enlightenment. But the passage is loaded with other cultural inflections that interact with each other. The "I" here is not a stable entity but a composite of cultural personae. He is the scientist analyzing past religions ("Magnifying and applying"). He is a man at a modern-day street auction outbidding the old religious "hucksters." He is the physiologist who has an almost mystical regard for the sperm. He is a carpenter taking "exact dimensions" of Jehovah and an artist who lithographs Kronos and puts Manito in his portfolio. And his gospel, as we learn in later lines, is that of the progressive scientist and Harmonialist, who sees holiness in the most apparently trivial things, such as a hair on the back of his hand or a mother with a baby at her nipple.

Such layering allows Whitman to interweave private desires with cultural images. The famous twenty-eight bathers scene, for instance, is a rich gathering place of cultural images and personal fantasies. The twenty-eight-year-old woman who lusts from behind the blinds of her fine house for the twenty-eight young men frolicking in the nearby stream is, on one level, a purified version of the wealthy masturbating woman, a common figure in reform tracts and pornographic novels of the day. The glistening sunlit water and the atmosphere of Edenic frolic give the scene an ennobling effect, distant from the sexual vampirism of, say, George Thompson's novel *New-York Life,* in which hundreds of wealthy women are described flocking to a dexterous doctor for "daily fingerings." Interwoven with Whitman's Edenic, sanitized version of the common theme of female masturbation are his own homoerotic fantasies. The "unseen hand" that strokes the men's bodies, as Michael Moon points out, might just as well be the hand of the male "I" as that of the voyeuristic woman. Added to both the homoerotic and heteroerotic themes here is the natural-health belief in water cure. Whitman was an ardent believer in regular swimming for both sexes, and the portrait of the bathers and the unseen woman bathing gleefully has a joyous, restorative effect.

This overlapping of meanings is visible virtually everywhere in the poem. When the "I" embraces the earth as his lover and exclaims, "We hurt each other as the bridegroom and bride hurt each other," he is communicating both Harmonial oneness with nature and erotic fantasy. The passage beginning "Is this then a touch?" can be read simultaneously as a poetic rendering of the Emersonian and Harmonial belief that every touch should thrill, a Grahamite diatribe on the perils of masturbation (since his "own hands" drive the "I" to madness), and a projection of homoerotic fantasy (especially in the original notebook version, with its line suggestive of anal intercourse: "Fierce Wrestler! do you keep your heaviest grip to the last? / Will you struggle even at the threshold with spasms more delicious than all before?").

The fact that neither "Song of Myself" nor many of its sections are reducible to a single meaning is a testament to Whitman's success in fusing disparate cultural and autobiographical elements at a time when America as a nation seemed on the verge of falling apart. Occasionally he becomes heavy-handed in his appeal for sectional unity, as when he pictures himself part of "an average unending procession, / We walk the roads of Ohio and Massachusetts and Virginia and Wisconsin and New York and New Orleans and Texas and Montreal and San Francisco and Charleston and Savannah and Mexico"—a rhetorical intermingling of North, South, East, and West that purposely imposes comradely unity on a highly disunified country.

But the unities asserted in "Song of Myself" are rarely as pedestrian or obvious as this. The caresser of life who flows comfortably in and out of identities, bringing health to all, announces togetherness in his very language. Slang words like "pave," "chuff," "slue," and "blab" come as comfortably from his lips as Swedenborgian, phrenological, or artistic terms. And all of them achieve striking new effects when they are combined by the all-fusing poet. As Whitman once wrote: "The great poet absorbs the identity of others, and the experience of others, and they are definite in him or from him, but he presses them all through the powerful press of himself." In "Song of Myself" Whitman eclectically absorbs the identity of others and presses them through the powerful press of himself in such a way that they shed their local, time-specific meaning and take on literary life.

The remaining eleven poems in the 1855 edition continue the all-fusing, all-absorbing strategy of "Song of Myself," though with diminished comprehensiveness and with only mixed success. A line from "A Song for Occupations" speaks for the whole volume: "The popular tastes and employments taking precedence in poems or anywhere." "A Song for Occupations" explicitly states one of Whitman's basic themes: since established institutions and laws have failed us, we should look to common humanity and its enjoyments to bind us. Allen Ascher has recently shown that writers like Cooper, Emerson, and Thoreau were struggling to come to terms with the decline of natural, moral-based law in America and the rise of morally dubious laws that defended the interests of the moneyed elite. The crisis over law became especially pronounced after the passage of the fugitive slave law and the Kansas-Nebraska Act, which seemed to invalidate all human laws and which impelled Emerson and Thoreau to reassert an organic, morally sound law allied with individual conscience and humanity.

Whitman does something very similar. He insists that law has little to do with rulers or legislators and much to do with the experiences and tastes of ordinary people living in a fundamentally harmonious universe. As he writes in "Great Are the Myths":

> Justice is not settled by legislators and laws. . . . it is in the soul,
> It cannot be varied by statutes any more than love or pride or the
>   attraction of gravity can,
> It is immutable. . . . it does not depend on majorities. . . . majorities or
>   what not come at last before the same passionless and exact
>   tribunal.
>
> For justice are the grand natural lawyers and perfect judges. . . . it is
>   in their souls,
> It is well assorted. . . . they have not studied for nothing. . . . the great
>   includes the less,
> They rule on the highest grounds. . . . they oversee all eras and states
>   and administrations.

Whitman here wrests the idea of law from existing power structures and plants it in the immutable universe, both in its spiritual and physical dimensions. He demands "natural lawyers and perfect judges" who "rule on the highest grounds" and "oversee all eras and states and administrations," largely because he finds none of these things in the political scene of the fifties. A new Union based on affirmative secular and religious laws must be found to supplant the lost Union based on failed rulers and unnatural laws.

Whitman's emphasis on the common denominators of experience—the earth, sleep, work, sex, and the appetites—shows him trying to regain fundamental laws that are unarguable and sound, not shifting and unfair. "The great laws take and effuse without argument," he writes in "Who Learns My Lesson Complete?" "I am of the same style, for I am their friend." He is making a strident call for the unification of humankind on the basis of natural law that is part and parcel of shared interests and common experiences.

The search for unifying phenomena outside of corrupt social structures leads in many directions. In "A Song for Occupations" the unifying factor is work; Whitman lists virtually every kind of work and worker in an effort to ennoble even the commonest of jobs. In "The Sleepers" it is the nightly act of sleeping, which is imagined as relieving all kinds of social and psychological ills. In "I Sing the Body Electric" it is the human body in its wondrous intricacy and fecundity. In "There Was a Child

Went Forth" it is the child's extraordinary sensitivity to the environment, which becomes a lifelong source of wonder and fear. In "Who Learns My Lesson Complete?" the unifying factor is the soul's immortality, which is said to parallel the unchanging laws of the universe, and in "Great Are the Myths," it is language, the overarching bridge between peoples.

Whitman's affirmations of unity in these poems are made with mixed success. The tiresomely inclusive catalogs of jobs in "A Song for Occupations" and the Ossianic exclamations of "Great Are the Myths" are counterbalanced by the masterfully phantasmagoric montage of personal and cultural images in "The Sleepers."

Skillful or not, all the poems reflect a fundamental faith in the power of the poet to restore equilibrium and connectedness to apparently disconnected phenomena. This faith in the poet's supreme power becomes the topic of an entire poem, "Song of the Answerer." Doubt does not enter this poem. The poet is said to encompass everything and set everything right. Because of this power, the poet can expect to be accepted universally. His healing power will spread through all society. As Whitman writes:

> Him all wait for.... him all yield up to.... his word is decisive and
>   final,
> Him they accept.... in him lave.... in him perceive themselves as
>   amid light,
> Him they immerse and he immerses them. [...]
>
> His welcome is universal, the flow of beauty is not more welcome or
>   universal than he is.

In 1855, Whitman felt America needed him, and he was there to supply the need. He firmly believed his country would absorb him as affectionately as he had absorbed it.

It was not long before he knew that he was terribly mistaken.

11

"THE MURDEROUS DELAYS": IN SEARCH OF AN AUDIENCE

T HE ANSWERER HAD SPOKEN. He had said his welcome would be universal. It was not. Therein lay a terrible problem.

Whitman's whole theory of poetry was based on the idea of the poet's social function and his reciprocal relationship with the mass of readers. Late in life, with the wisdom of hindsight, he would tell Traubel that from the start he should have traveled around reading and lecturing directly to the people instead of waiting for his poems to take effect. "I could, I should, have done it," he said. "I see now that it was my mistake: I needed to reach the people: I could have done so at once, following this method, instead of subjecting myself to the terrible delays—the murderous delays: but it's too late now." Another time he explained, "If I had gone directly to the people, read my poems, faced the crowds, got into immediate touch with Tom, Dick, and Harry instead of waiting to be interpreted, I'd have had my audience at once."

So caught up was he in such populist fantasies that he seemed to forget that the first edition of *Leaves of Grass* had gotten a fairly friendly response and that for years he had tried all kinds of gimmicks, including lecturing, to reach the people.

As it was, he cultivated in old age the myth that at the start he had been a lonely prophet reviled by his country. When he was correcting the proofs of the 1883 biography of him by his friend Richard Maurice Bucke, he let stand Bucke's report that the 1855 edition had met with nothing but rejection. "It was certain," Bucke wrote, "that the book quite universally, wherever it was read, excited ridicule, disgust, horror, and anger." Bucke insisted it was "considered meaningless, badly written, filthy, atheistical, and utterly reprehensible."

Whitman's own recollections about the reception of the first edition were hardly more positive. "It is tragic—the fate of those books," he said of the various states of the edition. "None of them were sold—practically none—perhaps one or two, perhaps not even that many." "Nobody would have 'em," he lamented, "for gift or price: nobody: some even returned their copies—editors—others. You can rely upon Dr. Bucke's book on all those matters: it is all verified."

All verified—but accurate? Not if we look firsthand at the book's early reception. Sales may have been lax, but surely not as dismal as Whitman recalled. In his 1856 open letter to Emerson Whitman had crowed, "I printed a thousand copies, and they readily sold." The same year, in an ad for the second edition, his publisher Fowler and Wells similarly said the first edition had "found purchasers, appreciators, and admirers."

Contrary to Whitman's old-age recollections, the 1855 edition was widely distributed and stirred a good amount of interest. Still, the sale of several hundred copies was not what he had had in mind when he had written of being absorbed by his country. Although the first edition got some good reviews, it rapidly fell victim to narrow interpretations. In the face of what amounted to the public's rejection of his poetry, Whitman resorted to various kinds of publicity stunts, some of them shady, in an effort to reach the mass audience. He also changed tactics in his poetry. The second edition of *Leaves of Grass*, published in August 1856, looked completely different physically from the first edition, and the poems it contained showed signs of genuine despair, as though Whitman already sensed his ultimate audience would have to be deferred.

The nation, in the meantime, continued to unravel. The nomination of yet another soft-spined Democrat, James Buchanan, threatened to worsen the problems of the house divided, especially since the corruption and proslavery compromises of previous administrations were outdone by his. Whitman still harbored a dream of rescuing his country, and he furiously continued writing poems. But he was also flailing about, exploring all kinds of avenues, sometimes in desperation, to gain a hearing.

The Answerer's confidence was shaken as the nation moved inexorably toward war.

The Reception of the 1855 Edition

LEAVES OF GRASS appeared on July 4, 1855, and two days later it was advertised for sale at Swayne's bookstore in Brooklyn and at Fowlers and Wells outlets in New York, Philadelphia, and Boston. It was withdrawn from the shelves of Swayne's within a week, but Fowlers and Wells continued to carry the book, as did the famous Old Corner Bookstore in Boston. It was also carried in England by Horsell and Shirefs, a progressive firm associated with Fowlers and Wells.

The book made its way into distinguished hands. Copies were sent to Emerson, Longfellow, and Whittier. Emerson, whose glowing letter to Whitman became his biggest promotional tool, spread the word in New England circles. When the reformer and liberal minister Moncure Daniel Conway visited him that summer, Emerson commended Whitman to him. In September, Conway became the first to visit Whitman in Brooklyn, anticipating later visits by Bronson Alcott, Henry David Thoreau, and, reportedly, Emerson himself. Emerson also alerted the famous Boston liberal William Henry Channing, who in turn introduced *Leaves of Grass* to his sister-in-law Mary Jane Tarr Channing and her sister Ellen (Nelly) Tarr O'Connor, who were staying in Providence with the women's rights leader Paulina Wright Davis. Through them the volume was made known to Nelly's husband, William Douglas O'Connor, a young radical firebrand who later became Whitman's close friend and ardent champion. Also caught up in the messianic spirit was the reformer and author John Townsend Trowbridge, who was in Paris when the first edition appeared and whose excitement was piqued by an American review of the volume that appeared in a French newspaper.

This was hardly disgust, horror, and anger, as Bucke would later call it. Shining like a dazzling rainbow over all positive responses to *Leaves of Grass*, of course, was Emerson's July 21 letter to Whitman. Among responses to the first edition, the letter was by far the most glowing and, in terms of Whitman's poetic aims, the most appropriate:

Dear Sir—I am not blind to the worth of the wonderful gift of "Leaves of Grass." I find it the most extraordinary piece of wit and wisdom that America has yet contributed. I am very happy in reading it, as great power makes us happy....

I give you joy of your free and brave thought. I have great joy in it. I find incomparable things said incomparably well, as they must be. I find the courage of treatment which so delights us, and which large perceptions only can inspire.

I greet you at the beginning of a great career, which yet must have had a long foreground somewhere, for such a start. I rubbed my eyes a little, to see if this sunbeam were no illusion; but the solid sense of the book is a sober certainty. It has the best merits, namely, of fortifying and encouraging....

I wish to see my benefactor, and have felt much like striking my tasks and visiting New York to pay you my respects.

R. W. Emerson

In its simple elegance, this is the Gettysburg Address of American literary commentary. If Lincoln's Gettysburg Address remade America, as Garry Wills says, Emerson's letter came close to making Whitman. It was constantly reprinted, quoted, and cited by Whitman's defenders, often with Whitman's encouragement. Its glow lingers over *Leaves of Grass* even to this day. Just as the Gettysburg Address soared above the details of battles or political squabbles and made an eloquent generalization about the goals of the nation, so Emerson's letter made a holistic, transcendental statement about Whitman's poetry. The first edition of *Leaves of Grass* had brought together all aspects of cultural experience into an organic whole, and its wholeness was matched by Emerson's response, which moved beyond details straight to the health-affirming, fortifying effects Whitman had tried to achieve.

The problem was, this was one of the last holistic responses Whitman got in his lifetime, from Emerson or anybody. Whitman had transformed the images of many different cultural-interest groups into something wholly new in an effort to unify America and change what he saw as its downward direction. But it was not long before the different interest groups seized upon specific aspects of *Leaves of Grass* and used them for or against Whitman, or for or against each other. Over time, the intricate tapestry of Whitman's poetry was unraveled into separate threads.

Emerson's letter itself rapidly fell victim to exploitation and infighting. Whitman kept the letter to himself for more than a month, savoring its contents as he spent much of the late summer in eastern Long Island, visiting his sister Mary in Greenport and roaming the shores and countryside as he had in youth. By the time he returned to Brooklyn in September, three reviews of *Leaves of Grass*, two positive and one mixed, had appeared, but the volume was very far from being absorbed by the country. Doubtless he read in the papers about the tremendous gathering of the Association of New York Publishers on September 27 at the Crystal Palace. "To American literature!" went the toast that opened the celebratory congregation of American publishers and authors.

In an orgy of enthusiasm and self-congratulation, publishers recited statistics about the amazing growth and influence of American books over the previous three decades. Whitman loved to contemplate such evidence of literature's cultural power, but he cannot have been cheered by the New York meeting. Everyone, it seemed, was there. Among the 650

invited guests were Irving, Bryant, Longfellow, Whittier, Alice and
Phoebe Cary, Susan and Anna Warner, and a host of others. But not
Whitman. Apparently, no one had thought to invite him. Giddy poems
were read aloud about the popularity of gory sensation novels, which
were said to be "teeming from the groaning press," and the surge in
other kinds of literature was described as well. But no mention was made
of the poetry volume that had appeared three months before and that
was intended by its author to be absorbed by America. Since America
wasn't listening, Whitman had to make himself heard.

Emerson's letter was a ready-made publicity tool. Although Tran-
scendentalism was not a popular movement, Emerson was a cultural
icon with instant name recognition. He was in such demand as a lecturer
that he commanded $250 per engagement. Whitman made Emerson's
letter known to an old newspaper friend, Charles A. Dana, editor of the
New York Tribune. Dana's generally positive review of *Leaves of Grass*
had appeared in the July 23 issue, and the paper had run ads for the
volume since July 6. Dana printed Emerson's letter in the *Tribune* on
October 10. Apparently Whitman did not tell him to do so, but neither
did he object, even though no authorization had come from Emerson.

Emerson's letter having entered the public arena, it was destined to
be used as a weapon by Whitman's defenders, and it was an important
part of the publicity apparatus of the second edition of *Leaves of Grass*,
quoted on the spine and reprinted entire in the appendix. Emerson's pri-
vate letter had become public hype. According to Moncure Conway,
"Emerson said that if he had known his letter would be published he
might have qualified his praise." In the meantime, his holistic enthusi-
asm for *Leaves of Grass* began to fade. Some of the friends to whom he
had recommended the volume objected to its sexual passages. Emerson
himself began to be bothered by the parts instead of seeing the whole.
When he mailed a copy to Carlyle in May 1856 he called it "a nonde-
script monster, which yet had terrible eyes and buffalo strength, and was
indisputably American." With cavalier indifference, he told Carlyle that
"if you think, as you may, that it is only an auctioneer's inventory of a
warehouse, you can light your pipe with it." Before long Emerson was
objecting to the sex passages in *Leaves of Grass*, which he thought might
be confused with a free-love document. By 1875 the poetry he had called
America's "most extraordinary piece of wit and wisdom" was not even
represented in *Parnassus*, his anthology of his favorite poetry that in-
cluded such unknowns as Walter Mitchel and James Gates Percival.

Nondescript monster. Auctioneer's inventory. Free-love document.
Emerson began to find cultural pigeonholes for poetry whose wholeness

he steadily lost sight of. Just as his letter had been co-opted as an advertising tool, so his response to *Leaves of Grass* began to show the partiality manifested by his friends and by many reviewers.

Among early reviewers, Whitman alone, in his three anonymously published self-reviews, presented a holistic vision of *Leaves of Grass*. It might seem odd today to think of an author writing complimentary self-reviews, planting them in friendly newspapers, and then repeatedly reprinting them in later promotional contexts. Before the Civil War, however, this kind of unabashed self-promotion was commonplace. P. T. Barnum reveled in his sobriquet the Prince of Humbug and popularized the flashy poster as a main means of advertising. The world's first advertising agency was founded in New York in the early 1850s, a decade that saw the emergence of the master of newspaper hype, Robert T. Bonner. When in June 1855 he lined up Fanny Fern to write for his New York *Ledger* at the unprecedented fee of one hundred dollars a column, he printed the sentence "Fanny Fern Writes for the New York Ledger!" ninety times without variation, using four whole columns. Whitman often saw the stocky, fair-haired Bonner on the street and described him in a *Life Illustrated* article as "the hero of unheard-of and tremendous advertising, who fires cannon, fills page upon page of newspapers, and— if he could—would placard the very walls of Paradise with hifalutin handbills, to sell that gorgeous and unprecedented sheet, the New York *Ledger.*"

Nor was it unusual then for advertising and promotion to involve crooked tactics. Reviews of plays and books were often supplied by promoters to the press, which printed them for a price. In the *Eagle* Whitman had noted with horror that most American theaters had paid "puffers" who regularly supplied the press with glowing reviews. At the time, he took a high-and-mighty stance: "The whole system of paid newspaper puffs should be discarded, entirely and utterly. There is hardly anything more contemptible." But the tide toward paid puffery was not to be stopped. It became common for book publishers to pay newspaper editors or reviewers for positive reviews. Even established critics like Rufus Griswold and E. P. Whipple wrote laudatory reviews for money, and in a time when newspaper editors made no more than policemen or bank clerks, they were natural targets of bribery. In December 1855 a writer for *Life Illustrated* generalized that the press "is not only willing, but anxious to be bribed" and, using italics to drive the point home, that *"comparatively few notices of new books are the absolute unbiased opinions of those who write the notices."*

Whitman did not have bribe money, but he had a message to communicate and friends in the press. Open to him were the columns of the

United States and Democratic Review, the *Brooklyn Daily Times,* and the *American Phrenological Journal.* The message of the reviews he wrote for these periodicals in September and October 1855 was essentially the same as that of the 1855 preface: a totally American poet, free of European conventions, had arrived to announce new possibilities of cultural togetherness and cohesion. The *United States Review* piece—beginning "An American bard at last!"—was especially comprehensive, mentioning many of Whitman's themes: intense Americanism, spiritualism and immortality, the cleanliness of sex and physiology, the poet's superiority to the president and any legislature. Whitman emphasized his central theme of unity with special vigor. He repeated the hopeful image from the preface of "the union always surrounded by blatherers and always calm and impregnable" and stressed the joining power of the poet: "He does not separate the learned from the unlearned, the northerner from the southerner, the white from the black, or the native from the immigrant just landed at the wharf." His *Daily Times* review was almost as comprehensive. No imitator is this poet, he proclaimed, no foreigner, large, lusty, "his physiology corroborating a rugged phrenology"—the later point underscored by a reprinting of his phrenological chart. Again stressing cultural unity, he called himself a bard "for the south the same as the north," adding another of his all-conjoining lists of states north and south.

If Robert Bonner was publicly repeating Fanny Fern's name ninety times, Whitman was hammering away with equal insistence at his message: Come together, America, through me. But a nation riven by sectionalism, class differences, and political factions was hardly prepared to become unified through poetry, no matter how comprehensive it was. Whitman's dream of being absorbed by his country faded as the months passed. No wonder he felt later that he had been totally rejected.

The image the public got of Whitman's poetry, however, was far from being uniformly hostile. Of the twenty-three reviews of the first edition ("reviews" meant to include Whitman's anonymous self-reviews and Emerson's letter printed in the *Tribune*), twelve were mainly positive, five mixed, and six mainly negative. The first really negative review, by Rufus Griswold in the *Criterion,* did not appear until November, five months after publication date.

Moreover, because the early reviewers were themselves part of the American culture that had produced *Leaves of Grass,* many of them heard contemporary inflections most twentieth-century critics have missed. Many saw that Whitman was mixing images from popular and elite culture. The earliest review, by Charles A. Dana, placed Whitman in the "class of society sometimes irreverently styled 'loafers'" but also saw Emersonian, Barnumesque, and oratorical sides to him, calling him "one of the modern 'prophets of the soul'" who at the same time would interest "lovers of literary curiosities" but sometimes had a "somewhat too oratorical strain." Five days later a reviewer for *Life Illustrated* likewise called Whitman a perfect loafer, but one with a thoughtful, philosophical bent. The third review, by Charles Eliot Norton in the September *Putnam's,* noted that Whitman's blending of contemporary voices created a new style. "[I]t is," wrote Norton, "a mixture of Yankee transcendentalism and New York rowdyism, and, what must be surprising to both these elements, they here seem to fuse and combine with the most perfect harmony." But Norton shied away from Whitman's mixture of polite and low language, noting that "the introduction of terms never before heard or seen, of slang expressions, often renders an otherwise striking passage altogether laughable."

Even reviewers who had a narrower understanding of Whitman's poetry still tended to identify it with current trends. Trying to substantiate the claim that it was "a mass of stupid filth," Rufus Griswold placed Whitman among a recently visible class of reformers (presumably the free lovers) who pretended to be pure but in fact were licentious. "These candid, these ingenuous, these honest 'progressionists,' . . . these men that have *come*—detest furiously all shams; 'to the pure all things are pure;' they are pure, and consequently, must thrust their reeking presence under every man's nose." An equally philistine but very different view was taken by the *Christian Spiritualist,* which praised Whitman as exemplifying one of "many varieties of Mediumship" along with Swedenborg and the spiritualists. Yet another contemporary twist was discovered by Whitman's first woman reviewer, Fanny Fern, who presented Whitman as a transformed Know-Nothing, intensely American but not anti-Catholic.

Foreign reviews, both positive and negative, tended to characterize *Leaves of Grass* as a typically outlandish product of an American culture full of freaks and marvels. William Howitt in the London *Weekly Dispatch* said the volume typified "American eccentricity in authorship" and was "so novel, so audacious, and so strange, as to verge upon absurdity." The London *Examiner* described Whitman as "a wild Tupper of the West," and the *Critic* put him in the company of America's Barnums, mermaids, sea serpents, and spirit rappers. In a squib called "A Strange Blade," the comic magazine *Punch* put *Leaves of Grass* "on a level with that heap of rubbish called *Fern Leaves,* by FANNY FERN, and 'similar' green stuff. The fields of American literature want weeding dreadfully." The London *Leader* found Whitman "one of the most amazing, one of the most startling, one of the most perplexing creations of the modern American mind; but he is no fool, though abundantly eccentric."

There were a few, to be sure, who damned or praised *Leaves of Grass* without mentioning any cultural forerunners. The Boston *Intelligencer* dismissed it as a "heterogenous mass of bombast, egotism, vulgarity, and nonsense" whose author must be "some escaped lunatic, raving in pitiable delirium." Edward Everett Hale, in a laudatory review close in spirit to Emerson's letter, admired the book's "freshness, simplicity, and reality," as enjoyable as a rest on a pleasant hillside in summer.

Such bifurcated responses were part of an ominous cycle of attack and defense that would gather momentum as the years passed and would become the chief focus of public discussion of Whitman. Any hopes he had of gaining widespread impact and getting holistic responses to his poetry would be seriously undermined by fragmented, partial readings, and in no area was the fragmentation so glaring as in the debate over his sexual themes. The early reviews set the tone of the debate.

On one side were Hale, Fern, and Whitman the self-reviewer, who insisted that *Leaves of Grass* was totally candid in its treatment of sex and the body but also totally pure. Hale wrote, "There is not a word in it meant to attract readers by its grossness." Fern insisted that Whitman's sexual frankness was infinitely preferable to much popular religious and reform literature, in which sex was insidiously cloaked by piety. Describing a widespread cultural phenomenon I identify in *Beneath the American Renaissance* as "immoral reform," Fern denounced the reader who would call Whitman gross and pointed to popular literature: "Let him look carefully between the gilded covers of books backed by high-sounding names, and indorsed by parson and priest, lying unrebuked upon his family table; where the asp of sensuality lies coiled amid rhetorical flowers." "I extract no poison from these Leaves," she wrote. Fern thus initiated what would become a major argument by Whitman's defenders: that his sexual openness was a healthy contrast to the furtive prurience of popular culture.

This was how Whitman expected to be seen, but in the early reviews contrary voices were raised. The loudest voices of opposition on this score were the fastidious Griswold, who categorized Whitman as a filthy free lover, and the reviewer for the *Intelligencer,* who thought Whitman "should be kicked from all decent society as below the level of a brute."

The controversy over Whitman's sexual themes, though still mild in comparison with later battles, did not bode well for the second edition of *Leaves of Grass.*

Depressions

WHITMAN HAD CONTINUED WRITING even as the early reviews appeared, and by spring 1856 he had produced twenty new poems and made some revisions of the earlier ones. He looked forward to publishing them under the auspices of the distributor of the first edition, but in September 1855 Orson Fowler left the company to pursue a solo career in sexual physiology, leaving it in the hands of his staid, quiet brother Lorenzo Fowler and the practical-businessman partner Samuel R. Wells. Even under this conservative management, the company planned to publish a second edition and by June 1856 had already bound a thousand-copy run that incorporated Whitman's new poems and his revised former ones as well as promotional matter. Then, shockingly, Samuel R. Wells tried to suspend publication.

Wells was feeling the pressure of the intensifying sex battle. Emerson's letter had been extremely heartening, and the early reviews were solid enough. But when Griswold's "mass of stupid filth" outburst appeared in November, followed by the mixed reviews from London and then, in May, the trashing by the *Intelligencer,* Wells had second thoughts about a second edition. On June 7, 1856, while visiting Boston, he sent Whitman a letter that must have devastated the poet. "We have concluded," Wells wrote, "that it is best for us to insist on the omission of certain objectionable passages in Leaves of Grass, or decline publishing it. . . . We must not *venture.*" Having made this prissy caveat, Wells did a clumsy turnaround and pretended Fowler and Wells was actually too daring a publisher for *Leaves of Grass.* "It will be better for you," he assured Whitman, "to have the work published by clean hands, i.e., by a house, not now committed to unpopular notions. . . . [A] more orthodox house would do better for you."

Evidently, Wells was trying to clean up the publishing firm's act. In the early fifties, under the impetus of the innovative Orson Fowler, the company had gone out on some precarious limbs, publishing, for instance, the socialist Charles Fourier and the free lover Marx Edgeworth Lazarus. *Leaves of Grass* had seemed to fit in with such experimental publications, but when some prominent reviewers starting calling it impure, the business-minded Wells decided to back off.

Since a second run was already stereotyped and bound, however, suspension of the edition was impractical. A deal was struck whereby Fowler and Wells would publish and distribute the edition but would keep its imprimatur off the title page. The firm would promote the volume, but Whitman retained copyright.

Whitman kept up a brave face in his new writings for the 1856 edition, but serious cracks would appear in the edition, pointing to a faltering of his poetic program. Absorption by the American public, so confidently anticipated in 1855, was obviously not forthcoming, at least in the foreseeable future. At the same time, American politics seemed, if anything, further removed than ever from the ideals Whitman associated with American democracy.

Disappointment over the lackluster public reception of the first edition seems to be registered in a note scribbled by Whitman during this interim period:

> Depressions
> Every thing I have done seems to me blank and suspicious.—I doubt whether my greatest thoughts, as I supposed them, are not shallow—and people will most likely laugh at me.—My pride is impotent, my love gets no response.—the complacency of nature is hateful—I am filled with restlessness.—I am incomplete.—

Whitman here was striking a disappointed, self-critical posture he would never totally surrender. Already, the gloom and self-questioning of later poems like "As I Ebb'd with the Ocean of Life" was manifesting itself. The phrases "people will . . . laugh at me" and "My pride is impotent, my love gets no response" communicate a pathetic feeling of sudden powerlessness and doubt in the face of public rejection. The statements "I am filled with restlessness.—I am incomplete" point to collapsed confidence and to a sense that much remained to be done to complete his poetic mission.

From a political and social standpoint, it was starting to look like an impossible mission. His private notes of later 1855 and 1856 were filled with bleak generalizations about politics and society. He saw ugliness on all levels of society, North and South, describing it in disjointed fashion: "Is this melange A [*sic*] crowd of attorneys, feverish southerners—owners of slaves, bleeders of the treasury, bullies without courage, angry dyspeptics from the north, supple human hinges from the same, are they this great America? this poor scum that has floated into the presidency—." He had once blindly accepted party principle, putting it above individuality. Now his attitude was exactly reversed. "Go back to first principles," he wrote, "—receive nothing through parties." The parties, he declared, "have no faith in man—they do not dream of any other way to success except schemings, caucuses, lying, not one lie, but all lies." The only remedies, he wrote, lay in returning to "first principles," in "throwing off authority," and in cultivating "countless breeds of great individuals, the eternal and only anchor of states."

Both the political problem and Whitman's proposed solutions had already been, as seen, the main bases for the 1855 edition of *Leaves of Grass*, but the political situation had become far more dire in the year following its publication. The marauding of Kansas by proslavery Missouri border ruffians in November 1855 was an ugly dress rehearsal for the bloody events of the following spring. On May 21 a posse of proslavery forces from Lecompton, Kansas, set out to arrest some free-state leaders in the town of Lawrence, setting fire to buildings and destroying two printing presses. Although no one was killed, the event was dramatized in the Northern press as "The Sack of Lawrence," with hyperbolic headlines reporting THE WAR ACTUALLY BEGUN—THE TRIUMPH OF THE BORDER RUFFIANS. The fact that President Pierce supported the proslavery Lecompton government fueled the North's rage.

In the meantime, blood was spilled on the floor of the Senate. On May 19 and 20 the Massachusetts Senator Charles Sumner gave a volatile speech calling for the admission of Kansas as a free state. Using vicious Lippardian rhetoric, he branded the Missouri invaders "murderous robbers . . . hirelings, picked from the drunken spew and vomit of an uneasy civilization." He impugned Senator Andrew Pickens Butler of South Carolina as a "polluted" public servant tied to the "harlot slavery." Two days later, the senator's cousin, Preston S. Brooks of South Carolina, strode into the Senate chamber while Sumner was quietly writing letters and, without warning, beat the confused, nearsighted Sumner with a gold-headed gutta-percha cane. After a brief struggle, Sumner, bleeding profusely, fell senseless to the floor. Brooks instantly became a hero in the South, a symbol of fearless revenge, while Sumner was hailed in the North as an actual victim of a Southern fire-eater.

"Bleeding Kansas" and "bleeding Sumner" made violence and sectional conflict seem the order of the day. That summer, much of the work on the second edition of *Leaves of Grass* behind him, Whitman poured out his own political venom in his prose tract "The Eighteenth Presidency!" In the aftermath of Sumner's "Crime Against Kansas" speech, savage rhetoric was in the air, and Whitman outdid Sumner and everyone else in the sheer abandon with which he used such rhetoric. Tumors, abscesses, pimps, skeletons, corpses' eyes, excrement, venereal sores— these were some of the epithets he hurled at party politicians. He sharply impugned President Pierce for supporting the proslavery Kansas government, and he demanded that not one more inch of slave soil should be added to America. He derogated the 1856 Democratic candidate, James Buchanan, as well as the nativist American Party candidate, Millard

Fillmore, giving tentative support to the Republican John Frémont. But he included a strong warning

TO FREMONT, OF NEW YORK

Whenever the day comes for him to appear, the man who shall be the Redeemer President of These States, is to be the one that fullest realizes the rights of individuals, signified by the impregnable rights of The States, the substratum of this Union. The Redeemer President of These States is not to be exclusive, but inclusive.

Whitman was bringing attention once more to a basic problem of antebellum politics: states' rights versus union. In the aftermath of Bleeding Kansas, the problem was messier than ever. Southerners, long the supporters of states' rights, ironically became the allies of federal power when Pierce endorsed Lecompton. Northerners were now generally disillusioned with the central government and wanted it to be redirected toward the antislavery cause. It would take a "Redeemer President," indeed, to settle the issue.

In the meantime, Whitman kept alive his utopian dream of some kind of compromise based on cultural unity. His projected Redeemer President would both recognize individual rights, "signified by the impregnable rights of The States" and would remain "not . . . exclusive, but inclusive." To describe the kind of inclusiveness he had in mind, Whitman pointed away from politics and, once again, to culture: to "the cheap book, the common newspaper," and all the modern inventions that he said "are interlinking the inhabitants of the earth together as groups of one family"; and especially to the "bravery, friendship, conscientiousness, clear-sightedness, and practical genius" of ordinary working-class Americans.

As though he were offering himself for the presidential nomination, he included an appeal "TO EDITORS OF THE INDEPENDENT PRESS, AND TO RICH PERSONS": "Circulate and reprint this Voice of mine for the working man's sake." He asked such persons to stereotype his pamphlet and "deluge the cities of The States with it, North, South, East, and West." Insisting that the great mass of Americans "are unsettled, hardly know whom to vote for, or whom to believe," he threw his hat into the political ring: "I am not afraid to say that among them I seek to initiate my name Walt Whitman, and that I shall in future have much to say to them."

By the summer of 1856, then, Whitman was looking for more than an audience: he was looking for a political constituency. Sheer fantasy, it seems in retrospect. But at the time, there was widespread disillusion with parties and the entire political process—a disillusion that would spark an unlikely enthusiasm for Frémont, the rough-hewn explorer with no political record. Who knows? Had Whitman won the support of the "rich persons" he was courting, maybe he would have leaped to national prominence too.

As it was, he had no access to the political power structures he painted so cynically in his pamphlet, which remained unpublished until after his death. But if he couldn't be the Redeemer President, he still envisaged large possibilities for a Redeemer Poet, who, after all, could be more inclusive than any president could hope to be.

The problem remained: how to win over the American readership. The style and format of the first edition had failed to do so. In 1856 Whitman decided to change his tack.

Amazing Changes

MOST STRIKING about the 1856 edition of *Leaves of Grass* is its difference in format and appearance from the 1855 edition. The new edition was a squat, chunky volume whose green exterior was ornamented by a gold "Leaves of Grass" in simple lettering on the cover and backstrip, where it was joined by Whitman's name and these words printed in gold leaf: "I Greet You at the Beginning of a Great Career/ R W Emerson." If the first edition had aspired to parlor-table elegance, this one tried to achieve both simple beauty and portability. He would once say that he wanted *Leaves of Grass* to be published as a pocket book, to be carried around everywhere: "That would tend to induce people to take me along with them and read me in the open air: I am nearly always successful with the reader in the open air." He also stipulated, "I want a beautiful book, too, but I want that beautiful book cheap: that is, I want it to be within reach of the average buyer."

A beautiful book within the average person's price range, able to be carried around: that's what the 1856 edition came close to being— though one would have to have ample pockets, like the oversized ones on Whitman's overcoats, to tote this 384-page book. Priced reasonably at a dollar, this edition was in line with standard poetry volumes by the likes of Longfellow and Whittier. With its relatively restrained exterior, normal size, and small but conventional typeface, it indeed had the look of a volume by one of the Fireside Poets.

More significantly, this edition, unlike the first, almost shouted that it was, above all, a volume of *poems*. Whereas the 1855 edition had included twelve free-flowing poems, untitled and unannounced, that might just as well have been rhythmic prose, the 1856 edition had thirty-two poems that were not only titled and announced in a table of contents but actually numbered 1 through 32, with page numbers announced on the title page. So intent was Whitman on presenting this as a volume of poetry that he now included the word "Poem" in the title of each piece. For instance, the first poem, later "Song of Myself," was "Poem of Walt Whitman, an American" and what would become "I Sing the Body Electric" was "Poem of the Body." His insistence on having "poem" in every title had some awkward results, as in "Poem of Apparitions in Boston, the 78th Year of These States" (later "A Boston Ballad") and "Liberty Poem for Asia, Africa, Europe, America, Australia, Cuba, and the Archipelagoes of the Sea" (later "To a Foil'd European Revolutionaire").

Why would Whitman, who in 1855 disguised the fact that his pieces were poems, now announce them as such to the point of clumsiness?

A part of the answer may be Henry Wadsworth Longfellow. In November 1855, while the first edition of *Leaves of Grass* was meeting mixed reviews and unspectacular sales, Longfellow's *Song of Hiawatha* appeared and quickly became a publishing phenomenon. Although Whitman saw Longfellow as a smooth imitator of European forms, he could not overlook the immense popularity of his poems. He once said he was "the expresser of common themes—of the little songs of the masses." By 1850 Longfellow earned nearly two thousand dollars annually from his poetry. His *Evangeline* (1847) sold more than thirty thousand copies in a decade, only to be outdone by *The Song of Hiawatha*, which sold ten thousand copies in a month and thirty thousand by the next June. Written in a catchy trochaic rhythm that would prompt Whitman to call it "a pleasingly ripply poem," *Hiawatha*, like most of Longfellow's works, showed that poems with traditional metrical patterns could be huge successes with the public.

Whitman, who thirsted for popular acceptance, thus had precedent in popular culture for presenting the 1856 edition as a collection of *poems*. He even began to make small concessions to popular tastes. His most popular poem during his lifetime would be his conventionally rhythmic eulogy to Lincoln, "O Captain! My Captain!" written in 1865. Although nothing in the 1856 edition came close to the conventionality of either "O Captain!" or Longfellow's poetry, Whitman used a trochaic metrical pattern in the opening lines of "Song of the Broad-Axe" and restored normalcy to his punctuation by getting rid of the odd ellipses of 1855 and replacing them with the standard commas and semicolons.

Another reason for the changes in the 1856 edition could be the popularity of Martin Farquhar Tupper's topic-oriented poems. Tupper's *Proverbial Philosophy* had contained prose-like poems about specific topics, as indicated in titles of individual poems such as "Of Prayer," "Of Friendship," "Of Humility," and "Of Rest." This categorization of poems by topic enhanced the usefulness of Tupper's volume for those who wanted guidance in specific areas. Whitman may have had a similar effect in mind when in the 1856 edition he presented poems about specific topics: "Lesson Poem," "Faith Poem," "Poem of Perfect Miracles," and so on. Since Fowler and Wells was a firm that published how-to books in various self-help fields, this kind of easily grasped classification would have made sense from a practical standpoint.

But the overriding reason for the changes in the 1856 edition would seem to be simply Whitman's sense that the public, which he had failed to reach in 1855, would have to be approached differently this time. The fact is, all six editions of *Leaves of Grass* were quite different from each other in format and appearance. Also, Whitman would keep reshuffling, recategorizing, and retitling his poems until settling on a final arrangement in 1881. His attitude seems to have been like Hawthorne's when he told his publisher he wanted *The Scarlet Letter* to appear in a volume along with some brighter tales, so that if he couldn't hit the public with one piece of "buck-shot" he would hit it with another. In 1855, Whitman had fired his poetic "gun" but had missed the target. In 1856 he fired again, from a different angle.

This time he loaded up with all kinds of buckshot. The 1856 edition offered something for everyone. Just by scanning the table of contents, the piously inclined reader could learn quickly that "Faith Poem" was on page 265. Women might feel impelled to turn to "Poem of Women," nature lovers to "Sun-Down Poem," children to "Poem of Remembrances for a Girl or a Boy of These States." Lovers of sensational literature would surely be intrigued by "Poem of the Propositions of Nakedness," and married couples might want to consult "Poem of Procreation." Everyone, presumably, would look at "Poem of You, Whoever You Are."

This was the old Whitman inclusiveness, but with a difference. The inclusiveness of the 1855 edition had been a self-assured, confident inclusiveness, as though all readers would fall willingly into the flow of the virtually undifferentiated poems and accept with wonder the totalizing experience Whitman offered. The inclusiveness of 1856 was scattershot, as though Whitman were dispensing topical poems for as many kinds of readers as possible.

This scattershot approach was visible in the appendix to the new edition. Titled "Leaves-Droppings," the appendix was a promotional section consisting of "Correspondence" (Emerson's letter and Whitman's public reply) and "Opinions. 1855–6" (a selection of reviews of the first edition).

Whitman's choice of reviews for reprinting in "Opinions" showed a deliberate outrageousness, as though he were trying to gain attention by stirring up trouble. He included his self-review in the *Daily Times* beginning with the controversial statement: "Very devilish to some, and very divine to some, will appear the poet of these new poems." He also included the *Christian Spiritualist* review, presenting him as an offbeat medium, and four quite mixed London reviews that stressed his outlandish, eccentric side. The appendix concluded with the damning Boston *Intelligencer* review that called him a brute and a lunatic.

The reprinting of such stinging, often negative commentary suggests that Whitman was testing out an advertising idea then quite new: controversy sells. The truth of the idea would strike home later on, when legal crackdowns on his poems resulted in surges in sales. In antebellum America there was ample precedent for the commercial exploitation of controversy. In the world of urban journalism in which Whitman was weaned, mud slung at oneself could be as effective an attention getter as that slung at others. James Gordon Bennett in his *Herald* gleefully reprinted epithets hurled at him by others, as when another paper called him a "horse-whipped, bribed, mendacious and miserable poltroon." The novelist and journalist George Lippard, likewise, loved to reprint nasty reviews of his novels to stir up interest. American popular culture was generating the commercialization of controversy that would become familiar in the era of Elvis, Madonna, and rap music.

The brashest—and most morally questionable—gimmick of the 1856 edition was Whitman's public letter of reply to Emerson. It was one thing for Whitman to reprint Emerson's letter, which by then was public knowledge anyway. It was quite another for him to include a public letter of reply to his "dear Friend and Master" presenting "thirty-two Poems" as a gift. In effect, Emerson's blessing was bestowed on twenty poems he hadn't even seen.

Whitman was beyond scruples. He felt his cause was worthy, and he would do anything in his limited power to push it. His open letter to Emerson was another effusion of his midfifties enthusiasm for his holistic poetic project. The message was the same as before: *Leaves of Grass* was above all a book for the masses, destined to be accepted by them because it emphasized all the positive aspects of American culture while stepping beyond failed political and social institutions. He put the message more baldly and sweepingly than ever, resorting to half-truths and wishful statements.

The first edition, he declared, had "readily sold." The second edition had been stereotyped (that is, put on plates for quick reproduction), so that rising public demand could be easily satisfied. The prospects were excellent that before long he would be totally accepted by the people:

> I much enjoy making poems. Other work I have set for myself to do, to meet people and The States face to face, to confront them with an American rude tongue; but the work of my life is making poems. I keep on till I make a hundred, and then several hundred—perhaps a thousand. The way is clear to me. A few years, and the average annual call for my Poems is ten or twenty thousand copies—more, quite likely. Why should I hurry or compromise? In poems or speeches I say the word or two that has got to be said, adhere to the body, step with the countless common footsteps, and remind every man and woman of something.

His populist fantasies were soaring to unrealistic heights. To say that the "average annual call" for his volume would surpass twenty thousand copies was self-delusion. Even Longfellow's *Hiawatha*, the biggest success story in antebellum poetry, would, despite its rapid initial sale, average under four thousand copies a year during its first thirteen years. But Whitman was not in the realm of reality. He was fantasizing again about being absorbed by his country, in any way. One was "making poems," a technological usage that summoned up mass production, as though he saw himself as a poetry factory forever stepping up output in order to satisfy broadening demand. He was also talking of "[o]ther work" that involved meeting "people and The States face to face." That is, a lecturing career was already on his mind. Either "in poems or speeches," he would inevitably get in "step with the countless common footsteps, and remind every man and woman of something."

The rest of the letter pointed readers once more away from established institutions to popular culture and universal principles. He summed up the political blight of the fifties with pithy cynicism: "The spectacle is a pitiful one. I think there can never be again on the festive earth more bad-disordered persons deliberately taking seats, as of late in These States, at the heads of public tables—such corpses' eyes for judges—such a rascal and thief in the Presidency." As for the churches, they were "one vast lie."

This was familiar rhetoric for Whitman, but his negativity was now deeper than before, his proposed solutions vaguer and less immediate. The ugliness he saw around him seemed more pervasive than ever. He saw it in literature ("There is no great author; every one has demeaned himself to some etiquette or impotence"), in manners ("The people, like a lot of large boys, have no determined tastes, are quite unaware of themselves"), in attitudes toward sex and love ("This tepid wash, this diluted, deferential love, as in songs, fiction, and so forth, is enough to make a man vomit"). What was needed, he indicated, was strong agitation and powerful imaginative reconstruction of American society. "Not a man faces round at the rest with a terrible negative voice," he wrote. He suggested he was such a one: "I love screaming, wrestling, boiling-hot days."

Along with sharp criticism, America needed a class of writers that would embrace the country and give it "a national character, an identity," creating "a new moral American continent" without which the physical one was "a carcass, a bloat." To illustrate the rising influence of literature, Whitman described the immense variety of recent popular writings. "All are prophetic; all waft rapidly on," he wrote. But all were just forerunners of the complete absorption of writers into society he foresaw: "Poets here, literats here, are to rest on organic different bases from other continents, not a class set apart."

The negativity and future-orientation of the open letter to Emerson reflect a poet who sensed with frustration that his dream of having widespread social impact would have to be deferred. The fantasy of mass acceptance of his poems was even more pronounced than before, but so was the stinging recognition of his actual rejection. Both the bright delusions and the dark reality were registered in polarities and mood swings that appeared in some of the new poems in the 1856 edition.

On the dark side were passages—and in the case of "Respondez!" a whole poem—in which the hopes and visions of the first edition were overturned. The utopian 1855 preface was now omitted, some of its lines dispersed in poems and its final line despondently rewritten: "The proof of the poet shall be sternly deferr'd till his country absorbs him as affectionately as he has absorb'd it." The addition of "sternly deferr'd" speaks volumes. Whitman now sensed that any reciprocal relationship between him and the public must be put off. In light of this, there may lurk real frustration behind the funny line: "Let him who is without my poems be assassinated!"

The poem in which this line appeared—"Respondez!"—gave vent to the "terrible negative voice" that Whitman told Emerson America needed. It was the most cynical poem Whitman ever wrote—indeed, the most cynical by any nineteenth-century American. It was humorous, but blackly, desperately so. In more than sixty scathing lines Whitman gleefully called for a complete reversal of roles in society. Murderers, infidels, obscene persons, and the diseased, he announced, should take over all political and social institutions. Atheism, obscenity, and materialism and racism must reign. Men and women were to be always distracted and depressed, unable to find happiness in themselves. Whitman reached to the depths of his nastiest Lippardian rhetoric to describe these role reversals:

> Let churches accommodate serpents, vermin, and the corpses of those
> who have died of the most filthy of diseases!
> Let marriage slip down among fools, and be for none but fools!
> Let men among themselves talk and think forever obscenely of
> women! and let women among themselves talk and think
> obscenely of men! [. . .]
> Let the earth desert God, nor let there ever henceforth be mention'd
> the name of God!
> Let there be no God! [. . .]
> Let all the men of These States stand aside for a few smouchers! let
> the few seize on what they choose! let the rest gawk, giggle,
> starve, obey!
> Let shadows be furnish'd with genitals! let substances be deprived of
> their genitals!
> Let there be wealthy and immense cities—but still through any of
> them, not a single poet, savior, knower, lover!
> Let the infidels of These States laugh all faith away! [. . .]
> Let the white person again tread the black person under his heel!
> (Say! which is trodden under heel, after all?)

On one level, these lines reflected the same instinct for attention-getting outrageousness that governed Whitman's choice of reviews for the appendix to this edition. They were part of the edition's scattershot effort to appeal to as many kinds of readers as possible: in this case, lovers of sensational literature and subversive reform rhetoric.

On another level, they revealed Whitman's profound disillusion with American society. They speak to the failure of the 1855 edition of *Leaves of Grass* to do its intended cultural work. From Whitman's perspective, anyone without his poems might just as well be "assassinated," for America without his poems seemed to him a wasteland. It was a nation out of touch with those all-healing first principles he had poeticized in the first edition, a nation more than ever in need of poetic reconstruction.

Despite his increased despair, Whitman felt he was the one who could accomplish this reconstruction. True, none of the new poems he wrote for the 1856 edition had the all-encompassing quality of his 1855 poem "Song of Myself," which had confidently fused virtually all types of cultural images. But not only did Whitman include "Song of Myself" and the other 1855 poems in the new edition, thus carrying forward his utopian experiment, but he added a number of poems that provided healing alternatives to all the defects he saw in the world around him. He continued to draw on affirmative cultural images he thought would have widespread appeal.

Two of the new poems, "By Blue Ontario's Shore" and "Song of the Broad-Axe," outlined the ideal nation. The former illustrated the poet's role in healing a fragmented America. "By great bards only can series of peoples and States be fused into the compact organism of one nation," went one line. This had been a main point of the 1855 preface, many lines of which were transposed into "By Blue Ontario's Shore." Most of the preface's cultural images—phrenology, physiology, progressive science, republican ideals, and others—were repeated, as was the description of the poet as "the equalizer of his age and land" who "supplies what wants supplying" and "checks what wants checking." This poem remained through subsequent editions Whitman's definitive social statement, to which he added topical references (about the Civil War, for instance) as time passed. In the 1856 edition it served as a kind of thesis poem, reminding readers of all the potentially unifying phenomena that might help heal the nation and the world. Other poems of the edition offered vivid symbols of such unifying phenomena.

One such unifying symbol was the broad-axe. In his notebook sketch toward "Song of the Broad-Axe" he told himself, "Make it an American emblem preferent to the eagle." The axe's connection to nature, to the past, to artisan labor, and to the construction of an ideal nation made it seem to him a superb symbol of unity. All these aspects of the axe come together in the poem's opening lines:

Weapon, shapely, naked, wan,
Head from the mother's bowels drawn,
Wooded flesh and metal bone, limb only one and lip only one,
Gray-blue leaf by red-heat grown, helve produced from a little seed
    sown.

A main point of the poem is that the axe, used for mainly destructive purposes in Europe and the past, is being applied to constructive uses in building a new democratic nation. The first word, "Weapon," is a reminder of the bloody past, vividly recalled later in the poem by the portrait of the European headsman with his dripping axe. But just as Whitman will write, "I see the headsman withdraw and become useless, / [. . .] I see the mighty and friendly emblem of the power of my own race, the newest, largest race," so the rest of the opening stanza stresses constructiveness and unity. The description of the construction of the axe (its head drawn from the earth, its limb produced by the little seed that grows into a tree) prefigures the later catalogs of artisan workers, close to nature and in love with their work, literally building America from the ground up, much the way Whitman thought the poet had to rebuild America in the 1850s. The association of the axe with the phallus (its "shapely, naked" head drawn from the "mother's bowels," as if after depositing the seed in intercourse) enforces the life-giving interpretation of the axe for America, just as in "By Blue Ontario's Shore" Whitman had the poet plunging his "seminal muscle" into his nation to produce a new America.

If in "Respondez!" Whitman had held a mirror up to the ugliest features of American life, in "Broad-Axe" he emphasized the brawn and creativity that went into building America. The dystopic reality of "Respondez!" is answered by its opposite: the utopian potential enunciated in "Broad-Axe." Whitman imagines a place

> Where the city stands with the brawniest breed of orators and bards,
>   [...]
> Where the men and women think lightly of the laws,
> Where the slave ceases, and the master of slaves ceases,
> Where the populace rise at once against the never-ending audacity of
>   elected persons,
> Where fierce men and women pour forth as the sea to the whistle of
>   death pours forth its sweeping and unript waves,
> Where outside authority enters always after the precedence of inside
>   authority,
> Where the citizen is always the head and ideal, and President,
>   Mayor, Governor and what not, are agents for pay, [...]
> Where speculations on the soul are encouraged,
> Where women walk in public processions the same as the men,
> Where they enter the public assembly and take places the same as
>   the men,
> Where the city of the faithfulest friends stands,
> Where the city of the cleanliness of the sexes stands,
> Where the city of the healthiest fathers stands,
> Where the city of the best-bodied mothers stands,
> There the great city stands.

This was a utopian vision produced by the problems and possibilities of the American 1850s. Since the president and other elected persons had proven themselves wanting, Whitman specifically indicts them and vigorously endorses the power of average men and women. Since human laws have proven corrupt, he encourages people to think lightly of laws and to follow "inside authority." He imagines a society without slavery and without sexual discrimination, one that breeds religions ("speculations on the soul"), sound parenthood ("the healthiest fathers," "the best-bodied mothers"), and a restored attitude to sex ("the cleanliness of the sexes").

The America Whitman envisaged here was light-years distant from the one he painted in "Respondez!" and in much of his journalism of the fifties. Having imagined this utopian nation in "Broad-Axe," he studied individual aspects of it in other new poems of the 1856 edition. The soul and its correspondences in the limitless universe were the focus of "Assurances," "Miracles," "Song of Prudence," and "Think of the Soul." Sex and parenthood were taken up in "Unfolded Out of the Folds" and were conjoined with Real Womanhood in "A Woman Waits for Me" and with same-sex affection in "Spontaneous Me." A general feeling of health and independence was communicated in "Song of the Open Road" and a longing for linkage to future generations in "Crossing Brooklyn Ferry."

Several of these poems hint of the personal and social ills that were the sole topic of "Respondez!" but they were rhetorically overcome, mainly by affirming the harmony between the physical and spiritual selves and the laws of nature. Negative moments remain, such as the "secret silent loathing and despair" in "Song of the Open Road" or the "guile, anger, lust, hot wishes I dared not speak" in "Crossing Brooklyn Ferry."

But Whitman puts to use his well-stocked arsenal of cultural images. For instance, in "Crossing Brooklyn Ferry" the grime and impersonality of city life, as well as the psychological "dark patches" at the center of the poem, are counteracted through several ameliorative devices: through distancing, as Brooklyn and Manhattan are viewed from the East River at sundown; through mystical time-space leaps, as the "I" communes with future generations; through affirmations from progressive science ("the float forever held in solution," "the simple, compact, well-joined scheme"); and through Harmonial or post-Swedenborgian images (the city and all its objects as "dumb, beautiful ministers" that "furnish [their] parts toward the soul").

The urgency with which Whitman described America's problems and proposed remedies in the 1856 edition suggests he was still buoyed by a belief that he could get a public hearing. When the edition appeared in early September, prospects seemed good that he would. In advertising the volume in *Life Illustrated* Fowler and Wells put a positive spin on the reception of the first edition and prophesied strong sales for the second. "It is evident," the ad said, "that the American people will give a hearing to any man who has it in him to reward attention. Walt Whitman's poems, the now famous 'Leaves of Grass,' would scarcely have thought to have become speedily popular.... Yet the 'Leaves of Grass' found purchasers, appreciators, and admirers. The first edition of a thousand copies readily sold." Fowler and Wells also ran ads for the second edition continuously from September 12 to October 4 in the *Tribune,* saying, "Dealers send in your orders. This book will always be in demand."

These exaggerations were typical of antebellum publicity, and they were about as far from reality as Whitman's dream of becoming the equalizer of his age and land. There is no way of testing Bucke's comment that the edition had "little or no sale." But it got only a smattering of reviews, all of them mixed. Whitman's exploitation of Emerson's letter and his reprinting of self-reviews shocked William Swinton, who in an unsigned review in the New York *Daily Times* noted with irony that "this self-contained teacher, this rough-and-ready scorner of dishonesty, this rowdy knight-errant who tilts against all lies and shams, himself perpetrates a lie and a sham at the very outset of his career." Likewise, the *Christian Examiner* called the printing of Emerson's letter "the grossest violation of literary comity and courtesy that ever passed under our notice," especially since the second edition contained new poems "which in their loathsomeness exceed any of the contents of the first," so that Emerson "is made to indorse a work that teems with abominations."

In the outrage over the second edition, reviewers did not mention specific poems, but doubtless they were bothered most by "A Woman Waits for Me" and "Respondez!" Whitman himself may have viewed "Respondez!" as a form of violent social bloodletting, but even those who saw flaws in American society were not ready to follow him to the depths of cynicism. He may have intended "Woman Waits" as an endorsement of healthy sex, but those outside reform circles were not prepared to accept the message. John Burroughs perhaps exaggerated when he recalled that in response to this poem "Every epithet of rancor and opprobrium was showered on the book and its author." But the least that can be said is that, despite the unifying images Whitman deployed in the second edition, the volume had little positive social impact. Reviewers saw that he was mixing negative and positive images, but they did not commend the tactic. The bemused Swinton called the edition a mass of "insolence, philosophy, tenderness, blasphemy, beauty and gross indecency." The *Canadian Journal* called it poetic and suggestive but also startling and somewhat ridiculous.

Having spoken again, the Answerer was even further from mass acceptance than before.

Man of the Fifties

HE MAY HAVE FAILED to reach the masses, but he was reaching some of the intelligentsia. In the fall of 1856, just after the second edition appeared, he was visited in Brooklyn by Bronson Alcott, Henry David Thoreau, and Sarah Tyndale.

The tall, thin Alcott arrived in Brooklyn on October 4 and visited the Whitman home, the middle tenement of an unimposing block of three frame dwellings far out on Classon Avenue, where the Whitmans had moved on May 1. Whitman looked to him like a rough satyr, broad shouldered, gray bearded, wearing an open-breasted red flannel shirt that exposed his brawny neck. Over this Whitman wore a striped calico jacket and coarse overalls. When they walked through Brooklyn together, he wore an overcoat with huge pockets into which he thrust his large hands. Cowhide boots and a slouched roundabout hat, which he wore indoors and out, completed the crude, insolent effect.

This was the Whitman of the individualistic, freewheeling midfifties, when idiosyncrasy in dress was a badge of honor. The same rebellion against convention that had produced the Bloomer outfit and the Kossuth hat was manifested in the poet's costume, which was a kind of caricature of working-class garb (see fig. 3, a photograph of Whitman taken around this time). As Alcott put it in his journal, "He wears his man-Bloomer in defiance of everybody, having these as every thing else after his own fashion."

Alcott had his own strange ways. The Transcendental reformer from Concord had long been a vegetarian. During his visit, Whitman's mother cooked a fine piece of meat and cut a thin slice for Alcott. When the dinner was over, the Whitmans were surprised to find that he had left the meat untouched and had eaten only the vegetables, bread, and cake.

Alcott found Whitman self-consciously lazy and slow, loving to stretch out on a couch for long talks. His deep voice was sharp but tender, his grayish eyes dull but wise. He was even a better listener than talker.

When Alcott visited Brooklyn again on November 10, he appeared with Thoreau and the Philadelphia abolitionist Sarah Tyndale. Whitman showed them his simple home, taking them up two flights of narrow stairs to his bedroom. Some books were scattered about the room. On the crude walls hung pictures of Hercules, Bacchus, and a satyr. In a corner was an unmade bed where Walt slept with his retarded brother Eddy; the pressure of their bodies could be seen on the bedding.

Whitman told them of his daily habits. He loved to bathe outdoors well into the winter, to ride the New York omnibuses, day and night, to go to the opera. He lived, he said with gruff mispronunciation, "to make pomes."

Thoreau and Whitman viewed each other with mutual fascination and suspicion. Alcott wrote that during the visit they acted wary of each other, "like two beasts, each wondering what the other would do, whether to snap or run." Whitman gave a copy of the 1856 edition of *Leaves of Grass* to Thoreau, who gave it a mixed commendation to his friend Harrison Blake in a letter of December 10. Thoreau wrote, "That Walt Whitman, of whom I wrote to you, is the most interesting fact at present." Thoreau was especially attracted by the courageous philosophizing of *Leaves of Grass*, which he called an incomparable sermon. Whitman's sex passages bothered him not for any intrinsic dirtiness but because he thought people weren't yet pure enough to read them properly. "It is as if the beasts spoke," he noted. As for Whitman's long catalogs, Thoreau found them tiresome: "By his heartiness & broad generalities he puts me into a liberal frame of mind prepared to see wonders—as it were sets me upon a hill or in the midst of a plain—stirs me well up, and then—throws in a thousand of brick." He also thought Whitman saw too much worth in common people.

This was a real point of disagreement between the two. Whitman was the archetypal fifties individualist, railing at the government and finding redemption in average Americans. As a rebel against authority, Whitman valued the anarchistic side of Thoreau, what he called "his lawlessness—his dissent—his going his own absolute road let hell blaze all it chooses." Whitman got an amusing look at this individualism during a later visit from Thoreau, who, finding Whitman was not home, went straight to the stove where cakes were baking and, without asking Mrs. Whitman, took one hot out of the oven.

Though attracted to Thoreau's self-reliant ways, Whitman thought him elitist. Both *Walden* and *Leaves of Grass* were very much products of the fifties, stemming from a disgust with the social and political status quo. But whereas Thoreau moved from disgust to isolationist individualism, Whitman moved from it to individualism coupled with radical democracy. Whitman would later say: "Thoreau's great fault was disdain—disdain for men (for Tom, Dick and Harry): inability to appreciate the average life."

If Thoreau was too detached from common life for Whitman, Alcott was too much in the clouds. When Alcott came for another visit in December, Whitman dined with him at Taylor's Saloon in Manhattan, discussing Emerson and politics. With his typical fifties hatred of social rulers, Whitman railed against "the pigmies assembled there at the Capitol." He said Emerson was America's best product, but he was not so kind about his dinner partner. As Alcott put it laconically in his journal: "Alcott, he fancies, may be somebody." Alcott's brand of Transcendentalism was too airy for Whitman, who once called him "a specialist," "a department man" who represented "pure thought, the poetic, the spiritual."

More to his taste than either Thoreau or Alcott was the woman who had accompanied them on the November visit, Sarah Tyndale. This portly, kindly woman was a vigorous activist in all kinds of reforms, principally abolitionism and women's rights but also Fourierism. She was the free-spirited radical woman of the fifties, a perfect fit for Whitman. She visited him several more times and sent her son Hector, a Philadelphia china importer, for a visit in February 1857. Whitman corresponded with her at least until that summer. He felt so at home with her that he kept her up-to-date on his personal life and literary activities.

His June 20, 1857, letter to her—the only surviving Whitman letter of note between August 1852 and January 1860—gives a valuable glimpse of his life at this time. He fondly recalled her visits and apologized for not having written sooner. "I am so non-polite," he explained, "—so habitually wanting in my responses and ceremonies. That is *me*— much that is bad, harsh, an undutiful person, a thriftless debtor, is me." He described his recent doings. Lately he spent an evening at the home of his good friend Abby Price. The wife of the owner of a Brooklyn pickle factory, Abby Price and her children, Helen, Emma, and Arthur were among his closest friends. In the Price home lived John Arnold with his daughter's family; Arnold was the Swedenborgian with whom Whitman had intense discussions. That evening they had a typical midfifties talk about Harmonialism and spiritualism. Whitman had recently attended a lecture by the golden-haired trance lecturer Cora Hatch, and they weighed her theory that spirit preceded matter against that of Andrew Jackson Davis, who thought it was the other way around.

Whitman also told Mrs. Tyndale of a meeting that day with the Brooklyn Dutch Reformed minister Elbert Stothoff Porter, who had read *Leaves of Grass* and said he hoped Whitman retained "the true Reformed faith" he must have inherited from his mother's Dutch ancestry. Whitman gave a humorous reply: "I not only assured him of my retaining faith in that sect, but that I had perfect faith in all sects, and was not inclined to reject a single one."

Next in his letter to Mrs. Tyndale he gave surprising news about his poetry. Since the appearance of the second edition of *Leaves of Grass* the previous fall, he had written nearly seventy new poems and was ready for a third edition. He was disgusted, however, with the way the first two editions had been published and received. "Fowler and Wells are bad persons for me," he said flatly. "They retard my book very much. It is worse than ever." He would try, he went on, to arrange for some other publisher to procure the plates, make the needed additions, and bring out a third edition. "Fowler and Wells are very willing to give up the plates—they want the thing off their hands," he added sourly.

He was prepared to change tack again. The new edition would have a hundred poems and nothing else, "no letters to or from Emerson—no notices, or anything of that sort." Once again, he was searching for the right format, the right arrangement that might make his poems amenable to the public. So dissatisfied was he with the response to the first two editions that he acted as though *Leaves of Grass* did not yet exist. Of the forthcoming edition he wrote: "I know well enough, *that* must be the *true* Leaves of Grass—I think it (the new Vol.) has an aspect of completeness, and makes its case clearer."

Mrs. Tyndale took the letter as a cry for help. In her July 24 reply she seconded his feeling that Fowler and Wells was not good for him. "I am sure they are not," she wrote, adding cryptically, "I can tell you more of their malpractice about it, when you come." She offered to lend him fifty dollars so that he could buy the plates. A week later, she said in another letter she was sending him the money through a friend and mentioned a couple of lesser publishers that might handle *Leaves of Grass*. A story had been spread by Alcott, she said, that Whitman was about to "publish another edition of Leaves of Grass, leaving out all the *objectionable* parts." "I with all my radicalism," she added, "would be delighted if some of the expressions were left out, the pictures are too vivid in some cases," since "the entire nakedness of the intercourse is rather calculated to increase libidinousness in weak minds which Heaven knows is frightfully rampant." She was probably objecting in particular to "Respondez!," believing its ironic valorization of obscenity and nakedness would be taken the wrong way by what she called "weak minds."

Whether or not Whitman received money from her, any plans for a third edition were soon squelched. Evidently, no publisher was ready to take on *Leaves of Grass* after the spotty reception of the second edition. Besides, two months after Mrs. Tyndale made her modest offer the economy went into a free fall, initiating a panic more severe and longer lasting than the one in 1854. With the publishing industry in the doldrums, controversial volumes of poetry were hardly in demand.

Whitman encountered financial setbacks and groped about for direction. His comment in his letter to Mrs. Tyndale that he was "an undutiful person, a thriftless debtor" was most likely a guilty reference to a run-in he had that month with the New York writer James Parton, the husband of Sara Parton (aka Fanny Fern). The previous winter Whitman had borrowed $200 from Parton and by June had still not repaid the loan. Parton tried to recover the money through his lawyer Oliver Dyer, who arrived at Whitman's Classon Street home on June 17. Since Whitman could not make the cash repayment, it was agreed he would hand over material goods worth $180. Among the things carted out of Whitman's home was a Jesse Talbot oil painting illustrating a scene from *Pilgrim's Progress,* supposedly valued at $400 to $500 but worth only $100 in the trade.

The Parton affair was a minor disturbance compared with the larger one of the failure of his poetry to have immediate social impact. Even as he was making plans for a third edition, he seriously contemplated going directly to the people by becoming a traveling lecturer. His visions of his prospective influence as a lecturer were as grandiose as had been his hopes as a poet. In sketching plans to become a "wander-speaker" in April 1857, he imagined just how powerful he could become: "That the mightiest rule over America could be thus.... That to dart hither and thither, as some great emergency might demand—the greatest champion America could ever know, yet having no office or emolument whatever,—but first in the esteem of men and women.... But to keep up living interest in public questions,—and *always to hold the ear of the people.*" Just as the year before he had thought of offering himself as an unofficial presidential candidate, he was now dreaming of taking control of America as a wandering speaker, rushing here and there to fix problems as they occurred.

This was no passing fancy. In July he wrote of his plans to become "a public Speaker, teacher, or lecturer." He actually printed a circular advertising "Walt Whitman's Lectures," stating that lecturing was to be "henceforth my employment" and that he would go "by degrees through all These States, especially the West and South, and through Kanada," charging just a dime's admission and distributing printed copies of each lecture to be "carefully perused afterward."

Sometimes his visions of power approached the messianic. It was in June 1857 that he identified as "the principal object—the main life work" the *"great construction of the new Bible*—the Three Hundred & Sixty Five." He expected the project would be done in two years. Presumably he expected to have completed by then 365 poems, largely of a religious or philosophical nature, to replace or complement the Bible.

Although composing new "Bibles" was not unusual in the era of *The Book of Mormon* and *The Great Harmonia,* it is surprising that Whitman would mention such a grandiose project and then drop it—unless the 1860 edition of *Leaves of Grass,* containing many new religious poems, can be seen as a kind of Bible.

The fact is, Whitman in 1857 was floundering. Having failed to get a hearing, he was looking for the right metaphor for the sort of work he was up to. Was it lecturing to the masses? Writing a new Bible? His uncertainty evidenced itself in a habit he developed of asking friends for criticism of his poetry. When in February he dined with Hector Tyndale, he asked him where his poems most needed improvement. Tyndale said, "In *massiveness,* breadth, large, sweeping effects, without regard to details." Whitman put the same question to others. One said he needed "finish and rhythms," another commented, "You have too much procreation."

Pedestrian advice, it all seems now. But that Whitman took some of it to heart is suggested by his later poetry, which, with some notable exceptions, was more windy, flaccid, less colorfully detailed and sexually charged than his earlier work.

In 1857 the poet without an audience was in need of a vocation. He found it in a field he had abandoned nine years earlier: newspaper editing.

The *Daily Times* and Bohemia

WHEN WHITMAN ASSUMED EDITORSHIP of the *Brooklyn Daily Times* in the spring of 1857, he was joining one of the best-run papers in the city. Founded as the *Williamsburgh Times* in 1848 by the English-born George C. Bennett, the paper got its new name when Williamsburgh consolidated with Brooklyn in 1855. The editorial and printing offices were on the second floor of a three-story redbrick building at 145 Grand Street, below a lodge room and above a hat store. A year after Whitman arrived, the paper moved to larger quarters near the ferries at 12–14 South Seventh Street, where printing was done on the first floor and editorial work on the second.

Besides overseeing the paper's contents, Whitman wrote from one to three columns of editorial matter, reviewed books and magazines, and selected the fiction that often ran serially on page one. A German who worked in the composing room, Frederick Huene, later recalled Whitman as a large, well-built man who tucked his trousers inside his boots, kept his heavy blue coat open at the chest, and wore a red kerchief around his neck. Whitman gave Huene a copy of *Leaves of Grass* to translate into German, but the translation did not do justice to the original, and the project was dropped.

As editor of the *Daily Times,* Whitman found himself in the anomalous position of one forced by circumstances to pander to the mass tastes while simultaneously denouncing these tastes in his editorials. He knew the American public loved sensations, so much so that he identified "intense love of excitement" as the nation's leading trait and generalized that the country could no more do without sensation than the drunkard could do without liquor. The *Daily Times* sold for two cents upon his arrival and a penny a year later. Like other penny papers, it was always well stocked with sensational fiction and news stories. The serial novels Whitman chose for reprinting were of the typical blood-and-thunder variety; titles included *The Specter's Visit* and *The Bond of Blood; or, the Death Secret.* The "Local Items" section of the paper kept sensation lovers satisfied. Typical columns had these headings: "Another Death from Burning," "Left His Wife," "A Carman Gets Inebriated," "Took Laudanum," and "Burglars Arrested." In one issue, posing as "Mr. Items," Whitman joked half-seriously that "unless a 'dreadful murder,' a 'disastrous conflagration,' or a 'gigantic burglary' should turn up soon, his occupation would be gone and himself forced to retire temporarily to the shades of private life."

If the fiction and local items were designed to answer the popular thirst for the sensational, Whitman's editorials had a different intention: to expose the evils of modern urban society. A subtle but definite change had occurred in his attitude toward America since he had written "The Eighteenth Presidency!" Then he had been disillusioned by political rulers but still clung to an idealistic faith in average men and women. Now both politicians and many ordinary Americans seemed to him almost beyond redemption. Whitman remained excited about certain aspects of contemporary life, but his excitement tended to be about things like modern inventions, sports, exercise, the water cure, Swedenborgianism, and spiritualism. Everywhere in modern society he saw corruption and rowdyism and noisy reforms. His indictment of city life and capitalistic society brought him quite close at times to a Southern agrarian point of view. Hence his oddly reactionary statements about slavery and African-Americans in the *Daily Times.*

Part of his disillusion with the masses was the rise of crime and what he perceived as widespread immoral behavior. In an August 5, 1857, article titled "What Are We Coming To?" he wrote:

The frightful increase of demoralisation and crime in our midst, during the last few years, is enough to shake the confidence of the most hopeful of enthusiasts and awaken the most earnest and prayerful solicitude of those who have the best interests of society at heart.

The morning newspaper is rapidly becoming a mere catalogue of horrors. From all over the country accounts come pouring in of crimes the most cold-blooded, of outrages the most unutterable. Justice seems asleep, and sin raises its unblushing face in bold defiance. Pervading all classes of society runs the poisonous virus of disbelief, of law-defying, God-defying vice—of that worst form of practical atheism, which makes illicit pleasure the sole end of existence, and which scornfully ignores the safe traditions of a better, a purer, and a wiser age.

Where shall we turn for evidences of a healthier state of things? Not, surely, to the young men and women who are growing up around us, soon to fill our places. . . .

A general laxity of morals—a general indifference to the old standards of right and wrong, by which our fathers regulated their lives, pervades all classes.

Having made this overall assessment of the age, Whitman turned in other editorials to specific problems. One area of his concern was health. American cities, he lamented, contained "multitudes of undeveloped, dyspeptic, stunted, cadaverous, bad-countenanced, bad-actioned, hardly-ever-well persons." Women were "spleeny, sickly, feeble," distant from their "stout, strong, happy and hearty" grandmothers. Young men were devoted to rowdyism and bad habits. "What is to be done," he asked, "with the hundreds of idle, dissolute young men in our midst, who defy the law, disturb the peace and quiet of the community, and make themselves generally a curse to themselves, and to peaceable and quiet citizens?" Relations between the sexes, he thought, were at a nadir. "We cannot take up a newspaper," he complained, "that we do not find it blackened and stained by some record of conjugal infidelity." The marriage institution, sacred in his eyes, was threatened. Divorce, infertility, and suicide were all on the rise. Also commonplace was abortion, which Whitman equated with infanticide.

Little help could be found from reform organizations, he believed, for they seemed to him disruptive and chaotic. "The cant of reformers is quite as barefaced and disgusting in its way as that of other descriptions of trade," he wrote. He watched with interest many reformers but couldn't help using words like "excrescences" and "amiable lunatics" to describe them.

Nor, he thought, could recourse be sought in political organizations.

The party that had once elicited his undivided loyalty had proven badly lacking on both the local and national levels. Tammany Democrats had brought to power Fernando Wood as mayor of Manhattan. Wood had won the mayoralty in 1854 on a promise to clean up New York, and indeed in his first term he launched a well-publicized vice campaign, closing saloons and brothels and cleaning the streets. But after he was reelected in 1856 he established himself as the boss of a political machine that thrived on bribery, extortion, and roughneck tactics. He took control of the city police force that had long catered to criminals and declared illegal a rival metropolitan police force established by the state. His enforcers were the brutal gangs of the "Bloody Sixth" ward, mainly the notorious Dead Rabbits, who used violence and intimidation to strengthen his political base.

Matters came to a head in 1857, shortly after Whitman came to the *Daily Times*. In the May 22 article "The Police Contest" Whitman took the state's side in the affair, denouncing Wood's "perverted despotic control over the police of New York" and his "rebellious defiance of law and violation of order." In later issues he harped on the despotism of Wood, who, he wrote, was establishing "an *imperium imperio*—a metropolitan city of which he should be the perpetual ruler, within limits of the empire state, but absolved from obedience to State law."

Violence peaked on July 4 and 5 when the Dead Rabbits (so named when a rival gang threw a dead rabbit into their midst) engaged in an all-out brawl with their arch-rivals, the nativist, anti-Irish Bowery Boys. Eight were killed and thirty wounded in the battle. Whitman reported the riot and on July 8 pronounced his former party "the Dead Rabbit Democracy." "Dead Rabbit" for him was a symbol of the anarchic condition of the Democrats. "The hungry hordes of office-seekers," he wrote, "the fighting men, the shysters, the proslavery crowders, the Brookses, the invaders of Kansas, and that strange gathering, the Cincinnati Convention of a year ago, with Mayor Wood, Alderman Wilson, etc., in New York City,—these now stand as 'the party.'" So violent did the political scene become that by November he could write, "Mobs and murderers appear to rule the hour."

On the national level, the Democratic Party disappointed him primarily because its concessions to the slave power had fueled the growth of the Republican Party. "Pierce created the Republican party," he noted, "by his concessions to the South. Buchanan has elevated it from a sectional to a national, from a defeated to a triumphant party, by following in the footsteps of his predecessor." Both "labored with might and main in the interests of slavery."

Despite such protests, he himself had taken a conservative turn on the slavery issue. The first two editions of *Leaves of Grass,* influenced in part by Kansas-Nebraska and Anthony Burns, had shown a radically democratic Whitman, ready to sympathize with fugitive slaves and recognize the nobility and humanity of blacks. Rising problems in the North, however, impelled him in the *Daily Times* to adopt a more pro-Southern stance. Indeed, his attitude toward the North was in some ways similar to that of the South's leading apologist, George Fitzhugh. In his books *Sociology for the South* (1854) and *Cannibals All!* (1857) Fitzhugh argued that Northern society was the site of growing class warfare, political malfeasance, and anarchic isms threatening social disarray. In contrast, he claimed, Southern plantation life was a model of cooperative, peaceful labor.

Whitman had been susceptible to such specious reasoning ever since he had unfavorably contrasted industrial society and slave society in *Franklin Evans.* As the problems associated with Northern urbanization became increasingly more apparent to him, he assumed some proslavery positions. Despite his dislike of Buchanan, he advocated in the *Daily Times* the annexation of Cuba, a main project of Buchanan that was dear to the South. Whitman's old hatred of abolition also resurfaced, as in a report of a reform meeting at which, he said, the most sensible speaker was a black man who claimed that loud-mouthed abolitionists had done more harm to his race than all the slaveholders of the South.

Whitman began to express the kind of racial attitudes that were all but universal among American whites. Most Northerners, even those opposed to slavery, assumed the inferiority of blacks, and many dreamed of an all-white society. In 1854 Lincoln had said of blacks: "A universal feeling, whether well or ill-founded, can not safely be disregarded. We can not, then, make them our equals." In his debates with Stephen Douglas he declared, "I have no purpose to introduce political and social equality between the white and black races. . . . I, as well as Judge Douglas, am in favor of having the race to which I belong, having the superior position." Whitman used similar language in the *Daily Times.* In May 1858 he supported a proposed prohibition of blacks from Oregon and predicted that such prohibitions would become common throughout the western states. Echoing his old Free-Soil argument, he wrote: "It will be a conflict between the totality of White Labor, on the one side, and, on the other, the interference and competition of Black Labor, or of bringing in colored persons on any terms." He added:

> Who believes that Whites and Blacks can ever amalgamate in America? Or who wishes it to happen? Nature has set an impassable seal against it. Besides, is not America for the Whites? And is it not

better so? As long as the Blacks remain here, how can they become anything like an independent and heroic race? There is no chance for it.

The blacks, he concluded, should be removed to "some secure and ample part of the earth, where they have a chance to develop themselves, to gradually form a race, a nation, that would take no mean rank among the peoples of the world."

Such statements reflect in part the recent Dred Scott decision, which denied American citizenship to blacks. "The social inferiority of the colored race," he wrote, "by this time is as well settled as the decision of the courts can make it." His idea that blacks should be relocated elsewhere was a reiteration of the argument that had been made by colonizationists for decades. The American Colonization Society had worked since 1817 for the removal of blacks to foreign shores, especially Liberia, in the belief that they could not successfully amalgamate with whites in America. Although endorsed by Henry Clay, Harriet Beecher Stowe, and other antislavery leaders—including, from a different perspective, African-Americans like Martin Delany and Henry Garnet, who wanted blacks to be free and independent in their own country—colonization had little success. By the late fifties fewer than five thousand American blacks had been removed to Liberia. Still, many clung to the idea of colonization with surprising tenacity. Lincoln, for instance, would hold until the second year of the Civil War that freed blacks should be relocated abroad.

Given the closeness of Whitman's and Lincoln's views on slavery, it is somewhat surprising that Whitman supported Lincoln's opponent, Stephen Douglas, in the Illinois Senate race of 1858. Whitman conceded that Lincoln beat Douglas in their debates that fall, but he applauded Douglas's victory in the November election. At the time, Douglas struck him as the most likely person to restore moderation in politics. In light of Whitman's growing conservatism on race matters, he was probably attracted to Douglas's advocacy of Herrenvolk democracy (that is, democracy for whites only). "Who would not rather now be Douglas, than be President?" he asked after the 1858 senatorial victory. "It affords him the opportunity of organizing a great middle conservative party, neither proscribing slavery, like [William Henry] Seward, nor fostering it, like Buchanan." The choice in the 1860 presidential race, he wrote, would be between two *D*'s—Douglas or Defeat. He declared: "Disunion is impossible; Defeat is unbearable; *ergo*, Douglas is inevitable."

"Disunion is impossible." There was the crux of the matter. His long-standing fear of abolitionists, fire-eaters, and ultraist reformers of all stripes was based on his overriding fear of disunion. In 1855 and '56 he had hoped union might be achieved through affirmative poetry featuring a powerful, all-embracing "I." In the 1860 edition of *Leaves of Grass* he would express this hope even more shrilly, though with less conviction than before. In the meantime, the North seemed to him crowded with rowdies and disunionists, and an equivocator like Douglas appeared to offer stability and hope for unity.

He also looked with increased fervor to unifying forces within culture. The main focus of his attention now were laborsaving inventions that promised to bring people together. The completion of the Atlantic cable in 1858 led him to philosophize about the unification of humanity through modern advances. "It is the sentiment of *union* that makes the popular heart beat and quiver," he wrote of the cable. "It is the union of the great Anglo-Saxon race, henceforth to be a unit, that makes the state throb with tumultuous emotion and thrills every heart with admiration and triumph." The railroad, the telegraph, and other mechanical contrivances symbolized for him unification. In the preceding twenty-five years, he wrote in 1858, we have "bound the sister-states together with innumerable iron-banded railways—built magnificent ocean steamers— . . . invented the photograph and the Lightning Press—introduced the pain-killing chloroform and a hundred lesser blessings that cannot be specified—and finally we have reached the crowning triumph of the age, and setting at naught both time and distance, have spanned the mighty deep and united two worlds with the electric Telegraph!"

As was true with several of his previous journalistic jobs, Whitman left the *Daily Times* under a cloud. He probably came into conflict with George Bennett over two of his controversial editorials, one arguing for the licensing of prostitution and another calling, albeit gingerly, for the right of women to experiment with premarital sex as men did. His editorship ended in June 1859.

Although his opinions on public issues of the late fifties can be traced in his *Daily Times* articles, his private life for this period is difficult to reconstruct. He continued to live with his mother and several siblings at the Classon Street house until May 1859, when they moved to a house at 106 Portland Avenue, where they lived in the basement while renting out the first floor and part of the attic to a tailor, John Brown, and his family. His brother Jeff, an assistant engineer at the Brooklyn Water Works, was married in February 1859 to Martha Emma Mitchell ("Mattie" or "Mat" to the family). They lived for a time on Fifth Avenue near Twelfth in Brooklyn but soon moved into the already-crowded Portland Avenue home, where they lived along with Mrs. Whitman, Walt, George, and Ed. To Jeff and Mattie were born two girls: in June 1860 the poetically named Mannahatta (called Hattie) and, three years later, Jessie Louisa.

Whitman himself began to have physical problems and perhaps suffered a psychological trauma associated with an ill-fated love affair. Evidence for both his physical and mental sufferings is scanty. No letters exist for the period, and Whitman's notebooks, which are fairly regular until the middle of 1857, are spotty for the late fifties. It seems that in the summer of 1858 Whitman had a "sunstroke," with symptoms of dizziness and faintness, probably associated with hypertension, that would plague him periodically during the Civil War and after.

The supposed love affair was long thought to have been with a woman, possibly the fair-haired, blue-eyed New York actress Ellen Grey, whose picture Whitman kept until his death. It may have been this picture Whitman showed Abby Price when she asked him around this time if he had ever been in love. He paused, then declared, "Your question, Abby, *stirs a fellow up*," handing her a picture of what Abby called "a very beautiful woman," whose name he didn't give.

Since Frederik Schyberg's 1933 study of Whitman, however, it has been commonly assumed that the painful involvement had been with a man. The evidence for this interpretation is a series of twelve poems Whitman wrote early in 1859 that traced a relationship involving love, renunciation, and loss. This cluster of poems, called "Live Oak with Moss," formed the basis for the homoerotic "Calamus" sequence, which appeared in the 1860 edition of *Leaves of Grass*. Signs of doomed love appeared in the "Calamus" poem "Sometimes with One I Love": "(I loved a certain person ardently and my love was not return'd, / Yet out of that love I have written these songs.)"

Barring the discovery of new evidence, the exact nature of Whitman's alleged love affair will remain a mystery. What is evident, though, is that in the wake of his exit from the *Daily Times* he was a man adrift, without any prospect of gaining an audience and with no faith in political institutions. In a troubled notebook entry of June 26, 1859, he warned himself: "It is now time to *Stir* first for *Money* enough *to live and* provide for *M*—*to stir*—first write stories, and get out of this Slough." The identity of "M" is unknown; guesses have included his mother, his sister Mary, or a male or female lover. He was back in the restless state of the pre–*Daily Times* days, reaching out in various directions. He sketched plans for a series of "Manhattan Lectures" and wrote an outline for a novel, *Proud Antoinette: A New York Romance of Today*. Obviously intended for the masses, this potboiler about a prostitute was, in his words, to have "Dialogue—animation—something stirring—."

He was disaffected and drifting, a perfect candidate for bohemia.

New York's bohemian culture had begun, significantly, in the dark year of 1854. The panic that fall had sped the financial ruin of the struggling young journalist William North, who committed suicide by swallowing prussic acid on November 14. North's death was a grisly initiation for a group of fifties dropouts who came to regard suicide as the preferred way of exiting life. The next suicide was the theatrical one staged by the novelist Henry W. Herbert (aka Frank Forrester). On May 18, 1858, Herbert invited his friends to a grand party and, when dinner was over, stood in front of a mirror and shot himself as the stunned group watched. Over the next two decades, the bohemians had no more suicides but did experience six premature deaths: one from alcohol, one after an overdose of hashish and opium, one from venereal disease, one from lockjaw, one from rabies, and one from tuberculosis brought on by living in a damp garret.

The group modeled itself after the Parisian Boheme Gallante of Théophile Gautier and his followers, who guzzled punch from skulls and knelt before Woman. The Parisian group was made known to Americans by Henry Clapp, Jr., a Nantucket-born radical author who spent several years in Paris and who pronounced himself a bohemian upon his return to America in the midfifties. Clapp was to be an important figure in Whitman's life. "You will have to know something about Henry Clapp if you want to know all about me," Whitman told Traubel.

Clapp's varied life symbolized the vagaries of antebellum reform. Born in 1814, Clapp became successively a Sunday-school teacher, a temperance lecturer, and an abolitionist. He also got involved in socialism, translating Fourier's works for Albert Brisbane. After living in France, he returned to Manhattan and joined Stephen Pearl Andrews's free-love league. In 1858 he indicted conventional marriage in his free-love book *Husband vs. Wife*.

By the time Clapp had established himself as the Prince of Bohemia, most of the reforms he had been associated with had fizzled in the political and social confusion of the late fifties. Wiry and haggard-looking, sarcastic and ebullient, the gray-bearded Clapp became the archetypal bohemian, lashing out at everything but standing for little besides a love of fine coffee, strong liquor, and lively repartee.

He occupied the head place at the long table that extended through the "cave" below the sidewalk in Pfaff's, the underground restaurant-saloon at 689 Broadway, just north of Bleecker Street. Run by Charles Ignatius Pfaff, a native of either Switzerland or southwest Germany, the restaurant started out as a dim, smoky room with just a table, a counter, a few chairs, and some barrels. It was on the seedy end of the scale of restaurants that filled the Bleecker Street area, then the theatrical and literary center of Manhattan.

Here gathered unconventional, arty types: the actress and author Ada Clare, the Queen of Bohemia, who loved to scandalize the respectable by flaunting her illegitimate son; the actress Adah Isaacs Menken, known for her many lovers and her role as the Naked Lady in a Broadway melodrama; the fictionist Fitz-James O'Brien, whose well-crafted horror stories were patterned after Poe's; Fitz-Hugh Ludlow, whose long book about his drug experiences, *The Hashish Eater* (1857) may be the most bizarre work by a nineteenth-century American; Artemus Ward, the comedian who punctured the era's bombastic oratory with his vernacular humor; the picturesque poet N. G. Shepherd and the Poesque tale writer Charles D. Gardette; and many other literary and artistic figures.

Including Whitman. "My own greatest pleasure at Pfaff's," he would recall, "was to look on—to see, talk little, absorb. I was never a great discusser, any way." What he witnessed at Pfaff's was little less than the last glorious gasp of antebellum America, with all its pleasures and many of its troubles. Like Whitman, most of the Pfaff patrons were disaffected Democrats, footloose rebels with laughter at their lips and gloom in their hearts. They were individualists replaying both the good and bad in antebellum life with a self-conscious frenzy. Trying to keep alive the participatory spirit that was rapidly fading in an increasingly commercialized, rigid American society, they made everyone who came through the door give a speech or joke or story. This was just a pale copy of the spontaneous playacting and storytelling Whitman had enjoyed in the thirties and forties. But then these were sadder days. Puffing furiously at cigars and chattering at each other as they drank, the bohemians seemed to Whitman a vestige of a communal culture of hearty spirits and shared good times. "Laugh on laughers!" he wrote in "The Two Vaults," his poem about Pfaff's. "Drink on drinkers! / Bandy and jest! / Toss the theme from one to another!"

But this was fun and activity without direction—most of all, without political direction. The bohemian, Clapp explained in his paper the *Saturday Press*, was the ultimate individualist, kicking off political authority and living for the moment. But what did the bohemian do about the intensifying slavery crisis? Virtually nothing. Like Whitman, the bohemians thought of themselves as opposed to slavery, but they had no sympathy for the abolitionists and Republicans who were fighting it. "We are opposed to slavery of every kind," Clapp wrote after Lincoln was elected in 1860, "but we are even more opposed to what is stupidly called anti-slavery, for the simple reason that it has no distinct aim or purpose, and consists of nothing but a series of noisy and unmeaning howls." Lincoln they derided as a pure humbug who, in Clapp's words, "has merely used the negro as a stepping-stone to power, and is now ready to kick him aside, and let him go to the devil."

This sort of criticism was disingenuous and could be more appropriately directed against the bohemians themselves than against Lincoln. It was they, not he, who had no distinct aim or purpose. Unable to cope with the national crisis, they were playing a desperate game of evasion. Their carefree, carpe diem attitude showed that fifties individualism had sunk toward anarchic decadence. Not surprisingly, Poe was their patron saint, and several of them cultivated melancholy. Ostensibly full of life, they in fact embodied death—the death of a culture headed toward an irrepressible conflict. Whitman caught the deathlike nature of the group in "The Two Vaults":

> The vault at Pfaff's where the drinkers and laughers meet to eat and
>   drink and carouse,
> While on the walk immediately overhead pass the myriad feet of
>   Broadway
> As the dead in their graves are underfoot hidden.

In the forced gaiety and underlying gloom of the bohemians, Whitman was witnessing antebellum culture in its death throes. It is no accident that he produced at this time two elegiac poems, "Out of the Cradle Endlessly Rocking" and "As I Ebb'd with the Ocean of Life," which would be the most powerful new pieces in the 1860 Leaves of Grass.

The former poem, under the title "A Child's Reminiscence," appeared in the December 24, 1859, issue of Clapp's Saturday Press. Clapp featured the poem on the front page, where it occupied two columns, and advertised it as a "wild and plaintive song" presented to readers "as our Christmas or New Year's present to them." The timing was appropriate, and so was the context. Appearing at the very end of the fifties, the poem integrated several devices of Whitman's earlier poems but pointed them toward death and gloom. Published in the journal of bohemia, it had an air of melancholy and loss; it even contained echoes of bohemia's guiding spirit, Poe.

The main narrative of the poem showed the kind of nostalgia for Whitman's Long Island childhood that would be visible in several poems of the 1860 edition. Indeed, Whitman may have been drawing on some primal memory in his portrait of a boy leaving his bed one August midnight, going to the "Paumanok" seashore, facing the moonlit waves, and tearfully thinking of a past May in which he witnessed two birds from

Alabama, at first joyfully united but then separated by death. Whitman once said that the Long Island seashore represented for him the boundary between life and death, and the poem summons up both the gloom and the pangs of awakening creativity that accompany a Long Island initiation to death. At the climax of the poem, the Paumanok waves whisper to the boy "the low and delicious word death, / And again death, death, death, death, death." The poet says he will never forget the word, "But fuse the song of my dusky demon and brother, / That he sang to me in the moonlight on Paumanok's gray beach, / With the thousand responsive songs at random, / My own songs awakened from that hour."

On one level a poem about his exposure to death in childhood, "Out of the Cradle" is simultaneously about Whitman's frustrations over the failure of his poetic project of the fifties. His strategy of fusing disparate cultural and personal images is still operating here, but differently from before. The italicized bird's song at the heart of the poem, directly connected to the Italian opera ("The aria sinking"), is fused with autobiographical memory and with popular cultural images ("Demon or bird!" for instance, recalling Poe's "The Raven"). But what begins as a poem of love and union becomes one of separation and isolation. The two "feather'd guests from Alabama" caroling love songs on Long Island's shores—the *"Two together!"* as *"Winds blow south, or winds blow north"*—are like Whitman in 1855, beckoning North and South to come together through his nation-binding poems. The he-bird left alone after his mate disappears, singing *"reckless despairing carols,"* is analogous to Whitman bereft of the audience he had dreamed of. The uselessness and pain resulting from Whitman's failed search for an audience are suggested in the lines, *"O throat! O throbbing heart! / And I singing uselessly, uselessly all night."*

The child's recognition that the bird, a "singer solitary, singing by yourself," is like "solitary me," with a "thousand warbling echoes" within him, brings attention to Whitman's sense of aloneness as a poet. His confidence that he is the all-embracing Answerer to whom all America will listen has been shaken. He is frightened by the idea that he might be a solitary singer in an unresponsive, divided nation. His extreme frustration, verging on utter confusion, is reflected in these lines that appeared in the early versions of the poem:

> O a word! O what is my destination!
> O I fear it is henceforth chaos!
> O how joys, dreads, convolutions, human shapes, and all shapes,
>   spring as from graves around me!

O phantoms! you cover all the land, and all the sea!
O I cannot see in the dimness whether you smile or frown upon me;
O a vapor, a look, a word! O well-beloved!
O you dear women's and men's phantoms!

The men and women whose love had seemed so real and so healing in
the first two editions of *Leaves of Grass* are now mere "phantoms"
crowding "all the land" in a nightmarish vision of chaos. With a para-
noia that points to Whitman's ambivalence about the reception of his
poetry, he wonders whether these phantom-people "smile or frown
upon me."

That they were frowning upon him is the bleak subtext of his next
great poem of the time, "As I Ebb'd with the Ocean of Life." Whitman
sent this poem for publication just a month after the appearance of "A
Child's Reminiscence," and it came out in James Russell Lowell's *Atlan-
tic Monthly* in April 1860 as "Bardic Symbols," a title showing that it is
above all about Whitman's bardic role, about his poetic mission. In the
poem he verges on admitting that this mission has been a failure and
that his aspiration of becoming the nation's bard is dead.

The setting is again the Long Island seashore, a setting whose auto-
biographical associations are deepened by the poet's references to the
island as his "father" and the ocean as his "mother." The melancholy
"I" of the poem is walking Paumanok's shore on a late autumn after-
noon, "gazing off southward," rather like Whitman in the late fifties, a
troubled Northerner with his eyes turned sadly south. But then the gaze
of the "I," "reverting from the south," turns downward to the "Chaff,
straw, splinters of wood, weeds, and sea-gluten" at his feet. He realizes
disconsolately, "I too but signify at the utmost a little wash'd up drift."
The proud, confident "I" of the 1855 edition has disappeared, leaving
just a self-doubting fragment of himself. The holistic poetic experiment
of 1855 has been threatened by the realities of misinterpretation and
neglect. Whitman wonders whether it was worth it to write poetry in
the first place:

O baffled, balk'd, bent to the very earth,
Oppress'd with myself that I have dared to open my mouth,
Aware now that amid all that blab whose echoes recoil upon me I
    have not once had the least idea who or what I am,
But that before all my arrogant poems the real Me stands yet
    untouch'd, untold, altogether unreach'd,
Withdrawn far, mocking me with mock-congratulatory signs and
    bows,

With peals of distant ironical laughter at every word I have written,
Pointing in silence to these songs, and then to the sand beneath.

The affirmative cultural images that had promised healing and tran-
scendence in 1855 now seem barren to him. Whitman's intended audi-
ence, far from absorbing him, has abandoned him. He feels he is mocked
with "mock-congratulatory signs and bows" and "peals of distant ironi-
cal laughter." He is left alone, doubting his poetic powers and everything
around him, able only to cling to his "father" the earth and his "mother"
the sea. He vividly contemplates his death: "(See, from my dead lips the
ooze exuding at last, / See, the prismatic colors glistening and rolling)."

The "prismatic colors" oozing from the decaying corpse, comparable
to the "thousand responsive songs at random" pouring from the death-
obsessed child in "Out of the Cradle," were like the poems that were
emanating from Whitman in the late fifties. He may have feared, after
the cool reception of the first two editions, that his mission as a holistic
cultural poet was in jeopardy, but he had not left off writing poetry and
in fact was carrying forward his plans for a third edition. In August 1859
he sent to his Brooklyn friends the Rome brothers a manuscript that
included the new poems he had written since 1856, with orders that the
poems be printed and returned to him in proof. Over the next six months
he wrote twenty-eight new poems.

He was still fantasizing about becoming a popular success, and his
dream of having social impact was still on a very high level. In an anony-
mous self-review in the *Saturday Press* in January 1860 he declared that
the earlier versions of *Leaves of Grass,* published by the author "in little
pittance editions, on trial," had just been enough "to ripple the inner
first-circles of literary agitation." With wishful bravura, he added: "The
outer, vast, extending, and ever-widening circles, of the general supply,
perusal, and discussion of such a work, have still to come. The market
needs to-day to be supplied—the great West especially—with copious
thousands of copies." Though terribly pained by his earlier failures, he
still had megalomaniac visions. He told himself in his notebook, "You
must become a force in the state—and a real and great force—just as
real and great as the president and congress—greater than they."

All this dreaming could have come to naught had it not been for a
great stroke of luck. On February 10, 1860, within two weeks of his send-
ing out the pessimistic "Bardic Symbols," he received an unexpected
offer from the Boston publishers Thayer and Eldridge. Richard J. Hin-
ton, who had been on the staff of the *Knickerbocker Magazine* when the
1855 edition had appeared, had introduced Whitman's poetry to the
young, energetic publishers, who specialized in antislavery and women's

rights publications. Seeing in Whitman a talented poet with a radical bent, they made him a wonderful offer:

> We want to be the publishers of Walt Whitman's Poems.... If you allow it we can and will put your books into good form, and style attractive to the eye; we can and will sell a large number of copies; we have great facilities by and through numberless Agents in selling. We can dispose of more books than most publishing houses.... Try us. You can do us good. We can do you good—pecuniarily.

Whitman himself couldn't have written the script better. "[A] large number of copies," "numberless Agents," "do you good—pecuniarily": these words were sweet to Whitman's ears. There was still a chance, it seemed, that he could deluge the country with "copious thousands of copies," as he had put it. He quickly negotiated the new edition, agreeing to a 10 percent royalty on all copies sold. By March 5 he was in Boston to supervise publication. The proofs printed by the Romes, along with Whitman's scribbled revisions and additional poems in longhand, provided the manuscript from which Thayer and Eldridge worked.

Whitman again had a controlling hand in virtually every aspect of publication. The appearance and contents of the new edition would show that he had not surrendered his idea of uniting his nation through poetry. The stakes were higher than ever. The corruptions of the Buchanan administration were unprecedented and would prove to be among the worst in American history. The fragmentation of the nation was evidenced by the fact that there were four presidential candidates in the 1860 race. The election of any of the candidates carried the threat of disunion, since each represented a different constituency and geographical section. Signs of the forthcoming calamity appeared in many of the new poems, which ranged from shrill cries for unity to private confessions of despair.

The Answerer's confidence had been challenged, but not undermined. With an established publisher behind him, he was ready to make another effort to make the nation hear him.

12

BROTHERLY LOVE, NATIONAL WAR: INTO THE 1860S

Y EAR OF METEORS! brooding year! [...] / O year all mottled with evil and good—year of forebodings!" So Whitman wrote in "Year of Meteors (1859–60)." An unusual meteor shower above Manhattan in November 1860 was, in his eyes, a metaphor for the thrilling yet ominous events of this period.

Among those mentioned in the poem was the raid by the radical abolitionist John Brown on the federal arsenal at Harpers Ferry, Virginia. The father of twenty, the bearded, tempestuous Brown had long been on the militant fringe of the antislavery movement. In mid-October 1859, he and a band of eighteen took over the Virginia arsenal with the plan of distributing weapons among slaves to incite insurrections throughout the South. This heroic, half-crazed scheme was quickly squashed after a battle in which federal troops led by Robert E. Lee killed ten of Brown's men, including two of his sons, and took Brown and the others into custody. The trial of Brown for treason became the focus of national attention, and when he was convicted and then hanged, he was widely seen as a Christ-like martyr in the North. Whitman eulogized him in "Year of Meteors":

> I would sing how an old man, tall, with white hair, mounted the
>   scaffold in Virginia,
> (I was at hand, silent I stood with teeth shut close, I watch'd,
> I stood very near you old man when cool and indifferent, but
>   trembling with age and your unheal'd wounds you mounted the
>   scaffold;).

Whitman, as usual, was taking poetic liberty: he was not "at hand" at the hanging of John Brown. He *was* at hand, however, when on April 4,

1860, the educator Franklin B. Sanborn, one of the "secret six" North-
erners who had backed Brown's raid, was brought to trial in Boston.
Sanborn later recalled the courtroom, mobbed with spectators, at the
rear of which on a high stool sat the tall, gray-bearded Whitman, wear-
ing a loose jacket and an open shirt. Whitman's eyes, intense under his
shaggy eyebrows, scanned the courtroom. He saw several who had come
to take action should the trial go the wrong way. There were his publish-
ers, Charles Thayer and William Eldridge, along with one of their au-
thors, James Redpath, whose biography of John Brown was one of their
most popular books. Also there was the journalist Richard Hinton, who
had recommended *Leaves of Grass* to Thayer and Eldridge, and, proba-
bly, William Douglas O'Connor, the blue-eyed firebrand whom the firm
was paying twenty dollars a week to write an antislavery novel, *Harring-
ton*, based on the Anthony Burns case.

In coming to Boston to supervise the printing of the third edition of
Leaves of Grass, he had arrived at the heart of antislavery activism. Thayer
and Eldridge were closely associated with abolition. In the back of their
store met an abolitionist society, the Black Strings. Whitman befriended
their most radical writers, Redpath and O'Connor, while he was in Boston.

Stirred as he may have been by his new antislavery associates, how-
ever, he was still far from being an abolitionist. He maintained a moder-
ate course on the slavery issue, much like the 1860 Republican candidate,
Abraham Lincoln. "I would sing your contest for the 19th Presidentiad,"
went another line in "Year of Meteors." Whitman was referring to the
unique presidential four-way race that year, which pitted Lincoln against
Stephen Douglas of Illinois, John Breckinridge of Kentucky, and John
Bell of Tennessee. The tall, gangly Lincoln was presented as a pristine
folk hero, devoted to preserving the Union and untainted by the corrup-
tions that had beset the Democratic party under Buchanan. Well into
the second year of his administration, Lincoln would insist that his main
goal was to save the Union.

Whitman in 1860 had a similar goal, but his strategy for saving the
Union still lay in the realm of poetry, not politics. His pleas for national
unity were more strident than before, his indictments of what he saw as
ruling-class evil more unsparing. Several of the new poems in the 1860
edition of *Leaves of Grass* were "program" pieces that directly com-
mented on the current social scene. At the same time, the edition re-
vealed the private, often tortured Whitman to a degree unseen in the
previous editions. Gone was the confident poet of 1855 who felt he could
transfigure America and himself in long, holistic poems. The 1860 edi-
tion showed an anxious Whitman trying to establish meaningful links
between private experience and public life.

An Elegant Book

WITH THE PROSPECT of *Leaves of Grass* coming out with a regular publisher, Whitman wanted to be absolutely sure everything went right this time. He spent three months in Boston, from March through May 1860. Even for one accustomed to controlling his publications, his experience with the 1860 edition was unusual. Thayer and Eldridge gave him a free hand in deciding on the contents and appearance of the volume. They didn't ask him what was going into it but just took him to the Boston Stereotype Foundry, where the plates were being prepared, and gave orders that his wishes be followed in the printing process.

Whitman established a daily routine. He took a morning walk, had coffee, went to the stereotype foundry until noon, walked again, and had a full dinner at 2:00 p. m. Boston struck him as both progressive and straitlaced. Blacks, he noticed, were more successfully integrated into mainstream society than they were in New York. Whitman loved Washington Street, with its varied pavement stones, its bustling groceries and stores, its fine trees and granite Custom House. He took amused pride in the fact that his distinctive appearance drew attention. "I create an immense sensation in Washington street," he wrote Abby Price. "Every body here is so like everybody else—and I am Walt Whitman!—Yankee curiosity and cuteness, for once, is thoroughly stumped, confounded, petrified, made desperate."

He renewed old acquaintances and made new contacts. Emerson, with whom he had dined in Manhattan several times in the late fifties and who may have visited him in Brooklyn, got him reading privileges at the Boston Athenaeum. The author John Townsend Trowbridge, who had been excited about his poetry since 1855, visited him in the stereotype foundry and the next day entertained him at his home in nearby Somerville. He found the poet dressed casually but neatly, with a huge cravat, tied in a loose knot, whose serpentine ends disappeared in his clothing. In a genial, low-key way, Whitman told the curious Trowbridge about some of the early influences on him: Brooklyn, Manhattan, Ossian, the Quakers, the opera, Emerson.

On Sundays Whitman sometimes went to hear Edward Thompson Taylor, the famous Methodist evangelist, at the Seaman's Bethel Chapel on the Boston waterfront. Father Taylor, whose colorful, vernacular sermons led Emerson to call him the Shakespeare of the American Pulpit, held fascination for many writers, from Dickens to Thoreau to Melville, who probably patterned Father Mapple in *Moby-Dick* after him. Whitman discovered in Father Taylor America's "essentially perfect orator," whose imaginative language and powerful delivery equalled that of his earlier pulpit hero, Elias Hicks.

Since he spent only two or three hours a day at the stereotype foundry, he had a lot of time on his hands. But boredom was just a minor irritant. He wrote his brother Jeff: "I am so satisfied at the certainty of having 'Leaves of Grass,' in a far more complete and favorable form than before, printed and really *published*, that I don't mind small things. The book will be a very handsome specimen of typography, paper, binding, &c.—and will be, it seems to me, like relieving me of a great weight—or removing a great obstacle that has been in my way for three years."

As this comment suggests, Whitman was again going for elegance. He took complete control of the book's typography, ordering typefaces and ornamental touches that the printers at first found "crazy" but that ultimately won them over. He proudly reported to Jeff that the foreman at Rand and Avery, his printers, declared it "the freshest and handsomest piece of typography that had ever passed through his mill."

This was the angle Whitman took in promoting the book. Thayer and Eldridge, trying to cast as wide a net as possible, wanted to try advertising it as *both* an elegant parlor-table volume and as a sensation book, but Whitman demurred. He protested when they came up with what he called "several tremendous puff advertisements—altogether ahead of Ned Buntline and the 'Ledger.'" He helped put together a promotional pamphlet, *Leaves of Grass Imprints*, issued as a free circular. The pamphlet contained twenty-five reviews of the first two editions, some negative, some positive, including Emerson's letter and Whitman's self-reviews. The back jacket of the pamphlet blazoned these words: WALT WHITMAN'S LEAVES OF GRASS. AN ELEGANT BOOK (see fig. 38A). There followed a paragraph, probably composed by Whitman, that emphasized the volume's fine appearance. "The typography will be found to vie in elegance with anything ever issued from the American or English press," the ad went. After enumerating the book's many physical virtues, it concluded: "The book, as a whole, will be found to be an ornament to any book-shelf or table; and as such the publishers confidently claim for it a recognition as one of the finest specimens of modern book making."

There was some truth to this. Physically, the 1860 *Leaves of Grass* strained toward respectability. It appeared in grayish-green cloth and later in reddish-orange and brown variations. Its nature themes were accentuated in small illustrations, appearing at several places in the book, of a sunrise, a globe half-hidden in clouds, and a butterfly on a pointed finger. The typeface was handsome, with elegant fonts used for the titles of poems and many decorative touches throughout. "Leaves of Grass" appeared in ornate, scriptlike lettering on the title page, opposite which was a picture of Whitman that was completely different from the insolent rough of the 1855 frontispiece. The new one, from an engraving by Stephen Alonzo Schoff after a portrait by Charles Hine, made Whitman look like a sort of refined artist, with a neatly trimmed beard and a billowing cravat (see fig. 4).

Whitman was making yet another attempt at appealing to mainstream readers. It looked as if he might succeed this time. Of William Thayer and Charles Eldridge, he wrote Jeff: "They are go-ahead fellows, and don't seem to have the least doubt they are bound to make a good spec. out of my book." "They expect it to be a valuable investment," he said, "increasing by months and years—not going off in a rocket way, (like 'Uncle Tom's Cabin.')." The special electrotype process used in printing the book, he told Jeff, would "wear well for hundreds of thousands of copies."

This was a familiar fantasy for him, but this time it seemed fantasy might be matched by reality. By June 14, after he had returned to Brooklyn, his publishers reported to him that the first printing of a thousand copies had nearly sold out and that a second one was printed and ready for binding. Although a couple of jobbers had refused to handle the book, the publishers were determined, in their words, to create "an overwhelming demand among the mass public, which shall sweep them and their petty fears on their resistless torrent." By late July, when sales had slowed a bit, they were ready to diversify the price of the book in order to reach both the elite and the mass readerships. They would raise the price of the original edition from $1.25 to $1.50, "because," they explained, "when you make a difference in price people all at once see a difference in quality which they were blind to before.... People *do* like to pay the cost of what they buy." In other words, they hoped to maximize the book's snob appeal. They also planned a cheaper edition, priced at a dollar, which they declared "must be the one to be universally sold."

The cheap edition never came off, but sales were reasonably good. John Burroughs's estimate that the edition sold some four to five thousand copies is probably accurate. Reviews were surprisingly strong. Whitman's name was kept before the public in other ways too. The *Saturday Press* ran twenty-five pieces by or about Whitman between December 24, 1859, and December 15, 1860. Parodies of Whitman's style started appearing regularly in papers as widely dispersed as the New Orleans *Delta* and the San Francisco *Golden Era.*

At least through the summer of 1860, Whitman could feel confident that his poetry was gaining visibility and having greater social impact than it had ever had. The social efficacy of his poetry, always important to him, was a paramount concern in 1860.

For this reason, many of the new poems had a stridency and obviousness that had been absent from the best pieces of the earlier editions. There were now 166 poems, 134 of them new, arranged for the first time in "clusters," or meaningful arrangements. Whitman found sensible, often poetic titles for some of the old poems: "Sun-Down Poem," for example, became the memorable "Crossing Brooklyn Ferry." But he had moved even further than before from the free-flowing 1855 format. The poems were no longer totally interconnected, as in 1855, nor presented as individual topic pieces, as in 1856, but were compartmentalized according to distinct subjects. Society and politics were the focus of the "Chants Democratic" cluster (numbered one to twenty-four), love between the sexes of "Enfans d'Adam" (numbered one to fifteen), comradeship and same-sex love of "Calamus" (numbered one to forty-five), and so on.

The 1855 edition had been a complex poetic carpet whose cultural and personal threads were interwoven so tightly that they were virtually inseparable. In the 1860 edition we begin to see the individual threads instead of the intricate weave. Many of the themes that had been *enacted* in the 1855 poems were overtly *discussed* in the 1860 poems, as though Whitman wanted to get his points across as clearly as possible, without layering or indirection.

An example of the new overtness is the poem that opened the 1860 edition, "Proto-Leaf," later retitled "Starting from Paumanok." This was the thesis poem of the 1860 edition, given its place of prominence because it enunciated the main points of the entire edition. The poem deals with Whitman's nostalgia for his Long Island childhood, his fantasies for an immense readership, and the different cultural phenomena he believed could hold America together, including religion, comradeship, respect for the body and sex, and appreciation for modern industry and technology. Whitman treats each subject in succession, as though eager to reach out in many directions to make linkages between himself and different aspects of American life. He states stridently many individual themes he formerly fused with confident ease and subtlety. He puts his favorite political themes directly:

> I will make a song for These States, that no one State may under any
>   circumstances be subjected to another State,
> And I will make a song that there shall be comity by day and by
>   night between all The States, and between any two of them,

And I will make a song of the organic bargains of These States—
And a shrill song of curses on him who would dissever the Union;
And I will make a song for the ears of the President, full of weapons
    with menacing points,

And behind the weapons countless dissatisfied faces.

Stripped of ornament, almost of poetry, his leading ideas stand out
in bare relief. The relaxed tone of 1855 is replaced by shrillness. "I will,"
Whitman constantly tells us. I will make sure that states' rights are per-
fectly balanced by comity between the states. I will write words that
undermine an incompetent president. I will curse all disunionists. He
pounds away at these themes here and throughout the 1860 edition. He
repeats the curse on disunionists in "Apostroph": "O a curse on him that
would dissever this Union for any reason whatever!" He returns to the
poor administrations of the fifties in "To the States, *To Identify the 16th,
17th, or 18th Presidentiad,*" in which he brands politicians as "scum float-
ing atop of the waters" and exclaims: "Who are they, as bats and night-
dogs, askant in the Capitol? / What a filthy Presidentiad! [. . .] Are those
really Congressmen? Are those the great Judges? Is that the President?"
His wishful declaration of perfect comity between fully independent
states is echoed in the many new poems that portray sympathetically
both Northern and Southern states, even to the point, in "Our Old Feuil-
lage," of depicting chattel slaves happily at work and embracing their
masters. In the latter poem, his search for any unifying element that
might defuse the slavery crisis leads to vague affirmation:

Down in Texas, the cotton-field, the negro-cabins—drivers driving
    mules or oxen before rude carts—cotton-bales piled on banks
    and wharves;
Encircling all, vast-darting, up and wide, the American Soul, with
    equal hemispheres—one love, one Dilation or Pride.

What this "American Soul" is Whitman doesn't say, but precision
doesn't matter for him as he gropes desperately for any kind of unifying
force. In "Proto-Leaf" he finds it variously in comradeship ("what alone
must finally compact these"), in religion ("the real and permanent gran-
deur of these States"), in material products ("Interlinked, food-yielding
lands!"), to name a few.

Just as his utopian affirmations were louder than before, so his nega-
tive comments on society and human nature were more glum. His most
negative poem prior to 1860—"Respondez!"—at least had been leav-

ened by humor. Several of the new poems, written in the bleak years after the 1856 edition, possessed no such leaven. In "I Sit and Look Out" he surveys all the sorrow and oppression of the world, "all the meanness and agony without end," which leave him silent. In "You Felons on Trial in Courts" he declares himself "ruthless and devilish" as any social outcast and asks: "What foul thought but I think it—or have in me the stuff out of which it is thought?" In "A Hand-Mirror" he says that all people who look at themselves frankly will see "Outside fair costume, within ashes and filth." The shrillness of both his utopian and negative verses point to the fact that he was reaching out in sympathy and identification to every aspect of humanity, good and bad. His dream of being universally accepted was stated baldly in "Proto-Leaf":

> Take my leaves America! take them South and take them North,
> Make welcome for them everywhere, for they are your own offspring;
> Surround them, East and West! for they would surround you,
> And you precedents! connect lovingly with them, for they connect
>   lovingly with you.

This was desperate self-promotion, but not nearly so desperate as his poem "Leaves of Grass. 20," in which he put his literary future totally in the hands of his readers:

> Whether I shall complete what is here started, [. . .]
> Whether I shall make THE POEM OF THE NEW WORLD,
>   transcending all others—depends, rich persons, upon you,
> Depends, whoever you are now filling the current Presidentiad, upon
>   you,
> Upon you, Governor, Mayor, Congressman,
> And you, contemporary America.

Was contemporary America hearing him yet? His whole poetic project, he was saying, depended on it. He directed every aspect of the 1860 edition—typography, binding, and contents—toward his overriding goal of reaching the public that had so far eluded him.

This goal controlled even the homoerotic "Calamus" cluster, which today seems the most daringly innovative and unconventional group in the 1860 edition. Because the issue of Whitman and homosexuality has been so hotly debated over the years, it merits special attention in the context of the "Calamus" poems.

"Calamus" Love

WHITMAN'S HOMOEROTIC themes have never been adequately placed in their nineteenth-century context. The notion some have of him as a lonely voice crying out in a wilderness of homophobia is misleading. There is reason to accept Whitman's declaration to John Addington Symonds that his poetry of same-sex love was to be "rightly construed by and within its own atmosphere & essential character."

Passionate intimacy between people of the same sex was common in pre–Civil War America. The lack of clear sexual categories (homo-, hetero-, bi-) made same-sex affection unself-conscious and widespread. There is evidence Whitman had one or two affairs with women, but he was mainly a romantic comrade who had a series of intense relationships with young men, most of whom went on to get married and have children. Whatever the nature of his physical relationships with them, most of the passages about same-sex in his poems were not out of keeping with then-current theories and practices that underscored the healthiness of such love.

Most important were the cult of romantic friendship, the phrenological notion of adhesiveness, and the idea of passional social bonding.

Romantic friendship was sanctioned by philosophy and practiced by many nineteenth-century Americans. Transcendentalism borrowed from European philosophy the notion that intimacy between people of the same sex by definition approached true love because it was untainted by sensuality. The German philosopher Johann Gottfried von Herder, in an essay included in Whitman's favorite philosophy anthology, Hedge's *Prose Writers of Germany,* wrote of friendship: "This relation is purer, and therefore, assuredly, mightier even than love." This outlook was echoed in America by Emerson, Thoreau, and Margaret Fuller. The Transcendentalist view was summed up in Emerson's essay "Friendship," which argued that true friends were bound by a special intimacy of the soul. "Friendship, like the immortality of the soul," Emerson wrote, "is too good to be believed." True friendship, in his eyes, was tender, challenging, often beyond words. It lifted people to the realm of spirit. "Should not the society of my friend be to me poetic, pure, universal, and great as nature itself?" he asked.

Several of Whitman's "Calamus" poems illustrate this philosophical view of friendship, most notably this one:

Primeval my love for the woman I love, O woman I love!
O bride! O wife! more resistless than I can tell, the thought of you!
Then separate, as disembodied or another born,
Ethereal, the last athletic reality, my consolation,
I ascend, I float in the regions of your love O man,
O sharer of my roving life.

Here, love for woman is found irresistible but finally on a lower plane than love between friends, which is an "[e]thereal" reality where the participants float as if "disembodied."

The idea of a sexual "identity" would not be formulated until Havelock Ellis and Freud. Same-sex friends often loved each other passionately. Before the 1880s, "lover" had no gender connotation and was used interchangeably with "friend." Emerson, for instance, used the words to mean the same thing, as when he wrote of his friends: "High thanks I owe you, excellent lovers, who carry out the world for me to new and noble depths." Throughout his poetry Whitman does the same. In one "Calamus" poem he writes, "And when I thought how my dear friend, my lover, was on his way coming, O then I was happy." In another he says his soul is "Wafted in all directions, O love, for friendship, for you." Similarly, the word "orgy" had no sexual association; it meant "party." When he writes, "I share the midnight orgies of young men" or imagines a "city of orgies, walks and joys" where "lovers, continual lovers, only repay me," he is imaginatively participating in the uninhibited gatherings that working-class comrades enjoyed.

Because relations between men and women were often characterized by exploitation and duplicity with the rise of capitalism, Whitman wanted to poeticize the candid, passionate same-sex friendship he saw everywhere in America. The problems with heterosexual love he had discussed in the *Daily Times*, evidenced by rising divorce and infidelity, were the same that impelled the free-love movement to call modern marriage "legalized prostitution." The intrigues surrounding seduction were at the center of what Whitman called "the love plot" of popular sensational writings of the day. He strongly protested against popular romances in the 1860 poem "Says," and he glorified the loving friendship he saw around him in American life. In his notebook he expressed his wish to find words for the "approval, admiration, friendship" seen "among the young men of these States," who he said had "wonderful tenacity of friendship, and passionate fondness for their friends, and always a manly readiness to make friends." He wanted to be the one who brought real-life friendship to the printed page. He noted in his

1856 open letter to Emerson: "As to manly friendship, everywhere observed in The States, there is not the first breath of it to be observed in print."

To some degree, this was an exaggeration. He was not alone in writing about fervent friendship. Because such friendship was not frowned upon, it made its way into popular poetry and fiction. Whittier, for instance, wrote several poems of love between friends. In the antislavery circles in which Whittier circulated, a discourse of same-sex affection developed that he put into verse. In a poem about his friend William Lloyd Garrison, Whittier wrote: "I love thee with a brother's love, / I feel my pulses thrill, / To mark thy spirit soar above / The cloud of human ill." Another reformer, Joseph Sturge, elicited these affectionate lines from Whittier: "I lean my heart unto thee, sadly folding / Thy hand in mine; / With even the weakness of my soul upholding / The strength of thine." Whittier wrote of the Quaker minister Daniel Wheeler: "O dearly loved! And worthy of our love!"

Still, Whitman's complaint about American writers' failure to express same-sex love is understandable, for such love was far more common in daily life than in literature. It was common among both men and women to hug, kiss, and express love for people of the same sex. Men often filled their diaries with lists of other men, as did Whitman. In a time when large families lived in small houses, brothers frequently slept with each other, as did sisters; Whitman's sleeping arrangement with Eddy was not unusual. In hotels and inns, complete strangers often slept in the same bed. Neither "to sleep with" nor "to make love to" had the sexual meanings they would take on in the 1890s.

Men often made strikingly ardent confessions of love to each other, as did women. Notable examples of intense male pairings were Abraham Lincoln and Joshua Speed, Daniel Webster and James Hervey Bingham, Emerson and Martin Gay, Henry Ward Beecher and Theodore Tilton. Usually, such relationships developed between young men who later had heterosexual relationships that led to marriage and children. Typical of such relationships was that between the Connecticut college students Albert Dodd and Anthony Halsey, who proclaimed their love for each other and slept together. As Dodd wrote: "Often too [Anthony] shared my pillow—or I his, and then how sweet to sleep with him, to hold his beloved form in my embrace, to have my arms about his neck, to imprint his face with sweet kisses."

Whitman gave a heightened version of this kind of comradely affection in several "Calamus" poems. In "Behold This Swarthy Face" he wrote: "Yet comes one a Manhattanese and even at parting kisses me lightly on the lips with robust love, / [...] We observe that salute of American comrades land and sea, / We are those two natural and non-chalant persons." Here he presents the custom of American males kissing each other as "natural." In "When I Heard at the Close of the Day" he communicates the kind of rapture of men in bed together that Albert Dodd felt with Anthony Halsey: "For the one I love most lay sleeping by me under the same cover in the cool night, / [...] And his arm lay lightly around my breast—and that night I was happy."

Did antebellum same-sex love involve sex? Certainly yes, if "sex" is defined as hugging and kissing. Most historians agree that genital sex was rare among romantic friends, who associated it with love between the sexes, as Whitman did when he specified that sex meant "the coming together of men and women." But romantic friends could have genital contact without necessarily feeling guilty. Recently unearthed letters of two of the "great men" of the South, James H. Hammond and Thomas Withers, suggest that sexual contact between men could be discussed openly and playfully, without any effort to hide it. With a breezy tone devoid of furtiveness, Withers in an 1826 letter asked Hammond if he had recently had "the extravagant delight of poking and punching a writhing Bedfellow with your long fleshen pole—the exquisite touches of which I have often had the honor of feeling?" Withers humorously recalls feeling defenseless before "the crushing force" of Hammond's "Battering Ram."

It could be, as Martin Duberman suggests, that this kind of genital frolic was a part of some same-sex relationships. The least that can be said is that women and men frequently showed various degrees of same-sex physical affection. Since romantic friendship was commonplace, ho-mosexual acts did not stir up much controversy, either with the public or with police. In investigating what he estimated as perhaps seventy-five thousand indictment papers in the New York district attorney's office dated 1796 to 1893, Michael Lynch found only about thirty indictments for sodomy (sometimes called the crime against nature or buggery). The so-called "inversion" that the late nineteenth century would associate with homosexuality was not yet a category used. There were no charges at all against males for other sexual acts, such as fellatio or frottage. Of the sodomy cases, only two, in 1847 and 1849, led to conviction; all the cases involved charges of force, violence, injury, or pain. Not until 1882 would "consenting to sodomy" be criminalized. Since there was no widely accepted concept of sexual types, sex between people of the same sex was not connected with a fundamental inclination or mind-set. In the massive range of court papers and news reports that he surveys, Lynch discovers that "there are no suggestions that sodomy is a threat to state or family, no appeals to an unnameable horror; not a phrase hints the impulse to sodomy is a medical matter or has to do with instinct, personality type, or any psychic disorder or anomaly," as would be true in some circles later in the century.

There is evidence that male prostitution occurred in some of the same areas as did female prostitution—along the Bowery and in the parks and on the wharves—but the public never got upset about it. The *New-York Sporting Whip* in 1843 denounced "leprous male prostitutes" in the Bowery Theatre, and four years later the *National Police Gazette* mentioned a brothel that was a "resort for male and female prostitutes of the lowest order"—a combination Whitman made in "Respondez!" with his reference to "the he-harlots and the she-harlots." But reports of forced sodomy did not get special attention in the press; they were reported along with other sensational news. Prostitution was of far greater concern to reformers and the public than were sexual acts between people of the same sex.

Despite his interest in advancing the cause of same-sex love, Whitman, like his contemporaries, protested when expressions of such love were forced or excessive. In the *Daily Times* he complained that the common custom of public kissing among women had gone too far. In an article called "Kissing a Profanation" he noted "the alarming increase, of late years, in the custom of kissing among ladies. It has rapidly usurped, indeed, every other mode of solicitation or parting ceremonial." "A kiss should not be deemed a mere unconsidered trifle to be rudely pitched," he wrote, but should be seen as "a sweet and holy token, beautiful and sanctified." Also in the *Daily Times* Whitman ran a paragraph titled "Revolting Developments" about "one of the most disgusting cases that has come to our knowledge for a long time," involving two naval officers who forcibly sodomized a young cabin boy. "The details are wholly unfit for publication," went the report, "and if they are true they exhibit a depth of depravity on the part of the two men, almost unparalleled."

It is unclear if Whitman wrote these moralistic words, but it would not be surprising if he did, since he often denounced certain kinds of behavior in his editorials and then sympathized with them in his poetry for purposes of cleansing or purgation. He did this with special frequency in the shrilly sympathetic poems of the 1860 edition, in which he lovingly embraces prostitutes, slave owners, and felons of all varieties. Although he does not directly refer to forced sodomy in his poems, he reenacts the sense of shame that might be felt by one who had committed the act. As seen, there is some evidence he himself had committed it, or at least been charged with it in his teaching days. If so, his apparent love-crisis of the late fifties may have triggered memories of pain or persecution that were registered in dark "Calamus" poems like "Trickle Drops": "Candid from me falling, drip, bleeding drops, / From wounds made to free you whence you were prison'd." In another poem he verbalizes the anxiety and isolation that accompanies same-sex love when it is frustrated: "Sullen and suffering hours! (I am ashamed—but it is useless—I am what I am;) / Hours of my torment—I wonder if other men ever have the like, out of the like feelings?"

Such tortured moments in the "Calamus" poems bring up the question of Whitman's sense of his own sexual identity. After repeated inquiries from John Addington Symonds about the possible homosexual meaning of "Calamus," Whitman confessed that perhaps the cluster "means more or less what I thought myself—means different: perhaps I don't know what it all means—perhaps never did know. My first instinct about all that Symonds writes is violently reactionary—is strong and brutal for no, no, no. Then the thought intervenes that I maybe do not know all my meanings." He specified, though, that the "Calamus" cluster "may be easily, innocently distorted from its natural, its motive, body of doctrine."

A main reason for the confusion of interpretations between Symonds and Whitman is that the former was working from a late-nineteenth-century European intellectual perspective on same-sex love, while Whitman retained an American working-class view of it. The people who most insistently connected Whitman with homosexuality in his lifetime, especially Symonds, were European thinkers aware of the medical "discovery" of homosexuality by the scientific community. The first medical case report of a homosexual came in 1869 in an article by Karl Westfal in a Berlin medical journal. Describing the impact of this article, Foucault writes: "The sodomite had been a temporary aberration. The homosexual was now a species." A species, we should add, for those aware of it. Scattered reports of what was called "sexual inversion" appeared in European medical journals through the 1870s and 1880s, but reports in America were scarce, and the word "homosexual" was not used in English until 1892, the year of Whitman's death. The idea of homosexuality as an underlying orientation did not take hold until the nineties. Symonds put his most pointed query to Whitman in medical terms. After Whitman wrote him that his "morbid inferences" about the "Calamus" poems were "damnable" and "disavow'd by me," Symonds wrote him back in exasperation, saying he was surprised Whitman was not aware that there were some people "whose sexual instincts are what the Germans call 'inverted.'" Symonds explained: "During the last 25 years much attention, in France, Germany, Austria, & Italy, has been directed to the psychology & pathology of these abnormal persons."

Whitman could not understand such language. He may not have known all his own meanings, as he put it, but he was ready to blurt "no, no, no" to Symonds because his meanings had little to do with the European medical ones. He may have had basic confusions about "Calamus" and his own sexual self, but these confusions emerged from the American working-class culture of comrades and romantic friends that had shaped him.

The division of "homosexual" and "heterosexual," introduced in medical circles in the 1890s, would not be commonly known by the educated public until the 1920s. Before then, American men who had sexual relations with other men were generally thought to be of two kinds: men with extremely powerful sex drives in whom the "masculine" element prevailed, making them want to have sex with either men or women; and "fairies" or "hermaphrodites" in whom the feminine element was excessively developed. The former were regarded as oversexed but normal males, while the latter, beginning in the late nineteenth century, were designated sexual inverts. Thus, the distinction was not between heterosexual and homosexual but rather between "manly" men and "feminine" men.

Where does Whitman fit on this scale? In his poems he typically posed as the extremely "masculine" man. His pose as one of the turbulent, drinking, fleshy working-class roughs places him in the realm of those sensual males who sometimes in real life loved both men and women without sacrificing their basic sexual identity. If in his poetry he liked to be the "robust" or "masculine" man, in personal life he had both "feminine" and "masculine" traits. On the one hand, some who knew him noted what struck them as "womanly" characteristics: his pinkish-white skin, his soft eyes, his pristine flowing beard, his generally gentle manner. Such characteristics led Edward Bertz to comment that "although many ignorant persons took Whitman for the most complete example of manliness, the poet was a woman in all respects except anatomy." Bucke captured Whitman's effeminate side in two passages in the original version of his 1883 biography of the poet, one calling him "motherly" (Whitman changed it to "paternal"), another describing him as a "sort of male castrato; a false soprano" (deleted by Whitman).

On the other hand, in his relationships with young men, Whitman liked to pose as a "masculine" authority figure, usually as a father or an uncle. It was this quality that led Peter Doyle and others to characterize him as a vigorous, intensely virile man. He assumed this "masculine" role in many of his relationships with young men, beginning, it seems, with his Long Island students and extending through the Civil War soldiers to Doyle and Harry Stafford after the war. His romantic friendships with these men were often ardently passionate and physical—perhaps, in some cases, sexual. An implied heterosexuality, however, was often part of these friendships. Whitman's close friend of the late fifties, Fred Vaughan, requested in 1862 that the poet attend his wedding and, a dozen years and four children later, reported in a letter to the poet, "My wife is loving, faithful, honest, true, and one you could dearly love." Whitman did not shy from mentioning the heterosexuality of his comrades. One, Bill Guess, he described as "fond of direct pleasures, eating, drinking, women, fun, &c." He said his best friend, Peter Doyle, was "a little too fond of his beer, now and then, and of the women." Although he frowned on promiscuity, he believed in marriage. He advised one of his soldier friends, Benton H. Wilson, "that it is every way the best & most natural condition for a young man to be married, having a companion, a good & affectionate wife." After the war he had a loving relationship with the farm boy Harry Stafford and then attended his wedding and befriended Harry's wife, Eva.

Poetry became his way of expressing every aspect of same-sex emotion, from "feminine" receptivity and gentleness to "masculine" turbulence and bravado. In early poems like "Song of Myself" and "The Sleepers" both sides of his nature merge so tightly that he can seem "masculine" in one line and "feminine" in another, though his self-conscious masculine voice presides. In the more compartmentalized 1860 poems, this fusion of voices unravels, and Whitman takes on different personae as a means of expressing different sides of himself.

In negotiating between personal and cultural definitions of same-sex love, the phrenological notion of adhesiveness was important to him. Phrenology came closer than anything else in his day to providing a system of the mind. Among the organs of the brain, the social ones of amativeness and adhesiveness were thought to have extraordinary power. Adhesiveness was not part of phrenology's scheme as elaborated by its founder, Franz Josef Gall, but was added in the 1820s by Gall's student, Johann Gaspar Spurzheim. Both amativeness and adhesiveness loomed large in the modernized phrenological system fabricated by Whitman's pseudoscientific mentors, the Fowlers. They wrote that when the organ of adhesiveness was large, one "loves friends with tenderness, and intense friendship will sacrifice almost anything for their sake." Those with large adhesiveness, Orson Fowler explained, "instinctively recognize it in each other; soon become mutually and strongly attached; desire to cling to the objects of their love; take more delight in the exercise of friendship than in anything else."

Intense love between people of the same sex, then, was sanctioned by the pseudoscientists who had read Whitman's skull and found him strong in this essential quality. For both the Fowlers and Whitman, adhesiveness had personal and social dimensions. Privately, it caused people of the same sex to be drawn to each other and love each other. Socially, it was a powerful force for cohesion. As the Fowlers explained, it had the power to "bind mankind together in families, societies, communities, &c.," and it created more social virtue than any other faculty.

Because comradeship and sexuality were closely fused in the 1855 edition, Whitman had not then referred to the separate categories of "adhesiveness" and "amativeness." Beginning with the topic poems of 1856, he began to find these categories useful. In the 1856 poem "Song of the Open Road" he announced: "Here is adhesiveness, it is not previously fashion'd, it is apropos; / Do you know what it is to be loved by strangers?" In the 1860 edition, adhesiveness becomes an important, socially condoned concept for communicating both personal love and social bonding. Since Whitman was now thinking more in categories than before, the phrenological terms took on new importance. In planning what would become the "Enfans d'Adam" and "Calamus" clusters, he wrote that the former would embody "the amative love of woman" and the latter "adhesiveness, manly love." This is how Whitman's defenders saw the two clusters. O'Connor, for instance, wrote that "Adam" celebrates "Love and Amativeness," while "Calamus" is devoted to "Friendship or Adhesiveness."

Although Whitman never categorizes erotic love neatly, in the 1860 edition he makes greater use of adhesiveness than previously. In "So Long!" he writes, "I announce adhesiveness—I say it shall be limitless, unloosened." Homoeroticism takes on both phrenological and religious meaning in these lines from "Proto-Leaf": "Not he, adhesive, kissing me so long with his daily kiss, / Has winded and twisted around me that which holds me to him, / Any more than I am held to the heavens, to the spiritual world." "O adhesiveness! O pulse of my life!" he exclaims in a "Calamus" poem, insisting that it must suffuse "these songs."

Because he thought amativeness sometimes involved duplicity and exploitation, as sensationalized in the popular love plot, adhesiveness seemed to him religious and moral. As he would explain in a note to *Democratic Vistas:* "It is to the development, identification, and general prevalence of that fervid comradeship, (the adhesive love, at least rivaling the amative love hitherto possessing imaginative literature, if not going beyond it,) that I look for the counterbalance and offset of our materialistic and vulgar American democracy, and for the spiritualization thereof."

Adhesiveness informed the 1860 poems even when it was not directly mentioned. Lorenzo Fowler had stipulated that people with large adhesiveness "would never choose a wilderness life, or the hermit's cell; but are unhappy if their friends are absent from them." This is the theme of the "Calamus" poem "I Saw in Louisiana a Live Oak Growing," in which Whitman describes a solitary tree "uttering joyous leaves all its life, without a friend, a lover near." Whitman adds, "I know very well I could not."

The fact that this live-oak tree, hung with moss, is in the South, and that the (presumably Northern) "I" of the poem carries a twig of it home to plant near his house reminds us of the political subbasis of many of the 1860 poems, including the "Calamus" cluster. This poem, among other things, gestures toward the unity of North and South. Some have distinguished between the private, confessional "Calamus" poems, which supposedly reveal an authentic Whitman, and public, programmatic ones, which sublimate or deflect his feelings.

But, given the cultural ideas of friendship Whitman accepted, this distinction is specious. The loving comradeship felt by romantic friends and described by phrenologists and reformers had a vital social dimension. Many reformers believed that, in the absence of reliable authority figures in government, love between friends was the only way society could hold together. The feminist and labor reformer Paulina Wright Davis spoke for many when she said in 1855, "We appeal to Fourier's principle of the 'oneness of the race' and human brotherhood as the grand superstructure.... We want associative, attractive and incorporated labor." Emerson in his 1838 "Address on War" discussed the use of private love as a means of social repair, arguing that real peace could be maintained not through laws or formal negotiation but through "private, dear and earnest love." This was also the philosophy of the era's most vocal pacifist, Elihu Burritt, the "Learned Blacksmith" from Worcester, who in his well-known newspaper *The Bond of Brotherhood* recommended private love as the key to universal peace.

Fourierists, free lovers, and Harmonialists strengthened the link between private and social love. For Fourier, love was the absolute mainspring of society. "Omniphily" was Fourier's name for the sudden spontaneous friendship that springs up between complete strangers; he believed that society should be reorganized so that omniphily could spread and, in his words, "every man, in all points of the globe, may suddenly find societies friendly to his taste." For the free lovers and Harmonialists, total individualism went hand-in-hand with social harmony, since both were based on free passional expression. As Thomas Low Nichols and Mary Gove Nichols wrote in 1854: "'Individual Sovereignty' is a true principle; but it is entirely consistent with the most beautiful social harmony, and can only be realized in a harmonic society." In the ideal society, the Nicholses continued, "the health of each member would be sustained by the loving magnetism of those with whom he was grouped."

Whitman had full exposure to all the current ideas on friendship, which took on particular meaning for him in the political and social crises of the late fifties. The subtle fusion of diverse cultural images that he had attempted in 1855 was replaced by overt insistence on national unity through magnetic, passionate friendship. The comradeship he saw everywhere among the working classes might, he hoped, save the Union. In discussing the "Calamus" poems with Traubel, he explained this comradely love: "It is one of the United States—it is the quality which makes the states whole—it is their thread—but, oh! the significant thread!—by which the nation is held together, a chain of comrades; it could no more be dispensed with than the ship entire. I know no country anyhow in which comradeship is so far developed as here—here, among the mechanic classes." Because he thought the health of the nation depended vitally on love between friends, he sometimes emphasized the political dimension of "Calamus." In the 1876 preface he said that "the special meaning of the 'Calamus' cluster of 'Leaves of Grass,' . . . mainly resides in its political significance. In my opinion, it is by a fervent, accepted development of comradeship, the beautiful and sane affection of man for man, latent in all the young fellows, north and south, east and west . . . that the United States of the future, (I cannot too often repeat,) are to be most effectually welded together, intercalated, anneal'd into a living union."

It is understandable that he made this political application of loving friendship with special fervency in the 1860 edition. Talk of a forthcoming "irrepressible conflict" filled the air. Abraham Lincoln had recently warned, "A house divided against itself cannot stand." Since Whitman had lost faith in the power of established institutions to unify the nation, he explored the possibilities of friendship offered by his culture. His "Calamus" poems were at once intensely "private," in the sense of retreating from institutions he thought were ineffective or corrupt, and "public," in the sense of replacing them with the kind of passionate friendship other reformers of the day were elucidating. The calamus plant, a tall, fragrant reed that grows by ponds and rivers, was a convenient metaphor. Its marginality reflected Whitman's attempt to remove himself from mainstream institutions; its pungent odor symbolized the beauty and pervasiveness of the comradeship he hoped would replace these institutions. In the words of the first "Calamus" poem, Whitman sought both "a secluded spot" apart "from all the standards hitherto published" and a place where he could project "types of athletic love" and "celebrate the need of comrades."

If the private moments in "Calamus" allowed him to verbalize all the nuances of same-sex passion, the public ones made explicit his effort to replace failed political strategies with new, comradely ones:

> States!
> Were you looking to be held together by lawyers?
> By an agreement on paper? Or by arms?
>
> Away!
> I arrive, bringing these, beyond all the forces of courts and arms,
> These! to hold you together as firmly as the earth itself is held
>   together. [. . .]
>
> There shall be from me a new friendship—It shall be called after
>   my name,
> It shall circulate through The States, indifferent of place,
> It shall twist and intertwist them through and around each other—
> Compact they shall be, showing new signs,
> Affection shall solve every one of the problems of freedom,
> Those who love each other shall be invincible,
> They shall finally make America completely victorious, in my name.
>   [. . .]
>
> I will make the continent indissoluble,
> I will make the most splendid race the sun ever shone upon,
> I will make divine magnetic lands.

This is the familiar plea for unity, but it is now heavy-handed. Whitman no longer attempts a wide-ranging fusion of cultural images but instead makes fusion and union themselves central topics. He announces "a continent indissoluble" and "divine magnetic lands," because he hopes the theories and practices of antebellum friendship can be arrayed against "all the forces of courts and arms" that have failed America. Several other "Calamus" poems have a similar message. One says "the brotherhood of lovers" is far worthier than "the President in his Presidency" or "the rich man in his great house." Another aims to establish "the institution of the dear love of comrades" throughout the land.

"I will make the continent indissoluble." Less than a year after these words were printed, the nation would be at war.

Onset of War

DESPITE HIS HOPEFUL PROCLAMATIONS of national unity through friendship, Whitman sensed that the full social impact of his poetry would be delayed indefinitely. Along with desperation and shrillness in the 1860 edition went a sense of finality and closure, as though he were actually thinking of leaving behind poetry altogether. In the last poem of the edition—"So Long!"— he said he was addressing readers "for the last time" and wrote: "My songs cease, I abandon them." The massive audience he had dreamed of was now placed vaguely in the distant future:

> See projected, through time,
> For me, an audience interminable.

As it happened, his hopes for gaining such an audience may have been strengthened by the reception of the 1860 edition, which was destined to be more widely and positively reviewed than all the other editions of *Leaves of Grass* published in his lifetime. Of the thirty-two known reviews of the edition, seventeen were mainly positive, eight were mixed, and seven were mainly negative. Some reviews generalized about the greatness of *Leaves of Grass*. The New York *Illustrated News* raved: "We find in it all sorts of marvellous insights and truths; the broadest intellectual and moral recognition and suggestions; and a culture which is up to the highest water mark to which the age has risen." Women were particularly responsive to the edition. Adah Isaacs Menken declared that Whitman was "centuries ahead of his contemporaries," and Juliette H. Beach pronounced his volume "the standard book of poems in the future of America."

But the controversy over Whitman's sex poems continued. Today, "Calamus" might seem the most daring and unconventional cluster in the 1860 edition, but because same-sex intimacy was then commonplace, it raised few eyebrows. "Enfans d'Adam" was a different story. One reviewer placed the "Adam" poems among the various kinds of popular pornography: "Until such time as the novels of a [Paul] de Kock find place upon parlor tables, and the obscene pictures, which boys in your city slyly offer for sale upon wharves, are admitted to albums, or grace drawing-room walls, quotations from *Enfans d'Adam* would be an offence against decency too gross to be tolerated." The London *Saturday Review* was astonished by the incongruity between the book's elegant appearance and what it saw as its scabrous contents: "Such books as this have occasionally been printed in the guise of a scrofulous French novel, on grey paper with blunt type, but this, we verily believe, is the first time that one has been decorated with all the art of the binder and the pressman. The odd thing is, that it irresistibly suggests its being intended for the luxurious and cultivated of both sexes." The strongest indictment came in a short poem in the comic weekly *Momus,* containing the lines:

> Humanity shrinks from such pestilent reekings
> As rise, rotten and foul, from each word, line and page,
> Of the foulness within [Whitman] the nastiest leakings,
> Which stamp him the dirtiest beast of the age.

Such outbursts led Whitman's supporters to insist on his purity with fresh fervor. A woman calling herself "C. C. P." wrote of *Leaves of Grass* in the *Saturday Press:* "I have read it carefully, and in reading, have found no page which made me blush, and no sentiment which might not be expressed by a pure man." Another woman wrote: "Walt ennobles everything he writes about." A reviewer for the Boston *Cosmopolite* explained: "It is the poet's design, not to entice to the perversion of Nature, which is vice, but to lead us back to Nature, which in his theory is the only virtue." The Brooklyn *City News* commented that Whitman treated sex "with unprecedented boldness and candor, but always in the very highest religious and aesthetic spirit."

These statements reflected Whitman's own feelings about the "Enfans d'Adam" poems, expressed to Emerson on Boston Common and often repeated. His intended combination of candor and purity had some amusing results, such as the love letter he received in July 1861 from a complete stranger, a Connecticut woman named Susan Garnet Smith. "Know Walt Whitman that I am a woman!" she announced. "I am not beautiful, but I love you!" She reported having read *Leaves of Grass* during a country walk, while the birds and bees were making love, and she found their natural sex enacted in Whitman's pure poetry. She made a proposition she assumed Whitman could not refuse:

> Know Walt Whitman that thou hast a child for me! A noble perfect manchild. I charge you my love not to give it to another woman. The world demands it! It is not for you and me, *is our child*, but for the world. My womb is clean and pure. It is ready for thy child my love. Angels guard the vestibule until thou comest to deposit our and the

world's precious treasure. . . . Our boy my love! Do you not already love
him? He must be begotten on a mountain top, in the open air. Not in
lust, not in mere gratification of sensual passion, but in ennobling pure
strong deep glorious passionate broad universal love. I charge you to
prepare my love.

On the envelope Whitman scribbled "? insane asylum," but years later
he had to agree when Traubel said the letter wasn't crazy, "it's Leaves of
Grass." After all, he always insisted on the cleanliness of his sex poems.

With the sex matter preoccupying many commentators, the gener-
ally positive response to the 1860 edition was vitiated. Even more
significant, Whitman's publisher fell on hard times. In October 1860
Whitman took up the matter of royalties with Thayer and Eldridge but
received a curt reply: "In regard to money matters, we are very short
ourselves and it is quite impossible to send the sum you name." They
predicted business would pick up after the elections in November, but
they were wrong. By January 10, 1861, for reasons not associated with
Leaves of Grass, they declared bankruptcy. Whitman received only $250
in royalties. The plates of the 1860 edition fell into the hands of the
Boston publisher Horace Wentworth, whom William Thayer called "my
bitter and relentless enemy."

Whitman's fantasy of flooding the market with "copious thousands
of copies," therefore, was not realized. In the meantime, the United
States, virtually disunited for years, had become officially so after the
election of Abraham Lincoln. On December 20 South Carolina seceded
from the Union, followed in rapid succession by Mississippi, Florida, Al-
abama, Georgia, Louisiana, and Texas. By February 7, a month before
Lincoln's inauguration, the Confederate States of America were formed.

Under these inauspicious circumstances, Lincoln made his twelve-
day journey in February from Springfield to Washington for the inaugu-
ration. He knew he was taking his life in his hands. Death threats
abounded as his train wended its way through the North, making whistle
stops in many cities. When he made his appearance in Manhattan on
February 19, Whitman watched him closely from the top of a stalled
omnibus. The city had strong reservations about the Illinois rail-splitter.
Only 35 percent of New Yorkers had voted for him in November, and
after the election Mayor Fernando Wood issued a proposal (never acted
on) that Manhattan should secede from the Union and become an inde-
pendent city-state. The air was heavy with hostility toward Lincoln the
day Whitman saw him. More than thirty thousand looked on in glum
silence as Lincoln emerged from his hack and walked up the steps of the
Astor House Hotel. Whitman was certain, as he later recalled, that

"many an assassin's knife and pistol lurk'd in hip or breast-pocket there, ready, as soon as break and riot came."

But, magically, riot did not come. Whitman had a kind of epiphany as he saw Lincoln handle the crowd. Tall and awkward, wearing a black suit and stovepipe hat, Lincoln coolly and curiously surveyed the silent throng. With that one look he seemed to quell all opposition. Then he turned and entered the hotel. This was not the kind of weak-kneed public official Whitman was accustomed to. There was majesty behind the bumpkin exterior. Whitman thought dimly that "four sorts of genius, four mighty and primal hands"—Plutarch, Aeschylus, Michelangelo, Rabelais—would be needed to limn Lincoln's portrait. He could hardly know then that it would take just one—Walt Whitman—to immortalize him in poetry.

Though struck by Lincoln's firmness, Whitman was far from thinking of him as a bright western star or an indomitable captain, as he would four years later. In early 1861 he was once more a man adrift, uncertain about his own and his nation's future. "Quicksand years that whirl me I know not whither," he wrote during this period. "Your schemes, politics, fail, lines give way, substances mock and elude me." Even though he had published three volumes of poetry, he felt his poetic project had not succeeded. In his notebook in April he sketched "Poem on the Incompleted," which reflected his sense of failure: "Always unfinished—always incompleted, / The best yet left—the road but fairly started." On May 31, his forty-second birthday, he wrote a new trial preface to *Leaves of Grass*, stating his work had hardly begun: "So far, so well, but the most and best of the Poem I perceive remains unwritten, and is the work of my life yet to be done. The paths to the house are made—But where is the house itself? At most only indicated or touched."

The Civil War would give him the sense of completion he lacked. He never forgot the day the war began. Around midnight on April 13, returning from a performance of Verdi's *A Masked Ball*, he was walking down Broadway when he heard the newsboys hawking extras and shouting the news of the bombardment of Fort Sumter in Charleston Harbor, South Carolina, by Southern forces. Whitman bought a paper, crossed the street to catch the lamplight outside the Metropolitan Hotel, and huddled with a gathering crowd that listened as someone read aloud the stunning news. A grim silence prevailed until the crowd dispersed. Within three days Lincoln called for seventy-five thousand troops.

Like many in the North, Whitman thought it would be a short war. His brother George, typically, signed on for a hundred-day stint with the Brooklyn Thirteenth Regiment. Whitman saw joyful, expectant, blue-clad troops marching through Brooklyn with ropes tied to their muskets, in his words, "with which to bring back each man a prisoner from the audacious South, to be led in a noose, on our men's early and triumphant return!"

Everything now seemed larger than life. On June 16 diplomatic princes from Japan arrived in Manhattan, greeted by harbor salutes and cheering crowds on Broadway. Sitting impassively in their open barouches, the bronze, bareheaded envoys symbolized for Whitman the meeting of East and West. "The sign is reversing, the orb is enclosed," he wrote in "A Broadway Pageant," "the ring is circled, the journey is done." Twelve days later nearly half a million New Yorkers greeted the tremendous steamship *Great Eastern* as it arrived after its maiden voyage from Southampton at the North River Dock at Bank Street. "Well-shaped and stately the Great Eastern swam up my bay, she was 600 feet long," he wrote. "Her moving swiftly, surrounded by myriads of small craft I forget not to sing."

He remained sanguine about the North's prospects in the war. On July 12 he blithely wrote his brother George: "All of us here think the rebellion as good as broke—no matter if the war does continue for some months yet."

Then came Bull Run. On July 21 Beauregard, Johnston, and Stonewall Jackson handed the Union army its first crushing defeat. The Saturday and Sunday of the battle had been parched and hot, a chaos of dust and smoke. After being routed, the worn, humiliated Federal troops retreated under a soaking rain. "Where are the vaunts, and the proud boasts with which you went forth?" Whitman wrote later. "Where are your banners, and your bands of music, and your ropes to bring back prisoners?"

In the aftermath of Bull Run Whitman penned a recruiting poem, "Beat! Beat! Drums," exhorting the Union to rise up in war. He read a draft of the poem at Pfaff's on September 27, and it was published in the *Boston Evening Transcript,* the *New York Leader,* and *Harper's Weekly.*

Meanwhile, he scratched out a living as a freelance journalist. In 1861 and 1862 he wrote a series of twenty-five articles, under the running title of "Brooklynania," for the *Brooklyn Daily Standard.* He had spent part of the summer of 1861 on the east end of Long Island, and he wrote of fishing and sailing off Greenport with some young women and a laughing minister. He described eating chicken, singing and telling stories, and falling asleep under a rolled sail. In the "Brooklynania" articles he roamed nostalgically over the previous thirty years, as though in eulogy of a culture that was disappearing with the onset of war. "Our city grows so fast," he wrote, "that there is some danger of events and incidents of more than ten years gone being totally forgotten." He discussed the early Dutch settlements on Long Island, the prison-ship martyrs, and life in early Brooklyn Village. He noted: "Brooklyn had such a rural character that it was almost one huge farm and garden in comparison with its present appearance."

Early Manhattan also preoccupied him. He recalled when the Bowery was a "shrubby, viny, orchardy, cabbagey road." He reviewed the colorful history of the Bowery Theatre, which had burned down four times between 1828 and 1845, and he fondly discussed the stormy melodramas and actors that had enthralled him as a youth. He remembered the time in 1849 when the Bowery b'hoy butcher Tom Hyer beat the ex-convict James "Yankee" Sullivan in a brutal boxing match. As though retracing some of his poetic roots, he said of the Bowery, "Things are in their working-day clothes, more democratic, with a broader, jauntier swing, and in a more direct contact with vulgar life" than on Broadway, "its high-bred, aristocratic brother, half-a-mile off." He affectionately described the Bowery dance halls and saloons, reeking with cigars and German lager, alive with chatter and activity. On a more sober note, he recounted the sufferings of the sick and wounded in New-York Hospital, including some of his stage-driver friends, with nicknames like Old Elephant, Dressmaker, Yellow Joe, and Broadway Jack.

If the culture he had known before the war was changing, so was his family. After the death of his father in 1855, he and other family members remained geographically close, but increasingly the family seemed a grim mockery of the stable stem families of former generations. In the early sixties, Whitman was living on Portland Avenue in Brooklyn with his mother and his brothers Jesse, Edward, and Jeff, along with Jeff's wife and their daughter Mannahatta (their other daughter, Jessie Louisa, was born after the poet moved to Washington). Jeff was the main breadwinner, earning ninety dollars a month as an engineer of waterworks; in 1860 and 1861 he was an assistant engineer in the departments of Brooklyn and Manhattan, respectively, and in 1863 he became the chief assistant engineer, under Moses Lane, of the Consolidated Sewer and Water Departments of Brooklyn. Nearby, at 105 Park Avenue, lived Walt's brother Andrew, a joiner, with his wife, Nancy, and their children, Jimmy and George. Walt's other brother, George, a cabinetmaker by trade, was off at war. His sister Hannah lived in Vermont with her artist-husband Charles Heyde, and Mary was still in Greenport with her husband and five children.

The family had an odd conglomeration of illnesses, physical and mental. Mrs. Whitman suffered from severe rheumatism in her arms and legs. The retarded, crippled Edward was a pathetic figure who needed constant tending. Andrew had a drinking problem and in 1863 developed a throat condition, probably tuberculosis, that killed him the next year. After his death his slovenly wife, Nancy, took to the streets, had her children beg, and apparently was a prostitute for a time. Jesse, an ex-sailor who worked as a loader in the Brooklyn Navy Yard, began in 1860 to show symptoms of a violent insanity attributed to a fall from a ship's mast years earlier. Walt committed him in 1864 to the Kings County Lunatic Asylum, where he died six years later of a ruptured aneurysm possibly brought on by syphilis he had reportedly contracted from an Irish prostitute.

Worst of all was the long-distance pain they all endured over the plight of the hapless Hannah. A big-boned, intelligent woman with gray eyes and a fine figure, Hannah had shown promise in youth. She had attended the Hempstead Female Seminary and subsequently taught school, substituting for Walt on occasion. Her problems surfaced after she married Charles Heyde in 1852. The pair lived successively in various Vermont villages until settling in Burlington; he eked out a meager living by selling his paintings and teaching art. Their marriage was a hellish melodrama played out before the whole Whitman clan. The neurotic Hannah dressed carelessly, never learned to cook, and kept a messy house. She was also the victim of constant verbal and physical abuse. In 1855, after three years of marriage, she reported to her mother that Charles "tells me to pack my damned duds and clear out." "There was never a woman as abused as I be," she lamented. Her thin, nervous husband took out all his frustrations on her. "Charlie has taken the greatest aversion to me no matter what I do is wrong," she wrote in 1861 after an incident in which he pushed her down, smashed her looking glass, and burned a book of poems he had given her. Mrs. Whitman cannot have been reassured by her saying that "sometimes he knocks me over chair and all, but never hurts me."

Walt spared no epithets in describing Heyde. He variously called him a whelp, a snake, a cur, "the bed-buggiest man on earth," "almost the only man alive who can make me mad." Ironically, Heyde showed appreciation of his poetry. About the 1860 edition of *Leaves of Grass* he wrote Walt, "I like the poems better than those first issued." Still, his appreciation did not run deep, for by 1870 he complained to Walt of the sexual imagery in the poetry: "The louse and the maggot know about as much about procreation as you do." Heyde violated every idea Walt had about the role of the husband and family member. His letters to the Whitmans were full of complaints about Hannah, as when he wrote, "She is, to me, a melancholy failure, in every particular, of a woman." He raised Walt's hackles when he blamed Hannah's shortcomings on her

mother, whom he called "a silly old woman" full of "wicked duplicity."
As an artist, Heyde was skilled but limited: he perversely painted over
and over again two Green Mountain peaks, Mount Mansfield and Cam-
els Hump. Eventually he fell into hallucinatory psychosis and died in a
Vermont insane asylum in 1892. Hannah, who in old age became a re-
cluse given to sitting in a dark room with the shades down, didn't die
until sixteen years later and was buried in the Whitman family vault.

Naturally, Walt was the one all the family members depended on for
emotional—and, in some cases as time passed, financial—support. After
all, he had announced himself in print as "the equable man" who could
handle all things "grotesque or eccentric." When he moved to Washing-
ton in 1863 he was constantly apprised of the deteriorating situations on
Portland Avenue and in Burlington. His mother assaulted him in un-
grammatical letters with graphic descriptions of Andrew's throat illness,
Jesse's violence, Eddy's helplessness, and Hannah's torments. With typi-
cal bluntness she wrote of Andrew's wife, Nancy, "i think she is about
the lazeyest and dirtiest woman i ever want to see[....] shes as ugly as
she is dirty i dont wonder he used to drink." At the same time, Jeff wrote
Walt about the insane crises of Jesse, whom he wished dead, and about
the querulousness and penny-pinching of their mother.

Walt not only felt the full weight of the family's sorrows but got an
intimate look at the war through his brother George. In September 1861,
after three months with the Brooklyn Thirteenth Regiment, George
joined the Fifty-first New York Volunteers under Colonel Edward Fer-
rero. Over the next four years he traveled more than twenty thousand
miles as a soldier and was in twenty-one general engagements or sieges.
His battles included Cedar Mountain, Second Bull Run, Chantilly, Antie-
tam, the Wilderness, Spotsylvania, and Cold Harbor. He served under
Burnside, McClellan, Pope, Hooker, Sherman, Grant, and others. Con-
stantly under fire, he gave vivid accounts of the war in his letters home.
He also kept a soldier's diary, which Walt considered one of the most
powerful records of the war. After Fredericksburg, a disastrous battle for
the Union, George wrote that "we had to advance in an open plain swept
on all points by their guns ... under a most terrible fire of Rifle balls,
Cannister, and Shell." An even-tempered, stolid man, George remained
remarkably self-possessed, as when he wrote from the Confederate mili-
tary prison at Danville: "I am in tip top health and spirits, and am tough
as a mule and shall get along first rate." His courage was rewarded by
frequent promotions. He rose from private to captain and finally to bre-
veted lieutenant colonel.

It is hard to overstate the importance of George's war experiences on
Walt's career as a writer. The war was at the very heart of his poetry,

Walt would later say. But it was mainly because of George that Walt got close to the war. Not only did George send home reports of his experiences, but his being wounded at Fredericksburg was what drew Walt to the front and then to Washington. On December 16, 1862, "G. W. Whitmore" appeared among the Fredericksburg casualties listed in the *New York Tribune.* Walt immediately started south to find George and assess the seriousness of the wound. After changing trains in Philadelphia, he was dismayed to find his wallet had been stolen; a friend would wryly comment that "any pick pocket who failed to avail himself of such an opportunity as Walt offered, with his loose baggy trousers and no suspenders, would have been a disgrace to his profession." Penniless and distraught, Whitman proceeded to Washington and, as he wrote his mother, "put in about three days of the greatest suffering I ever experienced in my life." He vainly searched the hospitals for George. At last he ran into his friends from Boston days, Charles Eldridge and William Douglas O'Connor. It was probably the latter who secured him a pass to travel by boat and train to Falmouth, where George's regiment was camped. One of the first sights that greeted him was a heap of amputated feet, legs, arms, and hands outside a camp hospital. He found George recuperating from a minor cheek wound caused by the fragment of an exploding percussion shell. While at Falmouth, he saw some of the war dead, including a soldier who prompted this line in draft: "Young man: I think this face of yours is the face of my dead Christ."

The Christ reference was apt, for Whitman himself was, in effect, resurrected by the war, just as he believed America was. He was aware that few knew the war as intimately as his brother George. He sang praise to George and his regiment in "Our Brooklyn Boys in the War," an article he wrote for the *Brooklyn Daily Eagle* soon after returning from Falmouth to Washington. He boasted that the regiment had been in the field fourteen months and had engaged in seven pitched battles, "some of them as important as any in American history." George Whitman, he noted, had risen to the level of captain and was one of only two hundred survivors of the original fifteen hundred volunteers.

When Whitman said good-bye to George and returned to Washington on December 28, he thought he might stay a few weeks. His stay, interrupted by periodic visits home, would last ten years. He discovered a new life mission in Washington, a mission closely tied to the war he said saved him. He wanted a government clerkship to support his main interest—volunteer nursing in the war hospitals—and so he asked Emerson to intervene on his behalf with powerful men in Washington, including Senator Charles Sumner and Secretary of the Treasury Salmon Chase. Emerson concurred, writing a form letter stating that Whitman was "a man of strong original genius, combining, with marked eccentricities, great powers & valuable traits of character." Sumner did not act on Emerson's recommendation, passing Whitman off to the New York senator Preston King, who thought that the white-bearded Walt looked suspiciously like a Southern planter and refused to help him. Whitman held on to the letter for Chase for a year until he got an entrée to him through his friend John Townsend Trowbridge, but Chase, as Whitman later recalled, "said he considered Leaves of Grass a very bad book, & he did not know how he could possibly bring its author into government service, especially if he put him in contact with gentlemen employed in the bureaus."

Although Whitman would not get a clerkship until 1865, he got a part-time job as a copyist in the office of the army paymaster, Major Lyman S. Hapgood, possibly through Charles Eldridge, who worked there. He supplemented his small salary by writing occasional war stories for newspapers. He worked only a few hours a day, spending much of his time in the Washington hospitals, of which there were around forty.

His living arrangements were modest. Failing at first to find a room, he was soon living in what he called "a werry little bedroom" on the second floor of a lodging house at 394 L Street, below his good friends William and Nelly O'Connor. He had breakfast with them at eight-thirty and dinner with them at four-thirty. When they took larger rooms down the street in June, the daily communal dining stopped, but he joined them for Sunday feasts and visited them often. "The O'Connor home was my home," he would recall; "they were beyond all the others—William, Nelly—my understanders, my lovers: they more than any others." At their home gathered many writers and reformers who had lively discussions of just about everything. Whitman was thus culturally and emotionally rich if economically straitened. By October he had moved into a third-story room at 456 Sixth Street, near Pennsylvania Avenue and not far from the Capitol. To his mother he called his new quarters "plenty big enough," but when Trowbridge visited him in December he found him "in a bare and desolate room up three flights of stairs, quite alone, with barely more than a bed, a cheap pine table, and a fireless sheet-iron stove." He ate simple meals of brown bread, tea, and fruit, using as plates scraps of paper he discarded after using.

His personal sufferings, however, seemed minimal compared with those he saw all around him among the soldiers. He wrote his mother that in view of those who had lived for months with "death and sickness and hard marching and hard fighting, . . . really nothing we call trouble seems worth talking about." All the torments and hopes he had long harbored were swept up in the drama of pain and glory that was the Civil War.

13

"MY BOOK AND THE WAR ARE ONE": THE WASHINGTON YEARS

To thee old cause! [...]
These recitatives for thee,—My book and the war are one,
Merged into its spirit I and mine, as the contest hinged on thee,
As a wheel on its axis turns, this book unwitting to itself,
Around the idea of thee.

"MY BOOK and the war are one." On the surface, the words seem badly mistaken. How could Whitman consider the Civil War central to *Leaves of Grass?* After all, most of his major poems had been written *before* the war. True, a few outstanding pieces of poetry and prose would come later, but the fact remains that by 1860 his main oeuvre was behind him.

It would be convenient to dismiss the statement as an aberration, but Whitman echoed it often. He told Traubel that the war was "the very centre, circumference, umbillicus of my whole career." In the 1876 preface to *Leaves of Grass* he highlighted the war: "[T]he whole book, indeed, revolves around that four years' war, which, as I was in the midst of it, becomes, in 'Drum-Taps,' pivotal to the rest entire."

Taken to mean "the war produced my best poetry," his declaration "My book and the war are one" makes little sense, even if we take into account his powerful Lincoln elegy and his vivid war vignettes in *Drum-Taps*. But interpreted as "The war was the culmination of my entire poetic mission," it makes perfect sense.

In his eyes, the Civil War accomplished for America what he had hoped his poetry would accomplish. It blew away many of the social ills that his early poetry had tried to rectify. It cleared the atmosphere like a thunderstorm, an image he liked to use for the war. It seemed to rid the North, especially Manhattan, of many of its prewar problems. It turned the fuzzy, shifting issue of states' rights versus national power into the crystal-clear one of *Secession* versus *Union*. It made most people in the Northern states rally around the ideal of union he had long cherished. It pulled together virtually all Americans, North and South, in a common action and a spirit of heroic self-sacrifice.

The war satisfied basic psychological needs as well. If Whitman's poetry had tried to answer America's thirst for violence and gore, the war made violence and gore everyday realities, ennobled by the cause behind them. If he had tried to make loving comradeship a national institution, the war endorsed his effort, since it sanctified comradeship in arms and gave him the tender "wound dresser" role that was both patriotic and emotionally satisfying.

The war also provided him with power structures he could finally believe in. Before the war, he had tried mightily to replace failed authority figures with a near-totalitarian poetic "I" who brought together many cultural materials. The war obviated the need for his totalitarian persona. In coming to Washington, he was entering the arena of government operations and what he called "the big men." Although not all government leaders were clean in his view, the important ones were—especially the most important one of all, Abraham Lincoln.

In Lincoln he found the Redeemer President he had sought. Many around him, including his brother Jeff, thought sourly of Lincoln, but Whitman defended him even when the war was going against the Union. The president embodied many of the qualities of the "I" of Whitman's early poetry: strength, tenderness, humor, tolerance, a penchant for popular enjoyments and entertainments. It is understandable that Lincoln inspired his most skillful postwar poem, "When Lilacs Last in the Dooryard Bloom'd," and his most popular one, "O Captain! My Captain!" Reifying Lincoln as the eternal "western star" and "my Captain," these poems signaled the advent of a new moral leadership and the retreat of the authoritarian "I" in Whitman's poetry.

To the end of his life, Whitman would idealize the Civil War, sometimes distorting it in the process. He could not be sure what the future would bring, but he could, and did, constantly relive his version of the war.

Welcome the Storm

THE NORTH, HE THOUGHT, was as much to blame for the war as the South. He explained his position in his essay "The Origins of Attempted Secession." "The Northern States," he wrote, "were really just as responsible for that war, (in its precedents, foundations, instigations,) as the South." "For twenty-five years previous to the outbreak," he explained, "the controlling 'Democratic' nominating conventions of our Republic ... were getting to represent and be composed of more and more putrid and dangerous materials." Launching into one of his name-calling tirades, he insisted that the antebellum political scene, "especially in New York and Philadelphia cities," was full of disunionists, infidels, "pimpled men," "scarred men," "skeletons," and so on. "Is it strange that a thunderstorm follow'd such morbid and stifling cloud strata?" he asked.

Worst of all, in his view, had been the disunionists, by whom he meant fire-eaters in the South and abolitionists in the North. If the issue of "*slavery and quiet*" had been put directly to the popular vote "as against their opposite," he argued, "they would have triumphantly carried the day in a majority of northern states." As it was, he said, disunion had as many adherents in the North as in the South. The Civil War, then, should be seen "not as a struggle of two distinct and separate peoples, but a conflict (often happening, and very fierce) between the passions and paradoxes of one and the same identity—perhaps the only terms on which that identity could really become fused, homogeneous and lasting."

His argument was in some ways naïve and in other ways perceptive. He seemed to forget that by electing Lincoln in 1860 the nation had voted, if not for "*slavery and quiet*," then at least for moderation on the slavery issue. Though morally opposed to slavery, Lincoln at first disavowed extreme stances. His initial objective was to preserve the Union as it was. He favored the fugitive slave law, gradual emancipation, and colonization. He wanted to remain friendly to the South. During his campaign, a poet praised him that "no Abolition force" had moved him "from safety's middle course." As late as 1862 he could write, "My paramount objective *is* to save the Union, and is *not* either to save or destroy slavery."

Still, Whitman was right to point out that some of the responsibility for the war lay with the North. During the three administrations of the fifties, which Whitman called "our topmost warning and shame," corruption had been rife, and disunion was increasingly talked of. Indeed, the two were connected: disunionists in both the South and the North advocated the dislodging of their sections from what they saw as a diseased national system. Even Mayor Fernando Wood, not known for his probity, brought up the corruption issue in his 1861 proposition that New York follow the South in seceding from the Union. "When disunion has become a fixed and certain fact," he wrote in his public document, "why may not New York disrupt the bands which bind her to a venal and

corrupt master—to a people and a party that have plundered her reve-
nues, attempted to ruin her commerce, taken away the power of self-
government, and destroyed the Confederacy of which she was the proud
Empire City?"

In this atmosphere, many saw the war as a necessary cleansing
agent. A Massachusetts congressman said that the war, for all its brutal-
ity, "was not a corrupter, but rather a purifier, of the moral character of
man; that peace was the period of corruption to the human race." Orestes
Brownson called the war "the thunderstorm that purifies the moral and
political atmosphere." Francis Parkman, using a Whitmanesque image,
declared that "like a keen fresh breeze, the war has stirred our clogged
and humid atmosphere." The Virginian Henry A. Wise gave the idea a
religious twist: "I rejoice in this war. . . . It is a war of purification. You
want war, fire, blood to purify you; and the Lord of Hosts has demanded
that you should walk through fire and blood."

For Whitman, too, the war was welcome:

War! an arm'd race is advancing! the welcome for battle, no turning
    away;
War! be it weeks, months, or years, an arm'd race is advancing to
    welcome it.

The uneasy peace of the fifties had represented, for him as for others,
a moral nadir in American life. The clean certainty of violent war ap-
pealed to him. At times he manifested an almost masochistic delight in
the violence, as in "Ship of Libertad," an uncollected poem written early
in the war:

Blow mad winds!
Rage, boil, vex, yawn wide, yeasty waves
Crash away—
Try at the planks—make them groan—fall around, black clouds—
    clouds of death.

Welcome the storm—welcome the trial—let the waves [sic]
Why now I shall see what the old ship is made of
Any body can sail with a fair wind, or a smooth sea [. . .]
I welcome the menace—I welcome thee with joy.

He was hardly alone in welcoming the war in poetry. Few American
poets, North or South, missed the chance to pen verses celebrating the
war. Everyone, it seemed, produced a rousing recruiting song compara-
ble to Whitman's "Beat! Beat! Drums!" Theodore Tilton's "The Great

Bell Roland," Whittier's "Following the Drum," Alice Cary's "Song for
Our Soldiers," Frederic Henry Hedge's "Our Country Is Calling," and
John Pierpont's "Forward!" and Charles Godfrey Leland's "Northmen,
Come Out!" were typical Northern poems. A verse from Hedge's poem
gives a flavor of the whole:

> Our country is calling! we come! we come!
> For Freedom and Union we rally;
> Our heart-beat echoes the beating drum,
> Our thoughts with the trumpets tally;
> Each bosom pants for the doomful day
> When the rebels shall meet us in battle array.

Two things made Whitman's recruiting poems stand out: they usu-
ally avoided partisanship, picturing the war spirit as a unifying rather
than divisive force; and they pointed to the war as a validation of free
verse. The lines from Hedge characterize most recruiting poems. The
rhyme scheme and metrical pattern are regular. The viewpoint is clear:
"we rally" for "Freedom and Union," panting for the "doomful day"
when "the rebels shall meet us in battle array." The pro-Northern stance
is exaggerated in Leland's "Northmen, Come Out!" in which the poet
vivifies the North's hatred of the aristocratic slave power by saying cotton
is "of kingly stock; / Yet royal heads may reach the block; / The puritan
taught it once in pain, / His sons shall teach it once again."

Partisanship went both ways. Southern recruiting poems shared the
militancy and jingoism of the Northern ones but turned them around.
Southerners maintained that they were patriotically reenacting the re-
belliousness of America's founding fathers. A typical Southern poem
drove the point home:

> Rebels! 'tis our family name!
> Our father, Washington,
> Was the arch-rebel in the fight,
> And gave the name to us—a right
> Of father unto son.

The Southern poems, like the Northern, reveled in the war violence,
sometimes becoming sadistic:

> Whoop! the doodles have broken loose,
> Roaring round like the very deuce!
> Lice of Egypt, a hungry pack;
> After 'em boys, and drive 'em back.

Bull-dog, terrier, cur and lice,
Back to the beggarly land of ice,
Worry 'em, bite 'em, scratch and tear,
Everybody and everywhere.

Whitman's recruiting poems have all the violence of the Northern and Southern ones, but they direct the violence toward affirmations of unity. The powerful "I" of his early poems that had tried to unify all cultural sections and levels was replaced by the totalitarian war spirit that, he believed, took control of virtually all Americans, bringing purgation and cleansing. The social purgation his early poetry had attempted—sometimes through violent images, sometimes through utopian ones—seemed to be happening before his eyes.

Since he thought the North needed cleansing just as much as the South, several of his poems pictured the war as cleansing the Augean stables of capitalism and urbanism. The war seemed to answer the problem of widening class divisions, since, at least in its early phase before conscription threatened to make it a "poor man's war," it pulled together people of all classes. In "First O Songs for a Prelude" Whitman describes the lawyer, the driver, the judge, and others of varied economic backgrounds melding as armed regiments: "How good they look as they tramp down to the river, sweaty, with their guns on their shoulders!" In "Beat! Beat! Drums!" the war is a "ruthless force" that bursts through everything and wrenches people from their peacetime pursuits. The inspiriting music of war blows "Through the windows—through doors," scattering the congregation, the scholars, the merchants engaged in their capitalistic double-dealing: "No bargainers' bargains by day—no brokers or speculators—would they continue?"

Whitman made a similar point in "Song of the Banner at Daybreak," a verse conversation among a pennant, a poet, a child, and a father. The flag in the poem is neither the Stars and Stripes nor the Confederate flag but an undescribed pennant beckoning both Northerners and Southerners to war. The child and the poet are dazzled by the flag and the war themes it represents; the stern father, in contrast, wants to look away from war to practical, materialistic things. The poem becomes a debate between the peacetime mentality of mercantile pursuits and the wartime one of unified martial action around a pennant. The latter wins the day. While the father calls attention to "the money-shops" of the city and the "dazzling things in the houses," the child insists that he likes neither money nor business but only the pennant that waves majestically over the whole land. The poet picks up the child's enthusiasm. He says that he has waited long for a unifying theme and that he has found it in the war: "My limbs, my veins dilate, my theme is clear at last, / Banner so broad advancing out of the night, I sing you haughty and resolute, / I burst through where I waited long, too long, deafen'd and blinded, / My hearing and tongue are come to me." The pennant is not partial to either side but is the "absolute owner of all," embracing both Northern and Southern states: it speaks of "my" Illinois, "my" Mississippi, "my" Missouri, and so on. The pennant is "an idea—furiously fought for" by both sides and thus has the kind of totalizing effect Whitman always hoped his poetry would have:

> The Continent, devoting the whole identity without reserving an
>   atom,
> Pour in! whelm that which asks, which sings, with all and the yield
>   of all,
> Fusing and holding, claiming, devouring the whole.

Whitman especially wanted to describe the war's transforming effect on Manhattan. His longtime ambivalence about what he had once called "that wicked city across the river" had come close in his late-fifties journalism to an all-out rejection of the city, which he had done his best to ennoble in poems like "Crossing Brooklyn Ferry" and "Mannahatta." He cannot have been pleased that by early 1861 the city had become a nest of Copperheads led toward disunion by Mayor Wood. All the more reason he was overjoyed when, after Fort Sumter, many Manhattanites, including Wood, jumped on the Union bandwagon. Although some New York newspapers opposed the war, most (including the *Tribune,* the *Times,* the *Evening Post,* and the *Sun*) strongly supported it, fanning the flames of Union sentiment with headlines like this one that ran for a week in the *Tribune:* "The Nation's War Cry: *Forward to Richmond! Forward to Richmond!*" The fact that the New York volunteers were among the first to march off to war thrilled Whitman: "O superb! O Manhattan, my own, my peerless! / O strongest you in hour of danger, in crisis! O truer than steel!"

The war seemed to him like a purifying fire that would burn away the city's problems. In his prewar poems he had used many strategies, including constant use of refreshing nature imagery, to cleanse the city imaginatively. Now he believed that the war was cleansing the city and that he need no longer retreat desperately to nature. In "Rise O Days from Your Fathomless Deeps" he begged the war to crash louder and louder to purge American cities of their prewar evils:

> Thunder on! stride on, Democracy! strike with a vengeful stroke!
> And do you rise higher than ever yet, O days, O cities!

Crash heavier, heavier yet O storms! you have done me good,
My soul prepared in the mountains absorbs your immortal strong
    nutriment,
Long had I walk'd in my cities, my country roads through farms,
    only half satisfied,
One doubt nauseous undulating like a snake, crawl'd on the ground
    before me,
Continually preceding my steps, turning upon me oft, ironically
    hissing low;
The cities I loved so well I abandon'd and left, I sped to the
    certainties suitable to me,
Hungering, hungering, hungering, for primal energies and Nature's
    dauntlessness,
I refresh'd myself with it only, I could relish it only,
I waited the bursting forth of the pent fire—on the water and air I
    waited long;
But I no longer wait, I am fully satisfied, I am glutted,
I have witness'd the true lightning, I have witness'd my cities
    electric,
I have lived to behold man burst forth and warlike America rise,
Hence I will seek no more the food of the northern solitary wilds,
No more the mountains roam or sail the stormy sea.

These lines re-create Whitman's prewar doubt, his retreat to nature
and his confidence that the war would purge the cities of their ills. His
"[o]ne doubt nauseous" had been that American cities would be lost in
corruption and capitalist sloth. He had then found solace in the "primal
energies" of nature. Now these primal energies were supplied by the war.
Witnessing "my cities electric," Whitman was exultant. He similarly
said of the city at the end of the poem:

Often in peace and wealth you were pensive or covertly frown'd amid
    all your children,
But now you smile with joy exulting old Mannahatta.

The war, in his view, not only purified America but also justified his
free poetic form. The explosive forces of war, he suggested, should never
be captured in traditional poetry. "No dainty rhymes or sentimental love
verses for you terrible year," he wrote in "Eighteen Sixty-One." "[D]id
you ask dulcet rhymes of me?" he asks in "To a Certain Civilian." "Did
you seek the civilian's peaceful and languishing rhymes?"
    He was using prowar enthusiasm to justify his unconventional poetic

form. The word he said summed up the war and the years leading up to it—"convulsiveness"—was becoming fused with patriotism in his verse. If before the war he had been a footloose individualist sneering at established institutions, now he was embracing the war, which permitted violent catharsis even as it strengthened institutions.

The Whited Sepulchre

"WHAT A CITY!" said the Union soldier Elijah Rhodes in describing Washington. "Mud, pigs, negroes, palaces, shanties everywhere."

By January 1863, when Whitman settled in Washington, the capital city was both a dazzling and a depressing place. Whitman took pleasure in the majestic government buildings, but only guilty pleasure. Witnessing the interior of the Capitol, with its costly frescoes, heavy chandeliers, and shimmering marbles, he described it oxymoronically as having "by far the richest and gayest, and most un-American and inappropriate ornamenting and finest interior workmanship I ever conceived possible." He knew the squalid and painful side of Washington too. Most of the city's streets were unpaved, leading him to report that "it is dusty or muddy most of the time here." Cows were herded by the thousands through the grubby streets. In an October 1863 article for the *New York Times* he recited all the usual complaints about Washington—it was dirty, frenetic, tiresome, politically corrupt—but added that now had arrived "the visible fact of this war, the ever-dearest fact to men, though the most terrible."

The war was certainly a visible fact in Washington. The city was rimmed with seventy-four forts and twenty-two batteries to ward off Lee's forces, often a real threat. Orderly, blue-clad regiments marching confidently southward regularly passed exhausted, bedraggled soldiers retreating to the city. Whitman arrived at a time when Union morale was low. The previous nine months had brought home the violence of the war to Northerners. A series of bloody battles in 1862—Shiloh, the Seven Days, Second Bull Run, Antietam, Fredericksburg—showed how terrible the carnage could get. Fredericksburg, the battle in which George had been wounded, was an egregious blunder by General Ambrose Burnside, who had ordered fourteen doomed assaults on Mayre's Heights, where Lee's forces, protected by a stone wall, mowed down Union troops at will, killing nearly thirteen thousand. Whitman called it "the most complete piece of mismanagement perhaps ever yet known in the earth's wars." But he noted the "unsurpassed gallantry" of the Union soldiers, whose bravery made him write: "Taking the army as a whole, it is almost certain that never did mortal man in an aggregate fight better than our troops at Fredericksburg."

If the war was "the most terrible" fact, it was nonetheless "the ever-dearest" one to Whitman. There was value for him in its very terror. For years he had been trying to come to terms with the American public's hunger for sensationalism, catering to this hunger in his journalism and poetry. Even before the war, in his 1860 poem "A Song of Joys," he had envisaged the purgative pleasures of war:

> To go to battle—to hear the bugles play and drums beat!
> To hear the crash of artillery—to see the glittering of the bayonets
> and musket-barrels in the sun!
> To see men fall and die and not complain!
> To taste the savage taste of blood—to be so devilish!
> To gloat so over the wounds and deaths of the enemy.

Now this "devilish" hunger for blood and gore was satisfied perpetually by the war. Many Americans reveled in the war as the greatest sensation in a culture known for its sensations. Beginning on April 14, 1861, when Bennett's *Herald* sold 135,000 copies with its report of the shelling of Fort Sumter, newspaper sales surged. To answer public demand for war stories, the *Herald* published three extra editions per day; other papers issued extra editions in the evening and on Sunday. The public actually became impatient during lulls in the warfare. An army colonel, Charles S. Wainwright, commented, "The public have got a taste for blood, and want more excitement. A week passed without reports of a battle with thousands killed and wounded—is very dull, rendering the papers hardly worth reading." Describing the popularity of war stories in the papers, Thomas Low Nichols wrote: "American life is a series of sensations, and a want of them will be an obstacle in the way of making peace. When it was feared and believed that General Lee might take Washington, Philadelphia, and even New York, there was no panic in those cities, nothing beyond a new sensation, which I believe they enjoyed as much as the spectators of Blondid and Leotard did their feats of daring and danger."

On some level, Whitman shared this sensational interest in the war. Hence his cavalier tone in a letter to his mother reporting an imminent invasion of Washington by Lee: "Well, mother, we are generally anticipating a lively time here or in the neighborhood.... I am getting so callous that it hardly arouses me at all—I fancy I should take it very quietly if I found myself in the midst of a general conflict here in Washington." Early in 1864 he told an official he had "a great desire to be present at a first class battle," and he got a pass to spend two weeks near the front at a field hospital in Culpeper, Virginia. From the front he wrote his mother: "I never cease to crave more & more knowledge of actual soldiers' life, & to be among them as much as possible."

So important was the war and its violence to his imagination that he would devote a disproportionate section of his autobiographical narrative *Specimen Days* to the war years. This disproportion has puzzled many readers. How could Whitman justify spending eighty-five chapters of *Specimen Days* on his war experiences, in contrast to just sixteen on his pre-1860 life, which would seem to have been the crucial period for the background of *Leaves of Grass?* Part of the answer lies in what Whitman saw as the war's purgative violence. "The real war will never get into the books," he wrote, referring to "the seething hell and the black infernal background of countless minor scenes and interiors." But he did what he could to record "the real war." It was the sheer tumult and adventure of the war that Whitman registered in *Specimen Days*. The agony of the wounded soldiers in the war hospitals; the demonic din of battles; the hellish war prisons North and South—these and other painful, violent details constituted a large portion of his autobiography.

American culture before the war had been filled with violence and sensationalism, much of it commercialized, as in the penny papers and freak shows, and much of it anarchic and senseless, as in blood-and-thunder novels and urban riots and street brawls. The war was a kind of massive bloodletting for a society that feasted on violence. Sometimes Whitman protested against the press's sensational handling of the violence. During the Wilderness Campaign in 1864, he wrote his mother that the papers were exaggerating casualty statistics in order to satisfy a blood-hungry public: "[T]he fighting has been hard enough, but the papers make up a lot of additional items.... (They, the papers, are determined to make up just anything.)" But he himself was not beyond sensationalizing the war. In *Specimen Days*, after recounting an especially gory incident in which Union troops shot to death nineteen Southern prisoners, he wrote: "Multiply the above by scores, aye hundreds, . . . light it with every lurid passion, the wolf's, the lion's lapping thirst for blood—the passionate, boiling volcanoes of human revenge for comrades, brothers slain—with the light of burning farms, and heaps of smutting, smouldering black embers—and in the human heart everywhere black, worse embers—and you have an inkling of this war." He captured the hell of war in some of the poems in *Drum-Taps*, as in "The Artilleryman's Vision":

> The skirmishers begin, they crawl cautiously ahead, I hear the
> irregular snap! snap!
> I hear the sounds of the different missiles, the short *t-h-t! t-h-t!* of the
> rifle-balls,
> I see the shells exploding leaving small white clouds, I hear the great
> shells shrieking as they pass, [...]
> And ever the sound of the cannon far or near, (rousing even in
> dreams a devilish exultation and all the old mad joy in the
> depths of my soul,)

Even that quintessential instance of undirected mob violence—the New York draft riots of July 1863—did not surprise or ruffle him. Under the new conscription law, Lincoln ordered up 300,000 troops, including 1,200 from Manhattan. The burden of the draft fell heaviest on the poor, most of whom could not afford the three-hundred-dollar fee required to buy a substitute. Working-class Manhattanites, mainly Irish, saw the draft as a tyrannical imposition by the government on behalf of black slaves, many of whom had been recently declared free under the Emancipation Proclamation. On July 13, two days after the list of New York draftees had been publicly read, furious mobs of poor whites rampaged through the city, killing blacks and destroying property. The riot lasted for several days and was not quelled until government troops were sent from Gettysburg. In all, at least eighteen blacks were lynched and scores more died in the violence. Possibly two thousand rioters died, and there was about five million dollars in property damage.

As though enjoying a sensational spectacle, Whitman maintained an amused distance from the riot and the angry reactions to it. From Washington he wrote his mother that he had been expecting the riot and that while "the feeling here is savage & hot as fire" against the rioters, whom most wanted shot or hanged, "I remain silent, partly amused, partly scornful, or occasionally put a dry remark, which only adds fuel to the flame." He said he didn't have it in his heart to condemn the poor people, though five weeks later he admitted that this scene of negrophobic violence had been "the devil's own work all through," and he expressed satisfaction at the government's crackdown on the rioters.

It was in the hospitals that he saw the results of the war's violence with special vividness. Most of the forty or so hospitals in Washington were improvised, single-story wooden sheds in which were crowded hundreds, sometimes thousands, of wounded soldiers in adjoining beds. Almost every day, in his off-hours, Whitman toured the hospitals, comforting the wounded and helping the doctors and nurses. He dispensed little gifts, often contributed by Brooklyn or Washington friends, such as stationery, stamps, oysters, candy, fruit, books, tobacco, and small sums of money. His flexible hours at the paymaster's office generally allowed him to go to the hospitals from noon to 4:00 p.m. and then again from six to nine. He spent most of his time in Armory Square Hospital, which had the worst cases. Altogether, he made some six hundred visits in three years, seeing between 80,000 and 100,000 soldiers.

The suffering he witnessed in the hospitals was on a scale unmatched in American history. More Americans died and were wounded in the Civil War than in all other wars *combined*. The final grim numbers were more than 610,000 dead and 425,000 with debilitating wounds. Whitman filled notebooks and letters with descriptions of soldiers afflicted with virtually every imaginable wound or with maladies like diarrhea and dysentery. He recorded his hospital visits in "The Wound-Dresser":

> To the long rows of cots up and down each side I return,
> To each and all one after another I draw near, not one do I miss,
> An attendant follows holding a tray, he carries a refuse pail,
> Soon to be fill'd with clotted rags and blood, emptied, and fill'd
>   again.

Whitman's hospital work has often been described, but his overwhelming attraction to it, even at the peril of his health, has not been satisfactorily explained. Like other aspects of the war, his hospital visits accomplished key things he had hoped his poetry would do. They validated his vision of the common man; they answered his need for an ideal family and for loving comrades; and they permitted full indulgence to his humanistic, magnetic medical ideas.

He had filled the first three editions of *Leaves of Grass* with fresh, Adamic common people whose goodness or picturesqueness was intended to counteract the governmental corruption that had contributed to the political crisis of the fifties. When he settled in Washington, he found corruption still rampant, but he also found that something wonderful was happening: the capital city was being flooded with thousands of young men—the wounded soldiers in the hospitals—who in a sense were accomplishing the very social cleansing he had designed his poetry to do. After only three weeks in Washington he wrote Emerson of his plans to write "a little book out of this phase of America: her masculine young manhood, . . . her fair youth—brought and deposited here in this great, whited sepulchre of Washington itself (this union Capital without the first bit of cohesion—this collect of proofs how low and swift a good stock can deteriorate—) Capital to which these deputies most strange arrive from every quarter, concentrating here, well-drest, rotten, meagre, nimble, and impotent, full of gab, full always of their thrice-accursed *party*— ... while by quaint Providence come also sailed and wagoned hither this other freight of helpless worn and wounded youth, genuine of the soil, of darlings and true heirs to me of the first unquestioned and convincing western crop, prophetic of the future, proofs undeniable to all men's ken of perfect beauty, tenderness and pluck that never yet race rivalled."

The contrast here was similar to that which had motivated the early editions of *Leaves of Grass:* beneath the "scum" of politicians lay the pure waters of common humanity. But there was a difference between poetic theory and actual events. Whereas in his earlier poetry Whitman had tried to flush out the impurities of the social scene through utopian poetry that extolled the average individual, now the flushing-out process seemed to him to be happening before his eyes. Thousands of average Americans were arriving at the very heart of the "whited sepulchre" where "rotten, meagre, nimble, and impotent" politicians still congregated.

The soldiers he saw in the war hospitals, he would say later, saved him and saved America by displaying all the qualities he associated with ideal humanity. "Saved" was his own word. He used it more than once in reference to the wounded soldiers. For him, the comparison of a fallen soldier to Christ in "A Sight in Camp in the Daybreak Gray and Dim" was no mere trope. Nor was it an accident that he called Bull Run "a crucifixion day" for Lincoln, or that when a dying New York soldier asked him to read aloud a Bible passage, he chose the story of Christ on the cross. Before the war, he had fallen into a deep cynicism about American society that his hospital experiences eradicated. As he told Traubel, "There were years in my life—years there in New York—when I wondered if all was not going to the bad with America—the tendency downwards—but the war saved me: what I saw in the war set me up for all time—the days in the hospitals." He said he was thinking of "not chiefly the facts of battles, marches, what-not—but the social being-ness of the soldiers" in the hospitals.

Generosity, tact, propriety, affection, and, always, toughness in the face of extreme suffering and impending death: these were the qualities he saw among the wounded. He recognized them instantly, from his earliest hospital visits onward. He had not been in Washington a month before he wrote Emerson, "I find the masses fully justified by closest contact, never vulgar, always calm, without greediness, no flummery, no frivolity—responding electric and without fail to affection, yet no whining—not the first unmanly whimper have I yet seen or heard,—always these young men meeting their death with steady composure, and often with curious readiness——." In "Song of Myself" he had written that it was just as lucky to die as to be born; this cheerful view of death was confirmed by everything he saw in the hospitals. Occasionally an irrepressible groan or scream sounded through the wards, but Whitman was amazed at how stoical the soldiers were. "Not a bit of sentimentalism or whining have I seen about a single death-bed in hospital or on the field," he wrote, "but generally impassive indifference."

He found the soldiers extremely tough and equally tender. It has become common recently to interpret Whitman's loving relationships with the wounded soldiers as a sublimation of homosexual desires that found expression in certain war poems, such as "Vigil Strange I Kept on the Field One Night" and "A Sight in Camp in the Daybreak Gray and Dim." A fuller explanation of these relationships is that they confirmed his belief in the prevalence and sanctity of same-sex love in America. Arthur Golden and Betsy Erkkila have found that in preparing the post-war editions of *Leaves of Grass* Whitman made his theme of comradely love *more*, not *less*, explicit than it had been in 1860. He did delete certain poems, such as "[Hours Continuing Long]," which involved private anguish or feelings of unusualness; but far from trying to hide his comradely images, he actually heightened them. What has not been mentioned is that the war validated his sense that same-sex affection was, as he had once said to Emerson, a common part of public behavior in America.

Newspaper reports and popular poems and songs dwelt on evocative scenes of soldiers cut off in their youth. Often these scenes were simultaneously erotic and pious: erotic in their accounts of the soldiers' physical and emotional attractions, pious in their suggestions that they were headed for a better world. One typical newspaper anecdote involved a handsome dying soldier who tenderly kissed a male friend, had a nurse write a letter home, and died without complaint. Another portrayed a wounded soldier named John who wrote his mother and fiancée and gave a loving good-bye to his friend Ned: "They kissed each other tenderly as women, and so parted; for poor Ned could not stay to see his comrade die." Yet another told of a soldier finding religion before death and giving thanks to the chaplain, who reported, "Suddenly he threw out his arms and clasped me tightly around the neck as I stooped over him."

Commentators frequently emphasized the physical beauty of the soldiers, who were domesticated for popular consumption and often called darlings. A correspondent for the *Cincinnati Gazette* wrote: "A remarkably sweet and youthful face was that of the rebel boy. Scarce eighteen, and as fair as a maiden, with quite small hands, long hair of the pale golden hue of auburn it changes to when much in the sun, and curling at the ends." The Congressman Albert Gallatin Riddle spoke of "our broad-browed, open-eyed youths, . . . pure as the mothers who bore them, and beautiful as their sisters in their homes."

Affectionate bonding between soldiers in the field was a common theme of popular war poems. "The Fallen Soldier" depicted the loving last moment of a soldier whose comrade reported: "You think them soft lips, but they changed without moan; / For I, who rode next him, sprang forward and clasped him, / And held both his hands to the last, in my own." Another poem, "Last Words," was the soliloquy of a dying soldier who asked his comrade to send love to his wife and then begged his friend: "Come nearer, closer, Charlie; / My head I fain would rest, / It must be for the last time, / Upon your faithful breast." One of the most popular songs in the last year of the war, Henry Tucker's "Somebody's Darling," encouraged a soldier to kiss and caress his dying comrade:

> Give him a kiss, but for Somebody's sake,
> Murmur a prayer for him, soft and low,
> One little curl from its golden mates take,
> Somebody's pride they were once, you know.
>
> Somebody's warm hand has often rested there,
> Was it a mother's so soft and white?
> Or have the lips of a sister so fair,
> Ever been bathed in their waves of light?
>
> (*chorus*)   Somebody's darling,
>   Somebody's pride,
>   Who'll tell his mother
>   Where her little boy died?

The eroticized language of same-sex affection, previously seen mainly in private letters or diaries, was thus part of public life during the war. It was a war of brutal violence but also of male bonding and loving comradeship. It was normal for a soldier to assume the role of parent, sibling, or spouse for a dying comrade. Since actual family members were rarely present to witness a soldier's death, fellow soldiers or other kindly disposed people filled familial roles, even to the extent of expressing deep affection. This was a role Whitman often assumed in the hospitals. He regularly wrote families or spouses about the condition of individual soldiers, and he thought of the soldiers as part of his family. In one letter he said that "often they seem very near to me, even as my own children or younger brothers." In another he described them as "so good, so sweet, so brave, so decorous, I could not feel them nearer to me if my own sons or young brothers." Doubtless his familial feelings toward them were enhanced by the fact that several members of his own family were in the throes of physical or emotional disintegration.

When he overtly displayed affection to his soldier-comrades, the public discourse of piety and domesticity that surrounded comradely love during the war tinged his attitudes. He had in the hospitals what he later called "the revelation of an exquisite courtesy—man to man—rubbing up there together: I could say in the highest sense, *propriety—propriety*, as in the doing of necessary unnameable things, always done with exquisite delicacy." He could hug and kiss the soldiers and feel he was on firm moral ground. He felt free to describe his loving relations with them unblushingly in his letters. He wrote of a Mississippi officer that "our affection is quite an affair, quite romantic—sometimes when I lean over to say I am going, he puts his arm, &c., quite a scene for the New Bowery." Of the soldier Lewis K. Brown he wrote: "Lew is so good, so affectionate—when I came away, he reached up his face, I put my arm around him, and we gave each other a long kiss, half a minute long."

Such love fell within then-current ideas of conventional behavior. Charles E. Benton, a veteran who knew him in the hospitals, found his displays of affection ideally suited to the emotional needs of the wounded soldiers. Like many of Whitman's contemporary defenders, Benton underscored the naturalness of his hospital activities and approvingly quoted these lines from Whitman's poem "The Wound-Dresser":

> I sit by the restless all the dark night, some are so young,
> Some suffer so much, I recall the experience sweet and sad,
> (Many a soldier's loving arms about this neck have cross'd and rested,
> Many a soldier's kiss dwells on these bearded lips.)

Whitman had long sought appropriate receptacles for his homoerotic feelings, ranging from sensational dark-reform fiction to poetry that drew from contemporary definitions of same-sex love. During the war he found that this love could be fused with public service, patriotism, and religion. His confessions of love to the soldiers often sounded at once passionate and pious. He proposed to Thomas P. Sawyer that they live together after the war, but that if "anything should go wrong, so that we do not meet again, here on earth, it seems to me, (the way I feel now,) that my soul could never be happy, even in the world to come, without you, dear comrade." He often acted as a spiritual or moral adviser to the soldiers, urging them to lead clean, temperate lives. He warned Lewy

Brown that he "must not go around too much, nor eat & drink too promiscuous, but be careful & moderate." During a busy visit to the New York area, he reported to Elijah Douglass Fox that he was tired of "suppers, drinking, & what is called pleasure," and that their friendship was far more worthy "than all the dissipations & amusements of this great city."

During the war, same-sex affection came to be widely seen as pious and improving. The homoerotic poems Whitman wrote after the war retained all the intensity of his prewar poems but put behind private psychological anguish. The war's violence and an ennobled homoeroticism went hand in hand for Whitman. The inner wounds he had described in tormented "Calamus" poems like "Trickle Drops" and "[Hours Continuing Long]" were outdone by the actual wounds he saw daily in the hospitals. His private bloodletting was absorbed into the mass bloodletting occurring all around him. He would look upon *Drum-Taps* as bloodier but also calmer than his previous poetry. On the one hand, he wrote, it was filled "with the unprecedented anguish of wounded & suffering, the beautiful young men, in wholesome death & agony, everything sometimes as if in blood color, & dripping blood." On the other hand, he said that in contrast to his previous work it lacked "perturbations," his word for comradely love when it became disproportionate or overheated. Whitman need not show anguish over his love of comrades, since such love was sanctified by the war and confirmed in popular poetry and journalism.

He could now pose as the comforting, pious wound dresser embracing the heroic, helpless soldiers. In "Vigil Strange I Kept on the Field One Night" he gave his version of the sentimental battlefield death, a common theme of the day. The poem mixes wartime violence, homoeroticism, and patriotic piety, as a soldier sits up all night with a mortally wounded comrade, devoting several "immortal and mystic hours" to his "son of responding kisses" whom he says he will meet in heaven. In "A March in the Ranks Hard-Prest" he gives grisly details of the death of a young soldier whom he affectionately tends until he is called to join his marching regiment.

In these and other poems in *Drum-Taps*, private feelings are subsumed to the larger purposes of the war. Homoeroticism was just one element of his psyche that was funneled into the war cause. Another was his conception of himself as a powerful healer. He had always mistrusted medical doctors, and he had assumed almost godlike healing powers in his prewar poems. The war intensified his distaste for conventional medicine and permitted him to test out his homespun ideas about healing. The massive numbers of wounded soldiers created huge difficulties for doctors at a time when medicine was still primitive. Surgeons performing difficult operations, often with ill-cleaned and imprecise surgical tools, had to rely on liquor or chloroform as painkillers. Maggots or worms often had to be dug out of festering wounds or flushed out with a whiskey compound that felt like boiling water when poured over wounds. Calomel, a chalky drug commonly prescribed in massive doses, probably did more harm than good, since it was a mercury-based compound that carried the risk of blood poisoning and organ damage.

Although Whitman sympathized with the overworked war doctors, he recognized their limitations and believed that his own magnetic powers were as effective as all their procedures. He wrote of the wounded soldiers: "I supply often to some of these dear suffering boys in my presence & magnetism that which doctors nor medicines nor skill nor any routine assistance can give." "I can testify," he averred elsewhere, "that friendship has literally cured a fever, and the medicine of daily affection, a bad wound." The almost shamanistic faith in magnetic healing he had displayed in his prewar poems he poured into his daily visits to the hospitals.

In these visits he exercised a personalism that contrasted with the cool professionalism of the nurses associated with the United States Sanitary Commission. Founded early in the war, the Sanitary Commission was the largest philanthropic organization in American history to that date. It brought to philanthropy a militaristic discipline and efficiency that contrasted with individualistic antebellum reforms and prepared the way for the "scientific" benevolence of the postwar period. Sanitary Commission nurses were trained to be coolheaded, even coldhearted. One woman associated with the commission advised all nurses to "put away all feelings. Do all you can and be a machine—that's the way to act; the only way." Whitman detested the Sanitary Commission's clinical, distanced attitude toward the soldiers. He wrote his mother in June 1863: "As to the Sanitary commissions & the like, I am sick of them all, & would not accept any of their berths—you ought to see the way the men as they lie helpless in bed turn their faces from the sight of these Agents, Chaplains &c. (*hirelings* as Elias Hicks would call them—they seem to me always a set of foxes & wolves)—they get well paid, & are always incompetent & disagreeable."

His hatred of the Sanitary Commission reflected his individualistic, anti-institutional bias, a holdover from the fifties, when he had castigated nearly all authority figures. He showed this bias in other ways too. The hierarchy and discipline of the army struck him as undemocratic. He wrote that the army needed to be "made ready to tally with democracy, the people—The officers should almost invariably rise from the ranks—there is an absolute want of democratic spirit in the present system & officers—it is the feudal spirit entirely—nearly the entire capacity, keenness & courage of our army are in the ranks."

Nevertheless, Whitman was in important ways capitulating to the kinds of institutions he had formerly met with resistance. In the anarchistic fifties he had proclaimed, "I celebrate myself." After the war he would celebrate a more impersonal "Oneself" and would become a kind of cultural institution. His transition from the individualist with the "barbaric yawp" to the Good Gray Poet feted by followers began during the war, a time when centralized institutions strengthened dramatically.

Among the Big Bugs

WHITMAN DRESSED DIFFERENTLY from before. That was the first thing John Townsend Trowbridge noticed when he visited Whitman in Washington late in 1863. The Whitman he had known in Boston three years earlier had still been an odd dresser, with colorful open-necked shirts and rough trousers. The Washington Whitman looked far more conventional (see fig. 43, a photograph from around this time). In Trowbridge's words, he was "more trimly attired, wearing a loosely fitting but quite elegant suit of black,—yes, black at last!"

Whitman took pride in the change of dress. Several months before Trowbridge's visit, he had boasted in a letter to his mother: "I have a nice plain suit, of a dark wine color, looks very well, & feels good, single breasted sack coat with breast pockets &c. & vest & pants." With "a new necktie, nicer shirts," he added, "you can imagine I cut quite a swell." He was participating in the movement to standardized male attire that began during the war years. The fifties, as mentioned earlier, had been a decade of experimentation and idiosyncrasy in male clothing styles, which had run the gamut from the hyperelegance of Broadway dandies to the studied casualness of dress reformers. The postwar years, with the rise of huge corporations and an ever-expanding middle class, would usher in the forerunner of the modern business suit: a dark coat and pants that "erased" the body and a plain white linen shirt. Only the colorful necktie would remain as a reminder of an earlier age's flamboyance.

Changing clothing styles signified larger changes in society and culture. During the war, the federal government, which had been relatively weak in the antebellum period, took on momentous new powers. At the same time, the economic institutions of the North gained muscle and verve from the war, setting the stage for the huge corporations of the Gilded Age.

Whitman's relationship with these governmental and economic institutions changed as surely as did his clothing style. In Washington he became financially dependent on the government he had formerly criticized. Swept up in the war spirit and the Union cause, he became, at times unwittingly, a partisan of centralized institutions and wartime leaders.

During his decade in Washington, from January 1863 to late spring 1873, Whitman became part of a government machine that sometimes appalled him but that supported his writing and his hospital work. From the start, he had to scrap for a government position, and his successive clerkships in the paymaster's office, the Interior Department, and the attorney general's office followed a slow but steady upward pattern. He became tied to the kinds of government officials he had once considered the epitome of moral degradation. As early as February 1863 he wrote his brother Jeff that he had already seen the Senate Foreign Affairs chairman Charles Sumner three times. Whitman reported, "[Sumner] says that every thing here moves as part of a great machine, and that I must consign myself to the fate of the rest."

The deterministic metaphor was appropriate, for it described what happened to Whitman, as to many others, during the war. Events began to move and control him, as he became absorbed into the mechanisms of the government and the war. He confessed his passivity in the wartime poem that began "Quicksand years that whirl me I know not whither," and he described the war's ruthless determinism in "Beat! Beat! Drums!" and other poems. In seeking government office, he affiliated with some who ran the government machine. "I am getting better and better acquainted with office-hunting wisdom, and Washington peculiarities generally," he wrote Jeff soon after his arrival. Not only did he find himself in the company of the kind of politicians he had once sweepingly dismissed, but he even liked some of them. After his interview with the New York senator Preston King, he wrote, "I like fat old Preston King, very much—he is fat as a hogshead, with great hanging chops."

He still saw corruption in government, but there was a crucial change in his attitude. Whereas in the fifties he had thought that corruption tainted all levels of government, including the executive branch, during the war he found subordinate officials often corrupt but higher ones, especially President Lincoln, basically sound and fully justified in their pursuit of the war. When in March 1863 he described to his mother the Union government's cruelty to Southern prisoners, he emphasized that it was the lower, not the higher, officials who were culpable. He wrote: "[I]t is not the fault of the President—he would not harm any human being—nor of [Secretary of State William Henry] Seward or [Secretary of War Edwin McMasters] Stanton" but rather of "the heartless mean-souled brutes that get in positions subordinate but where they can show themselves, and their damned airs and pomposity.... Meanwhile the great officers of the government have every minute occupied with pressing business, and these wretches have full swing." He made a similar point in a letter the same month to a New York friend, decrying the Congress but giving full support to the president. In Congress, he said, there was "much gab, great fear of public opinion, plenty of low business talent, but no masterful man," whereas "I think well of the President," and "I do not dwell on any of the supposed failures of his government."

His support of the higher levels of the Lincoln administration signaled a significant change in attitude from the antebellum years. Before the war he had not only been sour about the executive office but had failed to support Lincoln wholeheartedly. He had become an instantaneous Lincoln convert when he had witnessed the president-elect's masterful handling of the unfriendly Manhattan crowd in February 1861, and his support for Lincoln steadily intensified after that.

In supporting the Lincoln administration, even when he heard others criticize it, he was willingly giving himself over to the kind of firm, authoritarian government apparatus he had once held suspect. Early in the war, the president was widely regarded as "the unpopular Mr. Lincoln." As Whitman noted, "For two or three years he was generally regarded darkly, scornfully, suspiciously in Washington, throughout the North." A common complaint was that he was a tyrant who took the law into his own hands. Under the exigencies of war, Lincoln took several swift actions unprecedented in their decisiveness. He increased the size of the Union army without congressional approval. He promoted and signed into law the first federal income tax in American history. Under him the nation's first military drafts were enacted; first came the conscription law of August 1862 and then the Enrollment Act the next spring. Dramatically (and notoriously) he suspended the writ of habeas corpus in order to facilitate the arrest of persons suspected of disloyalty to the Union. The cancellation of the writ, proclaimed publicly in April 1861, led to the imprisonment of at least ten thousand suspected Copperheads, Northerners who supported the South. Although Lincoln was a latecomer to the idea of emancipation of the slaves, after the summer of 1862 he strongly supported the idea, and he wrote the Emancipation Proclamation, which was issued on January 1, 1863.

The common denominator of all these decisive actions was Lincoln's unwavering commitment to the war for the preservation of the Union. What his opponents saw as his tyrannical nature was nowhere more visible to them than in the simple fact of this overweening commitment. One Copperhead, Thomas Low Nichols, typically pointed up the seeming monomania of Lincoln's stance. "War for the Union!" Nichols wrote in sneering mockery. "Fraternity or death! Be my brother, or I will kill you! Unite with me, or I will exterminate you!" Because of his decisiveness, Lincoln was labeled by his opponents a "despot," as in the Illinois Democrat Andrew D. Duff's address titled "Footprints of Despotism, or the Analogy Between Lincoln and Other Tyrants."

Whitman supported Lincoln even at times when the cries of despotism were the loudest, as in early 1863, which brought the Emancipation Proclamation and the Enrollment Act, both widely unpopular measures. Whitman ardently praised Lincoln's draft law. In March he wrote Jeff that he hoped the government would "enroll *every man* in the land—I would like to see the people embodied *en masse.*" Although he didn't comment directly on Lincoln's most questionable act—the suspension of habeas corpus—he seems to have supported it, for he fiercely denounced Copperheads and gleefully recounted cases of their imprisonment or expulsion from Congress. He believed, as he put it, that "a rebel in the southern army is much more respectable than a northern copperhead." When in April 1864 the Copperhead Alexander Long was expelled from Congress, Whitman exulted: [T]hese are exciting times in Congress— the Copperheads are getting furious, & want to recognize the Southern Confederacy—this is a pretty time to talk of recognizing such villains, and after what has transpired the last three years."

In supporting Lincoln and the war cause while excoriating Copperheads, Whitman was turning from the nostalgic agrarianism of his prewar years and allying himself with the industrial, technological forces of Northern society. Copperheads were, in the main, backward-looking Democrats who wanted the war to cease so that the South's preindustrial agrarian society could be preserved. Whitman himself had shown such nostalgic longing for Southern culture in his 1860 poems "O Magnet-South!" and "A Song of Joys." The war exposed the illusoriness of this idealization of Southern life. The North's industrial economy thrived during the war, while the South's plantation-based one suffered. Inflation rates, held to a reasonable wartime rate of 80 percent in the North, soared to 9,000 percent in the South, as a billion and a half Confederate paper dollars came to have little value. At the start of the war the North had more than 88 percent of the nation's industrial capacity and more than two-thirds of its railroad density, and the wartime boom paved the way for the massive corporations and industries that came later. Two of Whitman's most famous postwar poems, "Passage to India" and "Song of the Exposition," would sing of the industrial and technological advances sped by the war.

A more basic aspect of his attraction to Lincoln and the war was the idea of Union. Whitman rarely used the phrase "the Civil War." Instead, he referred to "the Secession War" or "the Union War"—sometimes both in the same breath, as in his Lincoln speech where he checked himself: "The Secession War? Nay, let me call it the Union War." As was true with Lincoln early in the war, Whitman was fixated on the idea of the Union. Having long hated fire-eaters and abolitionists because they threatened to destroy the Union, Whitman was delighted when the war brought things to a head. "By that war," he wrote unequivocally, "*exit* Fire-Eaters, *exit* Abolitionists." The South's great sin, in his eyes, was secession; the North's greatest virtue was devotion to the Union. Lincoln, weaned in the Henry Clay school of nationality, epitomized this virtue above all for Whitman. In his oft-repeated Lincoln lecture, given from 1879 onward, Whitman said of Lincoln that "UNIONISM, in its truest and amplest sense, formed the hardpan of his character."

Lincoln's firm direction of the Union war cause was only part of what Whitman had in mind, but it was an important part. After the vacillations of the fifties, Whitman discovered in the Union cause something solid to believe in, something that seemed to him as fixed as fate. "To thee old cause!" Even in the darkest moments of the war, the cause kept him going. He was sorry in early 1863 when things looked bleak for the North, but he wrote, "I believe this Union will conquer in the end, as sure as there's a God in the heaven. This country can't be broken up by Jeff Davis, & all his damned crew." When his friend Lewis Brown was discouraged by bad war news, Whitman reassured him, "Lew, the *Union* & the *American Flag* must conquer, it is destiny—it may be long, it may be short, but that will be the result." The war cause made patriotism popular throughout the North. Flags flapped everywhere on city streets, and women proudly wore red-white-and-blue pins. Whitman caught the patriotic fever. He wrote his mother that after one was exposed to the sights of war, "the flag, the tune of Yankee Doodle, & similar things, produce an effect on a fellow never such before." The horrors of war sometimes overwhelmed him, but the cause remained for him an inexorable force. He admitted to his mother in July 1863 that "every once in a while I feel so horrified & disgusted—[the war] seems to me like a great slaughter-house & the men mutually butchering each other"; but he added, "then I feel how impossible it appears again, to retire from this contest, until we have carried our points."

Many things kept alive his belief in the Union and the war, including Lincoln's choice of generals. The tactical blunders of a Burnside or a McClellan were more than made up for, in his view, by the successes of Sherman and Grant, his favorite commanders. There was something Lincolnesque, on a minor scale, about the two. Both had rough-hewn characteristics: Sherman his rumpled blue uniform, his volcanic temperament, his constant curse words; Grant his scruffy appearance, his penchant for cigars and liquor. Still, Whitman saw the differences between them and admired them both. Sherman, who indulged in military show more than Grant, had, Whitman said, "something of grandeur, hauteur, haughtiness," as when he rode silent and stately in a military review Whitman saw in 1865. Grant, said Whitman, was "quite another man," one who "liked to defy convention by going a simple way, his own." "The real military figure of the war, counting the man in," he concluded, "was Grant, whose homely manners, dislike for military frippery—for every form of ostentation, in war and peace—amounted to genius."

What joined Sherman and Grant was their commitment to total, unrelenting war in the interests of the Union. In the last year of the war Whitman cheered in his letters as Grant moved steadily southward. In the dark spring of 1864 he wrote: "Others may say what they like, I believe in Grant & in Lincoln too—I think Grant deserves to be trusted, he is working continuously." When Grant began to flank Lee in May, Whitman noted, "Grant has taken the reins entirely in his own hands— he is really dictator at present."

The dictator reference is telling. Whitman found in Lincoln and his generals the kind of authoritarianism in the name of Union he had formerly designed his poetic persona to have. He dwelt on the decisive, commanding attributes of the North's war leaders, often ignoring their flaws in the process. In his mind, Grant was the steel-spined, common-man leader, not the heartless military butcher or, later, the incompetent president. Sherman was, in his words, "like a Norman baron, lord of many acres—with adherents, servitors," not the moody, nervous man who hated the sight of blood and who was afflicted by depression and alcoholism. Another Union general, Phil Sheridan, Whitman called "the Napoleonic figure of the war," forgetting that Sheridan's western campaigns against the Plains Indians were tainted by brutality and racism.

He overlooked these men's shortcomings because they served the Union and the most commanding figure of all, Lincoln. When Whitman said that Lincoln embodied "UNIONISM, in its truest and amplest sense," he was thinking not only of the war cause but of many other things besides.

My Captain

IN LIGHT OF the almost mythic stature Whitman assigned to Lincoln, it is perhaps fitting that the relationship between the poet and the president was long the stuff of myth. In *Personal Reflections of Abraham Lincoln* (1916) Henry B. Rankin told of an incident in 1857 when Lincoln in his Springfield law office picked up a copy of *Leaves of Grass,* began reading it to himself, and was so entranced after half an hour that he started over again, reading it aloud to his colleagues. Another anecdote, originally contained in an 1865 letter by a Lincoln aide and repeated by Whitman's followers, had Lincoln gazing out a White House window, spotting the hale, bearded Whitman walking by, and exclaiming, "Well, *he* looks like a *man.*"

There is no way of confirming either of these stories; probably both are apocryphal. Lincoln's reaction to Whitman or his poetry, if any, is unclear. But the kinship of spirits these stories suggest was very real, if we judge from Whitman's reaction to Lincoln. In Lincoln's life, Whitman saw the comprehensive, all-directing soul he had long been seeking. In Lincoln's death, he saw a grand tragedy that promised ultimate purgation and unification for America.

Whitman and Lincoln had much in common. Both rose to greatness from humble backgrounds, and both were largely self-taught. The cultural tastes of both ran the gamut from high to low. Like Whitman, Lincoln loved to recite Shakespeare and to hear grand arias but also had a weakness for minstrel shows and the songs of Stephen Foster. Whitman's favorite singing group, the Hutchinsons, helped elect Lincoln in 1860 by singing at Republican rallies, and during the war they entertained the Union troops. Both the president and the poet took delight in plays, even cheap melodramas and farces. There were temperamental similarities too: both were generally calm men given on occasion to explosions—of anger in Whitman's case, of laughter in Lincoln's. Both delighted in low humor and slang. Both had an amused curiosity about spiritualism: Whitman attended séances given by the medium Charles H. Foster in the sixties, and Lincoln attended séances in the White House ordered by his wife, Mary, after the death of their son Willie in 1862. Two of Whitman's favorite orators, Cassius Clay and John Hale, became part of Lincoln's administration, the former as minister to Russia, the latter as minister to Spain. Most importantly, both Whitman and Lincoln tried to cure America's problems through oratorical language. Whitman's quintessential work, *Leaves of Grass,* was a sprawling poetry collection that brought together cultural images in their variety and particularity. Lincoln's, the Gettysburg Address, was a terse, 262-word speech that soared beyond particulars into a transcendental realm of political abstractions. Both were written in the name of union, equality, and cultural retrieval.

Whitman saw Lincoln some twenty to thirty times in Washington. This was not unusual. Unlike today, when presidents are virtually inaccessible to average citizens except as images in the mass media, in those days they were available and visible in ordinary life. Even Lincoln, who had to be on guard because of death threats and the war situation, could be met personally by almost anyone, in the White House or at the Soldier's Home, his summer retreat three miles north of the city. Whitman didn't meet him, but he regularly saw him riding through Washington for business or pleasure. "I see the President almost every day," he wrote in the summer of 1863, when he lived near where Lincoln passed by en route to and from the White House. Lincoln appeared to him ordinary but impressive, riding comfortably on an easygoing gray horse or in an open barouche, escorted by twenty or so cavalry in yellow-striped jackets with sabers poised on their shoulders. Some afternoons he caught sight of the president and his wife, both in black, riding in their plain two-horse carriage on unescorted pleasure jaunts. "We have got so that we exchange bows, and very cordial ones," Whitman wrote of Lincoln, who once gave him a long, direct stare that Whitman felt was friendly but inexpressibly sad. "He has a face like a hoosier Michel Angelo," Whitman wrote, "so awful ugly it becomes beautiful, with its strange mouth, its deep cut, criss-cross lines, and its doughnut complexion" (see fig. 17). Whitman continued to spot Lincoln, as in March 1864 when the war-weary president, his sallow face creased with deep wrinkles, rattled by in his carriage after enduring the tedious ceremonies of the Second Inaugural.

No other human being seemed as multifaceted to Whitman as Lincoln. There was hardly a quality he did not attribute to the president. Lincoln, he said, had "canny shrewdness" and "*horse-sense*," as seen in the down-home stories he told to drive home his points. He seemed the average American, with his drab appearance and his humor, redolent of barnyards and barrooms. Whitman commented on the "somewhat rusty and dusty" appearance of Lincoln, who "looks about as ordinary in attire, etc., as the commonest man." He delighted in the ascendancy to power of one he called the embodiment of "the commonest average of life—a rail-splitter and a flat-boatsman!" He pointed to Lincoln's rural origins, which he thought made him totally American. His other cultural heroes paled in comparison. In contrast, Washington seemed "the first Saxon" and Franklin "an English nobleman," while Lincoln was "quite thoroughly Western," of the prairies and the outdoors.

Lincoln's homely, mysterious face, he thought, had never been captured by photographers or artists—indeed, could not be, since it was as ineffable as life itself. Funny and folksy, Lincoln nonetheless appeared basically sad; there was, Whitman wrote, "a deep latent sadness in the expression." He was both easygoing and tough: "generally very easy, flexible, tolerant, almost slouchy, respecting the minor matters" but capable of "indomitable firmness (even obstinacy) on rare occasions, involving great points," as when commanding his generals to win certain battles by any means. Lincoln was a family man—Whitman sometimes saw him with his wife or one of his children—but had an air of complete independence. "[H]e went his own lonely road," Whitman said, "disregarding all the usual ways—refusing the guides, accepting no warnings—just keeping his appointment with himself every time." He had tact and caution, Whitman emphasized, and his "composure was marvellous" in the face of unpopularity and the difficulties of war. Though grounded in everyday realities, he had what Whitman saw as a profoundly religious quality. His "invisible foundations" were "mystical, abstract, moral, and spiritual," his "religious nature" was "of the amplest, deepest-rooted, loftiest kind." Summing Lincoln up, Whitman called him "the greatest, best, most characteristic, artistic, moral personality" in American life.

In short, Lincoln, as Whitman saw him, was virtually the living embodiment of the "I" of *Leaves of Grass*. He was "one of the roughs" but also, for Whitman, "a kosmos," with the whole range of qualities that term implied. If *Leaves of Grass* and the Civil War were one, they particularly came together in Lincoln.

As impressive as Lincoln was in life, it was his death that represented for Whitman the transcendent, crucial moment in America's cultural life. John Wilkes Booth's murder of Lincoln in Washington's Ford Theatre on April 14, 1865, was for Whitman a culminating moment in history. There was good reason Whitman would give his "Death of Abraham Lincoln" speech over and over again in the last dozen years of his life. He became fixated on what he called "the tragic splendor of [Lincoln's] death, purging, illuminating all." The assassination, he declared, had unequaled influence on the shaping of the Republic.

Although Whitman was not in Washington at the time of the event, he had a vicarious presence at it. His close friend Peter Doyle was in Ford's Theatre the night of the assassination and gave him an intimate rendition of the tragedy. There were other associations too. John Wilkes Booth, the son of Whitman's favorite actor, Junius Brutus Booth, was a kind of inverse embodiment of many things Whitman had long held dear. A dashing actor with a large following, especially among starstruck women, Booth developed a melodramatic acting style that brought the emotional American style to a point of near frenzy. Whitman had seen Booth perform and thought he had moments of genius but lacked his father's subtlety. (He differed from Lincoln, who liked Booth's frenetic acting so much that he invited him to the White House; Booth did not accept the invitation.) A cocky man, Booth used as an advertising motto a line from Whitman's favorite play, *Richard III*—"I AM MYSELF ALONE"—which had all the assertiveness and independence of Whitman's poetic boasts.

But in Booth, independence was fused with a Southern states'-rights viewpoint. The Maryland-bred Booth considered the Union an imposture, Lincoln a grasping tyrant, and slavery a positive good. He was an ardent white supremacist who believed in the inferiority of blacks. By a cruel irony Whitman was probably unaware of, Booth was secretly engaged to Lucy Hale, the daughter of Whitman's favorite political speaker, John Hale. Booth had dined with Lucy the evening of the murder, and after she heard of Booth's deed she remained loyal to him, saying she would die with him even at the foot of a scaffold.

These associations between Whitman and Booth, some explicit and some buried, made the events of Good Friday, 1865, especially poignant to the poet. But it was the cultural meanings of the assassination that he stressed in his many retellings of the event. If he saw Lincoln's death as "purging, illuminating all," it was largely because many of the social phenomena underlying his own poetry came to a spectacular culmination in that one moment. Many of America's social problems were reenacted and resolved, he believed, and many of its possibilities were guided toward fruition.

Among the social problems, the political crisis of the 1850s, as always, loomed largest in Whitman's mind. He began his Lincoln lecture by reviewing the difficult social conditions during the decade before his election. "The hot passions of the South," Whitman recalled, "—the strange mixture at the North of inertia, incredulity, and conscious power—the incendiarism of the abolitionists—the rascality and *grip* of the politicians, unparallel'd in any land, any age," with "the Presidentiads of Fillmore and Buchanan" proving "the weakness and wickedness of elected rulers." These were the social and political problems *Leaves of Grass* had been designed to correct, but Whitman believed that only the death of the Redeemer President truly resolved them. In Lincoln's murder, he declared, "A long and varied series of contradictory events arrives at last at its highest, poetic, single, central, pictorial denouement. The whole involved, baffling, multiform whirl of the secession period comes to a head, and is gather'd in one brief flash of lightning-illumination— one simple, fierce, deed."

Far more than politics were involved, as Whitman told the story. Sensational news reportage, popular celebrations, acting and theater, music, audience involvement, mob violence—nearly all the cultural influences on *Leaves of Grass* were played out, in his retelling, the day of the murder. It had been a pleasant spring day in Washington. The city was in a festive mood in the aftermath of the Union's victory over the South. That afternoon, Whitman recalled, the popular Washington daily the *Evening Star* "had spatter'd all over its third page, divided among the advertisements in a sensational manner, in a hundred different places, *The President and his Lady will be at the Theatre this evening.*" The whole event, then, was surrounded by the hype and sensationalism typical of nineteenth-century America. Also typical was the scene that evening at Ford's Theatre, with the usual noisy crowds, "the usual cluster of gas-lights, the usual magnetism of so many people, cheerful, with perfumes, music of violins and flutes," everyone joyful about "the triumph of the Union." This was Washington by gaslight, an urban spectacle of the sort described at length by many antebellum journalists, including Whitman. Also typically, the president had come to see a farce, Tom Taylor's *Our American Cousin,* about an American bumpkin who becomes heir to an English fortune. In the midst of this absurd play, Whitman said, occurred "the main thing, the actual murder" of "the leading actor in the stormiest drama known to real history's stage." A muffled shot rang out, a man leaped from the railing of the president's box, catching his heel on a draped flag and falling twelve feet to the stage, snapping a leg in the process. Then the raven-haired Booth, "his eyes like some mad animal's flashing with light and resolution, yet with a certain strange calmness," faced the crowd and firmly cried, "Sic semper tyrannis" ("Thus it shall always be for tyrants"). He walked offstage, and then bedlam broke loose. Mrs. Lincoln wailed loudly, and the crowd surged forward, splintering chairs and flooding chaotically onto the stage amid the terrified actors, as in "some horrid carnival." The president's guard finally cleared away the crowds. Outside the theater, frenzied mobs came close to murdering several innocent people, including a man who barely escaped lynching, when policemen intervened.

These were the details Whitman loved to dwell on. The entire scene, he said, was a "sharp culmination, and as it were the solution, of so many bloody and angry problems." "Fit radiation—fit close!" he exclaimed. "How the imagination—how the student loves these things!"

Whitman loved to meditate on the event because so many personal and cultural threads were tied up in it. His retelling of it in his Lincoln lectures was really an imaginative reshaping, for many of the details he mentioned had, at best, only a tangential relation to the murder. But because the fifties crisis, sensationalism, crowd participation at theaters, acting style, oratory, and mob violence had fascinated Whitman and had undergirded *Leaves of Grass,* he included them in his story. He stretched the truth a bit. He didn't mention, for instance, that the Ford's Theatre shooting was a kind of afterthought for Booth, whose original plan to kidnap Lincoln and throw the country into open revolution had been foiled. But it was important to Whitman that the assassination was a theatrical event whose protagonists and setting all related to the theater, for theater and crowds had been important parts of his own shaping. This was for him the ultimate violent American melodrama whose villain was a caricature of bad acting, whose victim was the hero of the nation's greatest drama, and whose effect was audience frenzy on a massive scale. For Whitman, the theatrical trappings, like every other aspect of the event, had an inevitability. "Had not all this terrible scene— ... had it not all been rehears'd, in blank, by Booth, beforehand?"

Many violent, contradictory cultural elements Whitman had tried to harness and redirect in *Leaves of Grass* found their outlet in the tragic event that he would always believe offered a model for social unification. In Lincoln's death, he declared, "there is a cement to the whole people, subtler, more underlying, than any thing in written constitution, or courts or armies." The reminiscence of Lincoln's death, he noted, "belongs to these States in their entirety—not the North only, but the South—perhaps belongs most tenderly and devotedly to the South." Lincoln had been born in Kentucky, so that Whitman called him "a Southern contribution," and he had shown kindness to the South during the war—Whitman noted, for instance, that he avoided the word "enemy" in his speeches. Several of his generals, including Sherman and Grant, had ties to the South. In death Lincoln became the Martyr Chief, admired by many of his former foes.

Others at the time were also aware of the unifying effect of Lincoln's death. In a sermon nine days after the assassination, Henry Ward Beecher said, "[N]o monument will ever equal the universal, spontaneous, and sublime sorrow that in a moment swept down the lines and parties, and covered up animosities, and in an hour brought a divided people into unity of grief and indivisible fellowship of anguish."

In life and death Lincoln had, in Whitman's view, accomplished the cleansing and unifying mission he had designed for *Leaves of Grass.* It is not surprising that Whitman's writings changed dramatically after the war. Never again would he write all-encompassing poems like "Song of Myself" or "The Sleepers," for he believed that all cultural materials had been encompassed by Lincoln and the war. Although fresh social problems after the war would impel him to insist continually on the poet's vital social role, never again would he himself produce poems reflecting this mission in a large-scale way. His poetic output decreased, and he left it to other "bards" to resolve the problems he saw.

Since many of his poetic voices were effectively silenced after the war, it is fitting that he often used images of silence to describe reactions to Lincoln's death. He was home in Brooklyn on a two-week break from his Interior Department job when news of the assassination came. His mother served the breakfast she had prepared, but nothing was eaten, and "not a word was spoken all day." He later learned of a similar anecdote of silencing that he would incorporate into *Specimen Days*. Sherman's troops, returning from their victorious Georgia campaign, had been bellowing jubilantly during their homeward march until they heard of Lincoln's death, after which they were glumly silent for a week. "Hush'd Be the Camps To-day," one of Whitman's four poems on Lincoln, pictured the contemplative silence of grief-stricken soldiers.

In Whitman's best-known Lincoln poems, "O Captain! My Captain!" and "When Lilacs Last in the Dooryard Bloom'd," the silencing of his former poetic self is particularly noticeable. At first glance these poems seem to have little in common. "O Captain!" is a catchy, melodramatic poem, in conventional rhyme and meter, in which Lincoln is pictured as the fallen captain of the ship he has guided through the national storm. "Lilacs" is a free-flowing poem in which three images—the western star (Lincoln), the singing thrush (the poet), and the lilac (his poem offered in eulogy)—interweave with meditations on death and the war.

Despite their differences in style and tone, both poems signaled the passing of Whitman's poetry as it once was. Lincoln, as "My Captain" and the eternal western star, is the reified, autocratic self that Whitman's poetic "I" once embodied but was transferred to America's Martyr Chief, now the nation's main unifying symbol. Both poems concentrate on Lincoln and marginalize Whitman, presaging the poet's obsession with Lincoln in his later years. In "O Captain!" this fixation is visible in the image of the "I" staring relentlessly at Lincoln's bloody, pale corpse on the ship's deck amid celebrations heralding the ship's return to port. In "Lilacs," the poet calls himself "me powerless—O helpless soul of me" and marginalizes himself through the symbol of the "shy and hidden bird" singing of death with a "bleeding throat." No longer does Whitman's brash "I" present himself as the Answerer or arouse readers with a "barbaric yawp." In the war and in Lincoln, many of the nation's most pressing problems had reached painful resolution, changing the poet's role from that of America's imaginary leader to that of eulogist of its actual leader.

Of the two poems, "Lilacs" resonates most powerfully with autobiographical voices, even as it reenacts the nation's central tragedy. A month before the assassination, on a March evening in Washington, Whitman had been struck by the singular beauty of Venus sinking on the western horizon. The lilacs that year bloomed early due to an unusually warm spring. The hermit thrush also had real-life reference, for it was a common bird on Whitman's native Long Island; Whitman learned much about the bird from his naturalist friend John Burroughs.

These kinds of topical or autobiographical images had always been common in Whitman's verse, but here they were subsumed to the eulogy of Lincoln, whose death provided a fixation point for the poet and the nation at large. Whitman announces in the third line that he "shall mourn with ever-returning spring"—an accurate prediction, for many years later he would say that every spring brought Lincoln alive in his mind. Describing the nation's fixation on the fallen chief, he gives a long poetic version of Lincoln's funeral train. The image was appropriate, for the funeral train was a public phenomenon unprecedented in American history. Lincoln's coffin was carried in a black-draped train of nine cars on a 1,662-mile journey from Washington to Springfield, passing through many American cities, including Baltimore, Philadelphia, New York, Albany, Cleveland, Indianapolis, and Chicago. It was viewed by more than seven million Americans as it wended slowly on its circuitous route; four and a half million more saw Lincoln's body when it lay in state in Springfield.

Whitman converted the mass witnessing of Lincoln's funeral train into an all-absorbing ritual, as momentous and eternal as nature itself:

Coffin that passes through lanes and streets,
Through day and night with the great cloud darkening the land,
With the pomp of the inloop'd flags with the cities draped in black,
With the show of the States themselves as of crape-veil'd women
    standing,
With processions long and winding and the flambeaus of the night,
With the countless torches lit, with the silent sea of faces and the
    unbared heads,
With the waiting depot, the arriving coffin, and the sombre faces,
    [. . .]
With the tolling bells' perpetual clang,

Here, coffin that slowly passes,
I give you my sprig of lilac.

The American masses, crisply drawn and individualized in Whitman's earlier poems, are here an undifferentiated "sea of faces" and "unbared heads," all turned silently toward Lincoln's funeral train. Whitman's poetry, once savage and omnivorous, is now a frail sprig of lilac thrown onto a president's coffin. Self-assertive individuality is transformed into self-effacing grief. The poem has an abstract, generalizing quality; even Lincoln is not named or described. The death of hundreds of thousands of Americans in the war and the murder of the nation's leader impel Whitman to contemplate death generally. "Not for you, for one alone," he writes, "Blossoms and branches green to coffins all I bring." He especially has in mind the war dead: "I saw battle-corpses, myriads of them, / And the white skeletons of young men, I saw them, / I saw the debris and debris of all the slain soldiers of the war."

In his prewar poems, thoughts of death had inspired some negative lines, as in "Out of the Cradle Endlessly Rocking," in which the sad bird's song makes the listener wonder whether life is only "chaos." Now, death and nature, while still mysterious, have clearer referents than before, for the war has clarified them. There is a simplicity and transparency about the poem's three central symbols, as though the war and its tragic climax have brought things into focus. "I understand you," he writes of the thrush, and of the western star. "Now I know what you must have meant as a month since I walk'd." Death and nature become unambiguous in light of those who have sacrificed themselves for the ideal of union. Death no longer threatens to make life seem "a suck and a sell," as it did in "Song of Myself." It has become, in the words of the thrush's song, *"lovely and soothing death,"* a *"strong deliveress"* to be glorified above all else. The death of the soldiers and of Lincoln are to remain personal and cultural reference points, as perennial as nature's rhythms. Whitman ends by reaffirming Lincoln's centrality and by bringing together the three symbols in a proclamation of unity. He sings

For the sweetest, wisest soul of all my days and lands—and this for
his dear sake,
Lilac and star and bird twined with the chant of my soul,
There in the fragrant pines and the cedars dusk and dim.

The unity that "Lilacs" affirmed is baldly stated in Whitman's fourth Lincoln poem, a simple statement of just four lines:

This dust was once the man,
Gentle, plain, just and resolute, under whose cautious hand,
Against the foulest crime in history known in any land or age,
Was saved the Union of these States.

Salvation of "the Union of these States" by a plain person of varied qualities: this had been Whitman's original poetic goal, and it had been successfully accomplished by Lincoln.

Or had it been? Although Lincoln and the war would always be transcendent ideals for Whitman, he had to face the fact that the ideals were not matched by the realities of postbellum America. To the contrary, industrialization and the growth of centralized power structures brought new challenges for the poet intent on social salvation.

14

RECONSTRUCTING A NATION, RECONSTRUCTING A POET: POSTBELLUM INSTITUTIONS

THE VICTORY PARADE of the Armies of the East and West, which took place in Washington on May 22 and 23, 1865, was a peak experience for Whitman. Brilliant sunshine flooded the capital city as regiment after regiment of Union soldiers made a ritualistic, triumphant march before tens of thousands of cheering citizens who lined the wide avenues. The jubilation was fanned by news of the recent surrender of the last remaining Confederate troops in Texas. Whitman stood amid milling crowds near a reviewing stand where President Andrew Johnson sat, flanked by military and government leaders. Public buildings were still draped in black in eulogy of Lincoln, but for the first time since the assassination the city's flags were at full mast.

The parade, Whitman wrote his mother, was almost "too much & too impressive to be described." He told her of the ranks and ranks of war-torn soldiers, twenty or twenty-five abreast, moving steadily up Pennsylvania Avenue along Treasury Hill, around the White House and then out to Georgetown. It was for him a gleaming moment of social unity. Among the proud soldiers he saw battalions of blacks, carrying shovels and pickaxes, and Irish regiments merrily playing fifes. Among the generals, he took note of Grant, cantering slowly with his hat raised to the crowds, and Sherman, riding with quiet hauteur through the tumult.

The nation seemed emotionally joined in this transitional moment between war and peace. Grief over Lincoln's death was near-universal, and hopes for his successor were high. Whitman looked admiringly at President Johnson, whose huge brow, firm mouth, and well-built body gave him a look of plebeian toughness (see fig. 18). "I saw the president several times," Whitman reported to his mother, "stood close by him, &

took a good look at him—& like his expression much—he is very plain & substantial—it seems wonderful that just that plain middling-sized man, dressed in black, without the least badge or ornament, should be the master of all these myriads of soldiers, the best that ever trod the earth, with forty or fifty Major-Generals, around him or riding by, with their broad yellow-satin belts around their waists."

Whitman momentarily seemed to think Johnson was another Lincoln: a common-man president equipped to guide the nation through a difficult period. Time would challenge this belief. Johnson, lacking Lincoln's tact and flexibility, would rapidly come into conflict with Congress over key questions regarding the reconstruction of the nation. Should the South be treated leniently or harshly? What was to be done about the crucial issues pertaining to African-Americans? To what extent should states' rights, associated mainly with the Southern cause, be harnessed by the federal power represented by the victorious North?

Whitman had long been pondering similar questions and had written some of his major poetry in response to them. But his war experiences had changed him. Before the war he had been a poet driven by an impulse to rescue society: in his words, to supply what wanted supplying, to check what wanted checking. Into the vacuum created by the antebellum social and political crisis had rushed his gargantuan poetic "I," assimilating virtually every aspect of American culture in an effort to create a poetic model of democratic togetherness. The war had been for him a time of purgation and realization of many of the ideals he had offered in his early poetry. For the rest of his life, the war would remain for him a retrospective touchstone. It was, he wrote, "the Verteber of Poetry and Art, (of personal character too,) for all future America."

He would find, however, that the ideal nation made possible by the war was not mirrored by the reality of postbellum America. Neither the war nor his poetry had purified the political atmosphere. The Tweed Ring, the Crédit Mobilier, and other sordid operations, leading to the notorious corruption of Grant's administration, made Whitman believe, on some level, that America's problems were more dire than ever.

But he was more confident than before that these problems would disappear with time. He regained faith in the democratic political process, in part because the postwar administrations were directed by war leaders he instinctively venerated. He was able to overlook the foibles of Johnson and Grant because the former had been a staunch Unionist and the latter the North's greatest general. Also, Whitman got philosophical consolation from an intensified belief in Hegelianism and progressive evolution. With his poetic "I" no longer able to absorb and recycle massive amounts of cultural material, he looked to outside systems such as

Hegelian philosophy to resolve problems he had formerly tried to resolve in his poetry.

Although he believed more ardently than ever that America would be ultimately redeemed only through poetry, most of the poems he wrote after the war were brief vignettes or thoughts, as though his imagination had surrendered its all-encompassing posture on behalf of writing for the occasion. Several of his late poems actually celebrated the kinds of establishment people and things he had formerly regarded with defiant scorn. His change from rebellious individualist to Good Gray Poet was played out against the background of the rise of corporate capitalism and institutional organizations. Before the war, his temperament and poetry had reflected a free-flowing culture with few centralized institutions. After the war, such institutions confronted him, and much of his later life was defined by them. He faced a new repressiveness in sexual matters, evidenced in his being fired by the Interior Department in 1865 and later by the government-authorized Comstockery that lay behind the banning of the 1881 edition of *Leaves of Grass*. Although designed to suppress Whitman, these institutional actions actually aided his cause by arousing the loyalty of his followers and increasing his visibility. Ironically, the institutions aimed against him helped make him a cultural institution.

Although Whitman never surrendered his rebelliousness, he began to make dramatic accommodations to popular taste and established authority. His oft-repeated complaint that he was a persecuted, neglected poet was more a measure of his ambitions for popular acceptance than a reflection of fact. Not only did he continually reshape and repackage his oeuvre, but he went about the salesmanship of his writings and his image with new, businesslike fervor.

And he was very far from being neglected. According to my computation, of the 194 poems he wrote between 1867 and his death in 1892, a full 115 appeared in magazines or newspapers. Several enjoyed multiple reprintings. This 60 percent publication rate would please any writer, in his day or ours, especially since Whitman was also publishing a steady stream of prose essays in popular periodicals. His poetry increasingly appeared in popular anthologies, and there were four collections of his poems edited by others.

All along, Whitman, though beset by physical difficulties and troubled personal relationships, managed his career with the adroitness of a Gilded Age entrepreneur.

The Whitman Myth

IN THE LATE SIXTIES Whitman looked out on a cultural landscape in many ways different from the one he had surveyed a decade earlier. Among the losers of the war were the values of individualism, state autonomy, and local power. Among the winners were federalism, centralized control, technology, and industrialism. Not only did the powers of the federal government expand during the war, but several laws passed under Lincoln—particularly the National Banking Act and the chartering of the Union Pacific and Central Pacific Railroads—gave huge boosts to business. The Union's victory over the Confederacy set the stage for the passage of other laws that favored national and corporate power. The three amendments to the Constitution ratified between 1865 and 1869 strengthened the central government and, in the case of the Fourteenth Amendment, sped the rise of corporate capitalism. In his 1871 poem "Song of the Exposition" Whitman pictured postbellum America "With Victory on thy left, and at thy right hand Law; / The Union holding all, fusing, absorbing, tolerating all."

The spirit of centralization and organization affected many areas of American cultural life. Individualism, which in the fifties had fostered various forms of anarchism and bohemianism, later became largely coopted by capitalism in the popular apotheosis of the self-made man and the entrepreneur. Zany antebellum fads like Harmonialism and mesmerism were supplanted by more institutionalized mind-cure movements, ranging from Christian Science, with its highly structured church organization, to theosophy, New Thought, and Unity, all closely allied with consumerism. Urban conditions, though still grubby and chaotic, were being effectively dealt with by organizational entities such as New York's Metropolitan Board of Health, which in 1866 posted a momentous victory over cholera through improved sanitation, and the park movement, which established rural enclaves in many cities. Environmental regulation was also a priority of the powerful American Social Science Association, which stressed institutional change of the physical conditions of American life. Even radical reform was touched by the institutional spirit. American feminists, for instance, replaced the rather loose organizations of the antebellum period with the highly organized National Woman Suffrage Association and the competing American Woman Suffrage Association.

The intimate, communal culture Whitman had known before the war was giving way to one of passive spectatorship and efficiently managed spectacles. The postwar years brought the first college and professional athletic events witnessed in stadiums by large crowds. The grand three-ring circus replaced the small, chaotic circuses of former times. Plays and musical performances saw far less direct interaction between performers and audiences than previously.

The move toward organizational activity and institutions was widely noticed. "It is idle to cry out against organization," wrote one journalist in 1866. Another writer, in an article preceding Whitman's essay "Democracy" in the New York *Galaxy* for December 1866, wrote: "Just now the centralizing process seems in the ascendant; great cities are eating up small ones, and are growing greater; great nations are moving in the same direction, and great businesses, and great fortunes." The wartime spirit of discipline and organization was carried forward after the war by the Republican Party, which endlessly "waved the bloody shirt" (that is, revived patriotic memories of the Union war cause) and established machine politics through its associations with big business.

In this institutional, capitalistic environment, Whitman faced perplexing problems. On the one hand, he emerged from the war a government worker and an ardent celebrant of the war and its heroes, particularly Lincoln and Grant. Like the Republicans, he waved the bloody shirt vigorously until the end of his life. Also, he was enamored of the technological wonders, the city parks, and other aspects of late-nineteenth-century life. Sometimes he even said surprisingly positive things about big business. But how could he possibly be a business-boostering Republican? Many of his postwar writings reveal a genuinely ambivalent mentality, divided between technology and humanism, between capitalism and radicalism, between centralized institutions and residual individualism.

In the years immediately following the war, he was happy that many of his former friends had surrendered or modified radical views he had found extreme. He had always been uncomfortable with the fact that among his most loyal champions were abolitionists, whom he viewed as disunionists. His statement "By that war, *exit* Fire-Eaters, *exit* Abolitionists" had special meaning for him, since several of his closest friends had been ardent abolitionists who changed their views and lifestyles after the war. Their transformations were all the more meaningful to him since several of them transferred their ardor to the cause of Walt Whitman.

The most colorful convert was Count Adam Gurowski, a member of Whitman's Washington circle. Gurowksi, a translator for the State Department who had moved to America from his native Poland because of his radically democratic views, was like the protagonist of a Victorian melodrama, with a flowing cape, a saber cut on his cheek, and a green patch worn over one eye, highlighting the blue sparkle of the other. Moody and tempestuous, Gurowski sided through most of the war with the Radical Republicans in Congress who charged Lincoln with softness on the slavery issue. In his three-volume diary of the war, Gurowski branded Lincoln "the great shifter, the great political shuffler," slow to emancipate the slaves. His hostility toward Lincoln, however, dissolved partly after the Union successes of late 1864 and completely after the tragedy of Good Friday, 1865. Gurowski wrote: "This murder, this oozing blood, almost sanctify Lincoln. . . . The murderer's bullet opens to him immortality." In addition to embracing Lincoln, Gurowski became increasingly sympathetic to Whitman, with whom he had long, sometimes heated discussions at the O'Connors' gatherings. In the last volume of his diary he placed Whitman in the highest category of his three-rank breakdown of "Praise," "Half and Half," and "Blame," calling the poet "the incarnation of a genuine American, original genius." Whitman retained vivid memories of the count, whom he called "very crazy, but also very sane." Doubtless he thought the count "crazy" in his rabidly abolitionist phase and "sane" in his support of Lincoln and himself.

A number of others close to Whitman made the change from radicalism to respectability. Charles Eldridge, the radical publisher of the 1860 edition of *Leaves of Grass*, became first a government worker and then a lawyer, keeping in close touch with Whitman during the war and after. James Redpath, the abolitionist author of *The Public Life of Captain John Brown*, became the head of a lyceum bureau and then editor of the respectable *North American Review*, later accepting several of Whitman's articles for publication. Franklin B. Sanborn, the former associate of the abolitionist John Brown, favorably reviewed Whitman's *Drum-Taps*, was made the editor of the *Springfield Republican*, and in 1881 hosted Whitman in Boston. The journalist Richard J. Hinton, who had been another activist close to John Brown, met Whitman in a Washington hospital after being wounded in battle; so taken was he with Whitman and his work that he wrote pivotal articles in defense of the poet after the war.

Perhaps most striking of all was the change in Henry Clapp, the former Prince of Bohemia. In 1865 Clapp revived his experimental paper, the *Saturday Press*. New York's bohemian culture had been wiped out by the war, however, and the paper quickly failed. Within two years Clapp was working as a clerk in a New York public office, leaving himself open to the gibes of his former friends. When O'Connor met Clapp on the street in May 1867, he was amused to find, as he wrote Whitman, that Clapp was "becoming a respectable citizen. When once a man enters upon the downward path, &c . . . one can see as the guilty result of Bohemianism, a place on the Common Council or Board of Aldermen!"

O'Connor himself, however, was hardly one to laugh. He too had made a turn to respectability. A volatile man with a flair for invective, the wiry, blue-eyed O'Connor (see fig. 39) had been temperamentally suited to the reform movements of the seething fifties. The exigencies of family life—he and Nelly had two children, one of whom died prematurely—forced him into government work. Having written the abolitionist novel *Harrington*, he moved in 1861 with Nelly to Washington, where he became a clerk for the Lighthouse Board in the Treasury Department. He worked there for more than two decades. The flaming radical became a government drudge. The fervor he had formerly devoted to antislavery activism he now poured into endless discussions with Whitman and his circle.

Among the topics frequently discussed were abolitionism, women's rights, free love, and other radical causes. In these discussions, Charles Eldridge later recalled, Whitman came across as "one of the most conservative of men." This recollection seems to have been accurate, for Whitman himself remembered that he shied away from O'Connor's radical views. He explained later: "I fear'd his ardent abolitionism—was afraid it would keep us apart." Apparently, it *did* keep them apart for more than a decade; reliable evidence suggests that Whitman's estrangement from O'Connor in 1872 resulted from a disagreement over African-American suffrage.

But in the midsixties the split was far off. More devotedly than any of Whitman's other wartime friends, O'Connor became a convert to the Whitman cause. It was his timely aid in 1865–66 that the poet had in mind when he called him "a chosen knight: a picked man." The events that O'Connor helped set in motion in 1865 contributed greatly to America's acceptance of Whitman.

First, O'Connor gave Whitman practical help by using his connections to get the poet a government job. At the time, Whitman was on tenterhooks over the fates of his brothers Jesse and George. In December 1864 Jesse, who for more than a year had shown signs of violent insanity, had to be committed by the poet to the Kings County Lunatic Asylum. George had been captured in September in Virginia and was subsequently imprisoned in a Confederate prison at Salisbury, North Carolina, after which he was transferred to prisons in Richmond and then Danbury, Virginia. George's trunk had arrived in Brooklyn the day after Christmas, and Walt, home on extended leave, spent the day sorting out its contents with his mother and Eddy. The family was somewhat relieved on January 20 by a letter from George, dated November 27, assuring them of his health and good spirits. But it was not until Walt, with the aid of the *New York Times* editor John Swinton, arranged through General Grant a special prisoner exchange that George's return became a real possibility. After many anxious delays, George at last reached Brooklyn on March 18.

It was during this emotionally turbulent time that O'Connor approached an old friend, the lawyer J. Hubley Ashton, about Whitman's need for new employment. Ashton in turn spoke to the assistant secretary of the interior, William Tod Otto, who instructed Whitman to apply to him in writing. After applying and taking an examination, Whitman on January 24 assumed a first-class clerkship in the Interior Department's Bureau of Indian Affairs at a yearly salary of $1,200. Whitman had reason to be grateful to O'Connor. The flexible hours were to his liking, and his duties, consisting of copying reports and bids and sending them up to the Congressional Committee on Indian Affairs, were not onerous. On May 1 he was promoted to second-class clerk. He was impressed by the Native Americans who came to the office to negotiate for supplies, annuities, and treaty lands. Although later in life he would make prejudiced remarks about Native Americans, in 1865 he still possessed the democratic humanitarianism that had prompted his sympathetic portraits of the marriage of the trapper and the Indian in "Song of Myself" and of his mother's loving encounter with a squaw in "The Sleepers." He saw picturesque grandeur in the Indian chiefs, decked out in red facial paint, bear-claw necklaces, and headdresses. In his essay collection *November Boughs* he would write: "There is something about these aboriginal Americans, . . . something very remote, very lofty, arousing comparisons with our own civilized ideals—something that our literature, portrait painting, etc., have never caught, and that will almost certainly never be transmitted to the future, even as a reminiscence."

But his job at the Indian Affairs office was, in the long run, notable less for the sentiments it inspired than for the reputation it earned him after he was fired from it—a reputation engineered chiefly by O'Connor. In early May James Harlan, a senator from Iowa, assumed the position of secretary of the interior. Within a month, Harlan had compiled a list of some eighty clerks to be let go on reports that they were inefficient, immoral, or disloyal. Reportedly, Harlan made an after-hours visit to Whitman's desk and spotted a copy of the 1860 *Leaves of Grass*, heavily marked with the poet's editorial emendations, and decided that Whitman was among those who might injure the morals of the department. Whitman received his dismissal note on June 30.

H. L. Mencken, highlighting the importance of Harlan's dismissal of

Whitman to the history of literature, once remarked, "Let us repair, once a year, to our accustomed houses of worship and there give thanks that God one day in 1865 brought together the greatest poet America had produced and the world's damndest ass." He was only partly right. It was not Harlan's action that increased Whitman's visibility. Rather, it was O'Connor's response to the action. Upon hearing that Whitman had been fired, O'Connor stormed into the office of J. Hubley Ashton, now the assistant attorney general, asking him to intervene on Whitman's behalf. Ashton had an hour-long discussion with Harlan, who gave the opinion that Whitman "was wrong, was a free lover, deserved punishment, &c." and that he would not reinstate the poet even at the command of the president.

For the first time, *Leaves of Grass* had collided with governmental prudery. The inflammatory O'Connor was not about to let pass the opportunity for reprisal. Although he knew that Whitman, who was immediately transferred by Ashton to a clerkship in the attorney general's office, was safely employed, he was driven to avenge what he saw as an absurd injustice. The product of his vindictive rage was the brilliantly titled diatribe *The Good Gray Poet.* Written that summer and published the following January as a fifty-cent beige pamphlet, the work used Harlan's action to enhance Whitman's respectability. Harlan was a perfect scapegoat. A prominent Methodist and the former president of Iowa Wesleyan College, he had been one of the wealthiest members of the Senate before being appointed by Lincoln, a family friend, to his position at Interior. Whitman would recall: "He was of the sincere fanatic type, given to provincial views, ignorant of literature, in many ways that I consider essential ignorant of life." He represented the moral-police mentality that was part of the Republican sensibility. In his withering portrait of Harlan, O'Connor caricatured this aspect of the Republican outlook, shrewdly building up Whitman by emphasizing his wartime patriotism. Harlan became the narrow-minded, authoritarian watchdog victimizing the long-suffering Good Gray Poet, who had nobly served as a war nurse. As a poet, O'Connor insisted, Whitman was no more bawdy than any of the world's great geniuses, from Rabelais to Shakespeare, and at any rate was far more wholesome than the purveyors of the "anonymous lascivious trash" that infested America's cities.

There was a good amount of distortion in O'Connor's claims. As one of scores of people fired by Harlan, Whitman had not been singled out to the degree that O'Connor pretended. Also, his friend exaggerated Whitman's conventionality and minimized his eroticism. In fashioning Whitman for a middle-class readership, he was helping create what might be called the Whitman Myth: the image of the poet as a neglected genius who was thoroughly patriotic, personally exemplary, and almost spotless in his writings. Versions of the Myth would be pounded home time and again for the rest of Whitman's life, by the poet himself and by others. Like many myths, this one had certain elements of truth, but it presented a highly sanitized image of Whitman and overlooked the ways in which he had already enjoyed a fair amount of praise. O'Connor's greatest contribution to the Myth was the phrase "the Good Gray Poet," a sobriquet that would be echoed in newspaper headlines and interviews until Whitman's death. Even though O'Connor's pamphlet had only mixed reviews, its title remained a potent weapon always at hand for use by the poet's defenders. Whitman recognized O'Connor's shrewdness. "This was the hour for O'Connor," he said. "O'Connor was the man for this hour: and from that time on the 'good gray,' William's other name for me, has stuck—stuck."

Making Concessions

THE WHITMAN MYTH got another boost from the reception of the poet's new volume, *Drum-Taps*. A manuscript of some of Whitman's war poems had been completed as early as March 1863, and the following November he had written Eldridge: "I must bring out Drum Taps. I *must* be continually bringing out my poems—now is the hey day. I shall range along the high plateau of my life & capacity for a few years now, & then swiftly descend." These now-or-never words reflected not only worries over his health, already fragile, but also his urgent feeling that popular acceptance of his poetry was just around the corner.

Both he and O'Connor wanted to maximize the popular impact of *Drum-Taps*, but they had different ideas as to how that could be achieved. In a letter home in April 1864 Whitman announced his immediate plans for printing the volume, adding confidently, "I think it may be a success pecuniarily too." But wanting, as always, to maintain complete control over every aspect of publication, he planned to bring out the volume himself and sell it by his own exertions. O'Connor, in contrast, believed *Drum-Taps* might reach the popular market if an established publisher handled it. "I want it to have a large sale," he wrote Nelly, "as well I think it might, and I am afraid that his sort of private publication will keep it from being known as accessible to any considerable number of people."

Whitman, either unwilling or unable to find a major publisher, nonetheless was ready to make concessions to mainstream literary tastes. He wrote O'Connor in January 1865 that he considered *Drum-Taps* artistically superior to *Leaves of Grass* in part because "it delivers my ambition of the task that has haunted me, namely, to express in a poem ... the pending action of *the Time and Land we swim in*." He was pointing again to the historical roots of his poetry, always essential to him but not until now, he thought, fully realized. Stressing his cultural aims, he explained to O'Connor that *Leaves of Grass* was "intended to throw together for American use, a gigantic embryo or skeleton of Personality, fit for the West, for native models." He now saw, though, that this model personality for cultural use must be modified in order to win wide acceptance. As for *Leaves of Grass*, he said, "there are a few things I shall carefully eliminate in the next issue." But he planned to let stand some passages that "I should not put in if I were to write now," if only as "proofs of phases passed away." As for *Drum-Taps*, it "has none of the perturbations of Leaves of Grass."

Subtly but surely, the poet was changing his style in ways that would eventually contribute to the creation of the Whitman Myth. The poems in *Drum-Taps*—most of them patriotic, some of them using conventional rhythms—conformed more obviously to mainstream expectations than had any of the poems in *Leaves of Grass*. As seen earlier, even homoerotic poems like "Vigil Strange I Kept on the Field One Night" echoed the discourse of same-sex affection that had been popular during the war. However, the blatant eroticism of *Leaves of Grass* was circumvented, and poems like "O Captain!" and "Pioneers!" had a buoyant, driving militarism sure to please the postwar crowd.

Drum-Taps, containing fifty-three poems, was published in October 1865 as a thin, black-covered book by a small New York firm, Bunce and Huntington. A second issue, bound with an appended *Sequel to Drum-Taps* containing eighteen more poems, appeared a bit later from Gibson Brothers in Washington. Several reviewers noticed a striking change in Whitman's poetry. To be sure, those unaccustomed to his prose-poetry found *Drum-Taps* disagreeable. "It has been a melancholy task to read this book," wrote the young Henry James in the *Nation*. James's main complaint was that Whitman's verse was not poetry but "arrant prose," merely warmed-over Tupper. (Later he changed his opinion of Whitman.) Other reviewers, even hostile ones, noticed the patriotism and relative conventionality of Whitman's new stance. The *New York Times* and the Brooklyn *Daily Union* found Whitman's style odd but pointed to his war service as proof of his essential worth. William Dean Howells in the November *Round Table* found *Drum-Taps* unartistic but far superior to Whitman's previous poetry because of its avoidance of sex. "Whereas you had at times to hold your nose ... in reading 'Leaves of Grass,'" Howells wrote, there was not an indecent passage in *Drum-Taps*. (Like James, he later wrote more favorably of Whitman.) The omission of sexual themes was also noted by reviewers for the Boston *Radical* and the *North American Review*, both of whom found Whitman's war verse sonorous and thrilling. Predictably, reviewers gravitated to the more conventional-sounding poems: two reprinted "O Captain!"; one "Beat! Beat! Drums!"; and one "Pioneers!"

Although *Drum-Taps* did not become the best-seller O'Connor had envisaged, ten months after its publication Whitman heard from his publisher that sales were strong. But the volume's real impact was to be measured not in sales but in the contribution it made to the snowballing Whitman Myth. Not only had early reviewers discovered a new, sanitized Whitman, but the most influential review of all, by the poet's Washington friend John Burroughs (see fig. 40), was still in the works.

Gay Wilson Allen rightly notes that Burroughs's essay "Walt Whitman and His 'Drum-Taps,'" which appeared in the New York *Galaxy* in December 1866, was the first detailed appreciation of Whitman. Although in its calmness it was light-years distant from O'Connor's perfervid *Good Gray Poet*, the difference was mainly a tonal one that mirrored the divergent temperaments of the two Whitman comrades. The explosive, vigorous O'Connor contrasted sharply with the restrained, frail Burroughs. "William is always a towering force—he always comes down on you like an avalanche," said the poet, whereas John is "a milder type—not the fighting sort—rather more contemplative: John gives a little more for usual, accepted, respectable things." Given to "accepted, respectable things," the placid Burroughs was ideally suited to give the first full expression of the Whitman Myth in his review of *Drum-Taps*. It was his mildness, perhaps, that enabled him to accept Whitman's strong shaping hand: the review, like Burroughs's book that appeared the next year, was edited and partly ghostwritten by the poet. As such, it reveals how Whitman wanted to be seen by postbellum America.

All the major elements of the Whitman Myth were contained in the review. The starting point was that Whitman was almost totally neglected. "He has been sneered at and mocked and ridiculed," wrote Burroughs; "he has been cursed and caricatured and persecuted, and instead of retorting in a like strain, or growing embittered or misanthropic, he has preserved his serenity and good nature under all." The 1855 edition of *Leaves of Grass*, Burroughs continued, had been "still-born" and went unmentioned by reviewers for months, until Emerson's letter turned the tide a bit in the book's favor. But, Burroughs argued, Whitman owed no large debt to Emerson, since he read the latter's work only *after* the first edition appeared. Although subject to many interpretations, Whitman's poetry essentially "means power, health, freedom, democracy, self-esteem, a full life in the open air, an escape from old forms and standards." The tragic poems in *Drum-Taps* show the reflective Whitman, whose patriotic service as a war nurse was accomplished in spite of periodic illness. As for Whitman personally, wrote Burroughs, "with a large, summery, motherly soul that shines in all his ways and looks, he is by no means the 'rough' people have been so willing to believe. Fastidious as a high caste Brahmin in his food and personal neatness and cleanness, well dressed, with a gray, open throat, a deep, sympathetic voice, a kind, genial look, the impression he makes upon you is that of the best blood and breeding."

Burroughs's portrait, developed the next year in longer form in his *Notes on Walt Whitman, as Poet and Person,* was the image that would be repeated ad nauseam in the late nineteenth century and attacked with a vengeance by twentieth-century commentators, who in the aftermath of Freud preferred a neurotic, storm-tossed Whitman. The "real" Whitman seems to have lain somewhere between the two images. Burroughs failed to mention Whitman's churlish side—evidenced, for instance, by an incident on a Washington streetcar in which the poet reportedly got in an angry scuffle with a carpetbag senator—not to mention the anguish Whitman could express over his relationships with men like Peter Doyle and Harry Stafford. Also, to arouse sympathy for the poet, Burroughs stretched the truth. Contrary to Burroughs's claims, Whitman *had* read Emerson before 1855; *Leaves of Grass* did *not* go unreviewed in the early going (in fact, it got its first scathing notice *after* Emerson's letter was made public); and, above all, the response to Whitman had *not* been an unremitting torrent of abuse. Nor was Whitman quite as fastidious as "a high caste Brahmin" of "the best blood and breeding."

On the other hand, the twentieth century has been perhaps too strong in its dismissal of the Burroughs-O'Connor version of Whitman. If Whitman wanted his friends to emphasize his feelings of neglect, that was mainly because he never came close to having the kind of popular impact he dreamed of. Howells made this point when he wrote that Whitman ostensibly wrote for the masses, "Yet he is, perhaps, less known to the popular mind, to which he has attempted to give an utterance, than the newest growth of the magazines and newspaper notices." As for Burroughs's claim that Whitman was no rough but instead clean and wholesome, it had some validity with regard to the public, postbellum Whitman, with his simple woolen suits and sparkling white linen shirts. The many photographs taken of Whitman in the last three decades of his life bear little resemblance to the insolent rough of the 1855 engraving. Many of them show a respectable, avuncular Whitman (see, for example, figs. 44 and 45).

Numerous people who knew Whitman after the war used the words "clean" or "sweet" to describe him. Typically, when Richard Maurice Bucke met the poet in 1877, he found that Whitman's fresh suit, spotless shirt, and abundant white beard "exhaled an impalpable odor of purity. Almost the dominant initial feeling was: here is a man who is absolutely clean and sweet." In other words, Whitman not only helped fashion the Myth but, evidently, allowed it to affect his looks and behavior.

By the late sixties he was even allowing it to affect the presentation of his poetry, as is shown by his involvement with the first outside collection of his poems, the 1868 selection edited by the British poet William Michael Rossetti.

Theoretically, Whitman hated expurgation. "Damn the expurgated books!" he would exclaim to Traubel. "I say damn 'em! The dirtiest book in all the world is the expurgated book." He would always think of his treatment of sex as pure and natural. It was the censors, he thought, who had filthy minds.

But after the war he found himself confronted with new kinds of repressiveness in sexual matters. Harlan's drastic action against clerks suspected of immorality was emblematic of the institutional prudishness that arose in the postwar years. Several forms of sexual experimentation that had gone unchecked before the war now met with censorship or outright suppression. Street prostitution, which had been rampant before the war, became the target of several prolonged vice campaigns that closed brothels and made prostitutes wary. Free love, which had occasioned only a police raid or two before the war, now came under the moral ban, as evidenced by the arrest of the free-lover Ezra Heywood in the 1880s for defying the authorities by printing some of Whitman's sex poems. John Humphrey Noyes's Oneida community, where communal sex had been part of daily life since 1848, found itself after the war challenged by government and church authorities, contributing to its demise in the 1870s. Pornographic literature and entertainments, against which little organized action had been taken before the war, became the special target of the postwar vice campaigners, most notably Anthony Comstock, who helped pass obscenity laws used to suppress, among many other works, Whitman's *Leaves of Grass*.

Whitman, though strongly opposed to expurgation, had to face the realities of the postbellum moral environment. His careful tailoring of *Drum-Taps* and his aid in developing the Whitman Myth prepared him to make certain concessions in his dealing with the British publishers of his selected poems.

A positive British reception to Whitman had been initially prompted by an uneducated English cork cutter, Thomas Dixon, who had bought remaindered copies of the 1855 edition of *Leaves of Grass;* one of these copies made it through the author William Bell Scott to the Pre-Raphaelite poet William Michael Rossetti. In April 1866 Rossetti received a copy of *Drum-Taps* as well. Later that year, British interest was piqued by a piece in the *Fortnightly Review* by Moncure Daniel Conway, the former American abolitionist and Transcendentalist now living in London. Somewhat sensationally, Conway re-created two visits he had made to Whitman in Brooklyn. He soon received a letter from the poet's American champion O'Connor, who suggested that Hotten and Company, the publisher of Algernon Swinburne and other noted poets, would be an appropriate firm to approach about British publication of Whitman's poems. The next April, Conway sat in on a meeting of Rossetti, Swinburne, and John Camden Hotten in which it was decided that British publication was desirable but risky without expurgation.

International awareness of Whitman was greatly enhanced by Rossetti's July 1867 article on Whitman, which appeared in the London *Chronicle* and then was reprinted in several American periodicals. In the article Rossetti insisted that Whitman's flaws as a poet—occasional grossness and obscurity—were greatly outweighed by his originality and powerful rhythmic expression.

Everything pointed to a successful British publication. In August John Burroughs excitedly wrote Conway: "Our cause gains fast. The leaven is working and no mistake." The Whitman selection Rossetti was planning, however, was going to be heavily expurgated. Whitman at last had to face the prospect of a censored edition of his poems. This was no small matter. He often insisted on the centrality of the sex poems to *Leaves of Grass.* How could he possibly have anything good to say about Rossetti's *Poems of Walt Whitman,* which left out most of the "Children of Adam" and "Calamus" poems and even his signature piece, "Song of Myself"?

Surprisingly, he put up only mild, sporadic resistance to Rossetti's editorial changes. Over the years, his comments on the butchered edition swung between sullen resentment and absolute delight. Like his post-bellum response to established institutions in general, his feelings about this edition reveal conflicting pulls toward rebelliousness and conventionality.

He saw sales possibilities in the Rossetti volume, and in the end he didn't let his fear of expurgation stand in the way of potential popular acceptance. In October 1867 Conway wrote him that the edition would be "the best means of paving the way for a public demand for the entire work." Conway added, though, that Rossetti, uncomfortable with Whitman's references to "fatherstuff," onanism, venereal sores, and so on, wanted to make changes. Whitman immediately wrote back saying he didn't mind minor emendations. After learning more about the extent of the proposed changes, he wrote, "I cannot & will not consent of my own volition, to countenance any expurgated edition of my poems."

But consent he did. Moreover, he tried to use his connections to make the British edition another springboard for the Whitman Myth. He ghostwrote a letter from O'Connor to Conway insisting that the author of *Leaves of Grass* was no rough or vagabond but rather a person of "entire serenity & decorum, never defiant even to the conventions, always bodily sweet & fresh, dressed plainly & cleanly." He added: "All really refined persons, and the women more than the men, take to Walt Whitman. The most delicate & even conventional lady only needs to know him to love him." He resorted to more mythmaking again in a letter to Conway saying he was pleased with the forthcoming British volume because in America he had received just "one long tirade of shallow impudence, mockery, & scurrilous jeers." He amplified this now-familiar complaint into an outright lie in a letter to the publisher Hotten: "My book has never really been published here at all & the market is in a sort vacant of supplies."

With his eye on the market, he also gave in to Rossetti, to whom he wrote that, despite his qualms about expurgation, he wanted to go ahead with the edition. When the blue-covered, finely printed volume reached him in early March, he said nothing about the omission of "Song of Myself" and other major poems. He called it "a beautiful volume," and he waxed ecstatic in May when Hotten sent him a British review that Whitman called "a tremendous big favorable notice of my book, . . . one of the friendliest notices yet written."

The British edition did its intended work, opening the way to an acceptance of Whitman among many British literary figures upon whom he would often depend for support for the rest of his life. Occasionally Whitman griped about Rossetti's deletions, as in 1871 when he lamented "the horrible dismemberment of my book." But he would learn well the value of his British support, and he could not forget that it was Rossetti's scrubbed, polite Whitman that had been an important source of it. The volume was one more contribution to the myth that Whitman himself would vigorously push.

Undemocratic Vistas

THE CHANGING LITERARY AND MORAL CLIMATE was not the sole impetus behind Whitman's increasingly conventional posture. An equally powerful one was his participation in the Johnson and Grant administrations.

Whitman thought he saw in four presidents, starting with Lincoln, admirably average Americans who rose from obscure origins to rule with iron wills. In a late article he wrote: "The facts of rank-and-file workingmen, mechanics, Lincoln, Johnson, Grant, Garfield, brought forward from the masses and placed in the Presidency, and swaying its mighty powers with firm hand—really with more sway than any King in history, and with better capacity in using that sway—can we not see that these facts have bearings far, far beyond political or party ones?"

None of these presidents had a lowlier background or remained tougher as a ruler than Johnson, under whom Whitman served for two and a half years. Whitman's relationship to Johnson and his administration, which has received little attention in previous biographies, tells us much about Whitman's shifting political views and the resultant changes in his literary aims.

Whitman often shocked friends by defending Johnson. Few in his circle could understand his tolerance of the president known after the war for his leniency to the South and his white-supremacist views. Charles Eldridge recalled that Whitman "strenuously opposed the impeachment of President Johnson as an unwarranted attack on the independence of the Executive." Whitman once told a dubious Traubel: "Johnson was not a foul man—I knew all about him and I know that. All hands now see that the trial was a mistake—that he had done nothing impeachable—had done his best, according to his integrity: a real integrity, too, of his own order—an inherent integrity."

He may have been technically right that Johnson had done "nothing impeachable," but it is hard to think of Whitman, the archetypal democrat, seeing "inherent integrity" in Johnson, the foe of civil rights for African-Americans. Explanations of the anomaly can be found if we consider the contexts of Whitman's job in the attorney general's office, which he held from July 1865 to January 1872.

Whitman's job in the early going involved one of the most controversial of Johnson's policies: the pardoning of former rebels. After the war Johnson extended pardons to most ex-Confederates, the major exception being Southerners who possessed taxable property of twenty thousand dollars or more. The presidential mail was filled with pardon requests, and thousands of Southerners swarmed to Washington to be pardoned in person. Most pardons were handled through the attorney general's office. In August 1865, shortly after assuming his clerkship there, Whitman wrote his friend Alfred Pratt: "This is the place where the big southerners now come up to get pardoned—all the rich men & big officers of the reb army have to get special pardons. . . . I talk with them often, & find it very interesting to listen to their descriptions of things that have happened south." Some five thousand pardons, he noted, had already been issued through the office, though most had yet to be signed by Johnson. Eventually, Johnson would issue nearly fourteen thousand pardons to ex-Confederates.

His lenient pardoning policy outraged Southern freedmen and shocked even moderates. A convention of African-Americans in Virginia condemned the president, declaring that his pardons have "left us entirely at the mercy of these subjugated but unconverted rebels." During the impeachment trial one of the main charges made against Johnson was that under him "the pardoning power was prostituted, and pardons were issued in lots to suit rebels, thus grossly abusing that trust whose discreet exercise is so essential to the adminstration of justice." Whitman, among whose tasks as record clerk was processing pardons, aided his cause. He said later: "I was near him: my position in the Attorney General's Office placed me in daily contact with those who were close to him."

Near him and, overall, predisposed toward him. "What I hear & see about Andrew Johnson, I think he is a *good man*," he wrote Pratt. He also liked the attorneys general Johnson picked. Whitman served first under James Speed, who had been chosen by Lincoln and who was succeeded in July 1866 by Henry Stanbery, an Ohio lawyer close to Johnson. Within six months Stanbery promoted Whitman to a third-class clerkship at $1,600 a year—what Whitman called "a real good berth." "I like Mr. Stanbery," he wrote his mother. Years later he still felt strongly about him: "Stanbery was the man—and a real noble fellow he was, too— Western—not graceful in carriage, but with a fine face—a Lincolnish sort of man, though not Lincoln by any manner of means. He had much to do in the Johnson trial, and the big wigs valued his counsel highly." The New York lawyer William Evarts, who became attorney general in July 1868, Whitman remembered as "a very kind, friendly fellow," a man of "integrity: the sterling appeal to facts." Altogether, Whitman concluded in 1868, "I couldn't wish to have better bosses."

All this praise revealed a Whitman far more deferential to established authority than the one who a decade earlier had written that the president eats excrement and likes it. It is perhaps no accident that Whitman's near-totalitarian poetic "I," so prominent in his fifties poetry, virtually disappeared in his postwar verse. In the aftermath of Lincoln he began to have greater confidence in social leaders—even in Johnson and his henchmen.

When we recall these leaders' policies, we get a sense of his postwar priorities. Henry Stanbery was one of the architects of Johnson's Recon-

struction policy, which favored Southern whites. In 1867 Stanbery helped
Johnson prepare the veto of the congressional civil rights bill, arguing
that the federal government had no right to confer state citizenship on
blacks. Congress overrode the veto and later that year began the im-
peachment hearings at which Stanbery served on Johnson's defense
team. The leader of the team was William Evarts. When Whitman
stressed the superior qualities of Stanbery and Evarts, then, he was re-
vealing his strong support of Johnson's approach to Reconstruction.

Sympathetic to Johnson's defenders, Whitman was hostile toward
several of his enemies, particularly Radical Republicans who wanted to
punish the South and speed civil rights. "The republicans have exploited
the Negro too intensely, & there comes a reaction," he wrote his mother
in 1868. He was thinking especially of Supreme Court Justice Salmon P.
Chase, a leading Radical Republican who had tried in 1864 to snatch
the nomination from Lincoln and who was attempting the same against
Grant. Chase, Whitman wrote angrily, is "doing his best to injure the
Republican ticket—He is just the meanest & biggest kind of shyster—
He tried the same game at Lincoln's second nomination." Whitman
would recall him as "a bad, bad egg," "a trivial, damnable man" who
would have led America into chaos had he won the presidency.

How could Whitman possibly support the reactionary Johnson while
damning Chase and others who were on the cutting edge of civil rights?
A partial explanation lies in Johnson's humble background and populist
image. Whitman conceded to Traubel that Johnson lacked Lincoln's
"conscience" and "supreme reserve," but he insisted that "there was
something in Johnson which indicated the existence of democratic in-
stincts." The son of a hotel porter and a seamstress, Johnson had risen to
financial and political power without having attended school a single
day. In a sense, he was a figure of fantasy for Whitman, the self-made
and largely self-educated poet who imagined having tremendous social
power. Furthermore, Johnson had gained his power in a way that had
natural appeal for Whitman: by going directly to the people. A skilled
stump orator, Johnson gave stirring speeches throughout Tennessee that
earned him nine public positions, including governor, United States rep-
resentative and senator, military governor, and vice president.

Perhaps Johnson's main attraction for Whitman lay in his simultane-
ous devotion to the Union and to states' rights. Lincoln had selected him
as Tennessee's military governor and later as vice president because he
was a Southerner who nonetheless was completely devoted to the Union.
Like Whitman, Johnson regarded the South's secession as a terrible
crime but also had a near-mystical reverence for the Union and a funda-
mental sympathy for the South. As president, Johnson's main concern

was not with retribution but with restoring the Union by respecting the wishes of the individual Southern states. Johnson combined an old-fashioned Jacksonian states'-rights view with a Lincolnish, pro-Union one. Johnson's Republican foes, in contrast, were interested less in restoring state autonomy in the South than in establishing Republican control there.

Whitman, more worried than ever about the balance between the individual and the mass, felt this balance was more closely approached by Johnson than by the Radical Republicans. In *Notes Left Over* Whitman reiterated a long-standing conviction about the essence of America: "There are two distinct principles—aye, paradoxes—at the life-fountain of the States: one, the sacred principle of the Union, the right of ensemble, at whatever sacrifice—and yet another, an equally sacred principle, the right of each State, consider'd as a separate sovereign individual, in its own sphere." Either "the centripetal law" alone or "the centrifugal law" alone, he stressed, would be fatal to the nation.

So important was this balancing of the individual and the mass that he introduced the 1867 *Leaves of Grass* and all later editions with a poem that in its final version began:

> One's-Self I sing, a simple separate person,
> Yet utter the word Democratic, the word En-Masse.

In tone, this new opening was a far cry from the jaunty opening lines of the 1855 edition: "I celebrate myself, / And what I assume you shall assume." Both openings try to balance the individual and the mass, but the 1867 one is a generalized, abstract declaration, lacking the intimacy and casual bravado of the earlier one. The proud "myself" has become the vague "One's-Self," and the poet no longer prods the reader toward democracy ("what I assume you shall assume") but wants grandiosely to "utter the word Democratic, the word En-Masse." The easy personalism and self-confidence has disappeared, as Whitman's worry over the balance between the individual and the group takes on a note of desperation.

Seeking metaphors for the right balance became almost an obsession in his later years, but he could no longer rely on an all-powerful poetic "I" to achieve the balance. In *Democratic Vistas* (1871) he would powerfully describe the opposing principles of democracy and personalism, deferring final resolution of the two to a future race of "bards" he believed would ultimately emerge. In his other writings he groped for what he called "solutions of the paradox" of the contrasting tendencies. He seemed to find solutions everywhere but in himself. For instance, he would identify New York City as "the solution of that paradox, the eligibility of the free and fully developed individual with the paramount aggregate." At different times, he found further "solutions" in the railroad, in the Mississippi River basin, in the geography and people of the American West, to name a few phenomena he discussed in this way.

In the late sixties, the main solution he saw was the states' rights/ Union combination he found in the Johnson approach to Reconstruction. Indeed, he gave almost a gloss of Johnson's outlook when he wrote in *Democratic Vistas:*

> For it is mainly or altogether to serve independent separatism that we favor a strong generalization, consolidation. As it is to give the best vitality and freedom to the rights of the States (every bit as important as the right of nationality, the union,) that we insist on the identity of the Union at all hazards.

It was Johnson who had demanded "a strong generalization, consolidation" of presidential power in order to enforce "freedom to the rights of the States." It was Whitman who abstracted the principle of this policy and gave it lasting expression.

In siding ideologically with Johnson, however, Whitman faced the thorny problem of race relations. Johnson was a former slave owner who never shed his Southern white-supremacist convictions. Not only did he veto civil rights legislation and the Fourteenth Amendment, which gave blacks citizenship rights, but he was inflexible and heavy-handed. Nostalgic for the agrarian South of his youth, he believed whites should continue to hold social dominion over blacks, whom he considered inferior. "White men alone must manage the South," he told a friend. He made what has been called perhaps the most racist public statement ever by an American president when he declared that blacks had "less capacity for government than any other race of people."

Whitman's postwar statements on African-Americans and civil rights suggest that even in this area there were points of agreement between him and Johnson. Both had a long-standing antipathy to abolitionists, whom they regarded as extremists who endangered the Union. Both thought that keeping a balance between state and national power was more important than advancing the rights of minorities.

Whitman's racial views took a definitely conservative turn after the war. In his most radical phase, during the fifties, he had shared the fervent racial egalitarianism of Frederick Douglass, Samuel Ringgold Ward, and others who vociferously called attention to the humanity of African-Americans. In "I Sing the Body Electric" he had emphasized the "passions, desires, reachings, aspirations" of the auctioned slave, and in "Salut au Monde!" he had addressed the "black, divine-soul'd African, large, fine-headed, nobly-form'd, superbly destin'd, on equal terms with me!"

As a result of such exhilarating lines, Whitman has been rightly cherished as a great spokesperson for brotherhood and equality. There was a good reason abolitionists flocked to his cause. The ex-slave and feminist-abolitionist Sojourner Truth had such respect for *Leaves of Grass* that she thought God had written it. Whitman, for his part, in old age liked to quote from "old black Sojourner Truth," as he called her. One of Whitman's greatest champions late in life was Robert Ingersoll, a dyed-in-the-wool radical Republican who cited Whitman's poetry as the archetypal example of "Liberty in Literature," the title of a famous Philadelphia speech on Whitman that he gave in 1890. This was the aspect of Whitman that would later impress the Harlem Renaissance poet Langston Hughes, who wrote that Whitman's "all-embracing words lock arms with workers and farmers, Negroes and whites. Asiatics and Europeans, serfs, and free men, beaming democracy to all." More recently, the black poet June Jordan has identified Whitman as the one "white father" of a line of antiracist, antisexist writers including Pablo Neruda, Gabriela Mistral, Margaret Walker, and Edward Brathwaite. Just as Lincoln's highest message, especially at Gettysburg, was human equality, so Whitman's, in several key poems, was the dignity and togetherness of all races.

The fact is, though, that this message was far more prominent in his pre–Civil War poems than in his later ones. Over time, his outlook came to reflect the inconsistencies of the politics of the moment. Whitman admired the African-Americans who served in the Union army. Sometimes his comments on them were tinged with condescension, as when he wrote of a company of eighty-two black soldiers: "Certes, we cannot find fault with the appearance of this crowd—negroes though they be. They are manly enough, bright enough, look as if they had the soldier-stuff in them." But his respect for the pluck of black soldiers was unwavering, and he realized they were often underpaid. Witnessing the paying off of the First Regiment of U.S. Colored Troops on July 11, 1863, near Washington, he saw one company, offered just twenty-three cents a man, refuse the pay and march off angrily. He was genuinely moved by the courage of the black troops during the battles of Milliken's Bend, Vicksburg, Port Hudson, and especially in the failed assault on Fort Wagner in Charleston Harbor. The Kansas Colored Volunteers, a regiment of African-Americans and Native Americans, impressed him as "real warriors, in every respect, nothing to take them back." He extended a helpful hand to wounded black soldiers in the hospitals. Nearly a year after the war he was regularly visiting a ward of blacks at Harewood Hospital, reading or writing letters with several of them.

He was not able, however, to rise above the prevailing racial prejudices of his day, and he was temperamentally unequipped to ponder the legal and political ramifications of emancipation. A month after the Emancipation Proclamation went into effect, he wrote that Washington was filled with liberated blacks, "some with physiognomies of hogs or chimpanzees, others again, as dandified and handsome as anybody." Charles Eldridge recalled that in the Washington years Whitman had no black friends, adding: "Of the negro race he had a poor opinion. He said that there was in the constitution of the negro's mind an irredeemable trifling or volatile element, and he would never amount to much in the scale of civilization."

Whitman never said much about African-American suffrage, but when he did, his remarks were generally derogatory. In an essay on the suffrage question he sounded both nativist and racist: "As if we had not strained the voting and digestive calibre of American Democracy to the utmost for the last fifty years with the millions of ignorant foreigners, we have now infused a powerful percentage of blacks, with about as much intellect and calibre (in the mass) as so many baboons."

He left no complete record of his feelings about the failure of Johnson's Reconstruction plan and the rise to political power of hundreds of African-Americans in Southern states between 1866 and 1876. The fragmentary remarks that survive, however, show a negative response to the political participation of blacks. In a letter of 1868 he described crowds of blacks "yelling & gesticulating like madmen" after an election, adding that "they looked like so many wild brutes let loose." In 1875, at the height of postbellum civil rights and African-American power in the South, he expressed alarm over the number of black legislators in states like South Carolina, Mississippi, and Louisiana. He wrote that "the black domination, but little above the beasts—viewed as a temporary, deserv'd punishment for their [that is, Southern whites'] Slavery and Secession sins, may perhaps be admissible; but as a permanency of course is not to be consider'd for a moment."

As it turned out, the "black domination" *was* temporary; two years after he wrote this passage Reconstruction ended, and a long reactionary period of renewed white supremacy began in the South. The nostalgia for the antebellum South that swept the North after Reconstruction seems to be reflected in a note he wrote about what he called the "inexpressibly dear" South: "Tonight I would say one word for that South—

the whites. I do not wish to say one word and will not say one word against the blacks—but the blacks can never be to me what the whites are.... The whites are my brothers & I love them." In old age, Whitman would view white supremacy as a natural consequence of what he had come to regard as an incapacity for self-help among blacks. He told Traubel: "That is one reason why I never went full on the nigger question—the nigger would not turn—would not do anything for himself—he would only act when prompted to act. No! no! I should not like to see the nigger in the saddle—it seems unnatural.... Till the nigger can do something for himself, little can be done *for* him."

His racism was fueled by the so-called "ethnological science" that gathered strength during the war and gained wide acceptance during the postbellum years. Before the war, scientific racism had been most commonly promoted by phrenology, the pseudoscience that divided humankind into races and assigned a lowly position to blacks. Whitman kept in a scrapbook a phrenological chart in which an African-American was pictured in caricature and was assigned certain qualities considered by the phrenologists innate. Whitman seemed to have this typological view of blacks in mind when in the late fifties he scribbled down plans for a "*Poem of the Black person* / infuse the sentiment of a sweeping, surrounding, shielding, protection of the blacks—their passiveness—their character of sudden fits—the abstracted fit—."

One of the tragic ironies of the Civil War was that it freed enslaved African-Americans but doomed them to second-class status in the minds of many American scientists. During and after the war, there developed a theory of racial attrition that predicted the ultimate elimination of so-called "inferior" races. Scientists studied more than two thousand black soldiers and more than five hundred Native American ones, finding what they believed was solid evidence of the inferiority of these groups. The infusion into this racial theory of Darwinian thought, particularly Herbert Spencer's idea of the "survival of the fittest," as well as the eugenic belief in the ascendancy of "superior" races, introduced by Francis Galton in 1865, convinced many that certain racial groups would disappear in time.

Evidently, Whitman was among the convinced. Confused over the competing claims about African-Americans being made in the public arena, he turned to ethnological science for what he considered definite resolution of the racial issue. A recently unearthed Whitman manuscript, dating from the late 1860s, expresses his feeling about what seemed to him the inexorable, all-answering nature of the new "scientific" findings:

Of the black question

After the tender appeals of the sentimentalist, the eloquence of free-
dom's hottest orators, and the logic of the politico-economist, comes
something else to the settlement of this question—comes Ethnological
Science, cold, remorseless, not heeding at all the vehement abstrac-
tions of equality and fraternity, or any of the formulas thereof—unin-
fluenced by Acts of Congress, or Constitutional Amendments—by
noiselessly rolling on like the globe in its orbit, like the summer's heat
or winter's cold, and settling these things by evolution, by natural se-
lection by certain races notwithstanding all the frantic pages of the
sentimentalists helplessly disappearing by the slow, sure progress of
laws, through sufficient periods of time.

The "sentimentalists" referred to here may be popular writers like
Stowe or Whittier who were using sentiment to arouse antislavery feel-
ing. "Freedom's hottest orators" were either the abolitionists or Radical
Republicans like Thaddeus Stevens who were blasting Johnson. The log-
ical "politico-economist" may have been Thomas Carlyle, whose essay
"Shooting Niagara; and After?," well known to Whitman, attacked
African-American suffrage. The "Acts of Congress, or Constitutional
Amendments" were the recently passed civil rights laws on behalf of
blacks. Whitman sees ethnological science as a towering force that over-
whelms these competing claims about blacks, as a "cold, remorseless"
settler of all racial questions. His belief in the racial-extinction theory is
revealed especially in two previous versions of the manuscript that in-
cluded the phrase: "by certain races helplessly disappearing when
brought in contact with other races."

He echoed this outlook years later when he told Traubel: "The nig-
ger, like the Injun, will be eliminated: it is the law of races, history, what-
not: always so far inexorable—always to be. Someone proves that a
superior grade of rats comes and then all the minor rats are cleared
out." Small wonder that in the last decade of his life Whitman devel-
oped a close friendship with Daniel Garrison Brinton, the University
of Pennsylvania archaeologist and linguist who was one of the most
famous exponents of the racial-elimination theory. Whitman declared
Brinton "a master-man," one "of the school of the great modern scien-
tists and progressive metaphysicians." Brinton regularly visited the
poet in Camden, spoke at his funeral, and helped organize the Walt
Whitman Fellowship International.

How do we accommodate these attitudes into the overall picture of
him? Evidence of reactionary beliefs in great writers is always unset-

tling. In Whitman's case it is all the more so since he is widely beloved for his radical egalitarianism.

He was apparently swept up in the currents of the moment. The conclusions of ethnological science, which today seem as bogus and primitive as phrenology, then had widespread acceptance. A recent historian of the field generalizes that "the belief in the Negro's extinction became one of the most pervasive ideas in American medical and anthropological thought during the late nineteenth century." Whitman had an amateurish but ardent respect for science, and in the sixties he directed this fervor to the up-and-coming scientific strain of ethnology, particularly attractive to him since it seemed to use Darwin, whom he deified, to solve perplexing social problems.

As for Whitman's resistance to African-American political participation, that too was something he shared with many of his contemporaries. True, some public figures—Salmon Chase, Horace Greeley, Charles Sumner, for instance—supported the black vote out of principle. But others, such as Thaddeus Stevens, Benjamin F. Wade, George S. Boutwell, and Jacob Howard, advocated it mainly as a weapon to punish the South—the view Whitman assumed when he said that "black domination" was a temporary punishment for the South's "Slavery and Secession sins." A surprising number of otherwise forward-looking people were ambivalent about African-American voting. The two leading Radicals, Stevens and Sumner, called only for partial black suffrage. Lincoln had advocated the vote only for blacks who had served in the Union army and who were what he termed "very intelligent." The era's foremost abolitionist, William Lloyd Garrison, saw no advantage in granting blacks the vote. In general, the Northern public had far less interest in African-American suffrage than in establishing the Northern-controlled Republican Party in the South. Whitman's views on blacks and politics, like his acceptance of ethnological science, were thus in keeping with widespread opinion in his times.

On the racial issue, Whitman must be placed alongside other Americans whose best-expressed ideals held great potential for freedom but whose attitudes or behavior sometimes conflicted with these ideals. Jefferson's proclamations of human equality have profoundly inspired many radical movements that have benefited minorities; but Jefferson was a slave owner. The ambivalent racial attitudes of Stowe and Lincoln have been previously noted; but who contributed to liberty and equality more influentially than they?

The flowing, democratic interchange between Whitman's "I" and the people and things around him, so characteristic of his fifties poems, largely disappears from his more impersonal later poems. It is misleading to claim, as some have, that Whitman suffered a great loss of poetic power as he aged: a very late poem like "To the Sun-set Breeze," beloved by Whitman's contemporaries and by later readers such as Ezra Pound, suggests that his powers of language and poetic feeling remained strong.

What did change was his relation to American life. In the fluid, open culture of the midfifties, he exuded democracy from every recess of his soul, in every note of his musical tongue. In the institutional, systematized postwar culture, he made statements that were sometimes inconsistent with his earlier ones. Postbellum America was too complex, too big, too baffling for the "I" who had once announced himself the loving Answerer.

Taking Care of Business

THE DISAPPEARANCE of the old Whitman was graphically evidenced by his two main works of the late sixties: the 1867 edition of *Leaves of Grass* and the essays later expanded as *Democratic Vistas.*

In August 1866 Whitman took a leave from his Washington job to go to New York to supervise the printing of the fourth edition of *Leaves of Grass.* Once more, his hopes for success were high. This was to be, he assured his old friend Abby Price, "a new & much better edition of Leaves of Grass complete—that *unkillable* work!" He planned again to go directly to the people by arranging the printing and distribution of the volume himself. Coincidentally, President Johnson that month also decided to go directly to the people in his multicity speaking tour known as the "Swing Around the Circle."

Both attempts at the old-time populist salesmanship were disastrous. Johnson, as he traveled from city to city giving repetitive, ill-prepared speeches, alienated even many friends in his clumsy caricatures of the Radical Republicans, whom he called Judases. Likewise, Whitman, producing a drab book that fell into the hands of unprofessional book dealers, did little to advance his cause with the public he had long been wooing.

The publication history of the ill-fated 1867 edition is complicated. Whitman secured a Beekman Street printer, William E. Chapin, to print sheets that were bound and distributed independently. Whitman had gotten rid of the confusing array of cluster names of the 1860 edition, retaining only the "Enfans d'Adam" (now "Children of Adam") and "Calamus" titles, and had gone a long way to arranging his poems in what would be their final order. He soon prepared a second issue of the edition, with *Drum-Taps* and its *Sequel* as well as a new section, *Songs before Parting,* added at the end. The volume was to be bound by James Gray, but Gray went bankrupt, and the sheets fell to another binder and a New York distributing firm that later failed and was absorbed into the book dealership of Thomas O'Kane. In late 1873 Whitman, angered by O'Kane's failure to pay him royalties, gave the book over to Asa K. Butts and Company, which in turn went bankrupt, at which point the book became the property of the bookseller Charles P. Somerby. In 1876 Whitman demanded two hundred dollars in royalties from Somerby but got only ten dollars. The next year Whitman received notice of the bankruptcy of the man he now called "the rascal Charles P. Somerby."

Whitman kept up a chorus of wails and curses about what he saw as the nefarious intrigues of these booksellers, who actually were more victims of the economy than enemies of the poet. Limited publishing funds perhaps explain the remarkably plain format of the 1867 *Leaves of Grass.* With its unprinted grayish-brown wrappers and undistinguished typefaces, it was, in appearance, the polar opposite of the elegant 1860 edition. But more than just underfinancing accounted for the change. This was the first edition that omitted a picture of Whitman. The author seemed to be in retreat. His name appeared neither on the backstrip nor the title page.

The retreat of the former Whitman was evidenced by several new poems the edition contained. These poems were far less intimate and personal than his former ones. "Tears" is an agentless poem that refers to some "ghost" or "shapeless lump" sobbing on a beach at night; no person is described to flesh out the expostulation "Tears! tears! tears!" Equally unphysical is "The City Dead-House," in which an "I" views the body of a prostitute at a morgue—suggestive of the death of Whitman's erotic voice. Unlike the "I" who had announced himself "Walt Whitman, liberal and lusty as Nature" in the 1860 poem "To a Common Prostitute," the asexual, unnamed "I" in this poem contemplates the "fair house—that ruin!" that once was a prostitute. Even the body of a man fails to engage Whitman in a direct way. The short poem "The Runner" portrays a sinewy athlete but gives off no homoerotic sparks between an "I" and a "you." This kind of disembodied picture-poem, free of an absorbing "I," had arisen in *Drum-Taps* in pieces like "A Farm Picture" and "The Torch," which are like unconnected genre paintings. This muting of the personal self helps explain "When I Read the Book," which insists on the inherent flaws of biography. No "biography famous" comes close to capturing its subject; even of his own life the "I" of the poem knows "Only a few hints, a few diffused faint clews and indirections."

To say that Whitman was in retreat was not to say that he was backing down from his former stances. Although he deleted three particularly tortured, intimate "Calamus" poems and made a few other gestures toward conventionality, he retained the overwhelming majority of his poems with only slight revisions. He may have regarded some of these early poems, to use his words to O'Connor, as "proofs of phases passed away." But by keeping alive the poetic project he had begun in the fifties, he extended to postbellum America his prewar radical democracy and eroticism.

On the issue of blacks and slavery he sent mixed signals in the 1867 edition. He let stand the egalitarian racial passages in "Song of Myself" and "Body Electric." He strengthened the antislavery message of "By Blue Ontario's Shore," deleting the image of the "tremulous hands" protecting slavery and adding the warlike lines: "Slavery—the murderous, treacherous conspiracy to raise it upon the ruins of all the rest, / On and on to grapple with it—Assassin! then your life or ours be the stake, and respite no more." To reprimand the South for seceding, he also added a passage that would have pleased Thaddeus Stevens, calling the South "the menacing arrogant one that strode and advanced with senseless scorn, bearing the murderous knife, / [. . .] Today a carrion dead and damn'd, the despised of all the earth." But the new poems avoided the race issue, and Whitman removed these lines from the 1860 poem "Says": "I say man shall not hold property in man; / I say the least developed person on earth is just as important and sacred to himself or herself, as the most developed person is to himself or herself."

To isolate the racial issue, however, is misleading, since Whitman now had difficulty in addressing *any* social issue in poetry. His "I" no longer stretched and widened to embrace all facets of cultural experience. In the late sixties he began to view America's social problems as overwhelming, beyond immediate poetic repair. He would set forth his new approach to these problems in his essay *Democratic Vistas*.

It is well known that he wrote *Democratic Vistas* largely in response to Thomas Carlyle's article "Shooting Niagara; and After?" an acidic attack on republicanism. But Whitman's complex feelings about Carlyle and his revisions of the essays that fed into *Democratic Vistas* have not been probed satisfactorily.

Carlyle's special target in his essay was Disraeli's impending Reform Bill of 1867, the precursor of the 1884 Franchise Bill, that extended suffrage to wide sectors of the working class. In a larger sense Carlyle took aim at democratizing forces all over the world, symbolized particularly by what he called "Nigger emancipation" in America. Carlyle claimed that all worthwhile cultural values were being drowned in "swarmery," his word for the actions of people in swarms or mobs. Elitist and racist, Carlyle opposed suffrage for blacks. "One always rather likes the Nigger," he wrote superciliously, "evidently a poor blockhead with a good disposition, with affections, attachments." He found it insane that hundreds of thousands of "excellent white men" should have killed each other in America just to free "three million absurd Blacks" who are now "launched into the career of improvement,—likely to be 'improved off the face of the earth' in a generation or two!" Altogether, Carlyle expressed his disgust with "these ballot-boxing, Nigger-emancipating, empty, dirt-eclipsed days."

The fact that Whitman leaped to respond to Carlyle's overheated diatribe says much about his insecure feelings about American democracy in the postbellum years. In September 1867, a month after Carlyle's essay had appeared, Whitman wrote the first part of his response, an essay titled "Democracy," which appeared in the December issue of the New York *Galaxy*, edited by F. P. and W. C. Church. His second essay, "Personalism," appeared there the following May. The third, "Orbic Literature," was rejected by the Churches. After many revisions and additions, the three essays were eventually combined and published in 1871 as a seventy-five-cent green-covered pamphlet, *Democratic Vistas*.

We are so accustomed to reading *Democratic Vistas* in its final, entire form that we tend to forget that it was a patchwork document that changed dramatically over time. To be sure, the skeleton of Whitman's argument remained constant in the various reworkings between 1867 and 1871. Whitman countered Carlyle by admitting that many of his charges against democracy were true but that the shortcomings he enumerated could be overcome in several ways: by recognizing the worth of common people, dramatized especially in the selfless heroism of the Civil War soldiers; by cultivating both individuality and social unity; by having faith in the electoral process, a cleansing agent as antiseptic as nature; by permitting women to develop fully in many ways; by seeing that America is steadily developing through its current practical, business-oriented phase toward a time when great "bards" will arise, producing a true democratic literature that will instill much-needed religiosity and moral conscience into American life.

This was the main drift of Whitman's response to Carlyle. But his response was by no means uniform. Its emphases changed with Whitman's changing social environment. In a word, Whitman became more and more convinced that Carlyle was right in his worries over the dangers of democracy. The change becomes clear when Whitman's comments on America in his 1867 article "Democracy" are compared with those in the 1871 pamphlet *Democratic Vistas*.

In the early version, Whitman makes certain concessions to Carlyle but remains basically optimistic about current-day America. He parodies Carlyle's fear of "the rolling, mountainous surges of 'swarmery'" and asks him to "spare those spasms of dread and disgust." Despite lapses, Whitman says, American democracy is basically sound and will ultimately heal itself. The war had brought out the best in Americans; only previously, in the fifties, had social problems been widespread. "Once, before the war, I, too, was fill'd with doubt and gloom," he writes, recalling a man who had told him of his travels through America: "I have everywhere found, primarily, thieves and scalliwags arranging the nominations to offices, and sometimes filling the offices themselves. I have found the North just as full of bad stuff as the South."

This was Whitman's old complaint about the fifties social crisis. But in "Democracy" the complaint was retrospective, as though he thought America had left its main difficulties behind and was entering a new phase. In the four years between "Democracy" and *Democratic Vistas* his vision darkened measurably. In the later work, Whitman turned his "moral microscope" on current America and saw "a sort of dry and flat Sahara," with "cities, crowded with petty grotesques, malformations, phantoms, playing meaningless antics." If the United States continued in its current direction, he wrote, it might well end up "the most tremendous failure of time."

What explains his increasing sourness about America? For one thing, he was uneasy about the direction of Reconstruction. In the 1867 version he had noted "the din of disputation" around him: "Acrid the temper of the parties, vital the pending questions. Congress convenes; the President sends his message; Reconstruction is in abeyance." He was writing at the moment when the Republican-led Congress was preparing its strategy against Johnson that led over the next two years to the defeat of his Reconstruction plan and the subsequent extension of suffrage and civil rights to Southern blacks. As seen, Whitman was ambivalent about suffrage extension. He would feature this ambivalence in the third paragraph of the final version of *Democratic Vistas:* "I will not gloss over the appaling dangers of universal suffrage in the United States. In fact, it is to admit these dangers I am writing."

In his critique of America, he felt closer to Carlyle than to the Radical Republicans. He later told Traubel he preferred the Scot's criticism of America to that of the leading Republican, Salmon Chase. He declared: "Carlyle did not believe in our democracy—criticized it out of a divine belief. And I always welcomed his criticisms—always thought them valuable—do now: but Chase's, from the inside, were the most hateful, insidious, to be imagined." Over the years, he would conclude that Carlyle's bitter criticism of America was ultimately healthy. He made this clear in the final version of *Democratic Vistas*, explaining that at first he had been "roused to much anger" by "Shooting Niagara" but had "since read it again" and decided that Carlyle's "sharp cutting metallic grains, ... if not gold or silver, may be good, hard, honest iron." "What a needed service he performs!" he wrote later of Carlyle; and elsewhere: "His rude, rasping, taunting, contradictory tones—what ones are more wanted amid the supple, polish'd, money-worshipping, Jesus-and-Judas equalizing, suffrage sovereignty echoes of current America?"

It was not only the drift of Reconstruction that darkened Whitman's outlook; it was also his growing realization that political and social corruption had survived the war and had even worsened. In his more idealistic moments he looked back on the war as the purifying thunderstorm he had wanted it to be. In the 1876 preface to *Leaves of Grass* he would write that "the Secession War" cleared America of "death-threatening impedimenta." In a later essay he wrote of the war: "I have never had the least doubt about the country in its essential future since then." But the wording was cautious: he believed that the country "in its essential future" would succeed. *Democratic Vistas*, more strongly than any of his writings, shows that he was convinced that the present was in many ways bleaker than ever.

Between 1868 and late 1870, as Whitman was revising the essays that became *Democratic Vistas*, news of alarming malfeasance in high places began to come to view. A certain amount of corruption had plagued the Union war effort. Lincoln's War Department, for instance, was rotten under Simon Cameron, who gave lucrative government contracts to his business cronies in Pennsylvania. More ominous and longlasting was the alliance between business and government that took shape as the Crédit Mobilier, a dummy joint-stock company formed around the government-chartered Union Pacific Railroad, among whose stockholders were some influential congressmen. In New York City, the corpulent, cigar-chomping William Marcy Tweed took control of Tammany Hall in 1863 and established a carelessly organized but powerful ring of henchmen who made graft and vote buying a part of daily political life. By the late sixties, similar rings had arisen in many other American cities. The "machine politics" developed by the Republican and Democratic parties made corruption an institutional phenomenon.

As Whitman came to see the prevalence of the problem, he was devastated. He lamented in *Democratic Vistas:*

The spectacle is appalling.... The depravity of the business classes of our country is not less than it has been supposed, but infinitely greater.

The official services of America, national, state, and municipal, in all
their branches, except the judiciary, are saturated in corruption, brib-
ery, falsehood, mal-administration; and the judiciary is tainted. The
great cities reek with respectable as much as non-respectable robbery
and scoundrelism.

Contemplating the growing corruption, which steadily worsened un-
der Grant, Whitman would almost reach a point of suffocation. When
he revised his social-protest poem "Respondez!" for the 1871 edition of
Leaves of Grass, he added these despairing words:

Stifled, O days! O lands! in every public and private corruption!
Smother'd in thievery, impotence, shamelessness, mountain-high;
Brazen effrontery, scheming, rolling like ocean's waves around and
    upon you, O my days! my lands!
For not even those thunderstorms, our fiercest lightnings of the war,
    have purified the atmosphere.

These last words show bitter disillusion. The war, Whitman now re-
alized, had not done its supposed job of cleansing American life. Torn
between a lost ideal, the war, and an increasingly sordid present, Whit-
man turned hopefully to the future. No longer able to rely upon an all-
absorbing poetic "I," he looked now to outside systems for consolation.
Despite everything pushing him toward cynicism, he actually gained a
new source of optimism after the war in what might be termed "progres-
sive evolution," a combination post-Darwinian thought and Hegelian
idealism.

Whitman's interest in Hegel, dating at least from the fifties, intensi-
fied greatly in the late sixties as his relationship to American culture
changed. He discussed Hegel and other philosophers at length in his
notebooks. Compared with the other thinkers, he wrote, Hegel presents
"the most thoroughly *American point of view* I know." He could hardly
believe Hegel had not been born and raised in America. "Only Hegel,"
he emphasized, "is fit for America—is large enough and free enough."
With slight rewriting, we could say that by the late sixties America was
too "large" for Whitman, who now looked to the Hegelian dialectic for
solutions of cultural problems which his poetic "I"—itself once "large"
and "containing multitudes"—had formerly tried to solve.

Hegel's formula of thesis-antithesis-synthesis brought great consola-
tion to Whitman. It suggested that, no matter what, things would work
out in time. In *Democratic Vistas* he applied the formula in two ways.
There was the main tripartite division, established in the preparatory

articles, of "Democracy" (mass society), "Personalism" (the individual), and "Orbic Literature" (the all-resolving literary works of the future). Also featured was another trio of forces: first, the democratic political program, in part contradicted by the current corruption; second, the material wealth, prosperity, and laborsaving machines of modern America, in part spoiled by greed and materialism; third, "rising out of the previous ones, to make them and all illustrious, a native expression-spirit" of "original authors and poets to come." In both patterns, literary resolution is a dream for the future, not a reality of the present. Whitman now looked beyond himself as America's healer to "authors and poets to come."

When mentioning *Democratic Vistas* to friends, Whitman called attention to his debt to Hegel. To one he wrote that the essay projected "*moral purpose*, Hegelianism," to another that it was designed to produce a "new breed of authors, . . . Hegelian, Democratic, religious."

Hegel helped him come to terms with both Carlylean cynicism and Darwinian materialism. In *Specimen Days* he conceded that he had only a partial knowledge of Hegel, which he got secondhand through American sources, but that the German philosopher was crucial to his effort to strip Carlyle and Darwin of their potentially negative implications. He explained: "I am the more assured in recounting Hegel a little freely here, not only for offsetting the Carlylean letter and spirit—cutting it out all and several from the very roots, and below the roots—but to counterpoise, since the late death and deserv'd apotheosis of Darwin, the tenets of the evolutionists."

He did not, though, *reject* Carlyle and Darwin. Rather, his Hegelian outlook allowed him to *incorporate* them by giving them positive meaning. As mentioned, he often praised Carlyle as a trenchant critic of democracy's excesses. Darwin, in his view, held promise for democracy's future. Like other prominent Americans, such as Henry Ward Beecher, Whitman transformed Darwinian thought, ridding it of its pessimistic implications and making it an analogue for progress. "How can we ever forget Darwin?" he said to Traubel. "He was one of the *acme* men— he was at the top." For Whitman as for many other spiritual-minded postbellum Americans, neither Hegel nor Darwin was inconsistent with religious belief. Both offered large, overarching systems that, in his mind, made history a long-developing process slowly separating the evil from the good, the unfit from the fit, the imperfect from the perfect.

The grimmer side of Darwin, emphasized especially by Darwin's disciple Thomas Huxley, never posed a serious threat to Whitman's basically idealistic outlook. Even though Huxley presented a materialistic world operating by blind chance, Whitman read him avidly throughout his later years without losing faith in metaphysics and social improvement. Far from instilling doubt, evolution inspired hope in Whitman. He used "evolution" loosely to describe progress in almost all facets of life. When people in conversation reminded him of the nation's ills, one of his favorite rejoinders was that "no doubt America would evolute" to higher things. Literature, including his own poetry, was also for him part of a universal evolutionary process. "Evolution," he wrote, "is not the rule in Nature, in Politics, or Inventions only, but in Verse." To Traubel he declared: "*Leaves of Grass* is *evolution*—evolution in its most varied, freest, largest sense."

His evolutionary framework allowed him to deflect things to the future, and, simultaneously, to accept even the less promising facets of the present. *Democratic Vistas*, like a good portion of his postwar poetry, is future oriented. In it Whitman states unequivocally that "the fruition of democracy, on aught like a grand scale, resides altogether in the future." He says he writes "upon things that exist not" and travels "by maps yet unmade."

He defers not only social fruition but also personal fulfillment. His religious inclinations, strong from the start, became even more pronounced after the war as he embraced progressive evolution. In outlining a "model fit for the future personality of America" in *Democratic Vistas*, he said the most crucial element to be cultivated was a "primary moral element," a "penetrating Religiousness." In the seventies he declared that his whole literary career followed a prearranged, spiritualizing trend, with the early poems focusing on the body and the later ones on the soul. While it is doubtful he had ever had any such long-term plan, it is true that in his postbellum, evolutionary phase his mind often turned to what he saw as the soul's voyage to other spheres.

Evolutionism even opened the way to his acceptance of Gilded Age capitalism. His poetry of the fifties had been so antipathetic to the business culture that David Leverenz sees it as a conscious rebuff of capitalistic definitions of manhood. But after the war Whitman became far more amenable to capitalistic enterprise. The impetus given to industrialism by the war was inescapable. Whitman bore witness to the wartime boom. On a train north to Brooklyn in November 1863 he noticed that "the great cities & towns through which I passed look wonderfully prosperous,—it looks any thing else, but war—every body well drest, plenty of money, markets boundless & of the best, factories all busy." Later, he often noted the business expansion of the postwar years. America's total wealth swelled from $8.43 billion in 1850 to $48.95 billion in 1880, and its factory output from $1.06 billion to $5.56 billion in the same period. By 1880 Whitman could write: "In modern times the new word *Business*, has been brought to the front, & now dominates individuals and nations. . . . Business shall be, nay is, the word of the modern hero."

Although he continued to recognize the perils of capitalism, he placed business at the heart of his new outlook. "I perceive clearly," he wrote in *Democratic Vistas*, "that the extreme business energy, and the almost maniacal appetite for wealth prevalent in the United States, are parts of amelioration and progress, indispensably needed to prepare the very results I demand." He never thereafter gave up his basic belief in business, even in the face of sharp criticism from socialist friends. Material prosperity was now essential to his evolutionary program for America. As he put it to the Danish author Rudolph Schmidt in 1874, "I see that the only foundations and *sine qua non* of popular improvement & Democracy are *worldly & material success established first*, spreading & interweaving everywhere—*then* only, but surely for the masses, will come spiritual cultivation & art." It is understandable that many of his friends in the last decade of his life were businesspeople and lawyers.

Whitman's new blend of beliefs and attitudes—embracing evolution, religion, capitalism, and occasional racism—align in several ways with conservative thought of the day. His fantasy of a "class of bards" taking over America is analogous to the conservative notion of the American Social Science Association that a chaotic America must be directed by so-called best men. For all his talk about Personalism in *Democratic Vistas*, his model of "ensemble-Individuality" seems abstract. Hegelianism has always favored the state over the individual, and Whitman's ideal future authors sound almost like dictators: "I demand races of orbic bards, with unconditional uncompromising sway. Come forth, sweet democratic despots of the west!" His acceptance of evolutionary thought had political overtones as well. Evolutionary thought in the late nineteenth century became allied with racism and capitalism. Most evolutionists were racists, since they believed in the victory of so-called superior races in the struggle of life. When Herbert Spencer's notion of "the survival of the fittest" was applied to the economic jungle, it won disciples among American business magnates, including Andrew Carnegie, who had great admiration for both Whitman and Spencer.

Still, *Democratic Vistas* is in several ways a radical document. Its point about the potential sterility and dehumanizing nature of mass culture is acute. Its advocacy of a broad array of roles for women—as businesspersons, political participants, laborers, homemakers and mothers—was in line with the most progressive feminist thought of the time. Its call for constant self-questioning and activism on the part of all American citizens is inspiring.

More fully than any of Whitman's other postwar writings, *Demo-*

cratic Vistas embodies his conflicting tendencies toward conservatism and radicalism.

Personal Tensions, Public Poses

IF THE NATION'S PROBLEMS after the war had come to seem overwhelming to Whitman, so did his personal ones. The easy intertwining of the personal and the poetic that had characterized many of his prewar poems was especially difficult to sustain when his health and his relationships to family and friends were in the throes of change and, in several cases, deterioration.

During the sixties Whitman must have begun to see cruel mockery in his boasts of good health in several passages of his early poems. Although he would retain these lines in all the later editions of *Leaves of Grass,* and indeed add to them, they became less and less descriptive of his actual physical condition.

As early as the summer of 1858, he had suffered what he called a sunstroke but what was probably a small cerebral hemorrhage, the first of many strokes that eventually left him half-paralyzed. It was during the war that his health began to show real unsteadiness. He liked to brag about his ruddy complexion, full beard, and size (he then weighed more than two hundred pounds). But he periodically reported dizziness, trembling, fullness of the head. Shortly after he began his hospital visits, in March 1863, he reported to Jeff "a bad humming feeling & deafness, stupor-like at times, in my head, which unfits me for continued exertion." The next year he reportedly got a bad infection in his arm after being cut by a gangrenous scalpel while assisting in an amputation. In the spring of 1864, a terrible time in the hospitals, he was overcome by a "deathly faintness, and bad trouble in my head too," as he described it. He often felt faint during hot weather, having to carry a sunshade and take rests during walks. He was also plagued by severe colds and sore throats.

Some of his symptoms were signals of his later strokes, and perhaps of mercury poisoning from calomel. For the rest of his life, he would get from doctors as confusing an array of diagnoses as Tolstoy's Ivan Ilyich. The one that stuck in his mind was that the war had ruined his health. In September 1869, after suffering dizziness and sweating while on a visit home in Brooklyn, he was told by a doctor that "it is all from that hospital malaria, hospital poison absorbed in the system." The vague terms were typical of an age before germ theory, when atmospheric influences ("hospital malaria, hospital poison") were thought by many doctors to cause disease.

Whitman lived with the belief that the war had permanently hurt his health. If the war had not succeeded in purifying the social atmosphere, it had, he thought, succeeded in disabling him. He believed this even though his worst incident—the paralyzing stroke of 1873—came long after the war. "[T]hat secession war experience," he would tell a friend in 1890, "was a *whack* or series of whacks irrecoverable." As he put it the next year to another friend, "I am totally paralyzed f'm the old secession wartime overstrain—only my brain volition & right arm power left——." "I had to give up my health for it," he would conclude of the war; "my body, the vitality of my physical self, O so much had to go!"

His failing health doubtless contributed to the declining presence of the body and the ascendancy of the soul in his poetry. But it was not just his own periods of ill health he had to endure: it was those of his family members too.

After the war he continued to take periodic leaves to stay with his family in Brooklyn, and he kept up a steady correspondence with several family members. Too much has been made of Whitman's supposed alienation from his family. True, as he told Traubel, he felt like "a stranger in their midst" in terms of any deep understanding of his poetry. His mother and George had reportedly leafed through *Hiawatha* and the 1855 *Leaves of Grass* and, in George's words, "the one seemed to us pretty much the same muddle as the other."

But his family began to take real interest in his literary fortunes as his fame grew in the sixties. His mother liked sending him clippings about him from the New York–area papers. Her attitude toward his poetry was hardly as indifferent as legend has it. In late 1865 she reported to him her habit of reading in *Drum-Taps* every night before bed. Later she wrote that his poem "Whispers of Heavenly Death" was always at her bedside. When a friend asked to borrow it, as she wrote him, "i said no i would rather not let it go out of my hands." Hannah, too, was truly interested in his progress. "Mother," she wrote in March 1867, "will you ask Walt to be sure to send me all that is published about him. I was glad to get, & am much pleased with the last Leaves of Grass." Even the stolid George and the practical Jeff enjoyed reading the increasing number of pieces in the magazines by and about their brother. The whole family was ecstatic when Anne Gilchrist's piece praising him appeared in 1870 in the Boston *Radical*. The sixties were a time of closeness between the poet and his family, a time that prompted the kind of "tribal" loyalty he later confessed to.

But tribal loyalty had a price: vicarious suffering. He was still the emotional center of the family. His mother kept giving him news of the family's problems. At the end of the war, she, Eddy, and Jeff and Martha with their two children were still living on Portland Avenue, probably confined mainly to the first floor and basement, since they were renting out either the second floor or the back of the house. Her relationship with Jeff and Mattie, as she described it to Walt, was affectionate but subject to eruptions, mainly over money and the behavior of the children. Though basically optimistic, she complained constantly of rheumatism, lameness, and distress in her head.

When George was discharged from the army, he moped around the house, moody and distant, shell-shocked by the war and haunted by his six months in Confederate prisons. In time he recovered sufficiently to start a small building business, but Mrs. Whitman complained that, like Jeff, he could be stingy. (She regularly instructed Walt to "burn this letter" when she made such complaints.) The news from Burlington continued to be distressing: Hannah and her husband carried on their endless feud, and in December 1868 Hannah's thumb had to be amputated due to an infection. Also around that time Jeff's wife, Martha, whom Walt called his "Dear Sister," coughed up blood—an early sign of the agonizing illness, later diagnosed as cancer but probably tuberculosis, that led to her death in 1873. Andrew's widow, Nancy, heartily despised by the family, prostituted and begged on the streets with her three children, one of whom, her son Andrew, was run over and killed by a brewery wagon.

Walt took his relatives' troubles with apparent equanimity, but their dependence on him must have taken its toll. His mother often reminded him of his importance to her, as when she wrote, "i dont know what i would doo walt if it wasent for you to think of me it seems as if all the other sons and daughters has their own to attend to which is perfectly natural." When in March 1870 she learned that her oldest, Jesse, had died of a ruptured aneurysm in the lunatic asylum and was buried in a potter's field, she wrote Walt: "O walt aint it sad to think the poor soul hadent a friend near him in his last moments and to think he had a paupers grave." She was also wont to remind Walt that he alone had full sympathy for the retarded Eddy.

If he was experiencing pain in his family relations, he was hardly free of it in his friendships with men and women. In discussing these friendships, commentators have usually been preoccupied with the way he acted upon, or perhaps sublimated, his passion for young men, as opposed to his evasion of romantic involvements with the women who pursued him. What has been overlooked is the degree to which Whitman struggled to make both his homosexual desires and his heterosexual fears conform to the increasingly powerful Whitman Myth that he and others were cultivating.

Particularly revealing was his relationship with Peter Doyle, who came closer than anyone else to being the love of his life. (Doyle is pictured with the poet in fig. 41.) The Irish-born Doyle, the son of a blacksmith, was born in 1843 and was brought to live in America when he was eight. He lived in Virginia and worked in a Richmond iron foundry before joining the Confederate army. After the war he was a horsecar conductor on the Washington and Georgetown Railroad. One stormy winter night, in early 1865 at twenty-one he met forty-five-year-old Whitman on one of the cars. The poet was returning to his apartment after a visit with Burroughs and was sitting alone with a blanket around his shoulders. Doyle, who thought he looked like an old sea captain, was drawn to him. As he later recalled: "We were familiar at once—I put my hand on his knee—we understood. . . . From that time on we were the biggest sort of friends." For several years thereafter, Walt and Pete saw each other almost daily. They took long walks out the well-paved military roads toward Alexandria, with Walt singing tunes and reciting poetry, usually Shakespeare. Walt sometimes gave Pete a bouquet or had clothes made for him, and when he went on trips sent him newsy, affectionate letters.

That Walt was tortured for a time over his relationship with Pete doesn't mean, as is sometimes argued, that he was trying to "repress" his homosexual attraction to him. As many of his letters attest, he could kiss or spend the night with Doyle openly and without guilt in a culture that accepted intense same-sex passion. What he felt he had to guard against were homoerotic feelings that threatened to upset the equipoise and chasteness he prided himself on and which were important ingredients of the Whitman Myth. We have seen how in a famous diary entry of 1870 he used the phrenological self-help method to try to regulate his "feverish, disproportionate adhesiveness" and to overcome his torment by outlining "a superb, calm character." Just as he had determinedly avoided "perturbations" in his sixties poems, so he tried to keep them under control with Doyle.

He could even sound moralistic in his effort to maintain an emotional balance in himself and his friend. Hence his harsh reprimand when in August 1869 Doyle made some "proposition" that alarmed him. It is unclear whether the proposition related to Doyle's depressed, suicidal feelings over a recent skin rash or to a physical advance Whitman found offensive. "I was unspeakably shocked and repelled from you," the poet wrote, "by that talk & proposition of yours—you know what—

there by the fountain." He continued: "It seemed to me . . . that the one I loved, and who had always been manly & sensible, was gone, & a fool & intentional murderer stood in his place." Exploiting Doyle's Catholicism, he warned, "[D]on't let the devil put such thoughts in your mind again—wickedness unspeakable—murder, death & disgrace, & hell's agonies hereafter."

Whitman was struggling to make his relationship with Doyle conform with the moral and religious conventions that informed his own increasingly conservative self-image. He warned Pete to remain "manly & sensible," to overcome "wickedness unspeakable." When asked later whether Whitman had any bad habits, Doyle noted that he had stuck out in Washington by not smoking and by drinking only moderately. "Walt was too clean, he hated anything which was not clean. Not any kind of dissipation in him." Doyle recalled too Whitman's worship of Lincoln, his religiousness, his faith in an afterlife, his athletic abilities when he was healthy. The image that remained in Doyle's mind, then, was the patriotic, wholesome one that was being peddled by the poet's defenders. For Whitman, Doyle was a working-class gem with a few excusable flaws. Whitman described him to Traubel as "a great big hearty full-blooded everyday divinely generous working man: a hail-fellow-well-met—a little too fond of his beer, now and then, and of the women: maybe, maybe: but for the most part the salt of the earth."

Although passionately devoted to each other, Whitman and Doyle used a discourse of heterosexuality and familial love that heightened the conventional appearance of their relationship. If Whitman said Doyle tended to be a little "too fond . . . of the women," suggesting he was sometimes promiscuous, Doyle emphasized that Whitman, while not licentious, had strong appeal for both women and men. They traded stories about Whitman's reported romantic involvements with women. When the poet was visiting Providence in October 1868, he good-naturedly wrote Doyle of his conquests at parties: "I also made love to the women, & flatter myself that I made at least one impression—. . . . You would be astonished, my son, to see the brass & coolness, & the capacity of flirtation and carrying on with the girls." He added, on a proper note, that this flirtation was "all on the square" and that "they are all as good girls as ever lived." Doyle in turn ribbed Whitman about the report of a mutual friend, Jim Sorrill, about "that young Lady that said you make such a good bedfellow." In his reply to Doyle, Whitman included a note for Sorrill saying "the bedfellow business" was "all right & regular."

Doyle was subject to constant mood shifts, and Whitman in his letters played the consoling, wise parent figure. In the discourse of the relationship, Whitman was the "father" or "uncle," Doyle the "son" or "boy." In a letter of 1870 Whitman wrote: "Dear son, I want you to cast aside all irritating thoughts & recollections, & preserve a cheerful mind." Typical closing lines in his letters were: "Good-bye—my darling boy—from your comrade & father, / Walt."; or, "Here is a good buss to you, dear son, from your loving Father always—."

Was such conventional language, which also characterizes Whitman's letters to other young men, an exercise in sublimation or covering up? The evidence suggests that by the late sixties Whitman's public, conventional posture was infiltrating his unconscious, so that his private desires were largely verbalized in terms of the language of the Whitman Myth. Jacques Lacan brings attention to the crucial role of the signifier (the word or image) in the unconscious. Deemphasizing Freud's preverbal impulses, Lacan puts language at the very root of the psyche. Whitman, who was selling himself publicly as chaste, cheerful, avuncular, and patriotic, used these kinds of signifiers even in his private homoerotic letters. Whenever this self-image was threatened, as in the anxious diary entry or with Doyle by the fountain, he attempted to use conventional discourse to rectify the matter.

So successful was Whitman in defining his inner self by the image he was trying to cultivate that he and Doyle could actually feel like strangers to each other, even after years of intimate friendship. There is a note of genuine surprise, for instance, in an 1870 letter Whitman wrote Doyle from Brooklyn: "I never dreamed that you made so much of having me with you, nor that you could feel so downcast at losing me. I foolishly thought it was all on the other side." Doyle later said that Whitman had a "private border-line" over which no one could step: "He had a freezing way in him—yet was never harsh."

What Doyle sensed as a hidden private self, however, could just as well have been the merged "private-public" self Whitman was developing in the postwar years. Just as Whitman orchestrated Burroughs's and O'Connor's public presentation of his private behavior, so in private he tended to write publicly. His notebook entries on himself, which had never been very personal, began after the war to be increasingly made in the third person, many of them sounding like canned news reports. In a note of 1871 he wrote, "The newspapers still keep up their talk about Walt Whitman," emphasizing that he remained cheerful and manly despite their attacks. Even after his debilitating stroke in 1873 he had enough awareness of his public image to write of himself: *"Walt Whitman's case—Paralysis."* It's not enough to say, as some have, that Whitman became his own "press agent." True, he *was* that from the start, but after the war his "agent" (himself) became intertwined with his "press" (the image he and his friends were pushing).

Maneuverings

IF HE COULD RETREAT into the Whitman Myth in his love affairs with men, he could hide behind it in his relationships with women. The evidence about such relationships is scanty. On March 25, 1862, an Ellen Eyre had written him a letter that strongly suggests they had made love the previous night. That July Whitman mentioned in his diary a Frank Sweezey as "the one I told the whole story to, about Ellen Eyre." There was also Jim Sorrill's "bedfellow" comment and Whitman's old-age references to former girlfriends. Whatever the facts, a presumed heterosexuality was part of Whitman's self-image. In Camden he had on his mantelpiece a portrait of a woman he told his housekeeper was "an old sweetheart of mine." When the *New York Herald* reported in 1888 that Whitman had "never had a love affair," Whitman exploded in rage: "'Taint true! 'Taint true!"

A heterosexual posture was part of the emerging Whitman Myth. During and after the war he defended the marriage institution, opposed free love, and indicted adultery. He found the most famous adultery scandal of the period, the trial of Henry Ward Beecher for his alleged affair with his assistant's wife, "very coarse," though he believed Beecher was innocent. In a poem of 1865 he featured heterosexual fantasy: "Give me for marriage a sweet-breath'd woman of whom I should never tire, / Give me a perfect child, give me away aside from the noise of the world a rural domestic life."

However, critics like Emory Holloway who try to prove Whitman was fundamentally heterosexual have little to stand on. His basic attraction was to men, whatever flirtations or fleeting affairs he may have had with women. On the other hand, those who view his homosexuality in today's terms neglect to mention that Whitman, particularly in his late years, tended to define his relationships to *both* men and women in terms of the image of chasteness, piety, and manliness he was fabricating. Peter Doyle put his attraction to men and women on the same plane: "Towards women generally Walt had a good way—he very easily attracted them. But he did that with men too. And it was an irresistible attraction. I've had many men tell me—men and women."

Whitman's relationship with Anne Gilchrist (see fig. 31) tells us the most about the way he used the Whitman Myth to navigate what for him were the perilous waters of heterosexuality. Before he met her, he had already done a fair amount of navigating. It had been simple enough for him to evade Fanny Fern, who was married and probably did not pursue him, and to ignore the 1861 letter of Susan Garnet Smith, who had proposed to him a mountaintop mating. It was less easy, perhaps, for

him to put off Nelly O'Connor. Nelly had grown intimate with him dur-
ing the war years, and after the war she expressed her love for the poet
coyly but definitely in several letters, most overtly in one of November
20, 1870. Her marriage was in trouble from the midsixties onward, and
after 1872 she and her daughter, Jeannie, lived apart from William. Walt
seems to have handled the situation tactfully. Even though he did not
respond to her advances, he remained on friendly terms with her even
after he too broke with William.

Anne Gilchrist was a different matter. This determined English-
woman, a widow with three children, pursued Whitman in letters, and
in 1876 she moved to Philadelphia to be close to the poet, then living
in Camden. Usually, the relationship between Whitman and Gilchrist is
described as a kind of double failure: a failure on her part to win his love,
and a failure on his part to be able to respond intelligently to her ad-
vances. Actually, though, the relationship was ultimately a great success
for him in terms of the public (and self-) image he was developing. He
used the Myth to deflect her and, later, to incorporate her into his life.

This cat-and-mouse game proved easy enough for Whitman to play,
since from the start Anne Gilchrist swallowed the Myth whole. In early
June 1869 she borrowed from a friend the sanitized Rossetti edition of
Whitman and became instantly obsessed with the poetry. She had been
in a state of spiritual and emotional torment. Several years earlier she
had lost her husband, an intellectual who had written a biography of
Blake. She would later tell Whitman the marriage had been loveless and
its aftermath dreary. To her friend Rossetti she expressed her rapture
over Whitman's poetry in religious terms: "For me the reading of his
poems is truly a new birth of the soul." When Rossetti gave her a com-
plete edition of Whitman's poems, she became exultant: "I had not
dreamed that words could cease to be words, and become electric streams
like these." She found the "Calamus" poems and "Song of Myself" espe-
cially moving. Of the controversial poems on sex, she wrote, "Perhaps
they were indeed chiefly written for wives." In her article "A Woman's
Estimate of Walt Whitman," published the following May in the Boston
Radical, she expanded on her remarks to Rossetti, praising the freshness,
vigor, and joy of Whitman's poems. In particular, she defended what she
called "these beautiful, despised poems, the 'Children of Adam'" as com-
pletely pure.

She kept up the elevated rhetoric when she first wrote Whitman di-
rectly on September 3, 1871. Her emotional missive has often been called
a love letter, but it is far less erotic than pious. In describing to Whitman
the effect of his poems on her, she used the same sort of religious lan-
guage she had used with Rossetti: "It was the divine soul embracing

mine. I never before dreamed what love was like: nor what life meant. Never was alive before. No words but 'new birth' can hint the meaning of what then happened to me." She told him that now she understood "the divineness and sacredness of the Body," and she imagined him saying to her, "Bride, wife, indissoluble eternal!"

She was giving back to him what he had been spoon-feeding the public for years: the message that he and his books were chaste, religious, clean. Whitman had a tactical advantage. His books were a perfect screen. In a short letter of November 3 he wrote, "I too send my love," then quickly set up the screen: "My book is my best letter, my response, my truest explanation of all." He was using his "public-private self" to drive away potential involvement with a woman, just as with Doyle he had used it to perpetuate love with a man. When this approach failed— she continued to pursue him, even offering to bear him children—he decided to try detaching himself from the Myth:

> Dear Friend, let me warn you somewhat about myself—& yourself also. You must not construct such an unauthorized & imaginary ideal Figure, & call it W. W. and so devotedly invest your loving nature in it. The actual W. W. is a very plain personage, & entirely unworthy of such devotion.

Whitman surely knew that he himself had been more responsible than she in constructing an "imaginary ideal Figure" called Walt Whitman, but for the moment he was separating himself from it. In the meantime, he was constructing another imaginary ideal figure: Anne Gilchrist as the noble woman and the perfect reader of his poems. Right in the midst of his evasive maneuvering with her, he calmly wrote Rossetti: "Nothing in my life, nor result of my book, has brought me more comfort & support in every way—nothing has spiritually soothed me— than the warm appreciation & friendship of that true, full-grown woman—." He stayed on this tack when Anne Gilchrist moved to Philadelphia in September 1876, maintaining cordial relations with her and her children until she returned to England three years later. He continued to correspond with her thereafter, and to friends he always portrayed her as the apotheosis of womanhood. He waxed sentimental at her death in 1885, calling her "a sweet & rich memory—none more beautiful, all time, all life, all the earth—." To Traubel he described her as the ideal combination of wife, mother, and intellectual: "She was harmonic, orbic: she was a woman—then more than a woman."

Whitman succeeded in steering through the hazardous waters of all his personal relationships but one: that with William Douglas O'Connor.

In the five years after he wrote *The Good Gray Poet,* O'Connor had remained close to him and continued to be the chief architect, with Burroughs, of the Whitman Myth. The comparison of Whitman with Christ, later a common one in the poet's inner circle, was first made by O'Connor in his story "The Carpenter," published in the January 1868 issue of *Putnam's Monthly Magazine.* In the story, a carpenter spends Christmas Eve 1864 at the home of a farmer's family, which he finds riven by bitter rivalries. The family is symbolic of America with its sectional tensions, since part of the plot involves a son who had served in the Confederate army and who is alienated from his father. The carpenter, a kindly, bearded man with a powerful magnetic influence, heals the divisions in the family. Expressing the comradely love that Whitman thought the surest cure of social divisions, the carpenter warmly kisses one of the male characters and tells him to plant comradeship throughout America.

This mythic story of Whitman's power to resolve personal and social animosities proved sadly ironic, for such animosities led to his separation from O'Connor in 1872. The reason for the decade-long separation, which occurred sometime between August and December, has long been in question. A recent claim that the two had some kind of homosexual quarrel seems implausible, since there is no evidence Whitman ever had anything like a Doyle-type relationship with O'Connor.

A more likely scenario was an argument over civil rights, probably African-American suffrage. As Whitman was the first to admit, the civil rights issue was long a sore point between the two. O'Connor supported the vote for blacks out of principle. Whitman's ambivalence about the issue, discussed earlier, surfaced periodically in the postwar years and lasted into old age. Once when he was discussing black suffrage with Traubel, he said: "I know enough of Southern affairs, have associated enough with Southern people to feel convinced that if I lived South I should side with the Southern whites."

Whitman made this remark in 1890, long after Reconstruction had ended, but he had made similar comments earlier. It is understandable he would come into conflict with O'Connor in 1872, an election year when such issues were being raised, particularly by the Liberal Republican presidential candidate Horace Greeley, a strong advocate of civil rights. In the wake of the Fifteenth Amendment, which gave black men the vote, it would seem that the description of the quarrel by John Burroughs holds the most weight.

According to Burroughs, one day at O'Connor's apartment, during a discussion of this Amendment, "O'Connor became enraged at what Walt had said about the unfitness of negroes for voting." Burroughs reported that Whitman got "brutal and insulting," then grabbed his hat and left in a rage. The next day the two met on the street, and O'Connor passed by in glum silence, refusing to shake Whitman's extended hand. They didn't talk to each other again for more than ten years. This story, corroborated by Nelly O'Connor, may explain why years later, even after he had made up with O'Connor, Whitman often stressed the heatedness of his talks with his friend. "Yes," he told Traubel, "we had the hardest discussions in the old days—brutal ones, I should say," discussions in which "he would go for me in the fiercest way, denounce me—appear to regard me as being negligent, as shirking a duty."

If indeed the break with O'Connor was over African-American suffrage, we have another important piece of information about Whitman's complex relationship to America after the Civil War. He wrote Eldridge uneasily in 1873, "The union promises now to reconstruct— (after a violent and somewhat doubtful struggle.)" For him to talk of the painful and doubtful aspects of Reconstruction at a moment when government-authorized civil rights were moving swiftly is another sign of his ambivalence. Although he still thought of himself as America's poet, he had trouble coming to terms with many pressing political and social realities.

Distressed by widespread corruption, unsure about civil rights, he decided to become the celebrant of mainstream institutions, including one he had helped create: Walt Whitman.

15

THE BURDEN OF ATLAS:
THE NEW AMERICA

A S HE ENTERED the 1870s, Whitman still thought of himself as America's poet. His growing coterie of followers saw him as little less than the nation's savior. His loyal friend Burroughs wrote: "America, my country—I fear I should utterly despair of. He justifies it, redeems, it, gives it dignity and grandeur, bears it all on his shoulders, as Atlas the Earth."

But how was the poetic Atlas to carry the new America, the America of huge corporations, machines, robber barons, advertising agencies, department stores, and rampant consumerism?

There was a part of Whitman that was repelled by the new America. In some respects his attitudes toward the Gilded Age matched those of the era's protestors against capitalism. Like the farmers of the Grange movement, he nostalgically recalled a preindustrial America of small farms and homesteads. Like the reformers Henry George and Edward Bellamy, he was alarmed by class divisions and poverty. Particularly in the devastating years after the panic of 1873, he bore painful witness to the working-class miseries that contributed to burgeoning labor organizations and such protest movements as socialism and anarchism.

Still, he could not overlook the nation's rapid expansion and technological advance. The growth of America's population and industry was often, and justifiably, cited as a unique phenomenon. Between 1830 and 1880 America's population rose from thirteen to fifty million, a nearly 400 percent increase that dwarfed the 41 percent population increase in England and the 17 percent rise in France. Although America remained predominantly agricultural, the percentage of people living in cities of eighty thousand or more increased from just 6.5 percent in 1830 to 22 percent in 1880. In the three decades after 1850, a time when factory output in England doubled, American manufactures multiplied sixfold, a difference almost exactly duplicated by these countries' rise in total wealth. By the early 1880s, 128,000 miles of railways and 760,000 miles of telegraph traversed America—more mileage of each than in all of Europe. No other country had devised so many laborsaving machines and inventions as America. Among the nation's inventions were the first commercially successful steamboat, the first cross-Atlantic steamship, the cotton gin, the first practical mowing, reaping, and sewing machines, and many things related to electricity, including the Atlantic cable, the electric light, and the telephone. These facts were trumpeted with bumptious jingoism by the steel magnate Andrew Carnegie, who wrote in the mideighties: "The old nations of the earth creep on at a snail's pace; the Republic thunders past with the rush of the express."

The lure of capitalist expansion was not lost on Whitman, whom Carnegie considered America's greatest poet. When the bard wrote poems surveying American culture, he no longer produced lively collages of human beings in their personal and social relations, as he had in the fifties, but rather vistas of machines, inventions, and other engineering marvels. He saw the railroad not as the symbol of corporate exploitation, as did the Grange and other reform movements, but as the magical, muscular "type of the modern," allied in its roaring freedom, he thought, to his own poetry. The presidents who oversaw expansionist capitalism elicited from him not only repeated praise but also, in the case of Grant and Garfield, flattering poems. Like Simon Patten, the age's chief economic apologist of capitalism, Whitman thought he saw in modern industry new avenues toward intercommunication and linkage.

In contrast to other poets, such as Longfellow and Whittier, Whitman managed to assimilate modern technology and industry into several poems, most notably "Passage to India" and "Song of the Exposition." Having gained increased public visibility in the sixties, he was able in the seventies and early eighties to place his poems and prose in a number of mainstream periodicals. He was no longer shoved off to marginal sheets like the *American Phrenological Journal* or the *Saturday Press*, as had been true before the war, but now appeared in *Harper's*, the *New York Herald*, the *Century*, and elsewhere. He also gave well-publicized poetry readings, as at the 1871 New York industrial exposition, and, starting in 1879, the long-running series of Lincoln lectures that eventually made him a household name.

Nonetheless, he constantly presented himself as a writer almost totally neglected by his country. So powerful was the image of neglect he created that it persists even to this day, when many view him as a "solitary singer" distanced in many ways from mainstream culture. While it is true that, like most writers, he got his share of rejection slips and snubs from the literary establishment, it has not been adequately recognized that the neglect idea was largely a ploy he used to whip up support and speed his dreamed-of acceptance by the general public. In the seventies he became extraordinarily disturbed by the fact that even while he was being increasingly recognized abroad as the most distinctively American poet, this recognition was not coming from the American public, which still preferred Anglophile poets like Longfellow. As a result, he was a kind of entrepreneur of neglect, using his connections abroad to arouse sympathy in America.

Although the strategy failed to gain him a popular readership, it secured for him the kind of institutional recognition and support that would snowball in the eighties.

Sacred Industry

THERE WAS A KIND OF FAMILY LOGIC to Whitman's embrace of mainstream institutions. The two most artistically inclined members of his family, Hannah and Charles Heyde, seemed always on the verge of mental and financial ruin, while the two most practical ones, George and Jeff, were advancing in the areas related to the modern field of engineering. There was a close connection between engineering and capitalism. David Noble shows that "the history of modern technology is of a piece with that of the rise of corporate capitalism." The engineer, Noble points out, was "a new breed of man, the link between science and business." The American Society of Civil Engineers was founded in 1852, and by the eighties Thomas Edison had turned engineering into a business.

The engineer brothers were involved in one of the most important of the technological fields: public sanitation. Whitman had intended much of his poetry to have a cleansing effect on American society, but, from a practical standpoint, his brothers' engineering efforts came far closer to doing so than his writings.

Of the brothers, George was the least spectacular but ultimately the more successful financially. After a short time in the building business, in 1867 George became a pipe inspector for Moses Lane, the chief engineer for the Brooklyn Water Works. Also that year he was called to inspect pipes in Camden, New Jersey, and he worked part-time in both cities, boarding in Philadelphia until his marriage to Louisa Orr Haslam in April 1871. He and Louisa settled at 322 Stevens Street, Camden, where his mother and his brother Eddy joined them in August 1872. He continued inspecting water pipes in Camden and was soon made a mem-

ber of the New York Metropolitan Water Board. In time, George prospered; at his death in 1901 he left an estate of nearly sixty thousand
dollars, in those days a large sum. Although Walt once joked that George
cared more for pipes than poems, the poet over time became deeply indebted to him and Louisa, with whom he lived cheaply in Camden from
1873 to 1884.

Jeff was a naturally gifted engineer whose central role in public waterworks projects held appeal for Walt, who had hailed the Croton water
system in 1842 and Brooklyn's McAlpine water plan in the late fifties.
During the war, the poet's hospital work had been aided by contributions
from Jeff's associates at the Brooklyn Water Works, the first scientifically
engineered, coordinated system of sewers and waterworks in the country.
Not only had Jeff helped design the system, but in 1867 he was called to
St. Louis to construct a waterworks system for that growing city of
300,000. Walt called Jeff's new job, which paid $350 monthly, "a great
work—a noble position—& will give you a good big field." Jeff's wife,
Mattie, and their two children lived briefly in Towanda, Pennsylvania,
then returned to Brooklyn until they joined Jeff early in 1868 in St.
Louis. Jeff had an uncanny ability to survey a site for a reservoir without
using much mathematical calculation. He was also a technocrat who participated in the professionalization of his field. He was one of the first
members of the American Society of Civil Engineers, and, after completing his main work on the St. Louis project in 1871, he helped design
waterworks systems in five other midwestern cities as well. Upon his
death in 1890, his St. Louis project was hailed as "possibly the best designed, best constructed, and most practical system of Water Works of
any large city West of the Alleghanies." Although Walt didn't write Jeff
often after Mattie's death in 1873, he often hosted Jeff's daughters in
Camden and stayed several weeks with his brother on his 1880 western
trip.

More important to Whitman, though, than direct contact with Jeff,
was his overall interest in the kind of engineering accomplishments Jeff
and many others were achieving. The laying of the Atlantic cable had
inspired his enthusiasm in the fifties, and the subsequent completion of
the Suez Canal and transcontinental railroad increased his reverence for
engineering. These and other technological advances seemed to promise
the kind of cultural unification he had formerly hoped his poetry and
then the Civil War would accomplish. Each major feat of engineering
was a unifying phenomenon in a double way: in an age almost naïvely
wondrous of progress, it was greeted by mass celebrations; in an increasingly industrial society, it opened up new means of communication and
trade. For instance, when the Central and Union Pacific Railroads met

on May 10, 1869, near Promontory Point, Utah, virtually all Americans from the president to the young child were swept up in the enthusiasm over the event, which facilitated western trade and travel.

Whitman was coming to believe that the cultural unification he had been seeking might be achieved through the technological-industrial feats Americans were celebrating. He paid homage to these feats in three characteristic poems of the early seventies: "Passage to India," "The Return of the Heroes," and "Song of the Exposition." The poems gave technology an almost transcendental significance. More than two decades before the 1893 World's Columbian Exposition in Chicago, in which religion and technology were memorably joined, Whitman sang hymns to the modern age.

"Passage to India," completed in April 1870 and later featured as the first poem in an annex of the 1871–72 *Leaves of Grass,* is the quintessential statement of Whitman's relationship to the new America. Whitman would tell Traubel, "There is more of me, the essential ultimate me, in that than in any of the poems." This was not the "ultimate" Whitman of the fifties, sensuously caressing the world around him, but rather the one of the early seventies, praising technology and using it as a metaphor for eventual poetic and religious fruition. In *Democratic Vistas,* completed the same year as the poem, he pictured America evolving through its current business phase toward some literary and spiritual nirvana. This embrace of the industrial present and deferral of salvation was equally visible in the poem.

Engineering marvels preoccupy Whitman early in the poem. "Singing the great achievements of the present," he writes, "Singing the strong light works of engineers, / Our modern wonders." Bringing special attention to the Atlantic cable and the transcontinental railroad, he continues, "The New by its mighty railroad spann'd, / The seas inlaid with eloquent gentle wires." Technology's promise of cultural unity particularly intrigues him:

> The earth to be spann'd, connected by network,
> The races, neighbors, to marry and be given in marriage,
> The oceans to be cross'd and the distant brought near,
> The lands to be welded together.

Whitman's all-unifying "I" is nowhere to be seen: now he leaves it up to engineers and their ilk to take care of cultural cohesion. "A new worship I sing, [. . .] / You engineers, you architects, machinists, yours." He still insists on the poet's role in healing society, but he defers the poet's arrival to an undefined future:

After the great captains and engineers have accomplished their work,
After the noble inventors, after the scientists, the chemist, the
    geologist, the ethnologist,
Finally shall come the poet worthy that name,
The true son of God shall come singing his songs.

His choice here of modern precursors to the poet was telling. Four—
engineers, inventors, scientists, chemists—were partners in the emerg-
ing technological-industrial culture of capitalist America. One, the
ethnologist, parented the pseudoscientific racial-extinction theory that
Whitman embraced after the war. Given the earlier line about the
"races, neighbors" intermarrying and melding, one cannot help think of
the ethnologists' idea of so-called "superior" races gaining dominance
over others.

Whatever the racial theme, it is the religious one that Whitman fea-
tures in the second half of the poem, which optimistically envisages fu-
ture healing and spiritual liberation. William Leach demonstrates that
in the late nineteenth century a close connection developed between cap-
italistic culture and the healthyminded religions associated with the
mind-cure movement. Whitman, whom William James would later call
the archetypal poet of healthymindedness, makes this connection in
"Passage to India," moving from technological wonders to optimistic re-
ligion. When the future poet arrives, he assures us, all human woes will
disappear, and spiritual unity will be achieved: "All these separations and
gaps shall be taken up and hook'd and link'd together, / [...] Nature and
Man shall be disjoin'd and diffused no more, / The true son of God shall
absolutely fuse them."

Did Whitman see himself as the all-healing son of God? Not as
clearly as he once had. He would tell Traubel that the essence of "Pas-
sage to India" was "evolution—the one thing escaping the other—the
unfolding of cosmic purposes." The poem thus enforced his postwar be-
lief in progressive evolution. More specifically, it signaled, like his other
writings of the period, the departure of the former Whitman "I." The
"I" of the poem sings the technological present, anticipates a future
poet, and then expresses an urgent desire to escape to the spiritual realm.
The closing section of the poem projects the adventurous flight of "my
soul." There's a desperation in the call of the "I" for immediate with-
drawal from the world: "Away O soul! hoist instantly the anchor! / Cut
the hawsers—haul out—shake out every sail!" "Passage, immediate
passage! the blood burns in my veins!" demands the "I." He has no fear
of his venture into the spiritual world, for he is confident of the ultimate

meaning of things in a harmonious universe: "O daring joy, but safe! are they not all the seas of God?"

The poem's movement from rapture over technology to imaginings of spirituality suggests an underlying uneasiness, as though Whitman wants to exalt capitalistic America but also to escape it. This uneasiness is less visible in his two other technology poems, "The Return of the Heroes" and "Song of the Exposition." Both show Whitman trying to turn from the Civil War to the technological, business-oriented new America. In the latter poem he exclaims: "Away with themes of war! away with war itself!" In the former he writes, "Melt, melt away ye armies—disperse ye blue-clad soldiers," as he invites America to replace bloody conflict "With saner wars, sweet wars, life-giving wars."

The "saner wars" he now extols have to do with the machines and implements used by Americans in the industrial workplace. Even while he dismisses the Civil War, he extends its metaphors into the present, as did many of his contemporaries, from Republican leaders, who often expressed their support of capitalism in military terms, to Samuel Gompers with his "armies" of workers and Edward Bellamy with his vision of society organized as an industrial army. Like many other postwar Americans who waved the bloody shirt, Whitman devotes parts of both poems to recalling war scenes, at one point picturing the Union flag in battle as "a mere remnant grimed with dirt and smoke and sopp'd in blood." He could wave the bloody shirt with the most patriotic Republican.

He could also outdo any budding technocrat in his endorsement of the machine age. In "Return of the Heroes" he shouts orders to his own industrial army: "Toil on heroes! toil well! handle the weapons well!" The "weapons" are the machines that were gaining widespread use in postwar America:

> The human-divine inventions, the labor-saving implements;
> Beholdest moving in every direction imbued as with life the
>   revolving hay-rakes,
> The steam-power reaping machines and the horse-power machines,
> The engines, thrashers of grain and cleaners of grain, well separating
>   the straw, the nimble work of the patent pitchfork,
> Beholdest the newer saw-mill, the southern cotton-gin, and the rice-
>   cleanser.

He is praising here the mechanization of agriculture that swelled the production of farm products after the war. Even as America became increasingly urban, agricultural production soared, due largely to the expanding use of the mechanical instruments Whitman described.

That he also saw worth in many other kinds of machines is made clear in "Song of the Exposition." This poem, originally titled "After All, Not to Create Only," merits special attention because it was the first of many public performances to mainstream audiences that punctuated Whitman's later years. This performance was carried out very much within a capitalistic, institutional framework.

On August 1, 1871, the Board of Managers of the American Institute offered Whitman a hundred dollars plus travel and lodging to come to New York and deliver a poem for its Fortieth National Industrial Exposition. Within three days Whitman accepted. His poetry reading on September 7 was an important public event, covered in the New York papers. Biographers have tended to downplay the performance, characterizing it as poorly executed and generally lambasted. It is true that two New York papers, the *Times* and the *World,* said that Whitman's restrained delivery prevented his being heard in the noisy exposition room except by those in the first few rows. But, overall, the event was a publicity coup for Whitman, in both the short and the long run. The *Commercial Advertiser* emphasized that "the national poet" was greeted by long, loud applause. The *Evening Post* called Whitman "a good elocutionist," and in a piece titled "Our Great Poet" the *Globe* pointed out England's love of Whitman, asking: "What other American poet has been honored like this?" The managers of the institute were delighted, for on September 11 they sent him an official note thanking him for his "magnificent original Poem." The poem was printed in no fewer than a dozen newspapers, and it would remain a key reference point for capitalist-leaning advocates of Whitman.

Such advocates had reason to be pleased with the poem, the most glowing rendering of the industrial landscape by any late-nineteenth-century American poet. Whitman imagines the Muse emigrating from foreign lands like Greece and Europe to America: "For know a better, fresher, busier sphere, a wide, untried domain, awaits, demands you." Embracing even the most trivial technological devices, Whitman presents the Muse

> By thud of machinery and shrill steam-whistle undismay'd
> Bluff'd not a bit by drain-pipe, gasometers, artificial fertilizers,
> Smiling and pleas'd with palpable intent to stay,
> She's here, install'd amid the kitchen ware!

Greater than Egypt's pyramids or Greece's temples, he continues, are the products displayed at the modern industrial expositions, which are "Thy cathedral sacred industry." He imagines a cluster of "palaces" in which are shown all the latest inventions, many of which he lists by name. Praising the new industrial "army," he says that the war has gone, "And in its stead speed industry's campaigns, / With thy undaunted armies, engineering, / Thy pennants labor, loosen'd to the breeze." Once again, the real reward of modern technology for him is its promise of world unity:

> With latest connections, works, the inter-transportation of the world,
> Steam-power, the great express lines, gas, petroleum,
> These triumphs of our time, the Atlantic's delicate cable,
> The Pacific railroad, the Suez canal, the Mount Cenis and Gothard
>   and Hoosac tunnels, the Brooklyn bridge,
> This earth spann'd with iron rails, with lines of steamships treading
>   every sea,
> Our own rondure, the current globe I bring.

Whereas later poets like Allen Ginsberg would portray industrial America as a terrifying "Moloch," Whitman participated fully in his age's joy over smoke-billowing factories:

> Mark the spirit of invention everywhere, thy rapid patents,
> Thy continual workshops, risen or rising,
> See, from the chimneys how the tall flame-fires stream.

The poem closes with a patriotic paean to the Union and the flag. Just as "The Return of the Heroes" ends by picturing industrial activity going forward "under the beaming sun" of a "Maternal" America, so "Song of the Exposition" declares that industry is "All thine O sacred Union!" under "thou, the Emblem waving over all!"

Whitman had always sung praise to America's work, jobs, and inventions, but the differences between his prewar and postwar poems on the topic are striking. Those become clear if we compare the 1855 poem "A Song for Occupations" with the postwar poems. In 1855, the personal "I" is dominant, and the human reality of individual workers is supreme. Whitman begins "A Song for Occupations" on a highly intimate note ("Come closer to me, / Push close my lovers and take the best I possess"), and he goes on to describe a lively multitude of workers and jobs, ending with the affirmation that the individual behind the job is sacred above all.

The later poems, in contrast, reflect an age when workers had become increasingly dependent on machines and distanced from their employers. Instead of singing of individual laborers, Whitman now valo-

rizes "sacred industry." In 1855, warm affection and simple love of the
job fuse all; in 1871, modern technology and the Union are looked to for
fusion. Whitman's emphasis has shifted from workers to the workforce,
from individuals to industrial "armies." The earlier poem ends by as-
serting the supremacy of the human being; the later ones highlight the
machines that facilitate work and communication. Postwar America has
changed dramatically before Whitman's eyes and demands a different
kind of response than before. The new industrial revolution invites a
poetry that is vast, one that tries to come to terms with factories, corpora-
tions, and mechanical contrivances.

But Whitman was not up to the task. "Song of the Exposition" was
the final vast poem about American life he would ever write. He would
continue to treat America—its history, its leaders, its inventions—in in-
dividual poems, but never again would he write with the sweep he mani-
fested in "Passage to India" and "Song of the Exposition." He would
incessantly reshape *Leaves of Grass* and tailor his public image, but as a
cultural poet he showed signs of bafflement and exhaustion. Besides the
three large poems about technology, the 1871–72 *Leaves of Grass* in-
cluded forty-one other poems, many of them brief and all so varied as to
indicate a splintering of his poetic aims.

In August 1870 Whitman was on leave in Brooklyn supervising the
printing of the new *Leaves of Grass*. As usual, he was hopeful about the
forthcoming publication. In September he wrote a friend he had "been
engaged in electrotyping my book in better form" The result of his la-
bors, however, was another plain, self-effacing book. As in 1867, there
was no author's picture. The green cloth binding with *Leaves of Grass*
stamped on the spine was a small step toward elegance after the drab
1867 volume. For the 1871 version Whitman arranged the poems into
twenty-two groups, sixteen of them titled. There were twenty-four new
poems in the volume, in the annex *Passage to India*. Two expanded later
issues, made from the same plates with separately paginated annexes
titled *After All, Not to Create Only* and *As a Strong Bird on Pinions Free*,
included a total of sixteen new poems, including "Song of the Exposi-
tion." Of the 1872 version, Whitman boasted to Peter Doyle: "My new
edition looks the best yet— ... my books are beginning to do pretty
well—I send you the publisher's slip."

What Doyle could not know was that Whitman's new poems, though
sometimes powerful, showed a poet unsure of his direction. While the
poet had tightened the organization of the older poems, the new ones
were all over the place thematically. Most of them were short, with three
("The Untold Want," "Portals," and "These Carols") consisting of just
two lines. One picturesque vignette, "Sparkles from the Wheel," has a

disembodied "I" join some children who are watching a knife grinder whose whirring stone radiates sparks. Whitman's "I" has been reduced to a spectral spectator: "Myself effusing and fluid, a phantom curiously floating, now here absorb'd and arrested." The phantom image is significant, for several of the new poems are about spirituality and the afterlife. "Gliding O'er All" envisages "The voyage of the soul—not life alone, / Death, many deaths I'll sing." "Whispers of Heavenly Death" presents death as a new birth, and "Pensive and Faltering" calls the dead "Haply the only living, only real, / And I the apparition, I the spectre." These poems negate the living, breathing "I" and see the spiritual realm as the only sure reality.

It is fitting that one of the most memorable new poems, "A Noiseless Patient Spider," uses the ever-unreeling spider's thread as an analogue for the soul's launching into "measureless oceans of space" and "seeking the spheres to connect them." Whitman himself now seems to be dangling in space and looking for things to connect with. On the one hand, he produces an obsequious, procapitalist poem like "Outlines for a Tomb," eulogizing the millionaire philanthropist George Peabody as a "stintless, lavish giver" who funds the arts and feeds the poor. On the other hand, he has memories of his former rebellious self, though now it is almost lost in garbled syntax:

> Still though the one I sing,
> (One, yet of contradictions made,) I dedicate to Nationality,
> I leave in him revolt, (O latent right of insurrection!
>   O quenchless, indispensable fire!)

If it is unclear who wins in these lines—the insurrectionary self or Nationality—in most of the 1871–72 poems the latter definitely gets the nod. The suppression of the individual and the valorization of the mystical Union visible in the technology poems are also controlling factors in "Thou Mother with Thy Equal Brood": "I'd sow a seed for thee of endless Nationality, / [. . .] I'd show away ahead thy real Union, and how it may be accomplish'd." Confident lines, these, but laced with doubt. The "real Union" lies "away ahead," not in the present. As in *Democratic Vistas*, America's salvation lies in the indeterminate future. Looking into this future, Whitman sees a "larger, saner brood of female, male," and "sacerdotal bards, kosmic savans." He sees evil too: a "livid cancer" and "moral consumption" that threaten the nation's very life. But he asserts that the "Equable, natural mystical Union" will surmount all difficulties, going forward under its "natal stars, [. . .] Ensemble, Evolution, Freedom, / Set in the sky of Law." To drive home his point that America's only real hope lies in the future, Whitman concludes with these lines about his country, capitalizing all the letters of the main word:

> The Present holds thee not—for such vast growth as thine,
> For such unparallel'd flight as thine, such brood as thine,
> The FUTURE only holds thee and can hold thee.

Whereas in 1855 Whitman had believed his all-absorbing, equable "I" could absorb all his culture's images and offer healing by reveling in the miraculous present, now he looks to an abstract "mystical Union," guided by "Evolution" and "Law," which he hopes may bring future realization.

Events of the early seventies proved that this deferral of possibilities was understandable for a poet no longer able to absorb the "vast growth" of his nation. The papers were full of lurid accounts of political corruption in American cities, most notably that of Boss Tweed, who was exposed fully in 1870 and who would die in prison eight years later. Even worse was accumulating evidence of corruption in the Grant administration, emphasized by the president's opponents in the 1872 race. Whitman, who idolized Grant, never directly mentioned that the president's inefficiency perpetuated or gave rise to a series of corruption-related scandals, including Crédit Mobilier, the Whiskey Ring, and the Salary Grab. There were even reports of financial irregularities in the attorney general's office under George H. Williams, who became Whitman's boss in December 1871. Whitman's unwillingness to believe the worst of Grant is suggested in his aptly titled poem "Nay, Tell Me Not To-day the Publish'd Shame," which appeared in the New York *Daily Graphic* in March 1873. Whitman seems so overwhelmed by the growing spectacle of governmental corruption that he instinctively rejects it:

> Nay, tell me not to-day the publish'd shame,
> Read not to-day the journal's crowded page,
> The merciless reports still branding forehead after forehead,
> The guilty column following guilty column,
> To-day to me the tale refusing,
> Turning from it—from the white capitol turning.

Whitman turns from the numerous reports of governmental malfeasance to America's "million untold manly lives." He compares himself to "a determined diver" plunging to "the deep hidden waters"—that is, to the average, good American. He tried another metaphor in a slightly later poem, "Wandering at Morn," in which he writes desperately:

"Yearning for thee harmonious Union! [...] / Thee coil'd in evil times my country, with craft and black dismay, with every meanness, treason thrust upon thee." He compares America to a bird, feeding on "worms, snakes, loathsome grubs" but singing "sweet spiritual songs." If "vermin" can be "so transposed," he writes, then he can hope America's "future song may rise with joyous trills, / Destin'd to fill the world."

And so the wishful, future-pointing metaphors continued to trickle out of him. The poet whom John Burroughs saw as an Atlas holding up the nation was bending under the weight of modern-day America. In 1873, a fateful year for the nation and for Whitman, the weight came crashing down.

The Dark Years?

THE EVENING OF JANUARY 22, 1873, started out as a cozy one for Whitman. The poet had been recently transferred from the attorney general's office to the Treasury Department. His office in the Treasury building that night was cold, with the winter sleet pelting the windows. Whitman lit a fire, took up Bulwer-Lytton's potboiling novel *What Will He Do with It?* and stretched out on a couch. But a strange dizziness kept coming over him, and he had to lay the book down several times. For three years he had enjoyed fairly good health. In April 1870 he had gotten a bad infection from a thumb cut that took weeks to heal, but since then he had been bragging in his letters about feeling "sassy." As he struggled to pay attention to Bulwer's labored prose, he could have no way of foreseeing the calamity soon to follow.

After a while he left off reading and decided to return to his two-room apartment on Fifteenth Street NW. As he was leaving the Treasury building, a guard noticed that he looked ill and offered to escort him home. Whitman twice refused the offer but at last let the guard guide him through the storm with his lantern. Upon arriving home, Whitman immediately went to bed. He awoke in the middle of the night and found he couldn't move his left arm or leg. Thinking it would pass off, he fell back to sleep but in the morning discovered that his left side was almost totally immobile.

He lay for hours until friends arrived and called in a doctor, Beverly Drinkard. The calm, gentlemanly Drinkard had as small an understanding of strokes as did most doctors of the time. He assured Whitman that the problem was emotional and that recovery was not far off. Three days after the incident Whitman wrote his mother that he was temporarily laid up with "a slight stroke of paralysis, ... but the doctor gives me good

hopes of being out and at my work in a few days." But it would be three
months before he was back part-time at his Treasury desk. Whitman
later called Drinkard "the best Doctor that ever was," but there was little
the good doctor could do to relieve the dizziness and nausea the poet felt
when he tried to get up. Bedridden for weeks, Whitman was cheered by
regular visits from Nelly O'Connor, Pete Doyle, and Charles Eldridge.
But by April he could still barely walk a block without help. Later that
month Drinkard tried to relieve him with galvanic battery treatments,
rubbing his legs every other day with electrically charged handles that
Whitman said felt like "something pressing a sore." The treatment had
little effect and was soon stopped, after which Whitman was prescribed
some pills that were of little more use than the whiskey and buttermilk
Drinkard told him to drink.

To his mother Whitman tried to put the best face on his illness. She
had not been very happy since moving to Camden the previous August.
She complained, with little apparent justification, that George and Lou-
isa were parsimonious and inhospitable, and she reported that Eddy
missed his Brooklyn church. Although from afar she was unaware of the
severity of Walt's condition, she was devastated in late February by the
news from St. Louis of the death of Jeff's wife, Mattie. The news was
hardly unexpected, for Mattie had suffered bravely for years, living much
of the time on a prescribed diet of whiskey and raw oysters. Despite her
occasional differences with Mattie, Mrs. Whitman had developed a deep
emotional bond with her vivacious daughter-in-law, who had been press-
ing her to move with Eddy to St. Louis. After Mattie's death, she wrote
Walt, "i never had any one even my own daughters i could tell every
thing to as i could her." Walt too was deeply saddened by Mattie's death,
though he understated his grief in his letters to his mother, who was
showing signs of depression and physical debility. On May 1 she wrote
him, "i have not felt very well lately i am troubled." She was experienc-
ing appetite loss and trembling spells, though she still fantasized about
moving to Washington and setting up house with him. Two weeks later
he learned from Louisa that his mother was declining fast, and he rushed
to be at her bedside, arriving in Camden on May 20. Three days later
she was dead.

As bad as was Walt's paralysis, it was not as terrible a blow to him as
his mother's death. His friend Helen Price, who was among the thirty-
odd present at the funeral, noticed a muffled, thumping sound that regu-
larly broke the stillness of the service. She went into the next room and
saw the poet seated by his mother's coffin, his head bent and his cupped
hands pounding his cane on the floor. Louisa told Helen that he had

been there the whole previous night. Four months later Whitman wrote Helen's mother Abby that his mother's death was "the great dark cloud of my life—the only staggering, staying blow & trouble I have had—but *unspeakable*—my physical sickness, bad as it is, is nothing to it—." For years after his mother's death he slept on her pillow. He later wrote a poem about himself by his mother's corpse: "I sit by the form in the coffin, / I kiss and kiss convulsively the sweet old lips, the cheeks, the closed eyes in the coffin."

His mother's illness and death brought him even closer than before to several members of his family. In mid-May he had taken the precaution of making out a will, the first of three in a year and of several more later on. In this version, he left his $1,500 in savings to Eddy, gold rings to George, Jeff, Mary, and Hannah, and a gold watch and $89 to Pete Doyle. Shortly after his mother's death he received a compassionate note from Hannah: "I want to ask you dear brother to try not to grieve.... We all seem, Eddy and all, to depend on you so much, and next to dear Mother you are the very nearest to us." Nine days after the funeral he went to Washington, but he was weak and depressed, and after arranging with his landlord to retain just one of his rooms, he returned to Camden. His brother's house was on a block of brick homes with white marble doorsteps and white wooden shutters. Whitman moved into the rooms on the second floor where his mother had lived, using her furniture and, in his words, "living day & night in her memory & atmosphere." In October he moved with the family down the block to 431 Stevens Street, a new corner house where he chose a sunny, third-story bedroom facing south.

His health remained shaky, and doctors kept making guesses about his condition. Dizziness, faintness, vomiting, and slow locomotion were his main symptoms. A loud, blustery Philadelphia doctor, Matthew Grier, suggested in September that he had cerebral anemia, or insufficient blood to the brain, arising from "a long continued excessive emotion action generally." But before long Dr. Grier was insisting that the main problem lay in the intestines or stomach, while Dr. Drinkard changed his diagnosis to a malfunctioning liver. Whitman would not get a reasonable diagnosis until 1878, when Dr. S. Weir Mitchell, a specialist in nervous disorders, told him his paralysis resulted from a ruptured blood vessel in the brain. But Whitman continued to swing between various diagnoses and proposed remedies thereafter.

Given his recent losses and precarious condition, it is surprising Whitman did not fall into a complete mental slump. He later recalled the 1873–76 period as the darkest of his life, a time of ill health and utter neglect, and commentators in his time and ours have generally seen it as such. But his letters and other writings from this period paint a brighter picture.

He had no problem with his new surroundings. Soon after arriving in Camden, he wrote Doyle, "It has been a good move of me coming here." He had a positive attitude toward Camden that would later surprise his out-of-town friends. "Camden was originally an accident—but I shall never be sorry I was left over in Camden!" he told Traubel. "It has brought me blessed returns." He was curious enough about Camden and its environs to jot this note to himself:

MEMORANDA
   (Old & New) of
CAMDEN
   The Delaware River Region
& NEW JERSEY generally

Despite its reputation for drabness, Camden was much like the Brooklyn of Whitman's youth: a small but fast-growing industrial city linked by ferries to a major city across a beautiful river. Named after the British statesman Charles Pratt, Earl of Camden, who had sided with the American colonies in the Revolutionary War, the city had been incorporated in 1828, when its population of 1,143 was clustered near the ferries on the Delaware River. By the time Whitman moved there in 1873, its population had increased more than twenty-five-fold, to over 30,000. In the nineteen years he lived there, it would more than double, its growth spurred by its rapid expansion as a transportation and industrial center. It was a major railroad nexus. The Camden and Amboy Railroad was then the main rail link between Philadelphia and New York, and the Camden and Atlantic Railroad went east to Atlantic City. The incessant rumble of the city's freight and passenger trains was a nuisance to some, but Whitman loved it. "The trains of the Camden & Amboy," he wrote Doyle from his third-story room, "are going by on the track about 50 or 60 rods from here, puffing & blowing—often train after train, following each other—following each other—& locomotives singly, whisking & squealing, up the track & then down again—I often sit and watch them long—& think of you."

He could also hear the noise of many nearby factories. Several blocks away, at the foot of Stevens Street, was the Camden Iron Works, with six large foundries covering twenty acres. It was at this nationally known manufacturer of gasworks machinery and steam pipes that his brother George did most of his work. Also on Stevens was the imposing brick building of the Camden Tool and Tube Works. Some ten other machine- or ironworks factories were elsewhere in Camden, as well as a number of textile mills. Less than half a mile to the west of the Whitman house, along the Delaware shore across from Philadelphia, stretched a line of busy lumber mills that made a distant whirring sound.

Like the Brooklyn of old, Camden was in the midst of a building boom. Speculators bought large numbers of lots and built small frame or brick houses on them, hoping to turn a profit by selling or renting them. Though in 1876 Whitman would cry poverty to arouse sympathy, he had actually saved a good portion of his wages from the Washington years, and he had sufficient funds to try his hand modestly in real estate. In July 1874 he bought a lot on Royden Street for $450, hoping to put a house on it. His plan never reached fruition, for he sold the lot eight years later at a small profit. But he could not complain about his living arrangements. George and Louisa kept his rent low. For the whole period he boarded with them, from June 1873 to March 23, 1884, he paid them an average of $3.60 a week—about a third of what he would have had to pay had he rented a small house of his own. They gave him good food and companionship, and he in turn helped out with Eddy.

Given his relatively comfortable circumstances, what explains Whitman's marked shift as a poet? Since he was now living in a prototypical rising industrial city, why did he not continue writing hymns to the new America in the vein of "Song of the Exposition" or "The Return of the Heroes"?

A major reason for the change was that in 1873 the new America was threatened with ruin. In September the banking house of the financier Jay Cooke collapsed, and the country was thrown into what would prove to be its longest and most severe downturn until the Great Depression of the 1930s. Businesses failed by the hundreds. Steel production plummeted by 40 percent, and other basic industries operated at minimum levels. Bankruptcies and unemployment soared, and hordes of homeless tramps roamed the cities.

Whitman would not write again in detail on current America until the late seventies, and when he did he could only contemplate the devastating results of the depression. On an 1878 visit to Burroughs's upstate New York farm he encountered a tramp family whose look of "misery, terror, destitution" appalled him. The next year in "The Tramp and Strike Questions" he said the main issue of the time was "social and economic organization, the treatment of working-people by employers." He added glumly: "If the United States, like the countries of the Old World, are also to grow vast crops of poor, desperate, dissatisfied, miserably-waged populations, such as we see looming upon us of late years—steadily, even if slowly, eating into them like a cancer of lungs or stomach—then our republican experiment, notwithstanding all its surface-successes, is at heart an unhealthy failure."

In the meantime, the closest he could come to his former enthusiasm for the machine age was his poem "To a Locomotive in Winter," published in the February 19, 1876, *New York Tribune*. In describing the Camden trains to Doyle he had singled out the locomotives, and his poem takes a lyric view of the powerful engine with its black cylindrical body, gyrating sidebars, and smokestack belching gray-black clouds. There is no sign in the poem of the iniquities railroad companies had been charged with by the Grange movement, or of bitterness over the huge drop in railroad construction in 1874 that had created massive unemployment. Whitman was still able to assume his former transcendental stance toward a quintessential nineteenth-century machine. "Fierce-throated beauty!" he called it, and: "Type of the modern—emblem of motion and power—pulse of the continent, / For once come serve the Muse and merge in verse, even as here I see thee."

But "To a Locomotive in Winter" is an anomaly among Whitman's poems of the midseventies. It seems to have sprung almost impromptu from him one winter day while he did his habitual train watching in Camden.

In his other poems of the period he was far more ambivalent about the technological, industrial America he had once extolled. Between the fall of 1873, when the economic panic began, and the winter of 1875 Whitman wrote four major poems—"Song of the Redwood-Tree," "Prayer of Columbus," "Song of the Universal," and "Eidólons"—that showed his now-complicated relationship to the new industrial America. The first of these poems tried to transcend the new America with its problems; the second to register the anguish it was causing Whitman; the third to evade it through idealization; the last to make it disappear altogether.

Whitman wrote "Song of the Redwood-Tree" in late fall 1873 and submitted it to *Harper's Magazine*, which paid him his requested fee of one hundred dollars and published it in its February 1874 issue. In the poem, a dying redwood near the California coast is the vehicle for a utopian vision of a future America. Whitman now insists that the new America will be planted in the Far West, away from the East and its problems. In this 105-line poem only one line mentions industrial America. Whitman says that someday the West will have "Populous cities, the latest inventions, the steamers on the rivers, the railroads, with many a thrifty farm, with machinery." The rest of the poem determinedly avoids the industrial age, imagining "Lands bathed in sweeter, rarer, healthier air," lands fit for "The new society at last, proportionate to Nature." The poet dwells not on technological miracles but on nature and nebulous spiritual abstractions: the redwood tree sings of "occult deep volitions," of "average spiritual manhood," of an "unseen moral essence of the vast materials of America," of a "hidden national will lying in your abysms." Even the machine age becomes abstract, as he ends by saying: "I see the genius of the modern, child of the real and ideal, / Clearing the ground for broad humanity, the true America, heir of the past so grand, / To build a grander future." Now disinclined to revel in machines and industrial armies, Whitman looks vaguely back ("the past so grand") and vaguely forward ("a grander future"), hoping that an equally vague "genius of the modern" will nurture a totally new, transplanted America.

"Prayer of Columbus," also written in late 1873 and placed with *Harper's,* reveals an exhausted Whitman looking heavenward for solace. Columbus had appeared in the earlier poem "Passage to India" as "History's type of courage, action, faith," a heroic figure whose discovery of America led eventually to an age of useful technology. He appears in the new poem as "A batter'd, wreck'd old man" whose heroism lies only in his strong religious faith and his stoic endurance of bleak conditions. Whitman explained in the *Harper's* headnote that he was describing the nearly seventy-year-old Columbus, shipwrecked on Jamaica, confronted with mutiny, and destined for poverty and neglect upon his return to Spain. Whitman obviously identified with this man he describes as "Old, poor, and paralyzed." He told Nelly O'Connor he had "unconsciously put a sort of autobiographical dash" in the poem.

But he was not just drawing a self-portrait. In choosing the iconic American figure, he was reflecting on his own role as America's poet. Metaphorically, that role is as crippled as the battered Columbus of the poem. Reference to technology is reduced to a wishful line: "Haply the swords I know may there be turn'd into reaping tools." Columbus feels "rack'd, bewilder'd," and asks, "What do I know of my life? what of myself?," just as Whitman felt suddenly overwhelmed by the complexities of the new America. The poem ends affirmatively but vaguely, as Columbus sees "shadowy vast shapes" and hears "anthems in new tongues" saluting him from the future.

If "Prayer of Columbus" reflects Whitman's bewilderment and anxious hopes about his nation, "Song of the Universal" appeals to progressive evolution to resolve the nation's problems. On March 20, 1874, Whitman received an invitation to recite a commencement poem at Tufts College. He already had experience with this sort of event. Two years earlier he had recited a poem at Dartmouth. Reportedly the Dartmouth students had invited Whitman as a lark to flout the conservative faculty, though the poem he gave, "As a Strong Bird on Pinions Free" (later "Thou Mother with Thy Equal Brood"), was tame enough to satisfy the most pious don. If any of the Tufts students had hijinks in mind by inviting Whitman, they too were surely disappointed, for the poem that was recited in absentia (Whitman's poor health kept him away) had little to offer but windy generalities. Surely many in the audience groaned inwardly when they heard the gassy opening lines: "Come said the Muse, / Sing me a song no poet has yet chanted, / Sing me the universal."

From Whitman's standpoint, though, the generalities had crucial importance, for he was now seeking to soar above the pros and cons of American life and view them abstractly, from a height. His "keen-eyed towering science," overlooking "as from tall peaks the modern" and issuing "absolute fiats," is the progressive-evolutionary outlook he had gleaned from Hegel and Darwin. America's current problems? No need to worry about them, the poem assures us: they will go away in time, since the good will win in the end. Whitman writes: "For it the mystic evolution, / Not the right only justified, what we call evil also justified." What about political corruption? That too will pass. "Out of the bad majority, the varied countless frauds of men and states, / Electric, antiseptic yet, cleaving, suffusing all, / Only the good is universal." When Whitman writes, "And thou America," we think he is going to get down to the specifics of national life. But, instead, he floats his way through images of "immortality" and "Health, peace, salvation universal" until he dissolves everything in his last line, which proclaims "all the world a dream."

If this sounds like Mary Baker Eddy, it is no accident, for Mrs. Eddy's *Science and Health* was published less than a year after "Song of the Universal" had made its appearance in newspapers. Although there is no evidence that Mrs. Eddy and Whitman knew each other's work, both were important figures in the rising tide of healthyminded religiosity that William James in *The Varieties of Religious Experience* would call America's most distinctive contribution to American thought. Both Whitman and Mrs. Eddy denied the reality of social and individual evils at a time when such evils loomed particularly large on the American scene.

Whitman would go on to other phases, but he never totally left behind the healthyminded, metaphysical outlook. Nowhere is this outlook more visible than in "Eidólons," which appeared in the *New York Tribune* in February 1876. Whitman had always been fascinated by Swedenborg and his followers, and "Eidólons" appears to have been influenced by a post-Swedenborgian book, Balfour Stewart and P. G.

Tait's *The Unseen Universe,* which argues that everything on earth is exactly duplicated in a spiritual facsimile, what Whitman calls an "eidólon" (or phantom). More abstract even than "Song of the Universal," "Eidólons" insists on the ephemerality and ultimate unreality of the physical world and the permanence and true reality of the spiritual realm. Whereas in the technology poems of the early seventies Whitman presents industry as a precursor to spiritual truths, in "Eidólons" he highlights divine factories producing spirits:

> Ever the mutable,
> Ever materials, changing, crumbling, re-cohering,
> Ever the ateliers, the factories divine,
>   Issuing eidólons.

As for "The present now and here, / America's busy, teeming, intricate whirl," these too, no matter how distressing, are only "Today's eidólons."

If, as Galway Kinnell suggests, Whitman in Section 5 of "Song of Myself" descends Plato's ladder to earth, traveling from God down to mossy scabs and pokeweed, in "Eidólons" he reascends the ladder with a vengeance, dissolving the entire social and physical world into spirit. If Whitman could no longer sing of the self, the body, and the nation (once thoroughly combined in his poetry) he now felt he could literally soar away from them and watch them disappear behind him.

Besides, he had something more practical to attend to: his reputation.

Neglect, Imagined and Real

HE WAS UP in the clouds in his poetry but very much down-to-earth in the machinations he was using to push himself on the public. When in January 1874 a writer in the *Nation* wrote critically of his poetry, he penned an article of reply that he submitted through John Burroughs under his friend's name. The fact that he envied other writers' material success was suggested by his "Wealth of Poets," a press report of the 1873 period arguing that while Swinburne, Browning, and several others "have coined their genius into substantial guineas, dollars, or francs" from their writings, "Walt Whitman keeps up the tradition of narrow means and wide afflatus," having not earned "the first shilling of return from his poetic volumes." These exercises in subterfuge and prevarication apparently did not reach publication, but one that did—"Walt Whitman's Actual American Position," which he published anonymously in the *West Jersey Press* on January 26, 1876—outdid either of them in its shameless disregard for facts.

It is well known that the article, which Whitman sent to his British friends for reprinting, helped make the poet famous, since it prompted an international press war that hugely increased his visibility. It hasn't been recognized that the article is grossly untrue factually but, given Whitman's goals as a writer, largely true in spirit.

The article expanded on a point Whitman had been pressing for years in other contexts: that is, that he had been almost totally neglected by his country. From 1845 to 1855, he writes in the article, Whitman "bade fair to be a good business man, ... owned several houses, was worth some money and 'doing well.'" But then he "got possessed by the notion that he must make epics or lyrics, 'fit for the New World;' and that bee has buzzed in his head ever since, and buzzes there yet." But he met only with "a *howl* of criticism and the charge of obscenity." His attempts to write for the magazines have been "utter failures." All the established poets have studiously ignored him. He summed up his case with a categorical assertion: "The real truth is that with the exception of a very few readers, (women equally with men,) Whitman's poems in their public reception have fallen still-born in their country. They have been met, and are met to-day, with the determined denial, disgust and scorn of orthodox American authors, publishers, and editors, and, in a pecuniary and worldly sense, have certainly wrecked the life of their author."

This mixture of half-truths and outright lies doesn't merit a point-by-point rebuttal. The main facts can be stated simply: by 1876, *Leaves of Grass* had received far more positive than negative reviews; it had not fallen "still-born" with the public; Whitman, though hardly well off, was not poor; and his efforts to write for popular periodicals, far from being "utter failures," can be counted solid successes.

The latter point needs amplifying, since it is not sufficiently recognized how often Whitman appeared in American periodicals. Even in the difficult period after his stroke he did well in placing poems: in March and early April 1873, in the midst of his tragedies, he contributed four poems to the New York *Daily Graphic*. Early the next year he got the high royalties he demanded from *Harper's* for "Song of the Redwood-Tree" and "Prayer of Columbus." Between January 29 and March 7, 1874, he wrote seven articles on the Civil War for the *Weekly Graphic*. In February he sent President Grant some of the war articles, reminding the president that they had sometimes passed each other in Washington and exchanged salutes. The next month he received a cordial note from Grant's secretary, Levi P. Luckey, thanking him for the articles and "your very kind letter," and wishing him a speedy recovery from his illness. His Tufts poem, "Song of the Universal," had broad exposure, since it was printed in five major newspapers. Toward the end of '74 he printed two more poems in the *Daily Graphic*. The next year he collected his Civil War articles and published them as *Memoranda During the War*.

He was very far, then, from being an "utter failure" as a magazine writer. Also, as Ed Folsom has shown, he was appearing in a growing number of textbooks, handbooks, and anthologies. But almost to the end of his life, even after he began to get more requests for periodical contributions than his old brain could handle, he would keep insisting he was neglected. His high publication rate was particularly impressive in light of the fact that he actually wrote far more prose than poetry in these years, and most of that saw publication as well. This is not to mention the exposure he continued to get from reviews or articles on him. For instance, in the summer of 1874, supposedly a low point for him, James Thompson wrote seven laudatory articles about him for the *National Reformer*.

True, he had setbacks. He had trouble placing "Passage to India" and "Eidólons," though the latter did finally appear in the *Tribune*. He received a stinging review from the Scottish journalist Peter Bayne in the December 27, 1875, issue of the *Contemporary Review*. Bayne described Whitman as a typical American sensationalist who "must have his scores massacred, his butcherly apparatus of blood and mangled flesh," his "sensational subjects and fierce excitements." A harder blow came in 1875 with Emerson's omission of him in his poetry anthology *Parnassus*. Emerson's stated goal was to gather "all my favorites into one volume," but he had recently cooled on Whitman and left him out. On the other hand, Whitman was cheered that year by the Irish critic Standish O'Grady's article in the December *Gentleman's Magazine* commending Whitman as "the noblest product of modern times."

There are indications that even on the verge of writing the *West Jersey Press* lament Whitman was actually feeling chipper. Although he had suffered another stroke (a mild one, on the right side this time) on February 16, 1875, as the year went on, he was sounding happy about things. His sister Mary wrote him in March thanking him for his many letters and saying, "I often hear from you through the papers." Although he continued to smolder over what he saw as embezzlement on the part of the inept handlers of the 1867 *Leaves of Grass*, by November he could write a friend, "I feel yet about as cheerful & *vimmy* as ever, & may live several years yet." He was healthy enough to make it to Baltimore for a memorial for Edgar Allan Poe on November 17; though several leading poets were invited, he was the only one who attended.

Whitman, then, was hardly neglected, and in some ways he could claim to have been a real success. Why, then, his persistent claim of neglect? His friends sometimes wondered too. Traubel once asked, "Walt, don't you sometimes put that American neglect business a bit too strong?"

His feelings of neglect stemmed mainly from the fact that his reception didn't come close to matching his goal of having widespread cultural impact. This goal had become, if anything, more urgent for him after the war than previously. In the early seventies he had discovered the French sociological critic Hippolyte Taine, who argued for the social and historical embeddedness of literature. Taine would remain his favorite critic, one he echoed in his repeated calls for a historical understanding of his own work. He was interested, like Taine, in the way literature *grew out of* society and people, and also in its possibilities for *feeding back into* and *transforming* society and people. Robert Louis Stevenson noticed this in 1878 when he wrote of Whitman: "He was a theoriser about society before he was a poet. He first perceived something wanting, and then set squarely down to supply the want." Even though by the midseventies Whitman no longer felt capable himself of producing new, transforming works, he had his large body of earlier poems that he was continually readapting to suit the changing social scene.

Never losing his aim of having an impact on American society at large, he began describing the "I" of his poems as a model for all to follow. In an 1872 letter to Rudolph Schmidt he declared: "The main object of my poetry is simply to present . . . the Portraiture or model of a sound, large, complete, . . . intellectual & spiritual *Man*, . . . —& *Woman* also, a good wife, mother, practical citizen too—adjusted to the modern, to the New World, to Democracy, & to science." To Edward Dowden, a professor at Trinity College in Dublin, he wrote, "I seek to typify a living Human Personality." He agreed with Ruskin that *Leaves of Grass* was full of personal feeling but stressed that this personalism was presented "as a type however for those passions, joys, working &c *in all the race*, at least as shown under modern & especially American auspices."

But a model is only as effective as the number of people who observe it. By 1876 Whitman could claim to have a substantial following among intellectuals and literary types, mainly European, but only a tiny following in the American reading public. From this ambitious perspective, he was justified in claiming that his writings had fallen "still-born" in their public reception. The paradox of his reception had been noted by Standish O'Grady in his 1875 article: "The common people, whom he likes most, and who most like him, are not those who can comprehend or care for his poems.... It is the cultivated classes who receive and recognize him, and it is to them that he is beneficial."

What made the public's neglect especially painful for him was a growing recognition that he alone among leading American writers had fully absorbed the idioms and images of everyday Americans. He had assimilated popular culture but had produced poetry so varied and multivoiced that it could not be readily absorbed by the public, which gravitated toward simpler, more conventional writing. Edward Dowden had emphasized Whitman's unique Americanness in a shrewd article of July 1871. "Longfellow," Dowden wrote, "is one of ourselves—an European." His *Evangeline* is "an European idyll of American life," and *Hiawatha* "might have been dreamed in Kensington by a London man of letters." Irving and Bryant, argued Dowden, also have Anglophile styles; Lowell, on occasion, uses American idioms, but generally tends toward the British mode. Dowden conceded that Emerson was "a genuine product of the soil," but only Whitman was "a man not shaped out of old-world clay, nor cast in any old-world mould."

This was a perceptive comparison that spoke to Whitman's unique Americanness. But Dowden, with whom Whitman corresponded for years, had touched on a sore point. Although Whitman had proven himself a fully American poet, he was largely unread by the American public. In 1876 Whitman could draft a press release about his poems that included the wistful line: "Then Whitman has a fond confidence that he will yet be absorbed and appreciated by his country."

The public's neglect of him was all the more distressing for him because 1876 was the centennial year, a sacrosanct year for one who thought of himself as the national poet. Early in the year, plans were already established for the great Centennial Exposition in Philadelphia, a short ferry ride from Whitman's Camden. Whitman was not invited to write the Ode for the Centennial Exposition. But he put on an exposition of his own: one of himself. His plan was to generate publicity and then issue a Centennial Edition of his poems that would establish him at last as America's poet.

The plan worked about as well as could be expected, given that America was in the throes of the depression and had little time to think about its poets. The day his *West Jersey Press* article appeared, Whitman clipped it and sent it to Rossetti, asking him to have it printed in London. Rossetti printed excerpts of it on March 11 in the *Athenaeum*, adding the self-pitying comment from Whitman's letter that the poet's condition was "even worse than described in the article." Whitman also sent the article to other foreign friends, including the Irish professor Edward Dowden, the British poet Edward Carpenter, and the Danish writer Rudolph Schmidt, all sympathetic to him. Rossetti and Carpenter rushed into print in defense of Whitman, berating America for ignoring its finest poet. They were in turn attacked in *Harper's* by George William Curtis, who argued that Whitman was not impoverished and would get his due in time.

The cross-Atlantic war raged for months. Articles on the issue appeared in many leading periodicals: in England, in the *London Daily News* and the *Athenaeum;* in America, in the *New York Tribune,* the *Boston Evening Transcript, Appleton's Journal, Harper's, Scribner's,* and the *Herald.* Out of the woodwork came Whitman's estranged friend William Douglas O'Connor, who confirmed in the April 22 *Tribune* that the poet *was* poor and persecuted, an opinion seconded by John Burroughs in the same paper.

Whitman gleefully fanned the controversy. He planted a second article, in the May 24 *West Jersey Press,* contradicting denials in the American press of his poverty and distorting his self-portrait even more than before. "For twenty years," he wrote of himself, "he has been a continuous target for slang, slur, insults, gas-promises, disappointments, caricature—without a publisher, without a public—working away with composed and cheerful heart, as it were, in the darkness." To give an impression of conventionality, he printed his most popular poem, "O Captain!"

In England, meanwhile, Robert Buchanan was surprised to hear from Moncure Conway, who had visited Whitman in Camden, that the poet was not badly off. Conway publicly rebutted Buchanan and wrote Whitman, "It is ludicrously false for Buchanan to say you are in danger of starving, or that you have no appreciation in America (where books have been written about you, and you have enthusiastic admirers!)." Whitman was forced to backpedal with Buchanan. He wrote him, "Though without employment, means or income, you augur truly that I am not in what may be called pinching want—nor do I anticipate it."

The press war was wonderful publicity. Right in the midst of it, Whitman wrote complacently to Anne Gilchrist: "As to my literary situation here, my rejection by the coteries—& my poverty, (which is the least of my troubles)—I am not sure but I enjoy them all. Besides, as to the latter, I am not in want."

He had been trying since the fifties to translate controversy into good sales, and in 1876 the strategy began to work. As he made plans for his Centennial Edition, he first thought of producing a small, cheap pocket book with paper covers. But his plans changed, and he opted for an expensive edition to be sold by subscription. The Centennial Edition was a two-volume set consisting of the 1871–72 *Leaves of Grass* and a companion volume, *Two Rivulets,* that included *Democratic Vistas, Memoranda During the War,* "Passage to India," and assorted other poems. In a cluster called "Centennial Songs—1876" he reprinted "Song of the Exposition," "Song of the Redwood-Tree," "Song for All Seas," and "Song of the Universal." The price of the set was very high— five dollars per volume—but Whitman was now widely seen as a charity case, and requests for the volume steadily flowed in, particularly from abroad. The following June Whitman wrote to Doyle, "The new edition of my books I sell enough of to pay my way very nicely—so I get along all right in that respect—(I don't need much)—."

Perhaps the greatest irony about the Centennial Edition was that it helped establish him as America's poet at a time when he had virtually ceased dealing with American life in a comprehensive way. What better time was there to write a new vast poem for America than 1876, the occasion for celebrating not only the nation's independence but also the new America that modern technology was opening up? In October Whitman was taken for a tour of the Philadelphia exposition, where all the modern products were exhibited, but apparently he was not inspired to write another poem about the machine age. The best he could manage in the Centennial Edition was to reprint his former technology poems. He updated "Song of the Exposition" by adding the title *"(The Muse invited to Philadelphia.) / ... Applied to the Centennial, Phila., 1876."* and by briefly reviewing the century's industrial expositions, "culminating in this great Exposition at Philadelphia, around which the American Centennial at Philadelphia, with its thoughts and associations, cluster— with vaster ones still in the future."

Although his main technology poems were behind him, he would soon befriend the kinds of capitalists who were behind such technology. He was starting to become a celebrity. The events of the late seventies and early eighties would turn him into an American figurehead.

Visitors and Visits

IN 1876 WHITMAN made two contacts symbolic of things to come: with the Staffords, a New Jersey farm family; and with George W. Childs

and Henry Wadsworth Longfellow. The former contact represented con-
tinuity with the past in its domesticity, its rural simplicity, and its
working-class comradeship. The latter signaled Whitman's move toward
middle-class culture.

The visit of Childs and Longfellow in late June to Camden was in
itself undramatic, what Whitman called "a sort of one-horse visit." The
two men went to Stevens Street and, finding Whitman away, went to the
ferries, where they ran into him. But from a larger perspective their visit
was significant. It gave strong indication that the *West Jersey Press* ar-
ticle and the Centennial Edition had, at least in part, done their work:
they had made Whitman more available than before to the power bro-
kers of middle-class culture. Childs was a wealthy Philadelphia pub-
lisher whose mansion on Walnut Street was known for its expensive
artworks, its mahogany and satinwood paneling, and its white marble
hall. From 1876 onward he would be a sincere friend of Whitman. In
1878 he offered to publish a new edition of *Leaves of Grass,* an offer
Whitman refused because there was talk of expurgation, and throughout
the eighties he lent financial and moral support to the poet. In the late
seventies Childs was just one of many of the social elite who began to
rally to Whitman's cause.

As for Childs's companion that warm June day, his Camden visit also
had meaning. Longfellow, the Harvard professor and fireside poet who
had argued for years that American literature should be an extension of
European styles, was beginning to have a grudging respect for the author
so many Europeans had praised. Another conventional American poet,
Whittier, had reportedly once thrown his copy of *Leaves of Grass* into
the fire. Yet another, James Russell Lowell, had said Whitman was a
rowdy who belonged to the fire companies. In time, however, Whittier
and Lowell would come around to Whitman. Longfellow in 1876 had
already started to come. Whitman, for his part, would always harbor
some disdain for the fireside poets but also would say some surprisingly
positive things about them.

While the contact with Childs and Longfellow was a harbinger of
future directions, the one with the Staffords was a source of immediate
restoration and satisfaction. If moving to Camden had been much like
returning to old-time Brooklyn, visiting the Stafford farm at nearby
Glendale (Timber Creek, White Horse, and Kirkwood were Whitman's
other names for it) was like going back to the old Whitman homestead
at West Hills. The hard-luck, hardworking parents, George and Susan
Stafford, were not unlike Whitman's father and mother in the early days.
The large brood of children, five boys and two girls, were reminiscent of
the eight Whitman children. Whitman wrote a friend: "Does me good

to be with them all. Every thing is very old-fashioned, just suits me—good grub & plenty of it."

The Stafford farm, a short train ride east of Camden, was a rejuvenating place for Whitman, particularly in light of his acceptance of the medical theories of the day. Although he now consulted "regular" physicians for his health, he had as ardent a belief in bathing and outdoor exercise as he had in the fifties when he had been surrounded by hydropathists and health reformers like Trall and the Fowlers. Even his regular doctors, with their uncertainty about his condition, often advised him to expose himself to healthy environments.

That he found such a healthy place at Glendale is attested to by the amount of space he assigns to it in *Specimen Days*. The fact that he leaps in his autobiography from the Civil War to his Glendale days is, on the surface, bizarre, since he leaves out the intervening decade. But the juxtaposition of the war and Glendale permits him to move from scenes of purgative violence to those of tranquil restoration in nature. And the truncation of the 1865–75 decade allows him to sidestep the complex postwar social issues that left him ultimately baffled. The Glendale chapters in *Specimen Days* are simple, primitive, Edenic—and almost totally unconcerned with politics or society. If in poems like "Eidólons" and "Song of the Universal" Whitman dissolved the social scene into abstractions, at Glendale he put it aside on behalf of sensuous enjoyment of the physical world.

Whitman stayed with the Staffords for weeks at a time throughout the late seventies and early eighties. He hobbled down the dirt lane from the farmhouse to Timber Creek, stripping himself and rolling in the mud and water, or wrestling with a tough young sapling, or listening to the chorus of insects. At times he would declaim Shakespeare or other writers in a loud voice, as he had once done from the tops of Broadway omnibuses. Skilled at astronomy, he lay on his back for hours on warm nights identifying stars and constellations.

Did his days at Timber Creek actually improve his health? His references to ill health did decrease during his main years there, from 1876 to 1884. True, he had moments of suffering. In March 1878 he complained of rheumatic pain in his right shoulder. His long western trip in 1880 was interrupted by a spell of illness so severe he thought he was near death. By the early eighties, prolonged healthy periods were interrupted by brief, debilitating bad ones. However, during these years he was ambulatory with a cane and generally in good spirits.

Because he had aroused so much sympathy in 1876 by presenting himself as ill, poor, and neglected, he didn't waste much energy on publicizing his improved health. To the contrary, as he sketched plans for his autobiography he tested out several titles that highlighted his lameness, including *Idle Days & Nights of a Half-Paralytic* and *Little Loafings of a Half-Paralytic*. He continued to be the salesman of self-pity.

This "half-paralytic" in his "idle days & nights" kept a careful eye on his money. His daybooks make it clear that his earnings, while hardly princely, were higher than those of most Americans. The average annual salary for the American wage earner in 1875 was around $800. This was the reward most Americans could expect for working ten-hour days in factories, stores, and so on. Whitman was officially discharged from his Washington job in June 1874 and lived on his dwindling but solid savings until 1876, when the Centennial Edition brought in a flurry of contributions. Between then and his death seventeen years later he earned, without holding a job, an average of $1,270 annually. His money came mainly from magazine and book royalties, lecture fees, and contributions from friends. Not only were his rent and expenses held low on Stevens Street, but after 1884, when he moved into his own house, many of his daily costs were absorbed by his long-suffering housekeeper, Mary Davis; after his death she successfully sued his estate for lost money. Whitman's bank savings rose steadily, from $1,500 in 1873 to more than $3,600 in December 1882 to $7,379.02 at his death.

This half-paralytic was not only a careful bookkeeper but was surprisingly peripatetic, despite the image he sometimes projected of being housebound. During the eleven years he boarded with George and Louisa, he was out of town about a quarter of the time. He was gone twenty-six weeks in 1877, twenty-eight in 1879, and twenty-four in 1881. Many of his jaunts were weeklong stays with the Staffords or with Anne Gilchrist and her children at their residence at 1929 North Twenty-second Street in Philadelphia. In fall 1879 there was a nearly four-month journey west, which took him as far as Denver, and the next summer found him traveling through Canada.

Most precious of all were his stays at the Stafford farm. It was there that he wrote many sketches that went into *Specimen Days* and did much of the planning for the 1881 *Leaves of Grass*. It was there, most of all, that he spent many an hour with the Staffords' oldest child, Harry.

When Whitman met Harry Stafford in 1876, the eighteen-year-old was an errand boy for a Camden printer. Since arriving in Camden Whitman had met many young workingmen on the cars, the ferries, and the streets. He kept up a correspondence with Peter Doyle, but that relationship sputtered after his affection turned to Harry.

He found in him someone who was willing to fill the role of loving "son" or "nephew" that Doyle had once filled. The new relationship was reminiscent of the previous one. Harry was another unlearned, conventional young workingman who could share deep love with Walt but also keep up the discourse of piety, domesticity, and heterosexuality that were important parts of Whitman's self-image. When the deeply religious Harry once was upset by the arguments against religion by the agnostic Robert Ingersoll, Whitman sermonized to him: "True religion (*the most beautiful thing in the whole world,* & the best part of any young man's or woman's or boy's character) consists in *what one does* square and kind & generous & honorable all days, *all the time.*" Just as Whitman had enjoyed keeping up a semblance of heterosexuality with Doyle, so he could indicate to Harry that, despite his enfeebled condition, he was excited by women. Writing to Harry from Stevens Street, he described a full-figured teenage girl who lived nearby, adding wistfully, "O that I was young again!"

In some ways, Whitman was drawn more powerfully to Harry than he had been to Pete, since Harry was surrounded by relatives and thus could be more easily placed in a domestic framework. Just as Whitman lived always in his departed mother's atmosphere, so he liked to keep Harry framed in his mind with images of family. When planning visits to his New York friend John Johnston, he said he would be accompanied by Harry, whom he once called "my (adopted) son" and another time "my nephew." (To his close friend John Burroughs, who knew better, he called Harry his convoy.) In letters, Harry, like most of Whitman's other loving comrades, was his "son" or "boy." When the boy was disrespectful to his mother, Whitman scolded him, saying "there is not a nobler woman in New Jersey."

Whitman's most ardent extant profession of affection for Harry, in a letter of February 1881, was itself interwoven with family references. "Dear Hank, I realize plainly that *if I had not known you*—if it hadn't been for you & our friendship & my going down those summers to the creek with you—and living there with your folks, & the kindness of your mother, & cheering me up—I believe *I should not be a living man to-day*—I think & remember deeply these things & they comfort me—*& you, my darling boy, are the central figure of them all*—." Here his affection for his "darling boy" is mingled with memories of "your folks," "your mother," "them all."

The relationship was stormy, but Whitman, as ever, struggled to maintain equilibrium. In the fall of 1877, Whitman gave Harry a ring, then took it back, then gave it to him again, writing about the matter in cryptic notes to himself. Something occurred in late November that seemed to restore balance, for Whitman scribbled, "Down at White Horse—Memorable talk with H S—settles the matter." He later assured the boy that he had forgotten "the occasional ridiculous little storms &

squalls of the past" and expressed appreciation for the recent smoothness of their relationship. He apparently had few qualms about appearing as a witness to Harry's wedding to Eva Westcott before Camden's mayor on June 25, 1884. He thereafter stayed in touch with Harry and Eva, to whom a daughter was born in 1886, and often urged them to visit him as a family.

Whitman avoided prolonged involvements that threatened to escape the conventions of comradely love he had established for himself. He had a brief but intense relationship with Edward Catell, a semiliterate farmhand at the Staffords'. In the fall and early winter of 1876 Whitman enjoyed his evenings with Catell by Timber Creek, but something happened in the friendship that made him want to cut it off. By January 24, 1877, he was warning Catell not to see him any more, adding: "There is nothing in it that I think I do wrong, or am ashamed of, but I wish it kept entirely between you & me—&—I shall feel very much hurt & displeased if you don't keep the whole thing & the present letter entirely to yourself." Apparently the relationship stopped there.

The ideal of comradely love Whitman was developing in the seventies was one that was religious, hearty, nonintellectual, and socially cohesive. Although it was a direct extension of his earlier views of same-sex love, it was being readapted slightly as new pressures impinged on him. In April 1870 he received a letter from the writer Charles Warren Stoddard, who announced, "In the name of CALAMUS listen to me!" Stoddard, writing from the South Sea islands, described a tender, loving night he had spent with a native boy. Whitman's reply to Stoddard was ambivalent. He said he found the letter "soothing & nourishing after its kind" and that he approved of Stoddard's "emotional adhesive nature." He did not agree, though, with Stoddard's suggestion that such behavior could best occur outside of mainstream American society, for he added: "[B]ut do you know (perhaps you do,) how the hard, pungent, gritty, worldly experiences & qualities in American practical life, also serve? how they prevent extravagant sentimentalism?"

Whitman was directing Stoddard away from isolated, idyllic romance toward the working-class American comradeship he prized above all. It was evidently this devotion to working-class male love that made him want to ignore the persistent queries of the British intellectual John Addington Symonds. Although Symonds was married and had children, he was powerfully attracted to teenage boys and had several affairs with Swiss boys that may have involved sex. A prolific historian and critic, Symonds was aware of the medical studies of so-called sexual inversion pioneered in the sixties by Carl Ulrichs and Karl Westfal. Whether or not Whitman knew of these studies, he resisted the scientific, intellectual approach to comradeship. Significantly, the 1871 *Leaves of Grass,* published two years after Westfal's landmark medical article on congenital inversion, included Whitman's strongly anti-intellectual poem "The Base of All Metaphysics," which says that beneath "the Greek and Germanic systems" and all other sophisticated approaches lies "The dear love of man for his comrade, the attraction of friend to friend, / Of the well-married husband and wife, / Of children and parents, / Of city for city and land for land."

Perhaps because he was struggling to keep his idea of comradeship within the frame of American conventions, he didn't respond when Symonds tried to put categories on his idea of love between men. On February 7, 1872, Symonds wrote him that as a scholar he had "traced passionate friendship through Greece, Rome, the medieval and modern world," and when he started reading Whitman's poetry a few years previously, then did he "learn confidently to believe that the comradeship which I conceived on a par with the sexual feeling for depth and strength and purity and capability of all good, was *real.*" He said he was "burning for a revelation of your more developed meaning" of "Calamus." Whitman did not reply, and three years later Symonds reminded the poet he had "asked you questions about Calamus." Once again, Whitman did not answer and, as noted earlier, he rejected Symonds's suggestion in 1890 that "Calamus" was linked to the medical theories of the European intellectuals. Whitman told Traubel that Symonds "has a few doubts yet to be quieted—not doubts of me, doubts rather of himself. One of these doubts is about Calamus. What does Calamus mean? What do the poems come to in their round-up?"

More in tune with Whitman than the quizzical, probing Symonds was the British poet Edward Carpenter, who didn't try to put the "Calamus" poems into any of the new medical pigeonholes. In July 1874 Carpenter wrote Whitman: "I thank you continuously in my heart.... For you have made men not to be ashamed of the noblest instinct of their nature. Women are beautiful; but, to some, there is that wh. passes the love of women." Three years later Carpenter assured Whitman he did not find him an immoral writer: "I believe on the contrary that you have been the first to enunciate the law of purity & health which sooner or later must assert itself." Carpenter visited Whitman in Camden twice. In April 1877 he came to create with Whitman what he ambitiously called a new organic thought-center for the age. He visited Whitman again in 1884, and in the meantime published a poetry volume, *Towards Democracy,* which included the most Whitmanesque verse of the day, treating, among other things, working-class comradeship and brotherhood.

Carpenter's emphasis on the "purity & health" of comradely love was the line Whitman took in the seventies. When his Danish friend Rudolph Schmidt lamented the rising materialism of European society, Whitman said that America evidenced "the same *hardness*, crudeness, worldliness—absence of the spiritual, the purely moral," but "*Here*, it is much counterbalanced & made up by an immense general basis of the eligibility to manly & loving comradeship, very marked in American young men." Drafting a preface for a projected foreign edition of his 1876 *Leaves of Grass*, Whitman wrote that he saw "the peculiar glory of These United States ... more and more in a vaster, saner, more splendid COMRADESHIP, typifying the People everywhere." In the eighties, when for the first time homosexuality encountered a certain amount of organized repression by authorities, Whitman's ideas on comradely love nevertheless seemed sufficiently in accord with mainstream conventions to go uncensored by the moral police who cracked down on his heterosexual poems.

He would even be prepared for the latter crackdown, for he was developing a circle of friends and supporters in the literary and social establishment. The visit of George Childs and Longfellow to Camden was symbolic of respectable society's embrace of Whitman in the wake of the *West Jersey Press* affair and the Centennial Edition. It had been a brilliant stroke of Whitman to plant his article in the *West Jersey Press*, a staunchly Republican paper associated with big business and mainstream values. Bourgeois readers of the day, unaware that Whitman had written the article, might well have asked themselves, "If the conservative *West Jersey Press* can so strongly sympathize with Whitman, why can't we?" They would have been doubly won over by the vigorous endorsement of Whitman by his British friends.

When Whitman's Centennial Edition appeared, a number of the social elite subscribed to it. Among the many orders Whitman received was one from the wealthy Brooklyn society woman Laura Curtis Bullard, a feminist novelist and one of the cofounders of Manhattan's first large women's club, Sorosis. Whitman also made an important contact with John H. Johnston, the owner of a large Manhattan jewelry business. Whitman's long correspondence with Johnston began in April 1876. Starting the next year, the poet stayed at Johnston's home at 113 East Tenth Street during visits to New York and grew close to Johnston, his wife, and their son and daughter, who called him Uncle Walt. Whitman's entrance into respectable society was noted in March 1877 by the Camden *Daily Post:* "He visits New York after 5 years absence. High tone Society now takes him to its bosom." Through Johnston, Whitman met Richard Watson Gilder, an assistant editor at *Scribner's Monthly* and

later editor of its successor *The Century*, which published prose pieces by
Whitman in the eighties. His sister, Jeannette L. Gilder, whom Whitman
befriended in June 1878, was then with the *Herald* and in 1881 co-
founded and edited the *Critic*, another magazine friendly to Whitman.

As he was making new connections and reentering the public arena,
his family life was checkered. One of his comforts during the sometimes
bitter press battle over him had been tending George and Louisa's new-
born, Walter Orr Whitman. But the poet's little namesake died at eight
months on July 12, 1876. This death seemed all the more tragic to the
family when Louisa had a stillborn son the next year. The news from
Burlington continued to be worrisome. Heyde wrote that Hannah had
become so insanely jealous that she sniffed his clothes and hat for signs of
other women. Still, Whitman was cheered by long visits from his nieces
Mannahatta and Jessie, who came from St. Louis in July 1876 and stayed
at Stevens Street through October. They made visits again in 1877 and
'78, and at regular intervals after that.

He also renewed contact with his old Washington friend John Bur-
roughs, who had worked as a bank inspector for several years but was
now with his wife, Ursula, and their daughter on a farm at Esopus-on-
Hudson in upstate New York. Whitman and Harry Stafford paid them a
visit in March 1877. They went to Manhattan and then up the Hudson
to Esopus. Whitman loved the Burroughses' cottage, wreathed in honey-
suckle and wild rose, with its open view of the Hudson and a nearby
railway line he watched with his usual curiosity. Burroughs enjoyed
having the poet, though he was puzzled when Whitman and Stafford
wrestled and frolicked, acting, he thought, liked rambunctious boys.
Whitman was to visit Esopus twice more, and Burroughs regularly went
to Camden.

Although the calm, nature-loving Burroughs would remain a strong
source of support for Whitman until the end, it was a new friend the
poet made in the late seventies, Richard Maurice Bucke, that most vigor-
ously took up the poet's cause in the late years. A choleric man with a
full beard and a rasping voice, Bucke had nearly lost his life during a
Sierra hiking expedition in the fifties. One of his feet and several toes on
his remaining foot had to be amputated due to frostbite, but Bucke re-
mained a man of buoyant spirits and high energy who became a noted
alienist. His Mental Institution in London, Ontario, was one of the most
progressive of its kind, emphasizing work therapy and civil treatment of
the mentally ill. When Whitman visited the hospital in June 1881 he
called it "the most advanced, perfected and kindly and rationally carried
on, of all its kind in America." Bucke had first read *Leaves of Grass* in

1867 and had become an instant convert to Whitman, whom he revered as a prophet of the divine capabilities of humans, ideas he himself promoted in his books *Man's Moral Nature* and *Cosmic Consciousness.*

Bucke's first meeting with Whitman, in late 1877, was a sacrosanct moment for him. He was in Philadelphia on business and requested a meeting with Whitman but, getting no response, took the ferry to Camden and showed up at Stevens Street unannounced. He recalled Whitman lurching toward him with his cane, holding out a small, hairy hand to him. Bucke noticed the big fleshy ears, the thin wrinkles and red complexion, the ample snow-white beard, and the heavy-lidded eyes above which arched the high eyebrows. The poet's light gray suit and his sparkling white shirt added to the pristine effect. Whitman seemed to him, as he wrote later, "either a god or in some sense clearly and entirely preter-human."

Bucke was so enamored of Whitman's writings and magnetic presence that, despite his brittle temperament, he was like putty in the poet's hands. Whitman's relationship with Bucke provides more evidence of his attempt to make his image fit mainstream conventions, for the Whitman biography Bucke wrote in the early eighties was heavily edited by the poet. Even before Whitman rewrote it, Bucke's biography, though generally accurate, was another safe, sanitized representation of the poet's life and works. Whitman saw this instantly and did the kind of back-and-forth shuffle that characterized so many of his reactions in his late years. "The character you give me is not a true one in the main," he wrote Bucke, "—I am by no means that benevolent, equable, happy creature you pourtray [*sic*]—but let that pass—I have left it as you wrote."

In other words, although he saw through Bucke's idealizing portrait, he was content to let it stand. Moreover, he made it even more idealizing by deleting, among other things, Bucke's use of the words "motherly" and "castrato" to describe him, as well as a long passage in which Bucke had depicted the poet's loving encounter with a Canadian soldier. In the end, Whitman praised Bucke for having produced "a very creditable, serviceable book," though he might just as well have praised himself. After its publication in 1883, it remained for years the standard biography, the one Whitman later pointed to as the most honest record of his life, even though he had recognized and even added to its untruthfulness.

Conventionality and Comstockery

THE EVENTS surrounding the publication of the 1881–82 edition of *Leaves of Grass* show vividly the oscillation between conventionality and rebelliousness characteristic of Whitman's later years. It is well known that this, the definitive edition of *Leaves of Grass,* ran afoul of government authorities when published in Boston by James R. Osgood, after which it was reprinted by Philadelphia publishers. But this momentous episode in Whitman's literary career has never been placed adequately in its biographical and cultural context.

The real source of the Osgood edition was Whitman's increasingly conventional public posture in the late seventies, an image bolstered greatly by the Lincoln lecture he began giving in 1879. The first lecture was engineered by Whitman's new friends in the New York literary and social establishment. The poet had been invited to lecture on Lincoln in April 1878, but he was ill at the time and postponed his appearance until the following year. On April 14, 1879, before some sixty or eighty people at Steck Hall in Manhattan, Whitman sat on a chair and gave his scripted speech on Lincoln in a conversational tone. He ended by reciting "O Captain!" He stayed on for a month at the Johnstons' home, spending much of his time in Central Park. Although the park had been designed in the late fifties by Frederick Law Olmsted to provide "lungs" for the grubby city and diversion for its citizens, it was still so distant from working-class neighborhoods that it was used almost exclusively by the wealthy. Whitman noted the ashen-faced aristocrats rolling through the park in their carriages and wondered, "Why is it not a far more popular, free, average resort?" Yet he went to the park day after day.

The New York episode was typical of the late Whitman. There was a reminder of his working-class egalitarianism in his comment on the elitist Central Park. On the other hand, there were unmistakable signs of his recent attraction to established conventions: the long stay with the wealthy Johnston; the continual return to the park, in spite of his qualms about it; and, above all, the Lincoln lecture and recitation of "O Captain!"

Whitman's attitude toward "O Captain!"—his most conventional poem—was much like his attitude toward expurgation of his poetry. In theory, he was opposed to it, but in practice he often resorted to it to satisfy middle-class expectations. Supposedly, he was embarrassed by the poem, with its regular meter and melodramatic imagery. As he would say to Traubel: "I'm honest when I say, damn My Captain and all the My Captains in the book!" Nonetheless, he recited the poem time and again, almost always at the end of his Lincoln lecture, which he gave some nineteen times between 1879 and 1890.

Whitman's old-age obsession with Lincoln and his repeated recitation of a poem he supposedly hated revealed the side of him that looked increasingly to the past: mainly to Lincoln and the war, but also to assorted memories of persons and events that would appear collagelike in his prose collections *Specimen Days* and *November Boughs.*

When his eyes were not trained on the past, they looked to the future, which after 1879 appeared increasingly brighter to him, largely as a result of the two long trips he took at this time: his swing through the American Midwest in the fall of 1879 and his visit to Canada the following summer. The trips took him into vast frontier spaces that made him both freshly appreciative of agrarian life and hopeful about the commercial future.

The western trip was done under an institutional aegis, for Whitman had accepted an invitation by the Old Settlers of Kansas Committee to address the twenty-fifth anniversary of Kansas's territorial status. Accompanied by Colonel John Wien Forney, editor of the Philadelphia weekly *Progress,* Whitman started west by train on September 10. They passed through eastern industrial towns with their "smoke, coke-furnaces, flames, discolor'd wooden buildings, and vast collections of coal barges." Whitman waxed ecstatic when they reached the midwestern prairies: "I thought my eyes had never looked on scenes of greater pastoral beauty." After stopping over in St. Louis, he went on to Topeka, where he gave an impromptu speech on the grandeur of the prairies to a crowd of fifteen thousand. His trip took him to Denver, which he fell in love with, then south through the mountains to Pueblo, and east again to St. Louis, where he stayed with Jeff and his daughters until heading home on January 3.

He saw in the prairie states a rugged naturalness and, at the same time, an almost utopian promise for a new industrial future. The trip answered Whitman's love of primal nature and restored his hope for modern technology. The American economy was then on the rebound. Even as he traveled through the vast open lands that he thought were the basis for all future American poetry and art, he resumed his almost transcendental stance toward machines and business. He enthused over the swift, powerful train, which he called America's furthest "advance beyond primitive barbarism." He admired the large, bustling cities of Topeka and Lawrence. In Colorado he saw the steam sawmills, the smelting works, and the telegraph lines that, in his words, could carry "a message by electricity anywhere around the world!" When a St. Louis newspaperman asked him how a new western literature was to be found, he declared that America must first be developed "in products, in agriculture, in commerce, in networks of intercommunication," in "materialistic prosperity in all its varied forms." He wrote a poem, "The Prairie States," which captured what he felt was the unique promise of the developing frontier:

A newer garden of creation, no primal solitude,
Dense, joyous, modern, populous millions, cities and farms,
With iron interlaced, composite, tied, many in one,
By all the world contributed—freedom's and law's and thrift's
    society,
The crown and teeming paradise, so far, of time's accumulations,
To justify the past.

The prairie states for him were both pastoral ("A newer garden of creation") and freshly industrial ("Dense, joyous, modern, [...] / With iron interlaced").

He had a similar forward-looking experience on his Canada tour. On June 3, 1880, Whitman left Camden with Bucke for Niagara Falls and Canada, where he stayed with the Buckes in London, Ontario. Whitman toured Bucke's hospital and then embarked on a two-month, three-thousand-mile journey that took him down the St. Lawrence and up the Saguenay rivers, to Quebec and Montreal, and by August 14 back to the Buckes in Ontario.

His exposure to the wild Canadian countryside inspired poetic outbursts in his journal: "Land of pure air! Land of unnumbered lakes!" It also made him fantasize about an ideal agrarian society, "A race of 2,000,000 farm-families, 10,000,000 people,—every farm running down to water, or at least in sight of it." But, as in the prairie states, he saw young industrial towns that reinvigorated his respect for business. In outlining plans for a lecture in Ottawa he wrote that previous history was "dominated by one word, War," but "now *Business* does it all." Business, he wrote, was "an immense and noble attribute of man, . . . the tie and interchange of all the peoples of the earth."

At the same time that his positive feelings about the capitalist future were intensifying, he continued to establish his conventional posture through his Lincoln lectures, which were becoming real society events. Shortly before his Canada trip he had given his second Lincoln lecture, on April 15, 1880, at Association Hall in Philadelphia. He lectured and recited "O Captain!" before a reverent crowd of mainly snowy-headed men and women. To publicize the event Whitman sent the lecture to papers in Cincinnati and Chicago, and mailed copies of a Camden *Post* report of the speech to nearly two dozen friends. He was squeezing his already tired lecture for all it was worth.

He got his payoff the next year, when he gave the lecture for the third time in Boston. Arranged by the Papyrus Club, the event earned him $135 from an audience that paid a dollar apiece to hear him. Among those present were William Dean Howells, who had once attacked Whitman's poetry, Hawthorne's son-in-law George Parsons Lathrop, and many other society men and women. Whitman noted excitedly in his journal that "there never was a *more high toned crowd* collected in the town—full half were ladies, & I never saw finer ones." One of his listeners, the journalist Sylvester Baxter, later recalled Whitman's casual but neat suit, flowing collar and loosely knotted handkerchief, and his large, broad-brimmed hat. He sat before the crowd with a big stick and lectured in a voice Baxter called "high-pitched, but agreeable and without twang; a sort of speaking tenor." The day after the lecture, Whitman made a point of visiting Longfellow, who had visited him in Camden a second time in 1878. Two days later Whitman went a few miles out of town to the home of the wealthy art collector Quincy Shaw, whose Millet paintings thrilled him with their powerful depictions of French peasant life. Whitman left Boston on April 23, managing to escape, he joked, before being "killed with kindness, and with eating and drinking."

Everything seemed propitious for what truly signaled Whitman's entrance to the literary establishment: the publication of *Leaves of Grass* by a mainstream publisher. In the glowing aftermath of Whitman's Boston visit, James R. Osgood and Company, one of Boston's most prominent firms, offered to publish a new edition of his poems. The Maine-born James Osgood had worked in the fifties for Ticknor and Fields, the publisher of Longfellow, Whittier, Hawthorne, and others. Osgood in 1871 took over the firm and published a varied list of American and European authors, including James, Howells, George Eliot, and Arnold. He briefly joined forces with Henry O. Houghton and George H. Mifflin in the late seventies and then revived James R. Osgood and Company.

When Whitman was approached by Osgood not long after his Boston visit, he saw the opportunity of fulfilling his longtime dream of producing a portable, tasteful edition of *Leaves of Grass.* Desiring to present the poems as inoffensively as possible, he told Osgood to make the volume "markedly plain & simple even to Quakerness— ... no sensationalism or luxury—a well made book for honest wear & use & carrying with you." He wanted the margins narrow to keep the book fairly small and, as he put it, "as eligible as possible for the pocket, & to be carried about." He thought that at last he was producing an edition of his poems that average Americans might take around with them.

He knew he might have a problem with this rather stodgy publisher on the issue of his sex poems. He wanted to retain them but also to distance himself from them and from his rowdyish fifties persona as well. He wrote Osgood: "Fair warning on one point—the old pieces, the *sexuality* ones, about which the original row was started & kept up so long, are all retained, & must go in the same as ever." He was making a stand here but also gently removing himself from what he called "the old pieces" and "the original row" over them.

He also distanced himself from his main poem, which in the previous three editions had been titled "Walt Whitman" but was now changed to the more general "Song of Myself." He instructed Osgood to place the 1854 portrait of the loaferish young Whitman well inside the book on the page opposite "Song of Myself," as though the poem and the picture were discrete units, relics of another era. He was separating himself especially from what he now saw as his bygone bohemian self. His friend William Sloane Kennedy quoted him as instructing Osgood, "The portrait is required in the text to face page 29—in fact is involved as part of the poem." Kennedy himself expressed strong disapproval of the picture:

> It is to be hoped, nevertheless, that this repulsive, loaferish portrait, with its sensual mouth, can be dropped from future editions, or be accompanied by other and better ones that show the mature man, and not merely the defiant young revolter of thirty-seven, with a very large chip on his shoulder, no suspenders to his trousers, and his hat very much on one side.

Did Whitman share Kennedy's revulsion toward the 1854 picture? To Traubel, the poet would commend the portrait's naturalness but would criticize its rebellious, insouciant air. He said of the picture: "The worst thing about this is, that I look so damned flamboyant—as if I was hurling bolts at somebody—full of mad oaths—saying defiantly, To hell with you!" In showing dismay over the defiant picture, Whitman was eyeing his former self with old-age skepticism. He distanced himself even further from it by adding to the poem's opening section the passage that included the line, "I, now thirty-seven years old in perfect health begin." In 1881, readers knew well enough that Walt Whitman was neither thirty-seven nor in perfect health. By making this slight addition, Whitman was putting "Song of Myself" and its defiant persona in the past even while he included it in his volume.

He also added many buffer poems between the title page and the controversial "Children of Adam" cluster. In the 1867 edition he had put only three poems before this group. In 1871 and '76 he raised the number of preparatory poems to sixteen. In 1881 he used no fewer than twenty-six, the first twenty-four of which were grouped as "Inscriptions." These two-dozen short poems were of the safe variety, such as the patriotic "To Thee Old Cause," the metaphysical "Eidólons," and the calm "Me Imperturbe." Before getting to the sexual fire, the reader of the 1881 edition would have to pass through plenty of patriotic and religious mist.

Despite these precautions, the 1881 edition was headed for trouble with the moral police. But as he loafed by Timber Creek in the soft late-spring days planning the edition, Whitman can only have felt that his rising tide of respectability would carry him to a successful publication. He was determined to go to Boston to closely supervise publication of the volume. This was standard procedure for him but virtually unprecedented among Osgood's other authors, who left publishing up to the publisher.

Whitman made a nostalgic trip of it. On July 23 he met Bucke and another friend in Jersey City, then went east to Woodside, Long Island, where he stayed five days with his old friends Helen and Arthur Price. After that, he spent four days in the region of his birthplace at bucolic West Hills. It now seemed to him, as he wrote Harry Stafford, "the most beautiful region on earth." On August 1 he went to Manhattan for two weeks, touring the city again and raising a glass with the erstwhile leader of the now-defunct bohemia, Charles Pfaff. Then he took the shore route via Providence to Boston, arriving there on August 19.

He couldn't have hoped for more ideal conditions for bringing out his volume than those he found in Boston. Sylvester Baxter had arranged for him a sunny room at the Hotel Bullfinch on a quiet west-end street, where Whitman read proofs and entertained friends. He spent his mornings at the printing office of Rand and Avery, where he had a room of his own. He worked with the expert editor-proofreader Henry H. Clark, who had overseen books by Longfellow, Emerson, Stowe, and many others. Whitman spent his middays on Boston Common, then took the open cars out to South Boston, walked the waterfront at City Point, enjoying the harbor views. His visit was well publicized. On August 24 a long interview with the Good Gray Poet appeared in the *Globe*.

Early the next month his high mood was spoiled by news of the suicide of Beatrice Gilchrist, the talented, hardworking daughter of Anne Gilchrist. Another dark note was the death of President James Garfield, who had been shot by a political job seeker in Washington's Union Station. Whitman immediately wrote a poem, "The Sobbing of the Bells," which portrayed the assassination as a cause for national grief: "The passionate toll and clang—city to city, joining, sounding, passing, / These heart-beats of a nation in the night."

His spirits were lifted in mid-September when the journalist Franklin Sanborn took him to his spacious home in Concord, a forty-minute train ride west of Boston. At Concord Whitman took in the delicious autumn weather and the nostalgic atmosphere. On the evening of the seventeenth Sanborn's back parlor was filled with locals, including Bronson and Louisa May Alcott. They discussed Thoreau, passing around letters that shed new light on him. The aged Emerson was there, looking benign and saying little. Whitman now liked Emerson best this way: sweet, ethereal, acting almost lobotomized. The old sage was beyond saying anything good or bad about Whitman's poetry. Whitman said little too, preferring to sit for two hours and stare at Emerson's placid face. The next day he attended a dinner at Emerson's house, basking again in his silent presence. When Emerson died the next April, Whitman would lament, "So Emerson is dead—the leading man in all Israel." He would write an essay, "By Emerson's Grave," published in the *Critic*.

After the Emerson dinner Whitman toured Concord, walking through the Old Manse, viewing the Minute Man statue, spending time at Hawthorne's and Thoreau's graves in Sleepy Hollow Cemetery, and dropping a stone on the memorial pile where Thoreau's Walden cabin had stood.

Whitman finalized his contract with Osgood on October 1. The price of the edition was to be two dollars, with Whitman getting a twenty-five-cent royalty on each copy sold and Osgood agreeing to be his publisher for the next ten years. His work on the book completed, Whitman on October 15 held an open house for some three hundred friends and journalists, then left town a week later and, after stopping in Manhattan a couple of days, returned to Camden.

When the book was published in November, it was obvious that Whitman and Osgood had gone to great pains to make it as amenable as possible to middle-class tastes, without violating Whitman's principles. The jacket, which in different printings ranged from olive-brown cloth to light-brown leather with colored, marbled sides, was staid but had elegant touches. Whitman's signature was embossed in gold on the cover. On the spine appeared "Leaves of Grass" and his name, also in gold, as well as the pointed-finger-with-butterfly that Whitman had used in the fancy 1860 edition. There was a regularity and balance to the new volume's contents. The ungainly, rather chaotic annexes, which had been separately paginated in the previous two editions, were now integrated into the main body of the poems. Most of the poems in the volume appeared in organized, titled groups. Whitman had regularized the punctuation, replacing some odd dashes with commas. He had also done a fair amount of deleting or modification of sexual images that he thought might be found offensive. "Respondez!"—his most daring, flagrantly obscene poem—was removed and replaced by the short, tepid "Reversals" and "Transpositions."

As for the seventeen new poems in the edition, Whitman could safely believe none of them would raise eyebrows. Their topics included Ulysses S. Grant as democratic demigod ("What Best I See in Thee"), Hegelian optimism ("Roaming in Thought"), spirituality ("Hast There Never Come to Thee an Hour"), and the American midwest ("The Prairie States"). The only new poem that dealt with sex was "The Dalliance of the Eagles." But sex was so completely transposed to nature in this picture of two birds locked in "rushing amorous contact high in space" that Whitman may well have meant it to be an exaggerated presentation of his belief in the purity and naturalness of sex.

Eight of the first nine reviews of the 1881 edition were mainly positive. Whitman's friend Sylvester Baxter plugged the volume in the *Globe* as fresh, patriotic, and picturesque; he stressed that Whitman effectively conjoined evolutionary science and religion. The *Critic* and the *Springfield Republican*, also edited by friends of Whitman, found the volume candid rather than lewd and pointed to the Civil War poems as evidence of Whitman's nobility. The *Critic*, though, brought up an old sore point: "One great anomaly of Whitman's case has been that while he is an aggressive champion of democracy and the working-man, his admirers have been almost exclusively of a class the farthest possible removed from that which labors for daily bread by manual work. Whitman has always been truly caviare to the multitude."

Reviewers for the *New York Tribune*, the *Literary World*, and the *Chicago Tribune* found Whitman's poetry sometimes foul and formless but also brilliant and inventive. The *Liberty* praised Whitman as positive and original, and the Philadelphia *Times* saw him as intense and powerful. The first really negative review came in the December 15 *Nation* from Thomas Wentworth Higginson, who called Whitman indecent and inartistic. Higginson, who has gone down in literary history as the editor who took an ambivalent interest in Emily Dickinson's genius, was so conventional that he asserted that only "O Captain!" and just a few lines in Whitman's other poems would be remembered—a sentiment shared by a reviewer for the New York *Examiner.*

Altogether, though, it was not a bad crop of reviews. The mixture of praise and criticism was similar to that which had greeted the previous editions, though the balance had shifted definitely to the former. Whitman's family took real pride in his growing fame. Hannah, to whom he had sent the volume, reported excitedly that she and Charles were reading it aloud to each other. "Charlie sits here reading your book, he says this book is electrick [*sic*]," she wrote. "I believe every body under the sun knows of you, even persons that live far back in the country." She felt downright cocky: "Some want to see me, Walt Whitmans [*sic*] sister. I have not begun to put on airs yet, but I don't know but I should soon."

Whitman had become a powerful magnet. Drawn by him in January 1882 was the twenty-eight-year-old British aesthete Oscar Wilde. Having landed in New York on January 2 for a multicity lecture tour, Wilde quickly made plans to visit the poet he had been reading for sixteen years. Wilde lectured to an impressive Manhattan audience on the ninth and then headed south through New Jersey, telling a reporter on the train that he thought Whitman and Emerson had given more to the world than anyone else. Whitman was "so universal, so comprehensive," he said. In Philadelphia he was scheduled to lecture and be feted by a number of wealthy types, including Whitman's friend George W. Childs. Childs arranged a dinner and invited Whitman to come over from Camden, but the poet refused, citing the weather and his health. He said, though, that he would like to see Wilde and made himself available from 2:00 to 3:30 p.m. on the eighteenth.

The pallid, oval-faced, fleshy Wilde, dressed in a brown velvet morning suit, went to Camden with the publisher Joseph M. Stoddart. He loved the sunny parlor of the Stevens Street house, and he instantly won over Whitman by saying how much his poetry meant to him. Whitman opened a bottle of his sister-in-law's homemade elderberry wine, which Wilde drank eagerly despite its rancid taste. (Had it been vinegar, he said later, he would have gulped it down, he thought so much of Whitman.) Whitman took him upstairs to be on "thee and thou terms." The room was, typically, littered with manuscripts and papers, a bunch of which Whitman cleared off a chair to give his guest a seat. Wilde liked the view across the angular Camden roofs to the bristling masts that lined the Delaware. They talked animatedly about aestheticism, Swinburne and Rossetti, and Whitman's unconventional prosody, which he said came from his old printers' trick of trying to arrange words beautifully on a page, as if on a blank tombstone. Whitman disagreed with Wilde's art-for-art's-sake theories but genially told the younger man to "go ahead" with them.

Later on, this issue would create a real gap between them. Wilde, dedicated to standard poetic form, would write that Whitman would be recalled as a philosopher-prophet but not as a poet. Whitman would come out harshly against aestheticism in *November Boughs* in a passage Wilde took as a direct attack on him. To Traubel, Whitman would say Wilde was "a strong, able fellow" who wrote "lucid as a star on a clear night" but had "a little substance lacking at the root."

For the moment, though, mutual admiration got the best of literary differences. After drinking some milk punch that Whitman offered him, Wilde left buoyantly with two Whitman photos, one for him and one to be given to Swinburne. On March 1, Wilde, who had since gone on to other American cities, wrote Whitman that he had to see him again: "There is no one in this wide great world of America whom I love and honour so much." He returned to Camden in early May.

Did Whitman confess to homosexuality to Wilde on this second visit? Richard Ellmann writes that Wilde "would later tell George Ives, a proselytizer for sexual deviation in the nineties, that Whitman had made no effort to conceal his homosexuality from him, as he would do to John Addington Symonds." There is no way of telling what Whitman said or did. It's at least likely, given Wilde's sexual orientation, that Whitman confided in him about his deep love for young men. When a decade later this confession was told to "a proselytizer for sexual deviation," doubtless it was seen as a revelation of homosexuality, a term not used in English until the nineties. Some sparks seemed to have flown between the two men, for after their first meeting Whitman had written Harry Stafford: "Have you read about Oscar Wilde? ... He is a fine large handsome youngster—and had the *good sense* to take a fancy to *me*!"

Whatever confessions about male love Whitman made to Wilde, it was his heterosexual poems that were getting him into trouble that spring. In a culture that still accepted same-sex passion, the "Calamus" poems apparently had little shock value for the observant watchdogs of American morality. "Children of Adam" was a different story altogether.

On March 1, 1882, the Boston district attorney Oliver Stevens sent James R. Osgood an order to stop publication of *Leaves of Grass* on the grounds that it violated "the Public Statutes concerning obscene literature." Wishing to avoid a suit, Osgood sent Whitman Stevens's notice along with the list of poems and passages that were to be deleted or changed for publication to continue. Not surprisingly, "A Woman Waits for Me" was to be deleted entirely. More surprisingly, "To a Common Prostitute," which many saw as an updating of the Mary Magdalene story, was slated to go. Amazingly, "The Dalliance of the Eagles" was also to be removed. The fact that the innocent "Dalliance," about the mating of birds, was targeted while all but one of the "Calamus" poems were allowed tells us much about the era's moral tastes, which had become ridiculously prudish about heterosexual love but still permissive of same-sex affection. The only "Calamus" poem touched was "Spontaneous Me," but even in that poem it was images of masturbation and copulation, not homoerotic ones, that came under the moral ban. The rest of the list consisted of twenty-two deletions in some 150 lines of scattered poems, among them "I Sing the Body Electric," "The Sleepers," "Song of Myself," and "Unfolded Out of the Folds."

Whitman was willing to make some changes. Since he had already tailored the volume to middle-class readers, he wasn't going to let his supposed hatred of expurgation stop publication. He wrote Osgood that he would revise "Woman Waits," "Body Electric," and "Spontaneous Me." But when Osgood informed him that additional changes would be required, he wrote, "The list whole & entire is rejected by me, & will not be thought of under any circumstances." On April 9 Whitman noted tersely in his daybook, "Osgood gives up L of G." He immediately sent off his essay "A Memorandum at a Venture" to the *North American Review,* defending what he called his natural treatment of sex against the extremes of repressiveness and pornography. Osgood treated him civilly. He paid him $405.50 in royalties plus $100 in cash and gave him 225 copies of the book as well as the plates, which were used in subsequent printings of the poems.

The banning of the Osgood edition and the controversy it provoked was a culminating moment in America's cultural history. Before the Civil War there had raged lively but disorganized skirmishes between moral reformers and their opponents, particularly the free lovers. The opponents of moral reform insisted that the reformers, while pretending to be upright, were in fact salacious purveyors of the very pornography they ostensibly opposed. The battle was waged in popular newspapers and sensational novels, in which moral reformers were often caricatured as muckraking hypocrites.

After the Civil War, the stakes in the battle were raised significantly. Both moral reform and free love followed the general trend toward organization. In 1871 Anthony Comstock established the New York Society for the Suppression of Vice, a group he served until 1915 as the nation's leading foe of so-called social vice, which he seemed to see everywhere: not only in prostitution and pornography but in dime novels, nude statuary, and other apparently harmless things. He boasted that he had destroyed scores of tons of pornography. He got passed the kinds of antiobscenity laws that were used against the Osgood edition, and he was imitated by a number of vice campaigners who made the era one of organized prudery.

Comstock was a natural target for parody. The paunchy, bewhiskered zealot liked using disguises to snare his victims, posing variously as Edgewell (a free lover), Miss Anna Ray (three months pregnant and needing an abortion), and Mrs. Farnsworth (in search of a vaginal syringe). He had a well-known habit of enjoying forbidden pleasures before cracking down on them. In June 1878 he made headlines by entering a New York brothel, paying five dollars for the "Busy Fleas" show, and carefully watching three women disrobe and suck each other's private parts before he arrested them. It was this kind of lascivious repressiveness Whitman was opposing in "A Memorandum at a Venture" and in his direct comments on Comstock. Sarcastically labeling Comstock "Saint Anthony," Whitman told Traubel: "The psychology of that man would baffle devils; he haunts the purlieus of heaven with his crude philosophy: . . . he never yet has discovered the difference between virtue and vice: he is not so much a knave as an ass: he goes stumbling about as a bull in a china shop."

Was Comstock behind the Boston banning? Whitman and his friends sometimes thought so. The freethinking newspaper editor Benjamin Tucker, who angrily announced he would publish the banned *Leaves of Grass* even if it meant prison, wrote Whitman that Oliver Stevens was "a mere tool of Comstock." Others pointed to Thomas Wentworth Higginson or, more commonly, to a group of ministers led by the Reverend Baylies Allen, secretary of the Boston Vice Society. Actually, though, the matter is moot, for antiobscenity laws of the kind Comstock instituted, not individuals, were what killed the Osgood edition. As time passed, Comstock himself became implicated. Whitman informed a friend in July that *Leaves of Grass* was being banned from the mails "under the Comstock statutes." His old defender William Douglas O'Connor, reconciled with Whitman at long last, published an article on the poet in the *Tribune*, "Mr. Comstock as Cato the Censor," which in its original version tweaked Saint Anthony for his hypocrisy: "Mr. Anthony Comstock's hostility to the nude, of which an illustrious example was his famous prosecution of three unfortunate women whom he had hired to dance before him for over an hour, without clothing, in a New York brothel, appears to extend to the naked truth."

The free lovers also protested against the hypocrisy of the moral police. The Boston Free Love League on May 29 adopted a resolution saying that the crackdown on Whitman's poetry "shows the continuous lascivious stupidity voiced by pulpits and courts, the religio-political lewdness still mistaken for culture and purity." It was commonly thought that Comstock was behind the Boston postmaster Tobey's attempted banning from the mails of *This World*, edited by the freethinker George Chainey, who outspokenly defended Whitman. Comstock was also named as the hidden instrument behind the arrest of the free-love leader Ezra H. Heywood for publishing two "Children of Adam" poems in his paper *The Word*. After Heywood's arrest, Whitman wrote O'Connor, "the more I think of it, the more I am convinced it is Comstock's game." When Heywood was acquitted on all counts the following April, Whitman wrote snidely, "So A[nthony] C[omstock] retires with his tail intensely curved inwards," to which O'Connor replied that Comstock "ought to be nailed up, like a skunk to a barn-door, as an example to deter."

Although opposed to Comstock, Whitman was also hostile to the free lovers. As discussed earlier, there had been an affinity between Whitman and the loosely structured free love of the fifties; both criticized inequities in marriage and saw free, passionate choice as the only proper source of love. Given these affinities, it is not surprising that the Free Love League in 1882 would defend Whitman as chaste and would impugn the moral police as impure. But Whitman was now cautious of his public image in an increasingly conventional culture, and he was repulsed by the organized, institutional nature of postwar free love. He wrote O'Connor: "As to the vehement action of the Free religious & lover folk, in their conventions, papers &c in my favor—and even proceedings like these of Heywood—I see nothing better for yourself or your friends to do than quietly stand aside and let it go on—what do you think?" "I shall certainly not do anything to identify myself specially with free love," he wrote. O'Connor agreed, saying that though Heywood should be let alone, "I don't like the Free-Love theories at all."

The war between the moral reformers and free lovers was a battle of paper titans. The victor in the war was Whitman. Like previous wars over his poetry, this one aided his cause by stimulating sales and increasing his visibility. "The Leaves [of Grass] have had several set-tos with the state," he would tell Traubel, ". . . all of them serving to advance the book—Harlan's, to begin with, then Stevens', in Massachusetts, then that fool postmaster Tobey's." Bucke saw that the assault on the 1881 edition "immediately produced quite the opposite effect," and Whitman's enemy Baylies Allen lamented that "the book has been advertised more widely than ever by the attempt to suppress it."

The reaction they pointed to was confirmed by book sales. Not long after Whitman got his plates back from Osgood, he got an offer to publish from Rees Welsh, a Philadelphia firm that specialized in law tomes, secondhand books, and miscellaneous literature. Whitman worked out a good deal by which the firm would publish not only *Leaves of Grass* but also his prose writings, including *Specimen Days,* and Bucke's biography of him. Whitman also asked for an expensive edition of his poems "for holiday presents in handsome binding." Although nothing apparently came of the holiday book, due to the recent controversy the regular *Leaves of Grass* enjoyed its best sale ever. When the Rees Welsh edition appeared on July 18, the whole thousand-copy edition reportedly sold out in a day, and by August 13 a second printing of a thousand was nearly gone. On October 8 Whitman bragged "they are now in the fifth" printing. The next month, the firm's business manager, the thickset, bluff Scotsman David McKay, took over the firm's miscellaneous and second-hand list. On December 12 Whitman got from McKay a large royalty check of $1,230.78. Although sales declined after the novelty effect had worn off, Whitman emerged from the controversy well paid and famous.

In the midst of the excitement Whitman got a chance to relax with friends and family. In January 1882, shortly after Wilde's visit, his brother Jeff came to Camden for a short stay. In August Jeff's daughters Hattie and Jessie arrived on one of their customary visits, this time staying at Stevens Street nearly four months.

The following fall Whitman spent some of his royalties on a well-earned vacation in Ocean Grove, New Jersey. Along with John Burroughs, he took the Camden and Atlantic Railroad on September 26, 1883, and stayed in Ocean Grove at the comfortable Sheldon House until October 10. The continuous sound of the surf and the saline smell soothed him. While he was there he wrote a poem, "With Husky-Haughty Lips O Sea," which he later sold to *Harper's* for fifty dollars. In the poem, Whitman's "I" roves the shore, seeing in the ocean a metaphor for eternal beauty but also eternal torment. He pronounced himself "a kindred soul" to the angry ocean, whose splendor for him lay in its suggestion of unceasing tragedy: "(Naught but the greatest struggles, wrongs, defeats, could make thee greatest—no less could make thee,) / Thy lonely state—something thou ever seek'st and seek'st, yet never gain'st, / Surely some right withheld."

Was Whitman himself inwardly frustrated by some "right withheld"? Two private scribblings of the eighties suggest he was. There were signs of severe psychological tension within the superficially stable poet. "Why is it that a sense comes always crushing in on me, as of one happiness I have missed—life [*sic*], and one friend & companion I have never made?" he asked in his journal. He expressed ambivalence about his mental state to a friend in March 1884: "If I had not been born with a natural happy-tending disposition (I inherit it from my mother) the last few weeks—yes the last ten years—would have been unmitigated darkness & heaviness to me—As it is, the ennuyeed hours have been the rare exceptions—."

The last ten years. It was a large statement to say that a whole decade came close to being "unmitigated darkness & heaviness." To some degree, he was, as usual, reaching out for pity. But a hitherto-unnoticed change he made in the 1855 preface, which was republished along with other prose writings in 1882 by Rees Welsh, perhaps throws light on the statement. Whitman made only minor changes in the preface except for the last sentence, which now read: "The soul of the largest and wealthiest and proudest nation may well go half-way to meet that of its poets."

This was very different from the original, which had happily declared that the poet is absorbed by his country as affectionately as he has absorbed it. The Osgood edition had sold around 1,600 copies, the Welsh/McKay version about 6,000. That was not absorption by the country.

Whitman's new words diminished the self and amplified the nation: "[T]he largest and wealthiest and proudest nation"; "[M]ay well go half-way"; "The soul." The words were tentative, self-effacing, abstract.

Whitman had tried to carry the large, wealthy new America, and it had come close to crushing him. Now it would have to carry him.

16

THE POPE OF MICKLE STREET:
THE FINAL YEARS

I N M A R C H 1 8 8 4 Whitman bought his own house at 328 Mickle Street, Camden, for $1,750, of which $1,250 came from book royalties and $500 as a loan from his wealthy friend George W. Childs. It was typical that he got part of the money from Childs. Previous biographers have not noticed the degree to which Whitman in his last years became both financially and ideologically entangled with capitalists and social rulers. Nor have they sufficiently discussed the tensions, often over questions of power and money, between Whitman and his inner circle of followers, who are usually presented as almost obsequiously idolatrous of him.

These tensions also existed, to a great degree, within himself. How could the poet who had presented himself as a working-class rough conceivably align himself with money and power? But he was tempted to enjoy the fruits of his growing fame. It was during his last eight years that he won the support of Andrew Carnegie and several other capitalists. It was also during these years that his Lincoln lectures and birthday celebrations became big fund-raising events, that several authors who had once disdained him contributed to his support, and that he wrote poems praising the monarchs Queen Victoria and Emperor Frederick Wilhelm of Germany. And it was during these years that there appeared a Whitman cigar, a Whitman calendar, a Whitman tree, Whitman anthologies, a Whitman church, and various Whitman societies. The poet even fantasized whimsically about a Whitman popcorn.

Walt Whitman as capitalist commodity? The poet often put up lip-service resistance to his own commodification. But he let it happen, in some cases with enthusiasm. He detested the pirating of the 1860 edition of *Leaves of Grass;* but in these years he accepted royalties from it and refused to go to court about it. He said he was opposed to expurgated anthologies of his poems; but he consented to three during this period and even fantasized about a *Leaves of Grass, Junior* on his deathbed. He said he hated big affairs, but he accepted star billing at them, and he gladly accepted the proceeds they produced. He supposedly objected to a government pension for him, which was taken up in Congress, but he was disappointed when it didn't go through. He collected a substantial sum from contributors who wanted to buy him a country cottage, but he never bought the cottage, pocketing the money instead. And he continued to milk "O Captain!" and the Lincoln lecture for all they were worth.

He became more and more beloved by America even as he became less and less the poet of America. His name was a familiar one in newspapers, and toward the end he was assaulted by requests for autographs. But his poems now were thoughts, a few of them, like "Unseen Buds" and "To the Sun-set Breeze," exquisite, many of them nostalgic and self-pitying, and some, like "My Canary Bird," verging on the silly. In terms of placing his works in popular periodicals, this was by far his most successful period. Whitman, of course, kept saying he was neglected, but occasionally he forgot his line and said he couldn't keep up with the requests.

Shabby Digs, Rich Friends

IF CAMDEN had been an accident for Whitman, so, it seems, was Mickle Street. In August 1883 George and Louisa decided to leave Camden and move to a farm in the rural town of Burlington, New Jersey. Eddy had already been taken care of. In March 1881 he had been placed with the family of William V. Montgomery in Glen Mills, Pennsylvania. Whitman paid his sixteen-dollar monthly bill, then two years later transferred him to the farm of Margaret V. Goodenough in Moorestown, New Jersey, fourteen miles from Camden. When George and Louisa made plans to go, Whitman was unsure whether to accept their invitation to join them or move elsewhere. In late August he wrote a friend that he was going to move permanently from Camden, though he wasn't sure where.

As it turned out, he found a house of his own in Camden. It cannot have been called a bargain. He bought at a bad moment. Camden real estate prices, which had plunged during the 1873–79 depression, were now inflated. Fortunately for Whitman, he had just come off of good royalty years, and he had a useful connection in George Childs. He was able to buy the house in cash from Rebecca Jane Hare. The building was already rented to an elderly couple, a Mr. and Mrs. Alfred Lay, whom Whitman let stay on. He dined with them at first, but it soon became evident that cohabitation with a couple wasn't going to work in the cramped space of 328 Mickle. The Lays moved out the next January.

About then Whitman began having breakfasts with Mary Oakes Davis, a sea captain's widow who lived nearby at 412 West Street. The long-suffering woman, who had a history of nursing the elderly, had originally come to Camden to be with a friend, Mrs. Fritzinger, only to witness her death and that of her husband, Captain Fritzinger, whom Mrs. Davis cared for during his final illness. In the meantime, she was secretly married to a Captain Davis, who died at sea. Mrs. Davis inherited half of the Fritzingers' modest estate. The remaining share went to their sons, Warren and Harry, whom Mrs. Davis informally adopted.

Whitman had met Mrs. Davis in 1884, when he brought her clothes to mend. It was natural enough, with his family and the Lays gone, that he would dine with her. It soon seemed mutually advantageous that she move into Mickle Street as his housekeeper. His home at the time was only sparsely furnished. He reportedly told her: "I have a house while you pay rent; you have furniture while my rooms are bare; I propose that you come and live with me, bringing your furniture for the use of both." She moved in with him on February 24, 1885. She would be with him for more than six years, working for him without pay.

After she moved in, the house became a kind of combined dime museum and petting zoo. An animal lover, Mrs. Davis brought with her a cat, a dog, two turtledoves, a canary, a robin she had saved from a cat, and some hens she kept in an outhouse in the backyard. "We need but a snake—then our menagerie will be complete," Whitman once joked. Along with her pets and furniture, she brought along memorabilia like shells and curiosities from all over the world, including a model ship, which she hung in the front parlor much to Whitman's pleasure. Whitman had some memorabilia of his own. He added to the parlor a bust of Elias Hicks and a small seated sculpture of himself. He covered them with newspaper to prevent them from gathering dust; one day a visitor lifted the paper only to find there a thriving colony of ants.

The brown frame house, which faced north, was connected on its western side to a brick house that seemed to hold it up and was flanked on the east by a narrow alley that was closed from the street by a door. Three wooden steps without a banister led to Whitman's front door, which had to be closed in order for people to ascend the stairs to the second floor. On the ground floor were two small connecting rooms called the parlors, with a little kitchen in back. Upstairs there was a small back bedroom, where Mrs. Davis stayed, and a spacious room in front, which was Whitman's quarters.

The poet's room was large but simple, with uncarpeted plank floor, a small bed, and three windows facing the street. Near the middle window was a round table that Whitman used mainly for storage. But then, the whole room might have been called a storage bin since it was a sea of papers, books, and manuscripts (see fig. 47). The poet could easily pick out a document of choice from the chaos—which included, for instance, Emerson's 1855 letter to him—and he upbraided Mrs. Davis when she tried to tidy up, for he said then he couldn't find anything. Under the eastern window was a large square table at which Whitman worked. Typically he would tilt his big rocking chair back against the table and write with a mammoth quill pen as he held a pad on his knee. Against the western wall were two large wooden bedposts, between which were portraits of his mother and father.

Whitman had developed some rather bizarre habits. His three windows were shuttered, and, according to one report, he often left the western shutter closed and dark. The others he kept closed much of the time and only opened them slightly if he wanted to look out on the street. When he got a wood-burning stove in the room, he found it difficult to regulate. Usually he kept it roaring throughout the winter and spring, and, since he rarely opened the windows, visitors often complained of the insufferable heat. But there were times he forgot the stove altogether, and then the room could get frigid. "That's just the trouble—" he told Traubel. "I attribute a good deal of my cold, chilliness, discomfort, to the variable temperature: now it is hot, now cold—extremely hot, sweaty, roasty—then cold as ice."

Today, when Camden is a ghost of its former vibrant self, the Mickle Street area is virtually noiseless, a place where urban blight seems to get the best of urban renewal. In Whitman's time it was alive with sound. The poet was even closer to the railroad tracks than he had been at Stevens Street. Freight and passenger trains rumbled and screeched about a block away night and day. Below his window Whitman often heard the noise of children, who waited for the pennies he sometimes tossed down. They had a playful terror of his house, into which, they pretended, people entered, never to be seen again. Street vendors with rickety carts noisily hawked their cabbage or fish. Whitman remarked on "the vibrating voices of the loud-crying peddlers in the streets, quite a musical study, some of them have wonderfully fine organs as they peal and drawl them along." He also liked the nearby factory and shipping sounds, especially what he called "the great long *bur-r-r* of the Phila. whistles from factories or shores often & plainly here sounding." Also dear to him was the whistling buoy at a shipyard on nearby King's Point. Listening to its long, rising wail, he said, "It has a sound as if from Ulyssean seas."

There were less pleasant sounds as well. Nearby was a Methodist church whose bell clanged sharply and whose choir, which didn't seem to improve despite constant practice, was an "unsettling band of singers." As much as Whitman liked music, he came to detest the traveling bands that roamed Camden in warm weather. "Music is my worst punishment," he complained. "Oh! the bands out in the street—the drum and fife corps that go rattling and banging past: they beat my miserable head like hammers." The problem worsened when in 1888 a pianist took up daily practice sessions nearby. Also a nuisance to him was Mrs. Davis's spotted dog Watch, who more than lived up to his name by barking loudly at the least provocation. "He is the nastiest, noisiest, silliest, stupidest, horriblest dog that was ever born—a pest, a continual sore in my side!" Whitman declared. "He howls a hundred times a day, at all hours. In the night, too, generally about one o'clock when the rest of the world wants to keep quiet."

Mickle Street was then tree lined, and on the grassy sidewalk in front of his house was a tree Whitman sat under for hours in good weather. In back of the house was a middle-sized yard where a pear tree and a grape vine grew. Altogether, despite its industrial environment, Mickle Street had a rural feel. Whitman was a distinctive sight in the neighborhood as he walked to and from the horse-drawn streetcars, propped between his cane and Mrs. Davis, whose arm he gripped.

Like his doctors, Whitman had the idea cities got "malarial" in hot weather. In the eight years he was at Mickle Street summers were terribly hot and humid, especially those of 1886, 1887, and 1890. A real excitement occurred on August 3, 1885, when a cyclone roared through Camden, ruining more than six hundred homes and killing four people. Whitman's home barely avoided disaster. But the cyclone was an isolated incident. A more constant bother was the putrid odor given off by a fertilizer factory on the Philadelphia side of the Delaware. Whitman was also annoyed by a group of neighborhood women who, in order to taunt him, brushed puddles in front of his house with their brooms; he felt they were stirring up malaria. He cursed "the streets—the stinking reeking streets—Mickle street—sluttish gutters—women with hair a-flying—dust-brooms clouding the streets—confinement—the air shut off."

Still, he didn't think badly of Camden, as did many of his friends. Bucke, who called 328 Mickle "the worst house and the worst situated," urged him after his 1888 strokes to move to a nursing home in Baltimore.

Burroughs tried to tempt him away by offering him a cottage near Esopus. At one point Whitman actually got an invitation from a total stranger, a maker of beekeepers' supplies, to leave Camden and live with his family in Friendship, New York. But Whitman appreciated his easy access to the cars and ferries, and, as he put it to Traubel, "Every cock likes his own dunghill best."

Moreover, the house, like his half-paralysis, was always there to rely on whenever he wanted to drum up support. He called it his "shanty" or his "coop," as though he wanted to exaggerate its shabbiness. Even to this day, the image of the enfeebled Whitman living in shabby neglect lingers. We tend not to remember that he was befriended and in part supported by a number of the area's leading citizens.

He had made one important contact, with the family of the businessman Robert Pearsall Smith, in December 1882 when he was still on Stevens Street. Smith had married into the family that owned the Whitall-Tathum Company, a large manufacturer of glass bottles and containers in Millville, New Jersey. Smith had run the company for a while, then had become a touring religious evangelist before losing his faith, at which point he returned to the company. He and his family occupied a mansion at 1307 Arch Street in the Philadelphia suburb of Germantown. Smith encountered Whitman through his daughter Mary, who had read the poet at Smith College and grew so excited that she was determined to see him over her Christmas break.

Pearsall Smith was reluctant to accompany his daughter that winter day, and when he first arrived at Stevens Street he was aloof. Louisa Whitman, excited by the arrival of wealthy visitors, cried, "Walt, there's carriage folk come to see you!" When the visitors were taken up to the poet's den, it wasn't long before both sides were won over to each other. Walt was taken by the tall, lively, russet-haired Mary and by the serious Pearsall, who had a reflective side. Pearsall's churlishness quickly dissolved, and by the end of the conversation he was inviting Whitman to come and stay with them in Germantown. Whitman did his usual turnaround. At first he politely refused, but then, eyeing Smith's lavish carriage out front, changed his mind. He packed a bag and went off with them. He stayed in their mansion a whole month.

It was hardly the last time he accepted the generosity of the Smiths. Whitman was with them in Germantown on a regular basis, and when he was there he lived like a prince. He recalled later: "They treated me with peculiar consideration—made their home so much mine, its servants so much at my beck and call. . . . The house could not have been much more mine than if I had owned it." The Smiths were teetotalers, and Whitman while staying with them sometimes snuck out for a drink.

The poet didn't get along well with Robert's wife, Susan, who thought him too dismissive of church religion, but he was genuinely fond of the rest of the family, including Mary's sister Alys and their brother, Logan. When Whitman moved into Mickle Street, the three siblings bought him his big rocking chair and some pillowcases and afghans. Mary moved to England in 1885 and became a strong Whitman promoter there. She became an active feminist and fell in with a group of Fabians, among them George Bernard Shaw and Havelock Ellis, who talked of a forthcoming revolution of the workers of the world. Mary married a British socialite, and her relationship to Whitman cooled, possibly due to her radicalism. He warned her in one letter, "Don't invest thyself too heavily in those reforms or women's movements or any other movements over there—attend to *thyself* & take it easy."

But Whitman had enough other friendships going to keep him active and well entertained. Among his closest friends in the Mickle Street years was Traubel's brother-in-law Thomas B. Harned, one of Camden's leading lawyers, who had an elegant house on Sixth and Federal. Whitman had an open invitation to the weekly Sunday feasts at the Harned home. When he was feeling healthy, more often than not he joined Tom and Augusta Harned and their guests. As was his custom at gatherings, he usually chose to absorb what was going on around him rather than do much talking. He spent much of the time in a corner playing with the Harned children. When he was once asked to recite some of his own poems, he said he knew none of them—a candid response, apparently, since he said the same to others. (Here he differed from friends like John Townsend Trowbridge and Sir Edwin Arnold, who could recite pages of *Leaves of Grass* by heart.) Whitman sometimes felt he was being killed with kindness at the Harneds' lavish dinners, made festive by Madeira or champagne. But Harned was a lasting friend whose devotion to the poet stayed strong even after Whitman evidently exploited him financially in paying for his tomb.

Whitman had learned how to navigate in the new capitalistic environment, and he kept himself well stocked with friends who could help him out when necessary. Along with Smith, Childs, and Harned, there was James M. Scovel, another rich Camden lawyer at whose home Whitman often breakfasted. Of even more direct use to Whitman was Thomas Donaldson, a Philadelphia lawyer at whose house on Fortieth Street Whitman was a regular guest. Donaldson did the poet an important favor by securing him free ferry passes, and in 1885 he initiated a plan to buy Whitman a horse and buggy.

The horse-and-buggy campaign illustrated just how far Whitman's supportive network had spread by the mideighties. Some of his friends were informed by Mrs. Davis that Whitman felt confined by his physical condition, especially on Sundays when the cars didn't run. Some thirty people contributed to the purchase of a horse, a leather-lined phaeton, a whip, halter, and lap blanket. A total of $320 was donated by a large group of well-wishers, including Mark Twain, Whittier, and Oliver Wendell Holmes. This was one gift, evidently, Whitman did not help prearrange himself. He was sitting in his room on Mickle Street on September 17, 1885, when he looked out the window and saw a horse and buggy parked out front. He was dazed when he was told it was his. He immediately took to his new mode of transportation. Once hoisted onto the driver's seat, he displayed agility, and sometimes reckless speed, in guiding his horse, Frank, through the Camden streets. He was aided in his driving by a roguish teenager, William Duckett, who boarded for a while at Mickle Street. Although Whitman liked Duckett, who accompanied him on out-of-town trips like the one to Manhattan in April 1887, Mrs. Davis got into a financial dispute with the young man, who falsely claimed the poet had invited him to stay in his house for free. Whitman sold his horse, Frank, after five months and got a faster one, Nettie, but he had to give up the carriage after his strokes in June 1888.

Several other money-related matters were less pristine than the horse-and-buggy one. All of them reveal the double-natured aspect of the late Whitman, who betrayed contrary inclinations to principle and to lucre.

One of his ambivalent dealings was with Richard Worthington, a New York publisher who was trying to make money from the sale of a pirated printing of the 1860 edition of *Leaves of Grass*. Worthington had bought the plates of the 1860 edition at a publisher's auction for $200 and had started printing the volume and selling it in bookstores. When Whitman heard about the publication, he was, understandably enough, enraged. In 1880 he wrote Harry Stafford he planned to sue the "rascally publisher." The next year, as he was on his way north to oversee the Osgood edition, he had a half-hour meeting with Worthington in Manhattan, demanding that he stop publication at once. He continued to boil about the man he ironically labeled "Holy Dick." He seemed to be making a stand against literary pirating on principle, but, as in so many other cases, his principles proved more rubbery than his words. He actually accepted royalties from the pirated Worthington edition: $94.50 was paid to him by 1882, and some $50 more by 1888. Even more surprisingly, he never took the issue to court, even though his case against Worthington was solid. He told Traubel: "I am averse to going to law about it: going to law is like going to hell: it's too much trouble even if we win."

Once more, Whitman waffled. Perhaps he thought he received additional exposure through the pirated edition, and maybe he eyed more royalties in the future.

He waffled as well on a government pension for his support that was proposed in Congress. In December 1886, at the suggestion of Whitman's Boston friend Sylvester Baxter, a Massachusetts congressman proposed that Whitman be awarded a twenty-five-dollar monthly pension in reward for his service in the Civil War hospitals. Whitman, evidently loath to be seen as a freeloader off the state, made known his disapproval of the proposal, which was soon quietly dropped. But then he did a typical flip-flop. His indecision came through in this comment to a Philadelphia reporter: "I shall not be disappointed if it fails to pass, but if it does pass I will gladly accept it." After hearing in early March that Congress had gone out of session, he seemed disappointed: "The last closing days of Congress—great hubbub & confusion—not the least possibility of my pension bill passing."

He did a reversal as well, with far more diabolical overtones, over a group project to buy him a country house. Many of his friends shared his feeling that Camden was malarial, and a number of them wanted him to have a place he could go in sultry weather. In May 1887 the journalist and author William Sloane Kennedy started an active fund-raising campaign toward the purchase of a country home for the poet. Montgomery Stafford offered to donate a pleasant lot on Timber Creek where the cottage could be built. Whitman wrote Kennedy in June that "*there* I shall probably mainly live for the rest of my days—O how I want to get amid good air—the air is so tainted here, five or six months in the year, at best." Contributors to the project at first planned to build the house and then present it to Whitman as a surprise, but the press broke the matter, and a check for $323 was given to him instead, with an additional $465 sent later. Although he was given freedom as to the money's expenditure, it was generally understood that he would have the house built. But he never did. He accepted the cottage fund, then absorbed it into his increasing savings, evidently to the chagrin of several of his backers.

Nothing epitomized Whitman's ambivalence over the modern capitalistic environment more than his reactions to what was the crowning public event of his life: his 1887 Lincoln lecture at Madison Square Theatre in Manhattan. It is unknown whether he had given the Lincoln lecture in the four years after the 1881 Boston one, but in 1886 he gave the lecture four times and in 1887 twice, the main event being his April 14 appearance in New York.

This was a Barnumesque event on a high scale, arranged by two of the poet's wealthiest friends, the businessmen John Johnston and Robert

Pearsall Smith. Johnston took care of arranging the lecture itself, while Smith got a suite for Whitman at the luxurious Westminster Hotel, where a public reception was to be held afterward. To publicize the lecture, Johnston hired Major James B. Pond, a leading impresario of "Concerts, Lecturers, and All Descriptions of Musical, Lyceum and Literary Entertainments," as his letterhead put it. Major Pond hyped the event, which drew a large society crowd. In the audience were many of the day's rich and famous, including Andrew Carnegie, James Russell Lowell, Mary Mapes Dodge, Charles Eliot Norton, Mark Twain, and John Hay. William Dean Howells, who contributed his services, was so busy at the door collecting tickets that he didn't hear much of the lecture.

He missed a performance that today would probably seem like hokum but that was then taken as a moment of sacred patriotism. The backdrop to the stage was a domestic parlor scene, making Whitman look like an avuncular character in one of the sentimental novels of the day. The sentimental motif was carried to the end, for when Whitman had finished his melodramatic lecture and the inevitable "O Captain!" the flaxen-haired, six-year-old Laura Stedman walked onstage and handed the poet a bunch of lilacs, after which the curtain fell down to thunderous applause. The stage was inundated by many from the audience, mainly women, who thronged around him to congratulate him. The lecture netted him $600, with $350 coming from Carnegie alone.

The reception after the lecture was another society event, with many of the day's attendees plus others crowding into the Whitman suite at the Westminster Hotel to shake hands with the Good Gray Poet, who was never "gooder" or "grayer" than on that day of flatulent politesse. Whitman, dressed in conservative dark gray, was seated on a plush chair of red velvet. Known and unknown bigwigs strutted by, greeting him enthusiastically. There were, according to the newspaper reports, "Miss Breese, a wealthy society lady," "Mrs. Ward, a lovely lady of social prominence," and the Chevalier de Salas, who played a rare violin as Whitman watched. There were the philosopher John Fiske, the former secretary of the Legation in London E. S. Nadal, the widow of General George Custer, and so many others that it took thirty-eight column inches in the next day's New York *Sun* and twenty-six in the *Times* to describe the procession.

And what did the Good Gray think of all this? Again, he sent notably mixed signals. "It was too much the New York jamboree—the cosmopolitan drunk," he moaned to Traubel. Again: "first and last I opposed it—tried to beg off." But he had played his unctuous part to the hilt, and he told John Johnston that "the evening reception was the culminating hour of his life."

Quarrels, Recollections

W HICH WAS the real Whitman, the one who despised Worthington, nobly rejected the pension on principle, and detested the Lincoln lecture, or the one who embraced them all and perhaps even wanted more?

Some of his friends, drawn by his image as a maverick, were horrified when they suspected the latter might be true. No one was in for more of a surprise than Whitman's amanuensis from March 1888 onward, Horace Logo Traubel (see fig. 42).

Because of his faithfulness in taking down Whitman's words, Traubel, whose conversations with the poet now fill seven long volumes, has sometimes been pictured as the nineteenth-century equivalent of a tape recorder—appropriately located in Camden, later the home of RCA. But his relationship with Whitman was neither neutral nor always cordial. Certain tensions between them shed light on the poet's attitude toward power and authority.

Traubel, born in 1858, was the son of a German lithographer who had settled in Camden. He had gotten to know Whitman in the midseventies when the poet was living at 431 Stevens Street. He would sit with Whitman on mild summer evenings under the trees near the house and lose himself in endless conversations. He became, in a sense, one of the chief by-products of Whitman's growing fame, for on March 28, 1888, he began visiting the poet almost daily at Mickle Street.

The Northeast was then digging out from one of the worst blizzards in its history, and Traubel had to make his way through the snow to the poet's house. A short, blue-eyed man with wavy light brown hair and a mustache that didn't hide his boyish appearance, Traubel had quit school at twelve, worked as a printer and reporter, and a year after he began visiting Mickle Street took a job in a bank. He usually saw the poet in the late afternoon or early evening. Whitman would typically lie on his bed, with Traubel sitting near him on a couch, listening attentively as the poet talked in rambling fashion about everything under the sun. When he returned home after his visit with Whitman, Traubel hurriedly wrote down the day's conversation as fully as he could recall it. Although Whitman didn't realize the extent of Traubel's record, he knew the young man was taking notes and thoroughly approved of them.

He did not, however, concur with Traubel's radical political views. Traubel was a socialist of the Henry George variety who was appalled by the widening class divisions that accompanied capitalist expansion.

As seen, Whitman had written his major poetry at a moment when class divisions were extraordinarily high, and his fifties poems were full of compassionate portraits of populist types that attracted radicals like Traubel. But even in the fifties, Whitman had not joined socialist organizations like Lippard's Brotherhood of the Union or any of the utopian communities of the day. He even steered clear of labor organizations, though he saw their necessity. Traubel liked to see him above all as the poet of the working person, and Whitman occasionally obliged him with statements like, "Of course I find I'm a good deal more of a socialist than I thought I was: maybe not technically, politically, so, but intrinsically, in my meanings."

In the Marxist heyday of the 1930s, Newton Arvin wrote a whole book on the socialist themes in Whitman's work. But even Arvin found inconsistences in Whitman's position, and he overlooked substantial evidence that Whitman actually leaned just as strongly to capitalism as to socialism. When he used Traubel as a sounding board for his political views, the poet often met with hostility.

They came near to an outright fight over Andrew Carnegie. Whitman never got over the fact that the magnate had sent him $350 after the Lincoln lecture, even though Traubel reminded him that for Carnegie this was a trifling sum. He mentioned the contribution in no fewer than five letters, and he was grateful when Carnegie sent him another $50 later on. There were several reasons Carnegie contributed to Whitman's support. He shared with Whitman a love of the poetry of Robert Burns, he was a close friend of Whitman's favorite orator, Robert Ingersoll, and, most important, he considered Whitman America's greatest poet. Which body of Whitman's writings attracted him is unknown, but it was the procapitalist technology poems that most closely approximated his viewpoint. Carnegie's book *Triumphant Democracy* (1886) showcased all the kinds of technological marvels Whitman had in poems like "Song of the Exposition." When he heard that Whitman's British admirers, rallied by exaggerated stories of Whitman's supposed poverty in the *Pall Mall Gazette*, had raised over eighty pounds for him, he declared: "I felt triumphant democracy disgraced. Whitman is the great poet of America so far." America, he thought, must help out its finest poet.

Traubel and his radical friends did not have kind things to say about Carnegie, whom they considered an exploitative capitalist. But Whitman hated to hear Carnegie criticized. "I include Carnegie," he said flatly to a doubtful Traubel one day. Another time Traubel tried hard to convince Whitman of the sufferings of average workers in Carnegie's steel mills, but Whitman refused to criticize Carnegie. Traubel called it "treason" to the working person when Whitman said, "Carnegie showed himself so warm, generous, lavish towards me." The two came close to fighting, but they let the matter pass in a kind of sullen truce.

Whitman did lash out against the Philadelphia department store tycoon John Wanamaker, but that was largely because of Wanamaker's narrow religiosity and his prudish refusal to carry *Leaves of Grass* in his stores. In general, Whitman had kind things to say about the social elite. "I try to be just to the money folks: they are, many of them, very lovable, very human," he declared, though he said he didn't envy them their wealth. He used his egalitarian pose as a means of embracing both entrenched authority figures and their radical opponents, saying that while "I speak for Anarchists, socialists, George men, whatever you choose, I include as well Kings, Emperors, aristocracies, financial men."

He put muscle behind such statements by specifically defending two modern monarchs, Frederick Wilhelm I and Queen Victoria. Traubel wasn't the only one shocked by his defense of these two. So had been Anne Gilchrist, and so in fact were most of Whitman's friends. But defend them he did, even though it seemed to those around him the height of antirepublicanism. "You object to Emperor Frederick Wilhelm?" he asked Traubel. "Well—object: ... He is one of the very best Emperors in all history—tried to do right—makes a big strain to size up to the emperor ideal he has in his mind: why should we gag at it?" Queen Victoria, who remained dear to him because she prevented Europe from siding with the South in the Trent Affair during the Civil War, was also the subject of his praise.

He even wrote laudatory poems about these monarchs. "The Dead Emperor" was a eulogy for Wilhelm, who died in March 1888; the poet called him "a good old man—a faithful shepherd, patriot." His radical friends hated the poem. As Tom Harned later recalled, "His poem on the death of Emperor William I of Germany produced a storm of censure." In his 1890 poem "For Queen Victoria's Birthday" Whitman sent her "countless blessings, prayers, and old-time thanks" and in a footnote thanked her for her respect for the North during the war. Traubel thought Whitman was betraying his democratic principles. "Walt, you come damn near being a monarchist yourself with all this fol-de-rol about the Queen," he said.

In part, Whitman's defense of monarchs and businesspeople reflected his recognition of the inevitability of centralized power structures in the modern environment. The era's foremost defender of capitalism, William Graham Sumner, would declare in 1894 that since the rise of corporations and bureaucracies was inexorable, it was no use protesting against them; instead, they should be used for good purposes. This was similar to the attitude Whitman expressed to Traubel. He seemed slightly baffled but ultimately hopeful about the ubiquity of huge corporations and trusts. He said: "We seem to have entered an age, an atmosphere, of trusts, banks, stocks, capital—an overwhelming mass of it—but I am not clear what it all means. . . . Oh! they are here: the trusts! and yet it is all right: we must believe that it is all right: at least, we must believe that it is—and a thing that *is*, is, anyhow! and therein lies the seriousness of it always." He didn't like the way socialists automatically damned the wealthy, who, he believed, could work for good. Radicals didn't have a corner on social reform, he argued, for "everybody is occupied with it nowadays—even the millionaires, who if they have a few millions at death, leave a little of it—a million or so for ameliorative purposes."

Whereas he often defended capitalists and social rulers, he found himself having a mixed response to the radical activists of the day. He declared, "I am not asleep to the fact that among radicals as among the others there are hoggishnesses, narrownesses, inhumanities, which at times almost scare me for the future." He disapproved of the violent tactics of those behind the Haymarket bombing in 1886, and, unlike several of his friends, he thought it just when several convicted anarchists were hanged. When at the suggestion of his friend Sylvester Baxter he read the utopian socialist novel *Looking Backward* by Edward Bellamy, he was notably displeased with Bellamy's proposed classless society run efficiently by the state. In commenting on Baxter, Whitman dismissed Bellamy and others: "[Baxter] is very radical—progressive, he is enthusiastic over Bellamy's book. . . . But no—no—no—we are not going to be reformed in this way, by parcels—not by Henry Georgian Socialism, anarchism, Schools—any one agency."

This is not to paint the old Whitman as a naïve apologist of capitalism. Every once in a while one hears in his late years the kinds of searing critiques of American materialism he had launched in the dark middle section of *Democratic Vistas*. In an 1891 newspaper interview he declared, "I sh'd say we New Worlders are turning out the trickiest, slyest, 'cutest, most cheating people that ever lived." He used almost exactly the same words in a private jotting on America at the time. He wrote a cynical poem, "The Rounded Catalogue Divine Complete," in answer to an optimistic sermon that had claimed humanity was basically good, which said that in fact nineteen-twentieths of life was "The devilish and the dark, the dying and diseas'd, / [. . .] Newts, crawling things in slime and mud, poisons, / The barren soil, the evil men, the slag and hideous rot."

But there was something formulaic now even in his pessimism. A. James Reichley has pointed out that corruption in American government became far more deeply entrenched than previously once the Republican and Democratic parties established powerful political machines in the seventies and eighties. The question became, Reichley notes, not *whether* a political leader was corrupt but simply to what party that person owed his or her corruption. In the age of machine politics, individuals like Whitman had little recourse but to accept the flow of events while occasionally blasting out against them.

Tolerating a less-than-ideal status quo included, for Whitman, taking a positive stand on the postwar presidents, none of them cynosures and all of them involved in perpetuating machine politics. One can perhaps excuse his love of Grant, who remained an immensely popular leader even after the rottenness of his administrations was revealed. One might wonder why Whitman wrote three poems about Grant and one about his daughter Nelly's marriage, but even these poems can be viewed as *jeux d'esprit* in honor of the old war hero.

But what about his regard for Rutherford B. Hayes? This tool of the Republican machine had barely won the 1876 race and had thereafter overseen the end of Reconstruction and the resurgence of white supremacy in the South. How can Whitman have seen Hayes as a unifier of the nation? But he did. He was taken by the man's power as a stump speaker, which he believed might contribute to cultural cohesion. He wrote of Hayes in *Specimen Days:* "Underneath, his objects are to compact and fraternize the States, encourage their materialistic development, soothe and expand their self-poise, and tie all and each with resistless doubleties not only of inter-trade barter, but human comradeship." He repeated the point to Traubel, saying that he had read Hayes's speeches and found them "genial, good-natured, sensible, helping things along—South, North—especially South." It was ironic that he mentioned the bringing together of North and South as Hayes's strong point, because it was under Hayes that the South began its long plunge into the darkness of the caste system and legislated segregation that would last until the early 1960s. Whitman saw worth as well in Grover Cleveland, the pro-business Democrat elected in 1884 and nearly again four years later. Whitman said Cleveland "has done some honor to his office—has done his best: not your best or my best but his best."

His favorable attitude to less-than-stellar presidents reflects his renewed faith in the standard political process of democratic America. In his *Brooklyn Daily Eagle* days, as a loyal Democratic journalist, he had a basic faith in the "cleansingness" of the electoral process. In the fifties, his collapsed belief in the party system and presidential power had caused the incredible surge of his omnivorous, all-gathering poetic "I," creating his richest poetry. After the war, in the wake of Lincoln, his "I" was in retreat, and he looked again to the electoral process and American presidents to resolve social problems on a large scale. In his poem "Election Day, November, 1884," he celebrated Grover Cleveland's victory by saying that America's greatest "scene and show" was not any of its natural wonders, like Yosemite or Niagara or the Great Lakes, but rather "America's choosing day," creating "The final ballot-shower from East to West—the paradox and conflict, / The countless snowflakes falling." Battles between nominees, he argued, were healthy and held the prospect of change that would weed out all impurities from cultural life. Election day seemed to Whitman

>   the peaceful choice of all,
> Or good or ill humanity—welcoming the darkest odds, the dross:
> —Foams and ferments the wine? it serves to purify—while the
>   heart pants, life glows:
> These stormy gusts and winds waft precious ships,
> Swell'd Washington's, Jefferson's, Lincoln's sails.

As is suggested by this poem, when he wrote about America now, he praised its heroes and traditions in a straightforward way. He was light-years distant from the cocky, rebellious, tormented, erotic lover of American life that had made his fifties persona so multivalent. Whitman now penned uncomplicated, short poems in which America came out as a kind of smiling Greek goddess towering over humanity and time. Note, for instance, the images of solidity and permanence in his 1888 poem "America":

> Centre of equal daughters, equal sons,
> All, all alike endear'd, grown, ungrown, young or old,
> Strong, ample, fair, enduring, capable, rich,
> Perennial with the Earth, with Freedom, Law and Love,
> A grand, sane, towering seated Mother,
> Chair'd in the adamant of time.

There is no "I" in this poem; nor are there recognizable individuals either. There are only grandiose images and abstractions, as America is transformed almost literally into a huge, maternal Greek statue. Whitman wants to carve his love for his country in adamant, as though he were a Greek artist sculpting an art work.

The Greek reference is no accident, for he now liked to heighten the grandeur of America's cultural heroes with Greek references. In "As the Greek's Signal Flame" he hailed the octogenarian national poet Whittier as follows: "As the Greek's signal flame, by antique records told, / [...] So I aloft from Manahatta's ship-fringed shore, / Lift high a kindled brand for thee, Old Poet." In "The Wallabout Martyrs," the victims of the Brooklyn prison ships become "Greater than memory of Achilles or Ulysses" or than "tomb of Alexander." In "Death of General Grant" the plebeian president becomes one of "the lofty actors / From that great play on history's stage eterne," the "Man of the mighty days—and equal to thy days!" In "Washington's Monument, February, 1885," the first president becomes virtually a god: "Thou, Washington, art all the world's, the continents' entire—not yours alone, America, / [...] Wherever Freedom, pois'd by toleration, sway'd by Law, / Stands or is rising thy true monument."

Once again, the images are abstract, adamantine. There is a tremendous reification of America in these poems, as though Whitman sees his nation as a vast stone monument. It is fitting that in another poem of the period, "The United States to Old World Critics," he pictures America as an ever-growing building:

> Here first the duties of to-day, the lessons of the concrete,
> Wealth, order, travel, shelter, products, plenty;
> As of the building of some varied, vast, perpetual edifice,
> Whence to arise inevitable in time, the towering roofs, the lamps,
> The solid-planted spires tall shooting to the stars.

Whitman's procapitalist belief in material wealth as the precursor to America's growth is here conveyed in an image remarkably anticipatory of a skyscraper. Writing five years before the Chicago Columbian Exposition, which would celebrate the modern city, Whitman presents his nation as an ever-rising building.

If his relationship to America had grown more traditional and less personal, so had his poetic language. C. Caroll Hollis and others have noted that Whitman's language was far more abstract, formal, and conventional in the poetry he wrote after the war than it had been in his antebellum poetry. His changing language reflected various changing cultural phenomena. What Hollis calls a decline in oratorical "speech acts" in Whitman's poetry, including direct, personal addresses from an "I" to a "you," also occurred in the culture at large, as oratory and drama were becoming more and more involved in spectacle and less concerned with audience-performer interaction than before. Just after the Civil War, actors, lecturers, ministers, and other public performers became professionalized to a degree unknown before the war. The term "show business" began in the late sixties to be used widely to describe the commercialization of performance culture that has continued to broaden to this day. A main result of this process was the distancing between performer and audience, who before the war had been active coparticipants in virtually all aspects of performance culture. As ticket prices climbed for theaters, lectures, and celebratory dinners, rowdy, interactive working-class audiences started keeping away from performances like Shakespearean plays that formerly had been the scene of lively class interaction. Whitman, who followed the general trend by pricing his Lincoln lecture far too high for average working persons, also lost the slang-enlivened, dialogic idioms of his earlier poetry. He relied more heavily than before on formal, "poetic" language (such as "haply" for "perhaps," "list" for "listen," the stilted pronouns "thee" and "thou," and so on).

In part because he felt himself pulled inexorably by the stylistic and ideological magnet of capitalistic America, he looked back with nostalgia for what he recalled as a more boisterous, more richly human time. He wrote many articles on the actors, orators, preachers of his youth. His memories of Junius Brutus Booth, the quintessential antebellum audience-arouser, may have been piqued by an Osgood book, Asa Grey's *The Older and Younger Booths.* At any rate, in 1884 he wrote Booth's son, the Shakespearean actor Edwin Booth, asking for a photo of his father. He featured Junius Booth in his 1885 article "The Old Bowery," in which Booth stands out among many antebellum roaring performers Whitman describes as having appealed to all classes. This class-dissolving quality of antebellum performance was captured too in his 1887 newspaper piece "New Orleans in 1848," in which Whitman re-created lively, communal scenes such as General Zachary Taylor laughing unrestrainedly at a model artist show. Although Whitman's own poetry had largely lost its slang usages, he called slang the basis of all writing in his 1885 article "Slang in America." With Traubel he loved to use both African-American dialect and New York Bowery b'hoy slang. He spent far more time with Traubel talking of the old antebellum performers than of the more stiff, distanced performance scene of the modern day. He lost himself in memories of a communal, open culture that had largely disappeared.

Fame and Debility

IF A TIME can be pinpointed when Whitman became a real celebrity, the years 1887–88 must be that time. Ironically, it was also at that time that he became physically incapable of capitalizing fully on his celebrity status. At a moment when at last he might have caught the ear of America at large, he was beyond hope of addressing his nation in a vigorous way. No one saw the irony any more clearly than he.

The fact that Whitman was invited to give two Lincoln lectures in the spring of 1887, having already given four the year before, was a sign of his fame. His lecture before a Camden Unitarian group on April 5 was a modest affair, but the April 14 lecture in Manhattan was, as seen, one of the great public events of his lifetime.

Several visitors he had that summer and fall—the self-styled philosopher John Newton Johnson, the artists Herbert Gilchrist and Thomas Eakins, and the sculptor Sidney Morse—showed the mayhem celebrity could bring. Johnson was an old farmer and a homespun thinker from Alabama who had found spiritual consolation in Whitman after long, aimless wanderings through various philosophies. He was one of many who found Whitman's healthyminded faith a relief from the abysms of doubt. Whitman found him quirky. "He is the queerest, wildest, 'cutest mortal you ever saw—has a boy 12 years old named Walt Whitman," he wrote. He stayed in Whitman's house from May 18 through the third week in June.

While Johnson was expostulating in half-crazy fashion about philosophy, Whitman's head and bust were being eyed aesthetically by the ex–magazine editor and self-taught sculptor Sidney Morse, who shuttled back and forth between the parlor, where Whitman posed for him, and the backyard, where he pounded and shaped his clay models. Morse did several sculptures of Whitman before leaving in December to spend the holidays with his wife. Filling out the scene was Herbert Gilchrist, the artistic son of Anne Gilchrist, who was doing Whitman's portrait. Whitman disliked the proper, idealized portrait Gilchrist produced, whereas he was taken with the more gritty, realistic one done that fall by the Philadelphia artist Thomas Eakins. Having been introduced to the poet by the journalist Talcott Williams, the quiet, casual Eakins worked on Whitman's portrait from November 1887 to the following March. "I like Eakins' picture (it's like sharp cold cutting true sea brine)," Whitman commented. He saw in it "a poor old blind despised & dying king," though actually there was ruddiness and humor to the painting.

Just as he was gaining recognition from artists, he was learning the dark side of fame: rejection by a former friend. In August 1887 appeared Swinburne's recantation of Whitman in the *Fortnightly Review*. In the late sixties and early seventies Swinburne had been very sympathetic toward Whitman, praising his Lincoln elegy and writing a laudatory poem about him. But he had been fairly quiet about him since then, and Whitman was anxious enough about the matter to bring it up with

Wilde, who wrote ambivalently after his visit that Swinburne had not relaxed his admiration of Whitman's "noblest work." Whitman's increasing visibility probably impelled Swinburne to take a public stand on what he saw as the poet's vulgarity. "Mr. Whitman's Eve," he wrote prudishly, "is a drunken apple-woman, indecently sprawling in the slush and garbage amid the rotten refuse of her overturned fruit-stall: but Mr. Whitman's Venus is a hottentot wench under the influence of cantharides and adulterated rum."

Swinburne's recantation didn't make a dent in Whitman's growing fame. Like previous opposition to Whitman's verse, it may have actually increased it. At any rate, he still had strong friends among the British. In late December 1887 he got a friendly letter from the British author Edmund Gosse, who had visited him two years earlier at Mickle Street. Whitman appreciated Gosse's support but personally found him stuffy, too cultured for his taste. He was cheered that month by a visit from the British publisher Ernest Rhys, who went on to give a highly successful lecture on him in Manhattan in February.

His greatest publicity coup of the period was his being taken on as the unofficial poet laureate of the nation's most popular newspaper, the *New York Herald*. James Gordon Bennett, Jr., who had taken over management of the paper from his father in the sixties, invited Whitman to contribute to the paper's "Personal" column. Whitman wrote thirty-two poems and a number of prose pieces for the paper from January 21 to May 27, 1888. The new poems were little more than bits written about specific scenes or occasions, as indicated by some of their titles: "The First Dandelion," "From Montauk Point," "My Canary Bird," "A Carol Closing Sixty-Nine," "Old Salt Kossabone." He was now beyond even thinking about writing a sweeping, cohesive poem about America. His role combined the nostalgic storyteller, the benign nature poet, and the wallower in self-pity. He brought attention to his bad health. "As I Sit Writing Here" had him advertising his illness even while pretending to suppress it:

> As I sit writing here, sick and grown old,
> Not the least burden is that dulness of the years, querilities [*sic*],
> Ungracious glooms, aches, lethargy, constipation, whimpering *ennui*,
> May filter in my daily songs.

He was the famous sick old man, possessed of the opportunity to say something to America but with little new to say, and unequipped physically to bear the weight of fame. He seemed to see the worst coming, for in another *Herald* poem, "Queries to My Seventieth Year," he wondered whether the coming year would "cut me short for good? Or leave me here as now, / Dull, parrot-like and old, with crack'd voice, harping, screeching?"

He was right to worry. About a month after this poem appeared, Whitman suffered a series of strokes that nearly killed him and that left him in a precarious position for the rest of his life. On May 31 he attended a birthday reception for him at the Harned home, where there was much festivity and recitation of his poetry. Three days later he took a carriage ride to the Delaware shore in South Camden to watch the sunset. He apparently caught a cold, but, despite what his doctors later told him, that was probably unconnected to what occurred. That night he had a paralytic stroke and then had two more the next day. The first one left him sprawled on his bedroom floor for hours, almost totally helpless. He didn't call out for Mrs. Davis, for he was resolved to get through the problem himself. He managed to pull himself to the bed, but when he had his other incidents the next morning he lay speechless and nearly comatose for several hours. Traubel, who had been visiting him regularly since March, found that in the days just after the incident his mind wandered for the first time since he had known him.

Peter Doyle, now living in Philadelphia, made a rare visit on June 17, bringing flowers. The poet was confined to his bed and chair for weeks and to his room for the whole summer. He was saddened further by a deterioration of his brother Eddy's condition. Eddy was having epileptic seizures that, with his retardation and other handicaps, made him more helpless than before. On August 1, Louisa and the visiting Jessie placed Eddy in the insane asylum in Blackwoodtown, New Jersey. His expenses of fourteen dollars a month were still paid by Walt.

Now the poet himself needed constant care. From June 1888 onward his letters to Bucke were filled with reports of his wavering health. He developed, among other things, a bladder problem that caused leakages and had him up as many as fifty times a night. Eventually his urination was partly relieved by a catheter, but he suffered so badly from constipation that every bowel movement became an event to crow about to Bucke, who was duly informed of the shape and appearance of many feces.

Traubel procured him a succession of sturdy male nurses who aided the tireless Mrs. Davis. The first, W. A. Musgrove, served from mid-July to early November. Whitman liked the gruff Musgrove well enough, but Traubel found him surly and replaced him with Ed Wilkins, a dynamic, strong, ruddy young man Bucke had sent from Canada. He took up the violin, and Whitman good-naturedly put up with his endless amateurish screeching. Wilkins served Whitman a year but then left to attend veterinary school in Toronto. He in turn was replaced by Warren Fritzinger, the twenty-five-year-old adopted son of Mrs. Davis. Warrie, as Whitman called him, was as self-sacrificing as his mother. Although he was engaged to a woman for more than two years while tending to Walt, he almost never saw her at night because of his service to the poet. He took nursing classes in Philadelphia and also trained to be a professional masseur. The latter skill was a godsend to the poet, who found that Warrie's nightly "pummelings" of his body brought him great relief. A carpenter, Warrie helped around the house.

Well attended by nurses, Whitman was also coddled as a writer by sympathetic periodical editors and by his supportive publisher David McKay. After the original Rees Welsh printing of *Leaves of Grass* in 1882, McKay had reissued the volume under his own imprint in 1883 and '84. After that, so many of Whitman's poems and articles appeared in the popular press that in 1888 McKay worked with Whitman on a new poetry volume and a prose one too. Whitman had been working on these volumes in the late spring before suffering his strokes, and he continued with them despite his weakened health.

Whitman sometimes tried out his neglect complaint on Traubel, as when he said, "I have been and am rejected of all the great magazines." Traubel was right to raise his eyebrows at this tired lament. The two McKay volumes of 1888 show vividly that, far from being neglected, Whitman had been, if anything, spoiled by the press in recent times. McKay's new printing of *Leaves of Grass,* made from the Osgood plates, contained sixty-five recent poems grouped as an annex called "Sands at Seventy." Fifty-seven of these poems had already been published in magazines or newspapers—a remarkable publication rate of 88 percent. The second McKay volume that year, *November Boughs,* contained twenty prose articles, fifteen of which had been published in periodicals and one of which had appeared in a book on Lincoln. Given the fact Whitman still saw himself mainly as a poet, this 80 percent publication rate for the recent prose was particularly high.

Whitman got even more exposure that fall by bringing out a comprehensive edition of his writings with a Philadelphia printer, Ferguson Brothers. Called *Complete Poems and Prose of Walt Whitman, 1855 ... 1888/Authenticated and Personal Book,* the volume included all the recent poetry as well as *November Boughs* and *Specimen Days and Collect.* Sculpted almost completely by the poet himself, the book showed how he now wanted to present himself publicly. He featured the Good Gray Poet image in two prominently placed photographs, one of his old-age profile on the title page, with receding hairline and an ethereal look, and another of his aged face opposite *November Boughs.* The 1854 "loafer" portrait was still placed opposite "Song of Myself," as though the poem and its persona were of a different era. The "Walt Whitman" that appeared alone on the brown, chunky volume's spine was clearly intended to be associated with the old, benign picture on the title page.

Whitman's most important new work, his essay "A Backward Glance O'er Traveled Roads," which appeared in both the Ferguson and the McKay volumes, was his culminating statement on the historical embeddedness of his writings. The historical side of his vision was reflected in the nostalgic, anecdotal tenor of the new poems and essays, many of which re-created the scenes and people of his youth and young manhood. Whitman also highlighted history in an endnote to the *Complete Poems and Prose* in which he said that his poems were "created and formulated" not by "my pen or voice, or anybody's special voice" but rather by "the 33 years of my current time, 1855–1888, with their aggregate of our New World doings and people." Whitman here totally discounted the personal self on behalf of history.

He took a more balanced position in "A Backward Glance," in which the individual *and* history are presented as cocreators of his poems. Whitman sees in *Leaves of Grass* "my own physical, emotional, moral, intellectual, and aesthetic Personality, in the midst of, and tallying, the momentous spirit of its immediate days, and of current America." His poetry could be understood, he emphasized, only with reference to its "preparatory background." He reviewed central themes of his works and expressed thanks that the public's reception of him seemed to be warming. Although he made his usual complaint about the "mark'd anger and contempt" of his critics, he recognized signs of his growing fame: "I consider the point that I have positively gain'd a hearing, to far more than make up for any and all other lacks and withholdings. Essentially, *that* was from the first, and has remained throughout, the main object. Now it seems to be achiev'd, I am certainly contented to waive any otherwise momentous drawbacks, as of little account."

He was saying that finally his book, rooted totally in American life, was gaining a hearing, which had been his main goal from the start. He desired recognition so much that he put up with three new anthologies of his poetry that expurgated it far more drastically than had the 1868 Rossetti selection. These anthologies—edited, respectively, by Ernest Rhys, Elizabeth Porter Gould, and Arthur Stedman—tell us much about Whitman's hunger for fame, even at the expense of principle. They also shed light on late-nineteenth-century popular taste, which shied away from sex but still approved of comradely love.

Whitman's two-sided response to Elizabeth Porter Gould's *Gems from Walt Whitman* (1889) suggests just how much he was willing to put aside his qualms about expurgation in order to reach the public. Supposedly, he had a dim view of the Gould volume. He said, "These gems, sparkles, tid-bits, brilliants, sparkles, chippings—oh, they are all wearisome." He noted that "they might go with some books," but not *Leaves of Grass*. In other words, his was not the kind of volume that could be chopped up. But Gould chopped away furiously, and Whitman went along with her. When she sent him her manuscript in September 1887, he did not oppose her, writing in his daybook: "I consent." "I don't like the idea of having it done," he told Traubel, "but I like still less the idea of telling her not to." What he consented to was a spotless, desexed collection of poetic tidbits and hospital memorabilia of Whitman. Gould's thin, elegant book of Whitman excerpts, mainly about nature and religion, would have fit into the most pristine middle-class Victorian parlor, which was now what Whitman himself had his sights set on.

That the middle-class Victorian parlor could accept naturally Whitman's "Calamus" poems is suggested by Ernest Rhys's *Leaves of Grass: The Poems of Walt Whitman* (1886) and Arthur Stedman's 1892 collection of Whitman's *Selected Poems*. Like Gould, these other two editors carefully excluded the "amative" poems and passages they thought might offend middle-class readers. To avoid sex, Rhys omitted "Song of Myself" and all the "Children of Adam" poems. ("I am willing," wrote Whitman of the Rhys volume, despite his distaste for expurgation.) Stedman, likewise, omitted "Children of Adam" and heavily edited "Song of Myself." Both volumes emphasized the Whitman poems that were safely religious and patriotic. Significantly, many of the "Calamus" poems were deemed conventional enough to remain in these scrubbed, polite volumes. In fact, Rhys included nearly the whole "Calamus" sequence, and Stedman selected several, including the loving "When I Heard at the Close of Day" and "Whoever You Are Holding Me Now in Hand." That is, comradely love was still considered close to mainstream conventions.

Whitman was now trying in so many ways to appeal to these conventions that he even tolerated the commercialization of his name. Some today are shocked by the commercialization of Whitman, as in the Walt Whitman Mall in Huntington, New York, or the Walt Whitman Bridge connecting Philadelphia and Camden. But this commercializing process had begun in his time, and he was not totally opposed to it. When he saw the logo for the Walt Whitman cigar, he laughed, "That is fame!" and said of the picture of him on the logo, "It is not so bad—not as bad as it might be: give the hat a little more height and it would not be such an offense." He got a request from a Pasadena woman, Grace Ellery Channing, to publish a Walt Whitman calendar, with illustrated excerpts from his poems. She said the calendar, which would sell widely, would be "a means of disseminating and popularizing where we cannot reach in other ways." Whether or not the calendar appeared, there was a Walt Whitman tree dedicated in October 1889 by public-school students in Bath, Maine. The school's principal wrote Whitman asking him to give his blessing to "the grand work of tree-planting."

Perhaps the greatest mark of his growing celebrity status was the rapid rise of autograph requests he received in the mail. In 1889 he estimated that three of every five letters he received were autograph requests. In order to satisfy the public's hunger for his autograph, he included a facsimile of his scrawled name on all the McKay editions of his writings from 1888 onward. Though happy to print his autograph publicly, he rarely gave a private request any response other than tossing it in his stove. "You don't know, Horace," he said, "what a good investment that stove has been: I take a few of the autograph fellows, put logs on top of them, apply a match: then the fire is here. It is a great resource in trouble!"

Family and Friends

HE COULD NOT BE so dismissive of his family, which relied on him even more than before as his fame grew. Hannah and Charles Heyde, since their spurt of enthusiasm over the Osgood edition, had grown more and more pathetic—and progressively more fawning toward him. In the mideighties Hannah developed a bizarre habit of painting her dresses, body, and tablecloths bright red. Her mental condition improved somewhat after that, but physically she deteriorated due to the onset of jaundice. By November 1888 Heyde reported to Whitman that she was "extremely nervous, being weak from her prostrating sickness." She soon became thin and shrunken, with grayish skin and protruding bones. Heyde's paintings were selling poorly, so the indigent couple lived mainly off of their Burlington neighbors.

They also looked for help from their now-famous "Brother Walt." Heyde noted that Whitman had "good sympathizers, and those that appreciate your eminent talent, in advance of all others." Where there is fame, there must be money, Heyde reasoned. He assaulted Whitman with money requests, sweetening them with unctuous lead-ins like this: "Our dearly, first remembered, venerated brother Walt." Walt wasn't fooled by his sappy affection or his phony nostalgia, as when Heyde called his memories of old Brooklyn "brilliant stars, with one, yourself, supreme in the galaxy——." Whitman privately called Heyde "a perpetual filch, a damned mean lazy scoundrel," "the worst nuisance and worriment of my illness— ... always whining and squeezing me for *more money*—damn him—he ought to be crush'd out as you w'd a bed-bug." But Whitman felt a strong obligation to Hannah, to whom he wrote at least thirty-seven times in the last two years of his life. Despite his feelings about Heyde, he became a fountain of small bills to the suffering couple.

Concerned more than ever about his family in the wake of his 1888 strokes, he revised his will and made plans for his tomb, which was to house himself and several family members. In his will, which he twice revised and made final on January 1, 1892, he left one thousand dollars each to Hannah Heyde and Mary Davis, two hundred dollars to his sister Mary, his gold watch to Horace Traubel and his silver one to Harry Stafford, and the remainder of his estate, including the Mickle Street house and the bulk of his savings, to Ed. He explained, "First of all I want to protect Eddy. Eddy must be protected at all costs."

His tomb became a major concern, and another pretext for shady financial dealings on Whitman's part. Like much of his late writing, the tomb was an exercise in nostalgia. Among the things he recalled in his prose writings of the eighties was the large, cohesive Whitman and Van Velsor families of the distant past. Like many nineteenth-century families, his had been dispersed and darkened by tragedy. Jeff's relocation to St. Louis for professional reasons typified the geographical dispersal of the nineteenth-century family. The gap between him and Jeff had been bridged somewhat by the regular visits East by Jessie and Hattie, but then in 1886 Hattie died prematurely of enteritis. Walt expressed his grief over Hattie's passing in sorrowful letters to Jeff. Two years later Jeff made one of his rare visits to Camden, but in November 1890 Walt received the news of his death by typhoid pneumonia. Hannah, as noted, was a wreck, and the other sister, Mary, was a stout old woman who suffered terribly from rheumatism. Ed was doing relatively well at his insane asylum, but when Walt visited him he was confronted by a white-bearded man, with an uncanny resemblance to the poet, who could do little but sit in stony silence.

Surrounded by dispersal and collapse, Whitman wanted to create a monument of cohesion and strength. He was so famous now that several cities offered him burial sites, but he chose Camden's Harleigh Cemetery because of its association with his recent family life and its bucolic layout. Harleigh was the latest of many prominent examples of the rural cemetery movement in nineteenth-century America. The movement had begun with the establishment of Mount Auburn Cemetery in 1831 and Brooklyn's Greenwood Cemetery in the forties. The Harleigh Cemetery Association was founded in April 1885 to provide a pleasant, "natural" alternative to the city's old, traditional burial grounds, Camden Cemetery and Evergreen Cemetery. Harleigh, formerly the country seat of Isaac Cooper, one of Camden's leading citizens, was designed as a series of well-kept lawns and winding drives made interesting by trees and shrubbery. To maintain its appearance as a park, no fences or lot enclosures were allowed, nor were head- or footstones more than eight inches in height. Large monuments, however, were allowed.

In a cemetery impressive for its naturalness, Whitman wanted to create an impressive tomb, one that would bring together the family that life had separated. In December 1889 he went to Harleigh with the Harneds and chose a twenty-by-thirty-feet lot on a secluded slope. He contracted with a company to build a tomb that he helped to design. The tomb was a massive, tall structure with a peaked roof. It was about fifteen feet in height, fifteen in width, and twenty in depth. Constructed of Massachusetts granite totaling 72.5 tons, it contained six inner catacombs of white marble weighing 5.75 tons. Its sides and walls were lined with 15,500 hard bricks. The tomb seemed to give literal meaning to his flouting of death in "Song of Myself": "My foothold is tenon'd and mortis'd in granite, / I laugh at what you call dissolution, / And I know the amplitude of time." Eventually, the tomb housed not only Whitman but his parents, Hannah, George, Louisa, and Ed—all laid to rest under the "Walt Whitman" that was the only name on the structure.

Perhaps Whitman would achieve family togetherness in death, but, as usual, he risked alienating a friend over the question of money. The terms with his contractor had been vague. Whitman paid $1,500 over the course of the first year, but when in October 1891 he got a bill for an additional $2,500 he refused to pay it. He relied on his rich friend Tom Harned to clear up the matter. Harned negotiated the price down to $1,500 and paid the bill himself. Once more, Whitman fell back on a capitalist supporter to bear him through a thorny financial situation.

He had little now but shrewdness to carry him through, and he was ready to convert even private celebrations, like birthdays, into gold. When discussing money with Traubel he equivocated: "Of course I do not undervalue the canny qualities, either: the disposition to keep some background in goods, money: it has its place—but no first place—no superior place." No superior place, maybe, but Whitman, even in his diminished physical condition, exhibited some of the "canny qualities" needed to get it. His seventieth birthday celebration, as shown in the prologue to this book, was one of those fancy money-raising events that filled his late years. Unmentioned earlier was the degree to which Whitman saw the event as a commercial opportunity, even though it compromised his principles and was surrounded by tragedy.

In some ways, the seventieth birthday celebration could have been viewed as a dreary event by Whitman. Not only did he have mixed feelings about such affairs, but, as it happened, the event was darkened by tragedy. Three weeks before it, Whitman got word of the death of William Douglas O'Connor. After his reconciliation with O'Connor over the Osgood edition, Whitman had been on good terms with his old friend. O'Connor, still with the Light House Board in Washington, had visited Whitman for a few days in Camden in September 1885. The two corresponded with each other often over the next year and a half, then O'Connor had a stroke. Whitman, who had entered a new phase of debility after his own strokes, watched in sympathy from a distance as O'Connor developed painful symptoms of cerebral-spinal sclerosis, which killed him on May 9.

Whitman was also saddened by a larger tragedy that happened the very evening of his birthday celebration: the great Johnstown flood. The heavy clouds that brought showers to Camden that evening caused torrential rains and massive flooding after a dam collapse in the town of Johnstown in Cambria County, Pennsylvania. Some 2,200 people were killed in what Whitman called "the most signal & wide-spread horror of the kind ever known in this country." He commented to Traubel on the irony of the birthday festivities occurring just at the moment of this unprecedented disaster. He extended sympathy to the Johnstown victims in his poem "A Voice from Death," which included the lines:

> The household wreck'd, the husband and wife, the engulf'd forger in
>   his forge,
> The corpses in the whelming waters and the mud,
> The gather'd thousands to their funeral mounds, and thousands
>   never found or gather'd.

Not only was the birthday celebration framed by tragedy, but it was partly spoiled for him by the fact that no women had been invited to it. Whitman prided himself on being the poet of women. The feminist author Harriet Prescott Spofford had called him "the only poet who has done justice to women," a comment that he said "lubricates my soul like precious ointment." A Chicago newspaper editor, Helen Wilmans, in the early eighties had sent him what was both a love letter and a confession of the liberating effect of his poems, which she insisted had "done more to raise one from a poor working woman to a splendid position on one of the best papers ever published, than all the other influences of my life." Whitman counted women among his best readers. He discovered his birthday celebration was going to be an all-male affair too late, after all the formal invitations had been sent out. He approved of the event anyway but told Traubel it was against all his principles not to have women there.

In spite of his reservations, he was generally pleased with the event because of the publicity and contributions it generated. The five-dollar ticket price was high, and by early May enough payments had come in that Whitman could afford to buy a wheelchair. He had been largely housebound since his strokes the previous summer, so the chair provided a real sense of liberation. Whitman loved being wheeled down to the river, where he enjoyed the views of the boats and ferries, the Philadelphia skyline, and the sunsets over the Delaware.

The birthday celebration seemed to bring out the capitalist in him. Throughout the spring he had been preparing a new printing of his writings to be sold as a commemorative birthday edition. The volume, titled *Leaves of Grass,* "*Sands at Seventy,*" and "*A Backward Glance O'er Travelled Roads,*" was redundant, since it was virtually a repackaging of the *Complete Poetry and Prose,* which had just appeared the previous fall. But Whitman wanted to capitalize on mounting sympathy for him. Bound in limp black leather and printed on thin paper, the volume was, in his view, the epitome of what he had always wanted his books to be: both fancy and portable. It was a small printing of three hundred, but, priced high at five dollars, the book promised to turn a profit. Whitman found the volume "just as I wished!" and called it "the cream of all." Subtitled *Portraits from Life. Autography. Special Ed'n,* it revived Whitman's visions of popular success. Musing over the book, he told Traubel, "If a hustler got hold of Leaves of Grass, the book would make the fur fly in many places it don't touch at all."

With no professional hustler in sight, Whitman had to hustle on his own. He made sure with his contacts that the birthday feast was covered in all the Camden and Philadelphia papers, and he got a bonus when the *New York Tribune* ran a piece on it. The day after the event he praised it: "Everything seemed to pass off wonderfully well—everything." Trying to squeeze as much out of the birthday as possible, he gave consent to a volume edited by Traubel and others, describing it at length. Published by McKay, *Camden's Compliment to Walt Whitman* was put on sale for seventy-five cents in early June. Whitman kept track of its sale.

To say that Whitman sometimes compromised principles in the interest of money is hardly to say that he became amoral or totally manipulative. The fame that came to him was richly deserved and, despite all his efforts, only moderately rewarding financially. His yearly average of $1,270, though higher than the typical working wage, was still way below what popular writers of the era were earning.

Besides, the visibility that came with fame actually forced him to make a public stand on some key questions about his life and work.

Old Age's Lambent Peaks

IN THE LAST two years of his life Whitman was driven by circumstances to confront head-on several issues he had long been pondering: the meaning of the Civil War and Lincoln; the homosexuality question; religion and the afterlife; and the place of his writings in American culture.

Of all these issues, the Civil War was by far the clearest to him. Even though he suffered worse than ever from the effects of what he called his "war-paralysis," he revered the war and its president to an extent he never had. His utter devotion to Lincoln lay behind his determination to give his Lincoln lecture in 1890 despite miserable health. He had been invited to give the lecture that April at the Philadelphia Art Gallery, and he wasn't going to let his ruined state prevent him from appearing. As he explained to Traubel:

> I hope to be identified with the man Lincoln, with his crowded, eventful years—with America as shadowed forth into those abysms of circumstances. It is a great welling up of my emotional sense: I am commanded by it: only a severe chastisement could hold me from my contract.

His declarations that he hoped to be "identified" with the war and that he was "commanded" by his loyalty to Lincoln show how complete his devotion had become. His Art Gallery appearance, which he correctly predicted was his last Lincoln lecture, came off well, with a cordial crowd of sixty to eighty hanging on every word of his well-worn speech and the unkillable "O Captain!" So identified was he with Lincoln that Dodd and Mead that month offered him five hundred dollars to write a sixty-thousand-word book on the president. Whitman was seriously interested in the project but was too ill to follow up on it. It didn't seem to matter to him that the war had muffled some of the rebellious individuality that had prompted his greatest writing.

His readiness to be "commanded" by the war and its heroes was manifested in much of his late poetry. His poem "Interpolation Sounds," written in response to the recent funeral of General Philip Sheridan, described the warrior directing troops in battle. In a note to the poem,

Whitman gave an uncanny foretaste of the twentieth-century military-industrial complex when he said that Sheridan and other Civil War leaders had proved that America did not only have great rank-and-file soldiers: "But we have, too, the eligibility of handling and officering equal to the other. These two, with modern arms, transportation, and inventive American genius, would make the United States, with earnestness, not only able to stand the whole world, but conquer that whole world united against it."

America's military might and modern inventions gave him a vision of the nation's imperialistic domination of the world. He was broken physically, but he leaned on his war memories and the organizational strength they symbolized. In his autobiographical poem "My 71st Year," he pictured himself as a soldier reporting obediently to the Officer above:

> As some old broken soldier, after a long, hot, wearying march, or
>   haply after battle,
> To-day at twilight, hobbling, answering company roll-call, *Here*, with
>   vital voice,
> Reporting yet, saluting yet, the Officer over all.

In another poem, "A Twilight Song," his Mickle Street room seemed flooded with Civil War soldiers: "Even here in my room-shadows and half-lights in the noiseless flickering flames, / Again I see the stalwart ranks on-filing, rising—I hear the rhythmic tramp of the armies."

If his veneration of the war brought him closer than ever to mainstream conventions, so did his studied response to John Addington Symonds's questions about homosexuality. We have seen that Whitman had long tried, both in his private relationships and public statements, to make his homosexual urges conform as much as possible to permissible same-sex behavior in nineteenth-century America. That he was largely successful in doing so was suggested by the fact that even the most vigilant government censors and the most conventional poetry anthologists saw little that was out of the ordinary in his poems about male love. Furthermore, surprisingly few reviewers took issue with him on the point. True, Standish O'Grady in his otherwise positive 1875 review had complained that Whitman sometimes went too far in describing male friendship: "The emotion does not exist in us, and the language of the evangel-poems appears simply disgusting." But, in general, the reviews were notable for their lack of special commentary on the homoerotic poems.

In the eighties and especially the nineties Whitman faced a somewhat changed moral atmosphere regarding same-sex love. As Carroll

Smith-Rosenberg shows, even though deep same-sex affection would be regarded as normal and acceptable in wide areas of American culture until the 1930s, it was in the 1880s that a previously unseen self-consciousness about it arose in some circles. The idea of "sexual inversion" or "contrary sexual instinct" began to have currency among doctors and intellectuals.

Whitman had been trying in recent times to integrate same-sex love meaningfully into his vision of mainstream society. He had told an interviewer in 1880: "It pleases me to think also that if any of my works shall survive it will be the fellowship in it—comradeship—friendship is the good old word—the love of my fellow-men." He said to Traubel that he knew "no country anyhow in which comradeship is so far developed as here—here, among the mechanic classes." But he seemed also to have sensed a new repressiveness in these matters. There is no way of saying whether his mass destruction of private documents in the late eighties was connected to a suppression of evidence about his relations with men. But it was probably around this time that he exercised self-censorship in his diaries, especially in the 1870 Doyle passage, in which he changed pronouns and used a numerical code to cloak Doyle's identity.

Was Whitman's great secret connected to untold sexual liaisons? He mentioned the secret at least seven times to Traubel, who probably thought it had to do with illegitimate children, since one day Whitman said in response to his probing: "Still harping on my daughter." Such mentions of children, though, were almost certainly diversions from, rather than clues to, the real secret.

John Addington Symonds seemed to be on a hotter trail than Traubel in inquiring about homosexuality, though the answer he received led far away from any clear revelation about the "secret" Whitman. Actually, by the time Symonds queried Whitman directly about homosexuality, the public and private Whitman had become so conflated that such probings into the private Whitman were almost automatically doomed to failure.

Symonds himself had no clear ideas about homosexuality or about his own sexual identity. Married with four children, he struggled continuously to accommodate his attraction to young men into larger historical meanings of same-sex love. His obsession with such love in ancient Greek culture, studied most prominently in his 1883 book *A Problem in Greek Ethics,* lay mainly in the fact that the Greeks, in his view, elevated this love into chivalry, athleticism, and normal social behavior. Although versed in current medical theories about sexual inversion, he approached Whitman less as a proselytizer than as a student. What has not been recognized is the degree to which Whitman's firm rebuff of Symonds's inquiries, along with his overall stance on same-sex love, reverberated in medical circles, where his notions on the subject were regarded as wholesome and salutary.

To be sure, there was a part of Symonds that suspected Whitman was covering something up when he denied his homosexuality and especially when he claimed to have sired six children. He wrote Edward Carpenter, "I think [Whitman] was afraid of being used to lend influence to the 'Sods' [sodomites]. Did not quite trust me perhaps." As for the improbable story about the six children, Symonds thought Whitman "wanted to obviate 'damnable inferences' about himself by asserting his paternity."

But there was an equally strong side to Symonds that wanted to believe Whitman. Greek love, for Symonds, had been a socially acceptable love that, "though it was not free from sensuality, did not degenerate into mere licentiousness." Among Greek men, he wrote, "the tie was both more spiritual and more energetic than that which bound man to woman." This was how Symonds talked about Whitman when he discussed him publicly. The "Calamus" poems, he wrote, are "in a Dorian mood," illustrating a comradeship like that between Achilles and Patroclus or Orestes and Pylades. Although "there is indeed a distinctly sensuous side to [Whitman's] conception of adhesiveness," Symonds wrote, "he has nothing to do with anomalous, abnormal, vicious, or diseased forms of emotions which males entertain for males." Symonds quoted from Whitman's 1890 letter to suggest that the poet was "as hostile to sexual inversion as any law-abiding humdrum Anglo-Saxon could desire." For Symonds, "the democratic chivalry, announced by Whitman, may be destined to absorb, control, and elevate those darker, more mysterious abnormal appetites, which we have seen to be widely diffused and ineradicable in the groundwork of human nature."

Several others agreed with Symonds that Whitman's ideas on same-sex love ran counter to modern theories of sexual inversion. The term "homosexual," introduced in English in the 1890s and not used in the *New York Times* until 1926, did not gain widespread cultural use until the 1930s. In the meantime, the idea of sexual identity was embattled. Some who discussed Whitman in this context did not connect him with homosexuality. His close friend Edward Carpenter, who regarded the term "homosexual" as a monstrous combination of Greek and Latin (he preferred "homogenic"), believed, like Symonds, that Whitman was attempting to restore pure, chivalric Greek love as a social institution. To clear Whitman of what he called "morbidity," he cited a comment by Dr. Beverly Drinkard that Whitman had "the most natural habits, bases, and organization he had ever seen."

The British sexologist Havelock Ellis, who corresponded with Whitman and knew his work well, saw in Whitman a "latent and unconscious" homosexual instinct that was so handled that it could provide a model for sexual inverts. In his book *Sexual Inversion* Ellis argued that reading Whitman could help make an invert "healthy, self-restrained, and self-respecting," teaching "dignity, temperance, even chastity" like the Greeks. Ellis wrote: "The 'manly love' celebrated by Walt Whitman in *Leaves of Grass*, although it may be more doubtful for general use, furnishes a wholesome and robust ideal to the invert who is insensitive to normal ideals." With Whitman's help, Ellis concluded, the invert can learn "self-restraint and self-culture," particularly important because, in Ellis's eyes, "it is the ideal of chastity, rather than of normal sexuality, which the congenital invert should hold before his eyes."

When funneled back into medical circles, then, Whitman's treatment of same-sex love was seen mainly as a means of "controlling" or "elevating" homosexual desires instead of giving them unbridled expression. It is hard to say how Whitman's views were seen by practicing homosexuals, in part because there was no clearly defined gay culture at the time. In the nineties there arose clubs in American cities, such as the Golden Rule Pleasure Club in Manhattan, where sexual liaisons between males took place or were arranged. The roles usually assumed by the sexual partners were that of the "effeminate" man, called a fairy or queer, and the "trade," or the "masculine" man, who could have sex with fairies but was considered normal. There is only fragmentary evidence as to how Whitman was viewed by the fairies, who were most often associated with homosexuality. But in 1913 Harrison Reeves, an author inclined to categorize Whitman as homosexual, wrote with some dismay: "It is rather odd that homosexuals, at least in America, do not regard Whitman as one of themselves or brag about him."

It was left to Europeans of the early twentieth century to connect Whitman's Calamus feelings clearly with homosexuality. A 1905 article by the German critic Eduard Bertz was the first in a line of studies, extending through the 1933 biography by the Dane Frederik Schyberg to the 1954 book by the Sorbonne professor Roger Asselineau, that opened the way for the numerous psychosexual interpretations of modern times.

In his own day, however, Whitman had regulated his public image in such a way that many early gay commentators separated him from the so-called inversion associated with the evolving notion of homosexuality.

Dirt and Clouds

H E F A C E D an equally tricky challenge in the area of religion, for in 1890 his cause was taken up by America's leading agnostic, Robert Ingersoll. The stout, balding Ingersoll had been an Illinois lawyer who became a colonel in the Union army and then one of the leading orators of the postwar era. In May 1880 Whitman, at Dr. Bucke's invitation, went to Philadelphia to hear Ingersoll's speech "What Shall I Do to Be Saved?" Although he did not hear Ingersoll again until his 1890 birthday dinner, he mentioned the famous lecturer some sixty times to Traubel. His admiration for Ingersoll was almost unbounded. Whitman praised his "vital, manly, gigantesque powers." When Ingersoll lectured twice on his behalf in 1890, Whitman said, "I'm proud to have him associated with us. I think that Colonel Bob is a much vaster force in this, our time, land, than we are today willing to allow."

It was natural that Whitman felt an affinity with Ingersoll, whose mind-set was much like his. "Fearless, frank, eloquent, with a tongue of fire," Whitman said of him. "In all essential ways, Ingersoll's work and mine converge: I think even my intimate friends are disposed not to see this." Politically, both men were defined by the notion of liberty espoused by the North during the Civil War, though Ingersoll gave full support to Radical Republicanism, which Whitman shied away from. Philosophically, both rejected formal religion and espoused a humanistic faith that owed much to modern science. Just as Whitman had opposed theology and pronounced himself a "kosmos," so Ingersoll had rejected his childhood Calvinism and had found in Humboldt's *Kosmos* a revelation of the miraculous law underlying the physical universe. Both men saw Darwinian evolution as a source of hope, not pessimism. Also, both were boosters of American industrial expansion.

The sticking point between the two—and it was a major one—pertained to the afterlife. There has long been a division among Whitman commentators between those who emphasize the sensuous, earthly Whitman and those who see mainly his religious side. Ingersoll was in the former camp. In his lectures on Whitman he brought attention to the humanistic Whitman, the poet of the earth and political liberty.

The first lecture, given on the occasion of Whitman's seventy-first birthday, was an impromptu one. Because of the poet's worsening health, it was decided this birthday celebration would be more private than the previous one. But it was lavish enough. Held at C. H. Reisser's Restaurant in Philadelphia, the celebration featured a dinner of Delaware shad, chicken croquettes, and roast beef enjoyed by more than fifty of Whitman's friends—this time, men *and* women. The table was decorated with wildflowers and vines, and Whitman looked like a patriarch surrounded by his apostles. Several speeches were given, including Ingersoll's fifty-five-minute talk, which Whitman later called one of the greatest pieces of oratory he had ever heard. Ingersoll called Whitman the great poet of commonplace things and the physical world. Although he enjoyed the lecture, Whitman needled Ingersoll afterward, reminding him his poetry was as much about the spiritual as the physical world. "What would this life be without immortality?" he asked the agnostic. "What is this world without a further Divine purpose in it all?"

An even sharper contretemps arose after Ingersoll's next Whitman speech, "Liberty in Literature," given at Philadelphia's Horticultural Hall on October 21, 1890. Unlike the birthday talk, this was very much a staged affair, advertised well in advance. Whitman and Traubel worked closely with a professional promoter who had pushed Ingersoll for years, making him controversial and popular as "the Great Infidel." Ingersoll's notoriety helped generate publicity, for when two Philadelphia auditoriums refused to host the talk because of Ingersoll's infidelity, the press had a field day in reporting the controversy.

Whitman thought the battle over Ingersoll would ensure a large audience for the event. He was right. Between 1,500 and 2,000 people crowded into Horticultural Hall to hear Ingersoll defend the Good Gray Poet, who sat behind the lecturer onstage, flanked by friends. Whitman called the speech, which again stressed his physical themes, a "masterpiece of language, feeling, sense & utterance," "a bugle call, which will be heard all over this continent, perhaps across the globe." Whitman also appreciated the $869.45 the event netted him.

But the afterlife question still bothered him deeply. After the talk, he got into another public debate with Ingersoll about immortality. "O Robert! Robert!" Whitman cried. "Sometimes I think there is a great gap between us—between our thought, then again I wonder if there is any at all!" When Ingersoll thanked Whitman again for the human trend of his works, Whitman said, "But I, too, Robert go among the clouds!" Ingersoll retorted: "Yes, but you take a devil lot of dirt with you!"

The "great gap" that Whitman felt separated him and Ingersoll had to do with the abiding faith in immortality that brightened Whitman's final years. On this point, he was far closer to two of his recent British friends, Dr. John Johnston and J. W. Wallace, than to Ingersoll. If Ingersoll showed how Whitman could appeal to a Darwinian materialist, Johnston and Wallace showed how he could impart religious consolation so strong that it led to the founding of a Whitman "church." Johnston had sent Whitman birthday greetings in 1886, praising the poet as one "who has done so much to enrich my soul and to rescue my soul from its quagmire of Doubt and Despondency." As his friend Wallace later explained to Whitman, Johnston "owes to you entirely his spiritual enfranchisement from soul-benumbing scepticism, into which not without pain he had gradually fallen." Wallace himself found a healing power in Whitman that helped him relieve the pain he had endured over the recent loss of his mother.

Whereas Ingersoll was a fleeting acquaintance, Johnston and Wallace became so important to Whitman that in 1890 and '91 he sent sixty-three letters to the former and twenty-eight to the latter. He reveled in the religious veneration they and their friends in Bolton, England, felt toward him. Johnston visited Whitman in Camden in July 1890, and Wallace followed suit a year later. These were little less than religious pilgrimages. Johnston landed in Philadelphia on July 15, crossed over to Camden on the ferry *Delaware*, and stayed three nights at the West Jersey Hotel, spending his days with Whitman on Mickle Street. When he first saw Whitman, the poet was seated cross-legged on his large cane-runged rocker. The weather was blistering hot, and Whitman had his shirt open and his sleeves rolled up above his elbows, exposing skin of a delicate whiteness. Despite the heat, Whitman wasn't sweating. But even if he had, Johnston would have seen him as a miraculous being, for he looked on Whitman with the zeal of a convert. In Johnston's view, the white-maned, patriarchal Whitman "seemed to exhale sanity, purity, and naturalness." He had a magnetism, Johnston later wrote, "which positively astonished me, producing an exaltation of mind and soul which no man's presence ever did before." After his four days on Mickle Street, Johnston continued his pilgrimage, spending several weeks touring the old Whitman haunts in Brooklyn and West Hills.

Wallace's visit the next year followed a similar pattern. He arrived in Philadelphia on September 8, 1891, crossed to Camden, and stayed with Traubel while seeing Whitman during the day. Greeting Wallace, Whitman said with a laugh, "Well, you've come to be disillusioned, have you?" At first, Wallace *was* disillusioned. The poet's simple, infirm appearance didn't jibe with Wallace's view of him as "not only the greatest man of his time but for many centuries past."

But it wasn't long before he felt even more rapturous about Whitman than had Johnston. Although Wallace had never believed in spiritualism, while talking with Whitman he suddenly had a vision of his mother, who had died six years earlier. Wallace later wrote, "I seemed to see her mentally with perfect clearness, her face radiant with the joy of our realized communion." For him, it seemed "indisputable that Walt was somehow the link between us, and as if his presence had made the experience possible." In the afterglow of this mystical experience, Wallace followed Johnston's footsteps by touring the New York and Long Island areas where Whitman had been raised. In Brooklyn he met the quiet Scottish printer Andrew Rome, who took him to the little building on Cranberry Street where the 1855 *Leaves of Grass* had been printed. On October 15 he returned with Rome to Camden for another brief visit with Whitman.

Today, Whitman's relationship with Johnston and Wallace seems one of excessive adulation and cloying nostalgia. But not only did the two men suit perfectly Whitman's pious self-image, but so did the "church" they founded in Bolton. Whitman societies had already begun to appear as far away as Australia, where a devoted Whitman reader, Bernard O'Dowd, led a group of men and women that met Sundays to discuss Whitman. The poet praised O'Dowd's group but took even greater pleasure in the Bolton one because of its religious overtones. Some twenty men and women, led by Johnston and Wallace, convened weekly to discuss and read Whitman with religious intensity. Whitman gave the Bolton group his warm approval. He wrote Johnston in July 1891: "God bless the church & branch of the church (with candelabras blazing more fervidly than any) that is planted & grown in Bolton!"

The Bolton group signaled a larger phenomenon in Whitman's circle: the feeling that he was the new messiah. Whitman's growing fame, along with his self-conscious piety, made his followers feel they were in the midst of something momentous. Publicly, Whitman had come into his own. He could no longer seriously say that the magazines neglected him. In April 1890 he said that five years ago "the world did not want me. *Now*—hardly half a decade after, comes a multitude: comes cry and cry—after my power to respond is gone: after I am wrecked, stranded, left to look for the end—or near end!" His feebleness, though, didn't prevent him from keeping up a steady flow of poems and articles in magazines. He admitted to Traubel in October that "scarcely a day passes in which I do not receive a request with satisfactory honorarium to write for some leading magazine or newspaper." *Lippincott's Monthly Magazine,* for example, devoted nearly a whole issue to him in March 1891, with poems, a picture, and a biographical sketch.

His growing visibility electrified his followers and increased their sense that he was a kind of god. In the two decades after the poet's death, a group of critics would arise that dismissed Whitman's inner circle as "hot little prophets." The moment when the little prophets really crowed was in the last two years of his life. William Sloane Kennedy wrote Whitman shortly after Christmas 1890, asking with apparent seriousness, "Do you suppose a thousand years fr. now people will be celebrating the birth of Walt Whitman as they are now the birth of Christ? If they don't— the more fools they." Bucke used similarly grandiose terms when he wrote Traubel while visiting Bolton in July 1891: "I am more than ever (if that is possible) convinced that we are right at the centre of the largest thing of these late centuries. It is a great priviledge [sic] and will be ages from now a great glory to us."

Whitman felt somewhat embarrassed by such plaudits, but there was little he could do to stem his supporters' enthusiasm. It bubbled merrily at his final birthday dinner, held at the Mickle Street house on May 31, 1891. There was no question this time of a public banquet. Whitman had been feeling especially poorly of late, and just an hour before the dinner he thought the celebration would have to be called off. But he rallied, and Warrie lugged him downstairs ("like carrying down a great log," Whitman later wrote). The poet had all but lost his eyesight—he could see no more than ten feet—but he enjoyed himself immensely at the banquet.

Around thirty of his friends, including women, were seated at long tables that had been squeezed into his overheated parlors. Whitman quaffed iced champagne, and a dinner of salmon amd lamb was served. The air was heavy with adoration and nostalgia. Whitman begged his friends not "to lay it on too thick," but they laid it on anyway. One of them announced, "You are the greatest man of all this century and of all the world." Whitman tried to divert attention from himself by toasting Tennyson, Longfellow, and others, but his friends wanted to concentrate on him. Among the topics discussed were his Long Island background, his caution, and his belief in the historical roots of literature. He made the latter point strongly by saying that from the start his method had been "to equip, equip, equip from every quarter," from "science, observation, travel, reading, study," and then to "turn everything over to the emotional, the personality." Driving the point home that his work could only be understood historically, he declared that his poetry was simply "the utterance of Personality after—carefully remember that— after being thoroughly surcharged (if I may call it so) with all these other elements."

He had made the same point in his collection of essays that had appeared that month with McKay, *Good-Bye My Fancy.* This collection of recent articles and scraps, more than half of which had appeared in periodicals, drifted haphazardly over the historical and literary backgrounds of *Leaves of Grass,* commenting once more on the old actors, singers, writers, industrial expositions, and other early influences on him. In his lead essay, "An Old Man's Rejoinder," he reiterated his firm belief in history: "No great poem or other literary or artistic work of any scope, old or new, can be essentially consider'd without weighing first the age, politics (or want of politics) and aim, visible forms, unseen soul, and current times, out of the midst of which it rises and is formulated."

There was a roundedness to Whitman's last year, a sense that he was saying what he had to say and finishing what he had to finish. Truly remarkable, in this respect, was the timing of the final edition of *Leaves of Grass*. He had thirty-five recent poems, most of them periodical pieces, that he wanted to incorporate into his volume. He gathered them into an annex he called "Good-Bye My Fancy" to be added at the end of *Leaves of Grass*. Reflecting the otherworldly turn he had taken in recent years, more than half of the new poems were about religion or the afterlife.

The kind of religious images he now used—simple, hopeful— showed how his spiritual emphases had changed since the fifties. Then, his religious vision had reflected the zaniness of space-traveling trance lecturers, the erotic mysticism of Swedenborgians, the all-absorptive quality of mesmeric healers. Now, he had a simplified vision that was in line with the homogenized optimism of late-nineteenth-century movements like mind cure and liberal Protestantism. The weirdly magical, sometimes tortured seer of 1855 had become the positive thinker of 1891. He now sounded less like Andrew Jackson Davis than Mary Baker Eddy or a forerunner of Norman Vincent Peale. His optimistic statements to Traubel were often uncomplicated, straightforward. "Cheer! Cheer!" he said. "Is there anything better in this world anywhere than cheer—just cheer? Any religion better?—Any art? Just cheer!" Again: "I stand for the sunny point of view—stand for the joyful conclusions."

Simple too were most of the new poems. "Sail Out for Good, Eidólon Yacht!" pictured his soul as a "little white-hull'd sloop" about to "speed on really deep waters." He used the same nautical metaphor for his soul in "Ship Ahoy!" and "Old Age's Ship & Crafty Death's." In "Grand Is the Seen" he declared that as magnificent as is the physical world, the "unseen soul of me" is far more so. More subtle was his treatment of cheer in "Unseen Buds" and "To the Sun-set Breeze." The former poem sees the universe as full of "unseen buds," "Billions of billions, and trillions of trillions of them waiting, / [...] Urging slowly, surely forward, forming endless, / And waiting even more, forever more behind." "To the Sun-set Breeze" portrays the old, sick Whitman enjoying the soft wind that brings "occult medicines penetrating me from head to foot" and making him contemplate the soul.

There was in the poems not only a hopeful religious faith but also a sense of completion. The three-line poem "An Ended Day" summarized Whitman's outlook:

The soothing sanity and blitheness of completion,
The pomp and hurried contest-glare and rush are done;
Now triumph! transformation! jubilate!

Whitman had the satisfaction, rare among authors, of seeing his oeuvre gathered in what he regarded as definitive form. Having worked on the new volume throughout the fall of 1891, on December 6 he sent Bucke an advance copy, excitedly announcing, "L. of G. *at last complete*—after 33 y'rs of hackling at it, all times & moods of my life, fair weather & foul, all parts of the land, and peace & war, young & old—."

Finale

HIS COMPLETION of what later became known as the Deathbed Edition of *Leaves of Grass* was remarkably well timed, for it came just before his final collapse. Less than a week after he sent Bucke the volume, he wrote him again, complaining of "unmitigated belly-ache, fulness & soreness, & continual trouble & smartness & burning bladder & urethra—." Neither Whitman nor his doctors yet had a clear sense of what was behind his various symptoms. His prolonged bouts with constipation made one of his new doctors, Daniel Longaker, suspect a bowel blockage, but by October Longaker had changed his view. As Whitman reported to Bucke, "My disease is now called *progressive paralysis* with a more or less rapid tendency (or eligibility) to the heart." Bucke called this vague diagnosis "rubbish" and insisted "Paralysis *cannot* go to the heart."

Bucke was right to suspect Longaker's assessment, for Whitman's autopsy would reveal that his heart was one of his few healthy organs. He started failing rapidly in late November, and on December 18 he showed signs of bronchial pneumonia. His right lung collapsed, his pulse raced, his temperature soared, and what sounded like the death rattle set in. His doctors didn't think he would last five days. But he lingered three months, kept alive, those around him felt, by sheer willpower. By early January he couldn't turn in his bed, and he had hiccups that sometimes lasted for days. To Longaker's amazement, he rallied in mid-January, but as the weeks passed he lost flesh and strength. His left side had been helpless since his strokes, and by early March he had shooting pains in his right side. He could find no comfortable position in bed and had to be turned constantly. Although he had difficulty speaking, he remained interested in the news and literary gossip Traubel brought.

He was still deeply concerned about the public's reception of his poetry. Over the past three years he had lamented periodically that, despite his newfound fame, he was still largely unread by the masses. When Traubel reported to him on March 12 that the new edition of *Leaves of Grass* had almost sold out, Whitman asked eagerly, "Then we will have a little money next settlement?" He requested that McKay make the paper thin for the next printing of the volume. Even as his body was collapsing, he was vitally interested in the progress of Arthur Stedman's forthcoming anthology of his poems. He begged Traubel to instruct Stedman to call the anthology *Leaves of Grass, Junior.* Nothing so excited Whitman in his last days as his fantasy of this book. He was so interested in producing a popular version of his poetry that he not only threw to the winds his supposed qualms about expurgation but also offered a demeaning title whose silliness his friends immediately saw. Both Traubel and McKay disliked his proposal, but he clung to it stubbornly. A week before his death he told Traubel, "I want that to be the title: *Leaves of Grass, Junior,* with Junior spelled out, made unmistakable." Horace passed along the request to Stedman, though he privately advised him against using it and apologized for Whitman's intrusiveness. When Stedman rejected the idea, Whitman still demanded to see the proofs of the volume so that he could make any necessary changes. Traubel was exasperated, writing in his daily notes that Whitman "seems to forget A. S. edits the book—that we do nothing."

Traubel should have known better. *Leaves of Grass, Junior* was just one more effort on Whitman's part to tailor his image to suit the ever-elusive American public. *Of course* Whitman wanted to control Stedman's volume, just as he had been controlling and reshaping his public image from the start. His fantasy of popular acceptance lasted to the end.

In the last week of his life, though, Whitman had trouble focusing on his public image or anything else. His body shrank and caved in. His legs turned strange colors and became scaly. He coughed continually, and he was so weak he couldn't lift a knife or fork. His mood was brightened by a flood of telegrams and letters from well-wishers, including his sister Hannah, Ingersoll, Rossetti, and the Bolton group. When he joked with Traubel that he felt like "fifty thousand devils," his laughter dissolved into a raspy wheeze. By March 21 he was beyond joking: "I suffer all the time: I have no relief, no escape: it is monotony—monotony—monotony—in pain." But waves of excitement about *Leaves of Grass, Junior* still came over him. He said of Stedman's volume, "I am almost anxious to see it—it seems to bring us good news every way—but for *good luck*—we'll wait."

On March 25 he was transferred to a waterbed that had been brought in for his comfort. The waterbed helped somewhat. Whitman said he felt afloat "like a ship or a duck." Still, his only relief came when his body was shifted by Mrs. Davis or Warrie. He was shifted sixty-three times in his last twenty-four hours. But he made no complaints. He died with the stoic dignity of many of the Civil War soldiers whose deaths he had witnessed in the hospitals. By early afternoon on Saturday, March 26, he was sweating profusely. His breath came hard and fast. He murmured "shift" and "change" with his eyes closed. The last distinct words heard from him were "Warrie, shift." His breathing grew irregular, then stopped. At 6:43 p.m., he was pronounced dead by Dr. Alex MacAllister. At his bedside were MacAllister, Mrs. Davis, Warrie, Traubel, and Tom Harned. Outside, an early spring rain was falling as the dusk settled.

The autopsy revealed that Whitman's doctors had vastly underestimated the extent of his maladies. His body was riddled with tubercles and abscesses. An egg-sized abscess beneath his right nipple had completely eroded his fifth rib, causing the excruciating right-side pain he had complained of. His lungs had so deteriorated that it was estimated he had been surviving on one-sixteenth of his normal breathing capacity. A huge gallstone was found, as well as an enlarged prostate and a fatty liver. He had suffered, it seems, from almost everything but a heart problem. As stated in the autopsy, "The cause of death was pleurisy of the left side, consumption of the right lung, general miliary tuberculosis and parenchymatous nephritis."

Whitman would have enjoyed his own funeral, which, according to one report, was "wholly without parallel in America." It was a throwback to the spontaneous, populist celebrations of Whitman's youth, like the Lafayette excitement in 1825 or the noisy funerals Whitman had enjoyed at Greenwood Cemetery.

Whitman's body lay in an open oak coffin on March 29 in his house. The coffin was barely visible, covered as it was with flowers and wreaths sent from all over the world. Friends streamed in to view the gray-clad Whitman. The next day the public was invited. From 11:00 a.m. to 2:00 p.m. thousands of people filed into the modest house to take a last look at the familiar face. In the crowd were many of Whitman's working-class comrades, including Peter Doyle, as well as families and even street urchins, many of them drawn by the excitement of the occasion. Burroughs later wrote: "When I saw the crowds of common people that flocked to Walt Whitman's funeral, I said, How fit, how touching, all this is; how well it would please him. It is from the common people, the great army of workers, that he rises and speaks with such authority."

Whitman's coffin was taken in a carriage two miles down the Haddonfield Pike to Harleigh Cemetery. Spectators lined the road, and vendors sold fruit and wares. The scene at the cemetery had the atmosphere of an old-time tent meeting. Nearly four thousand people milled on the slope around Whitman's huge tomb as bands played. Food and drinks were served as a simple ceremony was conducted on a raised platform. Several of Whitman's friends gave speeches. Bucke and Harned spoke of Whitman's faith in immortality. Ingersoll praised him as the poet of nature and humanity.

The crowd, by all reports, was jubilant. Many present doubtless believed with Bucke that Whitman's soul was launched on cosmic seas. And doubtless others felt with Ingersoll that Whitman had made the earth and the body seem wholly new.

In death, Whitman touched the public that had eluded him in life. But this spontaneous show of affection cannot be confused with mass acceptance of his poetry. The two volumes of his poems that appeared shortly after his death—the Stedman anthology and McKay's new printing of the Deathbed Edition—sold decently but not spectacularly. Shortly after the poet's death a reviewer of the McKay edition noted the old irony about Whitman: "Songs which celebrate the toils and pleasures of the masses have thus far found small audience among the common people of the nation, being chiefly read by the cultivated few.... The poet of the people is neglected by the people, while the works of scholarly singers like Longfellow and Bryant find a place in every farmer's library."

Whitman had long been aware of his failure to gain popular acceptance, and toward the end of his life, despite his dream of popularity, he had seen that it might be very long before his poems were understood or accepted in the way he envisaged. In one of his last poems, "Long, Long Hence," he said recognition would come only after ages had passed:

> After a long, long course, hundreds of years, denials,
> Accumulations, rous'd love and joy and thought,
> Hopes, wishes, aspirations, ponderings, victories, myriads of readers,
> Coating, compassing, covering—after ages' and ages' encrustations,
> Then only may these songs reach fruition.

But it would *not* be hundreds of years before his songs reached fruition. In the century since his death he has reached "myriads of readers," and he has justifiably earned a secure place in the literary pantheon.

All great writing gains canonical status only over time, as it is observed by readers of various orientations and ideological viewpoints. The fact that Whitman in his own time appealed to both capitalists and socialists, to both religious types and materialists, foreshadowed the even richer multiplicity of appreciation that has greeted him in the twentieth century. No writer is regarded as more indisputably American than Whitman, yet no writer has reverberated on the international scene to the extent that he has. His liberation of the poetic line from formal rhythm and rhyme was a landmark event with which all poets since have had to come to terms. His equally bold treatment of erotic themes has provided a fertile field of interpretation and has contributed to the candid discussion of sex in the larger culture. The radically egalitarian nature of his poems, particularly those he wrote in his rebellious phase in the fifties, has consistently inspired progressives of all stripes. His boundless love and all-inclusive language, reflected in his extraordinary intimacy with his contemporary culture, makes his writing attractive and exciting for practically all readers.

The fact that Whitman was, as shown in this book, totally immersed in his times doesn't mean he was time-bound. To be sure, his ideas evolved in the course of his life, and sometimes they reflected cultural attitudes that have become outmoded. But if his weaknesses stemmed largely from his thoroughgoing participation in his contemporary culture, so did his strengths. At his best, he was the democratic poet to an extent never heretofore recognized, gathering images from virtually every cultural arena and transforming them through his powerful personality into art.

By fully absorbing his time, he became a writer for all times.

NOTES

Because Whitman constantly revised the punctuation, the titles, and, to a lesser degree, the wording of his poems in the various editions of *Leaves of Grass,* commentators are faced with the problem of which of the versions to quote from. I have chosen in almost all cases to use the poems in their final version, in the 1892 (so-called Deathbed) edition, which Whitman authorized as the definitive edition. However, since I am tracing the historical evolution of his poetry over time, I occasionally cite the poems as they originally appeared, particularly when I discuss the 1855 edition in Chapter 10 and the 1860 edition in Chapter 12. When citing the original versions, I indicate so in the text or the notes.

Changes in primary texts are indicated by brackets. There is one exception to this procedure: because Whitman's sentences (both in poetry and prose) are often extraordinarily long, I sometimes truncate a quotation and supply a closing period without bracketing it. Since Whitman sometimes used ellipses in his poetry and in the 1855 preface (varying between ellipses of two, three, four, five, six, seven, and eight dots), I bracket my own ellipses when quoting from the poems or the 1855 preface, in order to distinguish my ellipses from his. Elsewhere, I do not bracket ellipses.

Since there is no definitive edition of Whitman's newspaper and magazine writings, his journalism is a vexed issue. Some question the trustworthiness of the existing collections of the journalism, arguing that in some cases there is no final proof Whitman wrote a given piece. Others, in contrast, not only attribute the reprinted pieces to Whitman but point out that there is probably a large number of additional periodical writings by him that have yet to be identified. I steer a middle course on the issue. Like previous biographers, I work from the assumption, strongly supported by archival research, that the periodical pieces collected by Rubin, Rodgers and Black, Holloway, Adimari, Schwartz, Freedman, Christian, and Glicksberg are largely reliable. For additional journalistic pieces, I use, with caution, William White's "Walt Whitman's Journalism: A Bibliography," *Walt Whitman Review*, 14 (September 1968): 67–141. I try wherever possible to back up quotations from the journalism with corroborating evidence from other Whitman writings and from historical context.

Recent bibliographical information can be found in Joel Myerson, *Walt Whitman: A Descriptive Bibliography* (Pittsburgh: University of Pittsburgh Press, 1993) and M. Jimmie Killingsworth, *The Growth of "Leaves of Grass"* (Columbia, S.C.: Camden House, 1993). For archival information on Whitman's writings, see Myerson, ed., *The Walt Whitman Archive*, 3 vols. (New York: Garland, 1993). A useful recent contextual study is Ed Folsom, *Walt Whitman's Native Representations* (New York: Cambridge University Press, 1994).

Abbreviations for Frequently Cited Sources

BE	*Brooklyn Daily Eagle*
Brash	Thomas L. Brasher. *Whitman as Editor of the Brooklyn Daily Eagle.* Detroit: Wayne State University Press, 1970.
BT	*Brooklyn Daily Times*
C	Whitman. *The Correspondence.* Ed. Edwin Haviland Miller. 5 vols. New York: New York University Press. *Vol. I: 1842–67* (1961). *Vol. II: 1868–75* (1964). *Vol. III: 1876–85* (1964). *Vol. IV: 1886–89* (1969). *Vol. V: 1890–92* (1969).
CG	*Walt Whitman and the Civil War.* Ed. Charles Glicksberg. Philadelphia: University of Pennsylvania Press, 1933.
DN	Whitman. *Daybooks and Notebooks.* Ed. William White. 3 vols. New York: New York University Press, 1978. *Vol. I: 1876–Nov. 1881. Vol. II: 1881–91. Vol. III: Diary in Canada, Notebooks.*
FC	*Faint Clews & Indirections: Manuscripts of Walt Whitman and His Family.* Ed. Clarence Gohdes and Rollo G. Silver. Durham, N.C.: Duke University Press, 1949.
Feinberg	Charles E. Feinberg Collection, Library of Congress
GF	*The Gathering of the Forces.* Ed. Cleveland Rodgers and John Black. 2 vols. New York: G. P. Putnam's Sons, 1920.
H	*Walt Whitman, the Critical Heritage.* Ed. Milton Hindus. New York: Barnes & Noble, 1971.
InRe	*In Re Walt Whitman.* Ed. Horace L. Traubel, Richard Maurice Bucke, and Thomas B. Harned. Philadelphia: David McKay, 1893.
ISit	Whitman. *I Sit and Look Out: Editorials from the Brooklyn Daily Times.* Ed. Emory Holloway and Vernolian Schwartz. New York: AMS Press, 1966.
JM	*Whitman in His Own Time: A Biographical Chronicle of His Life, Drawn from Recollections, Memoirs, and Interviews by Friends and Associates.* Ed. Joel Myerson. Detroit: Omnigraphics, 1991.
LGC	Whitman. *Leaves of Grass, Comprehensive Reader's Edition.* Ed.

Harold Blodgett and Sculley Bradley. New York: New York University Press, 1965.

LV   Whitman. *Leaves of Grass, A Textual Variorum of the Printed Poems.* Ed. Sculley Bradley, Harold W. Blodgett, Arthur Golden, and William White. 3 vols. New York: New York University Press, 1980. *Vol. I: Poems, 1855–56. Vol. II: 1860–67. Vol. III: 1870–91.*

NF   Whitman. *Notes and Fragments.* Ed. Richard Maurice Bucke. 1899; rpt., Ontario: A. Talbot and Co., n.d.

NUPM   Whitman. *Notebooks and Unpublished Prose Manuscripts.* Ed. Edward F. Grier. 6 vols. New York: New York University Press, 1984.

NYA   *Walt Whitman of the New York Aurora.* Ed. Joseph Jay Rubin and Charles H. Brown. State College, Penn.: Bald Eagle Press, 1950.

NYD   Whitman. *New York Dissected.* Ed. Emory Holloway and Ralph Adimari. New York: Rufus Rockwell Wilson, 1936.

PW   Whitman. *Prose Works, 1892.* Ed. Floyd Stovall. 2 vols. New York: New York University Press. Vol. I: *Specimen Days* (1963). Vol. II: *Collect and Other Prose* (1964).

Trent   Trent Collection, Duke University Library

UPP   *The Uncollected Poetry and Prose of Walt Whitman.* Ed. Emory Holloway. 2 vols. Gloucester, Mass.: Peter Smith, 1972.

WCP   Whitman. *Complete Poetry and Collected Prose.* New York: Library of America, 1982.

WEP   Whitman. *The Early Poems and the Fiction.* Ed. Thomas L. Brasher. New York: New York University Press, 1963.

WLS   Florence Bernstein Freedman. *Walt Whitman Looks at the Schools.* New York: King's Crown Press, 1950.

WWC   Horace Traubel. *With Walt Whitman in Camden.* 7 vols. Vol. I (1905; rpt., New York: Rowman and Littlefield, 1961); Vol. II (1907; rpt., New York: Rowman and Littlefield, 1961); Vol. III (1912; rpt., New York: Rowman and Littlefield, 1961); Vol. IV (1953; rpt., Carbondale: Southern Illinois University Press, 1959); Vol. V (Carbondale: Southern Illinois University Press, 1964); Vol. VI (Carbondale: Southern Illinois University Press, 1982); Vol. VII (Carbondale: Southern Illinois University Press, 1992).

WWW   *Walt Whitman's Workshop: A Collection of Unpublished Prose Manuscripts.* Ed. Clifton Joseph Furness. New York: Russell & Russell, 1964.

Introductory Note

No one can/*WWC*, II: 116. do not take/*WWC*, IV: 41. In estimating/*PW*, II: 473. if he does not/*WCP*, p. 23. As explained in the introduction to the Notes, I bracket my own ellipses in quotes from the 1855 preface and Whitman's poetry. Ellipses in quotes from other sources are not bracketed. the part enacted/ *WWC*, VI: 251. Attracting [the nation]/*LGC*, p. 344.

Prologue

The main details of the seventieth birthday celebration are in *Camden's Compliment to Walt Whitman, May 31, 1889. Notes, Addresses, Letters, Telegrams*, ed. Horace L. Traubel (Philadelphia: David McKay, 1889). See also *WWC*, V: 235–53. **The proof of a poet**/*WCP*, p. 26. **I think of art**/*WWC*, IV: 4. **If Leaves of Grass**/*WWC*, IV: 43. **caviare to the multitude**/*Critic*, November 1881, in *H*, p. 183. **The people: the crowd**/*WWC*, III: 467.

1 / "Underneath All, Nativity"

convulsiveness/*WCP*, p. 775. **the safe traditions**/*BT*, August 5, 1857. **the primitive simplicity**/*BT*, May 28, 1857. **Underneath all**/*LV*, I: 206. **O, to go back**/"Song of Joys," *LV*, II: 335. **fond of**/*LV*, II: 273. **My tongue**/*LV*, I: 1. **My whole family**/*CP*, p. 693. **maternal nativity-stock**/*PW*, I: 23. **a stalwart**/ *NUPM*, I: 6. **Until about 1815**/For an account of the transition from subsistence culture to the market economy, see Charles Sellers, *The Market Revolution: Jacksonian America, 1815–1846* (New York: Oxford University Press, 1991), especially pp. 9–18. See also Harry L. Watson, *Liberty and Power: The Politics of Jacksonian America* (New York: Farrar, Straus and Giroux, 1990), pp. 55–58. For a discussion of pre-1815 signs of capitalism, see Gordon S. Wood, "Inventing American Capitalism," *New York Review of Books*, June 9, 1994, pp. 44–49. **The Whitmans on Long Island**/See Verne Dyson, *Whitmanland: West Hills Memories of the Poet & His Ancestors* (Brentwood, N.Y.: n.p., 1960). **owned Long Island**/In Katherine Molinoff, *Some Notes on Whitman's Family* (New York: n.p., 1941), p. 39. **My father's grandfather**/*DN*, I: 267. **where every spot**/*PW*, I: 7. **the most horrible excesses**/*NUPM*, I: 9. **See—as the annual**/ *LGC*, p. 299. **One pure, upright**/*WEP*, p. 99. **Now of the older**/*LGC*, p. 429. **The battle, the prison-ship**/*WEP*, p. 34. **Greater than**/*LGC*, pp. 510–11. **the haughty defiance**/*WCP*, p. 8. **Their influences**/Mann, *Lectures on Education* (1855; rpt., New York: Arno, 1969), p. 17. **There was a child**/"There Was a Child Went Forth," *LGC*, p. 364. **[T]he successive growth stages**/*PW*, I: 10. **Long Island Character**/*NUPM*, I: 320. **the island was worthy**/In John Johnston and J. W. Wallace, *Visits to Walt Whitman in 1890–91* (1917; rpt., New York: Haskell House, 1970), p. 134. **Me pleas'd**/"Our Old Feuillage," *LGC*, p. 174. **I write this**/*PW*, I: 353. **[E]ach man**/*LGC*, p. 83. **Starting from**/*LGC*, p. 15. **Sewanhacky**/These and other Native American etymologies are discussed in William Wallace Tooker, *The Indian Place-Names on Long Island* (New York: G. P. Putnam's Sons, 1911). **much which reminds**/In *Walt Whitman: The Measure of His Song*, ed. Jim Perlman, Ed Folsom, and Dan Campion (Minneapolis: Holy Cow! Press, 1981), p. 276. **We all kept**/*WWC*, V: 466. **the use of the negro girl**/Dyson, *Whitmanland*, pp. 16–17. **Whitman slaves grouped**/*WCP*, p. 694. **He was very genial**/*PW*, II: 580. **I must admit**/*WWC*, III: 43. **There are the negroes**/"Our Old Feuillage," *LGC*, p. 173. **The time of my boyhood**/ To Grace Gilchrist, in Bliss Perry, *Walt Whitman: His Life and Work* (Boston:

Houghton Mifflin, 1906), p. 19. **Education is something**/Orson S. Fowler, *Love and Parentage, Applied to the Improvement of Offspring* (New York: Fowlers & Wells, 1851), p. xi. **progeny inherits**/O. Fowler, *Love and Parentage*, p. 24. **Fowler devoted**/O. S. Fowler, *Hereditary Descent; Its Laws and Facts Applied to Human Improvement* (New York: Fowlers & Wells, 1847). **To him the hereditary**/*WCP*, p. 7. **parts of the greatest poet**/*WCP*, p. 20. **All that I am**/ In William Leach, *True Love and Perfect Union: The Feminist Reform of Sex and Society* (New York: Basic Books, 1980), p. 305. The discussion in this paragraph of rigid or distant fathers outside literary circles is indebted to Leach. **The father, strong**/"There Was a Child Went Forth," *LGC*, p. 365. **His relations**/*InRe*, p. 34. **My good daddy**/*WWC*, II: 175. **Brooklyn was in the early phase**/My information about early Brooklyn is derived from the following sources: Ralph Henry Gabriel, *The Evolution of Long Island: A Story of Land and Sea* (New Haven, Conn.: Yale University Press, 1921); Ralph Foster Weld, *Brooklyn Is America* (New York: Columbia University Press, 1950); R. F. Weld, *Brooklyn Village, 1816–1834* (New York: Columbia University Press, 1938); Henry R. Stiles, *A History of the City of Brooklyn*, 3 vols. (Brooklyn: n.p., 1867); H. R. Stiles, *The Civil, Political, Professional and Ecclesiastical History and Commercial and Industrial Record of the County of Kings and the City of Brooklyn from 1683 to 1884*, 3 vols. (New York: W. W. Munsell & Co., 1884). **were mortgaged**/*Complete Writings of Walt Whitman*, ed. T. B. Harned, R. M. Bucke, and H. Traubel (New York, 1902), IV: 17. **Go where you will**/In Sellers, *Market Revolution*, p. 138. **a firebell**/In Sellers, *Market Revolution*, p. 141. The following discussion of Andrew Jackson is informed by Sellers and by Watson, *Liberty and Power.* **were a decade**/Schlesinger, *The Age of Jackson* (Boston: Little, Brown and Co., 1945), p. 30. **the ideal woman**/"As at Thy Portals Also Death," *LGC*, p. 497. **The mother at home**/*LGC*, p. 365. **The best part**/ *WWC*, I: 11. **a poor, stunted boy** and **infernal, damnable**/*WWC*, I: 56. **lived in darkness**/*WWC*, II: 57. **wholly loyal**/*WWC*, III: 541. **The number of children**/Statistics in John D'Emilio and Estelle B. Freedman, *Intimate Matters: A History of Sexuality in America* (New York: Harper & Row, 1988), pp. 58, 173–74. **this alarming sterility** and **the procreative capacity**/*BT*, May 28, 1857. **We are under**/O. Fowler, *Love and Parentage*, p. 20. **something indescribable**/Clara Barrus, *Whitman and Burroughs, Comrades* (Boston: Houghton Mifflin, 1931), p. 15. **O the old manhood** and **O ripen'd joy**/*LGC*, p. 180. **hanging on**/*LGC*, p. 344. **doubtless comes**/*DN*, III: 658.

2 / *A Brooklyn Boyhood*

I was bred/*WWC*, III: 205. **preparatory and inauguratory life**/Horace Traubel, "Walt Whitman's Birthday," *Lippincott's*, August 1891, 233–34. **events and days** and **every aspect**/*BT*, June 3, 1857, in *UPP*, I: 2–3. **Brooklyn had such**/*Walt Whitman's New York: From Manhattan to Montauk*, ed. Henry M. Christian (New York: Macmillan, 1963), p. 147. **was fertile**/*Walt Whitman's New York*, ed. Christian, p. 12. **Indeed, it is doubtful**/*Walt Whitman's New*

York, ed. Christian, p. 57. **Between New-York**/Stiles, *History of the City of Brooklyn*, II: 52. **the Gomorrah**/*BE*, March 22, 1847. **state of Paumanok**/*Walt Whitman's New York*, ed. Christian, p. 106. **America's game**/*WWC*, IV: 508. **I celebrate**/"Song of Myself," *LGC*, p. 28. **Then we had various**/*Walt Whitman's New York*, ed. Christian, p. 63. **had an air** and **it was something**/*Walt Whitman's New York*, p. 64. **a big, good-natured** and **We need never**/*UPP*, I: xxvi, n. 9. **have written a word**/*WWC*, I: 10. **one deep purpose**/*PW*, II: 461. **Silent and amazed**/"A Child's Amaze," *LGC*, p. 275. **I never felt**/*WWC*, II: 500. **as a youngster**/Whitman, conversation with Traubel, February 26, 1891, from ms. conversations to be published as *WWC*, VIII; Feinberg. **Come, mother**/*PW*, II: 636. *What is the chief*/*PW*, II: 637. **in every blade of grass**/ In Bliss Forbush, *Elias Hicks, Quaker Liberal* (New York: Columbia University Press, 1956), p. 224. **heaven or hell is not a distant locale**/In Forbush, *Elias Hicks*, p. 166. **any more heaven or hell**/*LGC*, p. 30. **And the law of God**/In Forbush, *Elias Hicks*, p. 164. **the only real democrat**/*WWC*, II: 36. **anywhere—to no one place**/*WWC*, II: 51. **and O what pretty** and **The galleries**/*Walt Whitman's New York*, ed. Christian, p. 138. **How much I am indebted**/*WWC*, I: 96. **the richest vein**/*WWC*, I: 235. **an inexhaustible mine**/*PW*, II: 722. **Stop this day**/*LGC*, p. 30. **a great primitive poem**/*The Correspondence of Henry David Thoreau*, ed. Walter Harding and Carl Bode (New York: New York University Press, 1958), p. 445. **In explaining his use of free verse**/*WWC*, I: 163. **it is not metres**/Emerson, *Essays and Lectures* (New York: Library of America, 1983), p. 450. **cartloads** and **a most formative**/*WWC*, II: 553. **What is rhyme** and **I do in my** and **A great revolution**/John Neal, *Randolph* (n.p., 1823), II: 182, 184, 189. **was daily food**/ *WWC*, II: 445. **every atom belonging**/"Song of Myself," *LGC*, p. 28. **only the different**/Frances Wright [D'Arusmont], *Ten Days in Athens* (1822) rpt., *A Few Days in Athens* (New York: Arno, 1972), p. 178. **the beautiful uncut**/"Song of Myself," *LGC*, p. 34. **the resurrection**/"This Compost," *LGC*, p. 369. **I spent much**/*WWC*, I: 455. **had a long**/*PW*, II: 594. **affected me for weeks**/ *PW*, II: 593. **a rapid-running**/*PW*, II; 695. **The $2.5 million**/See Sellers, *Market Revolution*, p. 371. **The 200 newspapers**/See John D. Stevens, *Sensationalism and the New York Press* (New York: Columbia University Press, 1991), p. 14. **In the early village years**/Stiles, *History of the City of Brooklyn*, II: 133. **I like to supervise**/*WWC*, I: 194. **My theory is**/*WWC*, II: 480. **as carefully**/ Stiles, *History of the City of Brooklyn*, II: 211. **I am the poet**/"Song of Myself," *LGC*, p. 48. **the abolitionists of Brooklyn**/Stiles, *History of the City of Brooklyn*, I: 162. **the first totalitarian**/*Walt Whitman: The Measure of His Song*, ed. Perlman, Folsom, and Campion, p. 140. **What I assume**/"Song of Myself," *LGC*, p. 28. **The presence**/1855 preface, *WCP*, p. 10. **He does not stop**/1855 preface, *WCP*, p. 10. **Massive, yet most**/*BE*, June 3, 1846, in *UPP*, I: 118. **FIXED WILL**/*BE*, March 15, 1847. **Our Federal** and **The Union**/In Sellers, *Market Revolution*, p. 315. **But that nullification** and **beloved Union**/*NYA*, pp. 88, 93. **the nullification and**/*BE*, December 6, 1847.

3 /   Dark Passages

it involves so much/*WWC*, II: 511. hot wishes and the wolf/*LGC*, p. 163. a secret silent/*LGC*, pp. 157–58. So they go/*The Diary of George Templeton Strong*, ed. Allan Nevins and Milton Halsey (New York: Macmillan, 1952), I: 62. When the young/*WEP*, p. 327. has very little regard/*NUPM*, I: 5. a great dark cloud/*WEP*, p. 130. they found themselves/*WEP*, p. 133. Though a bachelor/*WEP*, p. 248. The other quotations in this and the following paragraphs are on pp. 248, 249. almost an observer/*PW*, I: 10. I look where the ship/*LGC*, pp. 428–29 *chance teachers*/*WLS*, p. 26. The shores of this bay/ *PW*, I: 11. We find 'e/New York *World*, July 2, 1887. Whitman clipped this article and kept it in his daybook. [B]y industry/*Long-Islander*, July 12, 1839. I have called/See David S. Reynolds, *Faith in Fiction: The Emergence of Religious Literature in America* (Cambridge, Mass.: Harvard University Press, 1981), chap. 2. No diseas'd person/*LGC*, p. 155. Putridity and privacy and seduction/*LGC*, p. 374. One of his Little Bayside students/See Horace L. Traubel, "Walt Whitman, Schoolmaster: Notes of a Conversation with Charles A. Roe," *Walt Whitman Fellowship Papers* 14 (Philadelphia, April 1895): 81–87. dozens of articles on education/Many of these articles are reprinted in *WLS*. Have you practis'd/"Song of Myself," *LGC*, p. 30. We consider it/*BE*, November 23, 1846, in *UPP*, I: 146. an entirely new system/*NUPM*, V: 1937. I teach straying/"Song of Myself," *LGC*, p. 85. He most honors/"Song of Myself," *LGC*, p. 84. public teacher/*NUPM*, IV: 1554. I would compose/*UPP*, I: 37. I loafe and invite/"Song of Myself," *LGC*, p. 28. looked like a convention and to take in/*Diary of G. T. Strong*, ed. Nevins and Halsey, I: 62, 94. New York may be classified/*New York Times*, March 5, 1856. I have sometimes and Give us the facilities/*UPP*, I: 44. would be entirely happy/In Schlesinger, *Age of Jackson*, p. 290. cut capers/In Arthur Golden, "Nine Early Whitman Letters, 1840–1841," *American Literature* 58 (October 1986): 349. Can we forget/*BE*, September 29, 1846. a well known loco foco/Quotations in this paragraph are in *Long Island Farmer*, October 6, 1840. Though parties sometimes/*WEP*, p. 13. carried into power/*UPP*, I: 51. the pupils had not gained/Whitney to Lotta Rees, letter of August 18, 1906; Walt Whitman Birthplace Association Library, Huntington, New York. warn't in his element/In Johnston and Wallace, *Visits to Walt Whitman*, pp. 70–73. In all the letters/All citations from the Woodbury letters are from Golden, "Nine Early Whitman Letters," pp. 342–60. Winter of 1840/*NUPM*, I: 217. because of his behavior/From notes of the Southold town historian Wayland Jefferson, in Katherine Molinoff, *Walt Whitman at Southold* (Smithtown, n.p., 1966). The main details in this paragraph are from the Molinoff pamphlet. had been in some and You mean that schoolteacher/Hummel, *Heritage* (New York: Frederick A. Stokes Co., 1935), pp. 252, 257. I am most sincerely sorry/Waldo to Cragin, letter in the estate of Arthur Fitzpatrick, Southold, N.Y. Have you heard/Waldo to Cragin, typescript of letter owned by Carl F. Baker, Northport, N.Y. **a living Whitman relative**/David T. Swertfager, the great-great-grandson of Whitman's sister Mary Van Nostrand, told me in a telephone interview of October 28, 1991, that he heard the story of Whitman's expulsion from Southold "from day one." The story had evidently been passed down through the family by his grandmother Zona Young Tuthill (1872–1956). David's wife, Nancy Merrill Swertfager (no relation to the poet), was unaware of the Southold story but did write me that Whitman "was considered the 'black sheep' of the family, but the real reason was not mentioned other than it was accepted that he was 'gay'" (letter of October 17, 1991). **Additional evidence**/Southold lawyer James Bitses tried to turn the Whitman schoolhouse into a museum but could not do so because the structure was, inexplicably, destroyed. Bitses wrote me on August 28, 1991, that the Sodom School had been bought around 1920 by Joseph F. Gradowski and used as a farm storage place. In June 1974 Bitses bought the twenty-by-forty-five-foot structure from Joseph's daughter Rose Gradowski for a dollar and formed the Walt Whitman Schoolhouse Restoration Society with the idea of opening a museum. To this purpose, Bitses turned over the school to Southold's Kiwanis Club, but several weeks later, in Bitses's words, "the turnbuckles that held the walls together were unscrewed and the walls fell outward, whereupon the roof ridge broke and the roof fell in. The building was bulldozed and hauled to the dump where it is now buried beneath forty feet of garbage." Rose Gradowski Oltmann of Saugerties, New York, confirmed to me in a letter of July 21, 1992, that her father and then she once owned the school, and that it was always said that Walt Whitman had taught there; but Mrs. Gradowski reported that the structure was destroyed by a Cutchogue contractor, Leander Glover, Jr., who found the building too fragile to move.

Pursuant to my article "Of Me I Sing: Whitman in His Times" (*New York Times Book Review,* October 4, 1992) I received an unsolicited letter of October 23, 1992, from an ex-Southolder, Philip M. Reinhardt, now of Brooklyn, who wrote of Whitman's having taught at the school known as the Sodom School. In Reinhardt's words, "The events leading to the school's name and date, were torn out of Southold's old archives by a group or person who believed that 'the good is intered [*sic*] with ones [*sic*] bones while the evil lives on.' The now unprovable rumor of the event is that Walt Whitman was tar [*sic*] feathed [*sic*] and run out of town on a rail." For further information about the Sodom School and its history, see the *Suffolk Times,* November 26, 1978; *Suffolk Times,* August 8, 1991; and the Mattituck *Traveler-Watchman,* August 8, 1991. **He would later confess to a friend**/Ellen O'Connor Calder, ms. "Personal Recollections of Walt Whitman"; Feinberg. This passage does not appear in the published version of the article in the *Atlantic Monthly,* June 1907. **I am confident**/*InRe,* p. 34. **The girls did not**/In Traubel, "Walt Whitman, Schoolmaster," p. 83. **They are apt to be eccentric**/*BT,* April 27, 1858, in *UPP,* II: 13. **I am still**/In Golden, "Nine Early Whitman Letters," p. 357. **Guilt and Wretchedness** and **When a man dies**/*Long Island Democrat,* August 11, 1840; in *UPP,* I: 35. **what I have termed "immoral reform"**/See David S. Reynolds, *Beneath the Ameri-*

"The Columbian's Song" (poem, 1840); "The Last of the Sacred Army" (tale, 1842); "The Child-Ghost" (tale, 1842; revised as "The Last Loyalist"); "Ode" (poem, 1846). **(6) POLITICAL:** "The House of Friends" (poem, 1850); "Resurgemus!" (poem, 1850); "Dough-Face Song" (poem, 1850); "Blood-Money" (poem, 1850). **(7) MORAL:** "A Legend of Life and Love" (tale, 1842); "The Play-Ground" (poem, 1846); "The Shadow and Light of a Young Man's Soul" (tale, 1848); "Lingrave's Temptation" (tale, 1848). **(8) BIBLICAL:** "Shirval: A Tale of Jerusalem" (tale, 1845). **blood and thunder romances** and **The public for whom**/*BT*, December 13, 1858, in *UPP*, II: 20–21. **one whose trade**/*WEP*, p. 10. **She clasped the cold neck**/*WEP*, p. 299. **with wild** and **his blood-shot eyes**/*WEP*, p. 290. **gained more by trickery** and **what base and cruel**/*WEP*, pp. 309, 314. The next two quotations in this paragraph are on p. 317. **My stories, I believe**/*C*, I: 26. **useless vexing strife**/Quotations in *WEP*, pp. 8–9. **Time levels all**/Quotations in *WEP*, pp. 14–15. **All, all know**/Quotations in *WEP*, pp. 16–17. **must sleep**/*WEP*, p. 23. **This brain**/Quotations in *WEP*, pp. 28–29. **wild, worn** and **classed with the**/Clark Jillson, *Sketch of M'Donald Clarke. "The Mad Poet"* (Worcester, Mass.: n.p., 1878), p. 5. **possessed all the** and **Whoever has the power**/*Aurora*, March 8, 1842, in *NYA*, p. 106. **Woman's nature**/*Poems of M'Donald Clarke* (New York: J. W. Bell, 1836), p. 47. **I cock my hat**/"Song of Myself" (original version), *LGV*, I: 25. **always wore a full cock'd hat**/*Poems of M. Clarke*, p. 29. **What prodigious queer**/*The Elixir of Moonshine; Being a Collection of Prose and Poetry, by the Mad Poet* (New York: n.p., 1822), p. 9. The quotations in the following paragraph are on pp. 77–78 and 105. **Of the griefs**/*WEP*, p. 26. **Only in the opening decades**/For a discussion of biblical fiction, see Reynolds, *Faith in Fiction*, chap. 5. **of middle stature**/*WEP*, p. 294. **Walking the old hills**/*LGC*, p. 64. **The memory of**/ and **The model of**/*WEP*, p. 95. **Everybody asked everybody**/T. L. Nichols, *Forty Years of American Life* (1864; rpt., New York: Negro University Press, 1968), I: 87. **It is very hard**/*WWC*, IV: 486. **Working class in origin**/For a fine account of the temperance movement and many other aspects of antebellum working-class life, see Sean Wilentz, *Chants Democratic: New York City and the Rise of the American Working-Class, 1788–1850* (New York: Oxford University Press, 1984). **Liquor consumption statistics**/Sellers, *Market Revolution*, p. 260. **A great revolution**/*WEP*, p. 236. **Yesterday was a great time** and **the immense number**/*NYA*, pp. 35, 36. **If the temperance doctrine**/Brooklyn *Star*, October 2, 1845. **A drunkard's breath**/*LGC*, pp. 268–69. **no rumdrinker**/*LGC*, p. 155. **pure** and **destitute of** and **more attacked**/Lippard, *The Quaker City* (1844–45; rpt., ed. David S. Reynolds; Amherst, Mass.: University of Massachusetts Press, 1995), p. 2. **It is true** and **want of polish**/*WEP*, p. 237. **written for** and **create a sensation**/*WEP*, pp. 127, 124. **versed in city** and **It was indeed**/*WEP*, pp. 128, 153. **gave a wild** and **hate and**/*WEP*, p. 133. **the very dreariest** and **far from agreeable**/*WEP*, p. 219. **a Popular** and **not written for** and **in the cheap**/*WEP*, pp. 124, 127. **It was damned rot**/*WWC*, I: 93. **something** *piquant*/*NYA*, p. 116. **secured the services** and **carry out**/*NYA*, p. 2. **a marked** and **a dash**/*NYA*, p. 4. **Among newspapers**/*NYA*, p. 12. The column of and **Cheap literature**/"A Song for Occupations" (original version), *LV*, I: 96. **a false villain**/*NYA*, p. 59. **Had it been**/*NYA*, p. 77. **a stupid** and **coarse, unshaven** and **[S]hall these dregs**/*NYA*, pp. 67. **Let us receive** /*NYA*, pp. 82–83. **an auctioneer**/*NYA*, p. 18. **horrible yet** and **crumbled ashes**/*NYA*, p. 37. **I am the mash'd**/*LGC*, p. 67. **amuse themselves** and **the mystery**/*NYA*, p. 21. **The butcher-boy puts off**/"Song of Myself," *LGC*, p. 39. **Petticoats— petticoats**/In Don C. Seitz, *The James Gordon Bennetts: Father and Son. Proprietors of the New York Herald* (Indianapolis: Bobbs-Merrill, 1928), p. 74. **the superiority** and **Scurrility**/*BE*, February 8, 1847, and February 26, 1847. **A reptile marking**/*NYA*, p. 115. **one of the most vain**/*NYA*, p. 111. **If ever any** and **In the west**/*NYA*, pp. 74, 58. **clergymen call**/*UPP*, I: 103. **the laziest fellow**/*NYA*, p. 12. **a small**/*NYA*, pp. 12–13. **There is in this city**/*NYA*, p. 13. **Any dead fish**/In M. R. Werner, *Tammany Hall* (New York: Doubleday, Doran & Co., 1928), p. 44. **I know perfectly well**/"Song of Myself," *LGC*, p. 77. **one of the human**/*The Subterranean*, September 9, 1843. **a man of original**/*BT*, March 18, 1859. **Turbulent, fleshy**/"Song of Myself," *LGC*, p. 52. **You there, impotent**/"Song of Myself," *LGC*, p. 74. **are not lascivious**/ *Sketches of the Speeches and Writings of Mike Walsh* (New York: Thomas McSpedon, 1843), p. 28. **What a career**/*BT*, March 18, 1859. **Whilst he puffs**/ *UPP*, I: 195. **the young shipbuilders**/*PW*, II: 595. **the New York Bowery** and **the splendid and**/*DN*, III: 669, 736. **The boy I love**/"Song of Myself," *LGC*, pp. 84–85. **the extravagance**/[A. S. Hill], *North American Review* 104 (January 1867): 302. **He is the**/*New York Examiner*, January 19, 1882. **The disorderly class**/Joel Tyler Headley, *The Great Riots of New York, 1712 to 1873* (New York: E. B. Treat, 1873), pp. 73–74. **How much of your**/Brooklyn *Star*, October 10, 1845. **Mobs and murderers,**/*BT*, November 7, 1857, in *ISit*, p. 43. **lawdefying loafers**/*BT*, February 20, 1858. **Already a nonchalant**/"By Blue Ontario's Shore," *LGV*, I: 204. **Arrogant, masculine**/"Song of the Broad-Axe" (1856 version), *LV*, I: 188–89. **the young man** and **class of society**/Charles A. Dana, *New York Daily Tribune*, July 23, 1855, in *H*, p. 22. **a perfect loafer**/ *Life Illustrated*, July 28, 1855. **The quality of**/Brooklyn *City News*, October 10, 1860. **Whitman is a rowdy**/*Boston Transcript*, July 3, 1888. **a compound of**/ Norton, *Putnam's Monthly*, September 1855, in *H*, p. 25, and letter to James Russell Lowell, September 23, 1855, in *H*, p. 30. **Walt Whitman**/This is the wording of the line in the first three editions of *Leaves of Grass*; see *LGC*, p. 52. **pull-down-and-build-over** and **Let us level**/*UPP*, I: 92, 93. **One journalist**/In *Harper's* 13 (1856): 272–73. See also Edward K. Spann, *The New Metropolis: New York City, 1840–1857* (New York: Columbia University Press, 1981), p. 158. **Everything in the streets**/Joel H. Ross, *What I Saw in New-York* (Auburn, N.Y.: Derby & Miller, 1851), pp. 178–79. **Unscrew the locks**/*LGC*, p. 52. **Imagine all the**/*Brooklyn Daily Advertiser*, June 28, 1851. **These domestic animals**/R. H. Collyer, *Lights and Shadows of American Life* (Boston: Brainard & Co., n.d.), p. 6. **Our city is literally**/*Brooklyn Evening Star*, May 21, 1846. **stately and**/*LGC*, p. 163. **The blab of the pave**/*LGC*, p. 36. **choice aboriginal**/*LGC*, p. 507. **the hill island** and **Hell Gate**/See W. W. Tooker, *In-*

June 4, 1847. **He has a splendid**/*BT,* January 8, 1859. **the hardy pioneers**/In Blue, *Free Soilers,* p. 295. **It would seem**/In Sellers, *Market Revolution,* p. 423. **I would preserve**/*Congressional Globe,* 29th Congress, 2nd Session, Appendix, pp. 317–18. **a question between** and **We call upon**/*BE,* September 1, 1847, in *UPP,* I: 208, 209–10. **George Fredrickson**/*The Black Image in the White Mind: The Debate on Afro-American Character and Destiny* (New York: Harper & Row, 1971), pp. 11, 41, 61–62, 67–68. **a physical difference**/Lincoln, *Speeches and Writings, 1832–1858* (New York: Library of America, 1989), p. 512. **he could call an adult black man "boy"**/See Philip B. Kunhardt, Jr., Philip B. Kunhardt III, and Peter W. Kunhardt, *Lincoln: An Illustrated Biography* (New York: Alfred A. Knopf, 1992), p. 88. **well taken care of**/*WEP,* p. 202. **Black and White Slaves**/*NYA,* p. 126. **We are all docile**/*WEP,* p. 44. **Things have come**/*WEP,* pp. 44–45. **Of olden time**/*WEP,* pp. 47–48. **Virginia, mother of greatness**/ *WEP,* pp. 36–37. **So fallen**/*The Complete Poetical Works of Whittier* (Boston: Houghton Mifflin, 1892), p. 186. **Fallen, fallen**/In Allan Nevins, *The Ordeal of the Union* (New York: Scribner's, 1947), II: 292. **Mikhail Bakhtin**/For Bakhtin's theory of the incorporation of popular idioms into literary texts, see especially *The Dialogic Imagination: Four Essays by M. M. Bakhtin,* trans. Caryl Emerson and Michael Holquist (Austin: University of Texas Press, 1981); Bakhtin, *Rabelais and His World* (Cambridge, Mass.: MIT Press, 1968); and Bakhtin, *Problems of Dostoevski's Poetics* (New York: Ardis, 1973). **Great writers penetrate**/ *Life Illustrated,* April 12, 1856, in *NYD,* p. 56. **As I show in**/See Reynolds, *Beneath the American Renaissance,* especially chaps. 2, 6, 7, and 15. **Nov. 26, '60—Lippard**/*NUPM,* I: 434. **Hurrah! The gallows**/Lippard, *The Quaker City,* p. 375. **Hurrah for Hanging!** and **Hurrah for Choking**/*UPP,* I: 97, 116. **Strangle and kill**/*UPP,* I: 103. **A coffin swimming**/*NUPM,* I: 131. **numberless agonies**/Quotations from "Resurgemus" are in *WEP,* pp. 38–40. **The romance is** and **I desire**/*C,* V: 282. **There is plenty**/Hannah Heyde to Louisa Van Velsor Whitman, letter of October 8, 1852; Feinberg. **There was a great boom**/*InRe,* p. 33. **that temper**/Quotations from Whitman's letter to Hale/in *C,* I: 39–40. **It is impossible**/BT, January 12, 1858. **the weakest**/*WWC,* III: 30. **perhaps the weakest**/*WWC,* III: 30. **My thoughts are murder**/"Slavery in Massachusetts," Thoreau, *Reform Papers,* ed. Wendell Glick (Princeton, N.J.: Princeton University Press, 1973), p. 108. **Clear the way there Jonathan!**/Quotations from "A Boston Ballad" (original 1855 version) are in *LV,* I: 147–49. **Agitation?**/In Paxton Hibben, *Henry Ward Beecher: An American Portrait* (1927; rpt., New York: The Press of the Readers Club, 1942), p. 187. **Only by unintermitted**/Phillips, *Speeches, Lectures, and Essays* (1884; rpt., New York: Negro University Press, 1968), pp. 52–53. **Agitation is the great** and **I glory in the name**/In Foner, *Free Soil,* p. 112. **Agitation is the test**/*NUPM,* I: 115. **I think agitation**/*WWC,* V: 529. **make every word**/*WCP,* p. 9. **sharp, full of danger**/*WWW,* p. 130. **I am he**/"By Blue Ontario's Shore," *LGC,* p. 342. **Let others praise**/"Myself and Mine," *LGC,* p. 237. **As circulation** and **Vive**/*PW,* II: 383, 386. **I have been wronged**/"Sleepers" (original version), *LV,* I: 116. **The President eats dirt**/*WCP,* p. 1310. **The State creeps**/In William E. Gienapp, *The Origins of the Republican Party, 1852–1856* (New York: Oxford University Press, 1987), p. 177. **As Mark Summers**/*The Plundering Generation: Corruption and the Crisis of the Union* (New York: Oxford University Press, 1987). **swarms of cringers**/*WCP*, p. 18. **Class differences**/Statistics in this paragraph are from Jeffrey G. Williamson and Peter H. Lindert, *American Inequality: A Macroeconomic History* (New York: Academic Press, 1964), especially pp. 36–37, 101, 141. See also James M. McPherson, *Battle Cry of Freedom: The Civil War Era* (New York: Ballantine, 1988), p. 25. **vast ganglions**/*WWW*, p. 57. **I see an aristocrat**/Uncollected ms. fragment, in *LGC*, p. 696. **The head of the**/*LGC*, p. 425. **Many sweating**/*LGC*, p. 77. **We don't know much**/*New Orleans Daily Crescent*, May 20, 1848, in *UPP*, I: 229. **intrinsically, in**/*WWC*, II: 4. **As socialism gave way**/For a good discussion of socialist and individualistic reform, see Carl J. Guarneri, *The Utopian Alternative: Fourierism in Nineteenth-Century America* (Ithaca: Cornell University Press, 1991). **absolute despot or sovereign**/See Madeleine B. Stern, *The Pantarch: A Biography of Stephen Pearl Andrews* (Austin: University of Texas Press, 1968), pp. 74–75. **This is preeminently** and **I claim individually**/Andrews, *Love, Marriage, and Divorce, and the Sovereignty of the Individual* (1853; rpt., Boston: Benjamin R. Tucker, 1884), pp. 34, 65. **I celebrate**/"Song of Myself," *LGC*, p. 28. **Going where I list**/"Song of the Open Road," *LGC*, p. 151. **Each man to himself**/"A Song of the Rolling Earth," *LGC*, p. 223. **Where outside authority**/*LGC*, p. 190. **The ten years ending**/In Leach, *True Love and Perfect Union*, p. 216. **Be radical, be radical**/*WWC*, I: 223. **I am somehow**/*WWC*, I: 166. **hot**/*WWC*, I: 363. **a higher law than**/In Robert T. Oliver, *History of Public Speaking in America* (Boston: Allyn and Bacon, 1965), p. 103. **Not even the**/Beecher, *Patriotic Addresses*, ed. John R. Howard (Boston: Pilgrim, 1887), p. 173. **MUST RUN-AWAY SLAVES** and **As to what**/*WCP*, pp. 1320, 1321. **a perfect and entire**/*WCP*, p. 1318. **the problem of two sets**/*PW*, II: 465. **He is the arbiter**/*WCP*, p. 9. **the union always**/*WCP*, p. 8. **I celebrate**/"Song of Myself" (original version), *LV*, I: 1. **A southerner soon**/"Song of Myself," *LGC*, pp. 44–45. **not be for the eastern**/*WCP*, p. 15. **slavery and the tremulous**/*WCP*, p. 8. **slavery would probably**/*BT*, May 14, 1857. **There are the negroes**/"Our Old Feuillage," *LGC*, p. 173. **The black with his**/*LGC*, p. 150. **I do not doubt**/"Faith Poem" (later "Assurances"), *LV*, I: 248. **No slaveholders**/In Kenneth M. Stampp, *America in 1857: A Nation on the Brink* (New York: Oxford University Press, 1990), p. 133. **He stands erect**/*The Life and Writings of Frederick Douglass*, ed. Philip S. Foner (New York: International, 1950), p. 130. **There swells and jets**/*LGC*, p. 99. **Never mind the man's**/Elisa Seaman Leggett, to Whitman, letter of June 22, 1881, Walt Whitman Collection, Library of Congress. **You will be**/*WWC*, IV: 429. **sympathy for** and **I too am**/In *Whitman: The Measure of His Song*, ed. Perlman, Folsom, and Campion, pp. 96, 351. **Old parties, old names**/In Gienapp, *Origins of the Republican Party*, p. 167. **has passed into**/*WCP*, p. 5. **fresh from the** and **a new man**/Quoted in Michael F. Holt, *The Political Crisis of the 1850s* (New York: John Wiley & Sons, 1978), p. 176. **I know that underneath**/*NUPM*, VI: 2148. **Eric Foner has shown**/See Foner,

Free Soil. **the true people** and **healthy-bodied**/*WCP*, p. 1308. **always most** and **a bound booby**/*WCP*, p. 1308. **3 million foreigners**/Statistics in Sydney Ahlstrom, *A Religious History of the American People* (New Haven, Conn.: Yale University Press, 1972), p. 749. **They elected eight**/See Taylor Anbinder, *Nativism and Slavery: The Northern Know Nothings and the Politics of the 1850s* (New York: Oxford University Press, 1992). **the great party**/*WWC*, III: 91. **America isolated** and **Bards for my own**/"By Blue Ontario's Shore" (1856 version), *LV*, I: 192. **Walt Whitman, an**/"Song of Myself," *LV*, I: 31. **An American bard** and **No imitation**/*InRe*, pp. 13, 23. **this glorious**/*NYD*, p. 147. **millions of ignorant**/*PW*, II: 762. **Beware** and **all this mummery**/*WWW*, pp. 41–42. **Pleas'd with the native**/*LGC*, p. 64. **See, in my poems**/"Starting from Paumanok," *LGC*, p. 27. **the white from the black**/*InRe*, p. 19. **to wrest the word "American"**/See "The Eighteenth Presidency!" where he writes: "Others are making a great ado with the word Americanism, a solemn and great word," and "are using the great word Americanism without yet feeling the first aspiration of it." *WCP*, p. 1315. **in the blood**/*NUPM*, I: 862. **empty flesh**/*WCP*, p. 1317. **from political hearses**/*WCP*, p. 1313. **no[t] the particular**/*NUPM*, VI: 2117. **We want no reforms**/*NUPM*, I: 145.

6 / American Performances

Lawrence Levine/*Highbrow/Lowbrow: The Emergence of Cultural Hierarchy in America* (Cambridge, Mass.: Harvard University Press, 1988). **Long Island clam dig**/*Long Island Farmer*, July 20, 1841, in *UPP*, I: 50. **absorbing theatres** and **everything, high**/*WWC*, I: 455. **Let's have it**/In Gene Smith, *American Gothic: The Story of America's Legendary Theatrical Family—Junius, Edwin, and John Wilkes Booth* (New York: Simon and Schuster, 1992), p. 82. **those long-kept-up tempests**/*PW*, II: 595. By contrast, he criticized a cold Brooklyn audience that made little noise. "You are not having daguerreotypes taken," he warned, "nor acting silent statues—and it comes over one like a chill to see so many persons perched, as it were, on their propriety, and every word in a low whisper" (*Brooklyn Star*, November 14, 1845). **His genius**/*PW*, II: 597. **He had much**/*WWC*, IV: 286. **THE MAD TRAGEDIAN**/In Smith, *American Gothic*, p. 17. **he stood out**/*PW*, II: 592–93. **I demand that**/*WWC*, VI: 141. **The words fire**/*PW*, II: 597. **When he was in a passion**/*WWC*, VII: 295. **inflated, stagy**/*PW*, II: 597. **favorite article**/Bell's article appeared in the *Nineteenth Century* (February 1878). Whitman clipped the article and scored and underlined several of its passages. **a night that formed**/*CG*, p. 54. **not only seized and awed**/*CG*, p. 56. **I have always had**/*WWC*, IV: 519. **No! no!** and **In my judgment**/*JM*, p. 33. **How often I**/*WWC*, II: 246. **Was he a sea captain?**/See *JM*, p. 33. **all things and all**/*NUPM*, I: 217. **this drama**/The quotations in this sentence are in *LGC*, pp. 381–82. **I do not ask the**/"Song of Myself," *LGC*, p. 67. **I become any presence**/"Song of Myself" (original version), *LV*, I: 59. **dashed strongly**/Gansevoort Melville's 1846 London journal; rpt., *New York Public Library Bulletin* (January 1966). **Miss Cushman is a**/Undated clipping, Har-

vard Theatre Collection. **I am the actor**/*LGC*, p. 426. **Play'd the part**/*LGC*,
p. 163. **knock'd us about**/*PW*, II: 695. **He liked**/See *PW*, II: 695; and *WWC*,
VI: 99. **a sudden revelation** and **power of**/*CG*, p. 55. *He is not an artist*/In
Montrose J. Moses, *The Fabulous Forrest: The Record of an American Actor*
(1929; rpt., New York: Benjamin Blom, 1969), p. 203. **This was both a
cultural**/See Peter G. Buckley, "To the Opera House: Culture and Society in
New York City, 1820–1860" (diss., State University of New York at Stony Brook,
1984). **After Booth**/*WWC*, VI: 303. **I watched his**/*WWC*, I: 456. **massive
freshness**/*BE*, December 22, 1846. **I could never enter**/*WWC*, VI: 141.
Mem[orandum]/Feinberg. **Such little reminders**/*WWC*, I: 365. **I feel I
cannot**/Moses, *Fabulous Forrest*, p. 226. **Macready's opening performance**/
A concise contemporary account of the riot is reprinted in "When 'Macbeth'
Shook the World of Astor Place," *New York Times*, January 12, 1992. **a sort of
American style**/*BE*, August 20, 1846, in *UPP*, II: 322–23. **permanently the
house**/George C. D. Odell, *Annals of the New York Stage* (New York: Columbia
University Press, 1928), IV: 551. **the character of the Bowery**/*PW*, II: 595.
completely nauseated/*Brooklyn Star*, October 27, 1845. The full quotation is:
"For what person of judgment, that has ever spent one hour in the Chatham
or Bowery theatres in New York, but has been completely nauseated with the
stuff presented there?" **Of all 'low' places**/*BE*, February 8, 1847, in *UPP*, I: 310.
as Richard Butsch shows/"Bowery B'hoys and Matinee Ladies," *American
Quarterly* 46 (September 1994): 374–405. **O Christ!**/"Song of Myself" (origi-
nal version), *LV*, I: 58. **You laggards there**/"Song of Myself," *LGC*, p. 71. **You
villain touch!**/"Song of Myself," *LGC*, p. 39. **It has always been**/*WWC*, VI:
457. **born, as it were**/"Democracy" (1867), in *Democratic Vistas, 1860–1880*,
ed. Alan Trachtenberg (New York: George Braziller, 1970), p. 359. **Edwin For-
rest, whose**/See Moses, *Fabulous Forrest*, p. 192. **a national and pervading**/
T. L. Nichols, *Forty Years of American Life*, I: 64. **politics seemed to enter**/
William E. Gienapp, "'Politics Seem to Enter Everything': Political Culture in
the North, 1840–1860," in *Essays on Antebellum Politics, 1840–1860*, ed. Wil-
liam, E. Gienapp et al. (College Station: Texas A & M University Press, 1982),
pp. 14–69. The statistics on antebellum voter turnout in this paragraph are
from this article. Twentieth-century voter-turnout figures are derived from the
Census Bureau (through 1984) and Voter Research and Surveys (1988 and
1992). **The lecture system**/*BT*, January 30, 1857. **When I was much
younger**/*WWC*, I: 5. **he had an idea**/*InRe*, p. 35. **American Lectures**/
NUPM, I: 314. **a public Speaker**/*C*, I: 45. **henceforth my employment**/
NUPM, IV: 1437. **the great cannon**/See Schlesinger, *Age of Jackson*, p. 84.
often—heard and **grandeur of manner**/*WWC*, III: 174. **Woe betide the
man**/Speech of June 17, 1843, celebrating the Bunker Hill monument, in *The
Great Speeches and Orations of Daniel Webster*, ed. Edwin P. Whipple (Boston:
Little, Brown & Co., 1923), p. 140. **as Garry Wills shows**/See *Lincoln at Gettys-
burg: The Words That Remade America* (New York: Simon and Schuster, 1992),
especially pp. 43, 56. **to write in the gush**/*WWC*, II; 26–27. **I like to read
them**/*WWC*, III: 375. **to speak as the spirit**/*A History and Criticism of Amer-*

ican Public Address, ed. William Norwood Brigance (New York: Russell & Russell, 1943), I: 170. **a great** and **majestic sweet**/*WWC*, VII: 107. **And I have seen poor**/*The Life of Cassius Marcellus Clay. Memoirs, Writings, and Speeches* (1886; rpt., New York: Negro University Press, 1969), I: 88. **yet ... I recall**/*PW*, II: 551. **the huge annual** and **I went frequently**/*PW*, II: 697. **to spout before**/In Richard H. Sewell, *John P. Hale and the Politics of Abolition* (Cambridge, Mass.: Harvard University Press, 1965), p. 6. **He was a stump orator**/Sewell, *John P. Hale*, p. 72. **as near my audience**/*Life of Cassius Marcellus Clay*, I: 88. **CLAY: You hiss**/*Life of Cassius Marcellus Clay*, I: 196. **Yes, the place**/*NUPM*, VI: 2234. **animated conversation**/In Oliver, *History of Public Speaking*, p. 237. **The Plymouth Church**/*Brooklyn Daily Advertiser*, June 6, 1850, in *UPP*, I: 235. **I want the audience**/In Oliver, *History of Public Speaking*, p. 376. **Do you suppose**/In *History ... of American Public Address*, ed. Brigance, p. 276. **He hit me so hard**/*WWC*, II: 471–72. **refreshing that his bold**/*UPP*, I: 235. **animated *ego-style*** and **direct addressing**/*NUPM*, VI: 2230; I: 409. **Come closer to me**/"A Song for Occupations" (original version), *LV*, I: 83–84. **He took his audiences by storm**/A good account of Clay's oratorical style is in Schlesinger, *Age of Jackson*, p. 83. **a splendid politician**/Comments on Clay in this sentence are in *NYA*, p. 88. **far more direct**/*WWW*, p. 34. **Be bold!**/*NUPM*, VI: 2232. **Not hurried gabble**/*NUPM*, VI: 2236. **O the orator's joys!**/"A Song of Joys," *LGC*, p. 181. **C. Caroll Hollis has shown**/*Language and Style in Leaves of Grass* (Baton Rouge: Louisiana State University Press, 1983). Another good discussion of style and language is Mark Bauerlin, *Whitman and the American Idiom* (Baton Rouge: Louisiana State University Press, 1991). **Christopher Burnam, likewise**/Christopher Charles Burnham, "An Analysis and Description of Walt Whitman's Composing Process" (diss., University of Rhode Island, 1979). **fitted for a Yankee**/In Harold Blodgett, *Walt Whitman in England* (1934; rpt., New York: Russell & Russell, 1973), p. 21. **was never so universally**/In Carl Bode, *The American Lyceum: Town Meeting of the Mind* (New York: Oxford University Press, 1956), p. 134. **The reader will always**/*PW*, II: 725. **Camerado, this**/"So Long!" *LGC*, p. 505. **Perhaps my dearest**/*PW*, II: 592. **My younger life**/*WWC*, II: 174. **I hear those odes**/*LGC*, p. 407. **the great, overwhelming**/*WWC*, V: 174. **As Robert Faner Notes**/Statistics in this and the following paragraph are from Robert D. Faner, *Walt Whitman and the Opera* (Carbondale: Southern Illinois University Press, 1951), p. 122. **their delight in music**/*WCP*, p. 6. **A taste for music**/*ISit*, p. 173. **I am a dance**/ *LGC*, p. 426. **Also that year Anthony Philip Heinrich**/Information in this paragraph comes largely from Robert Offergold, line notes to NW 7, *Gottschalk and Company. The Music of Democratic Sociability* (New York: New World Records, 1976), p. 1; discussed also in Charles Hamm, *Music in the New World* (New York: W. W. Norton, 1983), p. 227. *American opera*/ *NUPM*, I: 152. **For the first time** and **excel all the**/*Brooklyn Star*, November 5, 1845. The first quotation in the following paragraph is also from this article. **We have now**/*BE*, April 3, 1846. **a perfectly transparent** and **clearness, simplicity**/*NF*, p. 70. **Elegant simplicity**/*GF*, pp. 346–47. **perfect freedom** from/*Herald of Freedom*, December 9, 1842. **We like their music** and **genuine children**/In *There's a Good Time Coming and Other Songs of the Hutchinson Family as Performed at the Smithsonian Institution* (Washington, D.C.: Library of Congress, 1978), pp. 5, 12. **After the *staccatos***/*Birmingham Journal*, January 1846, in John Wallace Hutchinson, *Story of the Hutchinsons* (Boston: Lee and Shepard, 1896), II: 311. **are true sons**/*BE*, March 13, 1847. **The song seemed**/In Hutchinson, *Story of the Hutchinsons*, II: 298. **We're a band of brothers**/Song lyrics in *There's a Good Time Coming ... as Performed at the Smithsonian Institution*, p. 4. **Walt Whitman**/*LV*, I: 31. **almost miraculous** and **indeed an acquisition**/In Hutchinson, *Story of the Hutchinsons*, I: xvi, xv. **the woman the same**/"Song of Myself," *LGC*, p. 48. **cheer up slaves**/1855 preface to *Leaves of Grass, WCP*, p. 17. **I heard the soprano**/"I Heard You Solemn-Sweet Pipes of the Organ," *LGC*, p. 110. **[N]ow the chorus**/*LGC*, p. 449. **Indeed, their negro singing**/*Brooklyn Star*, January 13, 1846. **the famous band**/*BE*, April 28, 1847. **Then we had**/*WCP*, p. 1290. **our best work**/*WWC*, VI: 120. **They are heart songs**/*Life and Writings of Frederick Douglass*, ed. Foner, pp. 356–57. **pleasant scraps and airs**/in Faner, *Whitman and the Opera*, p. 63. **established favorites**/*New York Mirror*, April 29, 1845. **the boys whistled it**/George Frederick Root, *The Story of a Musical Life* (1891; rpt., New York: De Capo, 1970), p. 89. **Pianos and guitars**/*Albany Register*, September 1852, in Charles Hamm, *Music in the New World* (New York: W. W. Norton, 1983), p. 229–30. **Never before**/Hamm, *Music in the New World*, p. 231. **I hear America** and **singing with open mouths**/"I Hear America Singing," *LGC*, pp. 12–13. **a mass of**/*Brooklyn Star*, November 14, 1845. **a recent recording**/*There's a Good Time Coming ... as Performed at the Smithsonian Institution*. **to dazzle**/*Albion*, September 28, 1850. **The Swedish Swan**/*New York Evening Post*, August 14, 1851, in *UPP*, I: 257. **the *Italian opera***/*BE*, February 13, 1847. **the superbest**/*WWC*, II: 173. **The fresh, vigorous**/*UPP*, I: 257. **A tenor large and fresh**/*LGC*, p. 56. **How much from thee**/*LGC*, p. 523. **For me ... out of the**/*WWC*, IV: 286. **There was never**/In Odell, *Annals*, VI: 187–88. **Alboni's performances**/In Faner, *Whitman and the Opera*, p. 29. **every time she sang**/*PW*, I: 20. **She used to sweep**/In Johnston and Wallace, *Visits to Walt Whitman*, p. 162. **There is an indefinable**/In Odell, *Annals*, VI: 264. **Smile O voluptuous**/"Song of Myself," *LGC*, p. 49. **I hear the trained**/*LGC*, p. 56. **The teeming lady**/"Proud Music of the Storm," *LGC*, p. 407. **All persons appreciated** and **packed full**/*FC*, 19. For a recent discussion of Alboni's American tour, see John Dizikes, *Opera in America* (New Haven: Yale University Press, 1993), pp. 139–45. **All of the amusements**/*BT*, April 19, 1858, in *NYD*, pp. 217–18. **What a magnificent**/Quotations in this paragraph are in *Life Illustrated*, November 10, 1855, in *UPP*, I: 97–101. **Walt Whitman's method**/*Saturday Press*, January 7, 1860. **But for the opera**/John Townsend Trowbridge, "Reminiscences of Walt Whitman," *Atlantic Monthly* 89 (February 1902): 166. **As Robert Faner has shown**/Faner, *Whitman and the Opera*, chap. 5.

7 /   *"Sex Is the Root of It All"*

That's a New York reptile/*NYD*, p. 127. **the conventional one** and **by far the largest**/*PW*, II: 492. **a new departure**/Quotations in this paragraph are in *PW*, II: 493–94. **Gay Wilson Allen**/*The Solitary Singer: A Critical Biography of Walt Whitman* (New York: Macmillan, 1955), p. 64. **F. O. Matthiessen**/In *A Century of Whitman Criticism*, ed. Edwin Haviland Miller (Bloomington: Indiana University Press, 1969), p. 177. **Paul Zweig**/*Whitman, the Making of a Poet*, p. 12. **cataracts of trash**/*BE*, July 11, 1846, in *UPP*, I: 122. **he had sounded**/Burroughs, *Notes on Walt Whitman, As Poet and Person* (1867; rpt., New York: Haskell House, 1971), p. 81. **Yes, Women**/*Saturday Press*, June 2, 1860. **Henry Bryan Binns**/*Walt Whitman and His Poetry* (1915; rpt., London: George Harrap & Co., 1971). **Emory Holloway**/*Whitman; An Interpretation in Narrative* (New York: Alfred A. Knopf, 1926). **In your conception**/Symonds to Whitman, letter of August 3, 1890; Feinberg. **morbid inferences**/Quotations in this sentence are in *C*, V: 72. **Indeed, . . . I think**/*WWC*, VII: 338. **Sex is the root**/*WWC*, III: 452.**within its own**/*C*, V: 73. **James Miller's**/James E. Miller, Jr., "Walt Whitman's Omnisexual Vision," in *The Chief Glory of Every People*, ed. Matthew J. Broccoli (Carbondale: Southern Illinois University Press, 1973), pp. 233–59. Another rounded discussion of Whitman and sex is M. Jimmie Killingsworth, *Whitman's Poetry of the Body: Sexuality, Politics, and the Text* (Chapel Hill: University of North Carolina Press, 1989). For the specifically homoerotic elements in Whitman, see especially Moon, *Disseminating Whitman* and Robert K. Martin, *The Homosexual Tradition in American Poetry* (Austin: University of Texas Press, 1979), chap. 1. Martin expands upon, and slightly modifies, his views in "Whitman and the Politics of Identity," in *Walt Whitman: The Centennial Essays*, ed. Ed Folsom (Iowa City: University of Iowa Press, 1994), pp. 172–81. See also Byrne R. S. Fone, *Masculine Landscapes: Walt Whitman and the Homoerotic Text* (Carbondale: Southern Illinois University Press, 1992). **Attracting [the nation]**/*LGC*, p. 344. **the age transfigured**/*WCP*, p. 23. **Sylvester Graham**/His statistics are in Sellers, *Market Revolution*, p. 251. **Orson Fowler put the percentage**/*Amativeness; or Evils and Remedies of Excessive and Perverted Sexuality* (New York: Fowlers & Wells, 1844), pp. 14, 17. **Is this then a touch?**/*LGC*, pp. 57–58. **the sick-gray**/"The Sleepers" (original version), *LV*, I: 109. **a sickly, pale, shrivelled**/Graham, *A Lecture to Young Men, on Chastity* (Boston: Light & Stearns, 1837), p. 99. **Stephen A. Black and Edwin Haviland Miller**/Black, *Whitman's Journeys into Chaos: A Psychoanalytic Study of the Poetic Process* (Princeton: Princeton University Press, 1975), pp. 128–30; Miller, *Walt Whitman's Poetry: A Psychological Journey* (New York: New York University Press, 1968), pp. 76–78. **My hands are spreading forth**/"The Sleepers" (original version), *LV*, I: 112. **The young man that**/*LGC*, pp. 104–5. **Have you seen the fool**/*LGC*, p. 99. **A general laxity**/*BT*, August 5, 1857. **fearfully common**/Gove, *Lectures to Women on Anatomy and Physiology* (New York: Harper & Brothers, 1846), p. 177. **They fancy that they**/Thompson, *New-York Life: or, The Mysteries of Upper-Tendom Revealed*

(New York: Charles S. Atwood, 1849), pp. 78–79. **It is notorious**/*Life Illustrated*, December 15, 1855. **No man ever lived**/*JM*, p. 207. **speech and thoughts were**/*JM*, p. 247. **making frequent use**/*Brooklyn Star*, October 10, 1845. **indulging in** and **Profanity is**/*BE*, April 9, 1847. **vile, obscene stories** and **all in nature**/*JM*, p. 207. **In the pleantiful**/*NUPM*, IV: 1604. **the prolific brood** and **the same endless**/*PW*, II: 408. **all the literature**/*WWC*, IV: 119. **No one would more rigidly**/*WWC*, IV: 388. **Horrible—A Son**/*BE*, October 5, 1846. **Scalded to Death**/*BE*, December 23, 1847. CAPITAL FOUNDATION/*BE*, June 3, 1847. **he raved wildly about the Harper's Illuminated Bible**/See, for example, *BE*, March 9, 1846; March 25, 1846; and May 30, 1846. **always inculcate**/*BE*, May 31, 1847. **In tasty covers**/*BE*, May 31, 1847. **in exceedingly bad** and **revolting drunken**/*BE*, March 9, 1846. **the perfect cataracts**/ Quotations in this paragraph are in *BE*, July 11, 1846. **our country was flooded**/*Memoir and Select Remains of the Late Rev. John R. M'Dowall, the Martyr of the Seventh Commandment in the Nineteenth Century* (New York: Leavitt, Lord, & Co., 1838), p. 222. **libidinous books**/*New-York Sporting Whip*, February 11, 1843. See also Timothy J. Gilfoyle, *City of Eros: New York City, Prostitution, and the Commercialization of Sex, 1790–1920* (New York: W. W. Norton & Co., 1992), p. 133. **all the trashy and disgusting**/*Advocate of Moral Reform*, February 24, 1845. **The Ten Plagues**/Beecher, *Lectures to Young Men, on Various Important Subjects* (New York: Saxton & Miles, 1846), p. 211. **Within the last**/*BT*, December 4, 1857. **If there be**/*BT*, August 17, 1857. **George Thompson**/For a discussion of Thompson and other sensational writers, see Reynolds, *Beneath the American Renaissance*, chaps. 6 and 7. Of course, as I point out throughout that book, Thompson and others often sugarcoat their sensationalism with conventional moral endings to their novels. Christopher Looby, in reference to *The House Breaker* (one of Thompson's more obviously didactic works) argues that this "reactionary telos" in Thompson's fiction overwhelms its "insurrectionary and transgressive elements"; see Looby, "George Thompson's 'Romance of the Real': Transgression and Taboo in American Sensation Fiction," *American Literature* 65 (December 1993): 651–71. **How long must I** and **Each of the embryo**/Thompson, *Venus in Boston: A Romance of City Life* (New York: n.p., 1849), p. 93. **the crime of** *incest*/Thompson, *City Crimes; or, Life in New York and Boston* (New York: William Berry & Co., 1849), p. 131. **the anonymous lascivious** and **to rescue**/O'Connor, *The Good Gray Poet* (1866; rpt., Richard Maurice Bucke, *Walt Whitman* [1883; rpt., New York: Johnson Reprint Corp., 1970]), pp. 108, 118–19. **Of the morbid, venereal**/Burroughs, *Notes on Whitman*, p. 27. **a fully-complete**/*NUPM*, I: 413. **In my judgment**/*PW*, II: 767. **Great genius**/*WCP*, p. 19. **Away with old romance**/ *LGC*, p. 202. **Though the world is**/O. Fowler, *Love and Parentage*, p. 49. **Read no love-stories**/O. Fowler and L. N. Fowler, *Marriage: Its History and Ceremonies* (New York: Fowlers & Wells, 1847), p. 229. **The more perfectly scientific**/ Graham, *A Lecture to Young Men*, p. 9. **this vicious traffic**/In Leach, *True Love and Perfect Union*, p. 62. **Obscene novels** and **Still worse**/Trall, *Home-Treatment for Sexual Abuses: A Practical Treatise* (New York: Fowlers & Wells,

1853), pp. 45, 46–47. **As respects physiological**/*BE*, September 26, 1846. **The reproductive function**/Trall, *Home-Treatment for Sexual Abuses*, p. iv. **what steam power**/O. Fowler, *Sexual Science; Including Manhood, Womanhood, and Their Mutual Interrelations* (Philadelphia: National Publishing Co., 1870), p. 638. **Sex contains all**/"A Woman Waits for Me," *LGC*, pp. 101–2. **She is the pattern**/O. Fowler, *Sexual Science*, p. 638. **the vestibule**/Fowler, *Sexual Science*, p. 719. PASSION ABSOLUTELY/O. Fowler, *Sexual Science*, p. 680, in Madeleine B. Stern, *Heads and Headlines: The Phrenological Fowlers* (Norman: University of Oklahoma Press, 1971), p. 192. **Great God**/O. Fowler, *Sexual Science*, p. 712. **I prefer the**/*WWC*, II: 148. **We have scarcely**/*BE*, May 1, 1846. **sickly prudishness**/*UPP*, I: 191. **Clean and vigorous children** and **shall receive** and **Of the human form**/*WCP*, p. 19. **a poem in which**/*NUPM*, I: 304. **Who will underrate**/*ISit*, p. 113. **Exaggerations will be**/*WCP*, p. 19. The lines in "Suggestions" are: "That exaggerations will be sternly revenged in your own physiology, and in other persons' physiology also,/ [. . .] (For facts properly told, how mean appear all romances.)," *LV*, II: 437. **Welcome is every organ**/"Song of Myself," *LGC*, p. 31. **Perfect and clean**/"The Sleepers," *LGC*, p. 432. **Head, neck**/"I Sing the Body Electric," *LGC*, p. 100. **the amative part**/Burroughs, *Notes on Whitman*, pp. 27, 31. **belong in a** /*JM*, p. 289. **numerous class** and **not meant for obscenity**/*Saturday Press*, July 28, 1860. **I have always made**/*WWC*, IV: 386. **women, doctors**/*WWC*, IV: 392. **Of physiology from**/*LGC*, p. 1. **[O]nly when sex**/*NF*, p. 33. **essentially a woman's**/*WWC*, II: 331. **Whitman's athletic mothers**/In *Century of Whitman Criticism*, ed. Miller, p. 157. **G. J. Barker-Benfield**/*The Horrors of the Half-Known Life: Male Attitudes Toward Women and Sexuality in Nineteenth-Century America* (New York: Harper & Row, 1976). **the appaling depletion**/*PW*, II: 372. **alarming sterility**/*BT*, May 28, 1857. **W. W. himself**/*PW*, I: 10. **very far removed**/*BT*, August 5, 1857. **a healthy American female** and **of our fair-featured** and **The mothers of the next**/*BT*, August 18, 1857. **preformation theory**/See Peter J. Bowler, *Evolution: The History of an Idea* (Berkeley: University of California Press, 1989), p. 58. **This is not only one man**/"I Sing the Body Electric," *LGC*, p. 99. **a new, scientifically bred**/In Barker-Benfield, *Horrors of the Half-Known Life*, p. 301. **I pour the stuff**/"A Woman Waits for Me," *LGC*, p. 102. **[Y]our privilege encloses**/"I Sing the Body Electric," *LGC*, p. 97. **Unfolded out of the folds**/*LGC*, p. 391. **It is notorious**/*Life Illustrated*, March 20, 1858. **the artificial *deformity***/Trall, *The Illustrated Family Gymnasium* (New York: Fowler & Wells, 1857), p. 179. **Ann Douglas**/*The Feminization of American Culture* (New York: Alfred A. Knopf, 1977). **Barbara Welter**/*Dimity Convictions: The American Woman in the Nineteenth Century* (Athens: Ohio University Press, 1976). **Nina Baym**/*Women's Fiction: A Guide to Novels by and about Women in America, 1820–1870* (New York: Cornell University Press, 1978). **Jane P. Tompkins**/*Sensational Designs: The Cultural Work of American Fiction, 1790–1860* (New York: Oxford University Press, 1985). **Frances B. Cogan**/*All-American Girl: The Ideal of Real Womanhood in Mid-Nineteenth-Century America* (Athens: University of Georgia Press, 1989). **muscles like** and **I can** row/In Cogan, *All-American Girl*, p. 27. **know how to swim**/"A Woman Waits for Me," *LGC*, p. 102. **I say an unnumbered**/"Poem of Remembrances for a Girl or Boy of These States," *LV*, I: 253. **altogether among the women**/*WWC*, I: 78. **her majestic and Oh! it was sweet**/*WWC*, VII: 107. **Do you know**/*WWC*, II: 19. **a brilliant woman**/*WWC*, I: 80. **Oh! She was a splendid**/*WWC*, VII: 258. **Where women walk**/*LGC*, p. 190. **the payment for Women's**/*BE*, November 20, 1846. **a seamstress who supported**/*BE*, February 16, 1847. **a woman who had worked forty years**/*BE*, June 17, 1847, in *GF*, I: 158. **the miserably low rate**/*BE*, January 29, 1847, in *GF*, I: 148. **A wife could not**/For a discussion of American women and the law, see Miriam Gurko, *The Ladies of Seneca Falls: the Birth of the Women's Rights Movement* (New York: Macmillan, 1974), pp. 8–11. **he supported a proposed Canadian law**/*BE*, June 6, 1847. **No one is ignorant**/*Life Illustrated*, November 3, 1855. **was a free lover**/In Florence Bernstein Freedman, *William Douglas O'Connor: Walt Whitman's Chosen Knight* (Athens: Ohio University Press, 1985), p. 169. **an overmastering passion**/*JM*, p. 37. **single fools**/*BE*, April 1, 1846, in *UPP*, II: 101. **Young man reader**/*BE*, February 4, 1847, in *UPP*, II: 233. **When that**/*BT*, September 2, 1857, in *ISit*, pp. 113–14. **Anything like free**/*New York Times*, June 7, 1902. **all sorts of odd-fishes**/*BT*, June 29, 1858, in *ISit*, p. 45. **the marriage relation** and **a grand upheaval**/*ISit*, p. 46. **the contemptible lucubrations**/*BT*, September 14, 1858, in *UPP*, II: 8. **Free Lovers, Spiritualists** and **these heterogenous**/*BT*, September 21, 1858. **monotony, monogamy**/Lazarus, *Love vs. Marriage* (New York: Fowlers & Wells, 1852), p. 251. **Our whole existing**/Andrews, *Love, Marriage, and Divorce*, p. 19. **the passional theory**/In Edward K. Spann, *Brotherly Tomorrows: Movements for a Cooperative Society* (New York: Columbia University Press, 1989), p. 125. **There was a time**/*New York Criterion*, November, 10, 1855. **men and women associating**/Sarah Tyndale to Whitman, letter of July 1, 1857; Feinberg. **I am trying to**/Trowbridge, "Reminiscences," 164. **What is more subtle**/*LGC*, p. 164. **the dear love**/*LGC*, p. 311. **O to attract**/"A Song of Joys," *LGC*, p. 183. **I am he that aches**/"I Am He That Aches with Love," *LGC*, p. 109. **The great chastity**/"Spontaneous Me," *LGC*, p. 105. **Prostitution, in marriage**/Andrews, *Love, Marriage, and Divorce*, p. 19. **I only feel sure**/*WWC*, III: 439. **The numbers of brothels**/Statistics in this paragraph are from Gilfoyle, *City of Eros*, pp. 30–31, 59, 126. **are more or less familiar** and **the best classes** and **the custom is**/*NYD*, pp. 217–18. **You see the women**/*NYD*, p. 6. **degenerated into assignation**/*New-York Sporting Whip*, February 18, 1843. **males and females**/*New-York Sporting Whip*, February 11, 1843. **No one can walk**/*Diary of G. T. Strong*, ed. Nevins and Halsey, II; 57. **notorious courtesan** and **tawdry, hateful**/*NYD*, pp. 119–20. **If prostitution continues**/*BT*, June 20, 1857. **As Timothy Gilfoyle has shown**/*City of Eros*, pp. 138–40. **Abandoned females**/O. Fowler, *Love and Parentage*, p. 98. **Seduction; destitution**/Sanger, *History of Prostitution* (New York: Harper & Brothers, 1858), p. 676. **the great vice**/*ISit*, p. 118. **serpentine poison**/*WCP*, p. 21. **the treacherous seducer**/"I Sit and Look Out," *LGC*, p. 273. **The prostitute draggles**/*LGC*, p. 43. **You prostitutes flaunting**/"You cradle/"Song of Myself," *LGC*, p. 81. **an apex**/And quotations in the next sentence are in *LGC*, p. 81. **the different versions of his famous self-identification**/*LV*, I: 31. **I have the crazy notion**/In Douglas Botting, *Humboldt and the Cosmos* (New York: Harper & Row, 1973), p. 257. **the contemplation of all**/Humboldt, *Cosmos: A Sketch of a Physical Description of the Universe* (1845; rpt., New York: Harper & Brothers, 1858), I: 59. **harmoniously ordered** and **a harmony, or**/Humboldt, *Cosmos*, I: 24. **external manifestations**/Humboldt, *Cosmos*, II: 20. The next two quotations in this paragraph are in II: 19. **Humboldt, in his Kosmos**/Whitman's marginal notation to "Taylor's Eve of Conquest," *Edinburgh Review* 84 (April 1849): 192; Trent. **Who includes diversity**/*LGC*, pp. 392–93. **noun masculine or**/*DN*, III: 669. **I believe in Darwinianism**/Interview in the New York *Sun*, June 28, 1845, in *WWW*, p. 193. **When Spurzheim was in**/Martineau, *Retrospect of Western Travel* (London: Saunders and Otley, 1838), III: 201. See also Stern, *Heads and Headlines*. **If the professor**/*BE, March 10, 1846.* **Among the most persevering** /*BE*, March 10, 1847. **You are yourself**/In Stern, *Heads and Headlines*, p. 102. **the lawgivers** and **large hope**/*WCP*, pp. 15, 20. **Never offering others**/*LV*, I: 189. **I probably have**/*WWC*, I: 385. **[T]he expression of**/*LGC*, p. 94. **Some men**/O. S. and L. N. Fowler, *The Illustrated Self-Instructor in Phrenology and Physiology* (New York: Fowlers & Wells, 1852), p. 13. **The wolf, the snake**/*LGC*, p. 163. **TOTAL ABSTINENCE**/O. Fowler, *Amativeness*, p. 56. **I have resolv'd**/*NUPM*, I: 438. **When inflamed, fevered**/ O. Fowler, *Fowler on Matrimony: or The Principles of Phrenology and Physiology Applied to the Selection of Suitable Companions for Life* (Philadelphia: n.p., 1841), p. 5. **TO GIVE UP ABSOLUTELY**/*NUPM*, II: 888–90. **A Cool, gentle** and **to live a more**/*NUPM*, II: 887, 886. **I have always been very**/*WWC*, I: 282. **Extreme caution** and **Caution seldom goes**/*WCP*, p. 20. **Apart from the pulling**/"Song of Myself," *LGC*, p. 32. **Hurrah for positive**/*LGC*, p. 51. **one deep purpose**/*NUPM*, II: 461. **divine literatus**/*PW*, II: 365. **I am not prepared**/*WWC*, I: 149. **leading characteristic**/*JM*, p. 30. **had pretty vigorous ideas**/*Calamus: A Series of Letters Written During the Years 1868–1880 by Walt Whitman to a Young Friend*, ed., Richard Maurice Bucke (Boston: Laurens Maynard, 1897), p. 28. **a big valuable book**/*WWC*, IV: 239. **Each particle of matter** and **The eye**/Lavater, in Frederic H. Hedge, *Prose Writers of Germany* (Philadelphia: Porter & Coates, 1847), pp. 191, 198. **the relation between**/ *NUPM*, I: 258. **Emerson had opened up**/With Emerson, Whitman told Traubel, "all is fluid, uncertain," in *WWC*, III: 453. **held together by** and **one consistent** and **the most radical**/*NUPM*, I: 259, 260. **the vast all**/*LGC*, p. 274. **No terms are too high**/*BE*, June 28, 1847. **acting on** and **The truly great**/Channing, "Self-Culture," in *The Works of William Ellery Channing, D. D.* (Boston: American Unitarian Association, 1896), pp. 15, 13. **Ranting and**/ "Song of Myself," *LGC*, p. 79. **Introduce some scene**/*PW*, I: 99. **one essentially perfect**/*PW*, II: 549. **The new theologies** and **It is America**/*NUPM*, VI: 2043, 2099. **It was only fair**/*WWC*, I: 138. **The press is**/"The Present Age," in *Works of Channing*, p. 164. **our divine English**/In Blodgett, *Whitman* *in England*, p. 115. **I find letters**/*LGC*, p. 87. **a great absorber** and **his whole sermon**/*WWC*, II: 457. **John Herbert Clifford**/For his use of Whitman in the pulpit, see *WWC*, V: 333. **Magnifying and applying**/"Song of Myself," *LGC*, p. 75. **The time straying**/*WCP*, p. 9. **read these leaves**/*WCP*, p. 11. **The Great Construction**/*NUPM*, I: 353. **I too, following**/"Starting from Paumanok," *LGC*, p. 20. **No: tell me**/*Correspondence of Thoreau*, p. 445. **one of the richest**/ *NYA*, p. 106. For a useful discussion of the developing relationship between the two writers, see Jerome Loving, *Emerson, Whitman, and the American Muse* (Chapel Hill: University of North Carolina Press, 1982). **one of Ralph**/*BE*, December 15, 1857. **simmering** and **to a boil**/Trowbridge, "Reminiscences," p. 166. **The signs are**/*WCP*, p. 26. **a devout disbeliever**/New York *Sunday Times*, August 14, 1842. There is some discussion of mesmerisim in David Kuebrich, *Minor Prophecy: Walt Whitman's New American Religion* (Bloomington: Indiana University Press, 1989), p. 38. Kuebrich provides a fine overview of Whitman's religious vision in its cultural context. Also illuminating is George B. Hutchinson, *The Ecstatic Whitman: Literary Shamanism and the Crisis of the Union* (Columbus: Ohio State University Press, 1986). **between twenty and thirty thousand**/See Robert C. Fuller, *Mesmerism and the American Cure of Souls* (Philadelphia: University of Pennsylvania Press, 1982), p. 30. **He can change**/Dods, *The Philosophy of Electrical Psychology* (New York: Fowlers & Wells, 1850), p. 20. **Ever since** and **Electricity** and **the electricity**/ Dods, *Electrical Psychology*, pp. 19, 61, 71. **Magnetism, or electricity**/O. Fowler, *Love and Parentage*, p. 25. **I have instant**/*LGC*, p. 57. **O resistless**/ *LGC*, p. 91. **I sing the body**/"I Sing the Body Electric," *LGC*, p. 93. **a singular compound** and **wildness and** and **spreading with**/*BT*, May 28, 1857. **There can be no doubt**/*BT*, June 26, 1857. **spiritualist** and **the lawgivers**/*WCP*, p. 15. **I am the mate**/"Song of Myself," *LGC*, p. 35. **I know I am deathless**/ "Song of Myself," *LGC*, p. 48. **He is the true**/*InRe*, p. 19. **The poets are divine** and **convey gospels**/*LGC*, p. 481. **O! mediums!**/"Apostroph," *LGC*, p. 602. **Something unproved**/"A Song of Joys," *LGC*, p. 179. **the spirits of dear**/ "These I Singing in Spring," *LGC*, p. 118. **the rapt promises**/"As I Walk These Broad Majestic Days," *LGC*, p. 487. **his spiritual discoveries**/*BT*, June 15, 1858, in *UPP*, II: 16. **Born in 1686**/A comprehensive discussion of Swedenborg and his influence in America is provided in Marguerite Beck Block, *The New Church in the New World* (1932; rpt., New York: Octagon, 1968). **conjugial love**/For Swedenborg's doctrines of sex, see especially Emanuel Swedenborg, *The Delights of Wisdom Pertaining to Conjugial Love* (1768; rpt., New York: Swedenborg Foundation, 1928). **This age is**/*The Journals of Ralph Waldo Emerson* (Boston and New York: Houghton Mifflin, 1909–14), VIII: 477. **a very clear**/*BE*, May 25, 1846. **some beautiful idea**/*New Orleans Daily Crescent*, March 10, 1848, in *UPP*, I: 194. **the deepest and**/*BT*, June 15, 1858, in *UPP*, II: 18. **Another self**/*LGC*, p. 158. **[H]aving look'd at**/*LGC*, p. 23. **dumb, beautiful** and **none else** and **furnish your**/*LGC*, p. 165. **Nor my material**/*LGC*, p. 181. **For I know I bear**/*LGC*, p. 207. **Floyd Stovall's comment**/In Stovall, *The Foreground of Leaves of Grass* (Charlottesville: University Press of Virginia,

1974), p. 247. **Thank God for the**/Tyndale to Whitman, letter of June 24, 1857; Feinberg. **Partaker of influx** and **Through me the**/*LGC*, pp. 50, 52. **Here is the efflux**/*LGC*, p. 153. **The efflux of the soul**/"Song of the Open Road," *LGC*, p. 153. **I inhale with equal**/In Block, *New Church*, p. 138. **The smoke of my own**/*LGC*, p. 29. **I think Swedenborg**/*WWC*, V: 376. **When intelligence**/In Block, *New Church*, p. 142. **There is also ample**/Wilkinson, *The Human Body and Its Connection with Mann, Illustrated by the Principal Organs* (London: Chapman & Hall, 1851), pp. 347–48. **I believe in you my soul**/*LGC*, p. 33. **Foucault goes so far**/Foucault, *Language, Counter-Memory, Practice: Selected Essays and Interviews*, ed. Donald F. Bouchard (Ithaca: Cornell University Press, 1977), pp. 29–30. **We are all Lovers**/Harris, *An Epic of the Starry Heaven* (New York: Partridge & Brittan, 1854), p . 38. **In describing God**/See Block, *New Church*, pp. 32–33. **The great Camerado**/"Song of Myself," *LGC*, p. 372. **As God comes**/*LV*, I: 4. **Thou, thou the**/"Gods," *LGC*, p. 269. **The clairvoyant**/Davis, *Memoranda of Persons, Places, and Events ... in Magnetism, Clairvoyance, Spiritualism* (Boston: William White & Co., 1868), p. 284. **Between 1845 and '47**/Allan Nevins, *The Ordeal of the Union* (New York: Scribner's, 1947), I: 116. For other trance lecturers, see especialy the discussion in Ann Braude, *Radical Spirits: Spiritualism and Women's Rights in Nineteenth-Century America* (Boston: Beacon, 1989), pp. 20, 88–90. **there was no limit**/S. B. Brittan, introduction to Harris, *Epic of the Starry Heaven*, p. viii. **I am in a mystic**/*NUPM*, I: 194. **in a trance**/*WWW*, p. 191. **My ties and ballasts**/*LGC*, p. 61. **Walking the old hills** and **Speeding through**/"Song of Myself," *LGC*, p. 64. **seven spheres**/Harris, *Epic of the Starry Heaven*, p. 58. **Speeding amid the**/*LGC*, p. 64. **It avails not**/*LGC*, p. 160. **An unknown sphere** and **I depart from**/*LGC*, p. 506. **composed of magnetism**/Davis, *The Philosophy of Spiritual Intercourse* (New York: Fowlers & Wells, 1851), p. 20. **We shall know**/Lazarus, *Comparative Psychology and Universal Analogy* (New York: Fowlers & Wells, 1852), p. vii. **One of the most effectual**/Lazarus, *Passional Hygiene and Natural Medicine; Embracing the Harmonies of Man with His Planet* (New York: Fowlers & Wells, 1852), p. 194. **Press close bare-bosom'd** and **Smile O** and **You sea!**/"Song of Myself," *LGC*, p. 49. **A gigantic beauty**/*LGC*, p. 60. **Spirits who stand**/Harris, *Epic of the Starry Heaven*, p. 202. **Dazzling and tremendous**/"Song of Myself," *LGC*, p. 54. **I depart as air**/"Song of Myself," *LGC*, p. 89. **eyes dazzled** and **the fine centrifugal**/*LGC*, p. 161. **all men shall be**/Davis, *Philosophy of Spiritual Intercourse*, p. 176. **The Centripetal force** and **the Centrifugal force**/Lazarus, *Passional Hygiene*, pp. 107–9. **One of that centripetal**/"Song of Myself," *LGC*, p. 79. **He is the equalizer**/"By Blue Ontario's Shore," *LGC*, p. 347. **exact and plumb**/1855 preface, *WCP*, p. 12. **Of your soul**/"[Of Your Soul]," *LGC*, p. 653. **chaos or death**/"Song of Myself," *LGC*, p. 88. **I shall be good**/*LGC*, p. 89. **all who proclaim**/John Jay Chapman, in *Century of Whitman Criticism*, ed. Miller, p. 103. **The wretched features**/Quotations from "The Sleepers" are in *LGC*, pp. 424–33. **perhaps the only**/Editorial note to the poem, *LGC*, p. 424. **as in the rigmarole**/*Saturday Press*, June 30, 1860. **but perhaps not so**/*Critic* 15 (April 1, 1856): 171. **a** sign of the times/*H*, p. 84. rapt, absorbed and appeared like/*JM*, p. 29. indisputable that Walt/Johnston and Wallace, *Visits to Walt Whitman*, p. 99. quite determined/*C*, I: 43. a shallow thing, some little, and table rappings/ *C*, I: 208. we had a capital/*WCP*, II: 304. Nothing is ever really/"Continuities," *LGC*, p. 523.

9 / *Toward A Popular Aesthetic*

A third of his thirty-seven articles/Ruth L. Bohan, "'The Gathering of the Forces': Walt Whitman and the Visual Arts in Brooklyn," in *Walt Whitman and the Visual Arts*, ed. Geoffrey M. Sill and Roberta K. Tarbell (New Brunswick: Rutgers University Press, 1992), p. 2. slowly accomplishing/In Robert Taft, *Photography and the American Scene: A Social History, 1839–1889* (New York: Macmillan, 1938), p. 64. The photograph has this/*WWC*, IV: 125. In these *Leaves*/*NUPM*, IV: 1524. America produces and In daguerreotypes we beat/In Taft, *Photography and the American Scene*, pp. 72, 69. In New York/In Denise Bethel, "'Clean and Bright Mirror': Whitman, New York, and the Daguerreotype," *Seaport: New York's History Magazine* 26 (Spring 1992): 21. Another helpful discussion of Whitman and photography is Ed Folsom, "Whitman and the Visual Democracy of Photography," *Mickle Street Review* 10 (1988): 51–65. The implements/"A Song for Occupations" (original version), *LV*, I: 92. The camera and plate/"Song of Myself," (original version), *LV*, I: 18. You will see more *life*/This and the quotations in the next sentence are in *BE*, July 2, 1846, in *GF*, II: 113–17. The world will never die/Beecher, *Patriotic Addresses* (Boston: Pilgrim, 1887), p. 395. a capital artist/*Brooklyn Star*, February 20, 1846. We had many a talk/*WWC*, III: 552–53. illustrious Americans/My discussion here and in the following paragraph is informed by Alan Trachtenberg, *Reading American Photographs: Images as History, Mathew Brady to Walker Evans* (New York: Hill and Wang, 1989), pp. 43–63. Gabriel Harrison/Information on Harrison is derived largely from Stiles, *Civil ... History ... of the County of Kings*, II: 1152–56. New York has made over/In Bethel, "'Clean and Bright Mirror,'" p. 22. one of the best and perfect works/ In *Whitman and the Visual Arts*, pp. 6–7. they are honest/*WWC*, I: 131. You cannot look/In Trachtenberg, *Reading American Photographs*, p. 65. The well-taken photographs/"Song of Myself," *LGC*, p. 78. We could wish/*BE*, March 12, 1846; in *WLS*, p. 98. It is a well known/*BT*, November 10, 1858. Another very popular/Foster, *New-York by Gaslight*, ed. Stuart M. Blumin (1850; rpt., Berkeley: University of California Press, 1990), p. 160. In a little house/*LGC*, p. 642. I speak of art now/*Form and Function: Remarks on Art by Horatio Greenough*, ed. Harold A. Small (Berkeley: University of California Press, 1947), p. 5. The quotations in the remainder of the paragraph are on pp. 75, xvi, 120, respectively. a nuisance and distorts honest and shall receive/ *WCP*, p. 19. transparent, plate-glassy/*NF*, p. 70. The rhyme and uniformity/ *WCP*, p. 11. Stop this day/"Song of Myself," *LGC*, p. 30. we shall never again/*GF*, II: 362–63. That picture on the wall/*WWC*, II: 348–49. from the art side/*WWC*, II: 354. literally died/"Osceola," *LGC*, p. 550. I saw the marriage/*LV*, I: 11–12. His heads of negroes/*American Whig Review* 14 (August 1851): 124. Mount's "last" and/*New York Evening Post*, February 1, 1851, in *UPP*, I: 238. disliked abolitionism/As Elizabeth Johns shows, the Democrat Mount subtly criticized abolitionists and Whigs in several paintings; see Johns, *American Genre Paintings: The Politics of Everyday Life* (New Haven, Conn.: Yale University Press, 1991), especially pp. 34–35. Johns also points out that Mount, while generally successful in overcoming the period's racism (especially in a painting like *The Power of Music*), did occasionally fall into near caricature, as in *Rustic Dance*. I agree with this assessment, but I would add that Mount's African-Americans are always far more sympathetically portrayed than those in most other areas of popular culture. the Negro, on the other hand/*Life and Writings of Frederick Douglass*, ed. Foner, II: 298–99. the negro holds firmly/"Song of Myself," *LGC*, pp. 39–40. the most prominent painter/William H. Gerdts, *Art Across America: Two Centuries of Regional Painting, 1710–1920* (New York: Abbeville, 1990), I: 147. the desire to be entirely/In James Thomas Flexner, *Nineteenth Century American Painting* (New York: G. P. Putnam's Sons, 1970), p. 92. a follower of no school and of a strictly/W. Alfred Jones, in *American Whig Review* 14 (August 1851): 126, 122. one line genre word/Burroughs, *Walt Whitman, A Study* (1896; rpt., New York: AMS, 1969), p. 143. Two lovers out and Lovers Economical/Alfred Frankenstein, *William Sidney Mount* (New York: Harry N. Abrams, 1975), pp. 130, 174. The one-year wife/"Song of Myself," *LGC*, pp. 42–43. The connoisseur/*LGC*, p. 42. a death blow/In Miles Tanenbaum, "Walt Whitman and American Art" (diss., University of Tennessee, Knoxville, 1988), p. 48. Some of my discussion of Whitman and art is indebted to this dissertation. Flatboatmen make/"Song of Myself," *LGC*, p. 44. The western turkey-shooting/"Song of Myself," *LGC*, p. 42. the prince of and the best of/*BE*, November 18, 1847. all he does/*BE*, April 14, 1847. The American painters who developed luminist style/A good overview of luminism is John Wilderming, *American Light: The Luminist Movement, 1850–1875* (New York: Harper & Row, 1980), especially Barbara Novak's article "On Defining Luminism," pp. 23–29. Give me the splendid/"Give Me the Splendid Silent Sun," *LGC*, p. 312. Shot gold/*LGC*, pp. 530–31. Painters have painted/*LGC*, pp. 233–34. a sublime murkiness/ *PW*, I: 268. For a discussion of Whitman and Millet, see Laura Meixner, " 'The Best of Democracy': Walt Whitman, Jean-Francois Millet, and Popular Culture in Post–Civil War America," in *Whitman and the Visual Arts*, pp. 28–52. the untold something/*WWC*, II: 407. really only Millet/*WWC*, I: 7. Albert Boime/"*Leaves of Grass* and Real Allegory: A Case Study of International Rebellion," in *Whitman and the Visual Arts*, pp. 53–84. one sparkling fellow/*WWC*, II: 502. There is no hardness/*New York Evening Post*, February 1, 1851, in *UPP*, I: 258. A show of summer/"The Sleepers," *LGC*, p. 430. Abroad, a similar subject/*UPP*, I: 238. Libbey: he was/ *WWC*, II: 506. Among such people/*UPP*, I: 241. To the artist and [W]ith this freshness/*UPP*, I: 243. I think of few and all great rebels and Read how

slaves/*UPP*, I: 246. **They want a strong**/*UPP*, I: 236. **an edifice certainly**/
BT, June 5, 1857, in *ISit*, pp. 129–30. *New York, Great*/*PW*, II: 681. **the power
of Art**/*The World of Science, Art, and Industry Illustrated from Examples in the
New-York Exhibition, 1853–54*, ed. B. Silliman and C. R. Goodrich (New York:
G. P. Putnam, 1854), p. 15. **The cylinder press**/"A Song for Occupations" (orig-
inal version), *LV*, I: 92. **Phantoms, countless**/*LGC*, p. 645. **the young man**/
LGC, p. 647. **The Hudson River school**/Stebbins, "Luminism in Context," in
Wilderming, *American Light*, p. 218. **that which distorts**/*WCP*, p. 19. **I find I
incorporate**/"Song of Myself," *WCP*, p. 59. **awaken an interest**/*H*, p. 23.
aside from America/*H*, p. 27. **We had ceased**/*H*, p. 56. **Lawrence Buell**/
"Transcendentalist Catalogue Rhetoric," in *On Whitman: The Best from 'Ameri-
can Literature'*, ed. Edwin H. Cady and Louis J. Budd (Durham, N.C.: Duke
University Press, 1987), p. 117.

10 / "I Contain Multitudes"

We now say/*Life and Writings of Frederick Douglass*, ed. Foner, p. 283. **pimps**/
WCP, pp. 1310, 1313, 1314. **These States need one**/*NUPM*, VI: 2115. **The poets
I would have**/*NUPM*, I: 144. **I know nothing more**/*NUPM*, VI: 2147. **In re-
gard to intelligence**/*NUPM*, V: 1987. **What a progress**/This and quotations
in the next sentence are in *WCP*, p. 1329. **We need satisfiers**/*NUPM*, I: 96.
Merits and/*LGC*, p. 344. **One part does not**/*LGC*, p. 168. **as Ezra Greenspan
suggests**/*Walt Whitman and the American Reader* (New York: Cambridge Uni-
versity Press, 1990), p. 83. Greenspan usefully discusses Whitman in the con-
text of nineteenth-century publishing. **All publishers are naturally**/*Life
Illustrated*, May 31, 1856. **on very little different**/In Johnston and Wallace,
Visits to Walt Whitman, p. 41. **inlaid with gilding**/*BE*, October 21, 1846.
printed in a fine sort/*BE*, December 18, 1847. **In tasty colored covers**/*BE*,
May 31, 1847. **Within ten years** and **He studies the binding**/Beecher, *Star
Papers; or, Experiences of Art and Nature* (New York: J. C. Derby, 1855), pp.
250, 251. **People as a rule**/*WWC*, VI: 131. **I think an edition**/*WWC*, IV: 417.
We have met her Fern Leaves/*Norton's Literary Gazette* 3 (September 15,
1853): 154. Ronald Zboray provides a useful overview of the book trade in *A
Fictive People: Antebellum Economic Development and the American Reading
Public* (New York: Oxford University Press, 1993). **the cheap mass-papers**/
NUPM, VI: 2147. **the anatomist chemist**/*WCP*, p. 15. **With the merely
technical**/*Edinburgh Review* 84 (April 1849): 191; Trent. **a new spirit** and
Who does not/Prefatory matter to "Second State" of 1855 edition of *Leaves of
Grass;* Oscar Lion Collection, New York Public Library. **O thou that rollest** and
Rise, moon and **Father of heroes**/Macpherson, *The Poems of Ossian* (Philadel-
phia: Thomas Cowperthwait, 1839), pp. 166, 214, 330. Whitman owned this edi-
tion of Ossian, which is in Feinberg. **How misty, how windy** and **Don't fall**
and **Ossian must**/*NUPM*, IV: 1806–7. **warning to himself**/*NUPM*, I: 54. **all
marvelous**/Warren, *The Lily and the Bee: An Apologue of the Crystal Palace*
(New York: Harper & Brothers, 1851), p. 23. The following quotations in this

paragraph are on pp. 26, 67, and 71–72. **one of the rare men**/*BE*, February 20, 1847, in *UPP*, I: 136. **To watch the workings**/Tupper, *Proverbial Philosophy: A Book of Thoughts and Arguments, Originally Treated* (London: Joseph Rickerby, 1838), p. 113; Whitman's copy in Feinberg. **as his precursors**/*Fortnightly Review* (1887), in *H*, p. 204. **the same with which**/*Leader*, July 1860; rpt., *Saturday Press*, July 28, 1860. **It is more like**/*Nation*, November 16, 1865, in *H*, p. 112. **Mr. Tupper, his newspaper**/London *Saturday Review*, July 7, 1860. **a wild Tupper**/London *Examiner*, March 22, 1856. **rapt, weird**/*BE*, October 17, 1846, in *UPP*, I: 129. For a discussion of other British Romantic influences on Whitman, see Kenneth M. Price, *Whitman and Tradition: The Poet and His Century* (New Haven, Conn.: Yale University Press, 1990). **brought to a boil**/Trowbridge, "Reminiscences," p. 166. **nationality and true Americanness**/*United States Democratic Review* 20 (March 1847): 271; Whitman's clipped copy in Trent. **immune from democratic**/Michael Paul Rogin, *Subversive Genealogy: The Politics and Art of Herman Melville* (New York: Alfred A. Knopf, 1983), p. 73. **We cannot yet throw**/In Cecil B. Williams, *Henry Wadsworth Longfellow* (Boston: Twayne, 1964), p. 38. **without spasms and**/In *The Native Muse: Theories of American Literature*, ed. Richard Ruland (New York: E. P. Dutton, 1972), I: 305. **essentially the scholar**/*WWC*, III: 549. **want of racy** and **the poet of melody**/*PW*, I: 285. **calmness and solidity**/Lewis Leary, *John Greenleaf Whittier* (Boston: Twayne, 1961), p. 61. **very few strings**/*WWC*, VI: 294. **the disciples of form**/*WWC*, III: 84. **morbidity, abnormal beauty**/*PW*, I; 232–33. **belonged to the classics** and **marvelously well** and **after all his**/*WWC*, III: 515; II: 3. **Although we have** and **A wild strawberry**/*JM*, pp. 15, 322–23. **Irving Lewis Allen**/*The City in Slang: New York Life and Popular Speech* (New York: Oxford University Press, 1993). **Now-familiar slang**/See Luc Sante, *Low Life: Lures and Snares of Old New York* (New York: Farrar, Straus and Giroux, 1991), p. 78. **the lawless germinal**/*PW*, II: 572. **Kenneth Cmiel**/*Democratic Eloquence: The Fight over Popular Speech in Nineteenth-Century America* (New York: William Morrow & Co., 1990). **the best complete**/*BE*, October 9, 1847. **to conform to our uses** and **great dictionary** and **strong coarse**/*DN*, III: 810, 811. **Many of the slang words** and **The woman should reserve**/*DN*, III: 735, 712. **In the South** and **The nigger dialect**/*DN*, III: 730. **Shelley Fisher Fishkin**/*Was Huck Black? Mark Twain and African-American Voices* (New York: Oxford University Press, 1993). **Murray** and **I like limber**/*DN*, III: 666, 742, 746. **the moneymaker**/Quotations in this sentence are, respectively, in *LV*, I: 110, 116, 133, 67; and *WCP*, p. 18. **mean, angered**/*LV*, I: 151. **I knew of the agents**/*LGC*, I: 135. **a suck and a sell**/"Song of Myself," *LV*, I: 25. **Every thing I have done**/*NUPM*, I: 167. **The doubts of the daytime**/"There Was a Child Went Forth," *LV*, I: 151. **Roger Asselineau**/See *Walt Whitman: The Evolution of a Poet* (1954; rpt., Cambridge, Mass.: Harvard University Press. 1960). Asselineau writes that Whitman was "tormented, unstable, storm-tossed; his work allowed him to recover his equilibrium and achieve serenity" (II: 259). **an assertion of**/*BT*, December 17, 1856, in *ISit*, p. 186. **It would be a sacrilege** and **The Walt Whitman who**/

WWC, II: 78, 535. **this poet with his private soul**/*Whitman, A Collection of Critical Essays*, ed. R. H. Pearce, pp. 13–14. **Denis Donoghue**/*Connoisseurs of Chaos: Ideas of Order in Modern American Poetry* (1965; rpt., New York: Columbia University Press, 1984), pp. 24–25. **embody the rude materials**/*BT*, April 12, 1856, in *NYD*, p. 56. **I celebrate myself**/*LV*, I: 1. **We want no reforms**/*NUPM*, I: 145. **blood and thunder romances**/*UPP*, II: 19. **maimed and mangled** and **dabs of**/*LV*, I: 54, 58. **yields nothing for the seeker**/*WWC*, III: 396. **Crimes against persons**/Spann, *The New Metropolis*, p. 314. **Horrible murders, stabbings** and **Rowdyism runs rampant**/*Atlas*, August 13, 1854, and September 17, 1854. **crime-haunted** and **the revolver**/*NYD*, pp. 140, 43. **One touch of nature**/*BT*, September 22, 1857, in *ISit*, p. 71. **Greater than wires**/*NUPM*, I: 129. **The courage of present times**/*LV*, I: 50–51. **one of my changes** and **All these I feel**/*LV*, I: 52. **The play of shine**/*LV*, I: 2. **The sickness of one** and **Apart from**/*LV*, I: 5. **Battles, the horrors**/*LV*, I: 5. **Not a cholera patient**/*LV*, I: 59. **the burial lines**/*LV*, I: 101. **the strange melancholy**/Alexis de Tocqueville, *Democracy in America*, ed. J. P. Mayer (1835; rpt., Garden City: Anchor, 1969), p. 538. **a genuine sense of crisis**/Holt, *The Political Crisis of the 1850s* (New York: John Wiley & Sons, 1978), p. ix. **Our country seems**/*NUPM*, I: 216. **There is something radically**/*BT*, August 8, 1857. **Morality and talent**/*NUPM* I: 302. **the sick-gray faces** and **The putrid and serpentine poison**/"The Sleepers," *LV*, I: 109; and 1855 preface, *WCP*, p. 21. **This is a face of bitter**/*LV*, I: 134. **every organ** and **Copulation is no**/ "Song of Myself," *LV*, I: 4, 32. **Cushion me soft**/*LV*, I: 28. **To any one dying**/ *LV*, I: 63. **I am he bringing health**/*LV*, I: 83. **Clear and sweet**/*LV*, I: 4. **partaker of influx**/*LV*, I: 28. **many long dumb** and **I am afoot with**/*LV*, I: 32, 44. **I rise extatic**/*LV*, I: 59. **Magnifying and applying**/*LV*, I: 63–64. **daily fingerings**/Thompson, *New-York Life*, p. 78. **Moon**/*Disseminating Whitman*, pp. 41–42. **We hurt each other**/*LV*, I: 28. **Is this then** and **own hands**/*LV*, I: 39. **Fierce Wrestler**/*NUPM*, I: 78. For a perceptive discussion of this and other Whitman passages from a gay perspective, see Martin, *The Homosexual Tradition in American Poetry*, chap. 1. **an average unending procession**/*LV*, I: 60. **The great poet**/Whitman's marginal note to a clipped magazine review of R. M. Milnes's *Life of Keats*; Trent. **The popular tastes**/*LV*, I: 98. **Allen Ascher**/"'No Respecter of Persons': Law and the American Renaissance" (diss., Graduate Center of the City University of New York, 1991). **Justice is not settled**/*LV*, I: 158–59. **The great laws**/*LV*, I: 153. **Him all wait for** and **His welcome is universal**/*LV*, I: 138, 139.

11 / *"The Murderous Delays"*

I could, I should/*WWC*, IV: 467. **If I had gone directly**/*WWC*, IV: 392. **It was certain**/Bucke, *Walt Whitman*, p. 138. **It is tragic** and **Nobody would have 'em**/*WWC*, I: 92; VI: 289. **I printed a thousand**/*WCP*, p. 1326. **found purchasers**/*Life Illustrated*, August 16, 1856. **Dear Sir**/In *LGC*, pp. 729–30. **Garry Wills**/*Lincoln at Gettysburg*. **To American literature**/Details about the

convention are in *New York Times*, September 28, 1855. **Emerson said that/**
Autobiography, Memory and Experiences of Moncure Daniel Conway (1904;
rpt., Negro University Press, 1969), I: 217. **a nondescript monster** and **if you
think/***The Correspondence of Emerson and Carlyle*, ed. Joseph Slater (New
York: Columbia University Press, 1964), p. 509. **the hero of unheard-of/***ISit*,
p. 132. **The whole system/***BE*, February 12, 1847, in *UPP*, II: 317. **is not only
willing** and *comparatively few notices/Life Illustrated*, December 12, 1855.
An American bard at last/Quotations in this paragraph are in *H*, pp. 34, 39.
class of society/Quotations in this sentence are in *H*, pp. 22, 23. **[I]t is a mix-
ture** and **the introduction of terms/**In *H*, 25, 24. **a mass of stupid** and **these
candid/**In *H*, p. 32. **many varieties of/**In *H*, p. 82. **American eccentricity/**
In *NYD*, p. 166. **a wild Tupper/**London *Examiner*, March 22, 1856, 180. **on a
level/***Punch* 20 (April 26, 1856): 169. **one of the most amazing/**In *ISit*, pp.
167–68. **heterogeneous mass** and **some escaped/**In *H*, p. 61. **freshness,
simplicity/**In *H*, p. 49. **There is not a word/**In *H*, p. 51. **immoral reform/**
See Reynolds, *Beneath the American Renaissance*, chap. 2. **Let him look care-
fully** and **I extract no/***NYD*, pp. 163–64. **should be kicked/**In *H*, p. 61. **We
have concluded/**Samuel R. Wells to Whitman, letter of June 17, 1856; Fein-
berg. **Depressions/***NUPM*, I: 167. **Is this melange/***NUPM*, I: 285. **Go back
to first** and **have no faith in man** and **countless breeds/***NUPM*, I: 285, 286.
murderous robbers/In Nevins, *Ordeal of the Union*, II: 440. **TO FREMONT,
OF NEW YORK/***WCP*, p. 1321. **the cheap book** and **are interlinking** and
bravery, friendship/*WCP*, p. 1308. **TO EDITORS OF THE/**Quotations in this
paragraph are in *WCP*, p. 1323. **That would tend** and **I want a beautiful book/**
WWC, II: 175; IV: 20. **the expresser of common/***WWC*, III: 24. **a pleasingly
ripply/***NUPM*, V: 1730. **piece of "buck-shot"/**N. Hawthorne, *The Letters,
1843–1853*, ed. Thomas Woodson, L. Neal Smith, and Norman Holmes Pearson
(Columbus: Ohio State University Press, 1985), p. 307. **Very devilish to some/**
In *H*, p. 45. **horse-whipped, bribed/**Bennett reprinted these remarks several
times, in the October 3, 4, 7, and 17, 1836, issues of the *New York Herald.* See
Stevens, *Sensationalism and the New York Press*, p. 40. **I much enjoy making/**
WCP, p. 1327. **The spectacle is a** and **one vast/***WCP*, p. 1332. **There is no
great** and **the people, like** and **This tepid wash/***WCP*, pp. 1331, 1335. **Not a
man** and **I love screaming/***WCP*, pp. 1331, 1336. **a national character** and **All
are prophetic** and **Poets here/***WCP*, pp. 1336, 1333. **The proof of the poet/**
"By Blue Ontario's Shore," *LGC*, p. 351. **Let him who is/***LV*, I: 262. **Let
churches accommodate/***LV*, I: 262, 263, 264. **By great bards only/**This and
quotations in the rest of the paragraph are from "By Blue Ontario's Shore," *LV*,
I: 197, 198. **Make it an American/***NUPM*, I: 299. **Weapon, shapely/***LGC*, p.
184. **I see the headsman/***LGC*, p. 192. **seminal muscle/***LGC*, p. 344. **Where
the city stands/***LGC*, pp. 189–90. **secret silent loathing** and **guile, anger,
lust/***LGC*, pp. 157, 163. **It is evident/***Life Illustrated*, August 16, 1856. **Dealers
send in/***ISit*, p. 242. **little or no sale/**Bucke, *Walt Whitman*, p. 9. **this self-
contained teacher/***H*, p. 70. **the grossest violation** and **which in their loath-
someness** and **is made to/***H*, pp. 63, 64. **Every epithet of rancor/**Burroughs,

Notes on Walt Whitman, p. 19. **insolence, philosophy**/*H*, p. 69. **poetic and suggestive**/*Canadian Journal*, November 1, 1856. **He wears his man-Bloomer**/*JM*, p. 333. **to make pomes** and **like two beasts**/ *JM*, pp. 334, 336. **That Walt Whitman** and **It is as if** and **By his heartiness**/*Correspondence of Thoreau*, pp. 444, 445. **his lawlessness**/*WWC*, III: 375. **Thoreau's great fault**/ *WWC*, I: 212. **the pigmies** and **Alcott, he fancies**/*JM*, p. 337. **a specialist** and **a department**/*WWC*, V: 194. **pure thought**/*C*, I: 42. The quotations in the next five paragraphs are on pp. 43–45. **I am sure they are not**/Tyndale to Whitman, letter of June 24, 1857; Feinberg. **publish another edition**/Tyndale to Whitman, letter of July 1, 1857; Feinberg. **wander-speaker** and **That the mightiest**/*NUPM*, IV: 1554. **a public Speaker**/*C*, I: 45. **henceforth my employment** and **by degrees** and **carefully perused**/*NUPM*, IV: 1440. **the principal object**/*NUPM*, I: 353. **In** *massiveness* and **finish** and **rhythms** and **You have too**/*NUPM*, I: 351. **intense love of excitement**/*BT*, August 17, 1857. **unless a 'dreadful murder'**/*BT*, December 6, 1858, in *ISit*, p. 148. **The frightful increase**/*BT*, August 5, 1857. **multitudes of undeveloped**/*BT*, June 27, 1857. **spleeny, sickly**/*BT*, October 17, 1858, in *ISit*, p. 117. **What is to be done**/*BT*, July 26, 1858. **We cannot take up a newspaper**/*BT*, September 2, 1857, in *ISit*, p. 113. **The cant of reformers**/*BT*, April 19, 1858, in *ISit*, p. 44. **excrescences** and **amiable**/*BT*, June 29, 1858, in *ISit*, p. 46. **perverted despotic control** and **rebellious defiance**/*BT*, May 22, 1857. **an** *imperium imperio*/*BT*, June 18, 1857. **The hungry hordes**/*BT*, July 8, 1857, in *ISit*, p. 93. **Pierce created**/*BT*, April 2, 1858, in *ISit*, p. 94. **the most sensible speaker a black man**/*BT*, September 14, 1858. **A universal feeling** and **I have no purpose**/ Lincoln, *Speeches and Writings 1832–1858*, pp. 511, 521. **It will be a** and **Who believes that** and **some secure and**/*BT*, May 6, 1858, in *ISit*, p. 90. **The social inferiority**/*BT*, April 22, 1858. **Who would not rather**/*BT*, November 5, 1858, in *ISit*, p. 98. **Disunion is**/*BT*, August 2, 1859, in *ISit*, p. 185. **It is the sentiment**/*BT*, August 20, 1858, in *ISit*, p. 160. **bound the sister-states**/*BT*, August 9, 1859. **His brother Jeff**/For illuminating accounts and documents related to Jeff and Mattie, see *Dear Brother Walt: The Letters of Thomas Jefferson Whitman*, ed. Dennis Berthold and Kenneth M. Price (Kent: Kent State University Press, 1984); and *Mattie: The Letters of Martha Mitchell Whitman*, ed. Randall H. Waldron (New York: New York University Press, 1977). **Your question, Abby**/*JM*, p. 275. **Frederik Schyberg's 1933 study**/*Walt Whitman* (1933; rpt., trans. from Danish by Evie Allison Allen, New York: Columbia University Press, 1951). **I loved a certain person**/*LGC*, p. 134. **It is now time to**/ *NUPM*, I: 405. **Dialogue—animation**/*NUPM*, I: 403. **You will have to know**/*WWC*, I: 214. **My own greatest pleasure**/*WWC*, I: 417. **Laugh on laughers**/*LGC*, p. 660. **We are opposed** and **has merely used**/*Saturday Press*, November 17, 1860. **The vault at Pfaff's**/*LGC*, p. 660. **wild and plaintive song**/*Saturday Press*, December 24, 1859. **the low and delicious word** and **But fuse**/*LV*, II: 350, 351. **The aria sinking** and **Demon or bird**/*LV*, II: 349. **feather'd guests**/*LV*, II: 344. The remaining quotations in this paragraph are on pp. 345, 347, 348. **singer solitary**/*LV*, II: 349. The remaining quotations in this paragraph are on p. 350. **gazing off southward**/*LV,* II: 319. The remaining quotations in this paragraph are on pp. 319, 320. **See, from my dead**/*LV,* II: 322. **in little pittance**/Quotations from the self-review are in *Saturday Press,* January 7, 1860. **You must become a force**/*NUPM,* I: 417. **We want to be the publishers**/William Thayer and Charles Eldridge to Whitman, letter of February 10, 1860; Feinberg. **hundreds of thousands**/*C,* I: 52.

12 /   *Brotherly Love, National War*

Year of meteors/*LGC,* pp. 238–39. **I would sing how**/*LGC,* p. 238. **I would sing your contest**/*LGC,* p. 238. **I create an immense**/*C,* I: 50. **Emerson with whom**/The only evidence of Emerson's visiting Whitman in Brooklyn is the latter's old-age recollection of Emerson one day gently knocking at the Whitman home and announcing, "I came to see Mr. Whitman." See *WWC,* II: 130. **essentially perfect orator**/*PW,* II: 549. **I am so satisfied**/*C,* I: 50–51. **the freshest and handsomest**/*C,* I: 52. **several tremendous**/*C,* I: 53. WALT WHITMAN'S LEAVES/*Leaves of Grass Imprints. American and European Criticisms of "Leaves of Grass"* (Boston: Thayer and Eldridge, 1860), back jacket. The remaining quotations in this paragraph are also on the back jacket. **They are go-ahead** and **They expect it**/*C,* I: 52. **an overwhelming demand**/Thayer and Eldridge to Whitman, letter of June 14, 1860; Feinberg. **because ... when you make** and **must be the one**/Thayer and Eldridge to Whitman, letter of July 27, 1860; Feinberg. **I will make a song**/"Proto-Leaf" (1860 version), *LV,* II: 277. **O a curse on him**/*LV,* II: 291. **scum floating atop** and **Who are they**/*LV,* II: 414. **Down in Texas**/*LV,* II: 296. **what alone** and **the real and permanent** and **Interlinked**/*LV,* II: 278, 279, 285. **all the meanness**/*LV,* II: 329. **ruthless and** and **What foul thought**/*LV,* II: 325. **Outside fair costume**/*LV,* II: 433. **Take my leaves**/*LV,* II: 276. **Whether I shall**/*LV,* II: 331. **rightly construed**/*C,* V: 72. **This relation is purer**/Hedge, *Prose Writers of Germany,* p. 238. **Friendship, like** and **Should not the**/"Friendship" (1841), in Emerson, *Essays & Lectures* (New York: Library of America, 1983), pp. 343, 351. **Primeval my love**/"Fast Anchor'd Eternal O Love!" (originally "Calamus. 38"), *LV,* II: 403. **High thanks I owe**/"Friendship," Emerson, *Essays & Lectures,* p. 343. **And when I thought**/"When I Heard at the Close of Day" (originally "Calamus. 11"), *LV,* II: 381. **Wafted in all**/"Not Heat Flames Up and Consumes" (originally "Calamus. 14"), *LV,* II: 384. **I share the midnight**/"Native Moments" (originally "Enfans d'Adam. 8"), *LV,* II: 359. **city of orgies** and **lovers, continual**/"City of Orgies" (originally "Calamus. 18"), *LV,* II: 388. **approval, admiration** and **among the young** and **wonderful tenacity**/*DN,* III: 740–41. **As to manly friendship**/*WCP,* p. 1335. **In the antislavery circles**/For ardent same-sex relationships among abolitionists, see Donald Yacavone, "Abolitionists and the 'Language of Fraternal Love,'" in *Meanings for Manhood: Constructions of Masculinity in Nineteenth-Century America,* ed. Mark C. Carnes and Clyde Griffen (Chicago: University of Chicago Press, 1990), pp. 85–95. **I love thee with**/"To William Lloyd Garrison" (1832), in *The Complete Poetical*

Works of Whittier (Boston: Houghton Mifflin, 1892), p. 262. **I lean my heart/** "To My Friend on the Death of His Sister" (1845), in *Complete Poetical Works of Whittier*, p. 181. **O dearly loved/**"Daniel Wheeler" (1840), in *Complete Poetical Works of Whittier*, p. 182. **Men often made/**For intense male relationships, see especially E. Anthony Rotundo, "Romantic Friendship: Male Intimacy and Middle Class Youth in the Northern United States, 1800–1900," *Journal of Social History* 25: 1–25. See also Rotundo, *American Manhood: Transformations in Masculinity from the Revolution to the Modern Era* (New York: Basic, 1993). For relationships between women, see Carroll Smith-Rosenberg, *Disorderly Conduct: Visions of Gender in Victorian America* (New York: Alfred A. Knopf, 1985); and Lillian Faderman, *Surpassing the Love of Men: Romantic Friendship and Love Between Women from the Renaissance to the Present* (New York: William Morrow and Co., 1981). **Often too [Anthony]/**In Rotundo, "Romantic Friendship," p. 7. **Yet comes one/**Originally "Calamus. 19," *LV*, II: 389. **For the one I love/**Originally "Calamus. 11," *LV*, II: 381–82. **the coming together/** *WWC*, III: 452. **the extravagant delight** and **the crushing force** and **Battering Ram/**In Martin B. Duberman, "'Writhing Bedfellows' in South Carolina," in *Hidden from History: Reclaiming the Gay and Lesbian Past*, ed. Duberman et al. (Markham, Ontario: New American Library, 1989), p. 155. **Michael Lynch/**"New York City Sodomy, 1796–1873," paper presented at New York University, 1985, p. 3. Sadly, Michael Lynch's death from AIDS on July 9, 1991, prevented his completion of the book he was working on. Lynch entrusted Bert Hansen with publishing his historical research. **There are no suggestions/**Lynch, "New York City Sodomy," p. 19. **in not a single reference/**Lynch, "Urban Space and New York City Sodomy: 1830–1860," paper presented at Hofstra University, Hempstead, New York, 1985, p. 5. **leprous male/***New-York Sporting Whip*, February 11, 1843. **resort for male/***National Police Gazette*, June 12, 1847. **the he-harlots and/***LV*, I: 263. **the alarming increase** and **A kiss should not/***BT*, September 15, 1857, in *ISit*, p. 114. **Revolting Developments/***BT*, January 25, 1858. **Candid from me/**Originally "Calamus. 15," *LV*, II: 385. **Sullen and suffering/**"[Hours Continuing Long]" (originally "Calamus. 9"), *LV*, II: 379. **means more or less/***WWC*, I: 77. **may be easily/**In Jonathan Katz, *Gay American History: Lesbians and Gay Men in the U. S. A.* (New York: Thomas Y. Crowell, 1976), p. 344. **The sodomite had been/**Michel Foucault, *The History of Sexuality* (New York: Pantheon, 1978), p. 43. See also Bert Hansen, "American Physicians' 'Discovery' of Homosexuals, 1880–1900: A New Diagnosis in Changing Society," in *Framing Disease: Studies in Cultural History*, ed. Charles E. Rosenberg and Janet Golden (New Brunswick, N.J.: Rutgers University Press, 1992), pp. 104–33. **morbid inferences** and **damnable** and **disavow'd/***C*, V: 71. **whose sexual instincts** and **During the last/**J. A. Symonds to Whitman, letter of September 5, 1890; Feinberg. **Before then, American men/**My discussion here is informed by George Chauncey, *Gay New York: Gender, Urban Culture, and the Making of a Gay Male World, 1890–1940* (New York: Basic Books, 1994). **although many ignorant/**In Hendrik M. Ruitenbeek, *Homosexuality and Creative Genius* (New York: Astor-

Honor, 1967), p. 129. **motherly** and **sort of male**/Ms. draft of *Walt Whitman;* Trent. See Bucke, *Walt Whitman*, pp. xvi, 164. **My wife is loving**/Vaughan to Whitman, letter of November 1874; Feinberg. **fond of direct pleasures**/ *NUPM,* I: 200. **a little too fond**/*WWC,* III: 543. **that it is every way the best**/ *C,* I: 323. **loves friends with tenderness**/O. S. and L. N. Fowler, *Illustrated Self-Instructor in Phrenology,* p. 57. An interesting discussion of this subject is Michael Lynch, "'Here Is Adhesiveness': From Friendship to Homosexuality," *Victorian Studies* 29 (Autumn 1985): 66–96. **instinctively recognize it** and **bind mankind**/O. Fowler, *Phrenology Proved, Illustrated and Accompanied by a Chart* (New York: Fowlers & Wells, 1842), p. 65. **Here is adhesiveness**/*LGC,* p. 153. **the amative love** and **adhesiveness, manly love**/*NUPM,* I: 412, 413. **Love and Amativeness**/In Freedman, *William Douglas O'Connor,* p. 224. **I announce adhesiveness**/*LV,* II: 450. **O adhesiveness**/*LV,* II: 376. **Not he, adhesive**/"Starting from Paumanok" (original version), *LV,* II: 281. **It is to the development**/*PW,* II: 415. **would never choose**/L. Fowler, *Marriage: Its Histories and Ceremonies* (New York: Fowlers & Wells, 1847), p. 99. **uttering joyous leaves**/Originally "Calamus. 20," *LV,* II: 390. **We appeal to**/In Leach, *True Love and Perfect Union,* p. 203. **private dear**/*The Works of Ralph Waldo Emerson* (Boston: Houghton Mifflin, 1878), XI: 197. **every man, in all points**/ François Charles Marie Fourier, *Passions of the Human Soul* (London and New York: H. Bailliere, 1851), p. 317. **Individual Sovereignty** and **the health of each member**/T. L. and M. G. Nichols, *Marriage: Its History, Character, and Results* (Cincinnati: Valentine Nicholson & Co., 1854), pp. 416, 417. **It is one of the United**/*WWC,* VI: 342–43. **the special meaning of**/*PW,* II: 471. **a secluded spot**/Quotations in this sentence are from "In Paths Untrodden" (originally "Calamus. 1"), *LV,* II: 365. **States!**/"[States!]" (in 1860 edition only, as "Calamus. 5"), *LV,* II: 371–72. **the brotherhood of lovers**/"When I Peruse the Conquer'd Fame" (originally "Calamus. 28"), *LV,* II: 397. **the institution of the dear**/"I Hear It Was Charged Against Me" (originally "Calamus. 24"), *LV,* II: 394. **for the last** and **My songs cease**/*LV,* II: 449, 451. **See projected**/"Proto-Leaf," *LV,* II: 274–75. **We find in it all**/*Illustrated News,* June 2, 1860. **centuries ahead**/*New York Sunday Mercury,* June 10, 1860. **the standard book**/ *Saturday Press,* June 23, 1860. **Until such time**/*Saturday Press,* June 2, 1860. **Such books as this**/*Saturday Review,* July 7, 1860. **Humanity shrinks**/*Momus,* May 24, 1860, in *ISit,* p. 182. **I have read it**/*Saturday Press,* June 23, 1860. **Walt ennobles everything**/*Saturday Press,* June 23, 1860. **It is the poet's design**/*Cosmopolite,* August 4, 1860. **with unprecedented boldness**/*City News,* October 10, 1860. **Know Walt Whitman that I am**/*WWC,* IV: 312–13. The remaining quotations from this letter and Whitman's and Traubel's comments on it are also on these pages. **In regard to money**/Thayer and Eldridge to Whitman, letter of October 11, 1860; Feinberg. **my bitter and relentless**/ Thayer to Whitman, letter of April 19, 1861; Feinberg. **many an assassin's knife**/*PW,* II: 501. The quotation in the next paragraph is also on this page. **Quicksand years that**/"Quicksand Years," *LV,* II: 479. **Poem on the Incompleted**/*NUPM,* I: 439. **So far, so well**/*Whitman and the Civil War,* p.

135. **with which to bring**/*PW*, I: 26. **The sign is reversing**/*LV*, II: 517. **Well-shaped and stately**/"Year of Meteors," *LV*, II: 502. **All of us here**/*C*, I: 57. **Where are the vaunts**/*PW*, I: 27. **Our city grows so fast** and **Brooklyn had such a rural**/*Walt Whitman's New York*, ed. Christian, pp. 137, 147. **shrubby, viny** and **Things are** and **its high-bred**/*Whitman and the Civil War*, pp. 47, 48. **tells me to pack** and **There was never a woman**/Hannah Heyde to Louisa Van Velsor Whitman [hereafter cited in notes as LVVW], around 1855; Feinberg. **Charlie has taken**/Hannah Heyde to LVVW, letter of July 21, 1861; Feinberg. The next quotation is from a letter to LVVW of around 1861; Feinberg. **the bed-buggiest** and **almost the only man**/*FC*, p. 215. **I like the poems**/*FC*, p. 215. The following quotations in this paragraph are, respectively, on pp. 226, 218, 222. **i think she is about**/LVVW to Whitman, letter of December 1863; Trent. **we had to advance** and **I am in tip top**/*Civil War Letters of George Washington Whitman*, ed. Jerome M. Loving (Durham, N.C.: Duke University Press, 1975), pp. 76, 132. **any pick pocket**/Comment by Charles Eldridge, in Freedman, *William Douglas O'Connor*, p. 130. **put in about three days**/*C*, I: 58. **Young man**/*NUPM*, II: 513. **some of them as important**/*BE*, January 5, 1863. **a man of strong**/*C*, I: 65. **said he considered**/*NUPM*, II: 663. **a werry little bedroom**/*C*, I: 63. **The O'Connor home**/*WWC*, III: 525. **in a bare and desolate room**/Trowbridge, "Reminiscences," p. 167. **death and sickness**/*C*, I: 59.

13 /   *"My Book and the War Are One"*

To thee old cause/"To Thee Old Cause," *LGC*, pp. 4–5. **the very centre**/*WWC*, III: 95. **[T]he whole book**/*PW*, II: 469. **the big men**/*C*, I: 283. **The Northern States**/*PW*, II: 427. The following quotations in this paragraph are, respectively, on pp. 427, 428, 429. The quotations in the next paragraph are, respectively, on pp. 430, 426–27. **no Abolition**/In Werner, *Tammany Hall*, pp. 100–1. **My paramount objective**/Lincoln to Horace Greeley, letter of August 22, 1862; in *The Collected Works of Abraham Lincoln*, ed. Roy P. Basler (New Brunswick, N.J.: Rutgers University Press, 1953), V: 388. **our topmost warning**/*PW*, II: 429. **When disunion has become**/In Werner, *Tammany Hall*, p. 94. **was not a corrupter**/In Summers, *The Plundering Generation*, p. 295. **the thunderstorm that purifies** and **like a keen**/In George Fredrickson, *The Inner Civil War: Northern Intellectuals and the Crisis of the Union* (1965; rpt., New York: Harper & Row, 1968), pp. 71, 75. **I rejoice in this war**/In Charles Royster, *The Destructive War: William Tecumseh Sherman, Stonewall Jackson, and the Americans* (New York: Alfred A. Knopf, 1991), p. 266. My discussion of the war here is influenced by Royster's book, especially chap. 6. **War! an arm'd race**/"First O Songs for a Prelude," *LGC*, p. 281. **Blow mad winds**/"Ship of Libertad," *LGC*, p. 66. **Our country is calling**/Frank Moore, *Lyrics of Loyalty* (New York: G. P. Putnam, 1864), 23–24. The Leland poem quoted at the end of this paragraph is on p. 91. **Rebels! 'tis our**/Frank Moore, *Anecdotes, Poetry and Incidents of the War, North and South* (New York: n.p., 1866),

p. 32. The following poem is on p. 34. **How good they look**/*LGC*, p. 281.
Through the windows/*LGC*, p. 283. **the money-shops** and **dazzling things**/
LGC, p. 286. The following quotations in the paragraph are, respectively, on
pp. 290, 289. **that wicked city**/*BE*, December 6, 1847. **The Nation's War Cry**/
See Louis M. Starr, *Bohemian Brigade: Civil War Newsmen in Action* (New
York: Alfred A. Knopf, 1954), p. 35. **O superb!**/"First O Songs for a Prelude,"
LGC, p. 280. **Thunder on!** and **Often in peace**/*LGC*, pp. 292–93, 583. **No
dainty rhymes**/*LGC*, p. 282. **[D]id you ask dulcet**/*LGC*, p. 323. **What a city**/
In Geoffrey C. Ward, *The Civil War. An Illustrated History* (New York: Alfred
A. Knopf, 1990), p. 57. **by far the richest**/*C*, I: 75. **it is dusty or muddy**/*C*, I:
95. **the visible fact**/*New York Times*, October 4, 1863. **the most complete**/*C*,
I: 68. **unsurpassed gallantry** and **Taking the army**/*NUPM*, II: 508. **To go to
battle**/*LGC*, p. 180. **The public have got**/In Royster, *Destructive War*, p. 240.
Royster's discussion of sensational news and the war on pp. 240–42 is useful.
American life is a series/T. L. Nichols, *Forty Years of American Life*, I: 275.
Well, mother, we are/*C*, I: 110. **a great desire**/*C*, I: 193. **I never cease**/*C*, I:
198. **The real war**/*PW*, I: 116. **[T]he fighting has been hard enough**/*C*, I:
220. **Multiply the above**/*PW*, I: 81. **The skirmishers begin**/*LGC*, pp. 317–18.
the feeling here and **I remain silent**/*C*, I: 117. **the devil's own work**/*C*, I:
136. **To the long rows**/*LGC*, p. 310. **a little book**/*C*, I: 69. **a crucifixion day**
and **reading aloud a Bible**/*PW*, I: 30, 56. **There were years** and **not chiefly**/
WWC, VI: 194–95. **I find the masses**/*C*, I: 73. **Not a bit**/*PW*, I: 65. **Arthur
Golden** and **Betsy Erkkila**/Golden, "Whitman's Revisions in the *Blue Book*,"
in *Walt Whitman, A Collection of Criticism* (New York: McGraw-Hill, 1974),
pp. 127–31; Erkkila, "Whitman and the Homosexual Republic," in *Walt Whitman: The Centennial Essays*, ed. Folsom, pp. 153–71. **One typical newspaper
anecdote** and **They kissed** and **Suddenly he**/In Moore, *Anecdotes, Poetry… of
the War*, pp. 60, 62, 288. **A remarkably sweet** and **our broad-browed**/Frank
Moore, *The Rebellion Record* (New York: G. P. Putnam, 1861–63; Van Nostrand,
1864–68), VII: 32; in Royster, *Destructive War*, p. 250. **You think them soft** and
Come nearer/Moore, *Lyrics of Loyalty*, pp. 308, 317. **Give him a kiss**/Hamm,
Music in the New World, p. 250. **often they seem very near** and **so good**/*C*, I:
125, 188. **the revelation of an**/*WWC*, IV: 195. **our affection is quite**/*C*, I: 81.
Lew is so good/*C*, I: 91. **Charles E. Benton**/*As Seen from the Ranks: A Boy in
the Civil War* (New York: Putnam, 1902), pp. 193–96. **anything should go
wrong**/*C*, I: 93. The quotations in the next two sentences are from I: 120, 187.
with the unprecedented and **perturbations**/*C*, I: 247. **immortal and mystic**
and **son of**/*LGC*, p. 304. **I supply often**/*C*, I: 159. **I can testify**/*Walt Whitman's Civil War*, ed. Walter Lowenfels (New York: Alfred A. Knopf, 1971), p. 94.
put away all feelings/In Fredrickson, *Inner Civil War*, p. 90. **As to the
Sanitary**/*C*, I: 111. **made ready to tally**/*NUPM*, II: 662. See also II: 675. **more
trimly attired**/Trowbridge, "Reminiscences," p. 167. **I have a nice plain** and
a new necktie/*C*, I: 103. **[Sumner] says that**/*C*, I: 73. **I am getting better**
and **I like fat**/*C*, I: 74. **[I]t is not the fault**/*C*, I: 78. The following quotations
in the paragraph are from I: 83. **For two or three**/*Whitman's Civil War*, ed.

Lowenfels, p. 260. **The cancellation of the writ**/For a good discussion, see Mark Neely, Jr., *The Fate of Liberty: Abraham Lincoln and the Civil Liberties* (New York: Oxford University Press, 1991). **War for the Union**/T. L. Nichols, *Forty Years of American Life*, I: 3. **enrol every man** and **a rebel in** and **[T]hese are exciting**/*C*, I: 63, 133, 209. **Inflation rates**/For an account of the war economy, see J. M. McPherson, *Battle Cry of Freedom*, pp. 443–7, 816–19. **The Secession War**/*PW*, II: 502. **By that war**/*PW*, I: 312. **UNIONISM, in its**/*PW*, I: 98. **I believe this Union**/*C*, I: 92. **Lew, the Union**/*C*, I: 134. **the flag, the tune**/*C*, I: 209. **every once in a while**/*C*, I: 114. **something of grandeur**/Whitman, conversation with Traubel, February 12, 1891, from ms. to be published as *WWC*, VIII; Feinberg. The quotations in the next sentence are also from this conversation. **The real military figure**/*WWC*, I: 257. **Others may say** and **Grant has taken**/*C*, I: 213, 219. **like a Norman baron**/Whitman, conversation with Traubel, February 12, 1891, from ms. to be published as *WWC*, VIII; Feinberg. **the Napoleonic figure**/*WWC*, I: 257. **Well, *he* looks**/*WWC*, III: 179. **I see the President** and **We have got so that**/*PW*, I: 59, 60. **He has a face**/*C*, I: 82. **canny shrewdness** and ***horse-sense***/*PW*, II: 603. The remaining quotations in this paragraph, respectively, are on pp. 602, 604, 603. The quotations in the next paragraph are on pp. 602–3. **the tragic splendor**/*PW*, I: 98. **I AM MYSELF ALONE**/In Smith, *American Gothic*, p. 81. **The hot passions of the South**/*PW*, II: 498–99. **A long and varied series**/*PW*, II: 508. **had spatter'd all over**/*PW*, II: 503. The remaining quotations in this paragraph are on pp. 504–6. The quotations in the next paragraph are on p. 508. **Had not all this terrible**/*PW*, II: 505. **there is a cement**/*PW*, II: 508. The following quotations in this paragraph are on p. 498. **[N]o monument will ever equal**/Beecher, *Patriotic Addresses*, p. 705. **not a word was spoken**/*NUPM*, II: 764. **In "Lilacs"**/Quotations from this poem in *LGC*, pp. 328–37. **This dust was once**/"This Dust Was Once the Man," *LGC*, p. 339.

14 / Reconstructing a Nation, Reconstructing a Poet

too much & too impressive/*C*, I: 261. The quotation in the next paragraph is also on p. 261. **the Verteber of Poetry**/*Memoranda During the War & Death of Abraham Lincoln*, ed. Roy P. Basler (Bloomington: Indiana University Press, 1962), p. 4. **With Victory on thy left**/*LGC*, p. 203. **The intimate, communal culture**/A useful study of the phenomena discussed in this paragraph is in Alan Trachtenberg, *The Incorporation of America* (New York: Hill & Wang, 1982). See also L. Levine, *Highbrow/Lowbrow*. **It is idle to cry**/See Rembert W. Patrick, *The Reconstruction of the Nation* (New York: Oxford University Press, 1967), pp. 1–10. **Just now the centralizing**/*Galaxy* V (May 1868): 535. **By that war**/*PW*, I: 312. **the great shifter** and **This murder**/Gurowski, *Diary* (New York: Burt Franklin, 1968), III: 51, 398. **three-rank breakdown** and **the incarnation**/Gurowski, *Diary*, III: 310. For more on Gurowski's admiration of Whitman, see Freedman, *William Douglas O'Connor*, pp. 138–39. **very crazy**/*WWC*, I: 274. **becoming a respectable**/*WWC*, III: 522. **one of the most**

conservative/*New York Times*, June 7, 1902. **I fear'd his ardent**/*PW*, II: 690. **a chosen knight**/*WWC*, V: 165. **There is something about these**/*PW*, I: 578–79. **Let us repair**/Mencken, *Prejudices, First Series* (New York: Alfred A. Knopf, 1929), pp. 249–50. **was wrong, was a free lover**/*NUPM*, II: 798. **He was of the sincere**/*WWC*, I: 3. **anonymous lascivious trash**/O'Connor, *The Good Gray Poet*, reproduced in Bucke, *Walt Whitman*, p. 108. **This was the hour**/*WWC*, I: 3–4. **I must bring out**/*C*, I: 285. **I think it may be a success**/*C*, I: 210. **I want it to have a large sale**/W. D. O'Connor to Ellen O'Connor, letter of August 13, 1864; Feinberg. **it delivers my ambition**/*C*, I: 247. The remaining quotations in this paragraph are also on this page. **It has been a melancholy**/*Nation*, November 16, 1865, in *H*, p. 110. **Whereas you had**/*Round Table* 2 (November 11, 1865): 147. **Gay Wilson Allen**/*Solitary Singer*, p. 375. **William is always** and **a milder type**/*WWC*, I: 33, 334. **He has been sneered at**/*Galaxy* 2 (1866): 606. The following quotations in this paragraph are on pp. 608, 609. **Yet he is, perhaps**/*Round Table* 2 (November 11, 1865), 148. **exhaled an impalpable**/*Calamus*, ed. R. M. Bucke, p. 11. **Damn the expurgated**/*WWC*, I: 224. An interesting discussion of Whitman's ambivalence about censorship is Ed Folsom, "*Leaves of Grass, Junior:* Whitman's Compromise with Discriminating Tastes," *American Literature* 63 (December 1991): 641–63. **Our cause gains fast**/In *H*, p. 127. **the best means of paving**/Conway to Whitman, letter of October 12, 1867; Feinberg. **I cannot & will not**/*C*, I: 352. **entire serenity** and **All really refined**/*C*, I: 348. **one long tirade** and **My book has never**/*C*, II: 17. **a beautiful volume** and **a tremendous big**/*C*, II: 31. **the horrible dismemberment**/*C*, II: 133. **The facts of rank-and-file**/*PW*, II: 535. **strenuously opposed the impeachment**/*New York Times*, June 7, 1902. **Johnson was not a foul**/*WWC*, VI: 147. **This is the place**/*C*, I: 265. **left us entirely**/*Great Issues in American History: From Reconstruction to the Present Day, 1864–1981*, ed. Richard Hofstadter (New York: Vintage, 1983), p. 21. **the pardoning power was**/*Great Issues*, ed. Hofstadter, p. 38. **I was near him**/*WWC*, IV: 98. **What I hear**/*C*, I: 265. **a real good berth** and **I like**/*C*, I: 294. **Stanbery was the man**/*WWC*, VI: 147. **a very kind, friendly** and **integrity: the sterling appeal**/*WWC*, IV: 280, 403. **I couldn't wish**/*C*, II: 26. **The republicans have exploited**/*C*, II: 15. **doing his best to injure**/*C*, II: 35. **a bad, bad** and **a trivial, damnable**/*WWC*, VI: 39; V: 287. **there was something in Johnson**/*WWC*, III: 157. **The son of a hotel porter**/A useful recent biography is Hans L. Trefousse, *Andrew Johnson: A Biography* (New York: W. W. Norton, 1989). See also Eric L. McKitrick, *Andrew Johnson and Reconstruction* (Chicago: University of Chicago Press, 1960). **There are two distinct**/*PW*, II: 514. The quotations in the next sentence are on p. 513. **One's-Self I sing**/"Inscriptions," *LGC*, p. 1. **solution of that paradox**/*PW*, I: 172. **For it is mainly**/*PW*, II: 374. **White men alone** and **less capacity for government**/In A. James Reichley, *The Life of the Parties: A History of American Political Parties* (New York: Free Press, 1992), p. 132. **passions, desires** and **black, divine-soul'd**/*LGC*, pp. 99, 145. **Sojourner Truth had such respect**/The story of Truth's rapturous response to *Leaves of Grass* is told in a letter from Elisa Seaman

Leggett to Whitman, June 22, 1881; Walt Whitman Collection, Library of Congress. **old black Sojourner Truth**/*C*, IV: 370. **all-embracing words**/In *Walt Whitman: The Measure of His Song*, ed. Perlman, Folsom, and Campion, p. 96. The following quotation from June Jordan is from her essay in this volume, pp. 343–52. **Certes, we cannot find**/*PW*, II: 588. **real warriors**/*NUPM*, II: 637. **some with physiognomies**/*NUPM*, II: 557. **Of the negro race he had**/*New York Times*, June 7, 1902. **As if we had not**/*PW*, II: 762. **yelling & gesticulating**/*C*, II: 35. **the black domination**/*PW*, I: 326. **Tonight I would say**/*NUPM*, VI: 2160. **That is one reason**/*WWC*, VI: 323. **Poem of the Black person**/*NUPM*, IV: 1346. **there developed a theory**/See John S. Haller, Jr., *Outcasts from Evolution: Scientific Attitudes of Racial Inferiority, 1859–1900* (Urbana: University of Illinois Press, 1971); and Mark H. Haller, *Eugenics: Hereditarian Attitudes in American Thought* (New Brunswick: Rutgers University Press, 1963). **Of the black question**/Reprinted with commentary in Geoffrey Sill, "Whitman on 'The Black Question': A New Manuscript," *Walt Whitman Quarterly Review* 8 (Fall 1990): 69–75. The quotations in the next paragraph are from this article. **The nigger, like the Injun**/*WWC*, II: 283. **a master-man** and **of the school of the great**/*WWC*, I: 128; VI: 357. **the belief in the Negro's**/J. S. Haller, *Outcasts from Evolution*, p. 41. See also Fredrickson, *The Black Image in the White Mind*, p. 324. **very intelligent**/For the views of Lincoln and other political leaders on African-American suffrage, see R. W. Patrick, *The Reconstruction of the Nation*, pp. 23 and 53; also, McKitrick, *Johnson and Reconstruction*, pp. 53–56. **a new & much better**/*C*, I: 330. **the rascal Charles**/*C*, III: 42. **"Tears"**/*LGC*, p. 256. **"The City Dead-House"**/*LGC*, p. 367. **This kind of disembodied**/For a discussion of the changing pictorial nature of Whitman's verse, see Tenney Nathanson, *Whitman's Presence: Body, Voice, and Writing in 'Leaves of Grass'* (New York: New York University Press, 1992). **biography famous** and **Only a few**/"When I Read the Book," *LGC*, p. 8. **Slavery—the murderous**/*LV*, I: 196. **the menacing arrogant**/*LV*, I: 197. **I say man shall not**/*LV*, II: 436. **Carlyle's article**/Quotations in the following paragraph are from "Shooting Niagara" in Carlyle, *Critical and Miscellaneous Essays* (New York: AMS Press, 1969), pp. 3–30. **the rolling, mountainous** and **spare those spasms** and **Once, before the war**/*Democratic Vistas*, ed. Trachtenberg, pp. 357, 362. **a sort of dry** and **the most tremendous failure**/*PW*, II: 372, 363. **Acrid the temper**/*Democratic Vistas*, ed. Trachtenberg, p. 361. **I will not gloss over**/*PW*, II: 363. **Carlyle did not believe**/*WWC*, VI: 39. **roused to much anger** and **since read it** and **sharp, cutting**/*PW*, II: 375. **What a needed service** and **His rude, rasping**/*PW*, I: 250, 261. **the Secession War** and **death-threatening impedimenta**/*PW*, II: 473. **I have never had the least**/*PW*, II: 487. **The spectacle is appaling**/*PW*, II: 369–70. **Stifled, O days!**/*LV*, I: 261. **the most thoroughly *American***/PW, I: 262. **Only Hegel**/*NUPM*, VI: 2011. **rising out of the previous** and **original authors**/*PW*, II: 410. *moral purpose* and **new breed**/*C*, II: 151, 154. **I am the more assured**/*PW*, I: 260. **How can we ever**/*WWC*, II: 65. **Evolution ... is not**/*PW*, II: 675. *Leaves of Grass* **is** *evolution*/*WWC*, VI: 129. **the fruition of democracy** and upon things and by maps/*PW*, II: 390–91. model fit for and primary moral and penetrating Religiousness/*PW*, II: 397–98. David Leverenz/*Manhood and the American Renaissance* (Ithaca: Cornell University Press, 1989). the great cities & towns/*NUPM*, II: 540. America's total wealth/Statistics here from Andrew Carnegie, *Triumphant Democracy: or Fifty Years' March of the Republic* (London: Sampson, Low, Marston, Searle & Rivington, 1888), pp. 2, 149. In modern times/*NUPM*, III: 1078. I perceive clearly/*PW*, II: 384–85. I see that the only/*C*, II: 88. I demand races of orbic bards/*PW*, II: 407. a bad humming feeling/*C*, I: 79. deathly faintness/*C*, I: 231. it is all from that/*C*, II: 86. [T]hat secession war experience/*C*, V: 23. I am totally/*C*, V: 146. I had to give up/*Walt Whitman's Civil War*, ed. Lowenfels, p. 16. a stranger in their/*WWC*, III: 525. the one seemed to us/*InRe*, p. 36. i said no/LVVW to Whitman, letter of March 31, 1869; Trent; in *FC*, p. 201. Mother ... will you ask/Hannah Heyde to LVVW; in *FC*, p. 211. i dont know what i/LVVW to Whitman, letter of October 10, 1871; Trent. O walt aint it sad/LVVW to Whitman, letter of March 24, 1879; Trent. We were familiar/*Calamus*, ed. Bucke, p. 23. I was unspeakably/*C*, II: 84. Walt was too clean/*Calamus*, ed. Burke, p. 25. a great big hearty/*WWC*, III: 543. I also made love and all on the square and they are all/*C*, II: 62, 63. that young lady/Doyle to Whitman, letter of September 27, 1868; Morgan Library. the bedfellow business/*C*, I: 51. Dear son and Good-bye—my and Here is a good buss/*C*, II: 107, 125, 172. Jacques Lacan/For a good overview of Lacan's psychological theories, see Malcolm Bowie, *Lacan* (Cambridge, Mass.: Harvard University Press, 1991). I never dreamed/*C*, II: 101. private border-line and He had a freezing/*Calamus*, ed. Bucke, pp. 22–23. The newspapers still keep/*NUPM*, II: 897. *Walt Whitman's case*/*NUPM*, III: 936. Ellen Eyre/This letter is reproduced in Emory Holloway, "Whitman Pursued," in *On Whitman*, p. 106. the one I told/*NUPM*, II: 488. an old sweetheart/*WWC*, I: 389. 'Taint true/*WWC*, II: 425. very coarse/*C*, II: 219. Give me for marriage/"Give Me the Splendid Silent Sun," *LGC*, p. 312. Towards women generally/*Calamus*, ed. Bucke, p. 25. For me the reading/A. Gilchrist to William Michael Rossetti, letter of June 23, 1869; Feinberg. The following two quotations are from a July 11 letter from Gilchrist to Rossetti; Feinberg. these beautiful, despised/*The Radical* 7 (May 1870): 354. It was the divine soul and the divineness and Bride, wife/*C*, II: 135–36. I too send my and My book is my/*C*, II: 140. Dear Friend/*C*, II: 170. Nothing in my life/*C*, II: 161. a sweet & rich/*C*, III: 412. She was harmonic/*WWC*, IV: 93. his story "The Carpenter"/For a good discussion of this story, see especially J. Loving, *Walt Whitman's Champion*, p. 85; and Freedman, *William Douglas O'Connor*, pp. 209–12. A recent claim/David Cavitch, *My Soul and I: The Inner Life of Walt Whitman* (Boston: Beacon, 1985), pp. 181–83. I know enough of Southern/*WWC*, VII: 158. O'Connor became enraged/In Barrus, *Whitman and Burroughs*, p. 96. corroborated by Nelly O'Connor/In her version, the split resulted from a quarrel over the Fifteenth Amendment, "Walt taking the ground that the negroes were wholly unfit for the ballot, and Mr. O'Connor and others believing that the measure was the only one to adopt."

In *JM*, p. 211. **Yes ... we had** and **he would go for me**/*WWC*, VII: 189; III: 77–78. **The union promises**/*C*, II: 237.

15 /   *The Burden of Atlas*

America, my country/Barrus, *Whitman and Burroughs*, p. 300. **Between 1850 and 1880**/A. Carnegie, *Triumphant Democracy*, p. 2. The following statistics in this paragraph are, respectively, from pp. 149, 202, 12. The quotation at the end of the paragraph is on p. 1. **type of the modern**/"To a Locomotive in Winter," *LGC*, p. 472. **the history of modern** and **a new breed of man**/Noble, *America by Design: Science, Technology, and the Rise of Corporate Capitalism* (New York: Alfred A. Knopf, 1977), pp. xxiii, 33. **a great work**/*C*, I: 326. **possibly the best**/E. D. Meier, statement read before the St. Louis Engineer's Club, December 17, 1890; Feinberg. **There is more of me**/*WWC*, I: 166. **Singing the great achievements**/*LGC*, p. 411. Further quotations from "Passage to India" are from pp. 411–21. **evolution—the one thing**/*WWC*, I: 167. **Away with themes**/*LGC*, p. 201. Further quotations from "Song of the Exposition" are on pp. 195–205. **Melt, melt away**/*LGC*, p. 362. Further quotations from "The Return of the Heroes" are on pp. 358–64. **the national poet** and **a good elocutionist** and **Our Great Poet**/New York *Commercial Advertiser*, September 7, 1871; New York *Evening Post*, September 7, 1871; New York *Globe*, September 7, 1871. However, on September 8 the *New York Times* and the New York *World* commented that Whitman's voice did not project well in the noisy room. **magnificent original**/Board of Managers to Whitman, September 11, 1871; Feinberg. **been engaged**/*C*, II: 113. **My new edition looks**/*C*, II: 169. **Myself effusing**/*LGC*, p. 390. **The voyage of the**/*LGC*, p. 277. **Haply the only**/*LGC*, p. 455. **measureless oceans** and **seeking the spheres**/*LGC*, p. 450. **stintless, lavish**/*LGC*, p. 381. **Still though the**/"Still Though the One I Sing," *LGC*, p. 13. **I'd sow a seed**/Quotations from "Thou Mother with Thy Equal Brood" are in *LGC*, pp. 455–61. **Nay, tell me not**/*LGC*, p. 578. Quotations in the first two sentences of the next paragraph are also on p. 578. **Yearning for thee**/Quotations from "Wandering at Morn" are in *LGC*, pp. 399–400. **a slight stroke of**/*C*, II: 192. **the best Doctor**/*WWC*, IV: 472. **something pressing**/*C*, II: 215. **i never had any one**/LVVW to Whitman, letter of [Spring] 1873; Trent. **i have not felt**/LVVW to Whitman, letter of May 1, 1873; Trent. **Helen Price**/For her account of the funeral, see *JM*, p. 282. **the great dark cloud**/*C*, II: 242. **I sit by the form**/"As at Thy Portals Also Death," *LGC*, p. 497. **I want to ask you**/Hannah Heyde to Whitman, letter of June 7, 1873; Feinberg. **living day**/*WCP*, II: 231. **a long continued**/*C*, II: 240. **It has been a good**/*C*, II: 222. **Camden was originally**/*WWC*, II: 29. **MEMORANDA**/*NUPM*, III: 954. **Named after the British**/My main source of information about Camden and its history is George R. Prowell, *The History of Camden County, New Jersey* (Philadelphia: L. J. Richards, 1886). **The trains of the Camden**/*C*, II: 71. **misery, terror, destitution**/*PW*, I: 169. **social and economic** and **If the United States**/*PW*, II: 527, 528. **Fierce-throated beauty**/Quotations from the poem are in *LGC*, p. 472. **Populous cities**/Quotations from "Song of the Redwood-Tree" are in *LGC*, pp. 206–10. **History's type**/Quotations from "Prayer of Columbus" are in *LGC*, pp. 421–23. **unconsciously put**/*C*, II: 272. **Come said**/Quotations from "Song of the Universal" are in *LGC*, pp. 226–29. **Ever the**/Quotations from "Eidólons" are in *LGC*, pp. 5–8. **have coined their Walt Whitman** and **the first shilling**/*NUPM*, III: 961. **bade fair to be**/Quotations in this paragraph are in *West Jersey Press*, January 26, 1876. **your very kind letter**/*Memoranda During the War*, ed. R. P. Basler, p. 18. **as Ed Folsom has shown**/"'Affording the Rising Generation an Adequate Notion': Whitman in Nineteenth-Century Textbooks, Handbooks, and Anthologies," *Studies in the American Renaissance* (1991): 345–74. **must have his scores**/*H*, pp. 176–77. **all my favorites**/*Parnassus*, ed. Emerson (Boston: James R. Osgood, 1875), p. iii. **the noblest product**/"Walt Whitman, the Poet of Joy," *Gentleman's Magazine*, December 1875. **I often hear**/Mary Van Nostrand to Whitman, letter of March 16, 1875; Trent. **I feel yet**/*C*, II: 343. **Walt, don't you**/*WWC*, IV: 61. **Hippolyte Taine**/Whitman actually wrote an abridgment of Taine's *History of English Literature* sometime in the early 1870s. See *NUPM*, III: 1075. **He was a theoriser about**/*Century of Whitman Criticism*, ed. Miller, pp. 64–65. **The main object** and **I seek to typify** and **as a type**/*C*, II: 151, 154; III: 307. **The common people**/*Century of Whitman Criticism*, ed. Miller, p. 60. **Longfellow ... is one**/Quotations in this paragraph are in *H*, pp. 143–45. **Then Whitman has a fond**/*NUPM*, III: 977. **even worse than**/*C*, III: 20. **For twenty years**/*West Jersey Press*, May 24, 1876. **It is ludicrously false**/Conway to Whitman, letter of April 24, 1875; Feinberg. **Though without employment**/*C*, III: 47. **As to my literary situation**/*C*, III: 31. **The new edition**/*C*, III: 88. **(The Muse invited** and **culminating in this**/*LV*, III: 612. **a sort of one-horse**/*C*, III: 52. **Does me good**/*C*, III: 219. ***Idle Days*** and ***Little Loafings***/*NUPM*, III: 1061. **an average of $1,270**/See *Walt Whitman Review* 24 (March 1978): 36–37. **True religion** and **O that I**/*C*, III: 207, 216. **my (adopted)** and **my nephew**/*C*, III: 68. **There is not**/*C*, III: 211. **Dear Hank**/*C*, III: 215. **Down at White Horse**/*DN*, I: 54. **the occasional ridiculous**/*C*, III: 215. **There is nothing**/*C*, III: 77. **In the name of CALAMUS**/*WWC*, III: 444–45. **soothing & nourishing** and **emotional adhesive** and **[B]ut do you**/*C*, II: 97. **the Greek and Germanic** and **The dear love**/*LGC*, p. 121. **traced passionate friendship** and **burning for a revelation**/*WWC*, I: 73. **asked you questions**/*WWC*, I: 203. **has a few doubts**/*WWC*, I: 73. **I thank you continuously**/Carpenter to Whitman, letter of July 12, 1874; Feinberg. **I believe on the contrary**/Carpenter to Whitman, letter of January 3, 1876; Feinberg. **the same hardness**/*C*, II: 288. **the peculiar glory of These**/*NUPM*, IV: 1527. **He visits New York**/*DN*, I: 51. **the most advanced**/*PW*, I: 239. **either a god**/Bucke, *Walt Whitman*, p. vi. **The character you give me**/*C*, III: 266. **a very creditable**/*C*, III: 267. **Although the park had been**/See David Schulyer, *The New Urban Landscape: The Redefinition of City Form in Nineteenth-Century America* (Baltimore: Johns Hopkins University Press, 1986), p. 126. **Why is it not**/*DN*, I: 144. **I'm honest when I say**/*WWC*, II: 304. **smoke, coke-furnaces** and **I thought**/*PW*, I: 205, 206. **advance**

beyond and **a message by** and **in products**/ *PW*, I: 206, 212, 224. **A newer garden**/"The Prairie States," *LGC*, p. 402. **Land of pure air**/*DN*, III: 630. **A race of**/*DN*, III: 646. **dominated by one word** and **now** *Business* and **an immense**/*NUPM*, III: 1074. **there never was**/*C*, III: 323. **high-pitched, but**/ "Walt Whitman in Boston," *New England Magazine* (August 1892): 716. **killed with kindnesss**/*PW*, I: 269. **markedly plain & simple** and **as eligible as possible**/*C*, III: 226, 243. **Fair warning**/*C*, III: 224. **The portrait is required** and **It is to be hoped**/Kennedy, *The Fight of a Book for the World* (West Yarmouth, Mass.: n.p., 1926), p. 248. **The worst thing**/*WWC*, IV: 150. **I, now thirty-seven**/*LV*, I: 1. **the most beautiful region**/*C*, III: 237. **The passionate toll**/"The Sobbing of the Bells," *LGC*, p. 500. **So Emerson is**/*C*, III: 274. **rushing amorous contact**/*LGC*, p. 274. **One great anomaly**/*Critic*, November 5, 1881, in *H*, 183. **Charlie sits here** and **I believe** and **Some want to**/Hannah Heyde to Whitman, letter of November 1881; Feinberg. **so universal, so comprehensive**/Lloyd Lewis and Henry Justin Smith, *Oscar Wilde Discovers America* (New York: Harcourt, Brace, 1936), p. 65. The following account of Wilde's first meeting with Whitman in Camden is based mainly on this book. **a strong, able fellow**/*WWC*, V: 284. See also II: 192; III: 264–66. **There is no one**/*The Letters of Oscar Wilde*, ed. Rupert Hart-Davis (New York: Harcourt, Brace & World, 1962), p. 100. **would later tell George Ives**/Ellmann, *Oscar Wilde* (New York: Alfred A. Knopf, 1988), p. 171. **Have you read about**/*C*, III: 264. **The Public Statutes**/Stevens to Osgood, letter of March 1, 1882; Feinberg. **The list whole**/*C*, III: 270. **Osgood gives up**/*DN*, II: 289. **The psychology of that man**/*WWC*, IV: 92. **a mere tool**/Tucker to Whitman, letter of July 4, 1882; Feinberg. **under the Comstock statutes**/*C*, III: 295. **"Mr. Comstock as Cato the Censor"**/Feinberg; see J. Loving, *Walt Whitman's Champion*, p. 233. **shows the continuous lascivious**/Boston Public Library, *C*, III: 315. **the more I think**/*C*, III: 314. **So A[nthony] C[omstock]** and **ought to be nailed**/*C*, III: 338–39; *WWC*, IV: 91. **As to the vehement**/*C*, III: 314. **I shall certainly**/*C*, III: 315. **I don't like the**/In *C*, III: 312. **The Leaves**/*WWC*, I: 18. **immediately produced quite**/Bucke, *Walt Whitman*, p. 153. **the book has been advertised**/ Kennedy, *The Fight of a Book for the World*, p. 119. **for holiday presents**/*C*, III: 292. **they are now in the fifth**/*C*, III: 309. **a kindred soul**/Quotations from "With Husky-Haughty Lips O Sea" in *LGC*, pp. 517–18. **Why is it**/*NUPM*, III: 1099. **If I had not been born**/*C*, III: 366. **The soul of the largest**/Whitman, *Specimen Days & Collect* (Philadelphia: Rees Welsh, 1882), p. 275.

16 /   *The Pope of Mickle Street*

I have a house/Elizabeth Leavitt Keller, *Walt Whitman in Mickle Street* (New York: Mitchell Kennerly, 1921), p. 16. **We need but**/*WWC*, V: 491. **That's just the trouble**/*WWC*, VII: 422. **the vibrating voices**/*C*, IV: 369. **the great long**/ *C*, IV: 329. **It has a sound**/*WWC*, VII: 76. **unsettling band**/Keller, *Whitman in Mickle Street*, p. 1. **Music is my worst**/*WWC*, I: 361. **He is the nastiest**/ *WWC*, VI: 137. **the streets—the stinking**/*WWC*, V: 402. **the worst house**/

WWC, V: 181. **a total stranger**/See Harry L. Dwight to Whitman, letter of November 24, 1891; Feinberg. **Every cock**/In Johnston and Wallace, *Visits to Whitman*, p. 155. **Walt, there's carriage**/Robert Allerton Parker, *The Transatlantic Smiths* (New York: Random House, 1959), p. 44. **They treated me with**/ *WWC*, V: 52. **Don't invest thyself**/*C*, V: 26. **rascally publisher**/*C*, III: 198. **I am averse to**/*WWC*, I: 195. **I shall not be**/*Camden Courier*, January 21, 1887. **The last closing days**/*DN*, II: 410. *there* **I shall probably mainly**/*C*, IV: 100. **Concerts, Lecturers, and All**/*Memoranda During the War*, ed. R. Basler, p. 40. **Miss Breese**/New-York *Evening Sun*, April 15, 1887. **It was too much** and **first and last**/*WWC*, I: 65, 172–73. **the evening reception** /*Memoranda During the War*, ed. R. Basler, p. 40. **Of course I find**/*WWC*, II: 4. **Newton Arvin**/ *Whitman* (New York: Russell & Russell, 1938). **I felt triumphant**/*DN*, II: 414. **I include Carnegie**/*WWC*, III: 480. **treason and Carnegie showed**/*WWC*, IV: 254. **I try to be just**/*WWC*, IV: 467. **I speak for Anarchists**/*WWC*, V: 208. **You object to**/*WWC*, I: 81. **a good old man**/*LGC*, p. 533. **His poem on the**/ *Memoirs of Thomas B. Harned, Walt Whitman's Friend and Literary Executor* (Hartford: Transcendental Books, 1972), p. 34. **countless blessings**/*LGC*, pp. 620–21. **Walt, you come damn**/*WWC*, IV: 326. **We seem to have entered**/ *WWC*, IV: 470. **everybody is occupied**/*WWC*, VI: 46. **I am not asleep**/*WWC*, I: 22. **[Baxter] is very radical**/*WWC*, VI: 46. **I sh'd say**/*New York Herald*, March 15, 1891. **The devilish and**/*LGC*, p. 554. A. James Reichley/*The Life of the Parties*, pp. 142–44. **Underneath, his objects**/*PW*, I: 227. **genial, good-natured**/*WWC*, II: 556. **has done some honor**/*WWC*, I: 81. **The peaceful choice**/*LGC*, p. 517. **Centre of equal**/*LGC*, p. 511. "**As the Greek's signal flame**"/*LGC*, p. 533. **Greater than memory**/*LGC*, p. 510. **Thou, Washington**/*LGC*, p. 520. **Here first the duties**/*LGC*, p. 526. **Hollis**/*Language and Style in Leaves of Grass*. See also Burnham, "An Analysis . . . of Whitman's Composing Process." **He is the queerest**/*WWC*, IV: 94. **I like Eakins'** and **a poor old blind despised**/*WWC*, IV: 160, 163. **noblest work**/*Letters of Oscar Wilde*, ed. Hart-Davis, p. 100. **Mr. Whitman's Eve**/*Century of Whitman Criticism*, ed. Miller, p. 88. **As I sit writing here**/*LGC*, pp. 509–10. **Cut me short**/*LGC*, p. 510. **I have been and am rejected**/*WWC*, VII: 56. **created and formulated** and **my pen or voice** and **the 33 years**/*PW*, II: 733. **my own physical**/*PW*, II: 714. The remaining quotations in this paragraph are on pp. 713–14. **These gems, sparkles** and **they might go with some**/*WWC*, III: 395–96. **I consent**/*DN*, II: 438. **I don't like the idea**/*WWC*, I: 234. **I am willing**/ *C*, III: 407. **That is fame**/*WWC*, VII: 386. **a means of disseminating**/Grace Ellery Channing to Whitman, letter of July 7, 1888; Feinberg. **the grand work of**/S. K. McIlhaney to Whitman, letter of October 11, 1889; Feinberg. **You don't know, Horace**/*WWC*, IV: 351–52. **extremely nervous**/C. Heyde to Whitman, letter of November 1890; Feinberg. **good sympathizers**/C. Heyde to Whitman, letter of June 5, 1890; Feinberg. **brilliant stars**/C. Heyde to Whitman, letter of October 21, 1891; Feinberg. **a perpetual filch** and **the worst nuisance**/*DN*, II: 541. **First of all**/*WWC*, I: 308. **My foothold is tenoned**/*LGC*, p. 48. **Of course I do not undervalue**/*WWC*, VII: 447. **the most signal**/*DN*, II: 514.

The household wreck'd/*LGC*, pp. 551–53. the only poet who has done and lubricates my soul/*WWC*, III: 564, 335. done more to raise one/Helen Wilmans to Whitman, letter of May 21, 1882; Feinberg. just as I wished and cream of all/*WWC*, V: 237; VI: 130. If a hustler/*WWC*, VI: 130. Everything seemed to pass/*WWC*, V: 251. I hope to be identified/*WWC*, VI: 353. But we have, too/*LGC*, p. 546. As some old broken/*LGC*, p. 541. Even here in my/*LGC*, p. 549. The emotion does not/*Century of Whitman Criticism*, ed. Miller, p. 62. As Carroll Smith-Rosenberg shows/See *Disorderly Conduct*. It pleases me to think/*JM*, p. 22. no country anyhow/*WWC*, VI: 342. Still harping on my/*WWC*, II: 129. I think [Whitman]/J. A. Symonds to E. Carpenter, letter of January 21, 1893; in Katz, *Gay American History*, p. 358. wanted to obviate/Symonds, *Male Love: A Problem in Greek Ethics and Other Writings* (New York: Pagan Press, 1983), pp. 153–54. though it was not free/Symonds, *Male Love*, p. 8. The quotation in the next sentence is on p. 3. in a Dorian mood and there is indeed a distinctly and as hostile to sexual inversion/In Louis J. Bragman, "The Case of John Addington Symonds," in Ruitenbeek, *Homosexuality and Creative Genius*, pp. 105, 111, 113. the democratic chivalry/Symonds, *Male Love*, p. 102. Edward Carpenter/Katz, *Gay American History*, p. 363. morbidity and the most natural habits/E. Carpenter, *Iolaus: An Anthology of Friendship* (New York: Mitchell Kennerly, 1907), p. 189. latent and unconscious/H. Ellis and J. A. Symonds, *Sexual Inversion* (London: Wilson and Macmillan, 1897), p. 21. The remaining quotations in the paragraph are on pp. 146–47. the "effeminate" man and the "trade"/For a revealing account of these and other types, see Chauncey, *Gay New York*. It is rather odd that/In Numa Praetorius, "Storm Over Whitman," in Ruitenbeek, *Homosexuality and Creative Genius*, p. 127. vital, manly, gigantesque and I'm proud/*WWC*, VII: 13, 188. Fearless, frank and In all essential ways/*WWC*, VI: 141. What would this life be/*WWC*, VI: 447. masterpiece of language and a bugle call/*WWC*, VII: 223. O Robert! Robert!/Quotations in this paragraph are in *WWC*, VII: 225. who has done so much/Johnston to Whitman, letter of May 14, 1886; Feinberg. owes to you entirely/Wallace to Whitman, letter of May 18, 1887; Feinberg. seemed to exhale sanity and which positively astonished/Johnston and Wallace, *Visits to Walt Whitman*, pp. 34, 35. Well, you've come to be and not only the greatest/Johnston and Wallace, *Visits to Walt Whitman*, p. 90. The quotations in the next paragraph are on p. 99. God bless the church/*C*, V: 231. the world did not want me/*WWC*, VI: 374. scarcely a day passes/*WWC*, VII; 177. hot little prophets/The phrase was introduced in 1906 by Perry in *Walt Whitman: His Life and Work*. Do you suppose a thousand/Kennedy to Whitman, December 28, 1890, in *WWC*, VII: 397. I am more than ever/Bucke to Traubel, letter of July 18, 1891; Feinberg. like carrying down/*C*, V: 205. to lay it on/H. Traubel, "Walt Whitman's Birthday," *Lippincott's*, August 1891, p. 229. The other quotations in this paragraph, along with the description of the birthday party, are from this article, pp. 229–38, and from a typescript draft of the article by Traubel in Feinberg. No great poem/*PW*, II: 656. Cheer! Cheer!/*WWC*, I: 167. I stand for the sunny/*WWC*, II: 430. Little white-

INDEX

ILLUSTRATION CREDITS

Figure 1. Whitman in the early 1840s; daguerreotype, perhaps by John Plumbe, Jr. Courtesy of Gay Wilson Allen.

Figure 2. Whitman in July 1854: steel engraving by Samuel Hollyer from a daguerreotype by Gabriel Harrison (original daguerreotype lost). Frontispiece of the 1855 edition of *Leaves of Grass.* Courtesy of University of Iowa Special Collections.

Figure 3. Whitman, around 1860; photograph, probably by J. W. Black of Boston, firm of Black and Batchelder. Collection of Charles Feinberg.

Figure 4. Whitman in 1859: engraving by Stephen Alonzo Schoff from a portrait by Charles Hine. Frontispiece of the 1860 edition of *Leaves of Grass.* Courtesy Gay Wilson Allen.

Figure 5. Walter Whitman. Library of Congress.

Figure 6. Louisa Van Velsor Whitman. Library of Congress.

Figure 7. Whitman's birthplace, West Hills, New York. Library of Congress.

Figure 8. *Winter Scene in Brooklyn* (c. 1817–20); painting by Francis Guy. Courtesy of the Brooklyn Museum; Gift of the Brooklyn Institute of Arts and Sciences.

Figure 9. *New York, from Brooklyn Heights* (1837); painting by John William Hill. Courtesy of the New York Public Library.

Figure 10. *Walt Whitman's School at Southold, 1840;* painting attributed to William Sidney Mount. Current location unknown; photograph of painting courtesy of the Smithtown Library.

Figure 11. The Reverend Ralph Smith. Courtesy of the Smithtown Library.

Figure 12. *Mike Walsh at Tammany Hall in 1843;* engraving by S. H. Gimber. Collection of the New-York Historical Society.

Figure 13. *View of the Great Fire in New York, Dec. 16 & 17, 1835* (1836); aquatint by Nicolino Calyo, engraved by William James Bennett. Courtesy of the New York Public Library.

Figure 14. *Broadway, New York* (1836); etching by Thomas Hornor, engraved by John Hill. Courtesy of the New York Public Library.

Figure 15. Franklin Pierce. Library of Congress.

Figure 16. James Buchanan. Library of Congress.

Figure 17. Abraham Lincoln; photograph by Mathew Brady. Courtesy of the New York Public Library.

Figure 18. Andrew Johnson. Library of Congress.

Figure 19. Junius Brutus Booth. Courtesy of the New York Public Library.

Figure 20. Junius Brutus Booth as Richard III. Courtesy of the New York Public Library.

Figure 21. Edwin Forrest. Courtesy of the New York Public Library.

Figure 22. Edwin Forrest as Macbeth. Courtesy of the New York Public Library.

Figure 23. The Hutchinson Family Singers. Courtesy of the New York Public Library.

Figure 24. Marietta Alboni. Courtesy of the New York Public Library.

Figure 25. Elias Hicks. Courtesy of the Friends Historical Library, Swarthmore College.

Figure 26. Henry Ward Beecher. Courtesy of the New York Public Library.

Figure 27. Henry Ward Beecher preaching at Plymouth Church, Brooklyn. Courtesy of the New York Public Library.

Figure 28. Frances Wright; lithograph by Nagel and Weingaertner Lithography Company. National Portrait Gallery, Smithsonian Institution.

Figure 29. Lucretia Mott. Courtesy of the Friends Historical Library, Swarthmore College.

Figure 30. Sojourner Truth. Courtesy of the Friends Historical Library, Swarthmore College.

Figure 31. Anne Gilchrist. Library of Congress.

Figure 32. *New-York by Gas-Light. "Hooking a Victim"* (c. 1850); lithograph by Serrell and Perkins. Courtesy of the Museum of the City of New York.

Figure 33. *The Crystal Palace. New York* (1853); engraving by Samuel Capewell and Christopher Kimmel. Courtesy of the New York Public Library.

Figure 34. *Sleighing in New York* (1855); lithograph by Thomas Benecke, after a painting by D. Benecke. Library of Congress.

Figure 35. *The Trapper's Bride* (1837); painting by Alfred Jacob Miller. Courtesy of the Walters Art Gallery.

Figure 36. *Farmers Nooning* (1836); painting by William Sidney Mount.

The Collections of the Museums at Stony Brook, Gift of Frederick Sturges, Jr., 1954.

Figure 37. Front coverboard of the first issue of *Leaves of Grass* (1855). Courtesy of the New York Public Library.

Figure 38. Front and back jackets of the promotional pamphlet *Leaves of Grass Imprints* (1860). Library of Congress.

Figure 39. William Douglas O'Connor; 1887 photograph by Merritt and Wood. Library of Congress.

Figure 40. John Burroughs; photograph, c. 1870, by J. Golden. Library of Congress.

Figure 41. Whitman and Peter Doyle, c. 1869; photograph by M. P. Rice, Washington, D. C. Collection of Charles Feinberg.

Figure 42. Horace Traubel. Library of Congress.

Figure 43. Whitman, c. 1864; photograph, possibly by Alexander Gardner. Ed Folsom Collection.

Figure 44. Whitman in 1879 with Katharine Devereux Johnston and Harold Hugh Johnston; photograph by William Kurtz, New York. Ed Folsom Collection.

Figure 45. Whitman in 1878; photograph by Napoleon Sarony. Library of Congress.

Figure 46. Cigar box cover with Whitman logo. Library of Congress.

Figure 47. Whitman in 1891 in his upstairs bedroom at 328 Mickle Street, Camden; photograph by Dr. William Reeder, Philadelphia. Library of Congress.